FV.

MOTORCYCLE
OPERATION
AND SERVICE

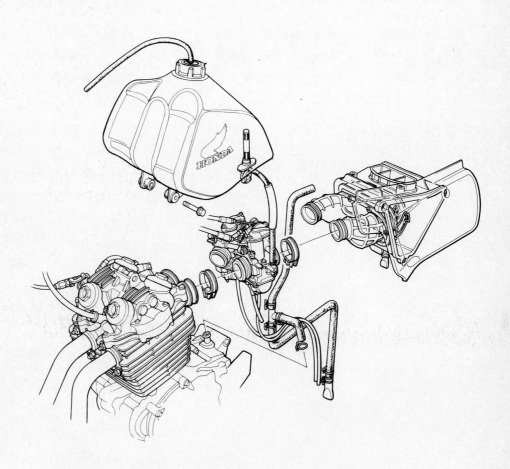

MOTORCYCLE OPERATION AND SERVICE

Jay Webster
California State University
Long Beach

Robert Putnam

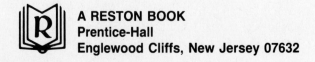

A RESTON BOOK
Prentice-Hall
Englewood Cliffs, New Jersey 07632

Library of Congress Cataloging in Publication Data

Webster, Jay.
    Motorcycle operation and service.

    ''A Reston book.''
    1. Motorcycles.   2. Motorcycles—Maintenance and
repair.   I. Putnam, Robert E.   II. Title.
TL440.W38   1986   629.2′275   85-19591
ISBN 0-8359-4669-X

A Reston Book
Published by Prentice-Hall
A Division of Simon & Schuster, Inc.
Englewood Cliffs, N.J. 07632

10   9   8   7   6   5   4   3   2   1

PRINTED IN THE UNITED STATES OF AMERICA

CONTENTS

Motorcycle Operation and Service is designed to meet the training needs of the student motorcycle technician. The purpose of the text is to help the motorcycle instructor present basic principles that are valuable in the instruction of students at various levels of training. The text can be used to train entry-level motorcycle technicians and to retrain and upgrade skills of practicing motorcycle technicians.

Motorcycle Operation and Service provides students with a foundation in the basics of motorcycle mechanics—with special emphasis in hands-on training. The principles of operation of motorcycle components are followed by the principles of maintenance, troubleshooting, and service. A motorcycle technician with a thorough understanding of operational concepts and service techniques will be better prepared to service the high technology motorcycles of the future.

The book is organized into 26 units. Units 1 through 5 provide the student with basic information required to work successfully in the shop. Units are devoted to motorcycle basics; safety; tools; measuring; and assembling and fastening devices. Units 6 through 10 focus on the two- and four-stroke motorcycle engine. The fundamentals of engine operation are presented first, followed by upper-end parts and construction. As soon as the student understands the parts and operation, units are presented on troubleshooting and service. There are troubleshooting and servicing units for both four- and two-stroke upper end. The engine lower end is presented in a unit, followed by a unit on lower-end troubleshooting and service.

The engine units are followed by engine accessory units. Units 12 through 21 present the operation, troubleshooting, and servicing of the accessory systems necessary for engine operation. There are units on the lubrication system; cooling system; exhaust system and turbocharging; fuel system; ignition system; battery and charging systems; and starting and accessory systems.

When the study of the engine and its accessory systems is complete, the transmission of power from the engine to the rear wheel is presented. The transmission of power is presented in Units 22 and 23. First the primary drive and clutch operation and service is presented, followed by the transmission and final drive. The last three units, 24, 25, and 26 are devoted to the motorcycle chassis systems. There is a unit on frames and suspension; brake systems; and tires and wheels.

A special effort has been made to make *Motorcycle Operation and Service* an effective learning tool. Illustrations provide direct visual correlation to the text material. Topics are developed from the simple to the complex following techniques that have been tested in the shop. Each unit begins with "Job Competency Objectives." These are specific measureable objectives designed to guide the stu-

PREFACE

dents' learning. Each unit has a set of "Key Terms" designed to help in the job of vocabulary development. Each unit ends with a set of "Checkup" questions to help the student and the instructor determine if the student understood the content of the unit. A set of "Discussion Topics and Activities" is provided in each unit for the student who is ahead of the rest of the class or who is interested in further study on a topic.

Job Sheets have been developed for each troubleshooting and servicing unit. The purpose of the job sheets is to help the instructor guide the student through the shopwork activities. Each job sheet specifies what reading the student should do before the job and provides blanks to fill in regarding the motorcycle and the time it takes to do the job. Each job sheet lists the special tools, equipment, parts, and materials necessary to complete the job. There is a space for the student to write in any reference to a manufacturer's shop manual. A specification section is provided so the student must look up and record any necessary specifications. The procedure section gives the basic steps for the completion of the job. There are checkpoints for the instructor to check the students' progress and blanks for the student to fill in the results of tests or measurements.

Jay Webster
Robert Putnam

MOTORCYCLE OPERATION AND SERVICE

The word *motorcycle* is a combination of the words *motor* and *bicycle*. The first motorcycles were just that—bicycles on which a backyard mechanic installed a small motor. The motorcycle has come a long way since those days, having evolved into a complex machine with many systems and thousands of parts.

Today's motorcycles are extremely powerful, more reliable, and easier to control than those of even a few years ago. New technology in motorcycle engine development, suspension design, and electronics has resulted in new levels of performance and reliability. The only negative effect of these developments is that the motorcycle is much more complex than it was in earlier times. A motorcycle technician must now have a good understanding of basic motorcycle systems and a good deal of experience servicing those systems. The purpose of this book is to help the beginning motorcycle technician understand the basic operating principles and servicing techniques of the motorcycle.

TYPES OF MOTORCYCLES

Over the years the number and types of motorcycles on and off the roads have increased. Today, there is a type of motorcycle for just about everyone.

The moped has become an increasing popular and fuel-efficient way to get around. The term *moped* is a combined form of *motor* and *pedal*. The moped (Figure 1–1) is a cross between a motorcycle and a bicycle, combining some of the better features of each. Like a bicycle, it is pedalable, easy to operate, highly maneuverable, and handily transportable by car. Like a motorcycle, it is motor driven, features handlebar acceleration, offers headlights, horns and turn signals, and demands little effort on the part of the operator. Mopeds often have a no-shift transmission; a low center of gravity for easier, safer balance; and a handy step-through design for easy mounting. They usually have a very small engine that is able to squeeze about 150 miles out of a gallon of gasoline. However, the rider often has to help the machine by pedaling on the steeper grades.

MOTORCYCLE BASICS

To many riders, off-road riding is what motorcycling is all about. Early motorcycle riders converted street bikes to off-road machines by removing their fenders and exhaust systems. These early conversions resulted in a sport that is now supported by all the major motorcycle manufacturers. As a consequence, the off-road or trail bike has evolved into its own kind of machine. These bikes (Figure 1–2) are extremely light and powerful and feature suspension travel and ground clearances that allow them to take the roughest terrain at high speed.

The technology developed in off-road motorcycles has expanded into three-wheel (Figure 1–3) and four-wheel (Figure 1–4) machines with fat tires for playing or working over any kind of terrain. These special-purpose machines use motorcycle engines and drive systems. They also often use motorcycle suspension systems.

The street motorcycle has evolved into today's superbikes (Figure 1–5), equipped with extremely powerful, highly advanced engines. Some are even equipped with turbochargers. These machines are designed for both rider comfort and clean aerodynamics, i.e., a ride with as much

Figure 1–1. A moped uses a small two-stroke engine and can usually be pedalled like a bicycle. (*U.S. Suzuki Motor Corp.*)

Figure 1–2. The off-road trail bike has maximum suspension travel for rough terrain. (*Kawasaki Motors Corp. U.S.A.*)

1

Figure 1–3. The three-wheel machine is a recent development. *(Kawasaki Motors Corp. U.S.A.)*

Figure 1–5. Today's street bikes have high-technology engines and are extremely aerodynamic. *(Kawasaki Motors Corp.)*

Figure 1–4. The four-wheel all-terrain machine is a variation of three-wheel bikes. *(U.S. Suzuki Motor Corp.)*

Figure 1–6. A motorcycle can be fitted with any number of accessories for touring. *(Harley-Davidson Motors, Inc.)*

reduction as possible in the drag created by pushing through the air. The level of technology of these machines increases with each yearly model.

Street machines can be equipped with any number of accessories for comfort and touring (Figure 1–6). To many people, the joy of motorcycling resides in comfortable, long-distance travel.

Some riders like both off-road and street riding. Consequently, many bikes are manufactured with off-road suspensions but are equipped with lights and other accessories for street riding (Figure 1–7).

BASIC MOTORCYCLE COMPONENTS

All types of motorcycle have the same basic components and systems. When you understand the basic operating principles behind these systems, you will be able to diagnose problems and make repairs on them.

Engine

The motorcycle engine (Figure 1–8) is a machine that converts heat energy to a form of power. All motorcycle engines operate on the principle of *combustion,* i.e., the ig-

Figure 1–7. This bike has maximum suspension travel for off-road riding but lights and exhaust for street operation. *(Kawasaki Motors Corp. U.S.A.)*

niting and burning of an air–fuel mixture to produce heat. The expansion of the air caused by the heat produces useful power.

There are, of course, many types and designs of engines. We shall consider both two- and four-stroke engines and their many design variations.

Figure 1–8. The engine supplies the power. *(Kawasaki Motors Corp. U.S.A.)*

Figure 1–9. Exhaust system. *(Kawasaki Motors Corp. U.S.A.)*

Figure 1–10. The fuel system provides fuel and air. *(Kawasaki Motors Corp. U.S.A.)*

Figure 1–11. The ignition system. *(Kawasaki Motors Corp. U.S.A.)*

Figure 1–12. The electrical system. *(Kawasaki Motors Corp. U.S.A.)*

In order to function, an engine requires a set of subsystems. A *lubrication system* circulates oil between the engine's moving parts in order to prevent the metal-to-metal contact which causes wear. Oil between moving parts allows the parts to move more easily because it lessens the friction between them. The lower the internal friction of an engine, the more power it can develop.

An *exhaust system* (Figure 1–9) provides a smooth flow of exhaust, maintaining maximum engine performance while minimizing the noise.

A *fuel system* (Figure 1–10) is used to store enough fuel for several hundred miles of operation, to deliver the fuel to the engine, and to mix the fuel with air in the proper amounts for efficient burning inside the engine.

An *ignition system* (Figure 1–11) is used to provide a high-voltage spark in each of the engine's cylinders so that the air–fuel mixture will explode. The ignition system distributes the high voltage to each of the cylinders at just the right time for a power stroke.

Electrical system

The electrical system of a motorcycle (Figure 1–12) powers all the electrical components of the machine. It consists of a battery that provides a source of stored energy that operates the electrical components of the motorcycle when the engine is not running.

The electrical system has several subsystems. The *charging system* restores the chemical energy used by the battery. It develops all the power required to operate the motorcycle's electrical system once the engine is running. The *electric starting system* allows the rider to use the energy stored in the battery to power a starter motor to crank the engine. *Electrical accessory systems* include headlights, turn signals, brake lights, and horns.

Figure 1-13. Drive train. *(Kawasaki Motors Corp. U.S.A.)*

Figure 1-15. The brake system. *(Kawasaki Motors Corp. U.S.A.)*

Figure 1-14. Frame and suspension. *(Kawasaki Motors Corp. U.S.A.)*

Figure 1-16. Tires and wheels. *(Kawasaki Motors Corp. U.S.A.)*

Drive train

After the engine develops its power, the power is delivered to the rear wheel of the motorcycle by an assembly of parts called the *drive train* (Figure 1-13). The components of the drive train are a set of primary gears: the clutch, used to connect and disconnect the engine's power from the drive train; the transmission, which provides the rider with a selection of different gear ratios to match engine power output with motorcycle speed; and a final drive that delivers the power to the rear wheel through a chain-and-sprocket or shaft assembly.

Frame and suspension

The motorcycle frame provides the basic foundation onto which the engine and drive train, as well as all the other components, are mounted. The frame works with the suspension system (Figure 1-14) to provide the rider with a smooth ride.

Brake system

The purpose of the motorcycle brake system (Figure 1-15) is to slow down the rotation of the wheels to allow the rider to slow down or stop the bike. Motorcycles may use a mechanical drum brake or a hydraulic disc brake.

Tires and wheels

The tire-and-wheel assembly of the motorcycle (Figure 1-16) supports the weight of the motorcycle and allows it to move down the road. The front tire and wheel provide directional control, while the rear tire and wheel deliver the engine's power to the road to push the motorcycle forward.

Each of the major motorcycle components is important to the operation and safe riding of the motorcycle. Accordingly, our study of motorcycles begins with units on safety and the use of tools and fasteners. From there, we proceed to a consideration of each of the above systems in detail.

In working on motorcycles, you will be using a number of tools and materials that can be hazardous if they are not handled properly. In various areas of work every year, more than two million people are injured and about 13,000 are killed because of occupational hazards. To many people, these statistics might seem to be just numbers. They are not just numbers, however, to the people who are part of those statistics—people who, for example, have lost an eye or a limb due to an on-the-job accident. Since safe work habits prevent accidents, it is important that you follow good work habits and be familiar with common safety practices in the shop. Remember: Safety is everybody's business! It's your life.

JOB COMPETENCY OBJECTIVES

When you finish reading and studying this unit you should be able to:

1. Demonstrate your knowledge of personal safety by working safely in the shop.

2. Demonstrate the safe use of common hand tools.

3. Recognize the possible hazards when using power tools.

4. Demonstrate the safe use of compressed air and parts-cleaning equipment.

5. Recognize the hazards in handling batteries.

6. Describe the safe handling of gasoline and how to extinguish a gasoline fire.

7. Explain how to ride a motorcycle safely in the shop.

PERSONAL SAFETY

Safety begins with you! Your personal appearance and behavior can prevent accidents from happening to yourself or to those around you (Figure 2–1). You must learn to practice personal safety in the way you look, dress, and act when you perform motorcycle repair work.

Personal appearance is an important part of personal safety. If you wear your hair long, you should be aware that it only takes an instant for it to get entangled in rotating machinery and yanked out by the roots. If you do have long hair, it should be either tied back or contained by a cap or bandana to prevent it from falling into your eyes and work.

What you wear is also important to your safety. Wear close-fitting clothing and keep it tucked in and buttoned or zipped up. Loose clothing, such as shirt tails, ties, lapels, cuffs, or scarves can easily get caught or wrapped up in machinery and cause serious bodily injury. It only takes a few moments to keep neat. Take the time.

Wearing jewelry can also be dangerous. It is best not to wear any at work. Jewelry can catch in rotating machinery,

UNIT 2

SAFETY IN THE MOTORCYCLE SHOP

Figure 2–1. Safety is everybody's business. *(U.S. Suzuki Motor Corp.)*

just as loose clothing can. And remember that metal jewelry is also a good conductor of electricity.

Always wear eye protection when you are doing any kind of job that may endanger your eyes. Always wear eye protection while using a grinder of any kind. Even if the bench tool grinder has its safety guard in position, wear eye protection. Wear eye protection when working around caustic fluids, such as battery acid or cleaning fluid. Your shop will have protective glasses or face shields (Figure 2–2). It is a good idea to wear the eye protection all the time you are in the shop.

Figure 2–2. Eye protection should be used when working in hazardous areas. Safety glasses or a safety shield is worn. *(Florin Limited)*

Foot protection is also a must. Heavy tools and motorcycle parts can easily be brushed off the work bench. Safety shoes with steel-capped toes can save a great deal of pain or even broken toes. Always wear safety shoes in the shop.

Gloves may be needed for inserting parts into a cold tank and then removing them, and for handling storage batteries.

Proper behavior can also help prevent accidents. Horseplay is not fun when it sends someone to the hospital. Such things as air nozzle fights or practical jokes do not have any place in the motorcycle shop. Remember, you are at work, and both work and safety are serious business.

To prevent injury to yourself or to your fellow workers, never use power machinery or attempt a repair job until you have received proper instructions from the appropriate authority. If you are in doubt, or if you are unfamiliar with a power tool or a repair process, ask for help. Never risk going ahead until you are sure.

You should also always pay attention to specific lifting and carrying rules. Lift with your legs, not with your back! Figure 2–3 shows the recommended lifting techniques. You may be as strong as an ox, but be careful when you lift. Even if your back muscles were made of steel, there would be a limit to the strain they could stand. Size up the load before you try to lift it, and get help if necessary. If

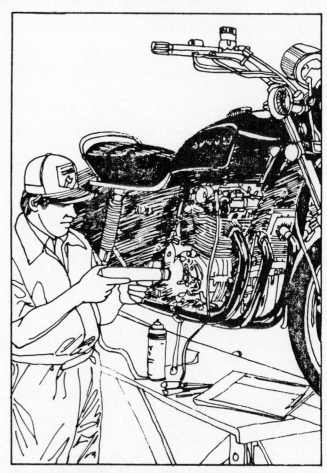

Figure 2–4. Keep your work area clean and well organized. *(U.S. Suzuki Motor Corp.)*

Figure 2–3. Lift heavy objects with your legs, not your back. *(Ford Motor Co.)*

you must lift the load alone, use your legs, not your back. Lift straight up by straightening your legs. Also, take care not to twist at your waist when lifting. Twisting while lifting can cause a severe injury to your back.

Personal housekeeping is very important. Always keep your personal work area clean and well organized (Figure 2–4). Have a place for each tool, and keep it there when not in use. Clean up all oil spills immediately, especially those on the floor. Do not allow machine parts, fasteners, or other debris to clutter up your work surface or to accumulate on the floor. Do not keep any oily cleaning rags around your work area because they are a fire hazard. Dispose of oily rags in a covered metal container provided for that purpose.

Be aware of your surroundings. Locate your work area in relation to key emergency points. Know where the nearest first-aid kit is located. If it is not properly stocked, tell your instructor. Usually, a list of the kit's contents is included inside the cover of the kit. Facilities for flushing the eyes should also be in or near the shop area.

Find out where the nearest fire extinguisher is located! A prominent red sign should mark the location of each fire extinguisher. Make sure you know how to use the fire extinguisher, and make sure you use the correct class of fire extinguisher. (Classes of fire extinguishers will be covered later.)

Find out where the nearest telephone is located. Make sure that the telephone number of a doctor, the nearest hospital, the fire department, the police department, and any other numbers you might call in an emergency are posted next to the telephone. If the numbers are not posted, talk to your instructor.

HAND TOOL SAFETY

Hand tools should always be in a sound, clean, workable condition. Greasy hand tools can easily slip out of your hands, causing skinned knuckles or broken fingers. Check

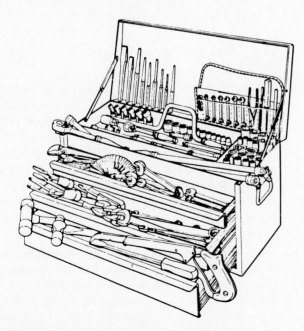

Figure 2–5. Keep your tools clean and organized. *(Ford Motor Co.)*

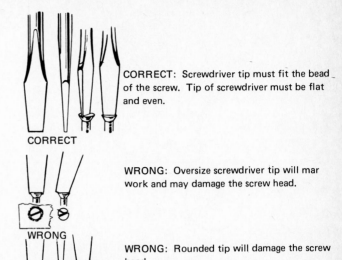

CORRECT: Screwdriver tip must fit the bead of the screw. Tip of screwdriver must be flat and even.

WRONG: Oversize screwdriver tip will mar work and may damage the screw head.

WRONG: Rounded tip will damage the screw head.

Figure 2–6. Use a correct-size screwdriver for the job. *(Stanley Works)*

all your hand tools for cracks, chips, burrs, broken teeth, and other dangerous conditions before you use them. If any defective tools are found, take them to your instructor so that no one can be injured using them. The basic rule for tool use is: Use the tool to do the job it is designed for.

A good motorcycle technician has a place where every tool is stored when it is not in use. You will save a lot of time if you have a well-organized tool chest. Each tool should be in its place, clean, and ready for use (Figure 2–5). Follow these basic rules for safe hand tool use.

1. When using any hand tool, keep your hands and the tool clean. Grease and oil on the tool or your hands can cause the tool to slip or your hands to slip off. Any slip can cause injury.

2. When using a screwdriver to tighten or loosen a screw, make sure that the blade of the screwdriver fits snugly in the screwhead slot. A blade that is too small will twist, and consequently damage and distort, the screwhead slot. A screwdriver of the wrong size can slip out and cut you. The top drawing of Figure 2–6 shows the use of the proper screwdriver tip. In the center drawing, the screwdriver tip is too wide and will scar the area around the screwhead; if the screwdriver is not held straight up, the blade tip will slip out of the screw slot and cause damage. The bottom drawing shows what will happen when a rounded tip is used.

3. Always use a screwdriver with its length perpendicular to the slot of the screw (Figure 2–7). This allows the tip to be fully seated, lessening the chance of slipping.

Figure 2–7. Hold the screwdriver straight up from the screw. Steady the tip with one hand and make sure the shank is perpendicular to the screw head. *(Hand Tool Institute)*

Figure 2–8. Never hammer on a hardened surface, such as another hammer. *(Snap-On Tools Corp.)*

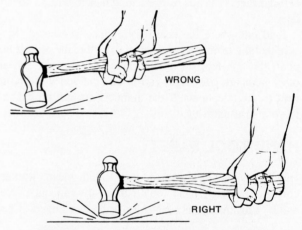

Figure 2–9. Use the hammer correctly. Grasp at the end of the handle as shown and hit squarely. *(Ford Motor Corp.)*

4. Use a pry or pinchbar for prying. Do *not* use a screwdriver. A screwdriver is designed for turning, not bending—with pressure, a screwdriver shank will bend. Also, since the tip of the screwdriver blade is hardened to keep it from wearing, it is brittle and may break, increasing the possibility of eye injury. If you must use a screwdriver for light prying, be sure you select one that is heavy enough to take the strain, and always wear safety glasses.

5. Do not carry screwdrivers, chisels, or open sharp-edged tools in your pockets. If you carry sharp tools in your hand, carry them with their cutting edges downward. Do not run while carrying any kind of tools. In fact, never run in the shop!

6. Before using any hammer, make sure that the head is securely attached to the handle. A loose hammer head can fly off its handle and cause serious injury.

7. Never strike a hardened-steel surface with a steel-headed hammer, and never strike any hammer with another hammer (Figure 2–8). Hardened steel is brittle and will splinter into steel particles that could easily put out an eye or inflict some other wound. Wear eye protection when hammering.

8. To use a hammer efficiently, you must learn how to hold it properly. Grasp the hammer near the end of its handle and place the head of the hammer on the object you want to strike. This will help your aim. Tap the object once or twice lightly, and then, when you are sure of your aim, hammer on the object. Hit the object square with the full striking force of the hammer (Figure 2–9).

9. Always hit with the striking face of the hammer.

Never strike with the side (cheek) of the hammer (Figure 2–10).

10. Always select the correct-size wrench to fit the bolt or nut you are working on (Figure 2–11). If you use a wrench with an opening considerably larger than the nut, you stand a good chance to round off the corners of the nut or bolthead. Use an inch-size wrench for inch-size bolts and nuts; use a metric wrench for metric fasteners. If the wrench slips, you face the danger of personal injury in the form of skinned or bruised knuckles, and possibly broken bones.

11. When using open-end wrenches, always pull the load (Figure 2–12). Pulling is much safer if something slips or breaks, because when you pull a wrench it is usually away from some obstruction. If you push it, it is often toward an obstruction which could jam your hand and knuckles if the wrench slips (Figure 2–13).

WRONG

Figure 2–10. Never strike with the side or cheek of the hammer head. *(Hand Tool Institute)*

RIGHT   WRONG

Figure 2–11. Use the correct size wrench: jaws must fit the nut or bolthead exactly. *(Sears, Roebuck and Co.)*

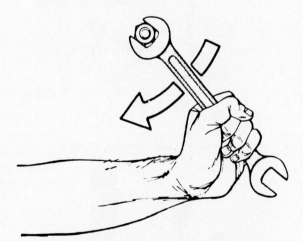

Figure 2–12. Pulling on an open-end wrench is safer than pushing it. *(Ford Motor Co.)*

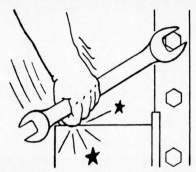

Figure 2–13. If you push a wrench, especially towards an obstruction, you may jam your fingers. *(Sears, Roebuck and Co.)*

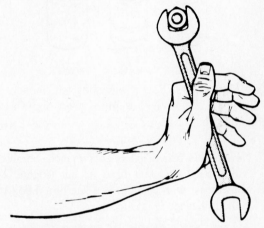

Figure 2–14. Correct method of pushing on a wrench. *(Ford Motor Co.)*

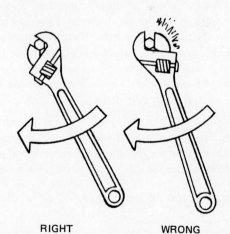

RIGHT   WRONG

Figure 2–15. Use an adjustable wrench so that the pull is on the fixed jaw, not the movable jaw. *(Sears, Roebuck and Co.)*

12. If you must push an open-end wrench toward an obstruction, do not wrap your fingers around the handle. Use the heel of your hand, as shown in Figure 2–14.

13. When using adjustable-end wrenches, observe the same precautions you would observe when using ordinary open-end wrenches. Adjust the jaws to fit snugly against the flats of the nut or bolthead, and then pull the wrench toward you, with the fixed jaw doing the pulling. If you try to pull with the adjustable jaw, and if the pull is too heavy, you may snap off the adjustable jaw (Figure 2–15).

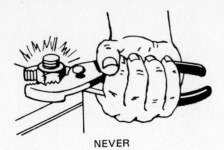

NEVER

Figure 2–16. Pliers will damage a nut or bolthead. *(Sears, Roebuck & Co.)*

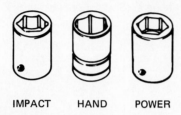

IMPACT   HAND   POWER

Figure 2–17. Socket wrenches: left, impact; center, hand; right, power. *(Snap-On Tools Corp.)*

14. Never use a pair of pliers as a wrench, because you will damage the bolt head or nut (Figure 2–16). Sometimes, with caution, you can turn a bolt or nut without damage if it is loose.

15. Always replace sockets that show cracks or wear.

16. When you use socket wrenches, never use hand sockets on power or impact wrenches. Figure 2–17 shows the difference between hand sockets and power and impact sockets. Hand sockets are nickel plated; power and impact sockets are made of black metal. Select the right-size socket for the job, and select only heavy-duty impact sockets for use with air or electric impact wrenches.

17. When using files, always use a handle on the tail end. This gives a good grip and avoids jamming the end into your hand. Never pry with a file: it is brittle and breaks easily.

POWER TOOL SAFETY

Power tools are tools which get their power from electricity, air, or hydraulic fluid. Use power tools only after you have received proper instructions on their use from the appropriate source. Follow these rules when using power tools.

1. If you are using an electrical power tool, make sure that it is properly grounded. Some electrical tools are double insulated and do not require separate grounding. Check the wiring for cracks in the insulation, as well as for bare wires. Do not use a defective tool, and never use electrical power tools while standing on a wet or damp floor.

2. Before turning a machine or electrical tool on, check to see that all safety guards are in place and properly adjusted. Never tie down or block a safety guard!

3. Before you plug in any machine or electrical tool, make sure the switch is off. Make all adjustments with the power off. If the machine or tool is running, let it come to a dead stop before making any adjustments. When you are through, turn it off for the next person.

4. If you are doing any power grinding, chipping, or sanding, always wear eye protection. In general, wear eye protection around machines and power tools.

5. When using power equipment on a small part, never hold the part in your hand because it could slip. Always use locking pliers or a clamp.

6. When operating a drill press, firmly secure the item to be drilled. Use either a clamp or a vise (Figure 2–18).

7. Do not use more extension cords than necessary; use

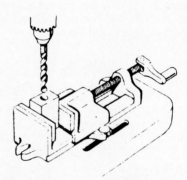

VICE USED TO SECURE OBJECT

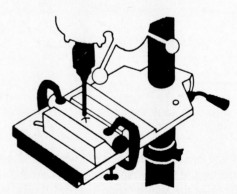

TWO C CLAMPS USED TO SECURE OBJECT

Figure 2–18. Always secure the object to be drilled, especially a small object. *(Top: Hand Tool Institute. Bottom: Sears, Roebuck and Co.)*

the electric outlet nearest the work area. Never string electric cords across pathways.

8. Always use machine guards, and make sure that they are working and correctly positioned.

9. When working with a hydraulic press, make sure that you are applying hydraulic pressure in a safe manner. Stand to the side, and remember to wear eye protection.

10. Do not touch any moving machinery parts. Remember that loose clothing can be dangerous around running machinery or tools.

11. Never try to slow down or brake a moving machine part or tool with your hand or other device. Let it stop of its own accord.

12. If the machine or power tool starts to smoke or make a strange sound, turn it off immediately.

13. Never walk away from a running machine or power tool. Always turn it off when leaving the area or when the job is completed.

COMPRESSED AIR AND PARTS CLEANING

Use only recommended solvents to clean parts. Never use gasoline because of the danger of fire or explosion. When using cold or dip tank cleaning solutions, be sure to wear eye protection, gloves, and a shop apron.

Compressed air is a very common source of injury. Always check the hose before using compressed air, because a badly worn air hose will burst under pressure. Replace a worn hose to prevent accidents. Check the air gauge; compressed air should never be over 30 pounds per square inch (psi).

Never pull the trigger when the gun is pointed directly toward anyone. You should especially never look into the discharge nozzle in order to find out if it is clogged. Never use compressed air to clean your clothes or parts of your body. Foreign matter may be forced into your skin or eyes.

Using compressed air to spin-dry bearings is extremely dangerous. For example, if you spin a wheel bearing with 30 psi of compressed air, you will spin it ten times faster than it would ever rotate inside the hub. This can cause the bearing to shatter and fly apart like shrapnel. Bearings should be cleaned in solvent and placed on a clean shop towel to air-dry. Avoid using compressed air to blow anything clean. If you do use air, wear eye protection and a respirator. Whenever possible, use a solvent wash or vacuum instead of blowing parts clean.

Do not use compressed air to clean brake parts when performing a brake job. There is always the possibility that harmful asbestos dust will be blown out. Always use a washer or vacuum to clean brake assemblies.

Always grasp the air hose firmly—sometimes it may kick or shake around. Never kink an air hose to cut off pressure.

When using compressed air to inflate a tire, turn your face and body away from the tire to protect yourself in the event that the tire explodes. Special tire safety inflation containers or cages are available to hold tires while they are being inflated.

FIRES AND FIRE PREVENTION

Before all else, know before a fire occurs where the fire extinguishers are and what types of fires they will put out. Figure 2–19 shows some typical signs that are used to identify the location of portable fire extinguishers, fire hoses, and fire alarms. By law, such signs need to be printed in red. Also, signs and fire equipment must be prominently located and easily accessible.

Some shops have a fire alarm box. In case of fire, warn the people in the area, pull the alarm box, and call the fire department. Because of the existence of combustible liquids, such as oil and gasoline, any fire in the shop can be serious. In case the shop needs to be evacuated, leave through the marked fire exits if they are not blocked off by the fire. (Fire exit signs are printed in black.) Act immediately to contain any fire!

All portable extinguishers are marked by class as follows.

Class A: Class A fire extinguishers are for ordinary paper and wood fires. The fire extinguisher

Figure 2–19. Red-colored signs are used to identify the location of fire extinguishers, fire alarms, and fire hoses. Fire exits are generally marked in black. *(Industrial Safety and Security Co.)*

Figure 2–20. Fire extinguishers are always marked by class: Class A, B, C, or a combination of classes. A Class B fire extinguisher is shown at left. *(Industrial Safety and Security Co.)*

must cool and quench the fire. The marking is an "A" in a triangle.

Class B: Class B fire extinguishers are for fires caused by flammable liquids such as oil and gasoline. The fire extinguisher must blanket or smother the fire. The marking is a "B" in a rectangle.

Class C: Class C fire extinguishers are for fires caused by faulty electrical equipment. The fire extinguisher must use a nonconducting agent to put out the fire. The marking is a "C" in a circle.

In the motorcycle shop, all of the above kinds of fires are possible. Normally, therefore, all three classes of fire extinguishers are available. Figure 2–20 shows the class markings used on fire extinguishers. You should be thoroughly familiar with these so that there can never be any doubt as to which extinguisher to use.

A multipurpose class ABC fire extinguisher is shown in Figure 2–21. These extinguishers are recommended for the motorcycle shop because they can handle all three classes of fire that may occur there.

In case of a fire, follow these steps.

1. Immediately warn other workers and students in the shop of the fire.

2. Pull the fire alarm, if there is one in the shop; if there is none, call the fire department.

3. If the fire is small, try to put it out with the appropriate fire extinguisher.

4. *Never* use water or a fire hose on a fire for which a class B or C fire extinguisher is required.

5. If the fire is large, leave the shop by the marked fire exits if they are not closed by fire. In any case, evacu-

Figure 2–21. A multipurpose Class ABC fire extinguisher is commonly used in the motorcycle shop. *(Walton Kidde, Division of Kidde, Inc.)*

ate the area immediately. Do *not* attempt to fight a large fire with portable fire extinguishers.

6. Direct firefighters to the area. Help the firefighters only if requested.

7. In case of a large fire, do not ventilate the area. Close doors and windows to prevent the fire from spreading.

8. Never return to a burning building for anything. Your life is too valuable!

9. Ventilate the area *after* the fire is out.

GASOLINE AND LIQUID FLAMMABLES

Never put water on a gasoline fire. Water just spreads the fire. Instead, use a class B or ABC fire extinguisher to smother the flames. A good rule is to call the fire department first and then attempt to extinguish the fire. But if it gets too hot or too smoky, get out! Never go back into a burning building for anything.

If you have to fight a gasoline fire, aim the fire extinguisher low at the base of the fire and stay with the fire until you are positive that it is out. Gasoline vapors can reignite very quickly if you do not get the fire thoroughly snuffed out.

The important fact to remember about gasoline is that liquid gasoline itself is not the real danger. Gasoline vapors are. So to avoid gasoline fires and explosions in the shop, you have to prevent gasoline vapors from escaping. The vapors are heavier than air and settle in low spots on the floor, where a lighted match or cigarette, or even an arc from an electric switch or motor can ignite them.

Gasoline vapors may be carried a considerable distance by the movement of air. Vapors are often ignited by a source such as a space heater or a pilot light on a water heater located at some distance from the gasoline source. Avoid the buildup of gasoline vapors in the shop, even if you think there are no sources of ignition.

Follow these rules when handling gasoline or other flammables.

1. Of primary importance, gasoline should be used *only* as a source of energy for a gasoline engine. It should never be used for any other purpose.

2. Never use gasoline to clean anything, including your hands. Kerosene or high-flashpoint solvents designed for cleaning parts should always be used to clean parts and tools only. Vaporized gasoline can ignite and flash back to the container you are using.

3. Clean up gasoline spills immediately. If gasoline is spilled inside the shop, open the doors and windows to get plenty of ventilation. Avoid any source of fire or spark, including the use of electric switches, until you get rid of the vapors. Small spills can be wiped up with rags, which then should be disposed of in an approved container. Large spills should be thoroughly flushed with water.

4. If there is a large gasoline spill, such as at the gasoline pump island, shut off the emergency switch to cut electric power at the pumps, and call the local fire department. Do not flush gasoline into the street without approval of the fire department.

5. Perform fuel system work only outside or in a well-ventilated area. When draining the carburetor or a fuel line, catch the gasoline in a container.

6. Gasoline-soaked clothes should be removed immediately and allowed to dry away from any source of ignition. The vapor can catch fire and the liquid can cause skin irritation.

7. Store gasoline only when absolutely necessary and only in an approved safety can (Figure 2–22).

Figure 2–22. Gasoline should be stored in a safety can. *(Eagle Manufacturing Co.)*

Figure 2–23. Oil, gasoline, and solvent-soaked rags should be stored in a metal oil waste can with a lid. *(Eagle Manufacturing Co.)*

8. Never smoke around gasoline. Remember that gasoline can be dangerous if allowed to vaporize around any source of ignition, including a lit cigarette, appliance pilot lights, and electric switches. Obey all *no smoking* signs.

9. Store flammables other than gasoline, such as paints, thinners, and solvents, in approved metal cabinets away from any source of heat. Never pour flammables or combustible liquids down the drain!

10. Store oily and gasoline-soaked rags in an approved metal container (Figure 2–23). When oily rags are left lying about, they could help start a fire. Also, oily rags can ignite by themselves by spontaneous combustion.

BATTERY SAFETY

The storage battery is potentially one of the most dangerous items around the shop. Normally, but especially when being charged, batteries give off explosive hydrogen gas that can be ignited by a flame or spark (Figure 2–24). Moreover, battery electrolyte is an acid solution that can cause damage to eyes and skin, as well as to clothing. The primary rule is to avoid any source of fire around batteries,

Figure 2–24. Storage batteries give off a highly explosive hydrogen gas, especially when being charged. Keep all fire or sparks away from the battery area. *(U.S. Navy)*

including a lit cigarette, cigar, or pipe, an open flame, and sparks from grinding or welding. Follow these precautions when servicing batteries.

1. Wear chemical goggles and neoprene gloves when servicing batteries.

2. Stand at arm's length when removing battery caps.

3. Handle the battery and its acid with care. Wash immediately any part of your body or clothing that comes in contact with battery acid or corrosion. If you get acid in your eyes, they should be washed with water for 15 minutes and you should immediately consult a physician.

4. Do not lean over batteries when making electrical or mechanical connections. Keep your head and body away from the battery as much as possible in case of explosion.

5. Use proper instruments for testing a battery.

6. Avoid overfilling a battery, especially if it is to be charged.

7. Use water and baking soda (a neutralizer) to clean off the top of a battery.

8. Wash your hands immediately after handling a battery.

9. Wear a face shield when using a battery charger.

10. Provide good ventilation when using a battery charger.

11. Remove the cell covers before charging a battery, unless the instructions for the covers say otherwise.

12. Keep open flames and sparks away from a battery. Do not smoke when charging a battery.

13. Turn off the charger before disconnecting its leads (wires) to the battery.

14. Replace the cell covers before moving a battery.

RIDING A MOTORCYCLE IN THE SHOP

You must take extreme care when riding a motorcycle in the shop. You must be particularly careful about other workers (and customers) in the shop. Ride slowly, carefully, and get someone to guide you if you cannot see a certain area or spot.

Never take it for granted that the brakes work. Always test them before starting a customer's motorcycle.

Exhaust gases contain a deadly poison, carbon monoxide, which you cannot see, smell, or taste. It does not take very much carbon monoxide to kill you. Whenever you have an engine operating inside the shop, be sure to attach one end of a flexible exhaust hose to the bike's exhaust pipes. The exhaust hose should lead outdoors or to the shop's ventilation exhaust system. Even if you are working outdoors, you shouldn't work around the exhaust pipe for any length of time while the engine is operating.

KEY TERMS

Compressed air: air under pressure, used to fill tires, to power tools, and to spray paint.

Eye protection: safety glasses or a face shield used to protect the eyes from hazardous substances or objects.

Fire extinguisher: a portable device designed to put out a fire.

Hand tools: tools that are guided and operated by hand.

Power tools: tools powered by electricity, compressed air, or hydraulic fluid.

Safety shoes: protective shoes with steel-capped toes.

Storage battery: a device that uses chemicals to create and store electrical energy.

CHECKUP

1. Describe two items of personal appearance which can affect safety.

2. What protective clothing should you wear for general safety in the shop?

3. Why is it a good idea to wear eye protection in the shop?

4. Why should hand tools be kept clean?

5. List three precautions to follow when using a screwdriver.

6. Why should a hammer never be used to strike a hardened-steel surface?

7. Why is it safer to pull rather than push on an open-end wrench?

8. Why should you wear eye protection when using power tools?

9. Describe three precautions to follow when using electrical equipment.

10. List two dangers involved in using compressed air.

11. Why should compressed air not be used to clean parts when doing a brake job?

12. What can happen if you use compressed air to blow dirt off your clothing?

13. Explain Class A, B, and C fire extinguishers.

14. List nine steps to follow in case of fire.

15. List ten precautions to follow when handling gasoline.

16. What are the two main dangers when handling batteries?

17. Explain how to safely ride a motorcycle in the shop.

DISCUSSION TOPICS AND ACTIVITIES

1. Develop a safety checklist for your shop area. Call all unsafe conditions to the attention of your instructor. Correct any hazards you find.

2. Make a safety inspection of your home work area and correct any hazards you find.

Almost all motorcycle repair operations require the use of hand or power-operated tools. Expert motorcycle craftsmen know their tools. They know how and why they work as they do, know the correct way to use them, and know how to take care of them. In this unit we shall describe the common tools used on most repair operations. Figure 3–1 shows a set of basic hand tools commonly used in motorcycle maintenance and repair. The many special tools required for specialized service jobs will be described in the sections on the specific servicing procedures.

JOB COMPETENCY OBJECTIVES

When you finish reading and studying this unit, you should be able to:

1. Describe the types and uses of screwdrivers.

2. Identify and explain the uses of the common wrenches.

3. Recognize and describe the uses for the common types of pliers.

4. Describe the correct hammer to use on different servicing procedures.

TOOLS

5. Explain the operation of a parts cleaning tank.

6. Demonstrate the ability to find specifications in a shop service manual.

SCREWDRIVERS

The purpose of a screwdriver is to drive and tighten, or to loosen and remove, screws. Many sizes and types of screwdrivers are required for the many types of screws found on motorcycles.

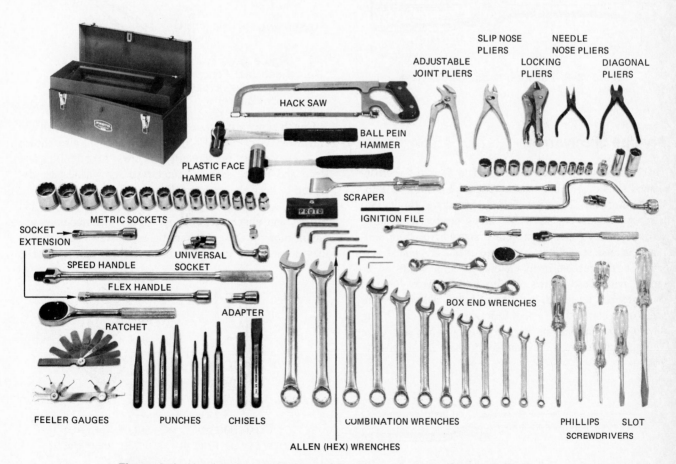

Figure 3–1. Hand tools commonly used in motorcycle work. *(Stanley-Proto Industrial Tools)*

17

Standard screwdriver

The standard screwdriver is used on screws and bolts with slotted heads. The part you grip and turn is the handle. The steel part extending beyond the handle is the shank, and the end of the shank is the blade (Figure 3–2). In standard screwdrivers, the blade is ground flat. Some screwdrivers have a round shank, others a square shank. The conventional screwdriver, with its wood or plastic handle and slim steel shank, is designed to withstand a great deal of twisting force—but only in proportion to its size.

Standard screwdrivers are sized by shank diameter and length. A commonly used standard screwdriver in motorcycle work has a ³⁄₁₆″ blade and a 4″ shank.

The square-shanked screwdriver is sometimes used with a wrench or locking pliers for additional leverage. The wrench or locking pliers are fitted to the square shank and used to help turn the screwdriver. Take care not to use excessive force in turning since the fastener or the screwdriver blade may be damaged. You should never use an ordinary pair of pliers since they will slip and mar the screwdriver shank.

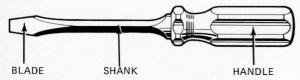

BLADE   SHANK   HANDLE

Figure 3–2. Parts of a standard screwdriver. *(U.S. Navy)*

Phillips screwdriver

The Phillips screwdriver is designed to fit into the cross-shaped slots of a Phillips screw. Figure 3–3 shows a Phillips screwdriver. The cross-shaped screwdriver tip fits into a screw with an x-shaped slot in its head. The Phillips screw was developed to prevent a screwdriver from slipping out and scratching a polished metal or painted surface. For this reason, many motorcycle components are attached with these screws. Phillips screwdrivers come in sets, grouped by length and size of blade. The blades are sized on a numbering system from zero to six, zero being the smallest and six the largest. Numbers two and three Phillips screwdrivers are commonly used in motorcycle work.

Figure 3–3. Phillips screwdriver fits into a phillips-head screw. *(U.S. Navy)*

Special-purpose screwdrivers

At first glance, Reed and Prince cross-slot screws are similar to Phillips screws, but, on close examination, you will find that they are different and require a different type of screwdriver. For one thing, the Reed and Prince slots are deeper and the walls separating the slots are tapered. Figure 3–4 compares a Reed and Prince with a Phillips screwdriver. Note the sharper point designed to fit into the deeper screw head. The screw heads are shown at the left in the figure. Clean the slots and use more pressure than usual when using Reed and Prince screwdrivers.

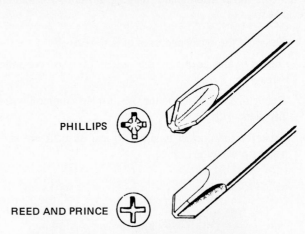

PHILLIPS

REED AND PRINCE

Figure 3–4. Phillips (top) compared to a Reed and Prince (bottom). The Reed and Prince has a much sharper point. *(Hand Tool Institute)*

Clutch screwdrivers are made for turning screws of the clutch-bit type (Figure 3–5). These screws are also known as "figure-eight" or "butterfly" screws. Like Phillips and Reed and Prince screws, clutch-type screwheads are designed to keep the bit from slipping off them.

There are many variations on the Phillips, Reed and Prince, and clutch screwdrivers. Many manufacturers use one or more of these different types of screws in parts that they do not want the consumer to tamper with. You have

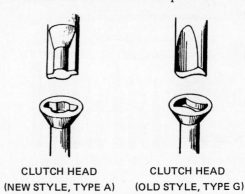

CLUTCH HEAD   CLUTCH HEAD
(NEW STYLE, TYPE A) (OLD STYLE, TYPE G)

Figure 3–5. Clutch-type screwdriver and screws. *(Hand Tool Institute)*

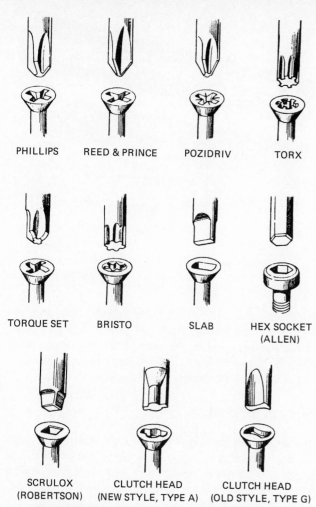

PHILLIPS REED & PRINCE POZIDRIV TORX

TORQUE SET BRISTO SLAB HEX SOCKET (ALLEN)

SCRULOX (ROBERTSON) CLUTCH HEAD (NEW STYLE, TYPE A) CLUTCH HEAD (OLD STYLE, TYPE G)

Figure 3–6. Different screw designs require different screwdrivers. *(Hand Tool Institute)*

to have a special screwdriver for these special screws. A selection of these different types of screwdrivers with their special screwheads is shown in Figure 3–6.

There are many screws on the typical motorcycle engine which are too tight to be removed by any of the foregoing screwdrivers. An impact driver (Figure 3–7) is a valuable addition to a motorcycle mechanic's tool kit. This device is used with screwdriver sockets. The correct-size socket is installed on the end of the impact driver, and the screwdriver tip is placed in the screw slot. A ball pein hammer is then used to strike the end of the impact driver. A cam action device inside the impact driver causes a turning motion when the hammer strikes the impact driver. The tool can be adjusted to loosen or tighten a screw. The combination of impact and twisting will usually loosen the most stubborn screws.

WRENCHES

Wrenches are used to hold, grip, and turn nuts and bolts. There are many different types of wrenches. In fact,

Figure 3–7. An impact driver is used to loosen or tighten very tight screws. *(Snap-On Tool Corp.)*

wrenches are the most common tools found in a motorcycle technician's tool box.

Wrenches are made in different sizes to fit the different sizes of bolts and nuts. The size of a wrench is usually stamped on the wrench end or handle. A fraction is stamped on if the size of the wrench is given in the inch system; for example, 5/16 indicates 5/16″. A whole digit number, such as 12, indicates that the size of the wrench is given in metric: 12 indicates a size of 12 millimeters. Some metric wrenches will have ''mm'' by the number, indicating ''millimeters.'' The wrench shown in Figure 3–8 has 14 stamped on it. This means that the opening of the wrench measures 14 millimeters across the flats and that it will fit on a bolt head or nut that measures 14 millimeters across the flats.

14 MILLIMETER
DISTANCE ACROSS FLATS

Figure 3–8. The wrench size is stamped on the handle. In this case a 14 represents 14 millimeters, the distance across the flats of the jaws.

Open-end wrench

The open-end wrench (Figure 3–9) has an opening at each end of the handle which fits over a bolt or nut. The opening is usually at an angle of 15 degrees to the handle, which makes turning in a tight space easier. Open-end wrenches are made in many different sizes and shapes; most have two open ends of different sizes.

Figure 3–9. An open-end wrench. *(Snap-On Tool Corp.)*

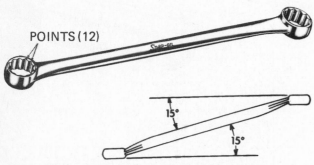

Figure 3–10. A box-end wrench with a 15-degree offset and 12 gripping points. *(Snap-*

Box-end wrench

The box-end wrench, or simply, box wrench (Figure 3–10) is made to fit nuts and bolt heads so that they will not slip off. These wrenches are usually two-ended, with different-size openings on each end. Frequently box wrenches are made with 10-degree or 15-degree offsets. Figure 3–10 shows a wrench with a 15-degree offset. Box wrench openings have 12 gripping slots, or points, for the nut. This is an advantage, since a handle movement of only 30 degrees is needed to get a new bite when turning.

Combination wrench

The combination wrench (Figure 3–11) has two types of openings, both of the same size. At one end of the handle, there is a box wrench for breaking tight nuts loose or pull-

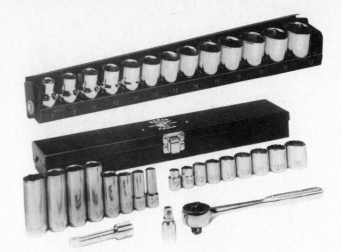

Figure 3–12. Sets of sockets or socket wrenches. The socket fits on a handle for turning. *(Klein Tools, Inc.)*

ing them tight. At the other end, there is an open-end wrench for fast turning. Each end is at a 15-degree offset to the handle, allowing the wrench to clear obstructions when its box end is used. The 15-degree angle on the open end is designed for turning in tight spaces.

Socket wrench

The socket wrench (Figure 3–12) is an improvement over the box wrench in that it will not slip off nuts or bolts and it can also be turned much faster with the aid of several types of handles. Socket wrenches are made in many different sizes to fit the many sizes of bolts and nuts. The term *socket wrench* is often shortened to *socket* in common usage.

Sockets are attached to their handles by a square hole at one end (Figure 3–13). These drive holes are made in different sizes. For small bolts and nuts, socket sets with a ¼″ square drive are useful. For general-purpose work, a ⅜″ drive set is popular. Heavier work requires a ½″ drive socket set; and there are even ¾″ and 1″ drive sets, made for very large nuts and bolts.

Sockets are made with different numbers of points. Figure 3–14 shows sockets that have six, eight, and 12 points. The more points a wrench has, the easier it is to slip it on a bolt or nut. More points also give a better grip when turning. The fewer the points, the more metal there is in the socket to support the bolt, and thus the stronger the socket is. Sockets with fewer points do not grip as well,

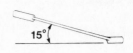

Figure 3–11. Combination wrench. *(Snap-On Tool Corp.)*

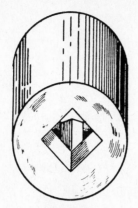

SOCKET END   DRIVE END

Figure 3–13. Socket wrench—12 points are shown on the socket end (left); a handle fits into the square hole of the drive end (right).

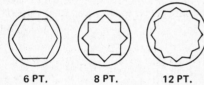

6 PT.   8 PT.   12 PT.

Figure 3–14. Sockets can have a different number of points; 6-, 8-, and 12-point sockets are shown. *(Stanley-Proto Industrial Tools)*

however, and require a greater handle movement to get a new bite. Most sockets have eight or 12 points; six-point sockets are used for heavy duty.

Sockets are available in long or short lengths. Long sockets are used for removing long, threaded parts such as spark plugs. Most standard bolts and nuts can be loosened with a short or shallow socket. A deep and a shallow socket are compared in Figure 3–15.

Some sockets are designed to be used with air or electric power. Sockets designed for use with impact wrenches are made of heavier material than those operated by hand. Only those special impact sockets can be safely used on power equipment. They can usually be identified by their dull gray finish in comparison to the bright chrome used on hand wrenches.

DEEP SOCKET WRENCH

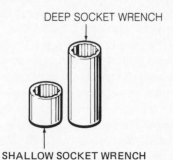

SHALLOW SOCKET WRENCH

Figure 3–15. Shallow and deep socket wrenches. *(U.S. Navy)*

Socket drivers

Various handles or drivers are used to turn the sockets. They are available in different lengths and with different-size drive ends. Handles with ¼″, ⅜″, and ½″ drive ends are commonly used.

Ratchet handles (Figure 3–16) are commonly used to drive sockets. The drive end of the ratchet snaps into the drive end of the socket. As mentioned, different-size drive ends are available. The ratchet handle moves back and forth to drive the socket. When the ratchet catch is snapped in one direction, pulling the handle will result in a tightening action and pushing the handle will simply return it to its starting position without putting force on or removing the socket from the nut or bolt. When the ratchet catch is snapped in the opposite direction, the result will be reversed: pushing the ratchet handle will loosen the nut or bolt and pulling the handle will bring it back to its starting position. This action is illustrated in Figure 3–17.

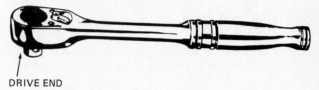

DRIVE END

Figure 3–16. The ratchet handle is a common socket wrench driver. *(Snap-On Tools Corp.)*

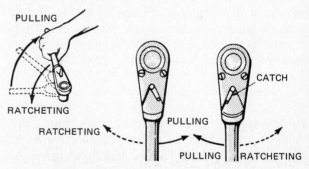

PULLING

RATCHETING

RATCHETING   PULLING

PULLING   CATCH

PULLING   RATCHETING

Figure 3–17. Ratchet handle operation. *(Ford Motor Co.)*

Ratchet handles come in a variety of sizes and lengths. Some are available with a swivel end to help get into obstructed areas. A selection of ratchet handles is shown in Figure 3–18.

A large number of other handles is available to drive socket wrenches. A typical collection of attachments is shown in Figure 3–19. A *speed handle* is shaped like a crank and is used to speed up the process of removing or installing a nut or a bolt. The *breaker bar* has a hinge that will permit driving at different angles. Its long handle lets the mechanic use a good deal of force to loosen a tight nut

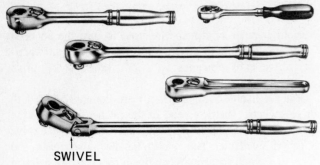

SWIVEL

Figure 3–18. Different styles and sizes of ratchet handles. *(Snap-On Tools Corp.)*

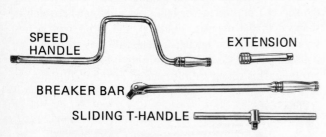

SPEED HANDLE

EXTENSION

BREAKER BAR

SLIDING T-HANDLE

Figure 3–19. Socket drivers and attachments. *(Snap-On Tools Corp.)*

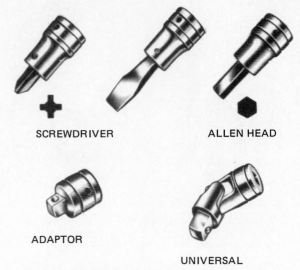

SCREWDRIVER   ALLEN HEAD

ADAPTOR

UNIVERSAL

Figure 3–20. Tools that can be driven by socket wrench handles. *(Snap-On Tools Corp.)*

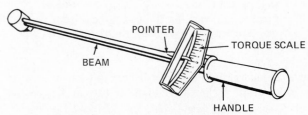

POINTER

TORQUE SCALE

BEAM

HANDLE

Figure 3–21. A torque wrench is used to tighten parts to the correct amount of torque. *(Stanley-Proto Industrial Tools)*

or bolt. The *sliding T-handle* will allow the socket driver to slide to any position along the handle.

An *extension* is also shown in Figure 3–19. Extensions are used to lengthen the distance between the handle and the socket wrench. They are available in different lengths. One end of the extension is connected to a handle or driver, the other to a socket wrench. The extension allows the socket to be used in an area where an ordinary handle would not have enough room to turn. Extensions are also shown in Figures 3–1 and 3–12 (bottom).

Other tools besides sockets can be driven by socket drivers. A collection of these is shown in Figure 3–20. An *adaptor* is used to connect sockets with attachments of different sizes. *Allen head* and *screwdriver sockets* are available for socket handles. The *universal joint* attachment permits a socket to be attached and driven at an angle where space is limited.

Torque wrench

Torque is the word applied to a turning or twisting force. Many motorcycle parts must be tightened to exactly the correct amount of torque. The wrench used to tighten parts to the correct torque is called a *torque wrench*.

One common type of torque wrench, shown in Figure 3–21, is equipped with a beam-and-pointer assembly. During tightening, the beam on the wrench bends as the resistance to turning increases. The pointer lines up with different readings on a torque scale to show the torque, or the

amount the beam is deflected. Another type of torque wrench has a ratchet drive head. Its adjustable handle and scale allows the motorcycle technician to adjust the wrench to a certain torque setting. A clicking signal tells the technician that the bolt or nut is tightened to that torque.

Torque is measured in several different systems. The most common English system units are foot-pounds and inch-pounds. There are 12 inch-pounds in a foot-pound. In the metric system, the most common torque measurements are Newton-meters or meter-kilograms. Figure 3–22 shows torque wrenches with different scales.

Recently, computer technology has been applied to the torque wrench. The electronic torque wrench (Figure 3–23) is a torque wrench with a built-in microprocessor memory. It has a pressure-sensitive keypad and a digital (LCD) readout. As a fastener is tightened, the torque is displayed on the window. There are three operating modes: a display mode in which the torque is shown, a memory mode in which the highest torque applied is shown, and a signal mode in which a buzzer sounds automatically when the selected torque is reached.

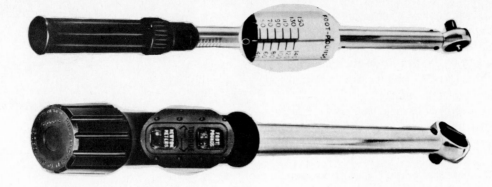

Figure 3–22. Inch-pounds or foot-pounds are used on English-system torque wrenches; Newton-meters or meter-kilograms are used on metric-system torque wrenches. *(Sears, Roebuck and Co.)*

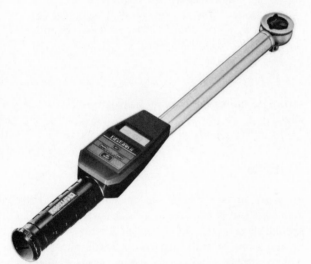

Figure 3–23. Electronic torque wrench. *(Sears, Roebuck and Co.)*

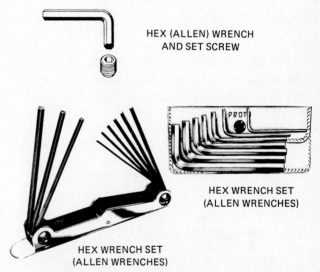

HEX (ALLEN) WRENCH
AND SET SCREW

HEX WRENCH SET
(ALLEN WRENCHES)

HEX WRENCH SET
(ALLEN WRENCHES)

Figure 3–24. Allen-head or hex key wrenches. *(Top: Sears, Roebuck and Co. Bottom: Stanley-Proto Industrial Tools)*

Allen wrench

Some parts of a motorcycle are connected with Allen head screws. Special Allen wrenches are provided to deal with them. The head of the screw has a hexagonal (six-sided) hole. Allen or hex wrenches are also hexagonal, with one long arm and one short arm as shown in Figure 3–24 (top). More leverage is obtained by inserting the short arm of the wrench into the screw head, but you must be careful not to strip the threads or break the screw of the wrench. Allen or hex keys often come in a set, as shown in Figure 3–24 (bottom). Both metric and English system screws and wrenches are used. Try different wrenches until one fits.

Adjustable-end wrench

The wrench shown in Figure 3–25 is called an *adjustable-end wrench*. The jaws of this type of wrench are adjustable

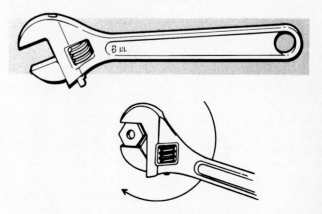

Figure 3–25. Adjustable-end wrench. *(Top: U.S. Navy. Bottom: Hand Tool Institute)*

within their designed limits. When using adjustable-end wrenches, you must be careful to observe the same precautions you would observe when using ordinary open-end wrenches: (1) adjust the jaws to fit snugly against the flats of the nut or bolthead, and (2) pull the wrench toward you, with the fixed jaw doing the pulling.

Once the nut or bolt is turning, you may "flop" the wrench to continue the turning. Keep checking each time you flop the wrench to be sure that the jaws still fit snugly around the nut or bolt. Remember that if you try to pull with the adjustable jaw, and the pull is too heavy, you may snap off the jaw.

Adjustable wrenches vary from about 4″ to about 20″ in length. The longer the wrench, the larger is the adjustment to the opening. For example, a typical 6″ adjustable wrench opens about ¾″ wide, while a 12″ wrench opens about 1⁵⁄₁₆″ wide.

Air impact wrench

The air impact wrench, or simply, impact wrench (Figure 3–26) is used to loosen large nuts and bolts which are very tight. Impact wrenches are power driven, usually by compressed air, although some are electrically driven. They vibrate or impact up and down as they loosen. By reversing a control on the driver, the wrench can be used for tightening. Special heavy-duty impact sockets must be used with impact wrenches. The torque on some impact wrenches can be increased or decreased at will. Impact wrenches can

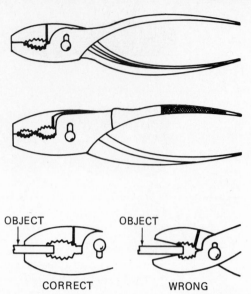

Figure 3–26. Air-operated impact wrench. *(Ingersol-Rand)*

Figure 3–27. Combination or slip-joint pliers. *(Top: Hand Tool Institute. Bottom: Sears, Roebuck and Co.)*

save time but can also cause damage to parts if they are allowed to overtighten them. Impact wrenches are best used for disassembly of large components.

PLIERS

Pliers are an extension of a technician's fingers. There are many types of pliers, and each has a special purpose. They should never be used in place of a wrench to loosen or tighten a nut. A craftsman knows which pliers to use for which purpose—and he or she never uses pliers when some other tool will do the job better.

Combination pliers

The pliers most commonly used in motorcycle work are the 6″ combination pliers (Figure 3–27). They have a slip joint or fulcrum to allow the jaws to open wide enough to grip large diameters and are consequently called slip-joint pliers. Two different adjustments are possible (Figure 3–27), bottom). Use the large adjustment for holding larger objects. Some combination pliers have a side-cutter arrangement for cutting wire or cotter pins. The better grades of combination pliers are made of drop-forged steel and can take a lot of hard usage.

Adjustable-joint pliers

Adjustable-joint or channel lock pliers (Figure 3–28) have jaws that can be adjusted to several different openings. They are useful for grasping and holding larger objects.

Figure 3–28. Adjustable-joint pliers. *(Hand Tool Institute)*

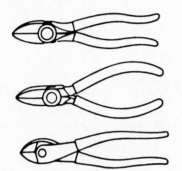

Figure 3–29. Diagonal cutting pliers. *(Hand Tool Institute)*

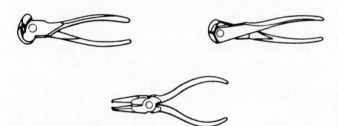

Figure 3–30. End cutting pliers. *(Hand Tool Institute)*

Diagonal pliers

Diagonal pliers (Figure 3–29) are made for the express purpose of cutting wires. For that reason, they have hard cutting edges.

End-cutting pliers

Often grouped with the diagonal pliers are the end-cutting pliers (Figure 3–30). These pliers permit you to cut very close to whatever object the wire extends out of.

Needle-nose pliers

Needle-nose or long-nose pliers (Figure 3–31) have long, slender, tapering jaws which are useful for gripping small objects. In selecting needle-nose and long-nose pliers for your kit, it is most important that the tips of the jaws be perfectly aligned. Some needle-nose pliers are equipped

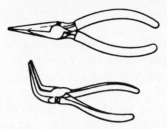

Figure 3–31. Needle-nose or long-nose pliers. *(Hand Tool Institute)*

with side cutters, while others are bent at right angles for hard-to-get-at places. As the jaws become longer and slimmer, more care must be used in handling them.

Snap-ring pliers

The two major types of snap-ring pliers are the inside and outside varieties (Figure 3–32). Inside snap-ring pliers have jaws that close and grip when the handles are closed (like an ordinary pair of pliers), and outside snap-ring pliers have jaws that open when the handles are drawn together. Regardless of how these pliers operate, they have one thing in common: the jaws of each are designed to safely engage the snap ring to be removed or installed.

Snap rings or lock rings are expandable rings which lock parts to shafts. Essentially, they are very powerful springs. If not handled with the proper tools and with adequate care, they can fly off their retaining grooves (or whatever else there is to retain them) and inflict severe damage or even personal injury. Always use the right tool to remove or install any part that has the potential for getting out of control.

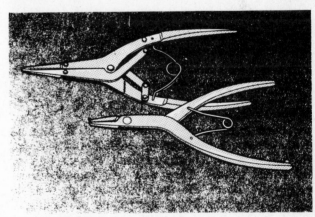

EXPAND EXTERNAL RINGS

COMPRESS INTERNAL RINGS

Figure 3–32. Inside and outside snap ring pliers. *(Top: Ford Motor Co. Bottom: Lisle Corp.)*

Locking pliers

Locking pliers (Figure 3–33) are compound-lever pliers that are clamped to the work. They can be adjusted to different sizes, and once clamped, they remain locked to the work after one's hands are removed. The adjustable lower jaw is retracted by an over-center spring when the locking handle is released. Adjustment of the size of the jaw opening is made by turning a screw at the end of the primary handle. Remember that locking pliers do not take the place of wrenches. However, they are often used to hold nuts which have had their corners rounded off by the misuse of wrenches.

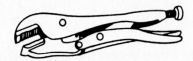

Figure 3–33. Locking pliers. *(Hand Tool Institute)*

HAMMERS

Hammers are often used incorrectly by many mechanics. For example, hardened-steel hammers are designed to drive on other tools such as punches and chisels. They are not intended to drive on motorcycle parts. Parts can quickly be damaged by using the wrong type of hammer.

Ball pein hammer

The ball pein hammer has a face that is square (at right angles) to the end of the handle, with the opposite end of the hammer head (the ball pein) rounded (Figure 3–34). The face of the hammer can be used for normal or light hammering operations. The ball pein is used to form and shape sheet metal or to pein over the end of a pin to form a rivet head, as shown in Figure 3–35. To form a rivet head from a straight pin, strike the end of the pin that is

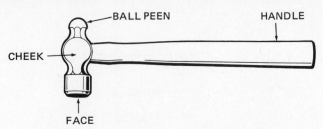

Figure 3–34. Ball-pein hammer. *(U.S. Navy)*

sticking up above the surface with the face of the hammer—just flatten it somewhat. Then turn your hammer over and go to work on the pin until it is properly rounded at its head.

Soft-face hammer

The soft-face hammer (Figure 3–36) has a softer head than the hardened-steel head of the ball pein hammer. Soft-face hammers are used to align or adjust parts that might be damaged by a hardened-steel hammer. The important thing to remember is that sometimes you must use a hammer made of material softer than the material you are working with. A hammer made of material softer than the material it is hammering will not damage that material because it can absorb the force of the impact instead of transmitting it to the material.

The most common soft-face hammers are made from plastic, rubber, and brass. Use brass and plastic hammers for tapping and aligning parts that will be harmed or distorted by steel hammers. Rubber mallets are the softest of

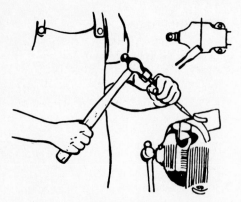

Cutting sheet metal with hammer and chisel

Figure 3–35. Using the ball-pein hammer. *(Left: U.S. Navy. Right: Stanley Works)*

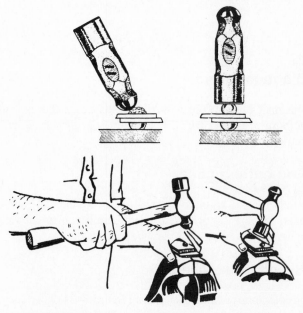

Support materials to be riveted. Flatten head with hammer face. Round head with the ball peen.

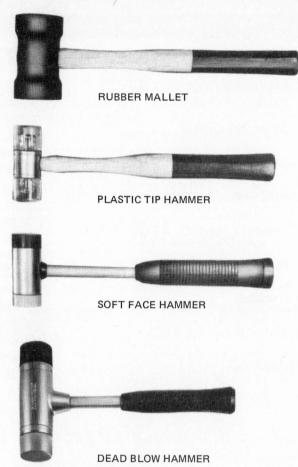

RUBBER MALLET

PLASTIC TIP HAMMER

SOFT FACE HAMMER

DEAD BLOW HAMMER

Figure 3–36. Soft-face hammer. *(Stanley-Proto Industrial Tools)*

Figure 3–37. Solvent parts washer. *(Graymills)*

all hammers, with the possible exception of leather or rawhide mallets.

The dead-blow hammer, shown in Figure 3–36 (bottom), is a type of soft-face hammer that allows you to exert a good deal of force on an object. The hammer head is filled with shot to increase the driving force and eliminate rebound. The dead-blow feature makes this hammer especially useful for loosening engine flywheels.

PARTS CLEANING EQUIPMENT

Parts cleaning is an important part of almost every motorcycle repair job. Parts must be cleaned to determine wear accurately and to prevent dirt from damaging the repair job.

Most motorcycle components are cleaned in a solvent cleaner like the one shown in Figure 3–37. The cleaning tank is filled with solvent which is pumped through a filter and then out of a nozzle. The nozzle stream is directed over the parts. The cleaning solvent thins and washes away grease, oil, and sludge.

SERVICE MANUALS

The service manual is one of the most important tools used by the technician in doing motorcycle repair. A service manual is used to locate specifications or ''specs''—the parts measurements recommended by the motorcycle manufacturer. The technician checks parts measurements against these specifications to determine what kind of servicing is necessary on the part. Service manuals also provide step-by-step procedures for doing motorcycle repair.

The motorcycle mechanic can find specifications and repair procedures in two types of service manual: the owner's manual and the shop service manual.

Owner's manual

An owner's manual (Figure 3–38) is a book that comes with any new motorcycle. It usually explains how to operate the motorcycle. In addition, many owner's manuals explain the basic services that should be performed periodically on the bike. They also typically provide troubleshooting procedures and specifications for common maintenance procedures.

Service manual

Manufacturers' service manuals are provided by motorcycle manufacturers primarily for motorcycle technicians who service motorcycles. The service manual covers one model

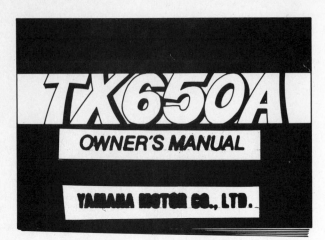

Figure 3–38. The owner's manual provides specifications, maintenance procedures, and troubleshooting help. *(Yamaha Motor Corp. U.S.A.)*

GROUP INDEX	
GENERAL INFORMATION	1
PERIODIC MAINTENANCE AND TUNE-UP PROCEDURES	2
SERVICING ENGINE	3
SHAFT DRIVE	4
FUEL AND LUBRICATION SYSTEM	5
FMISSION CONTROL & REGULATIONS	6
ELECTRICAL SYSTEM	7
CHASSIS	8
SERVICING INFORMATION	9
GS650GL	10

Figure 3–39. Typical index for a shop service manual. *(U.S. Suzuki Motor Corp.)*

of motorcycle in great detail, providing specifications, recommended maintenance, and service procedures.

The first step in using a shop service manual is to be sure that you have the correct manual for the motorcycle year and model you are working on. Usually, the paint and trim on the fuel tank will identify the model of the motorcycle. In some cases, you will have to check the engine or frame serial number. The shop service manual will describe where these numbers are located and how to interpret them.

Next, turn to the index (Figure 3–39), which lists the areas covered by the manual. If you want information on periodic inspection and adjustment, you turn to Section 2. If you need electrical service information, you turn to Section 6. Of course, the contents and organization of each manual differ.

Periodic maintenance information is often organized in the form of a chart like the one shown in Figure 3–40. The item to be maintained is listed along the left side. The work to be done on it is described under ''Remarks.'' The number of kilometers (or miles) between each service interval is charted to the right. For example, cylinder compression should be checked first (initially) at 3,200 kilometers and every 6,400 kilometers thereafter.

Specifications are also often organized into tables. A specification table for engine part tightening torque is shown in Figure 3–41. The part to be tightened is listed along the left side of the table. The thread diameter and part name are shown next, followed by the tightening torque. For example, the cylinder head on the engine shown in the figure uses a 6-millimeter (mm) bolt which should be tightened to 1.0 meter-kilogram (m-kg), or 7 foot-pounds.

It is a good idea to use a ruler or piece of paper as a guide when reading across the chart. Also, write down the

specification: if you rely on memory, you may make an error.

KEY TERMS

Adjustable wrench: a wrench that adjusts to fit bolts of different sizes.

Air impact wrench: a wrench powered by compressed air.

Allen wrench: a hexagonal wrench used to tighten or loosen Allen or hollow-head screws; a hex wrench.

Box-end wrench: a wrench designed to fit all the way around a bolt or nut.

Combination wrench: a wrench with one box end and one open end.

Combination pliers: pliers with a slip joint to allow the jaws to open wide for gripping large objects.

Diagonal cutting pliers: pliers with cutting edges on the jaw, often used for cutting cotter keys.

Hammer: a tool used to drive or pound on an object. Motorcycle hammers may have a hard or a soft head.

Open-end wrench: a wrench with an opening at the end which can slip onto the bolt or nut.

Owner's Manual: a manual supplied with a new motorcycle; includes maintenance and troubleshooting information.

Item	Remarks	Initial				Thereafter every		
		400 (250)	800 (500)	1,600 (1,000)	3,200 (2,000)	1,600 (1,000)	3,200 (2,000)	6,400 (4,000)
Cylinder	Check compression				O			O
Valves	Check/Adjust valve clearance			O	O			O
Cam chain	Check/Adjust chain tension		O					O
Spark plugs	Inspect/Clean or replace as required	O			O		O	
Air filter	Dry type — Clean/Replace as required			O		O		
Carburetor	Check operation/Adjust as required		O		O		O	
Brake system (complete)	Check/Adjust as required — Repair as required		O	O		O		
Clutch	Adjust free play		O		O		O	
Wheel and tires	Check pressure/Wear/Balance	O	O	O		O		
Fuel petcocks	Clean/Flush tank as required	O		O			O	
Battery	Top-up/Check specific gravity and breather pipe	O	O	O	O	O		
Ignition timing	Adjust/Clean or replace parts as required		O	O	O		O	
Lights/Signals	Check operation/Replace as required	O	O	O	O	O		
Fittings/Fasteners	Tighten before each trip and/or ...	O	O	O	O	O		
Generator brushes	Check brush wear/Replace if necessary							O

Figure 3–40. Typical periodic maintenance chart. *(Yamaha Motor Corp. U.S.A.)*

Part to be tightened	Thread dia. and part name	Tightening torque
Engine: Cylinder head and cylinder head cover	10 mm nut 8 mm bolt	3.8 m-kg (27 ft-lb) 2.2 m-kg (16 ft-lb)
Cylinder head	6 mm bolt	1.0 m-kg (7 ft-lb)
Cylinder head cover side	6 mm crown nut 8 mm crown nut	1.0 m-kg (7 ft-lb) 1.5 m-kg (10 ft-lb)
Spark plug	14 mm	2.0 m-kg (14 ft-lb)
Generator	12 mm nut	4.0 m-kg (29 ft-lb)
Stator coil	6 mm pan head screw	1.0 m-kg (7 ft-lb)
Governer	6 mm bolt	0.8 m-kg (6 ft-lb)
Valve clearance adjustment nut	8 mm nut	2.7 m-kg (20 ft-lb)
Cam chain tensioner cover	18 mm cap	2.2 m-kg (16 ft-lb)
Pump cover	6 mm pan head screw	1.0 m-kg (7 ft-lb)
Strainer cover	6 mm bolt	1.0 m-kg (7 ft-lb)
Drain plug	30 mm bolt	4.4 m-kg (32 ft-lb)
Filter cover	6 mm bolt	1.0 m-kg (7 ft-lb)
Oil filter	16 mm bolt	1.0 m-kg (7 ft-lb)

Figure 3–41. Typical specification table. *(Yamaha Motor Corp. U.S.A.)*

Pliers: a tool designed to grip objects.

Phillips screwdriver: a screwdriver with a point on the blade or tip used for driving Phillips screws.

Service manual: manufacturer's manual used by the motorcycle technician; includes specifications and repair procedures.

Socket handles and attachments: tools used to drive socket wrenches.

Socket wrench: a wrench that fits all the way around a bolt or nut; also called a socket, this wrench can be attached to or detached from a handle.

Torque wrench: a wrench designed to tighten bolts or nuts to a certain tightness or torque.

DISCUSSION TOPICS AND ACTIVITIES

1. Try to identify each of the common hand tools you can find in the shop.

2. Make a list of the most important hand tools for a motorcycle technician to have.

CHECKUP

Identify each of the tools shown by writing the names in the spaces provided.

1. _____
2. _____
3. _____
4. _____
5. _____
6. _____
7. _____
8. _____
9. _____
10. _____
11. _____
12. _____
13. _____
14. _____
15. _____
16. _____
17. _____
18. _____
19. _____
20. _____

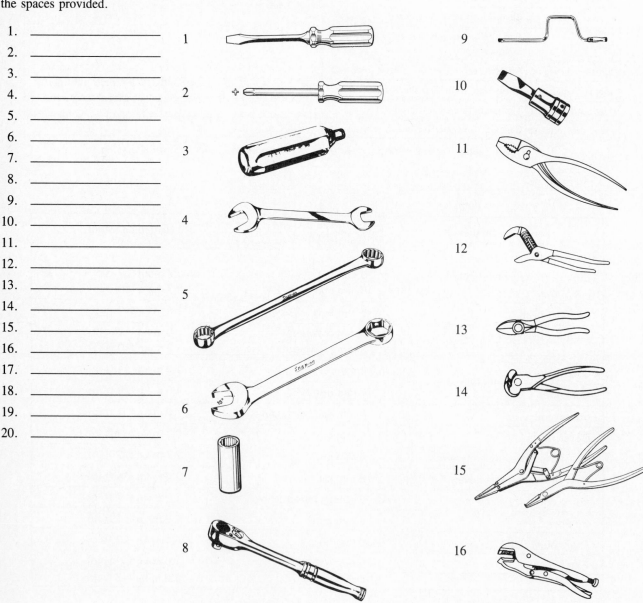

The motorcycle is manufactured to very precise tolerances that have to be maintained when it is repaired. One of the most important parts of any motorcycle repair or maintenance job is measuring. Measuring is done to determine wear and to check parts against specifications. A motorcycle technician must be able to understand measuring systems and use a number of measuring tools to make accurate measurements. In this unit, we shall describe the English and metric measuring systems and the use of English and metric measuring tools.

MEASURING

JOB COMPETENCY OBJECTIVES

When you finish reading and studying this unit, you should be able to:

1. Describe the units of measurement used in the metric measuring system.

2. Describe the units of measurement used in the English (customary) measuring system.

3. Explain how to convert between metric and English measuring units.

4. Demonstrate how to use a metric and English rule.

5. Demonstrate how to measure with a metric and English Vernier caliper.

6. Identify the parts of, and explain how to measure with, a metric and English outside micrometer.

7. Recognize and describe the uses of an inside micrometer, telescoping gauge and small-hole gauge.

8. Demonstrate how to use a feeler gauge to measure the space between two parts.

METRIC MEASURING SYSTEM

Currently, there are two measuring systems in common use. In the United States, the *English* or *customary system* which began in England has a long history and tradition. The *metric system* is the system in use in most of the world. Historically, motorcycles manufactured in England and the United States use English customary measurements. Those from Europe and Japan use metric measurements and metric tools.

In order to standardize the measuring systems of all industrialized countries, the United States, England, Canada, Australia, and other English-speaking countries are switching to the metric system. Eventually, only the metric measuring system will be in use. Until that time, the motorcycle technician must be able to use both measuring systems.

METRIC UNITS OF MEASURE

In the metric system, as in every system, there are seven common areas of measurement: length, mass, time, electric current, temperature, luminous intensity, and substance.

The most common unit of measurement used in motorcycle service work is length. In the metric system the basic unit of length is called a meter, from the Greek word *metron*, meaning measure. Meter is symbolized by the lowercase letter m.

Different sizes of units in the metric system are related by multiples of ten (Figure 4–1). This means that 10 meters equals a unit called the decameter, 10 decameters (100 meters) equals 1 hectometer, and 10 hectometers (1,000 meters) equals a kilometer. Still larger units and smaller units are defined in relation to the basic meter. The names for the different units are formed by a prefix to the word meter.

For motorcycle service, you will measure in millimeters and centimeters. The millimeter is $\frac{1}{1,000}$ of a meter and is symbolized by the lowercase letters mm. The centimeter is $\frac{1}{100}$ of a meter and is symbolized by the lowercase letters cm. From these definitions, 10 millimeters equals 1 centimeter. In the steel ruler shown in Figure 4–2, each mark at the top represents 1 millimeter. For more accuracy, half-millimeter divisions are shown at the bottom of the ruler. Most metric rulers today are marked in millimeters only, since that is considered to be the standard unit. As a motorcycle technician, you will work in millimeters

MULTIPLE OR SUBMULTIPLE	PREFIX	SYMBOL	MEANING
1000	kilo	k	ONE THOUSAND TIMES
100	hecto	h	ONE HUNDRED TIMES
10	deka	da	TEN TIMES
0.1	deci	d	ONE TENTH OF
0.01	centi	c	ONE HUNDREDTH OF
0.001	milli	m	ONE THOUSANDTH OF

Figure 4–1. Basic prefixes used in metric measure. *(Comteck)*

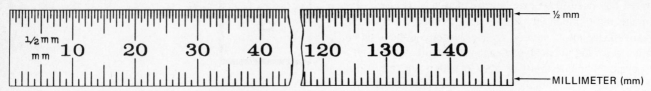

Figure 4–2. Millimeter rule. *(L.S. Starrett Co.)*

more than centimeters. The wrenches you use on the job are measured in millimeters.

The millimeter is the smallest standard unit of measurement of the metric system. In the shop, however, you may want to measure dimensions even smaller than 1 millimeter. This is made possible by subdividing the millimeter decimally into tenths or hundredths of a millimeter, usually written as decimal fractions, e.g., 0.1 mm or 0.01 mm. Note that the placement of the decimal point is very important: to indicate $^5\!/_{10}$ of a millimeter, you would write 0.50 mm; to indicate $^5\!/_{100}$ of a millimeter, you would write 0.05 mm. The difference between 0.50 mm and 0.05 mm is $^{45}\!/_{100}$ of a millimeter. Figure 4–3 compares the approximate positions of 0.05 mm and 0.50 mm on a metric ruler. Be careful when you read decimal parts of a millimeter.

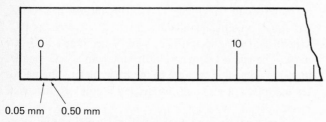

0.05 mm   0.50 mm

Figure 4–3. Position of 0.05 mm and 0.50 mm on a scale. *(Volkswagen of America)*

ENGLISH (CUSTOMARY) MEASURING SYSTEM

The basic unit of length in the English system is the inch. The inch can be divided into common fractional divisions or decimal fractional divisions, for example, ½ inch or 0.500 inch. Both mean half an inch.

In fractional division, we take the whole—one inch—and divide that in half, giving us two halves. Then we can divide one of the halves into two quarters; one of the quarters into two eighths; one of the eighths into two sixteenths; one of the sixteenths into two thirty-seconds; and one of the thirty-seconds into two sixty-fourths. That is about as far as we can go without using special measuring devices. Figure 4–4 illustrates this concept of fractional division.

The inch is divided into 16 parts on a normal inch rule, which is often 6 or 12 inches long. The rule shown in Figure 4–4 (bottom) is 6 inches long. The lines that go all the way across the rule divide it into 1-inch intervals. The next longest lines divide each inch into half-inch intervals. Each half-inch interval is then equally divided into quarter-inch intervals, each quarter-inch into eighth-inch intervals, and finally, each eighth-inch into sixteenth-inch intervals.

Many times, a division smaller than ¹⁄₁₆ inch is necessary for motorcycle service work. The machinist's precision steel rule shown in Figure 4–5 has one side of the rule divided into thirty-seconds of an inch and the other side into sixty-fourths of an inch. To use this rule, place one of its ends at one end of the length to be measured and then determine which of the marks on the rule most nearly lines up with the other end of the length to be measured. The numbers on the rule count off the number of ¹⁄₃₂-inch or ¹⁄₆₄-inch divisions.

Decimal rules are available which divide the inch into ten parts, i.e., into multiples of ten. Figure 4–6 shows a rule divided into tenths of an inch (top) and one divided hundredths of an inch (bottom).

You can convert inch fractions into decimals by dividing the bottom part of the fraction (the denominator) into the top part (the numerator). For example, if you wanted to convert the fraction ⁶¹⁄₆₄ to a decimal you'd divide 64 into 61 to get 0.9531 inch, which is read as $^{9,531}\!/_{10,000}$ of an inch. Given the right instruments, we can measure things in ten-thousandths of an inch rather than in the more cumbersome sixty-fourths of an inch. In general, more accurate measurements can be made using decimals than using inch fractions.

CONVERTING BETWEEN METRIC AND ENGLISH MEASUREMENTS

The motorcycle technician will probably be working on both English system and metric system motorcycles. Since measuring tools are very expensive, it may not always be that both metric and English measuring tools are available. Thus, you may have a specification written in millimeters and have tools that measure in thousandths of an inch.

You will need to know how to use a conversion chart. A conversion chart lists units of one system in one column and their equivalent units in the other system in another column.

Conversion or changeover from one system to the other may also be done through multiplying by a number called a *conversion factor*. Typical conversion factors are shown

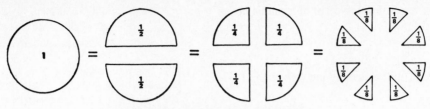

FRACTIONS ARE PART OF A WHOLE

$$\frac{8}{8} = \frac{4}{4} = \frac{2}{2} = 1$$

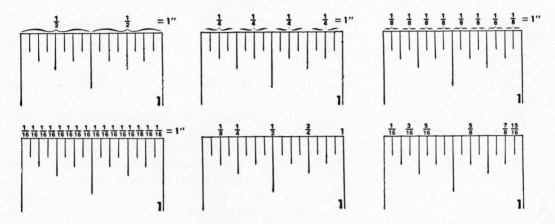

FRACTIONS

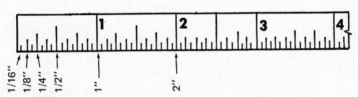

INCH RULE

Figure 4–4. Fractions in the inch system. *(Comteck)*

Figure 4–5. Precision machinist's steel rule. *(L.S. Starrett Co.)*

Figure 4–6. Decimal inch rule with 100 parts to the inch. *(L.S. Starrett Co.)*

in Figure 4–7. Thus, a specification of 10 mm can be converted to inches as follows:

Example:

Multiply the number of millimeters by the conversion factor, 0.03937.

$$10 \times 0.03937 = 0.3937$$

$$10 \text{ mm} = 0.33937 \text{ inch}$$

Similarly, 45 mm would convert to 1.772 inches (45 × 0.03937).

You can convert inches to millimeters by multiplying by 25.40, the number of millimeters in an inch. For example, 2¼ (2.25) inches would convert to 57.15 mm (2.25 × 25.40).

TO FIND		MULTIPLY	×	CONVERSION FACTORS
MILLIMETERS	=	INCHES	×	25.40
CENTIMETERS	=	INCHES	×	2.540
CENTIMETERS	=	FEET	×	30.48
METERS	=	FEET	×	.3048
KILOMETER	=	FEET	×	.0003048
KILOMETER	=	MILES	×	1.609
INCHES	=	MILLIMETERS	×	.03937
INCHES	=	CENTIMETERS	×	.3937
FEET	=	CENTIMETERS	×	.0328
FEET	=	METERS	×	3.281
FEET	=	KILOMETERS	×	3281.
YARDS	=	METERS	×	1.094
MILES	=	KILOMETERS	×	.6214

Figure 4–7. Converting from one system to another.

USING MEASURING TOOLS

We next describe the most common measuring tools used by the motorcycle technician. The type of measuring tool you choose to do your measuring is sometimes determined by how precise your measurement must be. Sometimes more than one kind of tool will do the job. In such a case, you may make the decision on the basis of what kinds of tools are available in the shop or which ones you like to use.

Rule

The rule (ruler) is the most common measuring tool and is used to make many measurements during motorcycle service work. It may be made of paper, wood, or plastic, but precision rules are made of steel. The rule is graduated, or divided, into a number of spaces. To use the instrument, place it next to the part being measured, being careful to align the end of the rule with the end of the part. Then

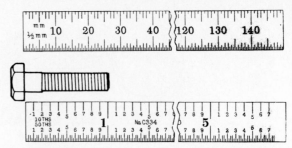

Figure 4–8. Measuring by rule: bolt length in 25.5 mm (top) or 1″ (bottom). (L.S. Starrett Co.)

compare the length of the part with the graduations on the rule.

Suppose, for example, that you wanted to measure the length of a bolt like the one shown in Figure 4–8 (center). You would place the end of the rule against the head of the bolt, as shown. For the millimeter rule, you count millimeter divisions over from the end of the rule until you get to the end of the bolt. The rule is marked off in 10-millimeter intervals. In the figure, the sum comes to 20 plus 5½, or 25.5, mm. For the inch rule, you read over in inches and fractions of an inch. As thus measured, the bolt is 1″ long.

Slide caliper

The slide caliper (Figure 4–9) is used for making both outside and inside measurements. Outside measurements can, of course, be made on any object but are most commonly taken on cylindrical objects such as a bolt shaft or a piston. Inside measurements are, as the name implies, made on the inside of an object, as, e.g., inside a cylinder opening. Any opening on the motorcycle engine can be measured, as long as the jaws of the slide caliper can fit in. The width of the caliper's closed jaws runs in two sizes: ⅛″ and ¼″ (6 mm only, for metric calipers).

The slide caliper shown in Figure 4–9 is based on the inch system. Readings can be made to a sixty-fourth of an inch. Figure 4–10 shows an inch caliper being used to take measurements.

In measuring, the jaws of the caliper fit around the object or into the opening to be measured. The front jaw is called the *fixed jaw;* the movable jaw slides to adjust to the size of the object. The bar with the moveable jaw has OUT/IN or OUTSIDE/INSIDE printed on its side to identify which scale is to be read for each type of measurement. You read up to the fixed-jaw bar for the inch scale.

A clamping screw is used to set the movable-jaw slide at any particular opening, which is very convenient. You merely set the slide caliper to fit the specific object, clamp the movable jaw with the clamping screw, and then bring the caliper up for reading. The clamping screw assures that

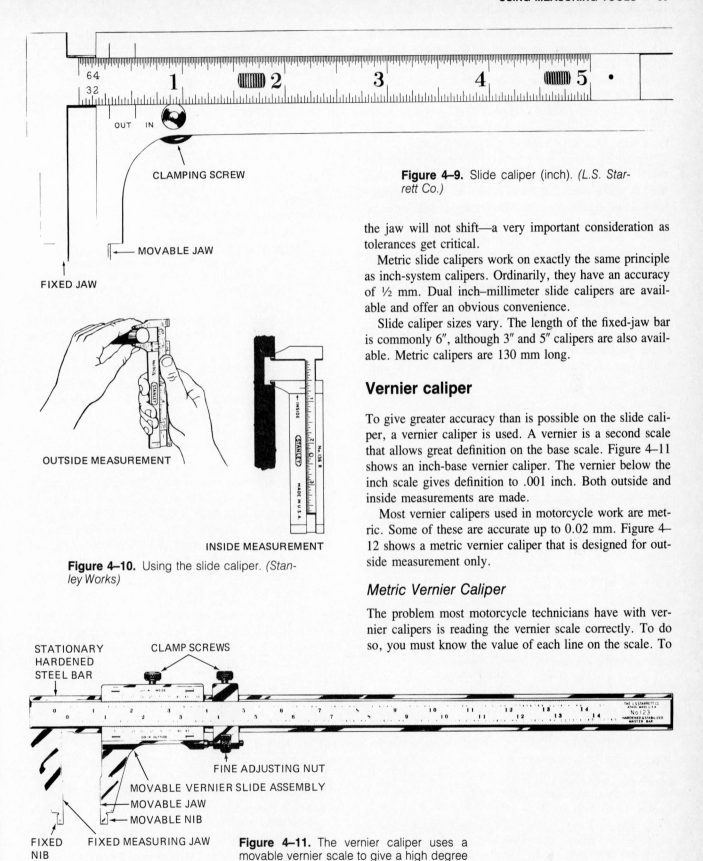

OUT IN

CLAMPING SCREW

MOVABLE JAW

FIXED JAW

Figure 4–9. Slide caliper (inch). *(L.S. Starrett Co.)*

the jaw will not shift—a very important consideration as tolerances get critical.

Metric slide calipers work on exactly the same principle as inch-system calipers. Ordinarily, they have an accuracy of ½ mm. Dual inch–millimeter slide calipers are available and offer an obvious convenience.

Slide caliper sizes vary. The length of the fixed-jaw bar is commonly 6″, although 3″ and 5″ calipers are also available. Metric calipers are 130 mm long.

Vernier caliper

To give greater accuracy than is possible on the slide caliper, a vernier caliper is used. A vernier is a second scale that allows great definition on the base scale. Figure 4–11 shows an inch-base vernier caliper. The vernier below the inch scale gives definition to .001 inch. Both outside and inside measurements are made.

Most vernier calipers used in motorcycle work are metric. Some of these are accurate up to 0.02 mm. Figure 4–12 shows a metric vernier caliper that is designed for outside measurement only.

Metric Vernier Caliper

The problem most motorcycle technicians have with vernier calipers is reading the vernier scale correctly. To do so, you must know the value of each line on the scale. To

OUTSIDE MEASUREMENT

INSIDE MEASUREMENT

Figure 4–10. Using the slide caliper. *(Stanley Works)*

STATIONARY HARDENED STEEL BAR

CLAMP SCREWS

FINE ADJUSTING NUT

MOVABLE VERNIER SLIDE ASSEMBLY

MOVABLE JAW

MOVABLE NIB

FIXED NIB

FIXED MEASURING JAW

Figure 4–11. The vernier caliper uses a movable vernier scale to give a high degree of accuracy to the main scale. *(L.S. Starrett Co.)*

figure out the line value, count the lines on the vernier scale, but *do not count the zero line*. The caliper shown in Figure 4–12 has ten lines on the vernier scale. Since the distance between each line on the main scale is 1.00 mm, to find the distance between each line on the vernier scale, you would divide 10 into 1.00 mm. Thus, each line on the vernier scale has a value of 0.10 mm. Each line on the main scale, of course, represents a full millimeter.

The setting shown in Figure 4–12 is for some value less than 1 mm. To get the exact reading, examine the vernier scale to find a mark that lines up with the main millimeter scale. In the figure, the eighth vernier scale mark is the one that so lines up. The setting shown thus represents 0.80 mm.

In Figure 4–13, the vernier zero falls between 3 and 4 mm. The full mm reading, therefore, is 3 mm. *Remember:* The vernier scale zero, not the end of the vernier scale, gives you the full mm reading. Then look along the vernier scale until you find a vernier scale line which lines up exactly with a main scale line. This is your decimal portion of the measurement.

In Figure 4–13 the vernier scale lines up with the main

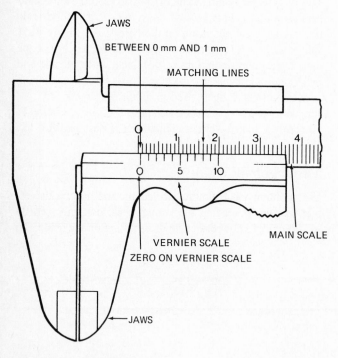

0.00 mm FULL READING
0.80 mm DECIMAL READING
0.80 mm TOTAL READING

Figure 4–12. Scales on a metric system vernier caliper. A reading of 0 mm is shown on the main scale, and the vernier scale decimal value is 0.80, for a total of 0.80 mm. *(Volkswagen of America)*

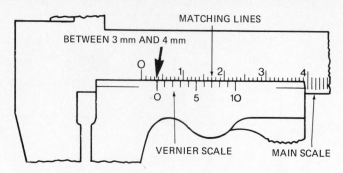

3.00 mm FULL READING
0.70 mm DECIMAL READING
3.70 mm TOTAL READING

Figure 4–13. The full reading on the main scale is 3 mm and the vernier decimal value is 0.70 mm, for a total of 3.70 mm. *(Volkswagen of America)*

millimeter scale at 7, representing 0.70 mm. The reading is therefore 3.70 mm: 3.00 mm full reading plus 0.70 mm decimal reading.

On the caliper shown in Figure 4–14, the full millimeter reading is 6 mm and the decimal reading is 0.30 mm. Thus, the total reading is 6.30 mm: 6.00 mm full reading plus 0.30 mm decimal reading.

Inch Vernier Caliper

English system vernier calipers are used in exactly the same way as metric system ones. The only difference is that the main and vernier scales are divided into parts of an inch instead of parts of a millimeter. Inches are numbered in sequence over the full range of the main scale on the bar. The bar is graduated into 20 divisions, each of which is a twentieth of an inch, i.e., 0.050 inch. The vernier plate is graduated in 50 parts, each representing .001 inch. Every fifth vernier line is numbered—5, 10, 15, 20,

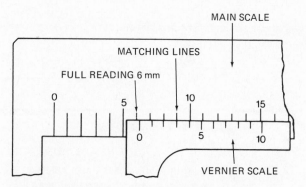

6.00 FULL READING
0.30 DECIMAL READING
6.30 TOTAL READING

Figure 4–14. The full reading is 6 mm and the vernier decimal value is 0.30 mm, for a total of 6.30 mm. *(Volkswagen of America)*

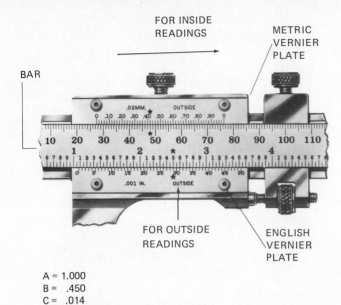

A = 1.000
B = .450
C = .014
TOTAL = 1.464

Figure 4–15. An English vernier caliper with a reading of 1.464 inches. *(L.S. Starrett Co.)*

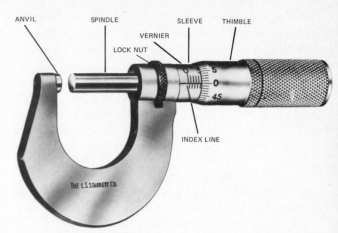

Figure 4–16. Parts of an outside micrometer. *(L.S. Starrett Co.)*

25 and so on to 50. This makes it easy to count the lines.

An example of an English system vernier reading is shown in Figure 4–15. The vernier plate has been moved to the right one and four-tenths plus one-twentieth (0.050) inches (1.450), as shown on the bar. The fourteenth line on the vernier slide exactly coincides with a line; therefore, you must add fourteen-thousandths of an inch to the reading on the bar. Your total reading is thus one and four-hundred sixty-four thousandths of an inch. In summary, to get your reading, add the following figures together:

The full reading on the bar	1.000
Additional reading past the inch	.450
Reading on the vernier plate	.014
Total reading	1.464

Outside micrometer

As we have seen, the caliper is really just a millimeter ruler (the main scale) with a device on it (the vernier scale) that allows you to accurately measure dimensions less than 1 mm or .025 inch long. Most measuring instruments will have just such an arrangement: one scale to obtain the full reading and another to accurately obtain the decimal reading.

Like the caliper, the micrometer is a refinement on the ruler. The purpose of both instruments is the same: to accurately measure dimensions. Like the caliper, the micrometer has two scales that must be read correctly.

The parts of an outside micrometer are shown in Figure 4–16. The measuring surfaces are at the ends of the sta-tionary anvil and the movable spindle. The spindle is actually an extension of a precision-ground screw which threads into the sleeve. Since the other end of the screw is attached to the thimble, turning the thimble moves the spindle toward or away from the anvil.

The part to be measured is placed between the anvil and spindle faces. The spindle is rotated with the thimble until the anvil and spindle both lightly contact the part to be measured. The measurement is read from the graduations on the sleeve and thimble. Always run the spindle up to the object being measured until it lightly touches; do not force the spindle against the object.

An example of a sleeve and thimble reading for a metric micrometer is shown in Figure 4–17. The full reading, or main scale, is provided on the sleeve. The sleeve is first divided into 25 equal divisions to indicate 1-mm gradua-tions. Then, each 1-mm graduation is subdivided into two equal divisions to indicate 0.50 mm.

The thimble is divided into 50 equal divisions, with ev-ery fifth line numbered. One complete revolution of the thimble moves the spindle 0.50 mm. Accordingly, one di-

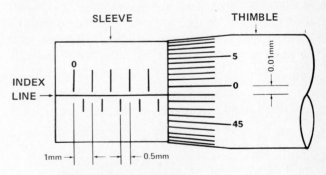

4.00 mm SLEEVE READING
0.50 mm SLEEVE READING
0.49 mm THIMBLE READING
4.99 mm TOTAL READING

Figure 4–17. Metric micrometer scales. A reading of 4.99 mm is shown. *(MTI Corp.)*

vision on the thimble is equal to one-fiftieth of 0.5 mm, or 0.01 mm, two divisions on the thimble equals 0.02 mm, three divisions equals 0.03 mm, and so forth.

In order to read a metric micrometer, add together the number of millimeters visible on the sleeve and the number of lines on the thimble that indicate hundredths of a millimeter. Do not omit the 0.50 mm graduation on the sleeve if it is visible. In Figure 4–17 the sleeve shows a reading of 4 mm and 0.50 mm; the thimble shows a reading of 0.49 mm. The total reading is therefore 4.99 mm.

Suppose now that you wanted to measure a motorcycle part. You place the part in the micrometer and turn the thimble until it closes on the part. The main and thimble scales might look like those shown in Figure 4–18.

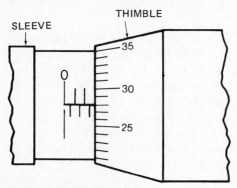

2.00 mm SLEEVE READING
0.50 mm SLEEVE READING
0.28 mm THIMBLE READING
2.78 mm TOTAL READING

Figure 4–18. A metric micrometer reading of 2.78 mm. *(Volkswagen of America)*

To read the measurement, start at zero on the main scale and count over to the last visible line above the index line. In the figure it is 2 mm. Then, look below the index line and see if a line is showing. In the figure one is, so 0.50 mm must be added to the first reading. Next, the thimble scale is checked. In the figure, the index line points to a line three lines past the twenty-fifth line, so 0.28 mm must be added to the first two readings. The part is thus 2.78 mm thick:

$$
\begin{array}{r}
2.00 \text{ mm from above the index line} \\
0.50 \text{ mm from below the index line} \\
+\,0.28 \text{ mm from the thimble scale} \\
\hline
2.78 \text{ mm}
\end{array}
$$

Inch Micrometer

The scales of an English system micrometer are shown in Figure 4–19. The English micrometer sleeve is divided into 40 equal parts, each of which is indicated by a vertical line. Each vertical line thus represents one-fortieth of an inch, or .025″, and every fourth line is marked by a longer

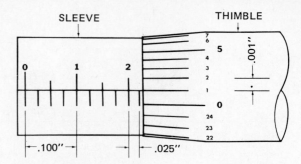

.200″ SLEEVE READING
.025″ SLEEVE READING
.001″ THIMBLE READING
.226″ TOTAL READING

Figure 4–19. The scale of an English micrometer with a reading of 0.226 inch. *(MTI Corp.)*

line and a number which designates some unit number of hundreds of hundred thousandths of an inch. More simply, the line marked ''1'' represents .100″, the line marked ''2'' represents .200″, and so forth.

The thimble is divided into 25 equal parts, and one complete rotation of the thimble coincides with the smallest division on the sleeve, or .025″. Thus, each division on the thimble is one twenty-fifth of .025″, or .001″.

In Figure 4–19, note that the thimble has stopped at a point beyond ''2'' on the sleeve, indicating an initial reading of .200″. Since one additional line is visible between the graduation numbered ''2'' and the edge of the thimble, a subsequent reading of .025″ is indicated. Finally, the line numbered ''1'' on the thimble coincides with the center line of the sleeve, meaning that another one-thousandth of an inch must be added to the sum of the first two readings. Thus, the total reading is .226″:

$$
\begin{array}{l}
.200″ \text{ from above the index line} \\
.025″ \text{ from below the index line} \\
\underline{.001″} \text{ from the thimble scale} \\
.226″
\end{array}
$$

Ratchet Micrometer

Most micrometers are adjusted against the surface of the part being measured by turning the thimble to tighten the spindle. It is important, of course, that you do not turn the thimble too tightly against the part. If the spindle is turned too hard, it will affect the reading of the measurement. Also, too great a pressure when turning the thimble could damage the tool. With practice, of course, you will learn just the right amount of pressure needed. To avoid this problem with pressure, and to guarantee that an accurate reading is taken, a special ratchet micrometer has been developed (Figure 4–20). After the spindle is moved against the part, the ratchet is turned to guarantee that the

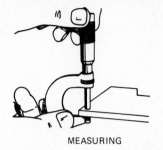

RATCHET

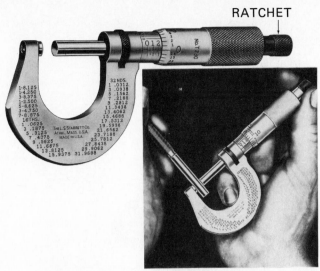

Figure 4–20. A ratchet micrometer guarantees that a given amount of pressure is always applied. *(L.S. Starrett Co.)*

required pressure is applied (bottom). The ratchet will not allow excess pressure to be transferred to the spindle.

Digital Micrometers

Inch and metric micrometers with a digital readout are also used today. Figure 4–21 shows a digital inch micrometer. Readings to thousandths of an inch are taken from the thimble and sleeve. Fast and very accurate readings can easily be taken.

Holding the Micrometer

When you use an outside micrometer, retract the spindle by turning the thimble. Hold the micrometer by the frame, as shown in Figure 4–22, and then turn the thimble with the thumb and index finger of the right hand. Now slip the part to be measured between the anvil and the spindle, and turn the thimble to the part until you feel a slight pressure against the part. If you have a ratchet micrometer, turn the ratchet stop (knurled knob) above the sleeve. This will al-

Figure 4–21. Digital micrometer. The Inch version is shown, but millimeter digital micrometers are also available. *(L.S. Starrett Co.)*

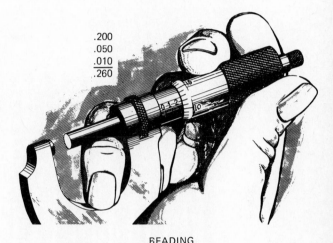

MEASURING

.200
.050
.010
‾‾‾‾
.260

READING

Figure 4–22. Holding the micrometer. *(U.S. Navy)*

low just the right amount of pressure to be exerted. Now you are ready to read the dimension value.

Dial indicator

A dial indicator is a precision measuring tool that is used to measure variations or runout on parts. It is often used for a comparison between two conditions, such as how much play there is when a crankshaft is fully against the front shoulder of the main bearing versus how much there is when it is fully against the rear shoulder of the main bearing.

Metric Dial Indicator

The metric dial indicator (Figure 4–23) has a dial-type gauge. Like the caliper and micrometer, it has two scales. A small inner pointer is used with the small inner scale to show the full millimeter reading. The outer pointer and scale are used to show the decimal part of a millimeter.

A plunger or tracer pin is connected to the scales by a set of gears inside the instrument. The plunger can move in and out and is used to "feel" movement in motorcycle parts. This means that the scales on the indicator must indicate in and out motion. This motion is passed to the scales by the plunger. The dial indicator is mounted on or

INNER POINTER

OUTER SCALE ADJUSTING KNOB

OUTER SCALE HUNDREDTHS OF A MILLIMETER

FULL MM INNER SCALE

TRACER PIN OR PLUNGER

MOUNTING ATTACHMENT

Figure 4–23. A dial indicator mounted to a cylinder head. *(Central Tool Company)*

near the part to be measured with a set of clamp attachments, as shown in Figure 4–23.

The tracer pin or plunger can move freely in or out, and as a result, the pointers will move clockwise or counterclockwise. As the tracer pin moves in, the outer pointer will move clockwise and the inner pointer will move counterclockwise (Figure 4–24), resulting in a higher value reading. As the tracer pin moves out, the outer pointer will move counterclockwise and the inner pointer will move clockwise, showing a lower valued reading.

The tracer pin is spring loaded so that its normal condition is fully extended. If you were to use the indicator under this condition, it would only indicate movement toward the indicator. (The tracer pin could only move inward.) You would then always have to start your measurement with the piece being positioned so that all movement would be toward the dial indicator. However, this is not always possible. To overcome the problem, you usually start your measurement with the tracer pin partially pushed *in*. This is called *preloading* the indicator. The amount of preload you put on the indicator depends on the amount of play you expect to find. You should preload to a little more than the expected measurement.

As the tracer pin moves in and out, the dial indicator will indicate some figure up the scale and then some figure down the scale. The total amount of movement is the difference between the lower valued and higher valued readings. Calculating this difference could be confusing and might result in an incorrect figure. Accordingly, to make it easier for you, the outer scale on a dial indicator rotates so that you can reposition the scale anywhere on the face of the dial.

To move the outer scale, loosen the outer scale adjusting knob and rotate the scale until the zero on the scale is aligned with the outer pointer. The zero is set when the tracer pin is at its lowest point. The knob is then tightened. By preloading the indicator and then *resetting* the outer scale to the zero on the lowest reading below the preload, the amount of play becomes the highest reading you can get on the dial indicator. You can then read directly from the scale.

Figure 4–25 illustrates how to read a metric system dial indicator. The outer scale is divided into 100 divisions, each of which represents one-hundredth of a millimeter (0.01 mm). Accordingly, the smallest amount of movement that the dial indicator can measure accurately is 0.01

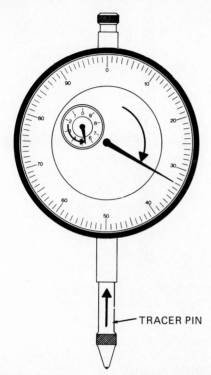

Figure 4–24. When the tracer pin moves up, the outer needle moves clockwise while the inner needle moves counterclockwise. *(Volkswagen of America)*

TRACER PIN

Figure 4–25. A dial indicator reading of 2.66 mm. *(Volkswagen of America)*

0.010″
0.002″
0.0005″
0.0125″ TOTAL READING

Figure 4–26. An English-system micrometer with a reading of 0.0125″. *(L.S. Starrett Co.)*

mm. The inner scale of a dial indicator is marked off in ten divisions, each representing one millimeter in length. To read the dial indicator, you first get the full millimeter reading from the small inner scale and then the hundredths-of-a-millimeter reading from the large outer scale. Note that one complete revolution by the outer pointer ($^{100}/_{100}$) equals 1 mm on the inner scale, so three revolutions are equal to 3 mm.

In Figure 4–25, the reading on the small scale is a little over halfway between 2 mm and 3 mm. The reading on the large scale is 0.66 mm. The total reading is thus 2.66 mm:

    2.00 mm inner scale reading
    0.66 mm outer scale reading
    2.66 mm

Inch Dial Indicator

The English system dial indicator works and is used in the same way as its metric system counterpart. English system dial indicators are usually classified as either thousandths (0.001″) or half-thousandths (0.005″) indicators. This information is marked on the face of the dial, as shown in Figure 4–26. The dial may be of the balanced type, in which the figures read both to the right and to the left of zero, or it may be of the continuous reading type, in which the figures read from zero only in a clockwise direction.

The dial is graduated so that each interval represents a definite movement of the plunger, which is designed so that it will move in and out. On thousandths type indicators, each graduation represents 0.001″.

The English system dial indicator shown in Figure 4–26 has its scale divided into large lines that represent .005″

and smaller lines that represent .001″. Each .001″ is further divided into two parts, each representing .0005″.

To read the dial indicator shown in Figure 4–26, count the last full number the needle has passed and multiply by one one-hundredths, resulting in a reading of .010. (Assume the needle has moved counterclockwise.) Then add the number of thousandths (2) multiplied by one one-thousandth (.002), and finally, add the number of half-thousandths (1) multiplied by one half-thousandth (.0005). The total reading is:

$$
\begin{array}{r}
0.010'' \\
0.002'' \\
+\,0.0005'' \\
\hline
0.0125''
\end{array}
$$

Inside micrometer

The inside micrometer is used to measure the inside of a hole, such as that formed by a hollow cylinder. As shown in Figure 4–27, measuring rods of different lengths and spacing collars are supplied with the micrometer. Different ranges of measurement are used by assembling different rods into the micrometer head. Widths from 2″ to 32″ and from 50 mm to 800 mm are available.

The scale on the inside micrometer works and is read exactly like that of the outside micrometer. Both metric and inch scales are available. It takes a little more practice to get an accurate measurement with an inside micrometer. It can easily be cocked in the bore and give an incorrect reading. For accurate measurement, make sure the micrometer is at right angles to the centerline of the bore. Then move one end back and forth slightly to get the maximum reading on the scales.

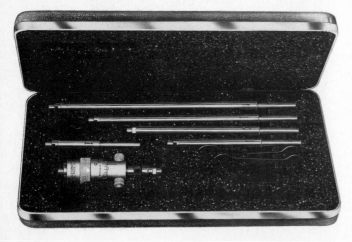

Figure 4–27. An inside micrometer set. *(L.S. Starrett Co.)*

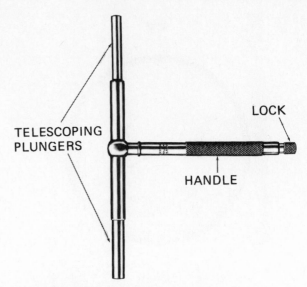

Figure 4–28. A telescoping gauge is used to measure the inside of a hole. *(L.S. Starrett Co.)*

Telescoping gauge

Like the inside micrometer, the telescoping gauge is used to measure the inside dimension of a hole. Telescoping gauges are made in sets to measure anything from very small to very large holes.

A telescoping gauge (Figure 4–28) has a handle which is attached to two spring-loaded plungers. A lock on the end of the handle is used to control the movement of the plungers. The gauge is placed into the hole and the handle is unlocked, permitting the plungers to expand to the size of the hole. When the proper feel is obtained, the handle is turned to lock the plungers in position. Figure 4–29 (top) shows a telescoping gauge being used to measure an opening. The exact size of the hole is found by removing the gauge and measuring across the ends of the plungers with an outside micrometer (Figure 4–29, bottom).

Small-hole gauge

When the hole you wish to measure is too small for an inside micrometer or telescoping gauge, you may use a small-hole gauge (Figure 4–30). The small-hole gauge has a split sphere whose diameter can be changed by means of an internal wedge which is made to slide up or down by turning the handle. The gauge is placed into the hole to be measured and adjusted to fit the internal dimension (Figure 4–31, top). After it is removed from the hole, an outside micrometer (Figure 4–31, bottom) is used to measure the diameter of the split sphere. The measurement is the hole size. Small hole gauges come in sets to cover various sizes of holes.

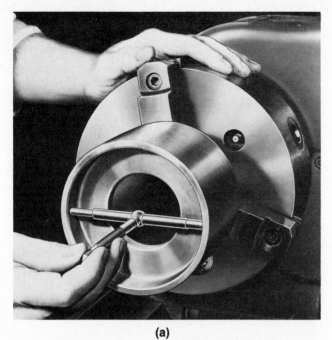

(a)

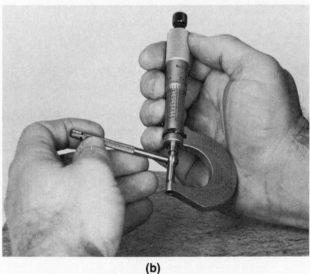

(b)

Figure 4–29. Telescoping gauge being used to measure an opening. The open gauge is then measured in a micrometer to establish the size of the hole. *(L.S. Starrett Co.)*

SPLIT SPHERE   HANDLE   LOCK

Figure 4–30. Small-hole gauges are used for holes too small to measure with other tools. *(L.S. Starrett Co.)*

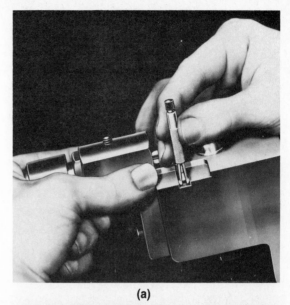

(a)

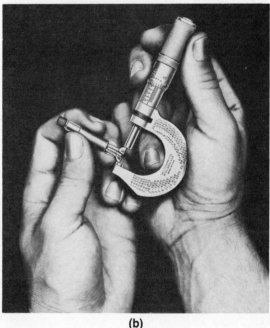

(b)

Figure 4–31. Small-hole gauge being used. *(L.S. Starrett Co.)*

Feeler gauge

Small spaces between parts can be accurately measured with a feeler gauge (Figure 4–32). This tool enables the motorcycle technician to measure valve clearances, spark plug gaps, ignition points, and so on. There are several types of feeler gauges, but they all consist of a number of metal blades of various thicknesses hinged in a holder like the blades of a penknife. The thickness is written on each individual blade. There are feeler gauge sets in metric (hundredths of a millimeter) and English (thousandths of an inch).

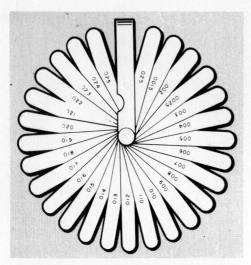

Figure 4–32. An inch feeler gauge set used to measure the space between two parts. (U.S. Navy)

The feeler gauge is used to measure a small gap between two pieces of metal by finding the blade or combination of blades which is a close fit for the space. The blade should slide in and out of the space, touching both sides at the same time without wedging or being forced. It should not be twisted or bent in slipping it in and out of a space. The blades should be wiped after every use with a clean oily cloth to remove dirt and prevent rust.

KEY TERMS

Caliper: sliding, two-part rule used for measuring openings and across parts.

Dial indicator: a gauge used to measure the contour, play, or runout of a motorcycle part.

English measuring system: one of the two main measuring systems in use in the world; based upon inch divisions of a foot.

Feeler gauge: a tool used to measure the space between two very close surfaces.

Inside micrometer: a tool used to measure the size of a hole, such as exists in a motorcycle engine cylinder.

Metric measuring system: One of the two main measuring systems in use in the world; based upon millimeter divisions of a meter.

Metric units: standard units based upon the meter and decimal multiples of the meter.

Outside micrometer: a tool used to measure the outside of an object such as a crankshaft or piston.

Rule: a flat length of metal divided into a number of measuring units.

Small-hole gauge: a tool consisting of a split sphere with an internal wedge used to measure the inside of a small hole such as exists in a valve guide.

Telescoping gauge: a tool with a spring-loaded piston that telescopes within a cylinder and is used to measure the inside of the cylindrical hole.

Vernier caliper: a measuring tool which uses two measuring scales, one on the main section and the other on a sliding vernier, which together provide a more precise reading than would be obtained on a single scale.

CHECKUP

1. What is the smallest unit of measurement commonly used in the metric measuring system?

2. What is the smallest unit of measurement commonly used in the English measuring system?

Convert the following metric measurements to English measurements.

3. 5 mm _____

4. 10 mm _____

5. 20 mm _____

Determine the length of each line alongside the metric rule, and record your measurements in the spaces provided below.

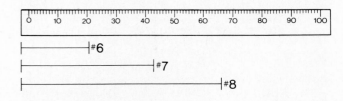

6. _____

7. _____

8. _____

What are the caliper readings in each of the following illustrations?

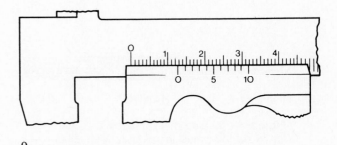

9. _____

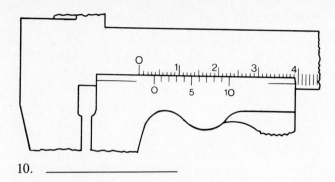

10. _____

What are the metric micrometer readings in the illustrations shown below?

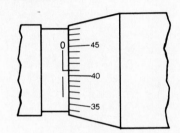

11. _____

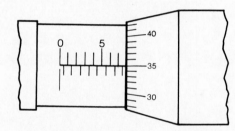

12. _____

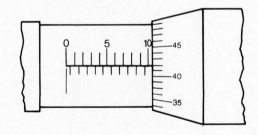

13. _____

What are the metric dial indicator readings in the illustrations shown below?

14. _____

15. _____

DISCUSSION TOPICS AND ACTIVITIES

1. Measure several common shop items. What is the smallest thing you can accurately measure?

2. How many different shop measuring tools can you use to measure one item? What measuring tool is easiest for you to use?

Every motorcycle component is assembled with a large variety of threaded and nonthreaded fastening devices. A look at the fasteners used just to mount the cylinder head on a typical engine (Figure 5–1) illustrates this important point. As a motorcycle technician, you have to know fastening devices as well as you know your tools. In this unit, we describe the common types of fasteners, as well as their size and designation systems.

JOB COMPETENCY OBJECTIVES

When you finish reading and studying this unit, you should be able to:

1. Identify the common types of threaded fasteners.

2. Describe the method used to determine the size of threaded fasteners.

3. Distinguish between different pitches of metric and English threads.

4. Explain the procedures used to repair threads and extract broken screws and studs.

5. Identify the types and uses of common nonthreaded assembling devices.

FASTENERS WITH THREADS

Fasteners with threads use the wedging action of a spiral groove, called a thread, to wedge two parts together. The common types of threaded fasteners are screws, bolts, studs, and nuts.

Machine screws

Screws are fasteners that fit in a hole. They fall into two very general categories: wood screws and machine screws. In motorcycle repair, we are interested only in machine screws. A machine screw is turned or driven into the threaded hole to hold or clamp two parts together, as shown in Figure 5–2. Note that the top part that is fastened is not threaded; the bottom part is threaded and holds the screw.

All machine screws have one thing in common: they do not taper. Except for their heads, their diameter does not change throughout their length. Since it does not taper, a machine screw can be used as a bolt, just by threading a nut on it. However, the converse is not true: some bolts, for example, "U" bolts, cannot be used as screws. Machine screws are identified by the shape of their heads, their diameter, and the type of thread that is formed on them. Figure 5–3 shows some common types of machine screw heads.

The most common type of screw used in motorcycle assemblies is the hex-head screw, which has a six-sided or hexagonal head (Figure 5–3, top left). The hex-head screw

ASSEMBLING AND FASTENING DEVICES

is driven or turned with the common wrenches, such as the box, open-end, combination, and socket wrench.

Many screws, such as the round, flat, oval, fillister, slotted truss, and Phillips screw, are designed to be turned with a screwdriver. A hollow-head or Allen-head screw is driven with an Allen or hex wrench. These latter types of screw are commonly used in motorcycle assemblies.

Set screws are a type of machine screw used to hold a part on a shaft. They go all the way through a part and set or pinch down on a shaft to hold the part on the shaft (Figure 5–4). Set screws on machinery often have a thumb head for easy removal. Flat, square, and Allen are common types of set screws. Set screws are classified by diameter, head, and point; thread size is also specified.

Bolts

Bolts (Figure 5–5) are threaded fasteners that are used with nuts, instead of threaded holes, to hold motorcycle parts together. None of the parts fastened together are threaded. Some bolt heads are flanged to give a wider holding surface.

Bolts are available with the same head shapes as described for machine screws. The most common type is a hex-head bolt. The basic difference between a bolt and a screw is that the bolt is used with a nut. You normally need two wrenches to tighten or loosen bolts, one to drive the bolt and one to hold the nut from turning.

Bolts are specified by diameter (in millimeters or fractions of an inch) and by length (millimeters or inches). The bolt is measured from the end to just under the head (Figure 5–6). Note that slotted, slant-head bolts are measured to the top of their head.

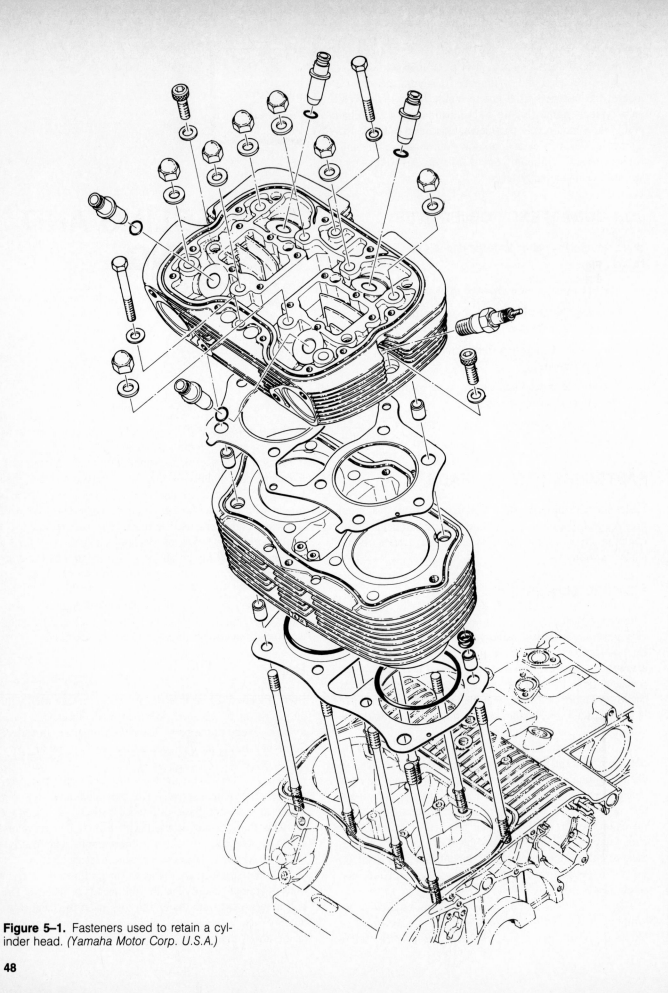

Figure 5–1. Fasteners used to retain a cylinder head. *(Yamaha Motor Corp. U.S.A.)*

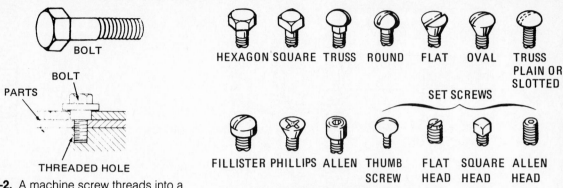

Figure 5–2. A machine screw threads into a threaded hole.

Figure 5–3. Common types of machine screw heads. *(Ford Motor Co.)*

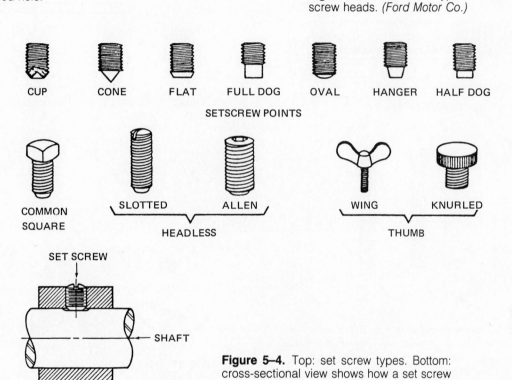

Figure 5–4. Top: set screw types. Bottom: cross-sectional view shows how a set screw is used to hold a part to a shaft. *(U.S. Navy)*

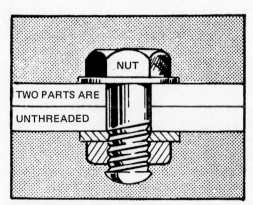

Figure 5–5. Bolts are used with a nut to fasten two or more parts together. None of the parts have threaded holes. *(U.S. Navy)*

Studs

Studs are fasteners with threads at both ends. One end of the stud fits into a threaded hole in a motorcycle part. Another motorcycle part fits over the stud, and the two parts are clamped together with a nut as shown in Figure 5–7. Studs are often used where the positioning of a part is important.

Nuts

Nuts are used to secure bolts that go through two or more motorcycle parts, none of which is threaded. Nuts are also used on studs to mount parts or components. The commonly used nuts are shown in Figure 5–8. The hex nut is

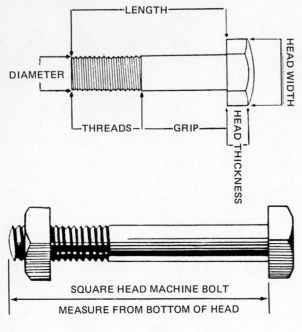

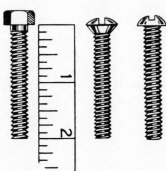

Machine bolts and screws are measured from end to under head. Slant head bolts and screws are measured to the top of the head.

Figure 5–6. Measuring machine bolts and screws. *(U.S. Navy)*

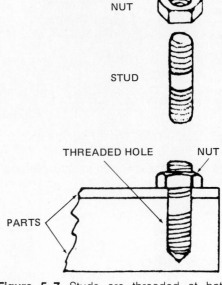

Figure 5–7. Studs are threaded at both ends. *(U.S. Navy)*

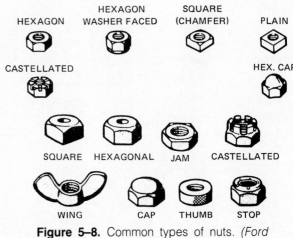

Figure 5–8. Common types of nuts. *(Ford Motor Co.)*

the most common type of nut used in motorcycle assemblies. Some nuts (and bolt heads) have a flange to increase their bearing surface (Figure 5–8, bottom).

If the nut is subject to vibration, as it is in a motorcycle wheel assembly, a castellated nut and cotter pin may be used. After the castellated nut is tightened onto the bolt or stud, a metal cotter pin is inserted through its slots and also through a hole that has been drilled in the stud or bolt. After the cotter pin is installed, it is bent around the nut as shown in Figure 5–9. The cotter pin prevents the nut from working loose.

Washers

Washers (Figure 5–10) are often used with bolts, screws, studs, and nuts. A flat washer is often used between a nut and a motorcycle part or under the head of a screw or bolt.

Figure 5–9. A castellated nut is used with a cotter pin. *(U.S. Navy)*

The washer helps spread out the clamping force over a wider area and also prevents machined surfaces from being scratched as the bolt head or nut is tightened.

Under severe vibration, nuts or screws can work themselves off the bolts or out of their threaded holes. This is prevented by the use of lock washers. Lock washers are designed to "bite" into both the nut and the surface the nut bears against. Shakeproof washers do the same and consequently also prevent the nut from loosening.

| FLAT WASHER | SPLIT LOCK WASHER | SHAKE PROOF WASHER |

Figure 5–10. Common types of washers. (U.S. Navy)

Fastener size and thread types

Motorcycles which are manufactured using the metric system have metric threads. Motorcycles manufactured using the English system use English thread types. The fasteners of one system cannot be mixed with those of the other system.

Metric system threads

Bolts in the metric system have threads cut to millimeter specifications. A common metric system bolt might be M12×1.75 (Figure 5–11). The M indicates that the fastener has metric threads. The first number is either the outside millimeter diameter of the bolt, screw, or stud or the inside diameter of a nut. Here, it is 12 mm. The second number, after the multiplication sign, is the pitch. The pitch is the distance between each of the threads, measured in millimeters. The larger the pitch number, the wider the spacing between the threads.

The length of the metric bolt or screw is measured from under the head to the end and is given in millimeters.

Japanese motorcycles have been manufactured using two different pitch dimension standards. The older system is termed JIS, for Japanese Industrial Standard. This system has been replaced by the newer ISO (International Standardization Organization) system used in other metric system countries. The differences in the dimensions of JIS bolts and ISO bolts are in the thread pitch, the width across the flat, and the thickness of the head. Because of the second item, metric wrenches are not interchangeable between the two systems.

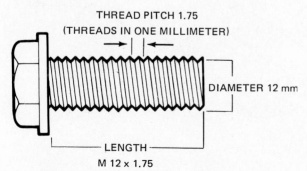

THREAD PITCH 1.75
(THREADS IN ONE MILLIMETER)

DIAMETER 12 mm

LENGTH

M 12 x 1.75

Figure 5–11. Measurements on a metric system bolt. A hex-head bolt, M 12×1.75 is shown. (Ford Motor Co.)

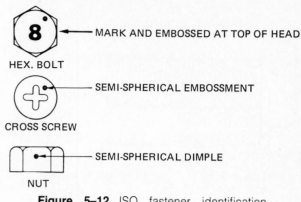

MARK AND EMBOSSED AT TOP OF HEAD

HEX. BOLT

SEMI-SPHERICAL EMBOSSMENT

CROSS SCREW

SEMI-SPHERICAL DIMPLE

NUT

Figure 5–12. ISO fastener identification marks. (Honda Motor Co., Ltd.)

ISO system fasteners are often identified with marks, as shown in Figure 5–12. Be sure you have the correct metric fastener for the job. Do not use JIS wrenches on ISO threads or ISO wrenches on JIS threads: you may damage the threads.

English system threads

Motorcycles manufactured using the English inch system use a thread designation system called the Unified System. The Unified System has two general types of threads, coarse and fine, denoted, respectively, by UNC for Unified National Coarse and UNF for Unified National Fine. The coarse thread has fewer threads per inch (larger pitch) than the fine thread and can be easily recognized. Trying to tighten a coarse-threaded screw into a hole with fine threads will damage the threads. Coarse threads are used in aluminum parts because they provide greater holding strength in soft materials. Fine threads are used in many harder materials, such as cast iron and steel. A UNEF thread (Unified National Extra Fine) is also made but is not used in motorcycle manufacture.

The size of a threaded English system fastener is designated in the same way as that of a metric system fastener. The many different sizes of bolts, screws, studs, and nuts are given in fractions of an inch. A typical designation is ½-20 UNF (Figure 5–13). The ½ represents a bolt, screw, or stud thread diameter of ½ inch; when applied to a nut, it refers to the size of the bolt that the nut fits. The 20 refers to the number of threads in every inch of length, and the UNF denotes Unified National Fine threads. All ½-inch Unified National Fine fasteners have the same number of threads (20) per inch. A Unified National Coarse thread fastener that is ½ inch in diameter would be designated ½-13 UNC. It would have only 13 threads per inch.

A distinction is made between bolts and nuts in regard to the location of their threads. Bolts are designated by the letter A to denote that they have external threads; nuts or

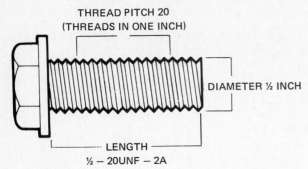

THREAD PITCH 20
(THREADS IN ONE INCH)

DIAMETER ½ INCH

LENGTH
½ — 20UNF — 2A

Figure 5–13. An English-system ½ 20 UNF bolt. *(Ford Motor Co.)*

threaded holes are designated by the letter B to denote that they have internal threads. Thus, a designation of ½-20 UNF-2A describes a bolt because of the A contained therein. The 2 preceding the A refers to the class of fit: threads in general use are normally designated by a 2. A designation of ½-20 UNF-2B describes a nut or threaded hole; again, the letter B designates internal threads.

The length of a bolt screw or stud may be given in the designation of a bolt—for example, ½-13 UNC-2A × 1 inch long. As in the case of metric bolts, the lengths of English bolts and screws are measured from the end to the base of the head.

Visually, UNF and UNC bolts and nuts look the same as their metric counterparts. The slight difference in size and pitch, however, make them incompatible.

Fastener strength or grade markings

Most threaded fasteners are selected according to motorcycle engineers' specifications that define required mechanical properties, such as tensile strength, yield strength, and hardness. These specifications are carefully considered in the initial selection of fasteners for a given application. To assure continued satisfactory motorcycle performance, replacement fasteners should be of the correct strength, as well as the correct nominal diameter, thread pitch, length, and finish, given in the specifications.

The strength of a threaded fastener is indicated by a marking system on the screw or bolt head and nut. The marks made are called *grade markings*. Metric fasteners use numbers to indicate their strength. The higher the number, the stronger the fastener is. Metric bolts are always numbered, while nuts may or may not be. Typical metric bolt and strength numbers are shown in Figure 5–14.

Grade markings on the heads of bolts show the quality for English system fasteners (Figure 5–15). A bolt with no marks on the head is of the lowest quality. Six marks are used for a grade-eight bolt, the highest quality bolt used on motorcycle parts. Nuts have a dot marking system. The more dots, the stronger the nut is.

Identifying fasteners

The many different types of threaded fasteners used on different manufacturers' motorcycles make it difficult for the motorcycle technician to select the correct fastener. A pitch gauge (Figure 5–16) is a useful tool in identifying fastener threads. The gauge has a number of blades with different-sized teeth. The thread size is written on the blade. By matching the teeth on the blade with the threads on a fastener, you can determine thread size. Pitch gauges are made for both metric and English threads. Figure 5–17 shows how the pitch gauge is used.

THREAD REPAIR

Threaded fasteners on motorcycle parts are often damaged by wear or abuse. You will consequently have to be able to use some thread repair tools such as taps, dies, helicoils, and screw or bolt extractors.

Taps

A tap (Figure 5–18) is a cutting tool used to make or repair inside or internal threads. Hand taps are used to cut or repair screw threads up to 25 mm (1 inch) in diameter in soft metals and plastics. A hand tap looks like a fluted screw;

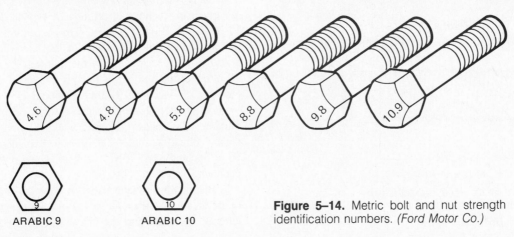

4.6 4.8 5.8 8.8 9.8 10.9

ARABIC 9   ARABIC 10

Figure 5–14. Metric bolt and nut strength identification numbers. *(Ford Motor Co.)*

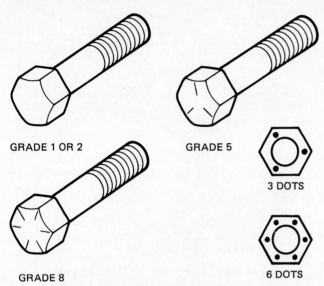

GRADE 1 OR 2   GRADE 5   3 DOTS

GRADE 8   6 DOTS

Figure 5–15. Grade system for English threaded fasteners. *(Ford Motor Co.)*

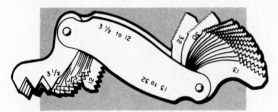

Figure 5–16. A pitch gauge is used to identify threads.

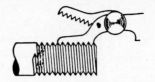

GAUGING EXTERNAL THREADS

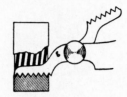

GAUGING INTERNAL THREADS

Figure 5–17. Using the pitch gauge for checking threads. *(U.S. Navy)*

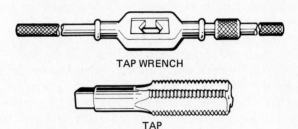

TAP WRENCH

TAP

Figure 5–18. Taps are used to make or repair internal threads. *(U.S. Navy)*

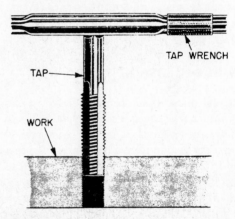

TAP WRENCH

TAP

WORK

Figure 5–19. Using the tap to thread a bored hole. *(U.S. Navy)*

it will cut its own threads in a hole of the correct diameter. There are many different sizes of taps. The size is indicated by numbers on the shank of the tap which show the diameter and pitch of the thread the tap will cut.

To repair an internal thread, select a tap with the same diameter and thread pitch as the damaged thread. Then clamp the square end of the tap shank in a tap wrench. Now place the tapered end of the tap in the hole, so that the tap is in line with the hole (Figure 5–19). Start the tapping by turning the wrench about a quarter of a turn—clockwise for a right-hand thread and counterclockwise for a left-hand thread. Then back the tap off about a third of a turn. Now turn the tap forward about half a turn, and back it off a quarter of a turn. This procedure provides a firm grip for the tap and allows the metal chips that are cut from the metal to be removed from the bottom of the tap, which does the actual cutting.

Dies

Dies (Figure 5–20) are used for cutting or repairing external threads. A die is held in a handle called a *die stock*. Cutting with dies is easier than tapping, but it still requires skill and practice. The rod to be threaded must be of the correct diameter. If is a little undersized, the result will be a sloppy fit in the tapped hole. Assuming that the rod is of the proper dimension, the end you are going to thread should be tapered, but only slightly. This allows the die to get a start on the rod.

Some dies are adjustable so that correct, slightly oversized, and slightly undersized threads can be cut. The adjustment is done by means of a screw. Once the adjustment is made, it will stay that way until it is purposely changed. When you are ready to start cutting a thread, mount the

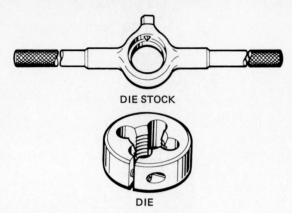

Figure 5–20. A die in a die stock is used to cut or repair external threads. *(U.S. Navy)*

required die in a die stock of the correct size. The sizes are marked on the die and correspond to the diameter and thread pitch of the thread to be cut.

When you look at the die, you will notice that the opening at the center of one face is just slightly larger than the opening at the other side. The larger of the two openings is the one with which you start the threading operation. The die-cutting procedure is similar to the tapping procedure. Be sure the rod to be threaded is at a right angle to the die. Start the die squarely over the rod, give it a quarter turn forward and back it off about one-eighth of a turn. Keep on turning and backing off, a little at a time, until you have cut the amount of thread you need (Figure 5–21). Dies are sometimes used to repair threads on a damaged bolt.

Screw thread inserts (helicoils®)

If an internal thread is too badly damaged, it can be repaired with a screw thread insert (Figure 5–22). A screw thread insert or helicoil® is a steel wire coil which is wound into the hole to form a new thread. A special helicoil® tap is used to prepare the hole for the thread insert. The helicoil® is then threaded into place with a special insert tool (Figure 5–23). The machine screw or bolt can then be installed by using the helicoil® for new threads.

Screw and stud extractors

Broken screws, studs, and bolts are common problems in motorcycle repair. If a screw or stud breaks off above the surface, you can usually grip it with locking pliers and unscrew it (Figure 5–24). If it breaks off flush or below the surface, it will be much more difficult to remove. If only a small stub remains above the surface, sometimes you can turn it by using a punch (Figure 5–25). Hit the punch with a ball pein hammer to turn the bolt or stud.

If no part remains above the surface, or if the fastener is frozen in the hole, you must begin by drilling a small

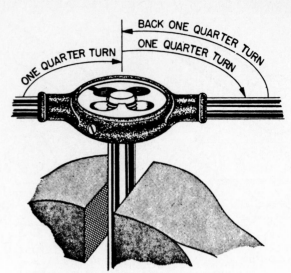

Figure 5–21. Using the die to cut threads on a rod or re-form damaged bolt threads. *(U.S. Navy)*

Figure 5–22. Badly damaged internal threads can be replaced by a screw thread insert or helicoil. *(Heli-Coil)*

hole in the exact center of the broken fastener (Figure 5–26). You then enlarge the hole by using a slightly larger drill. If necessary, do it again, until only a thin shell of stud or screw is left. Finally, force an extractor (Figure

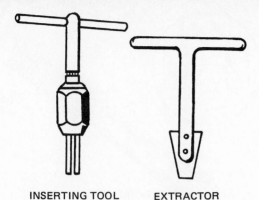

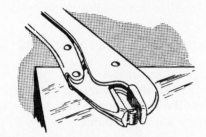

Figure 5–23. Screw thread insert tools.

INSERTING TOOL   EXTRACTOR

Figure 5–24. Using locking pliers to unscrew a broken bolt. *(U.S. Navy)*

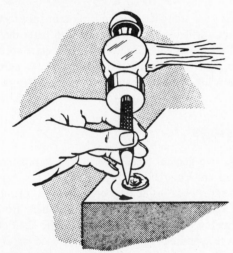

Figure 5–25. Using a punch and ball pein hammer to unscrew a broken bolt. *(U.S. Navy)*

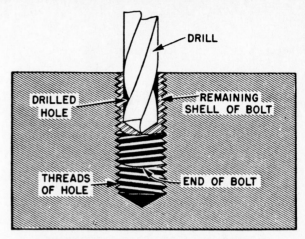

Figure 5–26. Drill out the broken fastener. *(U.S. Navy)*

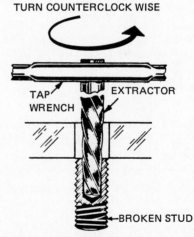

Figure 5–27. A bolt or screw extractor is used to remove broken bolts, studs, or screws. Different-size extractors are available. *(U.S. Navy)*

Figure 5–28. Fit the extractor in the hole bored in the broken fastener. Choose an extractor that fits the size of the hole. Turn counterclockwise to screw out the broken fastener. *(U.S. Navy)*

5–27) into the hole and turn it counterclockwise with a wrench (Figure 5–28). The extractor grips the inside of the hole and allows you to turn the broken fastener out. A tap wrench or a regular wrench is used to turn the extractor.

If an extractor is not available, drive the end of a diamond-point cold chisel into the hole and turn the chisel counterclockwise with a wrench (Figure 5–29). Remember, however, that a diamond-point chisel is not intended for this purpose, so do not apply excessive force. If the threads are rusted, apply a little penetrating oil, let it soak for a while, and try again.

A large broken stud or screw can also be removed with a round-nose chisel. Drive a hole in the center of the screw as before, and then, using a slightly larger drill, increase the inside diameter of the hole, being very careful not to touch the inside threads. Use a round-nose chisel to break

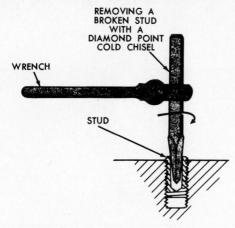

Figure 5–29. Using a chisel to remove broken screws. *(Ford Motor Co.)*

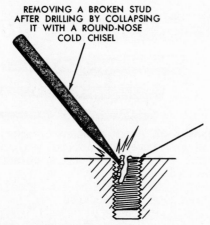

Figure 5–30. Using a chisel to break out a broken and drilled stud or bolt. *(Ford Motor Co.)*

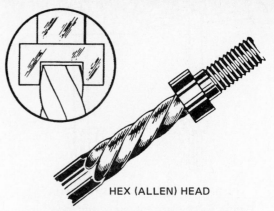

Figure 5–31. Extractor used to remove a damaged Allen-head screw. *(U.S. Navy)*

Nonthreaded assembling devices

Not all fastening devices use threads. Many motorcycle parts are assembled with nonthreaded fastening or assembling devices. The most common such devices are dowel pins, snap rings, keys, and splines.

Dowel pins

Dowel pins are straight or tapered, solid or split metal pins that fit into drilled holes to position two parts that fit together. Sometimes called roll pins, they require special pliers or a punch and hammer for removal. A number of dowel pins used to assemble a shifter are shown in Figure 5–32.

Snap rings

There are two general types of snap ring or retaining ring: expanding and contracting (Figure 5–33). The expanding type of ring is used inside the bore of a shaft, the contracting type around the circumference of the shaft. Both types are retained in grooves cut in the bore of the shaft or in the diameter. Expanding-type snap rings are used largely as retainers and are sometimes called circlips. As shown in Figure 5–33 (top), special snap ring pliers are used to remove and install the rings. Two snap rings are shown on the kick starter illustrated in Figure 5–34.

the stud threads out of the tapped hole and collapse the wall of the stud or screw to such an extent that it can be easily removed (Figure 5–30).

An extractor can also be used to remove Allen-head machine screws if their heads are stripped or damaged (Figure 5–31).

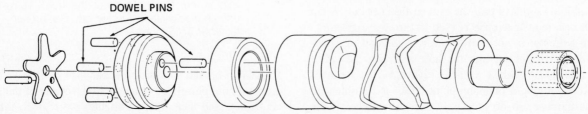

Figure 5–32. Dowel pins are used on this transmission shifter. *(Yamaha Motor Corp. U.S.A.)*

REMOVING OR INSTALLING
INTERNAL EXPANDING TYPE

REMOVING OR INSTALLING
EXTERNAL CONTRACTING TYPE

	BASIC *internal series* **N5000**		BOWED *external series* **5101**		REINFORCED CIRCULAR PUSH-ON *external series* **5115**		TRIANGULAR NUT *external series* **5300**
	BOWED *internal series* **N5001**		BEVELED *external series* **5102**		BOWED E-RING *external series* **5131** X5131		KLIPRING *external series* **5304** T5304
	BEVELED *internal series* **N5002**		CRESCENT® *external series* **5103**		E-RING *external series* **5133** X5133 • Y5133		TRIANGULAR PUSH-ON *external series* **5305**
	CIRCULAR PUSH-ON *internal series* **5005**		CIRCULAR PUSH-ON *external series* **5105**		PRONG-LOCK® *external series* **5139**		GRIPRING® **5555** D5555 • G5555
	INVERTED *internal series* **5008**		INTERLOCKING *external series* **5107**		REINFORCED E-RING *external series* **5144**		MINIATURE HIGH-STRENGTH *external series* **5560**
	BASIC *external series* **5100**		INVERTED *external series* **5108**		HEAVY DUTY *external series* **5160**		PERMANENT SHOULDER *external series* **5590**

Figure 5–33. Variety of snap rings. *(KD Tools)*

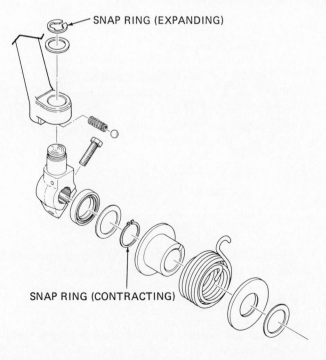

SNAP RING (EXPANDING)

SNAP RING (CONTRACTING)

Figure 5–34. Snap or retaining rings used on this kick starter. *(Yamaha Motor Corp. U.S.A.)*

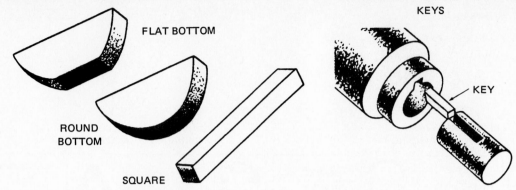

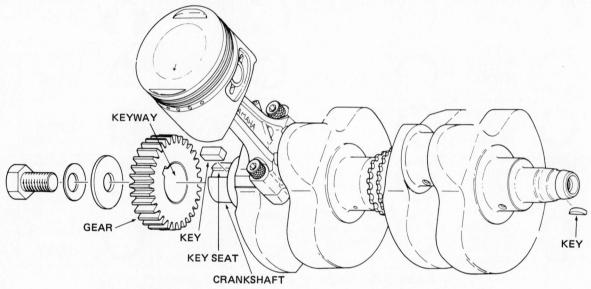

Figure 5–35. A key locks a gear to a shaft. *(U.S. Navy)*

Figure 5–36. A key is used at both ends of this crankshaft. *(Yamaha Motor Corp. U.S.A.)*

Both types of snap ring are made of spring steel and can cause severe injury if they are allowed to fly out of control when removing or replacing them. Always be sure to use the right tool on them. Retaining ring pliers are made for both internal and external rings.

Keys

Keys are small, hardened pieces of metal typically used with a gear to lock it to a shaft. Half of the key fits into a keyseat on the shaft; the other half fits into another slot called a keyway on the gear (Figure 5–35). A key is shown at both ends of the crankshaft depicted in Figure 5–36.

Splines

Another common method used to lock a part on a shaft is with splines. Splines are matching teeth cut on the two parts to be joined. In Figure 5–37, the external teeth or

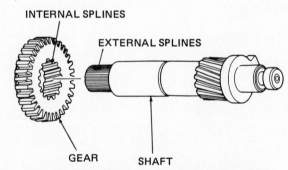

Figure 5–37. Matching splines lock a part to a shaft. *(Yamaha Motor Corp. U.S.A.)*

splines cut on the shaft slide into the internal splines on the gear. The two parts are then locked together.

KEY TERMS

Bolt: threaded fastener used with a nut to hold motorcycle parts together.

Die: tool used to cut threads on the outside of a fastener.

Dowel pin: a round metal pin that fits into drilled holes to position two parts that are to be mated.

Extractor: tool used for screwing out broken bolts, studs, or machine screws.

Grade markings: markings on threaded fasteners used to identify their quality and strength.

Key: a small, hardened piece of metal used to lock a gear to a shaft.

Machine screw: threaded fastener that screws into a threaded hole.

Nut: a small fastener with internal threads used with bolts and studs.

Pitch gauge: a tool used to measure the thread size of a threaded fastener or hole.

Set screw: machine screw that threads through one part to hold it to another part.

Snap ring: an internal or external ring used to hold motorcycle components together.

Splines: teeth cut into a shaft or gear so that they will fit and hold together.

Stud: a fastener with threads at both ends.

Tap: tool used to cut threads in a hole.

Washer: a fastener used with bolts, screws, studs, and nuts to distribute the clamping force in order to prevent fasteners from coming loose due to vibrations.

CHECKUP

Identify the types of screws shown in each of the illustrations below.

1. _____

2. _____

3. _____

   1   2   3

Identify the types of nuts shown in each of the illustrations below.

4. _____

5. _____

6. _____

   4   5   6

Identify the types of washers shown below.

7. _____

8. _____

9. _____

10. _____

  7   8

     9   10

Identify each of the measurements on the fastener shown below.

11. _____

12. _____

13. _____

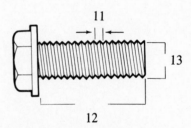

Identify the thread-repair tools shown below.

14. _____

15. _____

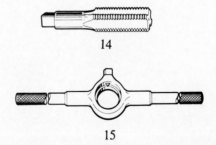

  14

  15

DISCUSSION TOPICS AND ACTIVITIES

1. Make a list of all the types of fasteners you can find on a shop motorcycle.

2. Measure a collection of shop fasteners and see if you can tell the difference between metric and English threads. Use a pitch gauge to check your results.

The motorcycle engine is a machine that converts heat energy into a form of power. All motorcycle engines operate on the basic principle of *combustion:* when fuel is mixed with air and burned, heat is produced. This heat develops useful power. In this unit, we look at the basic parts of the two- and four-stroke motorcycle engine and how they work together to develop power.

JOB COMPETENCY OBJECTIVES

When you finish reading and studying this unit, you should be able to:

1. Identify the basic parts and describe the operation of an internal combustion engine.

2. Describe the parts and operation of a two-stroke cycle engine.

3. Explain the operation and identify the parts of a four-stroke cycle engine.

4. Define the terms used to describe an engine's size and performance.

BASIC ENGINE PARTS AND OPERATION

On all motorcycle engines, combustion takes place inside the engine. This is why motorcycle engines are called internal combustion engines. An internal combustion engine is really just a container into which we put air and fuel and then start them burning.

The container used for burning the air and fuel in an engine is the *cylinder,* which is simply a metal tube closed at one end. The plug that fits inside the cylinder is a *piston.* There is a small space between the piston and the top of the cylinder where the burning takes place. This space is known as the *combustion chamber.* The basic parts required for internal combustion are shown in Figure 6–1.

Let's put several drops of gasoline into the space above the piston. As we move the piston up in the cylinder, the gasoline–air mixture in the combustion chamber is compressed. When the mixture is compressed as tightly as we

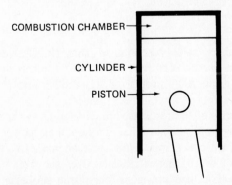

Figure 6–1. Basic parts for internal combustion. *(U.S. Navy)*

ENGINE FUNDAMENTALS

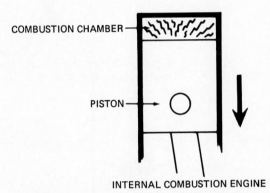

Figure 6–2. Combustion pressures force the piston down the cylinder. *(U.S. Navy)*

can get it, we start it burning with an electric spark. This combustion increases the pressure in the combustion chamber and pushes the piston down the cylinder with great force, as shown in Figure 6–2.

When the piston moves down the cylinder, power is produced. Our problem is to harness that power. Toward that end, a *connecting rod* is connected to the bottom of the piston, and as the piston is forced downward, the rod moves downward. This downward movement is changed to circular movement at the *crankshaft,* which is a shaft with its middle offset and its ends mounted so that it can turn freely. Since the lower end of the connecting rod is connected to the crankshaft and the upper end is connected to the piston (through a piston pin), the connecting rod can follow the crankshaft's motion. The parts that connect the piston to the crankshaft are shown in Figure 6–3.

If we want to have more than one piston movement down the cylinder, we have to bring the piston back up the cylinder. Thus, we need one more basic part, called the *flywheel.* The flywheel is a heavy wheel that is mounted on the end of the crankshaft, as shown in Figure 6–4.

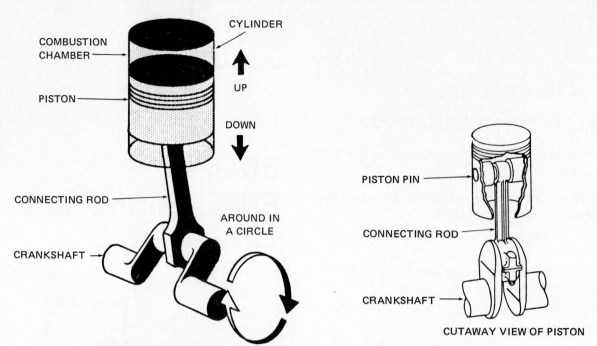

Figure 6–3. The piston is connected to a connecting rod which is, in turn, connected to a crankshaft. *(U.S. Navy)*

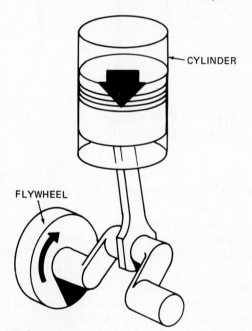

Figure 6–4. The flywheel keeps the crankshaft turning.

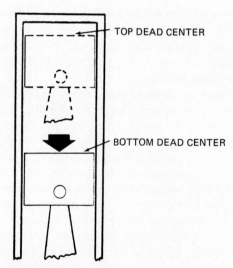

Figure 6–5. Piston movement from TDC to BDC or BDC to TDC is a stroke.

As the piston is forced down, both the crankshaft and the flywheel go around. Since the flywheel is heavy, it does not slow down easily. The momentum of the moving flywheel thus keeps the crankshaft turning, which in turn causes the piston to go back up to the top of the cylinder.

Piston movement in a cylinder is very important to engine operation. When the piston moves from the top of the cylinder, called *top dead center* (TDC), to the bottom of the cylinder, called *bottom dead center* (BDC), we say that one stroke has occurred (Figure 6–5). When the piston moves from BDC back to TDC, another stroke has occurred.

A series of strokes is used to develop power in a motorcycle engine. Engines that develop their power in two strokes are called two-stroke cycle engines. (A cycle is a series of events that is repeated over and over.) Engines that develop their power in four piston strokes are called four-stroke cycle engines. The next two sections deal with the operation of two- and four-stroke engines.

Figure 6–6. This competition dirt bike is equipped with a two-stroke cycle engine. *(U.S. Suzuki Motor Corp.)*

TWO-STROKE CYCLE ENGINE OPERATION

Many types of motorcycle are equipped with engines that operate on the two-stroke cycle principle. These engines are often called *two-cycle engines* or *two-strokers*. Many small street motorcycles and most off-road motorcycles (Figure 6–6) use two-stroke cycle engines. The principle of the two-stroke engine is that it takes two complete piston movements or strokes—one movement up and one movement down—to complete the cycle.

Two-stroke: basic parts

Regardless of whether a motorcycle engine is a two- or four-stroke cycle engine, it has the same two main sections (Figure 6–7): upper end (cylinder) and lower end (crankcase). The upper end houses the piston, the cylinder, and the top of the cylinder, called the cylinder head. The lower end supports the crankshaft. Since the engine is used to drive the rear wheel of the motorcycle, a clutch and transmission are necessary. The parts of the transmission and clutch fit into the lower end housing.

The two-stroke cycle engine uses the same basic parts described previously. As shown in Figure 6–8, there is a cylinder and a combustion chamber. A piston in the cylinder is connected to a crankshaft by a connecting rod. A flywheel is mounted to or combined with the crankshaft. There are two holes or ports in the cylinder: the exhaust port, to let the burned air–fuel mixture out, and the intake port, to let the fresh air and fuel in. A transfer passage connects the crankcase section to the cylinder section.

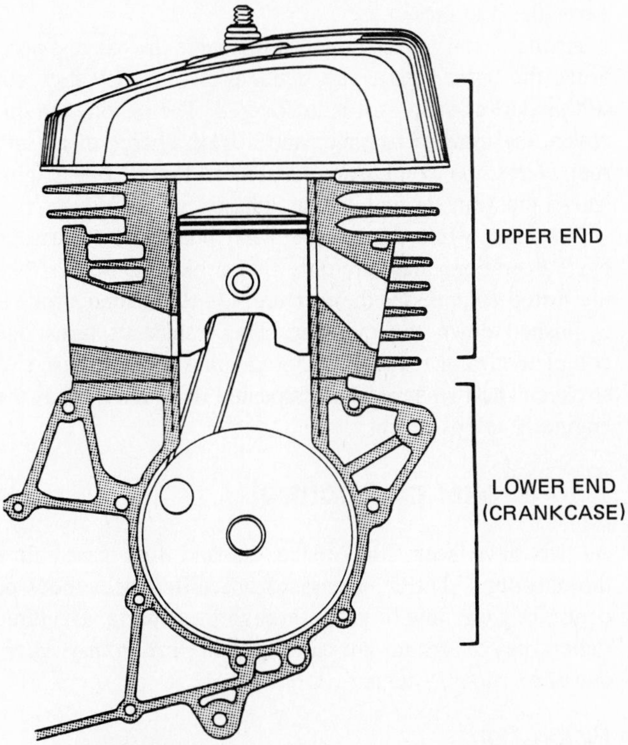

UPPER END

LOWER END (CRANKCASE)

TRANSMISSION

Figure 6–7. Three main engine sections of a motorcycle engine. *(U.S. Suzuki Motor Corp.)*

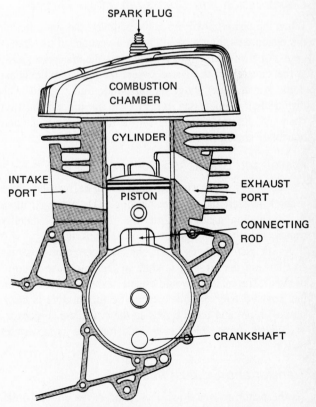

SPARK PLUG

COMBUSTION CHAMBER

CYLINDER

INTAKE PORT

PISTON

EXHAUST PORT

CONNECTING ROD

CRANKSHAFT

Figure 6–8. Basic parts of a two-stroke cycle engine. *(U.S. Suzuki Motor Corp.)*

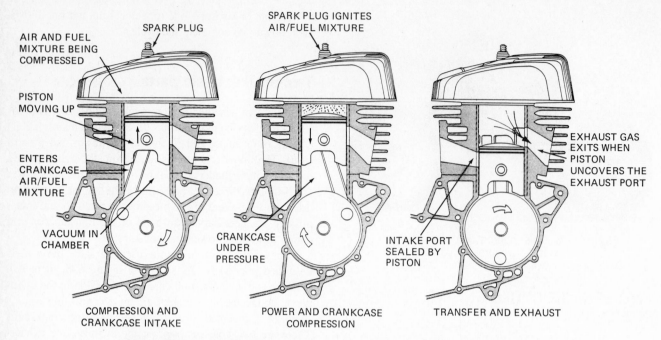

Figure 6–9. Two-stroke cycle. Compression and crankcase intake phase (left). Power and crankcase compression phase (center). Transfer and exhaust phase (right). *(U.S. Suzuki Motor Corp.)*

Two-stroke: how it works

Compression and Crankshaft Intake Phase

When the piston moves up in the cylinder, the space below the piston gets bigger, resulting in a vacuum in the crankcase. An air–fuel mixture is pulled into the crankcase, and, at the same time, the piston covers the intake and exhaust ports. Air and fuel above the piston are thus trapped. The piston then compresses the mixture in the combustion chamber. Figure 6–9 (left) shows this compression and crankcase intake phase.

Power and Crankcase Compression Phase

As the piston approaches its upward stroke, we introduce a spark to start the mixture burning. The burning causes the expanding gases to force the piston down, thereby transferring the piston's power to the crankshaft.

As the piston moves down, the crankcase area becomes smaller and the air–fuel mixture in the crankcase is compressed. The mixture would escape, except that the piston has covered over the intake port. So the mixture is compressed more and more tightly in the crankcase. Figure 6–9 (center) shows this power and crankcase compression phase.

Transfer and Exhaust Phase

As the piston moves down the cylinder, the air–fuel mixture in the crankcase is compressed because the piston makes the crankcase area smaller. The mixture cannot escape out of the crankcase anywhere except through the transfer passage, so it goes up the transfer passage and stands by until the piston moves down far enough to uncover the passage.

As the piston moves down, it uncovers the exhaust port. Since the burned gases are under pressure, they flow out of this port as soon as it is uncovered. The piston then uncovers the transfer passage, and a fresh charge of air and fuel enters the combustion chamber. Figure 6–9 (right) shows this transfer and exhaust phase.

Note that while there are several phases of two-stroke cycle operation, there are only two strokes. On one stroke the piston compresses the mixture. On the second stroke it is pushed down the cylinder. The crankshaft turns one complete turn or revolution (360 degrees) during these two strokes. The two strokes are repeated over and over as the engine develops power.

Two-stroke: port control

As we have seen, the intake air and fuel gases flow through ports. Different engines use different methods of controlling the flow of gases through these ports. The three main types of system are called *piston port, rotary valve,* and *reed valve* systems.

Piston Port

The piston port system is the most common method used to control air and fuel flow. This system was described in the discussion of two-stroke cycle operation. The lower

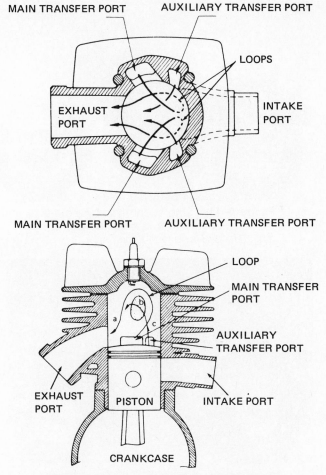

Figure 6–10. Loop scavenging on a piston port engine. *(Yamaha Motor Corp. U.S.A.)*

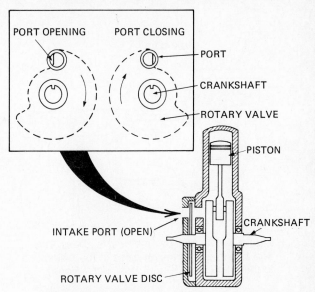

Figure 6–11. Operation of a rotary valve to control an intake port.

edge of the piston is used to open and close the intake port and transfer passage.

Most piston port systems make use of a cylinder porting arrangement that is designed to get the exhaust gases out completely without contaminating the incoming air and fuel charge. Such a technique is called *loop scavenging*.

In a loop scavenging system, a series of main and transfer ports are located around the cylinder. The main and auxiliary transfer ports on opposite sides are used to transfer two streams of air and fuel into the cylinder. The two main streams of fresh fuel meet at the cylinder wall opposite the exhaust ports and deflect upward. Then the streams deflect downward, forcing out the burnt gases through the exhaust ports. As shown in Figure 6–10, the streams create a loop as they flow through the cylinder.

Rotary Valve

Some engines use a rotary valve instead of the piston to control the flow of air and fuel into the crankcase. A rotary valve is an irregular-shaped disc that is mounted to the crankshaft. The shape of the valve is such that during part

of the crankshaft revolution it is open, allowing air and fuel to enter the vacuum of the crankcase. As the crankshaft rotates further, the larger part of the valve covers over the port and seals the crankcase (Figure 6–11).

Reed Valve

Another method used to control the intake port is a reed valve arrangement. A reed valve is a thin piece of metal that works like a hinge. Usually, several small reed valves are used together and mounted on a plate called the reed plate, as shown in Figure 6–12. A leaf-type spring is used to hold the valve in the closed position.

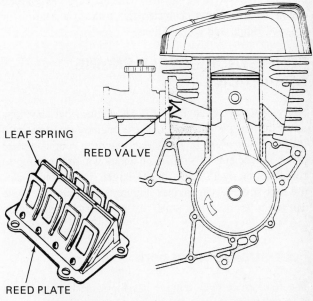

Figure 6–12. A reed plate with eight reed valves. *(U.S. Suzuki Motor Corp.)*

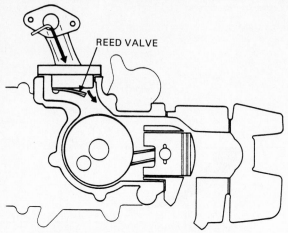

Figure 6–13. An open reed valve allows air and fuel to pass through holes in the piston to the crankcase. *(U.S. Suzuki Motor Corp.)*

Figure 6–14. Large street motorcycles are often equipped with a four-stroke cycle engine. *(Harley-Davidson Motors, Inc.)*

Figure 6–15. This small four-wheel quad runner has a four-stroke cycle engine. *(U.S. Suzuki Motor Corp.)*

When there is a vacuum in the crankcase, the reed valves hinge open because of the low pressure on the crankcase side. The air–fuel mixture is then pulled in through the open valve, and holes in the side of the piston allow the mixture to flow through the piston and into the crankcase, as shown in Figure 6–13. When the piston moves down, pressure starts to build up in the crankcase. This pressure pushes the hinged reed valve closed, and the mixture is trapped in the crankcase.

The main advantage of a two-stroke cycle engine is its simplicity. The two-stroker requires fewer parts to develop power than the four-stroker; it can therefore be lighter than the four-stroke engine. The two-stroke engine works best at high rpms and with unrestricted or unmuffled exhaust. The firing impulse of every crankshaft revolution results in the characteristic high-pitched buzzing noise two-stroke engines make. These characteristics make it a natural for off-road riding and competitions.

FOUR-STROKE CYCLE ENGINE OPERATION

Many motorcycle engines use an engine that develops power in four piston strokes. These engines are sometimes called *four-strokers* or *four-cycle engines*. Four complete piston movements or strokes, up and down, are required to complete the cycle. Most of the larger street motorcycles use four-stroke cycle engines (Figure 6–14), but the engine can also be used on small off-road machines (Figure 6–15).

Four-stroke: basic parts

The four-stroke cycle engine has the same basic parts as the two-stroke engine: a cylinder, piston, piston pin, connecting rod, crankshaft, and flywheel. However, instead of

having its transfer ports, intake ports, and exhaust ports located in the cylinder and crankcase, the four-stroke engine has its ports located above the piston in a component called the *cylinder head* (Figure 6–16).

One of the ports is used to let air and fuel in and is called the *intake port*. The other port, called the *exhaust port*, provides a passage for getting rid of the exhaust gases left after combustion. Opening and closing the ports is accomplished with valves.

In most engines, there are two valves above each piston (Figure 6–17). The valve used to control the inlet of air and fuel is referred to as the *intake valve*. The other, known as the *exhaust valve*, controls the escape of burned gases. The valves have a carefully ground taper called a *face*, which matches a carefully ground seat in the head. A strong spring called the *valve spring* holds the valve on its seat for an airtight seal.

The valves are opened by a camshaft and rocker arm assembly. The camshaft (Figure 6–18) is a shaft driven by the crankshaft, to which it is connected by a chain. Figure 6–16 shows the camshaft and chain. The camshaft has ec-

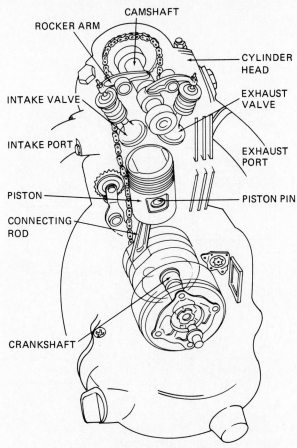

Figure 6–16. Basic parts of a four-stroke cycle engine. *(Honda Motor Corp., Ltd.)*

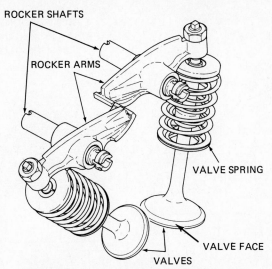

Figure 6–17. Two valves are located above the piston to control the intake and exhaust ports. *(Yamaha Motor Corp. U.S.A.)*

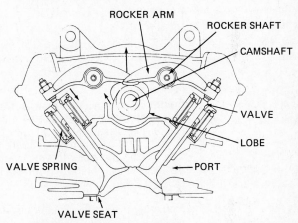

Figure 6–18. The camshaft and rocker arms open the valves. *(Yamaha Motor Corp. U.S.A.)*

centrics or lobes, one for each intake valve and one for each exhaust valve. A rocker arm is mounted on a rocker shaft above the camshaft. Figure 6–17 shows the rocker arms and shafts.

The rocker arm is essentially a lever with its free end resting on the camshaft lobe. As the high part of the camshaft lobe rotates under the free end of the rocker arm, the arm moves up. The center of the rocker arm is supported by the rocker shaft, which acts like a fulcrum or lever point. As the free end moves up, the other end of the rocker arm moves down, pushing on the end of the valve and thereby causing it to move off its seat and open the port.

Further rotation of the camshaft allows the low side of the cam to contact the rocker arm end, so that the arm is no longer being pushed down. The valve spring, which was compressed when the valve opened, closes the valve and pushes the end of the rocker arm (over the valve) back up.

Four-stroke: how it works

We are now ready to describe the action that occurs during one complete cycle of operation. We start with both the intake and the exhaust valves closed; the piston is as far up in the cylinder as the crankshaft and connecting rod will permit it to go.

Intake Stroke

The intake stroke (Figure 6–19, left, number 1) begins when the piston begins to move down the cylinder. This rapid movement of the piston creates a low-pressure area above the piston. If we open the intake valve above the piston, a mixture of air and fuel is forced into the cylinder, filling it. The piston has now completed one stroke from the top to the bottom of the cylinder, and the crankshaft has turned one-half turn, or 180 degrees.

Compression Stroke

As the piston starts up for the compression stroke, the intake and exhaust valves are closed. The piston travels up

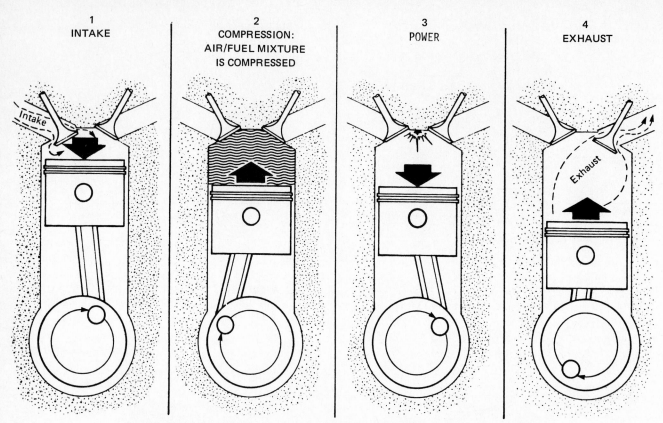

| 1 INTAKE | 2 COMPRESSION: AIR/FUEL MIXTURE IS COMPRESSED | 3 POWER | 4 EXHAUST |

Figure 6–19. Four-stroke cycle. (1) *Intake stroke:* piston moves down, causing air and fuel to enter the cylinder through the open intake valve. (2) *Compression stroke:* the piston moves up with both valves closed to compress the air-fuel mixture. (3) *Power stroke:* a spark from the spark plug ignites the air-fuel mixture, forcing the piston down the cylinder. (4) *Exhaust stroke:* the piston moves back up, forcing burned gases out of the open exhaust valve. *(Kawasaki Motors Corp. U.S.A.)*

as far as it can go, compressing the air–fuel mixture in the combustion chamber into a space about one-eighth of its former volume (Figure 6–19, number 2). The molecules of air are thus forced lightly together. The crankshaft has turned another 180 degrees, completing one revolution. During this phase, the intake and exhaust valves remain closed.

Power Stroke

As the piston nears its topmost point on the compression stroke, a spark from an ignition system is used to ignite the air–fuel mixture. Once ignited, the fuel burns quickly, causing a rapid rise in pressure in the cylinder. This rise in turn forces the piston down the cylinder on the power stroke and causes the crankshaft to rotate.

When the piston reaches the bottom of the cylinder, the power stroke is over. The crankshaft turns another 180 degrees during this stroke, and the exhaust and intake valves remain closed. The power stroke is shown in Figure 6–19 (number 3).

Exhaust Stroke

The exhaust stroke (Figure 6–19, right, number 4) begins as the piston again starts to move upward in the cylinder. This time, however, the exhaust valve is opened. Burned gases trapped in the cylinder are pushed out the exhaust port as the piston moves upward. The piston completes another stroke from the bottom of the cylinder to the top, while the crankshaft has turned another one-half turn or 180 degrees.

In summary, the four strokes of the engine are:

- *Intake:* The piston moves from the top of the cylinder to the bottom; air and fuel are pulled in through an open intake valve.

- *Compression:* The piston moves up, compressing the air and fuel trapped in the cylinder.

- *Power:* A spark from the ignition system ignites the air–fuel mixture, causing a rise in pressure which pushes the piston down.

- *Exhaust:* The piston moves up, pushing burned gases out of the cylinder through an open exhaust port.

These four strokes make up one complete cycle which is repeated over and over to develop power. Each cycle requires four strokes of the piston and two revolutions of the crankshaft.

Valve Operation

The operation of the valves in the four-stroke cycle is:

- *Intake:* The intake valve is pushed open by the camshaft.
- *Compression:* Both valves are held closed by the valve springs.
- *Power:* Both valves remain closed, held by the valve springs.
- *Exhaust:* The camshaft pushes the exhaust valve open.

The valves must open at just the right time in the four-stroke cycle. In order to time the valve openings so that they coincide with the piston strokes, the camshaft is driven by gears or a chain directly from the crankshaft. Since a valve must be open only during two strokes, intake and exhaust, the camshaft needs to rotate at only one-half the crankshaft speed. The gear or sprocket on the camshaft is thus twice as large as that on the crankshaft. Timing marks on the two gears or sprockets are used to make sure the camshaft and crankshaft are in the correct relationship. A cam chain and sprocket assembly are shown in Figure 6–20.

It should be obvious that the four-stroke engine has more parts and is heavier than the two-stroker. It has, however, a number of characteristics which make it a good choice for a street motorcycle: (1) It is much quieter than a two-stroke engine. (2) It can run at a lower speed for much longer. (3) It uses less fuel than the same size two-stroke engine. (4) It can be made to develop a great deal of smooth, quiet power.

ENGINE SIZE AND PERFORMANCE MEASUREMENTS

The engines so far described have a single piston and cylinder. Many motorcycles have a single-cylinder engine. Other motorcycles have engines with two (twin), three, or four cylinders. These multiple-cylinder engines may operate on either the four- or two-stroke principle.

When the engine has more than one cylinder, the crankshaft is designed so that at a given time different strokes are occurring in each cylinder. In a four-cylinder engine, one piston may be moving down on intake, another up on compression, another down on power, and another up on exhaust. A power stroke is always pushing on the crankshaft. These engines operate much more smoothly and can develop much more power than a single-cylinder engine.

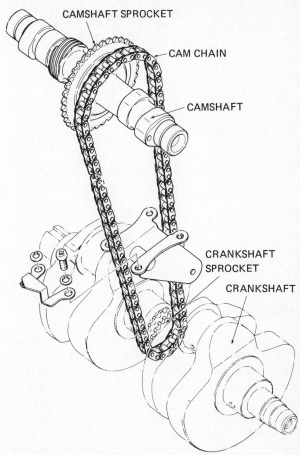

Figure 6–20. The camshaft is driven at half crankshaft speed by a sprocket and chain assembly. *(Yamaha Motor Corp. U.S.A.)*

We shall describe the designs and arrangements of these engines in a later unit.

Motorcycle engines are characterized by a number of size measurements and performance measurements, among which are *bore, stroke displacement, torque,* and *horsepower.*

Bore and stroke

The bore of an engine is a measurement of the diameter of its cylinder (Figure 6–21). The larger the bore, the more powerful the engine is. The stroke is the distance the piston moves from the bottom of the cylinder to the top, or from the top to the bottom. The size of the stroke is determined by the distance between the centerline of the crankshaft and the centerline of the connecting rod where it attaches to the crankshaft. The longer the stroke, the more powerful the engine is. The bore and stroke are given in millimeters, with the bore written first. For example, bore and stroke specifications may be 57 mm × 48.8 mm. Dimensions are always given in millimeters, regardless of where the motorcycle is manufactured.

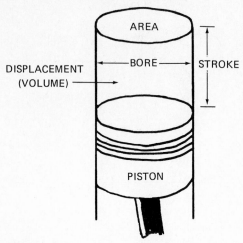

Figure 6–21. Engines are described by their bore and stroke.

Displacement

The displacement of an engine is the area or volume the pistons displace during one stroke (Figure 6–22). The bigger the displacement, the more air and fuel that are brought in on the intake stroke and the more the power that is developed. The bore and stroke of an engine are used to find its displacement. Displacement is measured starting with the piston at the bottom of the cylinder. The bigger the bore and the longer the stroke, the larger the volume or displacement. If the engine has more than one cylinder, the displacements of all the cylinders are added together to determine the total displacement for the engine.

The volume or displacement of a cylinder can be determined by the formula

$$\text{Displacement} = \pi R^2 S$$

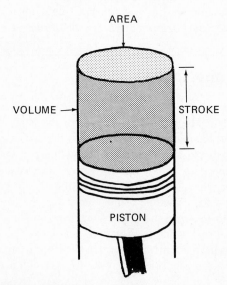

Figure 6–22. Displacement is the area or volume of the cylinder.

where π has the value 3.14, R is the radius (one-half the diameter) of the bore, and S is the stroke. Thus, if the bore and stroke specification is 57 mm × 48.8 mm,

$$\begin{aligned}
\text{Displacement} &= \pi R^2 S \\
&= 3.14 \times 28.50^2 \times 48.8 \\
&= 3.14 \times 812.25 \times 48.8 \\
&= 124{,}462 \text{ mm}
\end{aligned}$$

To change 124,462 mm to centimers, divide by 10; then divide by 100 to get cubic centimeters (cc). The result is 124.462 cc. Our engine thus has a displacement of 124.462 cc. Motorcycle manufacturers, however, use the next whole number, so this engine is described as a 125-cc engine.

Displacement is the most common way of describing a motorcycle engine. Common engine displacements are 50 cc, 80 cc, 125 cc, 250 cc, 500 cc, 550 cc, 750 cc, 1,000 cc and 1,150 cc. Figure 6–23 shows a three-wheeler with a displacement of 125 cc; Figure 6–24 shows a large two-wheeler with a displacement of 1,150 cc. Remember, if an

Figure 6–23. This small three-wheeler has an engine with a displacement of 125 cc. *(U.S. Suzuki Motor Corp.)*

Figure 6–24. This large street motorcycle has a displacement of 1150 cc. *(U.S. Suzuki Motor Corp.)*

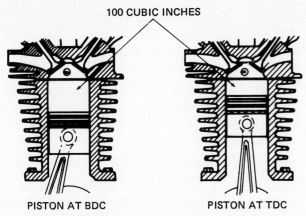

Figure 6–25. A compression ratio of 10 to 1.

engine has more than one cylinder, we have to multiply the displacement of one cylinder by the number of cylinders to get the total engine displacement.

Compression ratio

The compression ratio is a measurement that indicates how tightly the air–fuel mixture is compressed on the compression stroke. It is defined as the ratio of the volume of the cylinder when the piston is at the bottom of its stroke to the clearance volume, i.e., the volume of the small area above the piston when the piston is at the top of its stroke. For example, suppose the volume of the cylinder is 100 cubic inches when the piston is at the bottom of the cylinder. Suppose also that when the piston goes to the top of the cylinder, the air–fuel mixture is compressed into a clearance volume of only 10 cubic inches. (See Figure 6–25). Then the compression ratio is 10 to 1. Compression ratios for most current motorcycles are between 8 to 1 and 10 to 1.

Horsepower and torque

Motorcycle engines may be characterized by the amount of horsepower and torque they develop. *Power* is the rate or speed of doing some work. The type of power we use to describe an engine is *horsepower*. The unit of horsepower was developed a long time ago when man wanted to compare the work performed by steam engines to the work a horse could do.

The horsepower of an engine can be determined mathematically by measuring the engine's torque at any particular rpm (revolutions per minute) of the engine crankshaft. *Torque* is a rotary unit of force which measures turning or twisting effort. A mechanic using a wrench to tighten a bolt applies torque to the bolt. When the bolt is so tight that it no longer turns, the mechanic may still be able to apply torque. Thus, torque is a force that produces or tends to produce rotation.

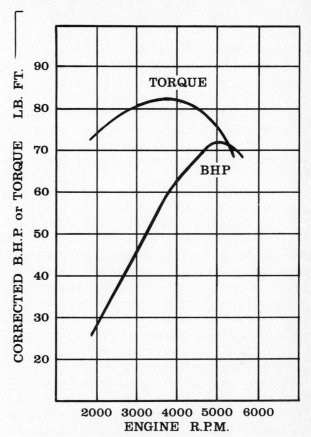

Figure 6–26. Engine torque and horsepower curve. (Harley-Davidson Motors, Inc.)

A device called a *dynamometer* is used to measure motorcycle engine torque and rpm and hence to calculate horsepower. There are many different ways of measuring horsepower. Horsepower measured at the flywheel of an engine is called *brake horsepower,* abbreviated BHP. The motorcycle engine is removed from the bike and installed on a dynamometer to measure BHP.

It is also possible to place the rear wheel of the motorcycle on a dynamometer and determine how much horsepower is being delivered to the road. This quantity is called *road horsepower,* or road HP. Road HP is always lower than BHP, because of frictional losses in getting the power from the engine to the rear wheel.

Torque measured on a dynamometer is recorded on a graph. Horsepower, calculated from torque and rpm, is also charted on a graph. The graph in Figure 6–26 shows horsepower figures along with values of torque in pound-feet. The bottom of the graph has engine speed in revolutions per minute. This graph allows both torque and horsepower to be compared to engine operating speed.

A horsepower and torque curve can be drawn from horsepower and torque measurements. When an operator observes a certain amount of torque on the dynamometer instruments at a particular rpm, the operator puts a mark on the graph that corresponds to the torque and rpm. When the test is complete, all the marks are connected together to form a curve.

The horsepower curve in Figure 6–26 is common to most engines. Horsepower does not start at zero because an engine will not run at zero speed. Therefore, the curve is cut off at the bottom. Horsepower increases as the engine speed and load increase. According to the graph, the engine shown in it reaches its maximum horsepower of 72 BHP at 5,000 rpm. An engine can run faster than this, but horsepower begins to decrease after reaching the maximum point.

The torque curve shows the load-carrying ability of the engine at different speeds in pound-feet or newton meters. The relationship between the torque curve and the horsepower curve shows how the engine will perform at different loads and speeds. The horsepower curve continues to climb as the engine speed increases, until maximum horsepower is reached. This is also true of the torque curve, but the torque curve will reach its highest point much earlier. Notice in Figure 6–26 how the torque curve drops after it reaches its peak point (maximum) at 4,000 rpm.

The torque of most engines varies widely over the normal range of crankshaft speeds. At very low speeds—200 to 300 rpm—an engine develops only enough torque to keep itself running. At these speeds, its horsepower is practically zero. As engine speed and load increase, torque increases to a peak. This is where the manufacturer rates the torque, very near the most efficient operating speed of the engine. At this point, the cylinder or cylinders are taking in the biggest and most efficient air–fuel mixture, and the exhaust gases in the cylinder are being forced out most effectively.

The torque curve drops off rapidly after its peak. At higher engine rpm, there is less time for the air–fuel charge to enter, and the exhaust gases to leave, the cylinder. This causes a weaker push on the pistons and consequently, less torque. Other factors which contribute to the drop in torque are internal engine friction and pumping losses. Power is wasted in an engine when it is pumping in air and fuel, and then exhausting it.

The horsepower curve is directly affected by the torque curve, since torque is one of the elements in the formula for horsepower. However, the horsepower curve does not directly correspond to the torque curve because it is also affected by another element, time. Recall that power is the speed or rate at which work is done. The horsepower curve is able to increase past the peak of the torque curve because the engine rpm increases beyond this point. Eventually, however, the torque drops off so much that even more rpm cannot hold the horsepower curve up.

KEY TERMS

Bore: a measurement taken across the diameter of a cylinder.

Bottom dead center (BDC): highest power of piston displacement.

Brake horsepower: horsepower measured at the engine's flywheel; abbreviated BHP.

Combustion chamber: part of the engine in which the burning of air and fuel takes place.

Compression ratio: the amount the air–fuel mixture is compressed during the compression stroke.

Compression stroke: that stroke of a four-stroke cycle engine during which the air is compressed.

Connecting rod: an engine part that connects the piston to the crankshaft.

Crankshaft: an offset shaft to which the pistons and connecting rods are attached.

Cylinder: a tube in which an engine's piston moves.

Displacement: the cylinder volume displaced by the pistons of an engine.

Engine: a machine that converts heat into a usable form of energy.

Exhaust stroke: that stroke of a four-stroke cycle engine during which the exhaust gases are pushed out.

Four-stroke cycle engine: an engine that develops power through four strokes of a piston.

Flywheel: a heavy wheel used to smooth out the power strokes.

Horsepower: a unit of power used to describe the power developed by an engine.

Intake stroke: that stroke of a four-stroke cycle engine during which air and fuel enter the engine.

Internal combustion engine: an engine in which the burning of fuel takes place inside the engine.

Piston: cylindrical metal part attached to the connecting rod; the piston slides up and down in the cylinder.

Power stroke: that stroke of a four-stroke cycle engine during which power is delivered to the crankshaft.

Stroke: the movement of the piston in the cylinder; the stroke is controlled and measured by the offset of the crankshaft.

Top dead center (TDC): lowest point of piston displacement.

Torque: a turning or twisting effort or force.

Two-stroke cycle engine: an engine that develops power in two piston strokes.

CHECKUP

Identify the basic parts of an engine by writing their names in the spaces provided.

1. _____

2. _____

3. _____

4. _____

5. _____

6. _____

7. _____

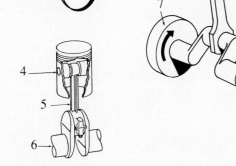

Describe the operation of each of the two-stroke phases shown below.

12. _____
    _____
    _____

13. _____
    _____
    _____

14. _____
    _____
    _____

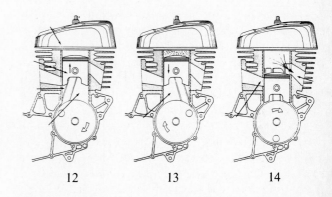

12   13   14

Identify the parts of a four-stroke cycle engine in the spaces provided.

15. _____

16. _____

17. _____

18. _____

19. _____

Identify the parts of a two-stroke engine in the spaces provided.

8. _____

9. _____

10. _____

11. _____

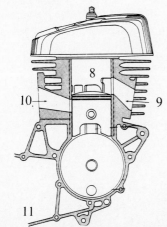

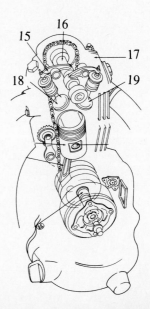

Explain the operation of each of the strokes of the four-stroke cycle engine shown below.

20. _____
_____
_____

21. _____
_____
_____

22. _____
_____
_____

23. _____
_____
_____

DISCUSSION TOPICS AND ACTIVITIES

1. Remove a cylinder head from a two-stroke cycle engine. Turn the engine over and identify each phase of operation.

2. Remove the valve cover from a four-stroke cycle engine. Turn the engine over and observe the valves opening and closing. Identify each of the four strokes.

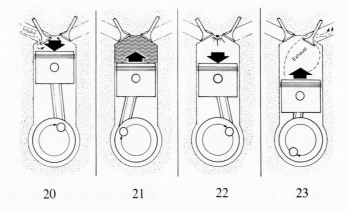

    20   21   22   23

As a motorcycle technician, you will be called upon to perform many engine servicing jobs. You not only need to understand how an engine works, but also how it is constructed. Engine construction is concerned with the different types and designs of engine parts and how they fit together to make an engine (Figure 7–1).

As detailed in the last unit, a motorcycle engine can be divided into two basic areas: the upper end and the lower end. The upper end consists of the cylinder, piston, and cylinder head. If the engine runs on a four-stroke cycle, the upper-end cylinder head includes the valves and the valve operating mechanism. The lower end includes the crankcase, the crankshaft, and the connecting rod. The two ends are designed so that the upper end can be separated from the lower end for servicing. In this unit, we describe the common parts and arrangements used in both two- and four-stroke cycle upper ends. The next unit discusses lower ends.

JOB COMPETENCY OBJECTIVES

When you finish reading and studying this unit, you should be able to:

1. Describe the common types of cylinder design and attachments.
2. Identify the different types of pistons used in two- and four-stroke engines.
3. Explain the purpose and operation of compression and the oil-control piston rings.
4. Identify the major parts of a two- and four-stroke cylinder head.
5. Identify the parts of a valve operating mechanism.

CYLINDERS

The cylinder (sometimes called the barrel) provides the opening in which the piston slides up and down and is made from an aluminum or iron casting (Figure 7–2). The cylinder walls are machined to very close tolerances. If the engine is of the single-cylinder variety, there is one individual cylinder. If the engine has two or more cylinders, both may be cast together in one part, as is the case with the twin cylinders shown in Figure 7–2.

If the engine is air cooled, cooling fins will be cast around the cylinder to remove heat. Liquid-cooled engines will have passages around the cylinder for coolant circulation.

The best surface for the sliding piston is cast iron. Many engines use a cast iron cylinder assembly. The problem with cast iron, however, is that it is very heavy. Hence, in order to reduce weight, it is necessary to cast the basic cylinder assembly from aluminum. Since aluminum is too soft for the actual cylinder walls, most aluminum cylinders are

UPPER-END PARTS AND CONSTRUCTION

fitted with a cast iron liner or sleeve. The aluminum is cast around the liner to make a tight bond, and the liner provides a cast iron surface for the piston to ride on. Aluminum makes an excellent conductor which removes heat from the cylinder.

Some engines use a thin layer of chrome applied directly to the aluminum cylinder. Chrome plating provides a very hard, long-wearing surface for the piston to ride on.

The cylinder must be held tightly to the crankcase because the forces of combustion tend to pull it off the crankcase. A common method of retaining the cylinder to the crankcase is to thread long studs into the crankcase. The cylinder fits over the studs, and the cylinder head and a nut hold the assembly together (Figure 7–3). Usually four studs are used on each cylinder.

Another common method is to form a flange around the bottom of the cylinder and use short studs or hex-head bolts to fasten the cylinder flange to the crankcase. The cylinder head is held in position with another set of studs or hex-head bolts. Figure 7–4 shows how four short studs with hex nuts are used to fasten the cylinder to the crankcase, and four more studs to fasten the head to the cylinder.

The barrel or cylinder used on a two-stroke cycle engine is made from the same material and is held in the same position as those described for the four-stroke cycle engine. The main difference is that the two-stroke barrel must have transfer and exhaust ports cast into it, as shown in Figure 7–5.

PISTONS

The piston's job is to transmit the force produced by burning fuel in the combustion chamber to the crankshaft through the connecting rod. The piston must be as light as

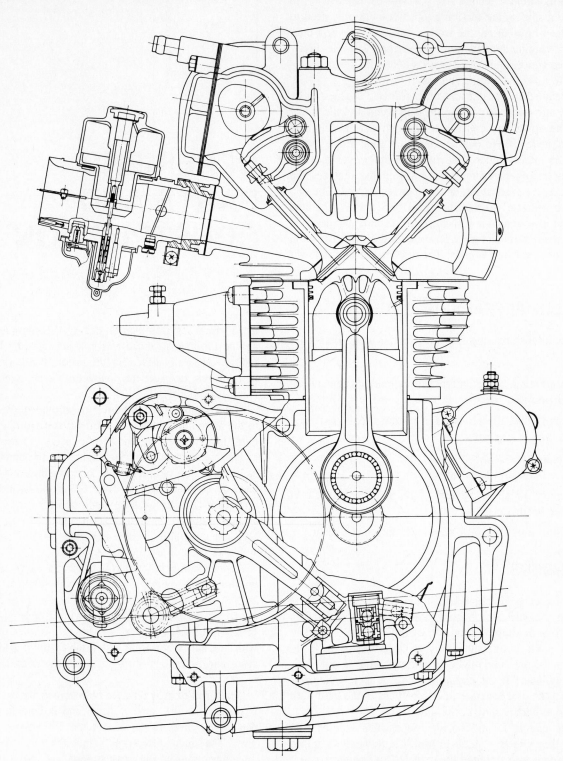

Figure 7–1. Engine construction is concerned with how the parts fit together to make an engine. *(Honda Motor Co., Ltd.)*

possible, but strong enough to withstand the great forces exerted on it.

Pistons are cast or forged from aluminum alloys, which makes them very light. The lighter the piston, the higher are the engine operating speeds. In casting, molten alumi-num is poured into molds. Cast pistons are less expensive to produce and are strong enough for most engines. In forging, aluminum is hammered into shape between two dies. Forging is more expensive, but provides a stronger and denser piston. Forged pistons are used in many en-

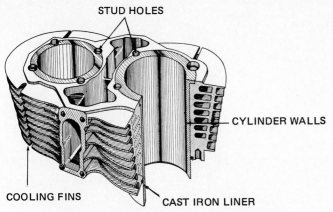

STUD HOLES

CYLINDER WALLS

COOLING FINS

CAST IRON LINER

Figure 7–2. Twin cylinders for a four-stroke cycle (one cylinder cut away). *(Honda Motor Co., Ltd.)*

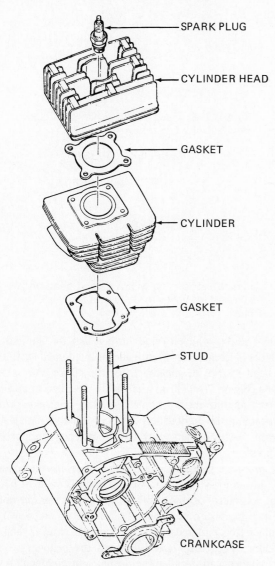

SPARK PLUG

CYLINDER HEAD

GASKET

CYLINDER

GASKET

STUD

CRANKCASE

Figure 7–3. Long studs are used to fasten the cylinder and cylinder head. *(Yamaha Motor Corp. U.S.A.)*

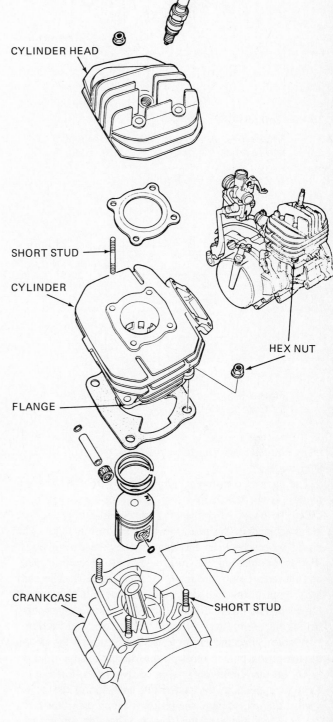

CYLINDER HEAD

SHORT STUD

CYLINDER

HEX NUT

FLANGE

CRANKCASE

SHORT STUD

Figure 7–4. Short studs or machine screws are used to fasten the flanged cylinder to the crankcase. Separate studs are used to fasten the cylinder head to the cylinder. *(Honda Motor Co., Ltd.)*

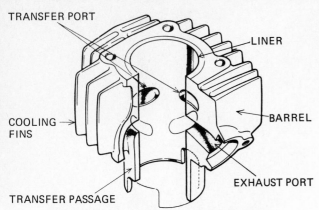

Figure 7–5. A two-cycle barrel or cylinder with ports cast in. (Honda Motor Co., Ltd.)

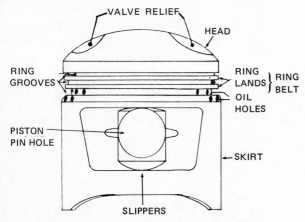

Figure 7–6. Parts of a piston. (Yamaha Motor Corp. U.S.A.)

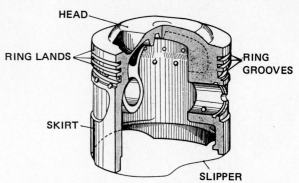

Figure 7–7. A sectional view of a piston. (Honda Motor Co., Ltd.)

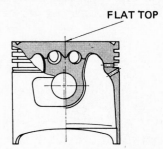

Figure 7–8. Piston with a flat-top head. (Honda Motor Co., Ltd.)

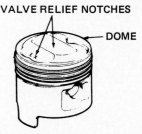

Figure 7–9. Piston with a domed head and notches for valve relief. (Honda Motor Co., Ltd.)

gines equipped with turbochargers (as we shall see in a later unit).

The parts of a piston are shown in Figure 7–6. The top of the piston, which may have many different shapes, is called the *head*. A number of grooves called *ring grooves* are machined in the piston to hold the piston rings. The raised spaces between the ring grooves are called *lands*. The area containing the rings and lands is the *ring belt*, and the area below the rings is called the *skirt*. The skirt area contacts the cylinder wall to guide the piston as it moves up and down. Areas of the skirt called *slippers* may be cut out to minimize cylinder contact area and friction.

A hole called the *pin hole* is bored through the piston for the piston pin. In most pistons the pin is supported directly on the aluminum surface of the piston. Since great force is applied to the piston pin area during the power stroke, the underside of the piston is supported in the wrist pin area by what are called *bosses*. These are shown in a sectional view of a piston in Figure 7–7.

The top of the piston may be of several different shapes. In many pistons the top is flat (Figure 7–8). Higher compression pressures can be achieved by using pistons with domed heads, which extend further into the combustion chamber. Notches are often made in the domed section of the head to provide clearance for the intake and exhaust valves (Figure 7–9). Piston heads are designed to burn the air–fuel mixture more completely. They often conform to the shape of the combustion chamber to move the air–fuel mixture past the spark plug more efficiently during combustion.

Two-stroke pistons (Figure 7–10) often have a rounded top. In addition, the skirt area of the piston may be cut away to control opening and closing of the transfer ports.

Since the piston must be able to move up and down the cylinder freely, it must be made slightly smaller than the cylinder. The small space between the piston skirt and the cylinder wall is called the *piston clearance*, which varies for different engines from .025 to .125 mm (.001 to .005 inch).

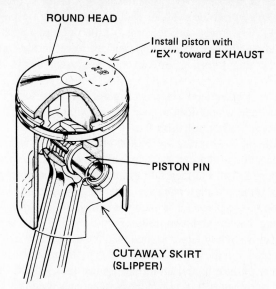

Figure 7–10. Two-stroke piston with a round head. *(Honda Motor Co., Ltd.)*

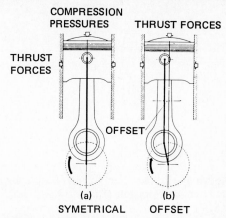

Figure 7–12. Piston pin offset controls thrust forces on the piston skirt. *(Honda Motor Co., Ltd.)*

If there is too much clearance, the piston will not be properly supported. It will make a knocking sound called *piston slap* as the skirt rattles against the cylinder wall. Piston slap can eventually lead to the breaking of the piston skirts.

If there is too little clearance, we can have another problem. As high combustion temperatures heat the piston, both it and the cylinder walls expand. Since an aluminum piston heats and expands at a much higher rate than the cast iron cylinder walls, if the piston has very little clearance to begin with, this expansion may cause it to become wedged in the cylinder. This phenomenon is called *piston seize*.

Most motorcycle engines solve the problem of piston seize by providing a piston skirt that is oval rather than round (Figure 7–11). An oval skirt prevents expansion across the larger diameter as the piston heats up. The result is a piston that gets round, increasing the area of skirt contact with the cylinder with increasing heat.

The piston skirt has the job of supporting and guiding the piston as it speeds up, stops, and reverses direction for each of the two or four strokes of the cycle. The direction

Figure 7–11. The oval piston skirt gets round as it heats up. *(Yamaha Motor Corp. U.S.A.)*

of the forces on the skirt area of the piston is different during each stroke. The piston in Figure 7–12(a) is on a power stroke. Notice the arrangement of the connecting rod and crankshaft. As the piston is forced down the cylinder with the rod in the direction shown, the crankshaft and rod will pull or thrust the piston to the left side of the cylinder.

The pin holes through the piston are often slightly offset to control the thrust forces on the piston (Figure 7–12 (b)). Piston pin offset reduces piston slap caused by the crossover action that results when the connecting rod swings from one side of the piston to the other. If the pin hole were located in the center, the piston would tend to get pulled to the left side during this crossover. Moving the pin toward the major thrust face causes the rod to pull the piston firmly against the right cylinder wall, reducing knocking.

PISTON RINGS

The piston rings are installed in piston grooves to provide a movable seal between the combustion chamber and the crankcase. The rings are made of cast iron or steel, so that they always press against the cylinder walls. Their main purpose is to prevent compression pressures from leaking around the piston into the crankcase.

In most two-stroke cycle engines, two rings are normally installed in the two grooves of the piston (Figure 7–13). A locking pin is installed in the groove to prevent the ends of the rings from rotating and catching in a transfer or exhaust port. The two rings are called *compression rings*. Both two- and four-stroke engines use compression rings.

Pistons used in four-stroke engines have three piston rings. The top two seal compression pressures, and the bottom one is used to control oil on the cylinder wall (Figure 7–14). As we shall see in a later unit, oil is mixed with gasoline in the two-stroke engine for lubrication. This

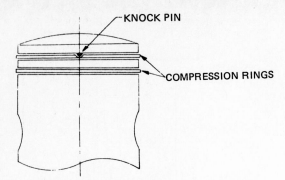

Figure 7–13. Two compression rings used on a two-stroke piston. *(Yamaha Motor Corp. U.S.A.)*

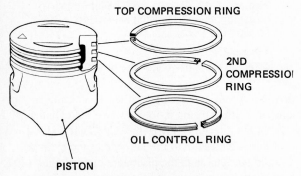

Figure 7–14. Two compression and one oil control ring used on a four-stroke piston. *(Honda Motor Co., Ltd.)*

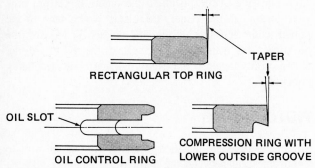

Figure 7–15. Cross-sectional view of three piston rings. *(Honda Motor Co., Ltd.)*

tips away from the cylinder wall, except during the power stroke. The lower outside corner of the ring has a positive contact with the cylinder wall, and the lower inside corner of the ring forms an effective blow-by seal in the ring groove.

The compression rings in Figure 7–15 use a tapered outer face which does a good job of wiping oil from the cylinder wall on the upstroke.

The oil control ring scrapes oil off the cylinder wall and directs the oil through the ring and into holes in the piston (Figure 7–16). Oil then flows through the piston holes and runs back into the crankcase. The oil control ring can be made in one piece, or it may be made up of an expansible spring spacer and two rails (Figure 7–17). The spring spacer is slightly larger around than the cylinder. When assembled on the piston and in the cylinder, the spring spacer pushes the rail uniformly against the cylinder wall.

A spring spacer or expander is sometimes used behind a piston ring to push it out against the cylinder wall with increased pressure. The two-stroke piston shown in Figure 7–18 has an expander behind the second ring.

Some two-stroke engines use a ring called a *keystone ring* (Figure 7–19, top), in which the top side of the ring slants or tapers down. The keystone design allows pressurized gases to force the ring against the cylinder wall before the gases get behind the ring. The sliding movement between the ring and piston breaks up the formation of car-

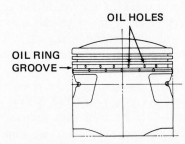

Figure 7–16. Oil scraped off the cylinder wall by the oil ring passes through holes in the piston ring groove. *(Honda Motor Co., Ltd.)*

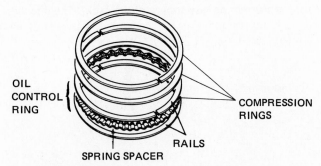

Figure 7–17. This set of piston rings has a three-piece oil control ring. *(Yamaha Motor Corp. U.S.A.)*

means that a two-stroke piston does not require an oil control ring.

A cross-sectional view of a set of piston rings is shown in Figure 7–15. Many top compression rings are rectangular in cross section, forming a simple mechanical seal against the cylinder wall. Since they are larger than the cylinder diameter, they push out against the cylinder wall to provide a seal when compressed in the cylinder.

A rectangular groove is cut on the lower outside or the upper inside edge of many piston rings, which causes the internal forces of the ring to be unbalanced. When the ring is compressed to fit in the cylinder, the top of the ring face

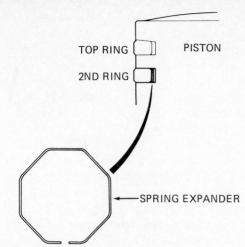

Figure 7–18. A spring expander may be used behind a piston ring to increase its sealing pressure. (Honda Motor Co., Ltd.)

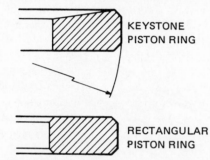

KEYSTONE PISTON RING

RECTANGULAR PISTON RING

Figure 7–19. A comparison between a rectangular (bottom) and keystone (top) piston ring. (Honda Motor Co., Ltd.)

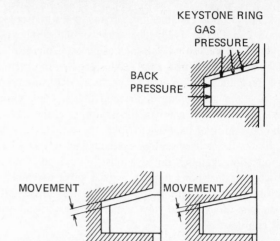

Figure 7–20. The keystone ring moves in its groove to prevent ring sticking. (Honda Motor Co., Ltd.)

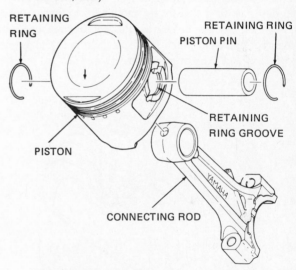

Figure 7–21. The piston pin is retained with two retaining rings or circlips. (Yamaha Motor Corp. U.S.A.)

bon that could cause ring sticking. Figure 7–20 shows a keystone ring, with tapered side.

PISTON PIN

The piston pin, often called a wrist pin, connects the piston to the connecting rod (Figure 7–21). Since the full force of the combustion pressure is transferred from the piston to the connecting rod through the piston pin, the pin is made of high-quality steel. To cut down on weight, it is usually tubular rather than solid.

Most engines use a free-floating method of installing the piston pin in the piston and connecting rod. In this method, the piston pin is slightly smaller than the holes in the piston and the connecting rod. It is therefore free to "float" or rotate in both parts, but it is prevented from slipping along its length by two retaining rings or circlips, one on each side of the piston. The retaining rings fit into grooves in the piston. The advantage of this design is that the pin could stick in either the piston or rod without locking up the assembly. The fit or clearance between the pin and rod

and the pin and piston is one of the closest and most precise in the engine.

CYLINDER HEAD

The cylinder head is an aluminum or iron casting mounted on top of the cylinder. A head gasket between the cylinder head and the cylinder forms a gas- and liquid-tight seal. Single-cylinder engines have a single cylinder head (Figure 7–22). Multiple-cylinder engines have either separate cylinder heads or two or more heads cast in one piece.

The combustion chamber above each piston is formed by the inside surface of the cylinder head. Each combustion chamber has a threaded hole for a spark plug.

The combustion chamber for a two-stroke cycle engine is shown in Figure 7–23. The shape of the combustion chamber is round, so we call the design hemispherical. In many engines, a "squish area" is designed on the perimeter of the cylinder. This area forces the air–fuel mixture to flow past the spark plug at the end of the compression stroke, making for a near-complete burning of the mixture at the beginning of the power stroke.

Cylinder heads used on four-cycle engines not only have a combustion chamber, but also must be equipped with intake and exhaust ports together with a valve assembly to control the ports. There are two types of valve assemblies in common use: pushrod valve systems and overhead camshaft engines.

In a pushrod engine, the camshaft is normally located in the cylinder head area between cylinders (Figure 7–24). It may also be located in the crankcase area. The camshaft operates a set of lower rocker arms which transfer camshaft movement through long hollow rods called pushrods. The pushrods then transfer the motion up to upper rocker arms which operate the valves. Pushrod engines use four valves per cylinder, which increases their ability to get air and fuel in and exhaust gases out.

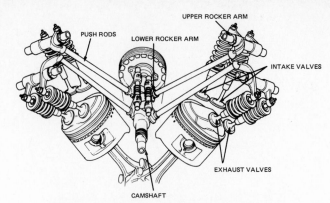

Figure 7–24. A pushrod engine with four valves per cylinder. *(Honda Motor Co., Ltd.)*

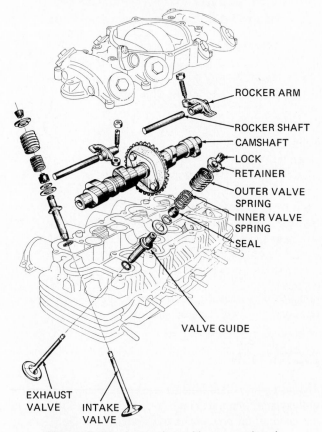

Figure 7–25. An engine with an overhead camshaft. *(Honda Motor Co., Ltd.)*

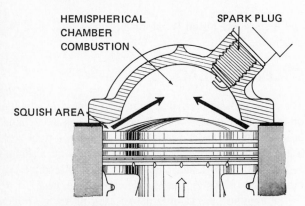

Figure 7–22. A cylinder head for a single-cylinder two-stroker. *(Yamaha Motor Corp. U.S.A.)*

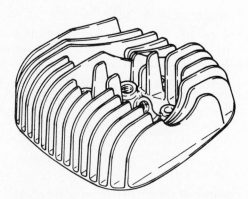

Figure 7–23. A hemispherical combustion chamber with a squish area. *(Honda Motor Co., Ltd.)*

The overhead camshaft engine uses one or two camshafts mounted on top of the cylinder head. Figure 7–25 shows a single overhead camshaft. Rocker arms mounted on rocker shafts transfer the camshaft motion directly to the intake and exhaust valves.

VALVES

The intake and exhaust valves both have a shaft called a *stem* that broadens into a large round valve head (Figure

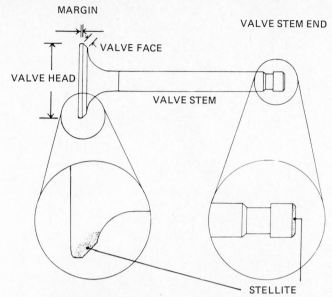

Figure 7–26. Parts of a valve. *(Yamaha Motor Corp. U.S.A.)*

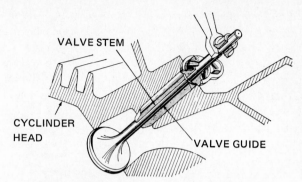

Figure 7–27. The valve guide is pressed into the cylinder head. *(Honda Motor Co., Ltd.)*

7–26) which has a precision-ground, tapered face that, when closed, seals against a seat in the cylinder head. When the face is pushed open by the rocker arm, gases are allowed to move around the valve head in or out of the cylinder.

Valves are made of very high-quality steel because they get very hot during combustion. The intake valve is usually larger in diameter than the exhaust valve because it must control the slow-moving, low-pressure intake mixture. Exhaust valves may be smaller because the exhaust gases leave the cylinder under higher pressures. Since the exhaust valve gets even hotter than the intake valve, it is made of even higher-quality steel. Stainless steel alloys are often used. The valve in Figure 7–26 has its stem end and valve face hardened by plating with a hard metal called stellite.

VALVE GUIDE

The valve stem is supported and guided in the cylinder head by a valve guide. Most engines use a guide that may be removed and replaced during an overhaul. Replaceable guides may be made of cast iron or a softer material such as bronze alloy. They are usually pressed into the cylinder head (Figure 7–27).

The clearance between the valve stem and the guide must allow free movement of the valve. It must also allow a small amount of oil to work its way between the stem and guide for lubrication. If there is too much clearance, oil from the rocker arm area could work its way down the stem and into the combustion chamber. This is especially a problem on the intake valve stem because there is a vac-

uum in the cylinder the entire time the intake valve is open.

VALVE SEAT

The valve seat is a precision-ground area at the entrance of the valve port. It may be a part of the cylinder head or a separate unit installed in the head with a press fit (Figure 7–28). If the cylinder head is made of aluminum, the seats must be made of cast iron or steel.

The angle ground on the valve seat matches the angle ground on the valve face, usually 45 degrees, although on some engines an angle of 30 degrees is used. Some engines also use an interference angle, which is a 1-degree difference in the seat and face angles. Thus, the seat may be ground to 46 degrees and the valve to 45 degrees. Or the seat may be ground to 45 degrees and the valve to 46 degrees. The interference angle provides a hairline contact

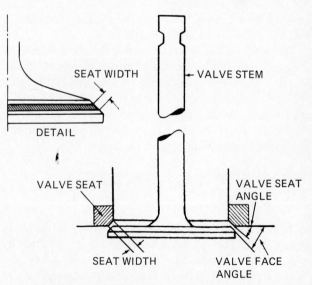

Figure 7–28. The valve seat, which may be a separate part of the cylinder head, matches the valve face. *(Detail: U.S. Suzuki Motor Co.)*

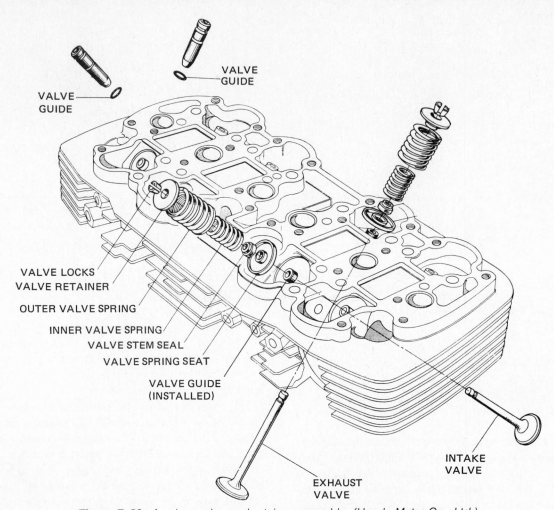

Figure 7–29. A valve spring and retainer assembly. *(Honda Motor Co., Ltd.)*

between the valve and seat for positive sealing and reduces buildup of carbon on seating surfaces.

The width of the seat is important for good sealing. If the seat is too wide, there is a greater chance of carbon buildup, preventing good seating. A wide seat also spreads the valve spring tension over a larger area, thereby reducing the seal. On the other hand, too narrow a seat will reduce heat movement away from the valve head and into the coolant passages near the valve seat.

VALVE SPRINGS, RETAINERS, AND SEALS

A typical valve-spring-and-retainer assembly is shown in Figure 7–29. The valves are held in the closed position by valve springs, which are coil springs on most engines. When extra sealing pressure is needed, two springs, an inner and outer one, are used.

The valve springs are held in position by a retainer. The bottom of the spring rests directly on the cylinder head or on a steel spring seat. The spring is compressed, and the

retainer is placed on top of it. Two split valve locks or keepers are inserted into grooves cut into the valve stem and fit into the retainer, locking the spring to the valve. A small "O" ring seal in a groove on the valve stem prevents oil from running past the lock-and-retainer-cap assembly down the valve stem.

Some engines use a torsion-bar-type valve spring (Figure 7–30). A torsion bar is a length of steel bar that is anchored at both ends in a holder. When the valve is pushed open, an arm attached to both the valve and torsion bar moves with the valve, twisting the torsion bar. When the lower part of the cam contacts the rocker arm, the torsion bar untwists and returns the valve to its closed position.

Rocker arms (Figure 7–31), which are usually made of cast iron, are mounted on and supported by a shaft connected to the cylinder head. Since the hole in the rocker arm is slightly larger than the diameter of the shaft, the rocker arm is free to rock up and down. The valve stem end of the rocker arm is usually adjustable for valve clearance.

The rocker arm changes upward movement to down-

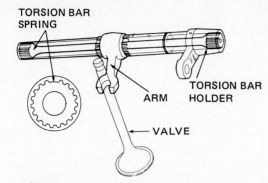

Figure 7-30. Torsion bar valve spring. *(Honda Motor Co., Ltd.)*

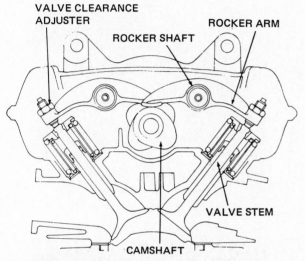

Figure 7-31. The rocker arm assembly opens the valves. *(Yamaha Motor Co., Ltd.)*

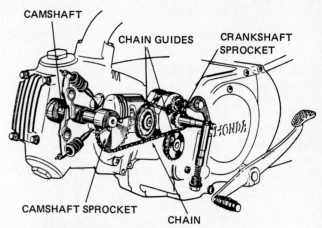

Figure 7-32. The camshaft is driven by a chain connected to the crankshaft. A single overhead cam is shown. *(American Honda Motor Co.)*

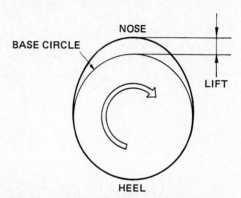

Figure 7-33. Parts of a camshaft lobe. *(Honda Motor Co., Ltd.)*

ward movement. If its pivot is in the center, a given amount of upward movement will result in exactly the same amount of downward movement, a relationship or ratio of 1:1. The pivot point of many rocker arms is off center to provide a ratio of about 1.4:1. That is, 1.4 times more downward movement than upward is provided so that the valve opens far enough for good engine breathing.

CAMSHAFT

The camshaft is mounted on top of the cylinder head in bearings, so that it is free to turn. A sprocket is attached to it so that it may be driven by a chain from the crankshaft (Figure 7-32). Tension wheels and chain guides are used to maintain proper chain tension and ensure quiet operation.

Each of the cam lobes is ground into a shape that provides the correct valve action. After grinding, the surface of the cam lobe is hardened to prevent wear. A typical cam (Figure 7-33) may be thought of as a base circle whose center is identical to or concentric with the center of the camshaft. A nose on the lobe sticks up past the base circle.

The extension of the nose beyond the base circle is called *lift,* and the lower part of the cam lobe is referred to as the *heel.*

KEY TERMS

Camshaft: a shaft with lobes that is used to open the valves at the proper time.

Cylinder head: a casting bolted to the top of the engine that contains the combustion chamber and, if the engine is a four-stroke cycle engine, the valves.

Piston rings: circular metal seals installed in grooves in the piston; used to seal compression pressure and, on a four-stroke engine, to prevent oil from entering the combustion chamber.

Pushrod: a rod used to transfer camshaft motion to the rocker arm.

Retainer: a washer-and-lock assembly used to hold the valve spring in position.

Rocker arm: a lever mounted on the cylinder head that pushes the valves open.

Valve: a device for opening and closing a port.

Valve guide: a part installed in the cylinder head to support and guide the valve.

Valve seat: the part of the cylinder head that the valve seals against.

Valve spring: a coil or leaf spring used to close the valve.

CHECKUP

Identify the two main sections of an engine by writing their names in the spaces provided.

1. _____
2. _____

Identify the parts of the four-stroke cylinder assembly by writing their names in the spaces provided.

3. _____
4. _____
5. _____
6. _____

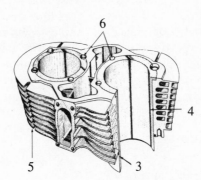

Identify the parts of the two-stroke cylinder assembly by writing their names in the spaces provided.

7. _____
8. _____
9. _____
10. _____
11. _____

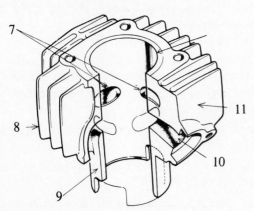

Identify the parts of the piston by writing their names in the spaces provided.

12. _____
13. _____
14. _____
15. _____
16. _____

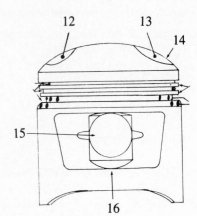

Identify the piston rings in the four-stroke piston by writing their names in the spaces provided.

17. _____
18. _____
19. _____

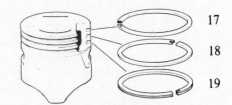

Identify the parts of the valve operating mechanism by writing their names in the spaces provided.

20. _____

21. _____

22. _____

23. _____

24. _____

25. _____

26. _____

27. _____

28. _____

29. _____

30. _____

DISCUSSION TOPICS AND ACTIVITIES

1. Disassemble the top end of a shop two-stroke engine and identify the parts.

2. Disassemble the top end of a shop four-stroke engine and identify the parts.

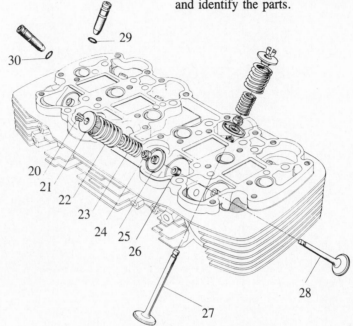

The top-end components in a two-stroke engine are subjected to a great deal of stress. Eventually the piston rings, piston, and cylinder wear out. If the owner takes reasonable care of the engine, the top end may last a long, long time. If, however, the owner abuses the engine by lugging (riding in too high a gear), overrevving, or riding in dirt with a missing, leaking, or improperly sealed air cleaner, the top end will have a very short life. Incorrect timing, incorrect fuel and oil mixture, and other tune-up problems can also lead to premature top-end failure. We shall discuss these tune-up procedures in a later unit. In this unit, we describe how to determine whether a top end needs servicing and how to perform the required services.

JOB COMPETENCY OBJECTIVES

When you finish reading and studying this unit, you should be able to:

1. Explain the problems related to two-stroke upper-end wear.

2. Measure the compression on a two-stroke engine.

3. Describe the disassembly, cleaning, measuring, machining, reassembly, and adjustment techniques required to service a two-stroke top end.

4. Disassemble and clean the components of a two-stroke upper end.

5. Measure a two-stroke cylinder for wear.

6. Measure the parts of a two-stroke piston, including piston clearance and piston rings.

7. Assemble the components of a two-stroke upper-end piston.

TOP-END TROUBLESHOOTING

Top-end problems usually show up as either low power or noise (or both). The best way to tell if the motorcycle has any of these problems is to test-ride the bike. Ride the motorcycle long enough to get it warm, and then listen carefully for abnormal noise coming from the cylinder area.

Piston and cylinder wall wear will eventually lead to too much clearance between the piston skirt and the cylinder (Figure 8–1). The piston will then begin to rock in the cylinder, and you will hear a clattering noise when you snap the throttle open. Wear on the sides of the piston rings and ring grooves will cause the rings to flutter up and down as the piston changes direction on each stroke, also causing a clattering noise.

Wear on the faces of the piston rings and scoring or scratching on the cylinder wall will result in a loss of compression pressure (Figure 8–2). When the compression pressure in the cylinder drops, the power output of the engine drops. At the same time, leaking piston rings cause a

UNIT

8

TWO-STROKE UPPER-END TROUBLESHOOTING AND SERVICING

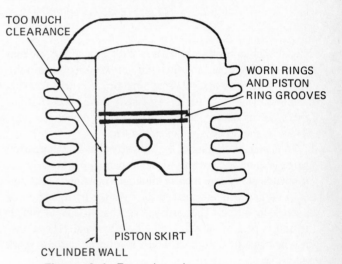

Figure 8–1. Excessive clearance causes engine noise.

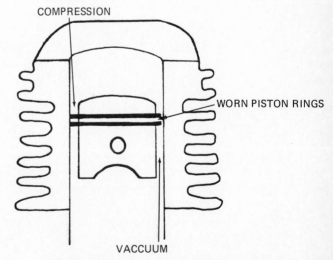

Figure 8–2. Loss of compression pressures past the piston rings means a loss of power.

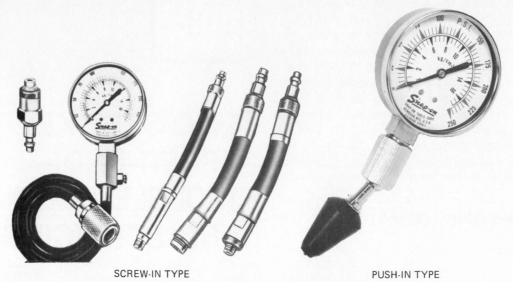

SCREW-IN TYPE   PUSH-IN TYPE

Figure 8–3. Compression pressure tester. *(Snap-On Tools Corp.)*

loss of vacuum in the crankcase. Without a strong vacuum in the crankcase, air and fuel will not be pulled in strongly enough on the crankcase vacuum phase. You will feel that the motorcycle lacks power, especially during acceleration. There are of course other causes of low power, so your next step should be a compression test.

Compression testing is performed with a compression gauge (Figure 8–3) whose scale is marked off in divisions of pounds per square inch or kilograms per square centimeter. The gauge is attached to the cylinder by a push-in or a screw-in fitting. The push-in type has a tapered rubber tip and is held in the spark plug hole by hand. The screw-in type has a flexible hose which is screwed into the spark plug hole.

For the compression test, the gauge is installed and the engine is kicked or cranked over. As the piston goes up, the pressure, which will be shown on the face of the gauge, should rise in the cylinder. You should compare your pressure reading with the compression specifications for the given type of engine. If you find a compression reading more than 1 kilogram per square centimeter (20 psi) below specifications, the problem could be worn rings or worn cylinder walls. Very low compression pressures can result from a hole in the head of the piston or a hole in the cylinder head gasket.

The following job sheet describes the steps to follow in performing a compression test. Be sure to look up the compression test procedure in the shop manual for the motorcycle you are working on. The job sheets are designed to guide you through the job, but you will still need the shop manual for detailed procedures.

Job Sheet 8–1

MEASURE TWO-STROKE COMPRESSION

Before you begin:

Read pp.

Make of Motorcycle _____ Model _____ Year _____

Time Started _____ Time Finished _____ Total Time _____

Flat-rate Time _____

Special Tools, Equipment, Parts, and Materials

Spark plug wrench
Compression tester
Torque wrench
Oil can

Reference

Manufacturer's Shop Manual _____

Specifications

Look up the compression pressure for this motorcycle and write it in the space below:

Compression pressure _____

Procedure

1. If the engine will run, warm it up to operating temperature.

2. With the engine turned off, remove the spark plug wires from each of the spark plugs. If the engine has multiple cylinders, position the wires so that they can be reinstalled correctly, or label them with masking tape. *(SAFETY CAUTION: Be sure you do not come in contact with the spark plug wires during cranking, or you could receive an electrical shock.)*

3. Wipe the area around the spark plug(s) with a cloth, and remove each spark plug.

4. After the plug(s) are removed, connect the compression gauge to a spark plug hole in the cylinder. Open the throttle all the way to get the most air into the cylinder.

5. Electrically crank or kick the engine over four to six revolutions, and observe the compression reading.

6. If the motorcycle has more than one cylinder, repeat steps 1–5 for each of the other cylinders. Be sure to crank the engine the same number of strokes for each cylinder being measured.

7. Record the compression pressure for each cylinder in the spaces provided below.

Cylinder   Compression
1   _____
2   _____
3   _____
4   _____

Instructor check _____

8. If you find a cylinder below specifications, squirt a small amount of oil into the cylinder and reset.

9. If you get a 20- or 30-percent higher reading, the problem is excessive top-end wear.

10. If there is no difference, the problem is a hole in the piston or head gasket.

11. If you find a pressure higher than specification, the problem is most likely a carbon buildup in the cylinder.

12. If the pressure is at least 120 psi or close to specifications, and you cannot get the engine started, the problem is in another area.

13. Reinstall and torque the spark plug(s).

14. Reconnect the spark plug wires to the correct spark plug(s).

NOTES

Instructor check _____   Date completed _____

TOP-END SERVICING

If your troubleshooting results in a problem's being discovered, then the top end must be serviced. Most technicians prefer to service the top end of a two-stroke engine with the engine in the bike. Usually the engine is not removed unless both the upper and lower ends are to be serviced.

The rest of this unit describes the basic steps of top-end servicing, as well as most motorcycle repair procedures.

Disassembly

The necessary exhaust and fuel ignition system components are disconnected from each cylinder. The cylinder head is removed by removing the nuts or cylinder bolts (Figure 8–4). The head gasket is removed, and then the cylinder assembly is removed from the crankcase. When you remove the cylinder, be sure to clean the area around the cylinder base to prevent dirt from falling into the

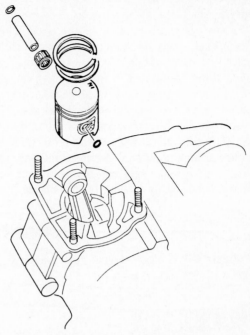

Figure 8–5. Remove the piston from the connecting rod. *(Honda Motor Co., Ltd.)*

crankcase. It is a good idea to cover the open crankcase with a clean cloth.

With the cylinder removed, the piston pin circlips can be removed so that the piston pin and the piston may subsequently be removed. The clips are removed with needle-nose pliers. The piston pin can then be pushed out, and the piston can be separated from the connecting rod, as shown in Figure 8–5. The rings can be removed from the piston ring grooves by prying them apart with your thumb and slipping them off by pushing up from the opposite side with your index fingers (Fig 8–6).

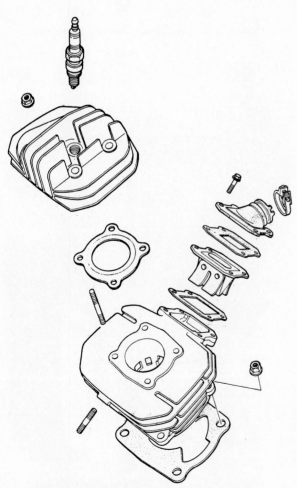

Figure 8–4. Cylinder head disassembly. *(Honda Motor Co., Ltd.)*

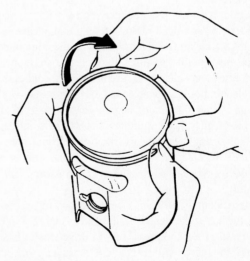

Figure 8–6. Open the rings with your thumbs and carefully slip off. *(Honda Motor Co., Ltd.)*

Cleaning

Each component must be thoroughly cleaned before you can determine its condition. Because two-stroke engines use an oil–fuel mixture, they develop a great deal of burned oil, called carbon. Carbon will be caked on the cylinder head, piston top, and cylinder exhaust parts.

A very useful tool for carbon removal is the carbon scraper, shown in Figure 8–7. A wire brush (Figure 8–8) is also useful for the purpose. Scrapers and wire brushes must be used very carefully on aluminum parts because these parts can be easily scratched and damaged.

Figure 8–7. Carbon scraper. *(U.S. Navy)*

Figure 8–8. Wire brush. *(U.S. Navy)*

Try to avoid using compressed air for cleaning parts because serious injury may result. For example, the solvent or dirt blown from the part can easily enter the eyes or lungs. The only safe way to use compressed air is with eye protection and a respirator. Never use an air blow gun to blow dirt off your skin or clothing; the air can force foreign particles into your skin.

Many engine parts are best cleaned in a solvent parts washer (described in Unit 3). The parts washer may be used to clean steel, iron, aluminum, or almost any material. The solvent will remove loose grease, oil, and sludge, but not carbon.

Carbon removal may be performed with a cold tank cleaner or a glass-bead blaster. A cold tank cleaner (Figure 8–9) uses a cleaning solution in which the components are soaked for a period of time. Because the solution is used without heat, the cleaner is referred to as a cold tank. Cold tank cleaning solutions are used to clean parts—e.g., pistons and other aluminum engine parts—made of nonferrous metal such as aluminum or brass. The solution in the tank is strong enough to remove carbon and paint. *(SAFETY CAUTION: Eye protection and rubber gloves must be worn when putting parts in or taking them out of the tank.)*

After cleaning parts in a cold tank, many shops clean them further with a glass-bead blaster (Figure 8–10). The bead blaster uses compressed air to drive small glass beads against the part. The beads are constantly recirculated through the cleaner, knocking off any particles of carbon or paint that remain on the part.

Figure 8–9. Cold tank cleaner. *(Kleer-Flo Co.)*

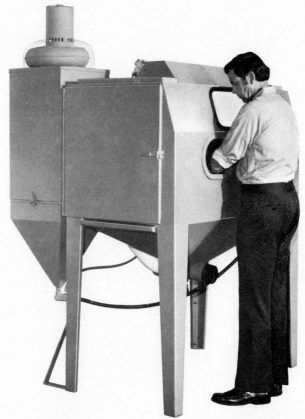

Figure 8–10. Bead blaster. *(Inland Manufacturing Co.)*

Inspection and measuring

After the parts are cleaned, they are inspected and measured for wear. The results obtained from inspection and measuring are then compared with specifications in the service manual so that you can determine whether the parts can be reused.

In two-stroke engines, maximum wear usually occurs in the upper area of the cylinder wall due to the side thrust of the piston. There is normally less wear in the adjacent areas that house the transfer and exhaust ports. Figure 8–11 shows the normal wear pattern.

Use a telescoping gauge and outside micrometer to measure each cylinder's bore diameter at three different depths and in two different directions, as shown in Figure 8–12. In measuring, you may find that the measurement taken in the upper part of the cylinder ("A" in Figure 8–12) is larger than that taken at, say, "C" in the figure. We call this *cylinder taper*. Cylinder taper is common because the top part of the cylinder runs hotter and is subject to more wear. If the measurement is larger at "B" than at "A" or "C," then warpage has occurred, caused by the heat at the exhaust ports. If you find a difference between "Y" and "X," you have a cylinder that is out-of-round. If your out-of-round, taper, or warpage measurement exceeds 0.05 mm (.0019″), the cylinder will have to be replaced, bored, or honed (to be explained later). Warpage can be extreme at areas of high heat, such as the exhaust port. Therefore, care must be taken during measuring.

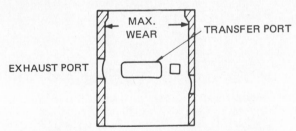

Figure 8–11. Areas of most wear in a two-stroke cylinder. *(Yamaha Motor Corp. U.S.A.)*

Use an outside micrometer to measure the outside diameter of the piston. The piston is cam ground or oval in shape, and its measuring point is at right angles to the piston pin holes, about ½″ from the bottom of the piston (Figure 8–13). Compare your measurement to specifications in the shop service manual. If the piston skirt is smaller than specifications, it should be replaced. If there is any evidence of cracks, deep scoring, or scratches on the piston, it will have to be replaced.

Compare the piston diameter to your cylinder bore measurements. The maximum piston diameter subtracted from the minimum cylinder diameter gives the piston clearance.

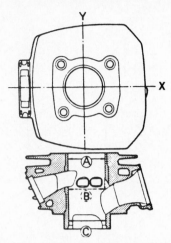

Figure 8–12. Where to measure the cylinder. Measure cylinder at four levels and in two directions. *(Honda Motor Co., Ltd.)*

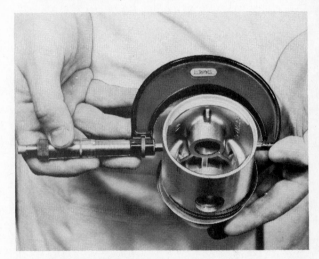

Figure 8–13. Measuring piston diameter. *(Harley-Davidson Motor Co., Inc.)*

If this clearance is larger than the manufacturer's specifications, the cylinder will have to be replaced, honed, or rebored to the next oversize, and a new piston will have to be installed.

Check the piston rings for scoring. If you find any severe scratches, replace the rings. Measure the piston rings for wear by placing each ring into the cylinder so that the ring is flat and parallel with the bottom edge of the cylinder. Then measure the clearance gap between the ring and the groove with a feeler gauge, as shown in Figure 8–14. If the clearance measurement is larger than the specifications, the ring must be replaced.

Make sure the piston ring grooves are clean and free of carbon. You can clean ring grooves with an old piston ring. Just break a used piston ring in two, and use the broken end. Be sure to wear eye protection when breaking the ring. Deburr any rough edges to avoid scratching the ring groove. Run the prepared ring around inside the piston

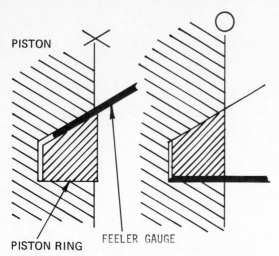

Figure 8–14. Measure ring clearance with a feeler gauge. Measure between the top of the ring surface and the groove. *(U.S. Navy)*

grooves to remove any carbon deposits that have formed.

After cleaning, install the ring or rings in the piston groove. Place a feeler gauge between each ring and the side of the piston ring groove, as shown in Figure 8–15. Keep trying feeler gauge blades until you get one that fits exactly. The measurement made is the piston ring side clearance. Check this measurement on the feeler gauge against the specifications. If too thick a feeler gauge fits into the groove, the ring or piston is worn excessively. Try the procedure again with a new piston ring. If specifications cannot be met and the space is still too large, replace the piston.

The piston pin must be checked for fit in both the piston and the connecting rod. Check the pin fit in the piston by applying a coat of oil to the pin and pushing it into the piston pin hole. The piston pin should fit snugly in its bore, so that it drags a little as you turn it (Figure 8–16). If the piston pin is loose, replace the pin and/or the piston.

To check the pin fit at the connecting rod, apply a light film of oil to the pin and bearing surfaces, and then install

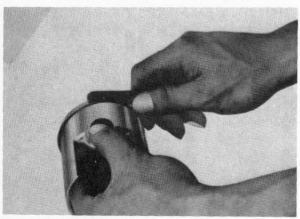

Figure 8–15. Checking piston ring side clearance. *(Yamaha Motor Corp. U.S.A.)*

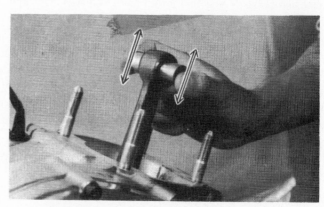

Figure 8–17. Checking piston pin fit in the connecting rod. *(Yamaha Motor Corp. U.S.A.)*

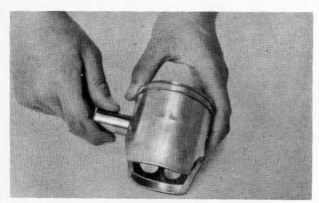

Figure 8–16. Checking pin fit in the piston. *(Yamaha Motor Corp. U.S.A.)*

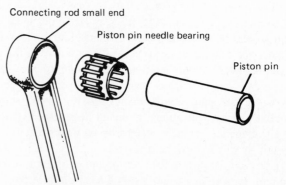

Figure 8–18. Piston pin and bearing assembly. *(Honda Motor Co., Ltd.)*

the pin in the small end of the connecting rod. Check for play, as shown in Figure 8–17. There should be no noticeable vertical play. If play exists, check the diameter of the small end for wear with a telescoping gauge and micrometer. Replace the pin and the bearing (Figure 8–18) or both, as required.

Machining

After you have determined the amount of wear and clearance between the piston and the cylinder, you are ready to decide what to do with the cylinder. If the clearance and condition of the parts are within acceptable limits, you can deglaze the cylinder.

The movement of the piston rings up and down in the cylinder polishes the cylinder surface. This polish or glaze must be removed so that new rings will wear in or "seat" quickly. Also, oil sticks better to a deglazed surface, preventing ring or piston scuffing.

Deglazing

Cylinder deglazing is done with a glaze-breaking tool (Figure 8–19) which uses spring-loaded, abrasive spheres. The abrasive end is about 220 grit, a medium-smooth abrasive. The deglazing tool is chucked in a slow-moving drill that operates at 300 to 500 rpm, and the cylinder is mounted on a fixture or in a vise. *(SAFETY CAUTION: Always wear eye protection when using a glaze breaker.)* As the cylinder rotates, the deglazer is moved up and down to make a cross-hatch pattern on the cylinder walls (Figure 8–20). A lubricant such as kerosene is often used during the deglazing operation. The cross-hatch pattern is important because oil sticks to the small oil grooves created by the cross hatching (Figure 8–21). If the cross-hatch pattern is too smooth, the rings will not wear or seat into the irregularities of the cylinder wall properly and quickly, without scoring or scuffing. If the cross hatch is too rough and too deep, the rings will wear out too fast.

When you finish breaking the glaze, use soap and warm water to wash the cylinders. Grit acts as a grinding compound and could quickly wear out the new rings. Soap and water is the only way to get the dirt and grit out of the tiny crevices that remain after honing. The soap collects around the dirt and grit, and the water then floats it all out. Kerosene or solvent would cause the grit particles to go right

Figure 8–19. Cylinder deglazing tool.

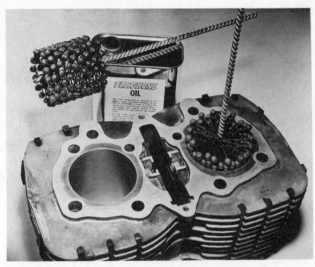

Figure 8–20. Deglazing the cylinder. *(The Carlson Co.)*

back into the crevices. After washing, the cylinders are wiped with a clean, oiled rag to prevent rusting.

Honing

If the cylinder has a small amount of taper or out-of-round, it can be honed. Honing is done with a cylinder hone (Figure 8–22) whose head holds two abrasive stones and two wipers. An adjuster at the top of the fixture is turned to expand the stones and wipers outward against the cylinder. The hone head is connected to a drive shaft, which is driven by an electric drill.

There are several different grits of honing stones available. Stone grits range from very rough (70 grit) to very smooth (600 grit). The piston-ring manufacturer usually specifies which grit is best for each particular ring. The speed with which the stones are rotated and pushed up and down also affects the finish. A slow-moving, ½-inch drill moved in and out rapidly provides the best results (Figure 8–23).

A coolant must be used during honing. Kerosene or honing oil is squirted from a squirt can onto the rotating stones. Honing oil flushes the loose abrasive and metal particles from the stones and cylinder wall, and it cools the cylinder.

Begin the honing operation in the bottom of the cylinder, using a firm cutting pressure. The pressure is adjusted by a control on the honing fixture. *(SAFETY CAUTION: Care must be taken not to allow the stones to come out of the top of the cylinder under power. The stones are not locked into the holder and could fly out, possibly causing injury. Always wear eye protection during honing.)*

As the cylinder is machined and the stones wear, you will have to expand the stones. Frequently remove the hone, and clean and measure the cylinder. As soon as the bottom measurement is close to the top measurement,

Figure 8–21. Deglazing creates a cross-hatched pattern on the cylinder walls. *(Sunnen Products Co.)*

Figure 8–23. Honing the cylinder. *(Sunnen Products Co.)*

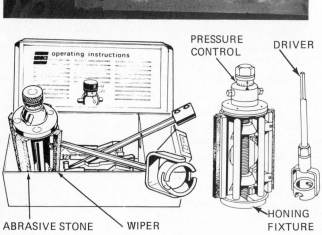

PRESSURE CONTROL

DRIVER

operating instructions

ABRASIVE STONE — WIPER

HONING FIXTURE

Figure 8–22. A hone is used to remove taper and out-of-round. *(Ammco Tools, Inc.)*

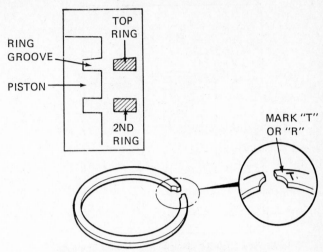

Figure 8–25. Piston ring placement diagram. *(Honda Motor Co., Ltd.)*

Figure 8–24. Cylinders can be bored for oversized pistons. *(Kwik-Way Manufacturing Co.)*

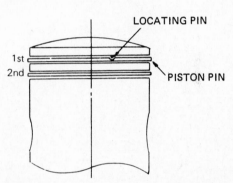

Figure 8–26. Piston ring gaps are aligned under the locating pins. There is a location pin for each ring. *(Yamaha Motor Corp. U.S.A.)*

stroke the stones through the entire length of the bore. Stop honing as soon as you remove all the taper and out-of-round. Be careful not to machine the cylinder too far oversize.

Boring

If the cylinder is scored or has too much taper or out-of-round, the cylinder can be rebored. Boring is usually done at a machine shop. In the boring operation, the cylinder is machined oversize with a tool bit driven by a tool called a *boring bar* (Figure 8–24). After boring, the cylinder is often polished with a cylinder hone to make a cross-hatch pattern. A new oversize piston is fitted to the oversize bore.

Reassembly

Install the piston rings on the piston by gently spreading them with your thumbs and sliding them into their grooves. Make sure that you put the correct ring in the correct groove and that you do not put the rings on upside down. Markings on a piston ring always face up, or towards the head of the piston. An identification drawing is usually provided with a new set of rings to show you the direction in which they should be installed (Figure 8–25). Be sure to align each piston ring end gap with the locating pin that is in the ring groove (Figure 8–26). The pin assures that the rings do not rotate in their grooves and catch in an exhaust or intake port.

Oil the piston pin needle bearing and insert the needle bearing into the small end of the connecting rod. Check the service manual for the correct instructions to install the piston. There are often marks on the head of the piston which point to the inlet or exhaust port side of the cylinder. When you are sure that the piston direction is correct, push the piston pin through the piston and connecting rod. Then install new circlips into each end of the piston.

Install a new cylinder base gasket in position, and coat the piston rings and cylinder wall with oil. Double check that the ring end gaps are in position on the locating pins. Slide the cylinder over the piston and, at the same time, squeeze the piston rings with your fingers. Then push the cylinder over the rings and into position (Figure 8–27), taking care that the rings do not catch on a port opening. Tighten the four cylinder base nuts or bolts. Next, install a new cylinder head gasket and place the cylinder head in position. Finally, install the cylinder head nuts or bolts and slowly tighten them with a torque wrench in a criss-cross pattern in stages, until you get to the specified torque.

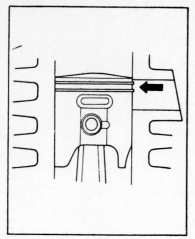

Figure 8–27. Replacing the cylinder. *(Honda Motor Co., Ltd.)*

Reassemble the exhaust system and any fuel system parts you have removed. Install and torque a new spark plug in the cylinder head.

Test ride and adjustments

Make sure that all the fuel lines are connected properly. Fill the fuel tank with the correct blend of premixed oil and fuel. Start the engine, and if there are no fuel, oil, or compression leaks, test-ride the bike. You must be careful how you ride the motorcycle while the piston rings are wearing in to the cylinder walls. This wearing in is called the *break-in period*. Do not allow the engine to lug down, but do not allow it to overrev either. Avoid long periods of idling or any other conditions which could cause the engine to overheat. The break-in period generally takes about one tank of fuel.

At the end of the break-in period, double check the cylinder head torque. Go back over all the fasteners you worked on, and make sure that everything is still tight.

Job Sheet 8–2

TWO-STROKE TOP-END DISASSEMBLY AND CLEANING

Before you begin:

Read pp.

Make of Motorcycle _____ Model _____ Year _____

Time Started _____ Time Finished _____ Total Time _____

Flat-rate Time _____

Special Tools, Equipment, Parts, and Materials

Carbon scraper
Solvent tank

Reference

Manufacturer's Shop Manual _____

Specifications

Procedure

1. Study the shop manual for the correct disassembly procedure.
2. Shut off the tank fuel supply and remove any necessary fuel system parts.
3. Disconnect the spark plug wire(s).
4. Disconnect the exhaust pipe(s).
5. Remove each cylinder head bolt or nut, working in a criss-cross pattern.
6. Remove the cylinder head and cylinder head gasket.
7. Clean the area around the base of the cylinder.

Instructor check _____

8. Remove the cylinder by pulling it up and over the piston.

9. Make a sketch of the direction of the piston in relation to the exhaust side of the engine in the space below. The sketch will help you in reassembly.

Instructor check _____

10. Remove the piston pin circlips and push out the piston pin. Separate the cylinder from the connecting rod.

11. Place a clean cloth over the open crankcase to protect it.

12. Carefully observe the position and any markings on the piston rings, and remove the rings from the piston grooves.

13. Clean and remove the carbon from the cylinder head, piston, and cylinder.

Instructor check _____

NOTES

Instructor check _____   Date completed _____

Job Sheet |8–3|

MEASURE TWO-STROKE CYLINDER(S) FOR WEAR

Before you begin:

Read pp.

Make of Motorcycle _____ Model _____ Year ____

Time Started _____ Time Finished _____ Total Time _____

Flat-rate Time _____

Special Tools, Equipment, Parts, and Materials

Telescoping gauge set
Outside micrometer set

Reference

Manufacturer's Shop Manual _____

Specifications

Look up the following specifications in the shop service manual:

Standard cylinder size _____ Oversizes _____ _____ _____

Instructor check _____

Procedure

1. Make sure that the cylinder is clean. Wipe it several times with a clean rag.

2. Use the correct-size telescoping gauge and outside micrometer to measure the unworn size of the cylinder. Make several measurements at the bottom of the cylinder, below the lowest point of piston ring displacement. Record these measurements below.

   Cylinder #
   1. _____
   2. _____
   3. _____
   4. _____

3. Compare the measurements of the unworn size of the cylinder to specifications to determine whether the cylinder is standard size or has been bored or honed oversize.

Standard size _____ Bored or honed oversize _____

Amount of oversize _____

Instructor check _____

4. Inspect the cylinder walls and indicate their condition below.

Smooth _____ Slightly scored _____ Rough _____

5. Determine the amount of taper in the cylinder by measuring the cylinder several times at the top, where wear is greatest. Calculate the taper by substracting the unworn size from the largest measurement at the top.

Cylinder #

	1	2	3	4
Largest top measurement	_____	_____	_____	_____
Unworn measurement equals	_____	_____	_____	_____
Cylinder Taper	_____	_____	_____	_____

Instructor check _____

6. Determine cylinder out-of-round by measuring the cylinder in the area of most wear in two directions. First measure the cylinder in the direction in which the crankshaft goes, and then measure it at 90 degrees to the crankshaft direction. Calculate out-of-round by comparing the difference between the two measurements.

Cylinder #

	1	2	3	4
Measurement with the crankshaft	_____	_____	_____	_____
Measurement against the crankshaft	_____	_____	_____	_____
Difference between the two measurements (out-of-round)	_____	_____	_____	_____

Instructor check _____

7. Compare the cylinder measurements against specifications to determine the type of cylinder servicing required.

Cylinder ready to rering _____

Cylinder requires deglazing _____

Cylinder requires honing _____

Cylinder requires boring _____

Cylinder damage beyond repair _____

NOTES

Instructor check _____

Date completed _____

Job Sheet   8–4

MEASURE TWO-STROKE PISTON, PISTON CLEARANCE, AND RINGS

Before you begin:

Read pp.

Make of Motorcycle _____ Model _____ Year _____

Time Started _____ Time Finished _____ Total Time _____

Flat-rate Time _____

Special Tools, Equipment, Parts, and Materials

Outside micrometer
Feeler gauge

References

Manufacturer's Shop Manual _____

Specifications

Look up the piston and piston ring specifications and record them in the spaces below:
Piston Diameter:

Standard _____ Oversizes _____ _____

Piston clearance _____

Piston ring side clearance _____

Piston ring end gap _____

Instructor check _____

Procedure

1. Make sure the piston is clean and free of carbon.

2. Inspect the piston head and skirt area. Is the piston:

   Smooth _____ Slightly scored _____ Rough _____

3. Use the correct-size outside micrometer to measure the piston diameter. Make your measurements at 90 degrees to the pin direction in the skirt area, about ½ inch (12 mm) from the bottom of the piston. Record your measurements below:

Cylinder   #1   #2   #3   #4

Piston
measurement _____ _____ _____ _____

4. Compare the piston(s) measurements with the specifications to determine whether the piston is reusable.
Piston(s) acceptable _____ Piston(s) unacceptable _____

5. Compare your piston measurement to the largest cylinder measurement to determine the piston-to-cylinder clearance.

Cylinder #   1   2   3   4

Cylinder
measurement
minus _____ _____ _____ _____

Piston
measurement
equals _____ _____ _____ _____

Piston clear-
ance _____ _____ _____ _____

6. Compare the piston to cylinder clearance with the specifications, and determine whether the clearance is:

Acceptable _____

Unacceptable _____

Instructor check _____

7. Place a new piston ring into the engine cylinder, and use the head of the piston to square it in the cylinder.

8. Use a feeler gauge to measure the space between the ends of the ring. Repeat this procedure for each ring and record your results below:

Piston #   1   2   3   4

Top ring end
gap _____ _____ _____ _____

Second ring
end gap _____ _____ _____ _____

9. Compare your measurements with the specifications to determine whether the end gap is acceptable.

Correct _____ Too small _____ Too large _____

Instructor check _____

10. Install the rings on the pistons in the correct direction.

11. Measure the piston-ring-to-piston-groove side clearance with a feeler gauge. Record your measurements in the spaces below:

Piston #   1   2   3   4

Side clear-
ance top ring _____ _____ _____ _____

Side clear-
ance second
ring _____ _____ _____ _____

12. Is the side clearance:

    Acceptable _____

    Too large _____

    Instructor check _____

13. Install the piston pin in the connecting rod and try to rock it up and down. Does it have:

    Movement _____ Zero movement _____

14. Install the piston in the piston and rock it up and down.
    Does it have:

    Movement _____ Zero movement _____

    Instructor check _____

NOTES

Instructor check _____   Date completed _____

Job Sheet 8-5

TWO-STROKE UPPER-END ASSEMBLY

Before you begin:

Read pp.

Make of Motorcycle _____ Model _____ Year _____

Time Started _____ Time Finished _____ Total Time _____

Flat-rate Time _____

Special Tools, Equipment, Parts, and Materials

Torque wrench
Gasket set
Spark plug

Reference

Manufacturer's Shop Manual _____

Specifications

Look up the following specifications:

Cylinder head torque _____

Spark plug torque _____

Procedure

1. Check to make sure that the piston rings are installed in the correct groove in the correct direction and that the end gaps have engaged the locking pins.

2. Check the shop manual for correct piston direction.

3. Install the piston pin through the piston and rod.

4. Install the piston pin circlips. *(NOTE: Put a rag over the open crankcase to catch any circlip that falls and prevent it from going into the crankcase.)*

Instructor check _____

5. Install a new cylinder base gasket.

6. Coat the piston rings and cylinder walls with oil.

7. Install the cylinder over the piston while compressing the rings with your fingers.

Instructor check _____

8. Install a new cylinder head gasket in position.

9. Start the cylinder head nuts or bolts by hand, and then tighten them in stages with a criss-cross pattern.

10. Tighten the nuts or head bolts to the proper torque with a torque wrench.

11. Install the exhaust and fuel system.

12. Install a new spark plug and torque it to specifications.

13. Check to make sure that all connections and fasteners are properly tightened.

NOTES

Instructor check _____   Date completed _____

KEY TERMS

Boring: machining a cylinder oversize with a boring bar for an oversize piston.

Deglazing: driving a set of abrasive balls around in the cylinder to remove the glaze left by the piston rings.

Honing: a machining operation in which expansible stones are used to remove taper and out-of-round from a cylinder.

Piston ring side clearance: the space between the side of a piston ring and the side of the groove the ring sits on.

Piston-to-cylinder clearance: the clearance or space between a piston skirt and the cylinder wall.

CHECKUP

1. What can happen if there is too much clearance between a piston and its cylinder?

2. What happens when an engine loses compression?

3. Describe how to check a two-stroke engine for compression.

4. Describe two ways of removing carbon from aluminum parts.

5. Describe how to measure a piston with a micrometer.

6. Explain how to measure a cylinder for taper.

7. Describe how to measure a cylinder for out-of-round.

8. How can you determine the piston-to-cylinder clearance?

9. Explain how to measure piston ring end gap.

10. Explain how to measure piston ring side clearance.

DISCUSSION TOPICS AND ACTIVITIES

1. Compare the performance of a two-stroke engine before and after a top-end service. How much did you gain in performance?

2. Measure the compression of a two-stroke engine before and after a top-end service. What, if anything, was the increase?

Upper-end problems in a four-stroke engine usually result in noise, loss of power, or excessive smoking (or any combination of these). The four-stroke cycle engine has valves which must seal to prevent loss of compression. If the valve faces and valve seats wear excessively, compression will be lost and the engine will lose power. The four-stroke cylinder and piston can wear, causing noise and eventual damage if the situation is not corrected. The four-stroke cycle piston oil control ring is designed to prevent oil from getting into the combustion chamber. A worn cylinder and/or oil control ring can allow excessive amounts of oil into the chamber, causing blue-white smoke to spew out of the exhaust and resulting in spark plug fouling and carbon formation in the combustion chamber. In this unit, we explain how to determine whether a four-stroke top end needs servicing and how to perform the required services. Figure 9–1 shows the major parts of the upper end of the four-stroke engine. Note how the cylinder head and cylinder fit on the crankcase. The camshaft and valves regulate the flow of the air–fuel mixture and the exhaust.

JOB COMPETENCY OBJECTIVES

When you finish reading and studying this unit, you should be able to:

1. Measure the compression pressure of a four-stroke engine.

2. Disassemble the top end of a four-stroker.

3. Inspect and measure the valve mechanism components for wear.

4. Measure and inspect four-stroke cylinders for wear.

5. Measure various features of the four-stroke piston, including piston clearance and piston rings.

6. Replace the valve guides in a cylinder head.

7. Resurface the valve faces.

8. Resurface and test the valve seats.

9. Reassemble the four-stroke top end.

TOP-END TROUBLESHOOTING

The first step in troubleshooting four-stroke top-end problems is to test-ride the motorcycle. Get the engine up to operating temperature and listen for abnormal top-end noise. If caused by too much piston-to-cylinder clearance, the noise will sound like a clatter as you snap the throttle open.

Another common noise on four-stroke engines is caused by the adjustable valve lash's leaving too much clearance in the valve operating mechanism. If the valve clearance is too large, a quite audible clicking noise will occur in the valve area of the cylinder head. (We shall describe how to check and adjust valve clearance later in this unit.) Noise

UNIT 9

FOUR-STROKE UPPER-END TROUBLESHOOTING AND SERVICING

in the valve area may be due to worn valve-adjusting components, worn valve guides, or a worn camshaft.

Look for a whitish-blue smoke coming out of the exhaust as you accelerate. White smoke indicates that excessive oil is getting up into the combustion chamber. The oil-control rings on the piston scrape excess oil off the cylinder wall and direct it through holes in the piston-ring grooves down into the crankcase. As the rings and cylinder become worn, the rings become less effective, allowing oil to pass them and leak into the combustion chamber, where the oil is burned.

Oil may also enter the combustion chamber through the intake valve guides. Oil is pumped into the area above the valve to lubricate valve parts. After lubrication, the oil drains back through return passages into the crankcase. If seals around the valve stems become worn, or if there is wear between the valve stem and the guide, oil can enter the combustion chamber between the guide and stem (Figure 9–2). Oil can also be pulled from worn exhaust valve guides into the exhaust system.

You can check for excessive oil in the combustion chamber by removing a spark plug and inspecting its firing end. If the end of the plug is caked with oil and carbon, you have found the problem (Figure 9–3). We shall consider how to "read" spark plugs in more detail in Unit 18.

If your test ride indicates that the motorcycle has less power than it should have, the problem can be too low a compression pressure. The four-stroke engine can lose compression from worn compression rings, worn and leaking valves and seats, a hole in a piston top, or a blown head gasket.

A compression test is performed to determine whether the engine has low compression, and if so, to pinpoint the source of the problem. The test is carried out with the testing mechanism described for the two-stroke engine, in essentially the same manner.

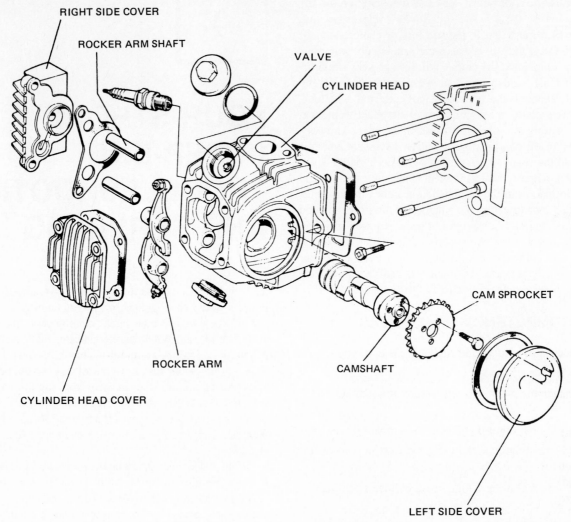

RIGHT SIDE COVER

ROCKER ARM SHAFT

VALVE

CYLINDER HEAD

CAM SPROCKET

CAMSHAFT

ROCKER ARM

CYLINDER HEAD COVER

LEFT SIDE COVER

Figure 9–1. Typical upper-end parts of a four-stroke engine. *(Honda Motor Co., Ltd.)*

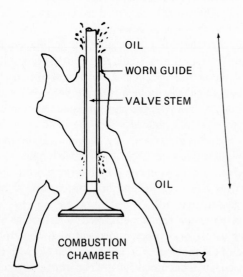

OIL

WORN GUIDE

VALVE STEM

OIL

COMBUSTION CHAMBER

Figure 9–2. Oil can enter the combustion chamber through worn valve guides.

Figure 9–3. A spark plug fouled with oil. *(Champion Spark Plug Co.)*

Job Sheet

MEASURE FOUR-STROKE COMPRESSION

Before you begin:

Read pp.

Make of Motorcycle _____ Model _____ Year _____

Time Started _____ Time Finished _____ Total Time _____

Flat-rate Time _____

Special Tools, Equipment, Parts, and Materials

Spark plug wrench
Compression tester
Torque wrench
Oil can

References

Manufacturer's Shop Manual _____

Specifications

Look up the compression pressure for this motorcycle and write it in the space below:

Compression pressure _____

Procedure

1. If the engine will run, warm it up to operating temperature.

2. Remove the spark plug wires from each of the spark plugs. If the engine has multiple cylinders, position the wires so that they can be reinstalled correctly, or label them with masking tape.
   (SAFETY CAUTION: Be sure you do not come in contact with the spark plug wires during cranking, or you could receive an electrical shock.)

3. Wipe the area around the spark plug(s) and remove each spark plug.

4. Connect the compression gauge to the cylinder. Open the throttle all the way to get the most air into the cylinder.

5. Electrically crank or kick the engine over four to six revolutions, and observe the compression reading.

6. If the motorcycle has more than one cylinder, repeat steps 1–5 for each of the other cylinders. Be sure to crank the engine the same number of strokes for each cylinder being measured.

7. Record the compression pressure for each cylinder in the spaces provided below:

Cylinder   Compression

#1   _____

#2   _____

#3   _____

#4   _____

Instructor check _____

8. If you find a cylinder below 20 to 30 percent of specifications, squirt a small amount of oil into the cylinder and reset. Write your retest findings in the spaces provided below:

Cylinder   Compression With Oil

#1   _____

#2   _____

#3   _____

#4   _____

9. If the oil increases the readings 20 to 30 percent, the problem is worn compression rings. (The oil you put in the cylinder temporarily sealed the worn rings.)

10. If the new readings are the same as the old, it is likely that valve sealing problems are present.

11. A reading lower than 30 percent of specifications indicates a hole in a piston or cylinder head gasket.

12. If you find a pressure higher than specifications, the problem is most likely carbon buildup in the cylinder.

Instructor check _____

13. Reinstall and torque the spark plugs.

14. Reconnect the spark plug wires to the correct spark plug.

NOTES

Instructor check _____   Date completed _____

TOP-END SERVICING

The steps used to repair four-stroke upper-end problems are about the same as those described for upper-end problems in two-strokers. The main difference is that the four-stroke upper end has valves and a valve operating mechanism that are serviced during a top-end overhaul. The servicing procedures, however, still involve disassembly, cleaning, measuring and inspection, machining, reassembly, and test-riding and adjustments.

Disassembly

The top end of a four-cycle engine can usually be serviced with the engine in the motorcycle; however, some technicians prefer to remove it. If the lower end is to be serviced at the same time, the engine must be removed from the bike. *(CAUTION: The many variations of valve components make it absolutely necessary that you locate and follow the specific step-by-step repair procedure in the shop service manual for the particular motorcycle you are working on.)*

You will usually need to remove the fuel tank if the engine is to be serviced in the frame. Remove the cylinder head cover(s). Loosen the cylinder head hold-down bolts in the order specified in the shop manual to prevent warpage of the cylinder head. Be sure to perform this operation while the engine is cold, in order to prevent warpage due to heat. Remove each cylinder head nut or bolt, and remove the camshaft holders. Finally, remove the springs and rocker arms by pulling out the rocker arm shafts (Figure 9–4).

When you reinstall the camshaft, it must be installed in the correct relationship to the crankshaft. We call this relationship *camshaft timing*. Marks called *timing marks* on

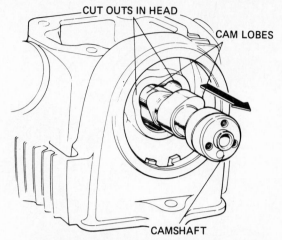

Figure 9–5. Remove the camshaft from the cylinder head. *(Honda Motor Co., Ltd.)*

Figure 9–6. Removing the cylinder head. *(Yamaha Motor Corp. U.S.A.)*

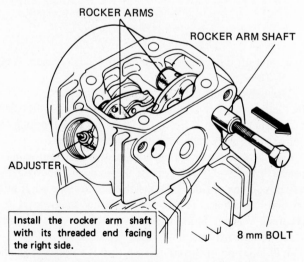

Install the rocker arm shaft with its threaded end facing the right side.

Figure 9–4. Removing rocker arm and springs. *(Honda Motor Co., Ltd.)*

the camshaft drive sprocket and crankshaft sprocket must be aligned during reassembly. Always make sure you can find these marks on the camshaft sprocket, and note how they should line up *before* you disassemble the sprocket from the chain. Check your shop service manual to avoid timing problems that may result from incorrect camshaft installation.

Remove the cam sprocket from the camshaft. Remove the cam chain from the sprocket and remove the camshaft (Figure 9–5). Line up the camshaft with the openings in the cylinder head.

Remove any necessary upper engine brackets, cam chain tensioner bolts, and exhaust pipes. Disconnect and remove the carburetors from the cylinder.

Remove the cylinder head by gently prying in its ribbed areas (Figure 9–6). Do not use too much force, or you might damage the fins on the cylinder head.

Remove any necessary cam chain tensioners and chain guides. Gently pry the cylinder away from the crankcase

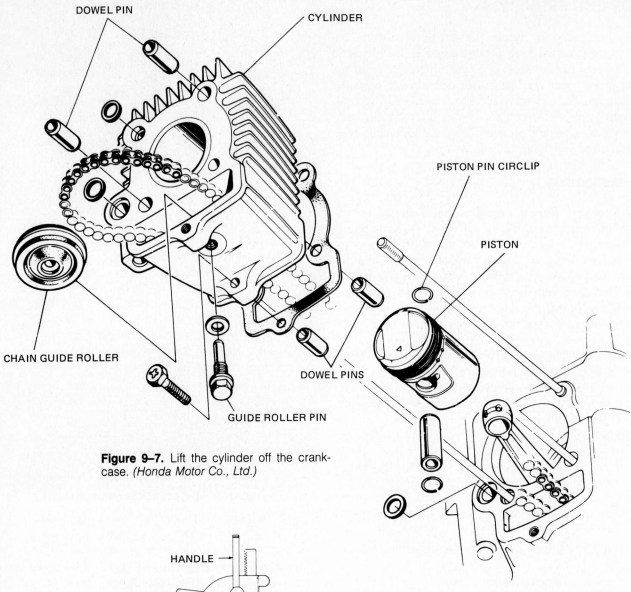

Figure 9–7. Lift the cylinder off the crankcase. *(Honda Motor Co., Ltd.)*

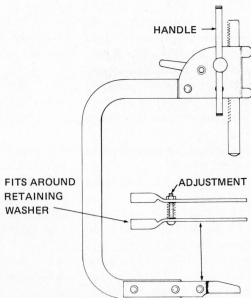

Figure 9–8. A valve spring compressor. *(Ammco Tools, Inc.)*

base, and lift the cylinder assembly off the crankcase (Figure 9–7).

The valves are removed from the cylinder head with a tool called a valve spring compressor (Figure 9–8). This tool, which is shaped like a C clamp, may have a long lever or gear for mechanical advantage.

Position the valve spring compressor over the cylinder head (Figure 9–9). The part of the tool that fits over the valve retaining washer is adjustable. Screws or wing nuts are used to adjust the tool so that it fits snugly over the retaining washer. Some tools have different-size adapters for different-size retaining washers.

With one end of the compressor firmly in place over the retaining washer and the other end against the valve, use the handle or lever to close the tool and compress the valve

Figure 9–9. Compressing the valve spring to remove the valve. *(Harley-Davidson Motor Co., Inc.)*

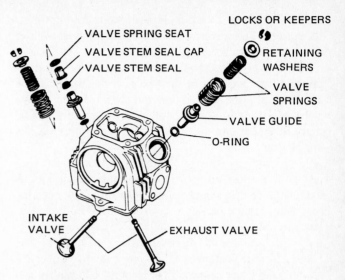

Figure 9–10. Typical valve assembly. *(Honda Motor Co., Ltd.)*

Cleaning

Clean each of the engine components as previously described for two-stroke engines. Make sure the holes for oil flow in the piston oil control ring groove are clear. Valves may be cleaned with a wire wheel mounted on a bench grinder. Hold the valve against the revolving wire brush until the carbon has been removed. The head, face, and stem must be cleaned throughly, particularly the area under the valve head. Carbon under the valve head prevents the flow of heat, which could result in the valve's overheating. *(SAFETY CAUTION: Eye protection must always be worn when using a wire wheel.)* Care must be taken not to catch the valve between the wire wheel and the tool rest on the grinder; if the valve is so caught, it could be pulled out of the operator's hand and hurled into the air. A bead blaster may also be used to clean valves.

Inspection and Measurement

Each of the valve's operating components has to be inspected and measured to determine whether it can be reused. Inspect the rocker arms in the camshaft contact area and the valve contact area (Figure 9–11). If the camshaft

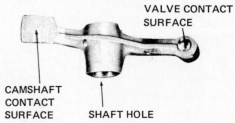

Figure 9–11. Rocker arm inspection and measurement areas. *(Yamaha Motor Corp. U.S.A.)*

spring. To prevent loss of tension, take care not to depress the valve spring any more than is needed to disassemble the valve. *(SAFETY CAUTION: Eye protection should be worn during valve disassembly, in case the tool slips and a keeper or spring is freed.)* Most tools have a mechanism that allows the tool to be locked in the position that results in optimal spring compression. With the spring thus compressed, remove the valve keepers or locks from the valve stem, always being careful to keep your fingers clear of the valve and spring, in case the tool slips. (A small magnet may be used to remove the locks.) Figure 9–10 shows a typical valve disassembly.

Valve parts should be reinstalled in their original location in the engine. Mark the parts or store them in marked boxes so that you can return them to their original location.

Remove the piston(s) by removing the piston pin circlips. Push the piston pin out of the piston, being careful not to drop the circlips into the crankcase. A clean rag placed in the crankcase opening will prevent anything from accidentally falling into the crankcase. Remove the piston rings from each of the piston grooves.

contact surface is scored or chipped, the rocker arm must be replaced. The valve contact end uses a screw-in adjuster which can be replaced if damaged.

Use a small telescoping gauge to measure the inside diameter of the rocker arm shaft hole. If the wear exceeds specifications, the rocker arm must be replaced. Some styles of rocker arm use a bushing in the arm that can be replaced. Make sure the oil feed hole in the rocker arm is not clogged.

If you find any damage on a rocker arm camshaft contact surface, make sure you look for similar damage on its camshaft lobe mate. Inspect each camshaft lobe for scoring or pitting. Use an outside micrometer to measure the distance from the cam lobe heel to the lobe, as shown in Figure 9–12. Compare this distance, called *cam height* or *lobe height,* to specifications, and if you find it to be below specifications, the camshaft lobe is worn excessively and the camshaft must be replaced or reground to specifications.

If, on the other hand, the camshaft meets lobe height specifications, check the camshaft for runout. Set the ends of the camshaft in V blocks, as shown in Figure 9–13, and mount a dial indicator next to the camshaft, with the

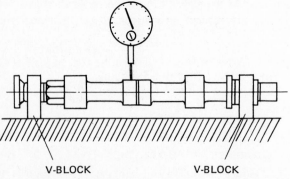

Figure 9–12. Measuring camshaft lobe height. *(Yamaha Motor Corp. U.S.A.)*

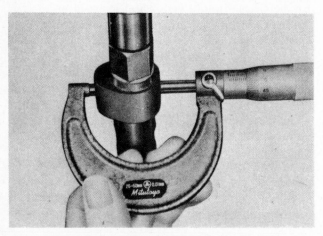

V-BLOCK   **V-BLOCK**

Figure 9–13. Measuring camshaft runout. *(Yamaha Motor Corp. U.S.A.)*

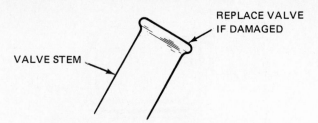

VALVE STEM

REPLACE VALVE IF DAMAGED

Figure 9–14. A mushroomed valve stem. *(Yamaha Motor Corp. U.S.A.)*

plunger contacting a machined surface in the center of the camshaft. Then preload the dial indicator and set its face to zero. Rotate the camshaft in the V blocks while you observe the dial indicator. If the camshaft is bent or has runout, it will be observable on the indicator. Compare any runout you find to specifications. If the runout exceeds specifications, you will have to replace the camshaft.

There are a number of checks to make on the intake and exhaust valves. Check the valve face and the stem end for wear. If the valve face and/or the stem end are pitted or worn, they will require regrinding, as described later. Inspect the end of the valve stem, and if it appears to be "mushroomed" or has a larger diameter than the rest of the stem, then the valve, valve guide, and oil seal should be replaced (Figure 9–14).

The amount of clearance between any valve stem and valve guide may be determined in any of a number of ways. One method is to use a small-hole gauge and an outside micrometer. First, make sure that the valve guide is perfectly clean. Then insert the "small hole" gauge into the valve guide and expand the gauge out against the guide until it fits snugly. Pull the gauge out of the guide and measure across the gauging surfaces with the micrometer. Record the measurement. Make three measurements of each guide altogether—at the top, middle, and bottom. Guides tend to wear more at the top and bottom than in the middle.

Use the outside micrometer to measure the valve stem for the valve that fits in the given guide (Figure 9–15). Make sure that your measurement is in the area of the stem that rides in the guide. The amount of wear is determined by comparing the largest valve guide measurement you found with the smallest valve stem measurement. The difference between them is then compared to the manufacturer's specifications to determine whether it is excessive.

Another, faster method for measuring valve guide openings is to use a valve guide dial gauge (Figure 9–16). This tool is adjusted so that the dial indicator reads zero at the standard valve guide size. The gauge is inserted into the guide, and, as the tool is pushed down the guide, the needle registers any oversize in the guide. The dial indicator gives very accurate readings.

Valve guide wear can also be measured with a dial indicator. A magnetic base or clamp is used to mount the dial

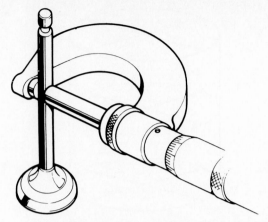

Figure 9–15. Measuring valve stem diameter. *(Honda Motor Co., Ltd.)*

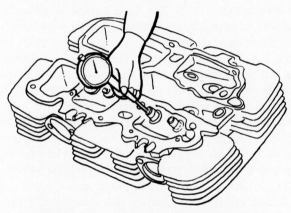

Figure 9–16. Measuring the inside diameter of the valve guide. *(Yamaha Motor Corp. U.S.A.)*

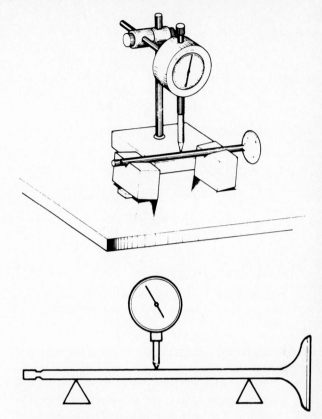

Figure 9–17. Checking for a bent valve. *(Kawasaki Motors Corp. U.S.A.)*

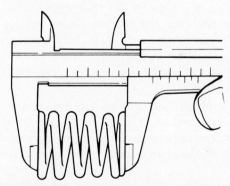

Figure 9–18. Measuring the free length of a valve spring. *(Yamaha Motor Corp. U.S.A.)*

indicator next to a valve, which is inserted into the guide and lifted slightly off its seat. The dial indicator, which has a plunger that is adjusted to contact the valve margin, is then set at zero, and the valve is rocked back and forth against the plunger. The reading on the indicator shows the amount of side-to-side movement, that is, the valve-to-guide clearance of the valve. This measurement is then compared to the manufacturer's specifications, and if excessive clearance is found, the guide and/or valve must be replaced.

A final check of the valve stems is to see whether, like the camshaft, they might be bent or have runout. Place the valve stem in two V blocks, as shown in Figure 9–17. Mount a dial indicator beside the valve, with the plunger on the valve stem, and preload and zero the dial indicator. Rotate the valve in the V blocks and observe the indicator. Any reading you get is runout. Compare the runout reading to specifications, and if it is larger, replace the valve.

Most engines use two springs of different sizes (see Figure 9–10) to prevent valve float, or surging. However, even though the springs are constructed of durable spring steel, they gradually lose some of their tension. This is evidenced by a gradual shortening of the length of the uncompressed spring called *free length*. Use a vernier caliper to measure the free length of the springs (Figure 9–18), and if the free length of any spring has descreased more than 2 mm (.08″) from its specifications, replace the spring.

Another symptom of spring fatigue is insufficient spring pressure. Spring pressure can be checked with a valve-spring compression-rate gauge (Figure 9–19). Test each spring individually. Place a spring in the gauge, and note the spring pressure (the torque on the torque wrench) when the spring is compressed to the installed length (with the

Figure 9–19. Checking valve spring tension. *(Chevrolet Motor Division, General Motors Corp.)*

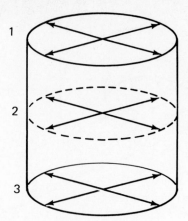

Figure 9–21. Measurement points for the cylinder. *(Yamaha Motor Corp. U.S.A.)*

valve closed). If the pressure does not equal the specified value, replace the spring.

After you have cleaned the cylinder head, you should check it for warpage against the manufacturer's specifications, which will usually be provided. The specification is typically around .03 mm (.001″). To check the head, place a precision straightedge across the head mating surface, as shown in Figure 9–20. Then select a feeler gauge that is the same thickness as the maximum warpage specification. Try to slide the feeler gauge between the precision straightedge and the cylinder head. If it fits, the cylinder head is warped beyond specifications and must be resurfaced or replaced.

The rest of the measurements are similar to those described for the two-stroke upper end. Inspect the cylinder walls for scratches. If vertical scratches are evident, the cylinder wall should be rebored, or the cylinder should be replaced.

Measure the cylinder with a telescoping gauge and outside micrometer in two directions at three different depths,

as shown in Figure 9–21. The value 3 is the unworn standard bore size. Usually, the cylinder will be worn more at level 1 than level 2, but in any event, any difference between 1 and 3 is cylinder taper. The maximum difference you get in the two directions shows the out-of-round. Compare your taper and out-of-round to specifications to determine how to service the cylinder.

Measure the outside diameter of the piston at the piston skirt. The measurement should be made at a point 7 mm (.28″) above the bottom edge of the piston. Place the micrometer at right angles to the piston pin (Figure 9–22).

The difference between your piston measurement and the largest cylinder measurement determines your piston-to-cylinder clearance. Compare the clearance to specifications to determine whether the piston and/or cylinder can be reused.

The piston ring must have the correct amount of side clearance. The ring groove should be cleaned of carbon, and then a new ring should be installed. Use a feeler gauge

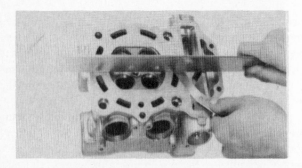

Figure 9–20. Checking the cylinder head for warpage. *(Yamaha Motor Corp. U.S.A.)*

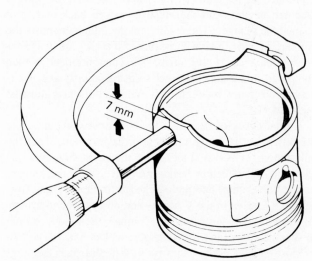

Figure 9–22. Measuring the piston. *(Honda Motor Co., Ltd.)*

Figure 9–23. Measuring piston ring side clearance. *(Harley-Davidson Motor Co., Inc.)*

Figure 9–25. Checking the pin fit in the piston. *(Yamaha Motor Corp. U.S.A.)*

Figure 9–26. Checking the pin fit in the connecting rod. *(Yamaha Motor Corp. U.S.A.)*

Figure 9–24. Measuring piston ring end gap. *(Harley-Davidson Motor Co., Inc.)*

to measure the space between the ring and the land (Figure 9–23). If a feeler gauge larger than specifications fits in between the ring and the land, the piston ring groove is worn excessively and the piston will need to be replaced.

Measure the end gap of each piston ring by inserting a ring approximately 20 mm (.8″) into the cylinder. Push the ring with the piston so that the ring will be at a right angle to the cylinder bore, and measure the ring end gap with a feeler gauge (Figure 9–24). If the end gap exceeds specifications, replace the whole set of rings. You cannot measure the end gap on the expander spacer of the three-piece-type oil control ring. If the oil control ring rails have an excessive gap, replace all three rings.

Lightly oil the piston pin and install it in the small end

of the connecting rod. Check the free play (Figure 9–25); there should be no noticeable vertical play. If any free play exists, check the connecting rod for wear, and replace the pin and connecting rod as required. Insert the piston pin in the piston and check the free play. None should be noticeable (Figure 9–26). If the piston pin is loose, replace the pin and/or the piston as required.

Machining

The cylinder machining techniques, such as deglazing, honing, and boring, are the same as those described in Unit 8 for the two-stroke engine. The four-stroke upper end, however, also requires that a number of machining techniques be performed on the valve operating mechanism. Let us examine these.

Most motorcycle cylinder heads have replaceable valve guides. If the valve guide clearance is excessive, the old guide is removed and replaced with a new one. To help remove the old guide, heat the cylinder head to 100°C (212°F). Use an oven to avoid any possibility of head warpage due to uneven heating. A valve guide driver is used to drive the old guide out and the new guide in (Figure 9–27). Make sure the new guide goes in to exactly the same depth as the old one.

The new valve guide must be finish-reamed to the correct size by driving a reamer through it (Figure 9–28). The size of the reamer used is determined by the size of the

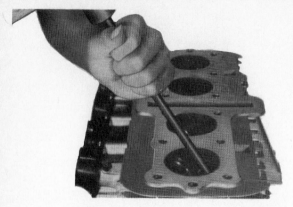

REMOVING

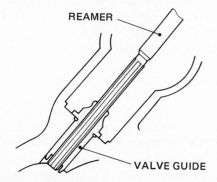

INSTALLING

Figure 9–27. Removing and installing a valve guide. *(U.S. Suzuki Motor Corp.)*

REAMER

VALVE GUIDE

Figure 9–28. The valve guide is finish-reamed to size. *(Yamaha Motor Corp. U.S.A.)*

valve stem and the recommended valve guide clearance. If the valve stem is not worn, a standard-size reamer may be used to establish the correct clearance. If the valve stem is worn, the valve guide will need to be reamed undersize for the correct clearance.

The valve seat is subject to severe wear. Whenever the valve is replaced or the valve face is resurfaced, the valve seat should be resurfaced. If a new valve guide has been installed, the valve seat must be resurfaced to guarantee complete sealing between the valve face and seat.

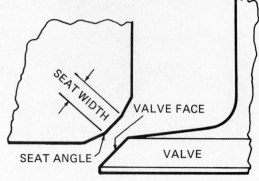

SEAT WIDTH

SEAT ANGLE

VALVE FACE

VALVE

Figure 9–29. Valve seat dimensions.

Valve seat resurfacing is done to establish the correct valve seat width and angle. The dimensions for a valve seat are shown in Figure 9–29. The angle of the valve seat matches the angle ground on the valve face and is usually 45 or 30 degrees. Some engines use an interference angle, in which there is a 1-degree difference between the seat and face angles. Thus, the seat may be ground to 46 degrees and the valve to 45 degrees; or the seat may be ground to 45 degrees and the valve to 46 degrees. The interference angle provides a hairline contact between the valve and the seat for positive sealing and reduces buildup of carbon on seating surfaces.

The valve width is also important for good sealing. If the seat is too wide, the valve spring tension is spread over too large an area, and the valve seat does not seat properly.

Valve seats can be resurfaced by grinding, cutting, or lapping. While popular for automotive valve seats, grinding is not often done on motorcycle cylinder heads. The most common procedures are cutting and lapping.

Valve Lapping

Lapping is a resurfacing procedure which is done either when the valve seat has very little wear or to improve the valve seat seal after cutting. An abrasive compound is spread on the valve face and valve seat, and the valve is placed down on the seat and rotated back and forth with a small suction cup unit with a handle (Figure 9–30). The abrasives in the compound remove metal from both the valve and the seat.

Lapping Procedure

Apply a small amount of coarse lapping compound to the valve face. Insert the valve into the head, and rotate the valve until the valve and valve seat are evenly polished (Figure 9–30). Clean off the coarse compound, and then follow the same procedure with a fine compound. Continue lapping until the valve face shows a complete and smooth surface all the way around. Clean off the compound material, and check for full seat contact, which is indicated by a grey surface all around the valve face. (The shiny surface turns grey from the adhesive.)

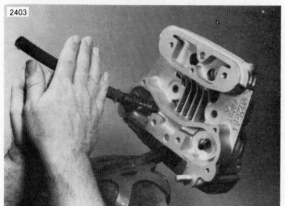

Figure 9–30. Lapping a valve seat. (Top: Yamaha Motor Corp. U.S.A. Bottom: Harley-Davidson Motor Co., Inc.)

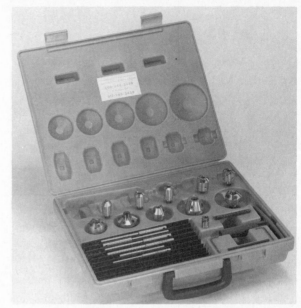

Figure 9–31. A valve seat cutter set. (Neway Manufacturing Co.)

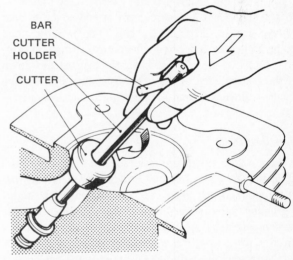

Figure 9–32. Cutting a valve seat. (Kawasaki Motor Corp. U.S.A.)

Valve Cutting

If the valve seat is worn or pitted, it can be resurfaced with a valve seat cutting kit (Figure 9–31). The cutter has a set of carbide blades which are rotated by hand in the seat with a T-handle. A pilot, which fits in the valve guide, is used to center the cutter. (NOTE: Since the cutter uses the valve guide for centering, you must replace any worn valve guides before cutting the valve seats.)

For cutting, a pilot of the correct size is installed in the valve guide, and a cutter of the correct diameter and angle is installed over the pilot. The cutter is driven by hand with a T-handle wrench. Apply steady, light pressure on the cutter directly downward to minimize the possibility of not having the seat be true to the guide (Figure 9–32). Excess pressure can cause the cutter to ''chatter'' and make the seat unsuitable for use. Just cut away the oxidized metal until new, solid metal is exposed. A good seat normally will have a brighter appearance than the surrounding metal.

When you have resurfaced the seat, measure the valve seat width with a vernier caliper. Apply mechanic's bluing dye (such as Dykem) to the valve face and valve seat. Then apply a very small amount of fine grinding com-

pound around the surface of the valve face, insert the valve, and move it quickly back and forth. Lift the valve, clean off all the grinding compound, and check the valve seat width. The valve seat and valve face will have removed the bluing wherever the two have come into contact with each other. Measure the seat width with vernier calipers; it should measure approximately 1 mm (.039″). The valve seat contact area should be one uniform width. If the valve seat width varies, or if pits still exist, further cutting will be necessary. Remove just enough material to achieve a satisfactory seat.

The valve seat contact area must be centered on the valve. If the valve face shows that the valve seat is centered on it, but is too wide, then lightly use both the 30-

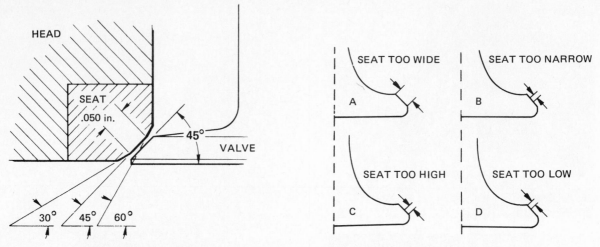

Figure 9–33. Seat contact areas on the valve. *(Left: Harley-Davidson Motors, Inc. Right: Yamaha Motor Corp. U.S.A.)*

and 60-degree cutters to reduce the seat width to 1 mm (.039″). [See Figure 9–33(a)]. If the seat is in the middle of the valve face, but is too narrow, use the 45 degree cutter until the width equals 1.0 mm (.039″). [See Figure 9–33(b)]. If the seat is too narrow and extends right up near the valve margin, then first use the 30-degree cutter and then the 45-degree cutter to get the correct seat width (Figure 9–33(c)). If the seat is too narrow and extends down near the bottom edge of the valve face, then first use the 60-degree cutter and then the 45-degree cutter (Figure 9–33(d)).

Valve Grinding

The faces of the valves are resurfaced on a valve grinder (Figure 9–34), which has two grinding wheels, one (the left) for grinding the valve face and the other (the right) for grinding valve stems, rocker arms, and other valve train components. *(SAFETY CAUTION: Always wear eye protection when using valve grinding equipment.)*

You first need to regrind and chamfer (angle the outside edge of) the valve stem tip. This is called *stemming the valve* and is necessary to ensure proper centering of the valve when it is chucked into the valve grinder. Clamp the valve on its stem in a V-bracket, and then advance the valve toward the side of the grinding wheel, using the micrometer feed. Coolant is pumped over the wheel and valve during grinding. When the stem end contacts the wheel, move the valve back and forth across the wheel side. Remove only enough metal to resurface the tip (Figure 9–35). After grinding the stem, put the valve in a chamfering fixture and advance it toward the wheel to grind a slight chamfer on the tip.

Install the valve in the chuck, which will grip the valve in the unworn part of the stem. Center the valve in the chuck off the valve tip. Loosen the Allen-head screw and pull the chuck stop out far enough to get the valve in. Then open the chuck sleeve and insert the valve far enough in so that the rollers will engage the stem just above the worn area. Push the chuck stop in until it contacts the end of the valve, and then tighten the Allen screw. Close the chuck sleeve so that it contacts the stem. Pull the lever back, close the chuck sleeve, and then back the sleeve off slightly. Press the valve firmly back into the aligner with a slight rotary motion, and release the lever.

Next, adjust the chuck to the correct angle. Specifications may call for the valves to be ground to 45 degrees or 30 degrees, or to an interference angle. Markings on the chuck carriage allow the chuck to be indexed to the correct angle. A hold-down nut is loosened and the chuck is moved into position; the hold-down nut is then retightened. Set the chuck carriage plate stop so that the valve face will reach the right edge of the grinding wheel, but will never go beyond it.

Using the feed wheel, advance the valve grinding wheel toward the valve until it just touches the valve. Begin grinding at the left side of the wheel. Using the carriage lever, move the valve slowly and steadily, right and left, across the wheel (Figure 9–36). Do not allow the valve to pass beyond either edge of the grinding wheel while grinding. Take light cuts, using the feed wheel to feed the grinding wheel up to the valve. Remove just enough material to make a clean, smooth face. When the valve face is trued, move it to the right with the carriage lever until the tip edge of the valve is flush with the right edge of the grinding wheel. Pause a second, and then, using the feed wheel, back the grinding wheel away from the valve—not the valve away from the wheel.

When you have resurfaced the valve face, measure each of the margins with a vernier caliper. The margin gets thinner each time the valve is ground. If there are deep pits in the valve face, or if the valve has been ground previously, the margin may be too thin. The sharp edge on a thin mar-

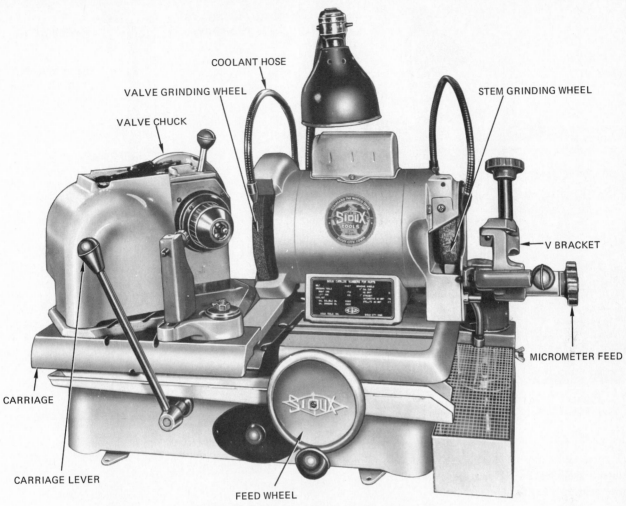

COOLANT HOSE

VALVE GRINDING WHEEL

VALVE CHUCK

STEM GRINDING WHEEL

V BRACKET

MICROMETER FEED

CARRIAGE

CARRIAGE LEVER

FEED WHEEL

Figure 9–34. Valve grinder. *(Sioux Tools, Inc.)*

Figure 9–35. Stemming the valve. *(Sioux Tools, Inc.)*

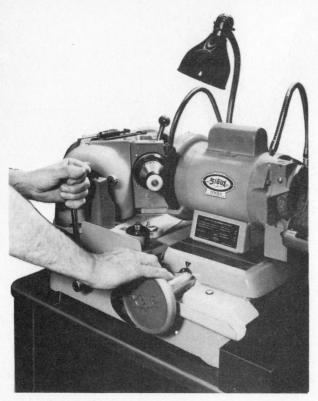

Figure 9–36. Grinding the valve face. *(Sioux Tools, Inc.)*

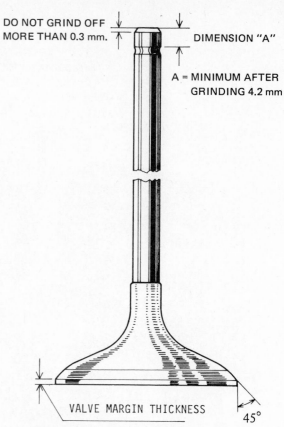

Figure 9–37. The valve margin must not be too thin after grinding, or else the valve will have to be replaced. *(Kawasaki Motors Corp. U.S.A.)*

gin leads to rapid valve burning. Measure the margin of each valve and compare your measurements to the manufacturer's specifications (Figure 9–37). Replace any valve whose margin is too thin.

Reassembly

Begin reassembling the top end by installing the new piston rings on the piston(s). All rings should be installed with the markings facing up. After installation, the rings should be free to rotate in the lands. Make sure you follow the installation diagram and get the correct ring in the correct groove (Figure 9–38). Space the piston ring end gaps 120 degrees apart (Figure 9–39). Make sure you do not align any of the gaps in the multipiece oil ring.

Install the piston(s) by installing the piston pin through the piston and connecting rod. Make sure that the pistons are installed in their original locations and oriented correctly. Piston orientation is often indicated by either an arrow pointing toward the engine front or the letters ''EX'' pointing to the exhaust valve side of the engine (Figure 9–40). Install new piston pin circlips in each piston.

Install a new cylinder base gasket on the crankcase. Install any oil control orifices or dowel pins to replace those that were removed during disassembly, and oil the cylinder walls and piston rings with clean engine oil. Install a piston ring compressor around each set of piston rings, and

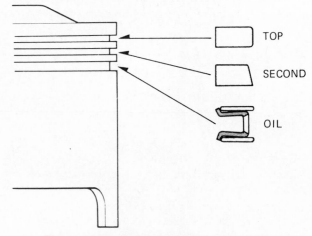

Figure 9–38. Install the piston rings in the correct groove. *(Honda Motor Co., Ltd.)*

squeeze the handle to compress the piston rings in their grooves. Have a helper push the cylinder in position over the pistons (Figure 9–41). When the rings enter the cylinder, remove the compressing tool. Install any chain guides or chain tensioners that you removed in order to remove the cylinder assembly.

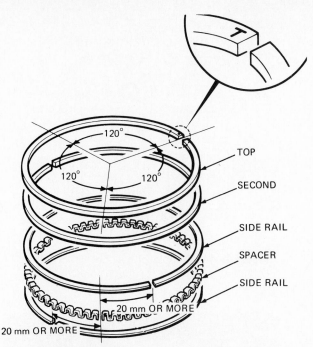

Figure 9–39. Piston ring end gap spacing. (Honda Motor Co., Ltd.)

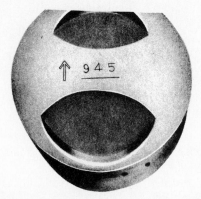

Figure 9–40. Piston markings show piston direction. The arrow points to the engine front. (Yamaha Motor Corp. U.S.A.)

Figure 9–41. Ring compressors used to install the cylinder assembly. (U.S. Suzuki Motor Corp.)

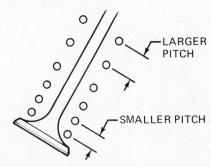

Figure 9–42. The tight coil on a valve spring goes toward the cylinder head. (Yamaha Motor Corp. U.S.A.)

Oil each of the valve stems and insert them into their valve guides. Then place a new stem oil seal over the valve stem. Install the valve springs with the tightly wound coil facing the cylinder head (Figure 9–42), and install the valve spring retainer. Compress the valve spring with the same tool you used to remove the valves.

To prevent loss of tension, do not compress the valve spring more than is necessary to install the valve locks. Install the valve locks or keepers. (CAUTION: Wear eye protection when doing this job.) Tap the valve stems gently with a soft hammer to seat the keepers firmly.

After all work has been performed on the valve and valve seat, and all head parts have been assembled, check for proper valve–valve-seat sealing by pouring solvent into each of the intake ports and then into the exhaust ports. There should be no leakage past the seat. To check, hold the cylinder head up and see whether solvent leaks from the port around the head of the valve. If fluid does leak, disassemble the machinery and lap the valves again with fine lapping compound. Clean all parts thoroughly, reassemble the parts, and check again with solvent. Repeat the procedure as often as necessary to obtain a satisfactory seal.

Oil the rocker shafts and rocker arms, and then assemble the rocker arms, springs, and shafts. Be sure that the rocker arms are correctly located and the cam holders are on the correct sides.

Install a new cylinder head gasket in position. Feed the camshaft drive chain through the cylinder head, and install the cylinder head in position. Replace any chain tensioner parts that were mounted in the cylinder head.

Lubricate the camshaft bearings and install the camshaft and camshaft sprocket. Carefully follow the cam timing in your shop service manual. The chain is installed over the camshaft drive sprocket when the timing marks on the crankshaft and camshaft sprocket are lined up properly (Figure 9–43). Place the timing chain on the sprocket while holding the sprocket. Tighten the sprocket mounting bolts to the specified torque.

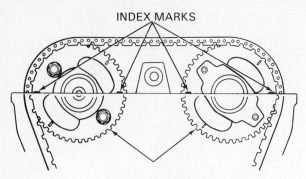

FRONT CYLINDER
CAMSHAFT SPROCKETS

Figure 9–43. Follow the manufacturer's directions for getting the cam in time with the crankshaft. *(Honda Motor Co., Ltd.)*

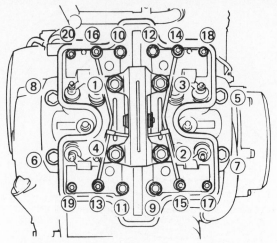

Figure 9–44. Sample of cylinder head bolt tightening sequence. *(Honda Motor Co.,*

Figure 9–45. Adjusting valve clearance. *(Yamaha Motor Corp. U.S.A.)*

Oil the camshaft and place the camshaft holders in position. Loosen and back off the valve adjusting screws on the end of each rocker arm. Start each cylinder head bolt, and tighten the cylinder head nuts or bolts in the specified sequence to the correct torque. Follow the tightening order found in the shop service manual. Figure 9–44 shows a sequence for one engine. Always follow the procedure in your shop service manual to adjust the tension on the camshaft drive chain.

You are now ready to adjust the valve lash or clearance, which is the space allowed for expansion in a valve train operating mechanism. If valve lash is too wide, there will be engine noise and wear on the camshaft and rocker arm contact faces. Eventually, valve timing is affected and the engine performs poorly. If valve lash is too close, then as the valve parts expand from heat, the valve may be prevented from closing tightly on its seat and sealing the combustion chamber. The immediate result of this situation is poor engine performance. But also, a valve held off its seat gets very hot because it is not able to move heat away from the valve head into the valve seat in the cylinder head. So the ultimate result can be a melted valve head, called a burned valve.

Before you start adjusting the valve lash, make sure you have the correct shop service manual procedure to follow. The shop service manual presents a step-by-step procedure for valve adjustment, as well as a set of clearance specifications. The latter is especially important because on some engines, intake and exhaust valves have different clearance specifications. The reason is that exhaust valve temperatures are higher than intake valve temperatures, and the two valves use different metals with different expansion rates. If specifications differ between the two, the exhaust valve clearance will normally be the larger.

The clearance must be measured when the rocker is resting on the heel of the cam (the valve is closed). The shop service manual will specify how to position the engine so that the valves are in the correct position for adjustment.

With most engines, you can rotate the engine and observe the cam and rocker arm. Stop rotating the engine when the heel of the cam contacts the rocker arm. A feeler gauge is selected that is the same as the clearance specification. Check the intake and exhaust valve clearance by inserting the feeler gauge between the clearance adjusting screw and the valve stem. Adjust by loosening the lock nut and turning the screw until there is a slight drag on the gauge (Figure 9–45). Tighten the locknut and recheck the clearance. Repeat the procedure for each valve.

Install a new gasket on the cylinder head, and install the cylinder head cover. Replace the exhaust, fuel system, and ignition components that were removed during disassembly. Refill the crankcase with oil, and then start the engine and check for leaks. Test-ride the motorcycle following the break-in procedure described for the two-stroke upper end. After riding the motorcycle, recheck all fasteners for proper tightening.

Job Sheet 9–2

DISASSEMBLE FOUR-STROKE TOP END

Before you begin:

Read pp.

Make of Motorcycle _____ Model _____ Year _____

Time Started _____ Time Finished _____ Total Time _____

Flat-rate Time _____

Special Tools, Equipment, Parts, and Materials

Valve spring compressor
Carbon scraper
Solvent tank

References

Manufacturer's Shop Manual _____

Procedure

1. Shut off the fuel valve and remove the fuel tank.

2. Remove the nuts or bolts and remove the cylinder head cover.

3. Look up the camshaft timing procedure in the shop service manual. Locate and identify the crankshaft and camshaft timing marks on your engine.

   Instructor check _____

4. Remove each cylinder head nut or bolt in the specified order.

5. Remove the camshaft holders.

6. Remove the cam sprocket from the camshaft.

7. Remove the camshaft.

8. Disconnect the exhaust pipes, ignition system, and fuel system from the cylinder and cylinder head assembly.

   Instructor check _____

9. Gently pry the cylinder head off the cylinder assembly.

10. Remove cam chain tensioners and guides as required.

11. Gently pry the cylinder assembly off the crankcase.

Instructor check _____

12. Use a valve spring compressing tool to remove the valves from the cylinder head. *(SAFETY CAUTION: Wear eye protection when using the spring compressor.)*

13. Mark and store each valve assembly so you can return it to the same location.

14. Remove the piston pin circlips and push each piston pin out. *NOTE:* Make sure the pistons have a direction mark, or make your own with bluing dye (Dykem).

Instructor check _____

15. Clean and remove the carbon from each engine component.

NOTES

Instructor check _____

Date completed _____

Job Sheet   9–3

VALVE MECHANISM INSPECTION AND MEASUREMENT

Before you begin:

Read pp. _____

Make of Motorcycle _____ Model _____ Year _____

Time Started _____ Time Finished _____ Total Time _____

Flat-rate Time _____

Special Tools, Equipment, Parts, and Materials

Outside micrometer   Vernier calipers
Small-hole gauge   Valve spring pressure tester
V-blocks
Dial indicator

References

Manufacturer's Shop Manual _____

Specifications

Look up the following specifications and record them in the spaces below:

Rocker arm inside diameter _____ Wear limit _____

Camshaft lobe height. Intake _____ Exhaust _____

Camshaft runout _____ Wear limit _____

Valve stem diameter _____ Wear limit _____

Valve guide diameter _____ Wear limit _____

Valve stem runout _____ Wear limit _____

Exhaust valve spring free length. Inner _____ Outer _____

Intake valve spring free length. Inner _____ Outer _____

Exhaust valve spring pressure _____ at _____

Intake valve spring pressure _____ at _____

Cylinder head warpage _____

Instructor check _____

Procedure

1. Inspect the rocker arm contact surfaces. Are they:

   _____ Pitted _____ Scored _____

2. Measure the inside diameter of each rocker arm and record your measurements below:

   Rocker arm inside diameter   Intake   Exhaust

   Cylinder #1   _____ _____

          #2   _____ _____

          #3   _____ _____

          #4   _____ _____

3. Compare your measurements with specifications to determine whether the rocker arms can be reused.

   Instructor check _____

4. Inspect the surface of the intake and exhaust lobes on the camshaft. Are the lobes:

   Smooth _____ Pitted _____ Cupped _____ Scored _____

   Instructor check _____

5. Inspect the surface of the camshaft journal. Is the journal:

   Smooth _____ Scratched _____ Scored _____

6. Use a micrometer to measure the lobe height on each intake and exhaust lobe. Record your measurements below:

   Cylinder   Intake   Exhaust

   #1   _____   _____

   #2   _____   _____

   #3   _____   _____

   #4   _____   _____

7. Compare your measurements to specifications. Are any of the lobes worn beyond specifications?

8. Use a set of V-blocks and a dial indicator to measure camshaft runout. Record your measurement below:
   Runout: _____

9. Compare your measurement with specifications. Is the runout within specifications?

   Instructor check _____

10. Inspect the inside of the valve guides. Are the guides:

    Smooth _____ Scratched or scored _____

11. Measure the valve guides with a small-hole gauge. Make a measurement at the top, middle, and bottom. Record the largest reading in the spaces provided under step 14.

12. Inspect each of the valve stems. Are the stems:

    Smooth _____ Scratched or scored _____

13. Use an outside micrometer to measure the stem of each intake and exhaust valve. Be sure to measure in the area where the stem rides in the guide. Measure the stem in three places and record the smallest measurement in the spaces provided under step 14.

14. Determine the intake and exhaust valve guide clearance by substracting the valve stem measurement from the valve guide measurement.

    Cylinder   Guide   Stem   Clearance

    #1   Intake   _____ _____ _____

            Exhaust   _____ _____ _____

#2	Intake	_____	_____	_____
	Exhaust	_____	_____	_____
#3	Intake	_____	_____	_____
	Exhaust	_____	_____	_____
#4	Intake	_____	_____	_____
	Exhaust	_____	_____	_____

15. Compare your clearance measurements with specifications to determine whether the valve guides must be replaced.

    Instructor check _____

16. Inspect the valve faces. Are the faces:

    Smooth _____ Pitted _____ Burned _____

17. Use V-blocks and a dial indicator to check each valve stem for runout. Record your measurements below:

Cylinder	Runout	
#1	Intake	_____
	Exhaust	_____
#2	Intake	_____
	Exhaust	_____
#3	Intake	_____
	Exhaust	_____
#4	Intake	_____
	Exhaust	_____

18. Compare your measurements with specifications to determine whether any valves are bent.

19. Use a vernier caliper to measure the free length of each valve spring. Record your results below:

Cylinder	Intake		Exhaust	
#1	Inner _____ Outer _____		Inner _____ Outer _____	
#2	_____	_____	_____	_____
#3	_____	_____	_____	_____
#4	_____	_____	_____	_____

20. Compare your free-length measurement with specifications and replace any springs that are shorter than specifications.

21. Adjust the valve-spring tension tester to the specified height for the valve springs.

22. Place a valve spring on the tester and compress it to the specified height. Read the tension scale on the tester. Repeat this procedure for each of the valve springs. Record your results in the spaces below:

Cylinder	Intake	Exhaust
#1	_____	_____
#2	_____	_____
#3	_____	_____
#4	_____	_____

23. Compare your readings with specifications and get new springs for the ones that test out below specifications.

    Instructor check _____

24. Use a precision straight edge and the recommended feeler gauge to check the cylinder head for warpage. Is the head:

    Warped _____ Flat _____

    Instructor check _____

NOTES

Instructor check _____   Date completed _____

Job Sheet

MEASURE FOUR-STROKE CYLINDER(S) FOR WEAR

Before you begin:

Read pp.

Make of Motorcycle _____ Model _____ Year _____

Time Started _____ Time Finished _____ Total Time _____

Flat-rate Time _____

Special Tools, Equipment, Parts, and Materials

Telescoping gauge set
Outside micrometer set

References

Manufacturer's Shop Manual _____

Specifications

Look up the following specifications in the shop service manual:

Standard cylinder size _____ Oversizes _____ _____ _____

Instructor check _____

Procedure

1. Make sure that the cylinder is clean. Wipe it several times with a clean rag.

2. Use the correct-size telescoping gauge and outside micrometer to measure the unworn size of the cylinder. Make several measurements at the bottom of the cylinder below piston ring travel. Record your measurements below:

Cylinder
#1   _____
#2   _____
#3   _____
#4   _____

3. Compare the unworn measurement with specifications to determine whether the cylinder is standard size or has been bored or honed oversize.

   Standard size _____ Bored or honed oversize _____

   Amount of oversize _____

   Instructor check _____

4. Inspect the cylinder walls and indicate their condition below:

   Smooth _____ Slight scoring _____ Rough _____

5. Determine the amount of taper in the cylinder by measuring the cylinder several times in its topmost inch (25 mm), where wear is greatest. Calculate the taper by substracting the unworn size from the largest measurement at the top.

   Cylinder

	#1	#2	#3	#4
Largest top measurement	_____	_____	_____	_____
Unworn measurement	_____	_____	_____	_____
Difference between the two measurements (cylinder taper)	_____	_____	_____	_____

   Instructor check _____

6. Determine cylinder out-of-round by measuring the cylinder in the area of most wear in two directions. First measure the cylinder in the direction the crankshaft goes and then at 90 degrees to the crankshaft direction. Calculate out-of-round by comparing the difference between the two measurements.

   Cylinder

	#1	#2	#3	#4
Measurement with crankshaft	_____	_____	_____	_____
Measurement against the crankshaft	_____	_____	_____	_____
Difference between the two measurements (out-of-round)	_____	_____	_____	_____

   Instructor check _____

7. Compare the cylinder measurements with specifications to determine the type of cylinder servicing required.

   Cylinder ready to rering _____

   Cylinder requires deglazing _____

   Cylinder requires honing _____

   Cylinder requires boring _____

   Cylinder damage beyond repair _____

NOTES

Instructor check _____   Date completed _____

Job Sheet

MEASURE FOUR-STROKE PISTON, PISTON CLEARANCE, AND PISTON RINGS

Before you begin:

Read pp.

Make of Motorcycle _____ Model _____ Year _____

Time Started _____ Time Finished _____ Total Time _____

Flat-rate Time _____

Special Tools, Equipment, Parts, and Materials

Outside micrometer
Feeler gauge

References

Manufacturer's Shop Manual _____

Specifications

Look up the piston and piston ring specifications and record them in the spaces below:
Piston Diameter:

Standard _____ Oversizes _____   _____

Piston clearance _____

Piston ring side clearance _____

Piston ring gap _____

Instructor check _____

Procedure

1. Make sure that the piston is clean and free of carbon.

2. Inspect the piston head and skirt area. Is the piston:

    Smooth _____ Slightly scored _____ Rough _____

3. Use the correct-size outside micrometer to measure the piston diameter. Make your measurements at 90 degrees to the pin direction in the skirt area about 12 mm (.5″) from the bottom of the piston. Record your measurements below:

Cylinder	#1	#2	#3	#4
Piston measurement	_____	_____	_____	_____

4. Compare piston measurements with specifications to determine whether the piston is reusable.

Piston(s) acceptable _____ Piston(s) unacceptable _____

5. Compare your piston measurements with the largest cylinder measurement to determine the piston-to-cylinder clearance.

Cylinder	#1	#2	#3	#4
Cylinder measurement minus	_____	_____	_____	_____
Piston measurement equals	_____	_____	_____	_____
Piston clearance	_____	_____	_____	_____

6. Compare the piston-to-cylinder clearance with specifications and determine whether the clearance is:

Acceptable _____

Unacceptable _____

Instructor check _____

7. Place a new piston ring into the engine cylinder and use the head of the piston to square it in the cylinder.

8. Use a feeler gauge to measure the space between the ends of the ring. Repeat the procedure for each ring and record your results below:

Piston	#1	#2	#3	#4
Top ring end gap	_____	_____	_____	_____
Second ring end gap	_____	_____	_____	_____
Oil control ring (if one piece)	_____	_____	_____	_____

9. Compare your measurements with specifications to determine whether the end gap clearance is acceptable.

Correct _____ Too small _____ Too large _____

Instructor check _____

10. Install the rings on the pistons in the correct direction.

11. Measure the piston-ring-to-piston-groove side clearance with a feeler gauge. Record your measurements in the spaces below:

Piston	#1	#2	#3	#4
Side clearance, top ring	_____	_____	_____	_____
Side clearance, second ring	_____	_____	_____	_____

12. Is the side clearance:

Acceptable _____

Too large _____

Instructor check _____

13. Install the piston pin in the connecting rod and try to rock it up and down. Does it have:

    Movement _____ Zero movement _____

14. Install the piston pin in the piston and rock it up and down. Does it have:

    Movement _____ Zero movement _____

                                              Instructor check _____

NOTES

Instructor check _____   Date completed _____

Job Sheet 9–6

REPLACE VALVE GUIDES

Before you begin:

Read pp.

Make of Motorcycle _____ Model _____ Year _____

Time Started _____ Time Finished _____ Total Time _____

Flat-rate Time _____

Special Tools, Equipment, Parts, and Materials

Oven
Valve guide driver
Valve guide reamer

References

Manufacturer's Shop Manual _____

Specifications

Look up the specification for the installed height of the valve guides for the engine, and write it in the space below:

Valve guide installed height _____

Instructor check _____

Procedure

1. Heat the cylinder head in an oven to 100°C (212°F).
2. Mount the cylinder head in a holding stand or support it on wooden blocks, to provide clearance for removing the guides.
3. Locate a valve guide driver that is the correct size for removing the guide.
4. Place the driver in the guide and use a hammer to drive the guide out.
5. Repeat steps 1–4 on each of the guides.

Instructor check _____

6. Locate a driver that is the correct size for installing the new guides.

7. Drive the new guide into the cylinder head. Use the measuring scale to measure the installed height. When the height you wrote in the specifications section is reached, stop driving the guide.

8. Repeat steps 6 and 7 for each of the other guides.

Instructor check _____

9. Measure the valve stem or look up specifications for the correct-size reamer for reaming out the valve guides. Write the size in the space below:

Reamer size _____

Instructor check _____

10. Attach a tap handle to the end of the reamer and drive the reamer through each guide.

11. Check each valve for correct fit after reaming. The valve should fit into the guide easily, but with very little side-to-side clearance.

NOTES

Instructor check _____   Date completed _____

Job Sheet   9–7

RESURFACE VALVE FACES

Before you begin:

Read pp.

Make of Motorcycle _____ Model _____ Year _____

Time Started _____ Time Finished _____ Total Time _____

Flat-rate Time _____

Special Tools, Equipment, Parts, and Materials

Valve grinder
Measuring scale

References

Manufacturer's Shop Manual _____

Specifications

Look up the following specifications for the engine and record them in the spaces below:

Intake valve face angle _____

Exhaust valve face angle _____

Intake valve minimum margin _____

Exhaust valve minimum margin _____

Instructor check _____

Procedure

1. Mount the stem of one of your valves in the V-bracket of the valve grinder. *(SAFETY CAUTION: Always wear eye protection when using the valve grinder.)*

2. Turn on the machine and adjust the coolant flow over the grinding wheel.

3. Advance the valve stem toward the wheel and grind just enough material off the stem to resurface it.

4. Install the valve stem in the fixture and chamfer the tip.

Instructor check _____

5. Repeat steps 1–4 for each of your valves.

6. Adjust the valve grinding chuck to the correct angle for grinding the valves. Inspect the valve-face grinding stone. If it appears to require truing, check with your instructor.

Instructor check _____

7. Adjust the chuck sleeve and chuck stop to accept the valve stems.

8. Install a valve in the chuck and adjust the carriage plate stop to prevent the valve neck from contacting the grinding wheel.

9. Turn on the grinder and adjust coolant flow over the grinding wheel.

10. Move the valve into grinding position and slowly bring the grinding wheel into contact with it.

11. Move the valve back and forth over the grinding wheel. Be sure not to let the valve face pass beyond the grinding wheel edge.

12. Move the grinding wheel toward the valve in small increments until the face is smooth and shiny all the way around. Be careful to remove the minimum amount of metal.

13. Back the grinding wheel away from the valve and then move the valve carriage back out of the way.

14. Use a measuring scale to determine whether the margin is still an acceptable width.

Instructor check _____

15. Grind each of the other valves and record the margin measurements in the spaces below. Valves with thin margins must be replaced:

Cylinder	Intake	Exhaust
#1	_____	_____
#2	_____	_____
#3	_____	_____
#4	_____	_____

Instructor check _____

NOTES

Instructor check _____   Date completed _____

Job Sheet 9–8

RESURFACE AND TEST VALVE SEATS

Before you begin:

Read pp.

Make of Motorcycle _____ Model _____ Year _____

Time Started _____ Time Finished _____ Total Time _____

Flat-rate Time _____

Special Tools, Equipment, Parts, and Materials

Valve seat cutter set
Measuring scale
Solvent
Lapping compound
Valve spring compressor

References

Manufacturer's Shop Manual _____

Specifications

Look up the following specifications for the engine and record them in the spaces below:

Intake valve seat angle _____

Exhaust valve seat angle _____

Intake valve seat width _____

Exhaust valve seat width _____

Instructor check _____

Procedure

1. Install a valve cutting pilot in the guide of the intake valve seat.

2. Select a valve cutter of the correct angle and diameter and install it on the pilot.

3. Cut the valve seat just enough to remove all the pits.

4. Measure the seat width and compare it with specifications. If the seat is too wide, install a narrowing cutter on the pilot and cut the seat until it is the correct width.

Instructor check _____

5. Repeat the grinding and narrowing procedure for each of the other valve seats.

6. Measure and record the width of each of your valve seats in the spaces provided below:

Cylinder	Intake	Exhaust
#1	_____	_____
#2	_____	_____
#3	_____	_____
#4	_____	_____

Instructor check _____

7. Use the spring compressor to install the valves, valve springs, and retainers. *(SAFETY CAUTION: Wear eye protection.)*

Instructor check _____

8. Pour solvent around each of the valve heads and watch for leaks into the intake exhaust or port.

Instructor check _____

9. If there is a leak, disassemble the valve.

10. Place a small amount of valve lapping compound on the valve face and seat. Use a valve lapping cup to lap the valve into the seat.

11. Clean the lapping compound off the parts.

12. Reassemble the valve and check it again for leaks.

Instructor check _____

NOTES

Instructor check _____   Date completed _____

Job Sheet 9–9

REASSEMBLE FOUR-STROKE UPPER END

Before you begin:

Read pp.

Make of Motorcycle _____ Model _____ Year _____

Time Started _____ Time Finished _____ Total Time _____

Flat-rate Time _____

Special Tools, Equipment, Parts, and Materials

Piston ring compressor
Feeler gauge
Gasket set
Piston ring set

References

Manufacturer's Shop Manual _____

Specifications

Look up the following specifications and record them below:

Cylinder head nut or bolt torque _____

Intake valve clearance (lash) _____

Exhaust valve clearance (lash) _____

Procedure

1. Install the piston rings on the piston. Observe the markings to get the correct ring in the correct groove right side up.

2. Space the end gaps of the rings 120 degrees apart.

Instructor check _____

3. Install the pistons on the connecting rod using new circlips. Be sure that the pistons are in their original location and point in the correct direction.

Instructor check _____

4. Install a new cylinder base gasket.

5. Oil the piston rings and cylinders.

6. Compress the piston rings with one or more compressors and push the cylinder over the pistons.

7. Install chain guides or tensioners if required.

8. Install a new cylinder head gasket in position.

Instructor check _____

9. Place the cylinder head in position on the cylinder.

10. Install the camshaft in place.

11. Rotate the crankshaft into position for camshaft timing.

12. Align the timing marks on the camshaft sprocket and install the sprocket and chain in the camshaft. Tighten the sprocket bolts to the correct torque.

Instructor check _____

13. Back off the adjustment screws on each of the rocker arms.

14. Oil the camshaft and install the camshaft holder in position.

15. Start all the cylinder head nuts or bolts and tighten them in stages. Follow the tightening order in your shop service manual.

16. Adjust the tension on the camshaft drive chain.

17. Rotate the engine into position on the intake and exhaust valve rocker arm on the heel of the camshaft.

18. Using the correct feeler gauge between the rocker arm and valve stem, adjust the rocker arm to set the valve clearance.

19. Repeat steps 17–18 for each rocker arm.

Instructor check _____

20. Install a new gasket on the cylinder head cover, and install the cover. Tighten the cover nuts or bolts to the specified torque.

21. Install the exhaust, fuel, and ignition system components.

NOTES

Instructor check _____   Date completed _____

KEY TERMS

Valve clearance: space or lash left in the valve train to allow for heat expansion.

Valve clearance adjustment: the setting of the valve lash to the correct specifications.

Valve guide clearance: the space between the valve stem and the valve guide.

Valve margin: the width of the unground head of the valve that is reduced during each valve face grinding.

Valve seat angle: the angle of the valve seat that must match the angle of the valve face.

Valve seat width: the width of the valve seat that gets wider during valve seat cutting.

Valve spring free length: The length of a valve spring when it is not compressed.

Valve spring tension: the amount of pressure developed by the valve spring when it is compressed to a specified amount.

CHECKUP

1. List three symptoms of upper-end problems.

2. Describe how to troubleshoot a cylinder by observing a spark plug firing end.

3. How can you use a compression test to determine whether an engine has a ring or valve problem?

4. Why should you locate the cam and crankshaft timing marks before disassembling the engine?

5. What should you look for when inspecting a rocker arm for wear?

6. What measurements should you make on a camshaft?

7. Describe how to determine whether valve guides are worn.

8. How can you determine the amount of piston-to-cylinder clearance?

9. Explain how to remove and replace valve guides.

10. Why must valve guides be replaced before valve seats are resurfaced?

11. How can you check a valve for sealing after lapping?

12. Why is valve seat width important to good valve sealing?

13. What two measurements are made on valve springs?

14. Why is the margin that is left on a valve after resurfacing important?

15. Why must the camshaft and crankshaft be aligned during reassembly?

DISCUSSION TOPICS AND ACTIVITIES

1. Measure the compression of a four-stroke engine before and after top-end servicing. What are your results?

2. Compare the power of a four-stroke engine before and after top-end servicing. Did the power improve noticeably?

In the discussion of engine parts and construction in Unit 7, the engine was divided into two basic areas: the upper end and the lower end (Figure 10–1). The lower end of the engine consists of a crankcase, crankshaft, connecting rod, crankshaft bearings, and connecting rod bearings. There are a number of types and designs of each of these components. In order to be able to troubleshoot and service lower ends for both two-stroke and four-stroke engines, a basic understanding of lower-end components is required. Accordingly, in this unit we describe the parts and construction of engine lower ends.

JOB COMPETENCY OBJECTIVES

When you finish reading and studying this unit, you should be able to:

1. Describe the purpose and types of crankcases.
2. Identify the parts of a crankshaft.
3. Explain the different crankshaft designs required for different cylinder arrangements.
4. Identify the parts of a connecting rod.
5. Describe the different types of bearings used in an engine.

CRANKCASE

The crankcase is the aluminum case or housing that supports the crankshaft and houses all the lower-end components. It must be made in two parts so that it can be disassembled for installation of lower-end components.

Many smaller single- and twin-cylinder engines have a crankcase which is divided or split vertically (Figure 10–

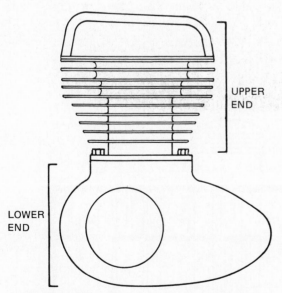

Figure 10–1. Upper and lower ends of the engine.

ENGINE LOWER END

2). A side cover or covers on either side can be unbolted to remove the crankshaft and connecting rod assembly. The dividing line between the two parts of the crankshaft is rarely down the center of the engine, because the center is an area of high stress.

Large multicylinder engines have a crankcase which is split horizontally, as shown in Figure 10–3. With a horizontal split, the dividing line may be, and usually is, down the center of the crankshaft. The two crankcase halves are machined to accept the crankshaft bearings and transmission components (to be discussed subsequently). Oil passages are cast and drilled throughout the crankcase to carry oil to each of the parts (Figure 10–4). (Oil flow is discussed in a later unit.)

CRANKSHAFT

The crankshaft converts the up-and-down motion of the piston or pistons to rotary motion to power the rear wheel of the motorcycle. Motorcycles use one of two different types of crankshaft. Most of the larger, four-stroke cycle engines use a single-piece crankshaft, i.e., a crankshaft that is cast or forged from one piece of metal. Most two-stroke engines use a crankshaft that is built up from a number of smaller parts.

Regardless of the design, all crankshafts have certain parts in common. A single-piece crankshaft for a two-cylinder (four-stroke) engine is shown in Figure 10–5. This crankshaft has two offsets, called *throws,* to which the connecting rods are attached. The throws are placed directly in line with the cylinders.

Each of the throws has a precision-ground surface called a *journal* where the connecting rod is mounted. Crankshafts also have precision-ground journals which rotate in main bearings located in the crankcase. The crankshaft in Figure 10–5 has three main bearing journals. The more main bearings the crankshaft has, the better is its support.

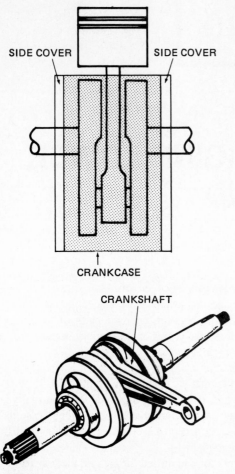

Figure 10–2. A crankcase can be divided (split) vertically. *(Bottom: Honda Motor Co., Ltd.)*

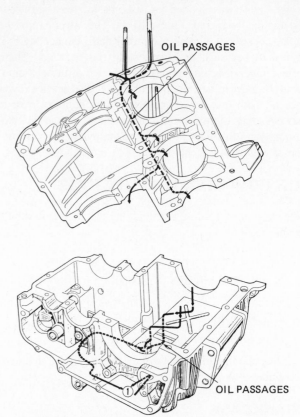

Figure 10–4. Oil passages are cast and drilled in the crankcase halves. *(Honda Motor Co., Ltd.)*

The crankshaft throws, with their connecting rods and piston assemblies, are very heavy, and the rapid rotation of the crankshaft increases the force that their weight exerts even further. Since the increased force tends to bend or twist the crankshaft out of shape, heavy counterweights are attached to the crankshaft opposite the throws to balance the weight of the piston and connecting rod assembly when the crankshaft is rotating. Most motorcycle engines combine the flywheel and counterweights into one part.

As shown in Figure 10–5, the four-stroke crankshaft drives the valve operating mechanism by means of a chain. A camshaft drive sprocket is attached to the end or the cen-

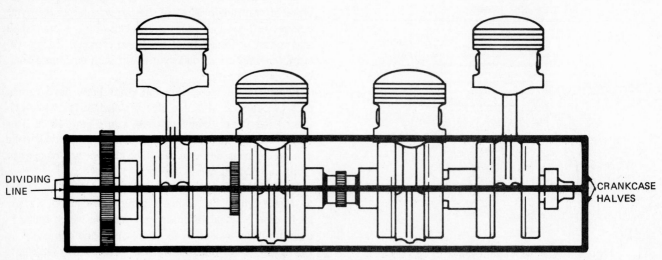

Figure 10–3. A crankcase can be divided (split) horizontally.

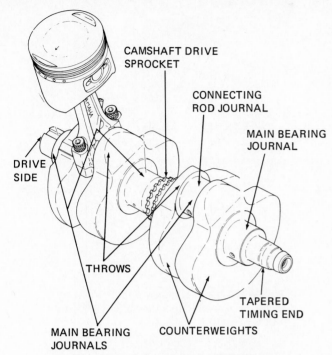

Figure 10–5. Crankshaft for a two-cylinder engine. *(Yamaha Motor Corp. U.S.A.)*

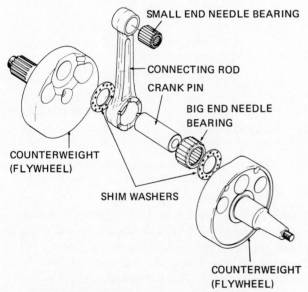

Figure 10–6. An exploded view of a built-up crankshaft. *(Yamaha Motor Corp. U.S.A.)*

ter of the crankshaft. One end of the crankshaft, called the drive side, is used to deliver power to the clutch and transmission. The other end is used to drive accessories, such as the alternator. Since ignition components may be located at this end, it is often called the timing end.

A multipiece or built-up crankshaft for a two-cylinder (two-stroke) engine is shown in exploded view in Figure 10–6. The counterweights have a shaft attached to their centers, which form the crankshaft main bearing journals.

The offset connecting rod journals are machined as separate parts called *crank pins*. Each crank pin is pressed through the two counterweights and fits through the center of a connecting rod bearing, which in turn fits inside the big end of the connecting rod. The built-up design allows the use of a caged needle or roller bearing for the connecting rod which is required for the speed and lubrication requirements of a two-stroke engine.

The spacings of the throws on a multicylinder-engine crankshaft are designed to allow a different stroke to occur in each cylinder at a given time. There is a wide variety of cylinder arrangements and crankshaft throw designs in use.

The most common motorcycle engines have one, two, or four cylinders. Crankshafts for single-cylinder engines are simple, having just one throw and a main bearing journal at either end. (Figure 10–7).

Figure 10–7. Crankshaft for a single-cylinder engine. *(Honda Motor Co., Ltd.)*

Figure 10–8. Twin side-by-side or in-line cylinders. *(Kawasaki Motors Corp. U.S.A.)*

Two- or twin-cylinder engines can have their cylinders arranged either side by side (called *in-line*; see Figure 10–8) or in a V-shape (Figure 10–9). These engines have their crankshaft throws arranged so that one piston at a time provides a power stroke. Most two-stroke twins have a crankshaft whose two throws are set 180 degrees apart, as shown in Figure 10–10. The reason is that a two-stroke twin with a 180-degree crankshaft has one piston going down on a power stroke while the other is going up, thus making the engine operate very smoothly.

Figure 10–9. Twin with cylinders arranged in a V-shape. *(Harley-Davidson Motors, Inc.)*

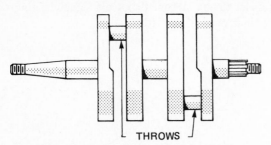

THROWS

Figure 10–10. Two-stroke twin with throws 180 degrees apart. *(Honda Motor Co., Ltd.)*

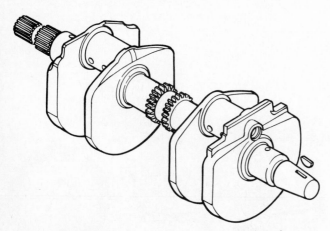

Figure 10–11. A 360 degree crankshaft used on a four-stroke twin. *(Honda Motor Co., Ltd.)*

Many in-line, four-stroke cycle engines use a crankshaft whose throws are arranged as shown in Figure 10–11. In this arrangement, both pistons go up and down together. On the way down, one piston is on a power stroke, the other on intake. On the way up, one is on exhaust and the other on compression. Since the four-stroke engine has a power stroke every two crankshaft revolutions (720 degrees), a four-stroke twin can have a power stroke every 360 degrees of crankshaft rotation. We call this arrangement, appropriately, a 360-degree crankshaft.

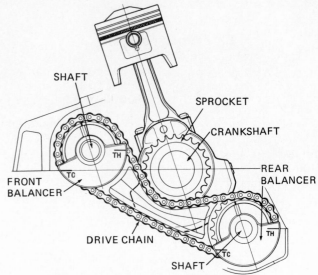

SHAFT

SPROCKET

CRANKSHAFT

REAR BALANCER

FRONT BALANCER

TH

TC

DRIVE CHAIN

TH

SHAFT

TC

Figure 10–12. Counterbalancers attached to the crankshaft to reduce vibration. *(Honda Motor Co., Ltd.)*

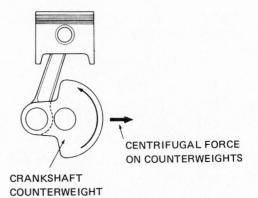

CENTRIFUGAL FORCE ON COUNTERWEIGHTS

CRANKSHAFT COUNTERWEIGHT

Figure 10–13. Centrifugal force acts on the crankshaft counterweights. *(Honda Motor Co., Ltd.)*

The four-stroke twin with a 360-degree crank is not a smooth engine because both pistons go up and down together, setting up vibrations in the engine. One solution to this problem is to use counterbalancers attached to the crankshaft (Figure 10–12). A chain from the crankshaft is attached to two counterbalancers which are supported on shafts in the crankcase. As the crankshaft turns, the chain drives the balancers.

The counterweights on the counterbalancer are designed to balance the inertial forces on the crankshaft as it revolves. They do a good job of balancing the inertial force at top dead center (TDC) and bottom dead center (BDC), but they create a corresponding horizontal imbalance of their own at 90 degrees before top dead center and 90 degrees after top dead center due to centrifugal force (Figure 10–13). The balancers as a unit are designed to counteract

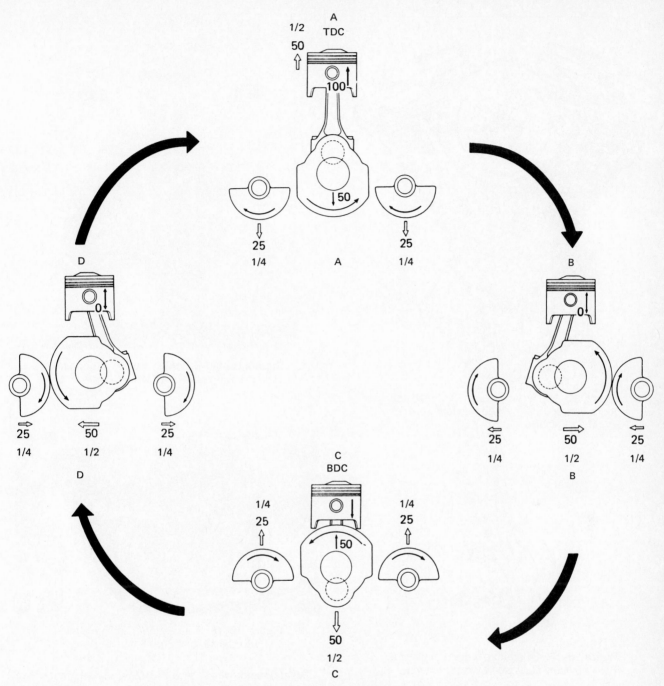

Figure 10–14. Operation of the counterbalancers. *(Honda Motor Co., Ltd.)*

the centrifugal force, including the inertial force created by the rotating mass.

The operation of the counterbalancers is shown in Figure 10–14. At TDC, the counterweight creates a centrifugal force to neutralize one-half of the inertial force. The remaining inertia will be totally balanced by two balancers. Thus, each balancer counteracts one-fourth of the total inertia (Figure 10–14).

As the piston moves down the cylinder, the inertial force is balanced by the counterweight, as shown in Figure 10–14(b). However, the centrifugal force acting on the counterweight is still present. Thus, the centrifugal force on the balancers is required to cancel this remaining force.

At BDC (Figure 10–14(c)), the centrifugal force on the counterweight neutralizes one-half of the downward inertial force. The other half is neutralized by the two balanc-

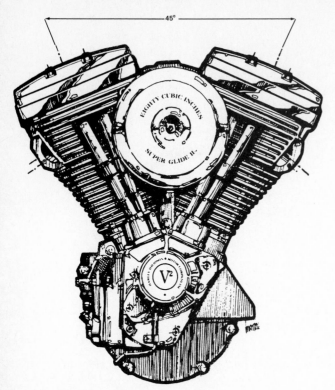

Figure 10–15. A V-twin with a 45-degree angle between the cylinders. *(Harley-David-son Motors, Inc.)*

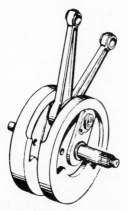

Figure 10–16. Single-throw crankshaft for a V-twin. *(Harley-Davidson Motor Co., Inc.)*

Figure 10–17. Motorcycle with an opposed cylinder arrangement. *(BMW of North America, Inc.)*

Figure 10–18. Four-cylinder in-line engine. *(U.S. Suzuki Motor Corp.)*

ers (one-quarter each). The piston then moves back up the cylinder (Figure 10–14(d)), whereupon the centrifugal force on the counterweight is balanced by the balancers.

The V-twin engine design made popular by Harley-Davidson typically uses two cylinders which have an angle of 45 degrees between them (Figure 10–15). The crankshaft throw to which two connecting rods are attached is shown in Figure 10–16. The V shape allows the engine to be narrower than the side-by-side engine, allowing, in turn, for a decrease in frontal area and less air drag as the motorcycle moves through the air.

Several motorcycles, such as BMW, use an arrangement in which the cylinders lie flat or are horizontal. Since there is one cylinder on each side, we call this an *opposed cylinder arrangement* (Figure 10–17). The crankshaft throws are 180 degrees apart, as shown in Figure 10–10. The opposed cylinder arrangement gives a very smooth-operating engine, but does not provide for good streamlining or good ground clearance when turning corners.

Four-cylinder in-line motorcycle engines have their cylinders arranged side by side (Figure 10–18). The four small cylinders provide for more power strokes spaced closer together, making for a very smooth-running engine. The crankshaft for a four-stroke, four-cylinder engine is

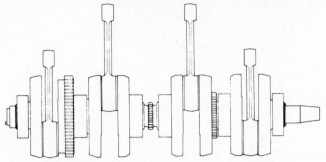

Figure 10–19. Crankshaft for a four-stroke, four-cylinder engine. *(Kawasaki Motors Corp. U.S.A.)*

shown in Figure 10–19. Two sets of throws are arranged 180 degrees to two other throws, allowing a different stroke of the four-stroke cycle to occur in each cylinder at any given time. There is always one piston delivering power, one exhausting gases, one drawing in the air–fuel mixture, and one compressing the air–fuel mixture. The main disadvantage to this type of engine is its large number of parts and large frontal area.

CONNECTING ROD

The connecting rod connects the piston to the crankshaft and may be either cast or forged. Many engines use a cast iron connecting rod, which is inexpensive to produce. Other engines use connecting rods forged from aluminum, which is lighter than cast iron but more expensive. The connecting rod usually has an I-beam cross section to combine high strength with low weight.

The parts of a connecting rod are shown in Figure 10–20. The end of the connecting rod through which the pis-

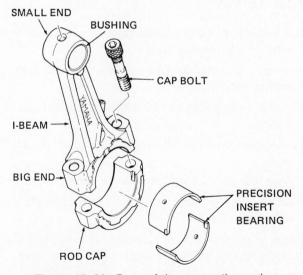

Figure 10–20. Parts of the connecting rod. *(Yamaha Motor Corp. U.S.A.)*

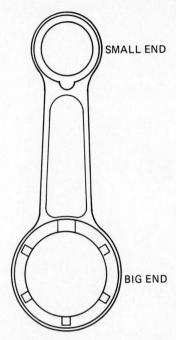

Figure 10–21. Two-stroke connecting rods do not have a removable cap. *(Honda Motor Co., Ltd.)*

ton pin fits is called the small end. If a free-floating pin is used, this end will usually be fitted with a piston pin bushing. The other end of the connecting rod is called the big end. It is fitted with a removable cap so that it may be bolted around the crankshaft throw.

Precision insert bearings (see next section) may be used on four-cycle engines. They are held in the connecting rod and connecting rod cap with locking grooves. In most engines, the cap is held with bolts and nuts. The bolts must be of very high quality to withstand the high loads. Self-locking nuts are often used to prevent loosening by vibration.

Connecting rods for two-stroke cycle engines have the same basic parts as a four-cycle rod. The main difference is that the large end does not have a removable cap (Figure 10–21). Instead, the crankshaft crankpin is designed to slide through the big end after a bearing is installed in the rod. (See Figure 10–6.)

BEARINGS

Wherever moving parts meet in an engine, there is a resistance called friction which causes heat and wear and reduces the power output of the engine. The wear due to friction may be reduced by making the moving parts that touch or slide against each other out of different materials. Copper, tin, or lead against cast iron or steel causes less friction then steel against steel or cast iron against cast iron. Bearings are used at all major points in an engine to

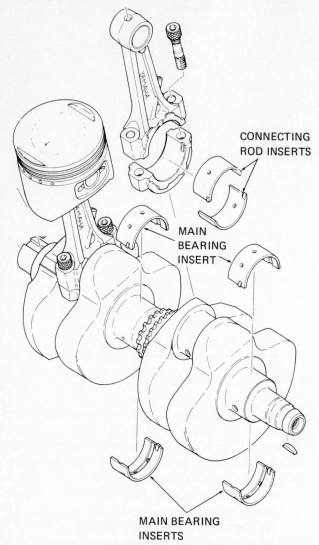

CONNECTING
ROD INSERTS

MAIN
BEARING
INSERT

MAIN BEARING
INSERTS

Figure 10–22. Precision insert bearings used on the connecting rod and main bearing journals. *(Yamaha Motor Corp. U.S.A.)*

reduce friction. They are always made of a material different from that of the parts they support.

Most four-stroke cycle engines use a type of bearing called a *precision insert* at the big end of the connecting rod to support the crankshaft in the crankcase (Figure 10–22). Any insert bearing used on a connecting rod or main journal is made up of two pieces, each having a steel (or sometimes bronze) backing. One of any number of special bearing alloys called the *bearing lining material* is molded to the backing. No one bearing lining material will do every job better than any other such material. Most of the time many materials—tin, lead, copper, cadmium, aluminum, and silver—are used in combination, or *alloyed*.

Precision insert bearings are held in the crankcase or connecting rod by spread and by a locking lip. *Spread* refers to the bearings' being slightly larger than the cap or housing in which they fit, so that they will snap into place.

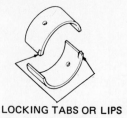

LOCKING TABS OR LIPS

Figure 10–23. Locking tabs or lips keep the bearing in place. *(Yamaha Motor Corp. U.S.A.)*

The locking lip of the bearings fits into a slot in the housing (Figure 10–23).

Many smaller four- and two-stroke engines use a ball-type bearing to support the crankshaft (Figure 10–24). Ball bearings have an inner race or cup which fits over the crankshaft and an outer race which fits into the crankcase. Both races have channels in which a number of balls revolve, allowing almost friction-free rotation of the two races.

Many two-cycle engines use needle bearings to support the big and small ends of the connecting rod (Figure 10–25). A needle bearing is an outside race or cage which holds a set of long thin rollers called needles. The inside surfaces of the needles ride directly on a crankpin or piston pin.

Bushings (Figure 10–26) are used at the piston end of the four-stroke engine's connecting rod and rocker arms. A bushing is a small, full-round sleeve that is pressed into place in a hole or bore; it may be machined on the inside diameter to "fit" a shaft. Bushings act as a kind of bearing to reduce friction.

KEY TERMS

Ball bearing: a type of bearing which uses two races separated by a number of balls.

Bearing: a part used to reduce friction and wear between moving parts.

Bushing: a sleeve that fits into a hole or bore and acts as a bearing.

Crankcase: the part of the engine that supports the crankshaft.

Journal: the part of a shaft on which a bearing is installed.

Needle bearing: a bearing which uses a caged set of rollers called needles.

Precision insert bearing: a bearing made in two half-round pieces that are inserted between a part and a journal.

Throw: the offset part of the crankshaft to which the connecting rod is attached.

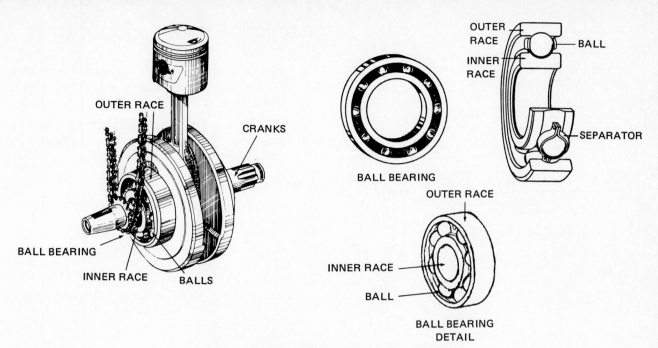

Figure 10–24. Ball bearing used to support a crankshaft. *(Honda Motor Co. Ltd. Detail: The Torrington Co.)*

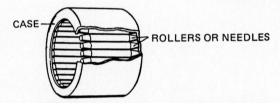

Figure 10–25. Needle bearings are used on two-stroke connecting rods. *(U.S. Navy)*

Figure 10–26. A bushing is a full round sleeve that is pressed into place in a part.

CHECKUP

1. In which two ways are crankcases divided?
   Identify the parts of the one-piece crankshaft by writing their names in the spaces provided.

2. _____

3. _____

4. _____

5. _____

6. _____

7. _____

8. _____

   Identify the parts of a built-up crankshaft by writing their names in the spaces provided.

9. _____

10. _____

11. _____

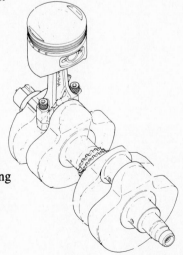

12. _____

13. _____

Identify the parts of a connecting rod by writing their names in the spaces provided.

14. _____

15. _____

16. _____

17. _____

18. _____

19. _____

20. _____

DISCUSSION TOPICS AND ACTIVITIES

1. Examine all the crankshafts you can find in the shop. Can you determine the kind of engines they were removed from?

2. What is the smoothest-operating engine you have experienced? What were the number of cylinders and the crankshaft design for this engine?

The lower end of a motorcycle will generally withstand more miles and abuse than the upper end. When the upper end is being serviced, the technician must decide whether the engine should be removed from the motorcycle and the crankcase disassembled or split. Splitting the case to service the bottom end takes a great deal more time than a top-end job; thus, it is very important that you know how to determine whether the bottom end should be serviced. In this unit, we describe the troubleshooting procedures necessary to determine whether a bottom end is worn excessively, and the servicing procedures for repairing a worn bottom end.

JOB COMPETENCY OBJECTIVES

When you finish reading and studying this unit, you should be able to:

1. Pressure-check a two-stroke crankcase.

2. Disassemble the engine's lower end.

3. Inspect and measure a crankshaft for wear.

4. Inspect and measure the connecting rods for wear.

5. Reassemble the engine's lower end.

LOWER-END TROUBLESHOOTING

The crankcase on a four-stroke engine has oil in it. Accordingly, damaged gaskets, seals, or sealing surfaces may leak oil into the lower end. Two-strokers do not have oil in the engine part of the crankcase, but have transmission oil in the transmission section. Hence, the main leakage problem that may arise in a two-stroke engine is a pressure leakage from the crankcase.

In both four- and two-stroke engines, lower-end problems usually show up as abnormal noise from the lower end. This noise or knocking may occur if an engine is excessively worn or has internal damage. An experienced motorcycle technician learns to tell the cause of an engine problem by the sound it makes. One helpful tool used to diagnose engine noises is the stethoscope. The technician uses this tool to listen to engine noises just the way a physician listens to a patient's heart. The ear pieces are placed in the ears, and the pick-up end is placed on various parts of the engine. If the noise is most audible in the cylinder head, the problem may be a faulty camshaft or rocker arm. If the noise seems to be most audible at the crankcase, the problem most likely involves a main or connecting rod bearing. A technician's stethoscope is shown in Figure 11–1.

If you do not have a stethoscope available, you can use a screwdriver to help you isolate a noise. Place the blade of the screwdriver on the part of the engine you want to hear. Then put your ear against the screwdriver handle.

LOWER-END TROUBLESHOOTING AND SERVICING

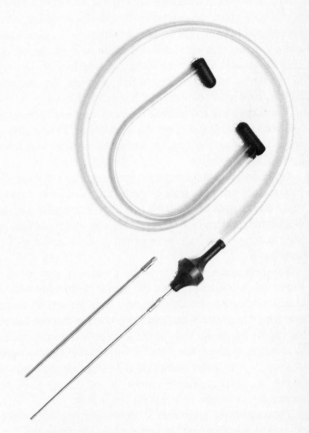

Figure 11–1. A stethoscope is used to listen to engine noises.

The sound will travel through the screwdriver much as it does in a stethoscope.

Noises isolated at the top of the engine are most likely from the valve train. Noise at the valve train may be due to worn valve-adjusting components, worn valve guides, incorrect valve lash, or a worn camshaft.

When you listen at the bottom end, a light metallic knock that becomes worse when the engine is under a light load may be caused by the connecting rods. Connecting rod noises may be caused by insufficient oil supply, low oil pressure, thin or diluted oil, excessive bearing clearance, connecting-rod journals being out-of-round, or misaligned connecting rods.

Main-bearing knocking, indicating that the bearing clearance is too great, usually occurs only when the engine is under a heavy load. When the engine is loaded, the sound changes from the light knocking of the connecting rod to a heavy "thump." Main-bearing noises may be caused by insufficient oil supply, low oil pressure, thin or diluted oil, excessive bearing clearance, excessive end play, or crankshaft main-bearing journals worn out-of-round.

Any time you disassemble the top end for service, there is a simple check to determine the condition of the connecting rod bearing. Grab the connecting rod in your hand and try to move it up and down while holding the crankshaft stationary. Do not rock the rod side to side; just try to move it up and down. If you feel any play, the connecting rod bearing or the crankshaft journal is worn.

The connecting rod bearing usually wears out faster than the bearings which support the crankshaft. If you find a worn connecting rod bearing, the cases must be split for a bottom-end overhaul.

Oil leaks from the crankcase area can mean that crankcase sealing surfaces, seal, or gaskets are damaged. Sometimes an oil leak can only be cured by a complete engine disassembly. Many times, however, the source of the oil leak is minor and can be repaired without splitting the crankcase.

The best thing to do is to be absolutely sure of the source of the oil leak. Clean the engine thoroughly with a chemical cleaner or steam cleaner. Run the engine up to operating temperature and carefully observe the outside of the engine for the oil leak. If the leakage is from the crankcase sealing surface, the problem will require a bottom-end disassembly. In most cases you will find that the leakage is just in some accessory mounting, or it may even be something as simple as a leaking drain plug.

The two-stroke engine must develop a pressure in the crankcase when the piston comes down to force the air–fuel mixture up the transfer passage. Also, the engine must develop a vacuum in the crankcase when the piston moves up to draw air and fuel into the crankcase. A leak in the crankcase can prevent a pressure or vacuum from forming and cause poor engine performance.

If you suspect a leak, you can apply soapy water to the suspected area. A leak will show up as bubbling soap suds. Larger motorcycle repair shops will have a tester designed to test for air leaks.

The most common air leakage problem is with the crankshaft seals. The crankshaft seals fit around the rotating crankshaft and keep the pressure in the crankcase. They are subjected to continual wear from the spinning crankshaft. Most two-stroke engines will have one of the crankshaft seals (usually the one on the clutch side of the engine) retaining the crankcase pressure while keeping out the transmission oil. When the seal starts to leak, the engine will both pull in transmission oil and blow pressure into the transmission. The transmission can thus be drained without the rider's knowing it. Hard starting and poor performance combined with black, oily spark plugs indicate a bad clutch-side seal.

In some cases, the crankshaft seals can be replaced without disassembling the engine. In most cases, however, replacement means splitting the case to remove the old seals and install new ones.

LOWER-END SERVICING

In order to service the parts inside the lower end, the crankcase has to be split. You must always find and follow the crankcase disassembly procedure in the shop service manual. The engine will have to be removed from the motorcycle, as will all components attached to either end of the crankshaft. Similarly, the top end has to be removed as described earlier, and then each of the studs, bolts, or machine screws holding the two halves of the crankcase have to be removed. A good service manual is a must to locate all the crankcase fasteners.

Disassembly and cleaning

When splitting singles with vertical-parting crankcases, you can usually get them to part if you strike the left-hand crankshaft end against a wooden bench. Figure 11–2 shows a split vertical crankcase. Horizontally split crankcases are split by gently tapping on parts of the lower half of the case. Figure 11–3 shows a split horizontal crankcase. Any hammering must be done with a plastic hammer or a metal hammer on a piece of wood. Never try to pry a crankcase apart with a screwdriver; you will ruin the sealing surface of the crankcase halves and cause oil leaks.

When you separate a vertical crankcase, look carefully for any spacers or shims which may be used to control crankshaft end play. Be certain to note their location and be very careful not to mix them up.

On multicylinder engines, you will have to remove the bolts which hold the crankshaft main bearings, called the bearing-holder bolts (Figure 11–4). In most engines you will also have to remove the camshaft chain guides and, if present, counterbalancer assemblies.

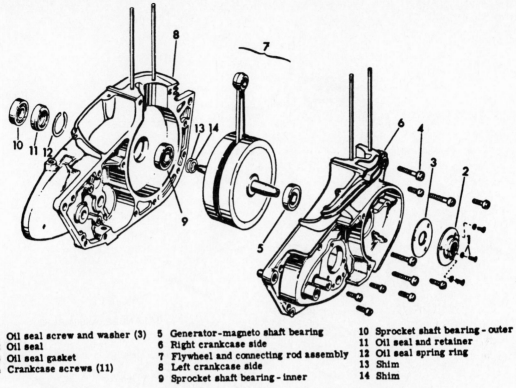

1 Oil seal screw and washer (3)
2 Oil seal
3 Oil seal gasket
4 Crankcase screws (11)

5 Generator-magneto shaft bearing
6 Right crankcase side
7 Flywheel and connecting rod assembly
8 Left crankcase side
9 Sprocket shaft bearing - inner

10 Sprocket shaft bearing - outer
11 Oil seal and retainer
12 Oil seal spring ring
13 Shim
14 Shim

Figure 11–2. Split vertical crankcase assembly. *(Harley-Davidson Motors, Inc.)*

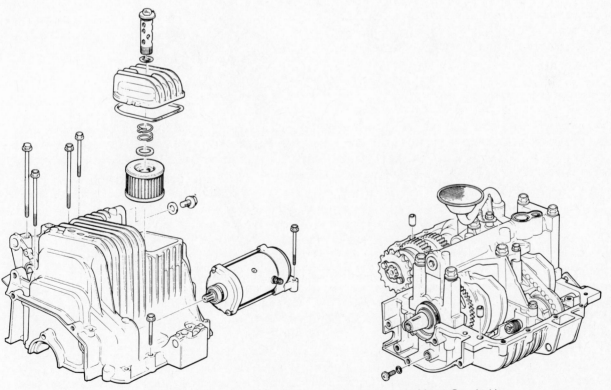

Figure 11–3. Separating crankcase halves. *(Honda Motor Co., Ltd.)*

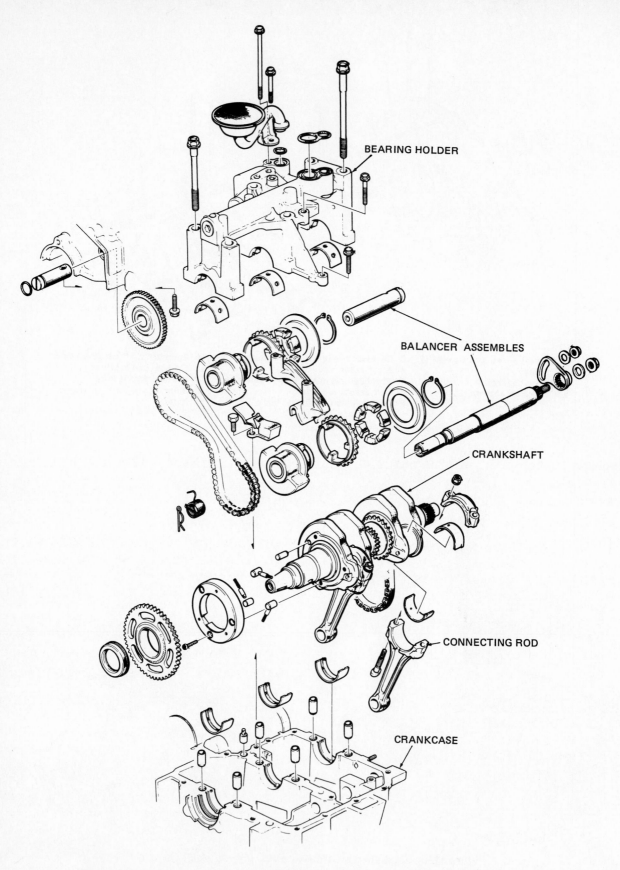

Figure 11–4. Disassembling the multicylinder crankcase parts. *(Honda Motor Co., Ltd.)*

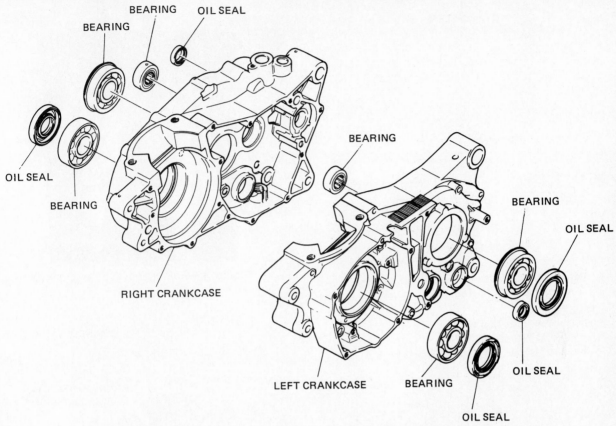

Figure 11–5. Bearings and seals in a vertically split crankcase. *(Yamaha Motor Corp. U.S.A.)*

Before you remove any connecting rod caps, carefully observe each connecting rod for factory match marks indicating their position. Not all engine manufacturers mark the connecting rods. It is extremely important to stamp unmarked connecting rods on both the cap and rod during removal. Use a hammer and punch to mark the cap and rod. You can mark one mark for #1, two marks for #2, and so on. Remove the connecting rod cap nuts and then the rod caps. Take care not to scratch the crankshaft journals with the rod cap studs.

The halves of vertically split crankcases contain a number of ball bearings and oil seals (Figure 11–5). Remove the seals and discard them. Remove the bearings and place them in containers marked to identify each bearing. Identification is important for later inspection and possible reuse.

Clean all the crankcase components in cleaning solvent, and allow them to air-dry on a clean rag. After any ball or needle bearings have been cleaned, they should be reoiled to prevent rusting.

Inspection and measurement: Built-up crankshaft

Many small two-stroke engines use a built-up crankshaft. A number of checks can be made to determine whether this type of crankshaft must be disassembled for parts replacement. You can measure connecting rod axial looseness at the small end to determine the amount of wear in the big end (the crank pin and big end bearing). Hold the big end stable to prevent it from sliding, and then rock the small end as shown in Figure 11–6. If the play exceeds 2 mm (.08″), the big-end bearing is worn. You can judge this by eye or feel.

Check for the correct connecting rod big-end side play (Figure 11–7). Slide the big end to one side and insert a feeler gauge between the crank counterweight (flywheel) and the rod big end. Compare your measurement with specifications. In most cases, it should be between .3 mm (.012″) and .6mm (.024″). If it exceeds the latter value, the connecting rod big end should be closely checked for excessive wear. In addition, total crankshaft width should be measured.

If either measurement is beyond the specification, the crankshaft must be disassembled for parts replacement. Remove the pump drive gear, pump gear locating pin (located in a hole in the shaft), thick washer, primary drive gear, and square primary drive gear key if they occur on the particular model you are working on. Both gears are a slip fit on the crankshaft end, but the gear puller (Figure 11–8) may be able to be used to aid in their removal. *Do*

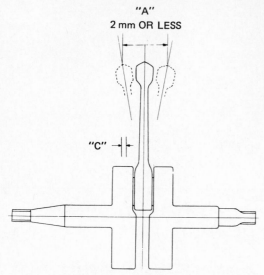

"A"
2 mm OR LESS

"C"

Figure 11–6. Checking the big-end bearing *(Yamaha Motor Corp. U.S.A.)*

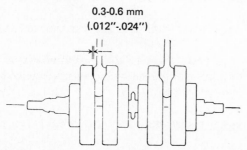

0.3-0.6 mm
(.012"-.024")

Figure 11–7. Measuring big-end side clearance. *(Yamaha Motor Corp. U.S.A.)*

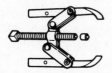

Figure 11–8. Claw puller used for pulling gears. *(Harley Davidson Motors, Inc.)*

Figure 11–9. Pressing out the crank pin. *(Yamaha Motor Corp. U.S.A.)*

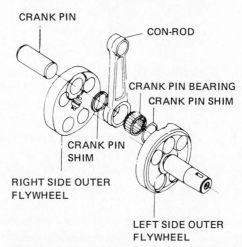

CRANK PIN

CON-ROD

CRANK PIN BEARING
CRANK PIN SHIM

CRANK PIN
SHIM

RIGHT SIDE OUTER
FLYWHEEL

LEFT SIDE OUTER
FLYWHEEL

Figure 11–10. Disassembled crankshaft. *(Yamaha Motor Corp. U.S.A.)*

not use a screwdriver or chisel to pry the gears off, as gear teeth can be chipped.

Use a hydraulic press to press off the left-hand crank counterweight (flywheel). This pressing procedure requires a crankshaft support fixture (available from each motorcycle manufacturer). A length of pipe with an inside diameter wide enough to slip the crank into can be used. Pipe ends should be squared and filed smooth. Cut a slot the entire length of the pipe wide enough for the connecting rod to fit through. Drop the crank into the fixture, place support plates beneath the left-hand outer crank wheel, and push the crank pin out of this wheel (Figure 11–9).

Remove the connecting rod and rod bearing, lift the remaining crankshaft section up, place a support plate beneath the right-hand crank counterweight (flywheel), and press the crank pin out of the supported wheel.

Finally, support the left hand counterweight (flywheel) and press out the crank pin. Figure 11–10 shows a disassembled crankshaft.

If any evidence of damage is found on the crankpin or big-end connecting rod bearing, both bearing and crankpin are normally replaced. These are usually sold as a kit along with the shims or thrust washers on each side of the rod.

To reassemble the crankshaft assembly, support the right-hand outer crank counterweight (flywheel) with the pin installed; then install the rod bearing and connecting rod, with the crank pin pointing up. Position the left-hand counterweight (flywheel) over the pin, use a machinist's square or straightedge to accurately line up both wheels, and tap the left wheel down onto the pin to prevent the wheel from moving out of alignment.

Press the left-hand counterweight (flywheel) straight down onto the pin until you reach the specified width. The wheel must be pressed straight down, or the pin will enter the hole on a slant, resulting in damage.

Lay a straightedge across both counterweights (flywheels) at two points 90° opposite the crank pin. Both wheels must be parallel to each other. If they are not, tap the high wheel with a brass hammer. Finally, align each crank half before pressing both halves together.

Inspection and measurement: One-piece crankshaft

After the parts of the one-piece crankshaft are cleaned, they can be inspected and measured for wear. Carefully check each journal for any signs of scoring. Place the crankshaft on a bench under a strong light, and look over each main and connecting rod journal for any signs of scoring. The slightest score on a crankshaft journal can shorten the life of a new main or connecting rod bearing.

If the journals pass a visual inspection, they should be measured. Crankshaft journals are measured with an outside micrometer (Figure 11–11). Select a micrometer with the correct size-range for the journals to be measured.

Look up the specifications for main bearing and connecting rod journal diameters in the shop manual, and write them down for reference. Wipe the journals with a clean rag to make sure that they are free of oil and dirt. Also, wipe off the measuring surfaces of the micrometer to make sure there is no dirt on them to cause an error in the measurement.

Start at the front of the crankshaft and measure the diameter of the connecting rod journal for cylinder number 1. Make the measurement about 6 mm (.25″) away from the end of the journal, to ensure that the micrometer does not measure the small radius, called a fillet, where the journal meets the throw. Record this measurement. Make and record another measurement at the other end of the journal. Make and record two more measurements of the same journal at 90° from the first two measurements.

Should you find a difference between a measurement taken at one end of the journal and one taken at the other end, the journal is probably tapered. If you find a difference between two readings taken at 90° from each other, the journal is out-of-round. Connecting-rod journals usually wear out-of-round, because of the way the connecting rod applies force to the crankshaft. Repeat the measurement procedure for each of the other connecting rod journals, and record all of your measurements. Repeat this same procedure for each of the main bearings, and record these measurements.

After you have completed your measurements, determine the maximum out-of-round and maximum taper for the worst journal. If the taper or out-of-round is larger than

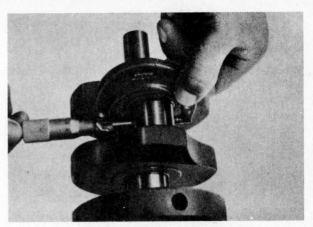

Figure 11–11. Measuring a crankshaft journal. *(Yamaha Motor Corp. U.S.A.)*

.03 mm (.001″), the crankshaft will have to be reconditioned. The crankshaft may also be worn undersize. To find out whether it is, compare your smallest journal measurement with the crankshaft journal specifications from the shop manual. A journal that is worn under this specification by .03 mm (.001″) will also have to be reconditioned.

The big-end bore made when the rod cap is attached to the big end of the connecting rod (where the insert bearing fits) is called the *saddle bore*. This area often wears out-of-round, because during the power stroke, the top of the saddle bore is placed under a severe load. Since the bottom of the saddle bore is not under much load, we call it a no-load area. The uneven load application eventually stretches the saddle bore out-of-round. A new insert bearing installed in a stretched saddle bore will have a very short service life.

The saddle bore is measured for out-of-round by means of a telescoping gauge and an outside micrometer (Figure 11–12). Choose a telescoping gauge that will fit into the saddle bore and expand out against the cap and rod. Place the telescoping gauge into the saddle bore in a direction 90 degrees from the cap mating surfaces, and expand the gauge until there is a light drag against the saddle bore. Then tighten the handle and remove the gauge. Measure across the gauge with an outside micrometer, and record the measurement. Then place the gauge back in the saddle bore in a direction 90 degrees from the first measurement. Make sure the gauge does not contact either the mating surface between the rod and cap or any bearing lock grooves, and make and record a measurement with the saddle bore in the new direction.

The difference between the two measurements is the out-of-round. Any measurable out-of-round means that the connecting rod has to be replaced. Check the specifications in the shop's service manual.

Carefully inspect the sealing surfaces of each of the crankcase halves. Minor dents or scratches can be removed

Figure 11–12. Measuring the big end of the connecting rod for stretch.

by using valve lapping compound and a flat surface like a large piece of glass. Put the lapping compound on the scored surface and place the crankcase on the glass. Move the crankcase back and forth, holding it flat on the glass. Change from coarse to fine lapping compound as the scratches are polished away.

Reassembly: Lower end

To begin reassembling the lower end, select the correct-size main bearing inserts. You must select main bearings that match the crankshaft diameter. If the crankshaft has been ground undersize, the main bearings will have to be thicker to make up the space. These thicker bearings are called undersize because they are used with an undersize crankshaft. Bearing size is usually printed on the bearing box and on the back of the bearing. Always check the shop manual for the types and identification of available undersize bearings.

Put the new main bearing inserts into the bearing holder and into the crankcase half. Be sure to wipe the caps and housings perfectly clean and dry first; the backs of the main bearing inserts should never be oiled or greased. Place the crankshaft in the crankcase on the new main bearing inserts.

You are now ready to measure the oil clearance between the crankshaft and the main bearing inserts. Proper lubrication and cooling of the bearing depend on correct crankshaft oil clearances. Scored bearings, a worn crankshaft, excessive cylinder wear, stuck piston rings, and worn pistons may result from too small an oil clearance. On the other hand, if the oil clearance is too great, the crankshaft may pound up and down, overheat, and weld itself to the insert bearings.

Fine plastic string called *plastigauge* is used to measure the oil clearance between the insert bearing and the crankshaft. The plastigauge is relatively long and has a small di-

ameter. Wipe the crankshaft and insert bearing free of oil, cut a length of plastic string about 3 mm (⅛″) shorter than the bearing, and set the string on each bearing inside surface.

Position the bearing holder over the crankshaft, and tighten the bolts to the recommended torque wrench reading. Be careful not to turn the crankshaft when you remove the bearing holder; the plastic string will have been squashed between the crankshaft and the main bearing insert. You can now determine the clearance, using the width scale on the string package. Match the stripes on the package with the flattened string (Figure 11–13). Each stripe has a clearance measurement printed on it. When the correct stripe is found, read the measurement. This is the clearance between the main bearing insert and the crankshaft main bearing journal. If you measure a clearance larger than .08 mm (.003″), then the crankshaft is worn or the bearings are the wrong size.

If the clearance is acceptable, the main bearing inserts are ready for final assembly. Remove the bearing holder and lift the crankshaft back out of the cylinder block. Oil each of the main bearing inserts in the crankcase with engine oil or an assembly lubricant. Assembly lubricant has the consistency of thick grease and will not leak out of the bearing. If the engine is not to be started for a period of time after overhaul, assembly lubricant should always be used. Lubricate each of the main bearing inserts in the bearing holder, and each crankshaft journal. Then gently set the crankshaft into the main bearing inserts. Install the bearing holder and tighten the bolts to the final torque value specified by the manufacturer.

The connecting rod big-end clearance is checked in the same way. Install a new insert bearing in each rod cap and rod, and put a piece of plastigauge on each crankpin, avoiding the oil hole. Install the bearing caps on the correct crankpins, and torque them to specifications. Remove the caps and measure the compressed plastigauge on each crankpin (Figure 11–14). The clearance should be less than

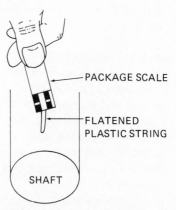

Figure 11–13. Compare the flattened plastigauge string to the scale on the package.

Figure 11–14. Checking connecting rod bearing oil clearance. *(Yamaha Motor Corp. U.S.A.)*

.08 mm (.003″). If the clearance is larger, the crankshaft is worn or the bearings are the wrong size.

Oil the insert bearing and the connecting rod journal with clean oil. Install the rod cap in the correct position, always double-checking the factory match numbers. Install and tighten the connecting rod cap nuts to specifications. Repeat the procedure for each of the connecting rods.

Install any new seals or ball bearings which fit in the crankcase halves, and then coat the sealing surfaces of the crankcase halves with the recommended type of sealant. Install any counterbalancers, chain guides, or cam chains removed during disassembly. Push the crankcase halves together and install all studs, screws, and bolts. Finally, tighten all fasteners to the recommended torque in the recommended sequence.

Job Sheet   11–1

DISASSEMBLE LOWER END

Before you begin:

Read pp.

Make of Motorcycle _____ Model _____ Year _____

Time Started _____ Time Finished _____ Total Time _____

Flat-rate Time _____

Special Tools, Equipment, Parts, and Materials

References

Manufacturer's Shop Manual _____

Procedure

1. Use the shop service manual to locate all the fasteners that are holding the crankcase halves together.
2. Remove all the aforementioned fasteners.

Instructor check _____

3. Using a block of wood or a plastic hammer, split the crankcase halves.
4. *(NOTE: Do not use a screwdriver or prybar on the crankcase sealing surfaces.)*
5. On a vertically split crankcase, observe, mark, and store any spacers or shims on the crankshaft.

Instructor check _____

6. On a horizontally split crankcase, remove the bolts which hold the bearing holder. Then remove the bearing holder.

7. Check each connecting rod for factory numbers and match marks. Mark the rods with a punch if they are not marked.

Instructor check _____

8. Unbolt the rod caps and remove the rods.

9. Clean all parts in cleaning solvent for inspection and measurement.

NOTES:

Instructor check _____ Date completed _____

Job Sheet 11-2

INSPECT AND MEASURE THE CRANKSHAFT

Before you begin:

Read pp.

Make of Motorcycle _____ Model _____ Year _____

Time Started _____ Time Finished _____ Total Time _____

Flat-rate Time _____

Special Tools, Equipment, Parts, and Materials

Outside micrometer

References

Manufacturer's Shop Manual _____

Specifications

Look up the following specifications for the engine and record them in the spaces below:

Connecting Rod Journal:
Standard diameter _____   Maximum taper _____
Maximum out-of-round _____   Undersize _____

Main bearing journal:
Standard diameter _____   Maximum taper _____
Maximum out-of-round _____   Undersize _____

Instructor check _____

Procedure

1. Wipe the crankshaft bearing journals and the main bearing housings with a clean rag.

2. Inspect each crankshaft connecting rod journal. Are the journals:

    Smooth _____   Slightly scored _____   Rough _____

3. Inspect each main bearing journal on the crankshaft. Are the journals:

Smooth _____ Slightly scored _____ Rough _____

4. If you find any scoring, the crankshaft will have to be reconditioned. Check with your instructor.

Instructor check _____

5. Select an outside micrometer with the correct range for measuring the connecting rod journals.

6. Use the correct-size outside micrometer to measure each connecting rod journal. Make at least two measurements in a horizontal direction and at least two in a vertical direction. The maximum difference between these two measurements is the out-of-round. Write in your results below:

Connecting Rod: #1 _____ _____ _____ _____

#2 _____ _____ _____ _____

#3 _____ _____ _____ _____

#4 _____ _____ _____ _____

Maximum out-of-round _____

Maximum taper _____

Maximum undersize _____

Instructor check _____

7. Make the same measurements on each of the main bearings and record your measurements in the spaces below:

Main Bearing #1 _____ _____ _____ _____

#2 _____ _____ _____ _____

#3 _____ _____ _____ _____

#4 _____ _____ _____ _____

Maximum out-of-round _____

Maximum taper _____

Maximum undersize _____

8. Compare your measurements with specifications. If any of your measurements are beyond specifications, the crankshaft must be reconditioned.

Instructor check _____

NOTES

Instructor check _____   Date completed _____

Job Sheet |11–3|

INSPECT AND MEASURE CONNECTING RODS

Before you begin:

Read pp.

Make of Motorcycle _____ Model _____ Year _____

Time Started _____ Time Finished _____ Total Time _____

Flat-rate Time _____

Special Tools, Equipment, Parts, and Materials

Outside micrometer
Telescoping gauges
Torque wrench

References

Manufacturer's Shop Manual _____

Specifications

Look up the following specifications for your engine and record them in the spaces below:

Maximum saddle bore out-of-round _____

Saddle bore diameter _____

Rod cap nut torque _____

Procedure

1. Remove all the bearing inserts from the connecting rods, and install the caps on the rods. Be sure to match the cap number with the rod number.

2. Place the rod in a connecting rod vise. Position the nuts and then torque them to specifications.

3. Select a telescoping gauge and outside micrometer of the correct size to measure the saddle bore.

4. Place the telescoping gauge in one of the saddle bores in a direction 90° from the cap mating surfaces. Tighten the gauge, and then remove it.

5. Place the gauge back in the saddle bore about 90° from the first measurement. Make sure you are not contacting the mating surfaces. Make another measurement.

6. Repeat these measurements for each connecting rod, and write them in the spaces below:

   Connecting rod:

   #1 _____ _____

   #2 _____ _____

   #3 _____ _____

   #4 _____ _____

7. The difference between the two measurements is the amount of out-of-round. The difference between your largest reading and the specifications is the amount of oversize. Determine the out-of-round and write it in the space below:

   Out-of-round _____

8. Compare the out-of-round measurements with specifications to determine whether the connecting rods should be replaced.

Instructor check _____

NOTES

Instructor check _____   Date completed _____

Job Sheet   11-4

REASSEMBLE THE BOTTOM END

Before you begin:

Read pp.

Make of Motorcycle _____ Model _____ Year _____

Time Started _____ Time Finished _____ Total Time _____

Flat-rate Time _____

Special Tools, Equipment, Parts, and Materials

References

Manufacturer's Shop Manual _____

Specifications

Look up the following specifications for your engine and record them in the spaces below:

Bearing holder torque _____

Main bearing oil clearance _____

Connecting rod nut torque _____

Connecting rod bearing oil clearance _____

Instructor check _____

Procedure

1. If you are working on a vertically split crankcase, install new bearings in the crankcase and install the crankshaft assembly.

2. If you are working on a horizontally split crankcase, begin by determining the crankshaft main bearing oil clearance.

3. Clean each bearing cap and housing, using a clean rag.

4. Place a mean bearing insert in each of the main bearing housings in the crankcase.

5. Place a main bearing insert in each of the main bearing positions of the bearing holder.

6. Carefully lift the crankshaft into position in the crankcase.

7. Cut a length of plastigauge and lay it on each main journal.

8. Install the bearing holder and torque the cap bolts to specifications. Remove the bolts and remove the bearing holder.

9. Compare the flattened plastigauge string to the stripes on the plastigauge package to get the clearance measurement. Write the clearance measurements in the spaces provided below:

Main Bearing #1 _____

           #2 _____

           #3 _____

           #4 _____

10. Compare your oil clearance measurements with specifications. If your measurements are larger or smaller than the specifications, check with your instructor.

Instructor check _____

11. Wipe assembly lubricant on each bearing insert and main bearing journal.

12. Place each main bearing cap in the correct location and direction.

13. Tighten all the bearing holder bolts to the correct torque in the correct sequence.

14. Check the crankshaft for free rotation. If it does not turn freely, check with your instructor.

Instructor check _____

15. Place an insert bearing in the rod cap. Cut a length of plastigauge and position it on the connecting rod journal.

16. Place the cap in position on the rod and tighten the cap nuts to specifications. Remove the cap and measure the width of the flattened plastigauge using the stripes on the package.

17. Repeat the procedure for each connecting rod and piston assembly, and record your results below:

Connecting Rod #1 _____

           #2 _____

           #3 _____

           #4 _____

18. Compare your clearance measurements with specifications. If your clearances are larger or smaller than the specifications, check with your instructor.

Instructor check _____

19. Coat each insert bearing and journal with lubricant.

20. Install each bearing cap and torque the nuts to specification.

21. Install any new seals that are required on the crankcase halves.

22. Replace any counterbalancer assemblies, chains, or chain guides that have been removed during assembly.

23. Put the recommended sealer on the crankcase sealing surfaces.

24. Push the cases together and tighten all fasteners to the recommended torque in the recommended sequence.

Instructor check _____

NOTES

Instructor check _____　　　　　　　　　　Date completed _____

KEY TERMS

Connecting rod bearing oil clearance: the space between the connecting rod journal and the connecting rod precision insert bearing; measured with plastigauge.

Crankshaft out-of-round: a condition in which a crankshaft journal has worn in an egg-shaped manner.

Main bearing oil clearance: the space between the crankshaft main bearing journal and the main bearing precision insert; measured with plastigauge.

Plastigauge: a plastic string placed in between an insert bearing and a journal to measure oil clearance.

Saddle bore out-of-round: the stretch or egg-shaped wear that occurs to the big end of the connecting rod.

CHECKUP

1. Describe how to troubleshoot an engine for abnormal noise.

2. Explain how to check a lower end by moving the connecting rod.

3. Explain how to check a lower end for an oil leak.

4. How can a pressure tester be used to locate a two-stroke crankcase vacuum leak?

5. Explain the steps to follow in splitting crankcase halves.

6. Why should you never use a screwdriver to pry crankcase halves apart?

7. Explain how to measure big-end side clearance.

8. How is a built-up crankshaft disassembled?

9. What new parts are normally installed on a built-up crankshaft?

10. Explain how to reassemble a built-up crankshaft.

11. How is a connecting rod journal measured to determine out-of-round?

12. How is a connecting rod measured to determine whether the saddle bore has stretch?

13. Explain how to measure the crankshaft main bearings.

14. How can minor scratches be removed from the sealing surface of a crankcase?

15. How is the connecting rod bearing oil clearance measured?

DISCUSSION TOPICS AND ACTIVITIES

1. Measure a connecting rod saddle bore with an insert bearing installed, and then measure the crankshaft journal the rod fits on. How can you determine the oil clearance?

2. Measure the oil clearance of the same rod and crankshaft with plastigauge. How does this oil clearance measurement compare with your first one? Which method do you think is more accurate?

Oil is circulated between moving parts of the engine to prevent the metal-to-metal contact which causes wear. Oil between moving parts allows them to move easily, with less friction. The lower the internal friction of an engine, the more power it can develop. The circulating oil cools the engine by carrying heat away from hot engine components; it also cleans or flushes dirt and deposits off the engine parts. Finally, oil circulated on the cylinder walls seals the rings, improving the engine's compression. We call the components used to circulate oil the *lubrication system*. In this unit, we describe the types and operation of two- and four-stroke lubrication systems and how to service them.

JOB COMPETENCY OBJECTIVES

When you finish reading and studying this unit, you should be able to:

1. Explain the relationship between lubrication and friction.

2. Describe the parts and operation of a wet and a dry four-cycle lubrication system.

3. Describe the parts and operation of a premix and an oil injection two-cycle lubrication system.

4. Change the oil and filter element on a four-cycle engine.

5. Prime the oil injection pump on a two-cycle oil injection system.

FRICTION AND LUBRICATION

One of the main purposes of the lubrication system is to reduce friction. Friction is a resistance between two objects that are moving against each other. If you push a book along a table top, you will notice resistance due to friction. The rougher the table and the book surface, the greater the friction, because the two surfaces tend to lock together. If a weight is placed on the book, it takes even more effort to move it across the table. This illustrates two important points about friction: (1) The smoother the two surfaces of the objects, the less the friction. (2) As the amount of pressure between two objects increases, the friction between them increases.

We want to reduce the amount of friction in an engine as much as possible since the lower the friction between engine parts, the more power the engine can develop. Also, friction between two surfaces causes them to heat and, consequently, to wear. The heat generated by friction may be demonstrated by simply rubbing your hands together fast. The friction between the skin on your hands causes the skin to get hot.

We cannot eliminate friction completely, but it can be reduced so that longer engine life may be expected. If we

LUBRICATION SYSTEM OPERATION AND SERVICING

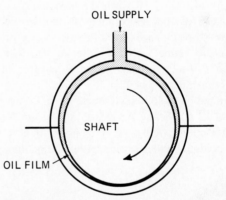

Figure 12–1. An oil film between the shaft and bushing prevents metal-to-metal contact.

were to pour a slippery liquid such as oil on a table top, our hypothetical book would move across the table with very little resistance. The oil would form a thin layer called a *film* under the book, lifting the book off the table surface, and thereby reducing the friction between the book and the table. In a similar manner, we use a film of oil to reduce metal-to-metal contact between engine parts. As an example, consider a shaft supported by a bushing (Figure 12–1) that is slightly larger than it. The slightly larger size of the bushing leaves a small space, usually about .05 to .08 mm (.002 to .003″), that we can fill with oil. Oil is directed under pressure into the oil clearance area of the bushing, whereupon the oil pressure and the rotation of the shaft cause a film of oil to form and wedge between the shaft and the bushing. The shaft thus rests not on the bushing, but on the film of oil, leaving no metal-to-metal contact. Hence, the friction has been reduced as much as possible.

177

FOUR-STROKE LUBRICATING OIL

Lubricating oil is a chemically complex fluid that is refined from petroleum or synthetic materials. The oil used in a motorcycle engine must have the correct viscosity and service rating.

The *viscosity* of an oil is the thickness or thinness of the oil. A fluid with a high viscosity is very thick. Low-viscosity fluids are thin. High-viscosity fluids flow sluggishly. Oils used in engines must flow freely in cold conditions, but be thick enough during times of high temperature.

The Society of Automotive Engineers (SAE) has set up standards for oil viscosity. Thin oil receives a low viscosity number, like SAE 20, while thicker oil receives a higher number, like SAE 40 OR SAE 50. The viscosity number is printed on top of the oil can (Figure 12–2). The motorcycle owner's manual usually specifies which viscosity should be used.

Many motorcycles use SAE 30 in the summer and SAE 20 in the winter. A multiple-viscosity oil like SAE 10-40 flows freely like SAE 10 when the weather is cold, but protects like SAE 40 when it is hot. A motorcycle ridden in different climates needs a multiple-viscosity oil. Note that a viscosity rating with a W after it, like SAE 20W, means that the oil with that rating is capable of cold- (winter-) temperature operation.

Also printed on the oil can is an engine oil's *service rating* (Figure 12–2). Serice ratings, set up by the American Petroleum Institute (API), are a measure of how well a given oil holds up under severe servicing conditions. The

Figure 12–2. The viscosity and service rating are printed on an oil can.

VISCOSITY

SERVICE RATING

ratings are designated by the letters SC, SD, SE, or SF for gasoline-powered engines. Currently, SC is the lowest rating, SF the highest. The following list describes the API ratings.

- *SC*. Oils designed for SC service provide minimum control of high- and low-temperature deposits, wear, rust, and corrosion in gasoline engines.

- *SD*. Oils designed for SD service provide more protection against high- and low-temperature engine deposits, wear, rust, and corrosion in engines than do SC oils. SD oils may be used when API Engine Service Category SC is recommended.

- *SE*. Oils designed for SE service provide more protection against oil oxidation, high-temperature engine deposits, rust, and corrosion in engines than do either SC or SD oils. SE oils may be used when either SC or SD classifications are recommended.

- *SF*. Oils developed for SF service provide increased oxidation stability and improved antiwear performance relative to oils that meet the minimum requirements for API Service Category SE. SF oils also provide protection against engine deposits, rust, and corrosion, and may be used when any of the classifications SE, SD, and SC are recommended.

TWO-STROKE LUBRICATING OIL

In the discussion of engine operation in Unit 6, it was mentioned that air and fuel enter the crankcase of the two-cycle engine and then move up the transfer port into the cylinder. Most two-cycle engines are lubricated by bringing oil into the crankcase along with the air and fuel. To bring it in, the oil must be mixed with the gasoline. This mixing can be done outside or inside the engine, as we shall see later.

Two-cycle lubricating oil (Figure 12–3) is a special type of oil that mixes with the gasoline and stays mixed for a long time. The mixture is different for different engines. Some engines use 15 parts of gasoline for each part of oil. Others use a 25-to-1 mix, i.e., 25 parts of gasoline to one part of oil. There is always more gasoline than oil in the mixture.

FOUR-STROKE LUBRICATION SYSTEMS

Four-stroke cycle engines use a lubrication system in which oil is directed under pressure to the parts that require lubrication. There are two basic types of these pressure lubrication systems: *wet sump* and *dry sump*.

A dry-sump lubrication system uses two pumps and a separate tank on the motorcycle to store the oil. One pump forces oil through the engine parts and the other pump re-

Figure 12–3. Two-cycle lubricating oil must mix with gasoline. *(Chevron Chemical Co.)*

turns the oil to the oil tank. The parts of a dry sump system are shown in Figure 12–4. The oil tank is usually located above the engine, so oil flows by gravity into the high-pressure pump, which forces the oil through the engine parts for lubrication. The lubricating oil then runs down to the bottom of the engine into an area called a sump. The scavenger pump then pulls the oil out of the sump and re-

turns it to the oil tank. The system is called a dry-sump system because there is only a small amount of oil in the sump. The dry-sump system has the advantage of providing a large supply of oil because more oil can be stored in the tank than in the lower end of most small-engine crankcases.

In the wet-sump system (Figure 12–5), the oil is stored in the bottom of the crankcase. The one pump required in the system picks up oil from the bottom of the crankcase and delivers it to the components that require lubrication. After lubrication, the oil runs back into the crankcase by gravity, to be stored for later use.

Both the wet- and dry-sump systems have about the same lubrication system components and internal oil flow route. Each system has an oil strainer pressure pump, oil filter, and drilled oil flow channels and galleries.

The oil that enters the pump first passes through a wire-screen oil strainer, which prevents any large particles of foreign material from entering the lubrication system. The pressure oil pump causes the oil to flow throughout the engine, resulting in a pressure buildup. While there are many different types of pumps, the rotor pump is used on many engines. In wet-sump systems, it is common to have both the pressure pump and the scavenger pump in one housing.

The rotor-type pump is mounted on the bottom of the crankcase and driven from the primary shaft through a

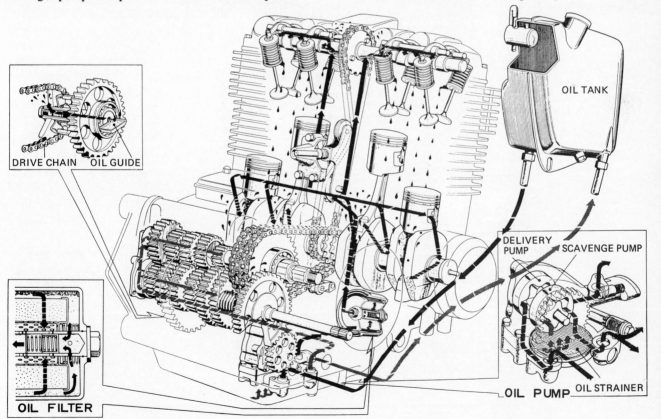

Figure 12–4. A dry-sump lubrication system. *(Honda Motor Co., Ltd.)*

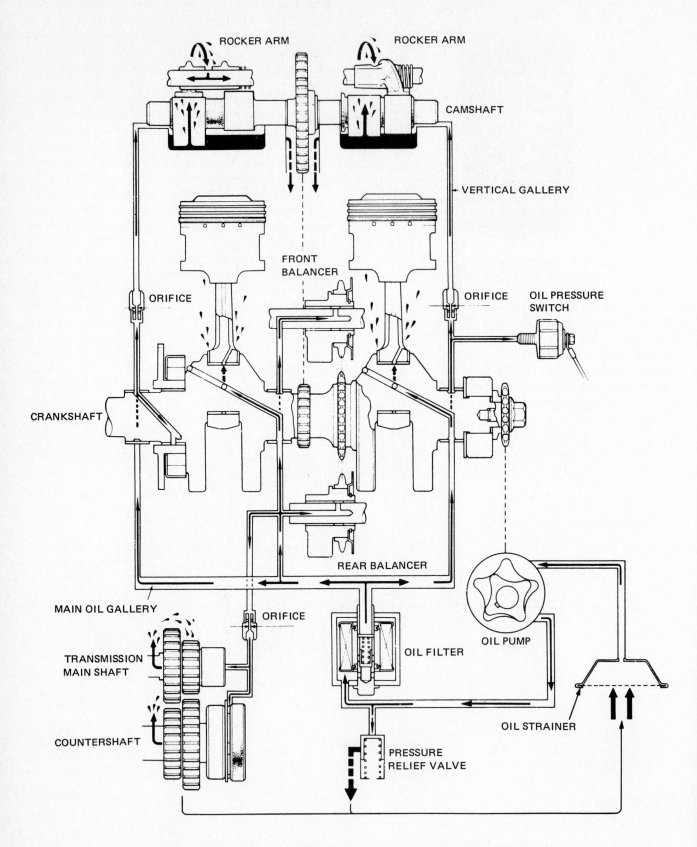

Figure 12–5. Typical wet-sump lubrication system. *(Honda Motor Co., Ltd.)*

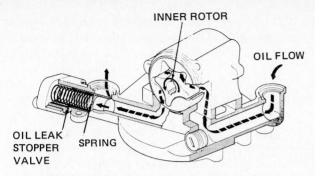

Figure 12–6. Rotor-type oil pump. (Honda Motor Co., Ltd.)

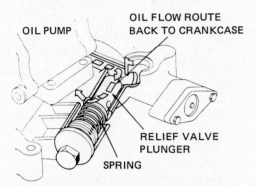

Figure 12–7. The relief valve prevents too high a pressure. (Honda Motor Co., Ltd.)

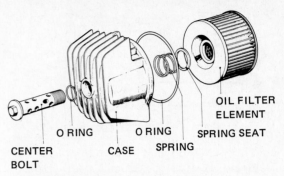

Figure 12–8. Oil filter assembly. (Honda Motor Co., Ltd.)

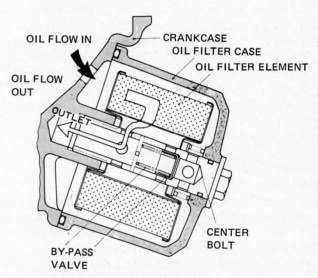

Figure 12–9. Cross-sectional view of an oil filter. (Honda Motor Co., Ltd.)

gear. The pump shown in Figure 12–6 consists of both the delivery and scavenger pumps, a leak stopper valve, and a relief valve. The pump is made up of an inner rotor driven by the engine and an outer rotor driven by the inner rotor. As the rotors turn, the lobes separate, causing a partial vacuum. Oil is pulled in and carried around between the rotor lobes until it is forced through the outlet.

During engine operation, the oil pressure opens the oil leak stopper valve to maintain oil flow, and when the engine stops, the valve closes to prevent flow from the oil tank. The leak stopper valve is used only in wet-sump systems.

The rotor pump has a relief valve assembly mounted on its outlet side (Figure 12–7). The purpose of the relief valve is to prevent too high a pressure from forming in the system. The unit consists of a small plunger backed up by a calibrated spring. If the pressure becomes too high, the plunger is pushed into position to release pressure, sending some oil back into the crankcase. As soon as the pressure returns to normal, the relief valve spring repositions the plunger.

After the oil passes through the pump and relief valve, it goes to the oil filter assembly (Figure 12–8). The function of the filter is to clean the oil before it reaches the engine parts. The filter assembly is typically mounted onto the crankcase, where it is accessible for replacement. The filter element is housed in a removable case sealed with a

large "O" ring. A center bolt and "O" ring hold the case to the crankcase.

The oil filter element is shown in cross section in Figure 12–9. The filter element is made from paper. When oil is routed through the treated paper that the element is made of, any dirt and acids in the oil stick to the outside of the paper, and only clean oil gets through. After the oil goes through the filter element, it returns to the crankcase to be circulated into the engine components.

After a period of use, the oil filter element may become clogged with materials that have been filtered from the oil. If oil no longer passes easily through the element, it no longer gets to the engine parts. To prevent this problem, a bypass valve is located inside the filter assembly. When the filter element becomes clogged, the pressure inside the canister increases and pushes open the bypass valve. The oil then goes around the filter and directly into the main oil gallery.

Some engines use a centrifugal type of oil filter (Figure 12–10), consisting of a set of vanes attached to a rod driven by the engine. When the engine is running, the

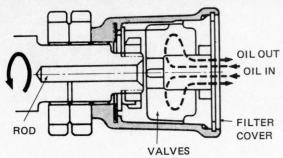

Figure 12–10. A centrifugal-type oil filter. *(Honda Motor Co., Ltd.)*

vanes spin. Oil enters the filter and is picked up by the spinning vanes, whereupon foreign matter such as metallic dust and carbon particles are separated from the oil by centrifugal force. The cleaned oil is fed to the engine parts through the outlet port in the center section of the filter cover.

When the oil leaves the filter assembly, it enters the oil passages of the crankcase, flowing into several long channels called *galleries*. From the main gallery, oil flows to oil clearance areas at main bearings. The crankshaft is drilled from the main journals to the connecting rod journals to promote oil flow.

The connecting rods are sometimes drilled lengthwise up to the piston bushing so that oil may reach the piston bushing area. Oil is sent up vertical galleries in the cylinder head to the camshaft and rocker arms.

After the oil has passed through those parts of the engine that require lubrication, it falls or runs down the inside of the engine back to the sump. Oil that makes its way out of each of the connecting rod bearings is thrown off the crankshaft, splashing up on the cylinders and lubricating them, as well as the piston and ring assembly. Excess oil picked up by the oil control ring passes through oil holes in the piston, from where it is allowed to fall back to the sump. The path of oil flow for typical engines is shown in Figures 12–11 and 12–12.

An oil pressure switch (see Figure 12–5) is part of the lubrication system. This switch is connected to a warning light usually mounted near the tachometer. The oil pressure warning light warns the rider of low oil pressure. Current for the indicator light is provided from an ignition switch terminal. In order to have a complete circuit, the oil pressure switch must provide a path to ground. The oil pressure switch unit, mounted on the crankcase, senses engine oil pressure, and if the pressure drops below a safe level, the sending unit provides a ground and a completed circuit lights the oil pressure indicator light.

If the oil level is too low, the pump will not be able to provide enough oil for lubrication. Oil level is measured with a dipstick inserted into the crankcase sump or oil tank. The higher the oil level, the higher the oil will come

up on the dipstick. Markings on the dipstick show whether there is enough oil. The dipstick on the oil tank is usually made as part of the oil tank cap, as shown in Figure 12–13.

TWO-STROKE LUBRICATION SYSTEMS

There are two basic types of lubrication system used on two-stroke engines. The *premix* type uses gasoline and oil mixed together in the motorcycle fuel tank. The *oil injection* type mixes oil with the air and fuel as they enter the engine.

The premix lubrication system is the simplest type and does not require any special components. The rider simply adds the correct amount of two-stroke oil to the fuel in the fuel tank and shakes the bike to mix up the fuel. Some motorcycle shops sell fuel already mixed with oil.

The premix encounters the air moving through the carburetor and mixes with it to form the final air–fuel mixture (Figure 12–14). The air-laden mixture is forced into the crankcase and goes through the crankcase bearings, connecting rod large ends, and cylinder, thereby lubricating each component.

While the premix system is simple, it has several disadvantages. If the rider mixes the prelube incorrectly and does not add enough oil, the engine parts will not receive enough lubricant and can quickly wear out. On the other hand, if too much oil is added, the engine will smoke and excessive carbon will build up on engine parts. Eventually, the spark plug will be fouled with carbon and the engine will run poorly.

To avoid these problems, many two-stroke motorcycles, especially those used on the street, have a separate tank for oil and an oil injection system of metering the oil into the engine in just the correct amount. A pump is used to force oil from the oil tank into the crankcase and to control the amount of oil delivered (Figure 12–15). The pump forces oil from the oil tank into the crankcase in exact proportion to the engine speed and load, resulting in reduced oil consumption and less carbon buildup in the combustion chamber.

An oil pump for an oil injection system is shown in Figure 12–16. The pump is mounted at the top of the crankcase with a screw. The pump drive gear, which is press fitted to the engine crankshaft, rotates the drive shaft. The cam drive gear at the other end of the drive shaft rotates the cam gear. The pump itself consists of a plunger, a valve, a pump body, and springs. Two-stage cams, inside and outside, are formed on the side surface of the cam gear. The inside cam is for the plunger, the outside one for the valve. The valve and plunger are held against the cam surfaces by means of the springs so that they move up and down in the pump body as the cams rotate according to the rotation of the cam gear.

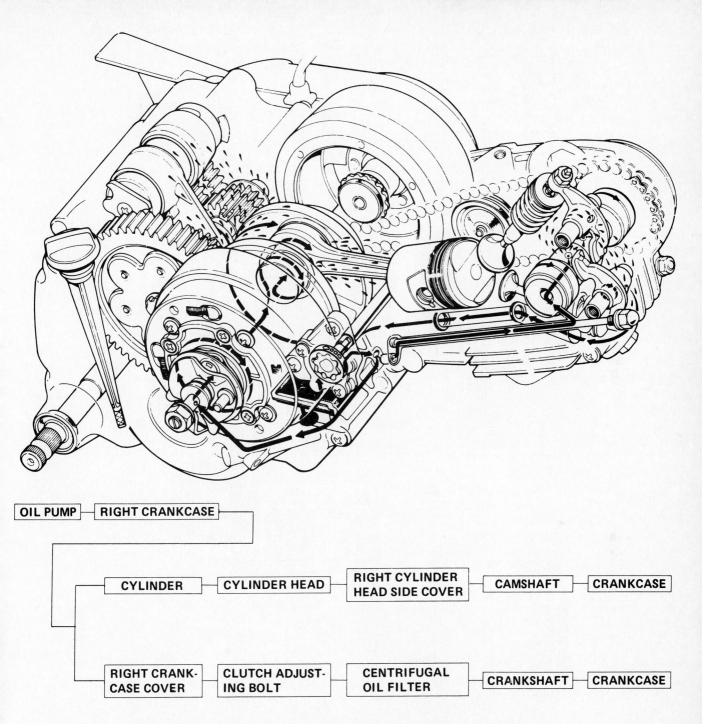

Figure 12–11. Oil flow in typical motorcycle engines. *(Honda Motor Co., Ltd.)*

The operation of the valve and plunger is shown in Figure 12–17. At point A, the valve is at bottom dead center, blocking the discharge port and the pump port. At point B, the intake port opens, and oil flows into the pump housing due to the creation of a vacuum as the plunger goes down.

At point C, the end of the intake stroke, the valve starts rising in the body, blocking the inlet port. As the valve rises further, the pump housing opens to the discharge port

(point D), and the plunger is pushed up by the cam. Oil is then forced into the inlet pipe, overcoming the check valve spring force (point E). Lubricating oil flows through the system as shown in Figure 12–18.

Some oil injection systems control the flow of oil with the accelerator grip as well as with engine speed. As shown in Figure 12–19, the oil pump is driven by the engine through a reduction gear and is connected to the car-

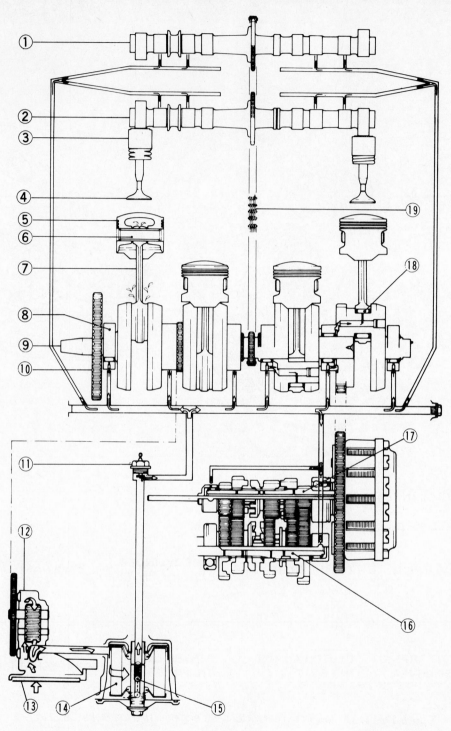

1. Camshaft
2. Camshaft
3. Valve Lifter
4. Valve
5. Piston
6. Piston Pin
7. Connecting Rod
8. Main Bearing
9. Crankshaft
10. Starter Gear
11. Oil Pressure
     Switch
12. Oil Pump
13. Oil Screen
14. Oil Filter
15. Bypass Valve
16. Output Shaft
17. Drive Shaft
18. Big End Bearing
19. Camshaft Chain

Figure 12–12. Oil flow in motorcycle engine. *(Kawasaki Motors Corp. U.S.A.)*

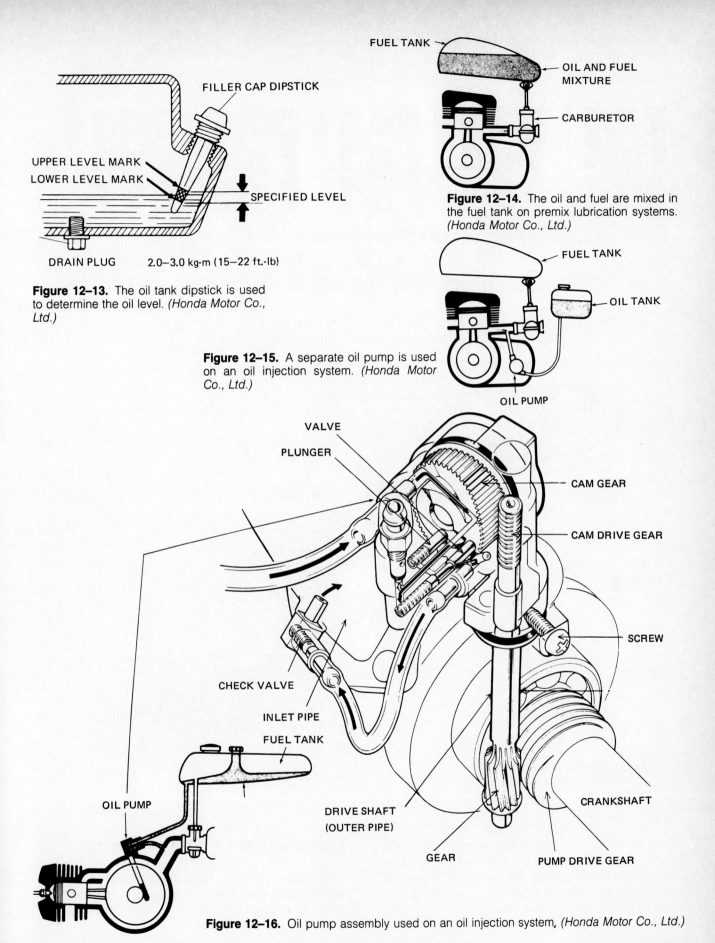

FILLER CAP DIPSTICK

UPPER LEVEL MARK
LOWER LEVEL MARK

SPECIFIED LEVEL

DRAIN PLUG   2.0–3.0 kg-m (15–22 ft.-lb)

Figure 12–13. The oil tank dipstick is used to determine the oil level. *(Honda Motor Co., Ltd.)*

FUEL TANK
OIL AND FUEL MIXTURE
CARBURETOR

Figure 12–14. The oil and fuel are mixed in the fuel tank on premix lubrication systems. *(Honda Motor Co., Ltd.)*

FUEL TANK
OIL TANK
OIL PUMP

Figure 12–15. A separate oil pump is used on an oil injection system. *(Honda Motor Co., Ltd.)*

VALVE
PLUNGER
CAM GEAR
CAM DRIVE GEAR
SCREW
CHECK VALVE
INLET PIPE
FUEL TANK
OIL PUMP
DRIVE SHAFT (OUTER PIPE)
GEAR
CRANKSHAFT
PUMP DRIVE GEAR

Figure 12–16. Oil pump assembly used on an oil injection system. *(Honda Motor Co., Ltd.)*

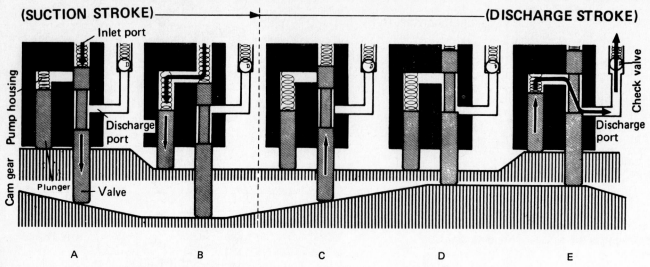

Figure 12–17. Operation of the oil injection pump. *(Honda Motor Co., Ltd.)*

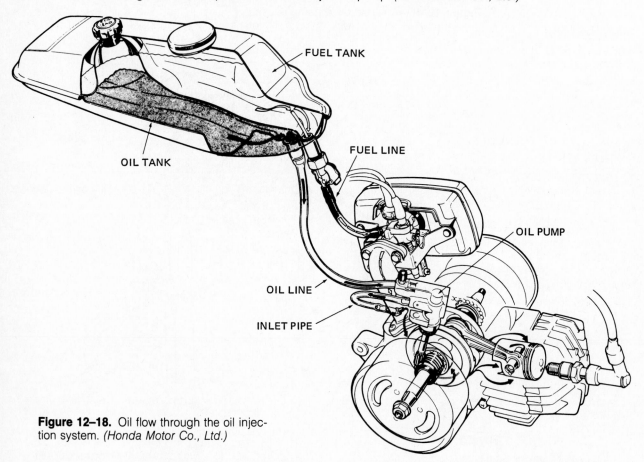

Figure 12–18. Oil flow through the oil injection system. *(Honda Motor Co., Ltd.)*

buretor throttle cable controlled by the throttle hand grip. The pump automatically regulates the volume of oil according to the engine speed and throttle valve opening, thus pumping the optimum amount of oil for engine lubrication under any operating condition.

LUBRICATION SYSTEM SERVICING

Servicing the four-stroke lubrication system involves draining the engine oil and changing the filter. The oil and filter should be changed regularly. Note that the intervals sug-

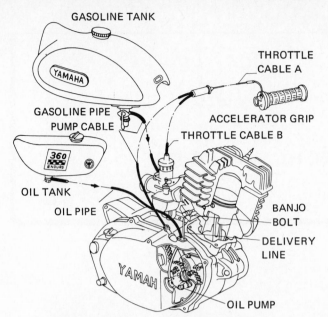

Figure 12–19. An oil injection pump connected to the accelerator grip. *(Yamaha Motor Corp. U.S.A.)*

gested by the motorcycle manufacturer should be considered the maximum; you can add many miles to the life of the engine by changing the oil even more frequently. Oil should definitely be changed more frequently if most of the riding is done in traffic or under conditions in which a lot of dirt is likely to enter the engine.

Oil should be drained when it is hot. If the engine is cool, the oil will be too thick to drain well, and particles of dirt and water will have time to stick to parts of the engine. Oil is best changed after a long ride.

The oil can be drained into a flat pan. If the bike has a wet sump, place the pan under the crankcase drain plug. If the motorcycle has a dry sump, you will have to drain both the sump and the tank. You can make a cardboard flume, tape it under the oil tank drain plug, and direct the oil into the oil pan. Install the drain plugs and torque them to specifications.

To change the filter, place a pan under the filter cover, remove the center bolt or side bolts, and pull off the oil filter cover. Clean the cover thoroughly in solvent and allow it to dry. Remove the old filter element and replace it with a new one. Then remove the old ''O'' rings and install new ones. Replace the cover and install and tighten the center bolt (or bolts) to the correct torque.

Add the correct amount of recommended oil to the crankcase or oil tank. Start the engine and observe all drain plugs and filter case for leaks.

Two-stroke oil injection systems do not require changing the oil because oil is consumed in the engine. If the oil pump or an oil line is removed from the engine, or if the rider allows the tank to run dry, air will get into the oil lines and oil pump. This air must be removed before the pump will operate properly. The procedure to remove the air is called *bleeding* or *priming* the pump. Usually, the engine is turned off and the oil delivery line at the pump is loosened while the throttle is held open, allowing oil to run from the tank to the pump. Always follow the exact priming procedure outlined in the shop manual.

TROUBLESHOOTING

Various troubleshooting procedures are recommended in different shop service manuals. Of course, any checklist is only a diagnostic guide—it is never foolproof. Often, two and even three conditions can be causing the problem. One manufacturer[1] recommends the following sequence for some of the models:

LUBRICATION SYSTEM

Oil Does Not Return to Oil Tank
1. Oil tank empty.
2. Scavenger pump gear key sheared.
3. Oil feed pump not functioning.
4. Restricted oil lines or fittings.
5. Restricted oil filter.

Engine Uses Too Much Oil or Smokes Excessively
1. Breather valve incorrectly timed.
2. Piston rings badly worn or broken.
3. Valve guides or valve guide seals worn.

Engine Leaks Oil from Cases, Push Rods, Hoses, Etc.
1. Loose parts.
2. Imperfect seal at gaskets, push rod cover, washers, etc.
3. Restricted oil return line to tank.
4. Restricted breather hose to air cleaner.

Excess Oil Out of Crankcase Breather (Air Cleaner)
1. Oil not returning to oil tank.
2. Oil lines or passages restricted.
3. Gearcase cover gasket not sealing.
4. Leakage between passages and pockets in gearcase cover and gearcase.
5. Restricted oil return line to tank.

Excess Oil Out of Crankcase Breather When Starting Engine
1. Oil pump check ball stuck open.
2. Poor seal between feed and return gears in pump.

[1]Harley-Davidson Motor Co., Inc.

Job Sheet |12–1|

CHANGE FOUR-STROKE OIL AND FILTER

Before you begin:

Read pp. _____

Make of Motorcycle _____ Model _____ Year _____

Time Started _____ Time Finished _____ Total Time _____

Flat-rate Time _____

Special Tools, Equipment, Parts, and Materials

Torque wrench
Drain pan
New filter element
Oil

References

Manufacturer's Shop Manual _____

Specifications

Look up the recommended amount of oil required for this engine when the oil and filter are changed. Record the amount in the space provided below:

Capacity _____

Look up the following torque specifications:

Oil tank drain plug _____ Crankcase drain plug _____ Oil filter case center bolt _____

Instructor check _____

Procedure

1. Does this motorcycle have: (check one)

    wet sump _____ dry sump _____

    Instructor check _____

2. Warm the engine to normal operating temperature.

3. Place a pan under the crankcase drain plug.

4. Remove the plug and allow the oil to drain. *(SAFETY CAUTION: Be careful—the oil is hot.)*

5. If the motorcycle has an oil tank, construct a flume out of cardboard, position it under the oil tank, and direct the oil through the flume and into the oil pan.

6. Remove the oil pan drain plug and allow the oil to drain.

7. While the oil is draining, locate the filter. Put a pan under the oil filter case to catch the oil that will come out.

8. Remove the filter center bolt and the filter case.

9. Remove the old filter element and compare it to the new one. Are they the same?

Instructor check _____

10. Clean the oil filter case assembly in cleaning solvent and allow it to dry.

11. Wipe the area the filter is mounted on in the crankcase with a clean rag.

12. Using new ''O'' rings, install the new filter element and filter case.

13. Torque the filter case center bolt to specifications.

14. Add the recommended amount of the correct type of oil to the crankcase or oil tank.

15. Start the engine and check for oil leaks.

Instructor check _____

16. Turn the engine off and check the oil level with the dipstick.

NOTES

Instructor check _____   Date completed _____

Job Sheet $\boxed{12-2}$

PRIME A TWO-STROKE INJECTION PUMP

Before you begin:

Read pp.

Make of Motorcycle _____ Model _____ Year _____

Time Started _____ Time Finished _____ Total Time _____

Flat-rate Time _____

Special Tools, Equipment, Parts, and Materials

Two-stroke oil

References

Manufacturer's Shop Manual _____

Specifications

Procedure

1. Look up the procedure for priming the pump on this model motorcycle in the shop manual.

2. Remove the oil injection pump cover.

   Instructor check _____

3. Bleed the oil inlet line by loosening a bleeder screw on the line at its connection on the pump or by removing the line.

4. Allow the oil to flow out of the bleeder hole or the line until all air bubbles stop.

5. You may have to hold the pump open by hand and turn the pump plunger by cranking the engine.

   Instructor check _____

6. Retighten the bleeder screw or line connection.

7. Bleed the outlet lines by loosening the connections at the engine.

8. Crank the engine and allow it to run at low RPM for a short period of time until all the air is expelled.

Instructor check _____

9. Retighten all line connections and refill the oil tank, if necessary.

10. Reinstall the oil pump case cover and tighten the screws to the correct torque.

11. Check the system for oil leaks.

NOTES

Instructor check _____   Date completed _____

KEY TERMS

Dry-sump system: a four-stroke lubrication system with a separate oil tank and a scavenger pump to return oil to the tank after it has been used in the engine.

Lubrication: reduction of friction in an engine by the provision of oil between moving parts.

Lubrication system: a system designed to provide oil to the engine's parts.

Oil: petroleum- or synthetic-based fluid used to provide lubrication.

Oil filter: a device to filter out dirt and other foreign matter from oil.

Oil injection system: a two-cycle lubrication system in which oil from a separate oil tank is injected into the engine and mixed with the air and fuel.

Oil level indicator: a dipstick inserted into the oil pan to measure the oil level.

Oil pump: a device used to circulate oil to the moving parts of an engine.

Premix lubrication system: a two-stroke lubrication system in which oil is mixed with the fuel in the gasoline tank.

Relief valve: a spring-loaded valve used to regulate the pressure in the lubrication system.

Service rating: a system of rating how well an oil stands up under wear and tear; established by the American Petroleum Institute.

Viscosity: the thickness or thinness of an oil.

Wet-sump system: a four-cycle lubrication system in which oil is stored in the crankcase of an engine.

CHECKUP

1. Why must the oil used in a two-stroke engine mix well with gasoline?

2. What is the purpose of a scavenger pump on a dry-sump system?

3. What is the purpose of a relief valve on an oil pump? Identify the parts of the oil filter assembly by writing their names in the spaces provided.

4. _____

5. _____

6. _____

7. _____

8. _____

9. _____

10. _____

11. What is the purpose of the oil filter?

12. What happens when the oil filter element becomes clogged?

13. How does a two-cycle premix lubrication system work? Identify the parts of the two-cycle oil injection system by writing their names in the spaces provided.

14. _____

15. _____

16. _____

17. _____

18. _____

19. _____

20. _____

DISCUSSION TOPICS AND ACTIVITIES

1. What type of lubricating system is used on most two-stroke engines under conditions where dirt may easily enter the engine? Why is this system used?

2. Using a shop four-cycle engine, try to trace the flow of lubricating oil through the lubricating system.

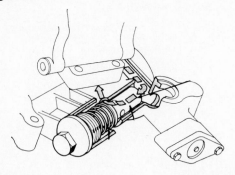

The combustion that takes place in the motorcycle engine cylinders generates a great amount of heat. Most of this heat is used to push down the pistons, but a part of it goes into the engine parts. Thus, a cooling system is required to remove excess heat that might damage these parts. The heat generated by combustion may be removed by either air cooling or liquid cooling. In this unit, we describe the operation and servicing of the cooling system.

JOB COMPETENCY OBJECTIVES

When you finish reading and studying this unit, you should be able to:

1. Explain how heat is removed from air-cooled engine parts.

2. Describe the parts and operation of a liquid cooling system.

3. Explain the procedure used to locate a cooling system problem.

4. Pressure-test a liquid cooling system.

5. Drain and refill coolant, and debug a radiator.

AIR COOLING SYSTEMS

Most motorcycles, and all two-strokers, use an air cooling system. In such a system, components which get the hottest, such as the cylinder and cylinder head, have cooling fins formed around their outsides (Figure 13–1). The purpose of these cooling fins is to direct the greatest amount of air into contact with the greatest amount of hot metal. When the engine is running, heat builds up in the cylinder head and cylinder and then moves out into the cooling fins. Aluminum, an especially good conductor of heat, is used wherever possible. Air flows around the cooling fins and carries away the heat, as shown in Figure 13–2.

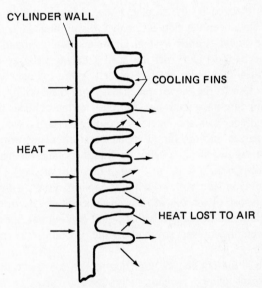

Figure 13–2. Heat passes into the cooling fins, and air carries it away.

Air is directed around the cooling fins by the natural draft. As the motorcycle moves, it pushes through the air (Figure 13–3), causing the air to flow over the motorcycle and through the cooling fins. There is a natural flow of air as long as the motorcycle is moving. However, when the motorcycle is running but not moving, there is no flow of air, and parts can overheat. When riding or testing an air-cooled motorcycle, you should avoid long periods of running the engine with the bike stopped.

LIQUID COOLING SYSTEMS

The advantage of an air cooling system is that it is simple: as long as there is adequate air flow over the motorcycle, the air cooling system can prevent engine parts from overheating. However, large V-twin motorcycles have a built-

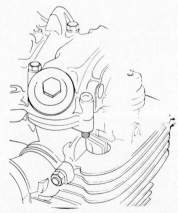

Figure 13–1. Cooling fins are formed on the outside of the cylinder and cylinder head. (Honda Motor Co., Ltd.)

COOLING SYSTEM OPERATION AND SERVICING

Figure 13–3. Movement of the motorcycle through the air creates a natural draft flow over the engine. *(Yamaha Motor Corp. U.S.A.)*

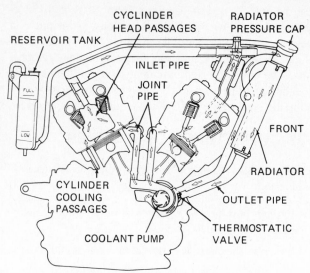

Figure 13–4. Parts of the liquid cooling system. *(Yamaha Motor Corp. U.S.A.)*

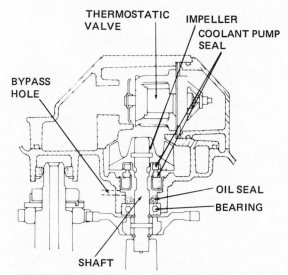

Figure 13–5. Sectional view of coolant pump. *(Yamaha Motor Corp. U.S.A.)*

in cooling problem: some of the air flow to the rear cylinder is blocked by the front cylinder. Liquid cooling systems have been developed to solve this problem.

The liquid cooling system circulates liquid around hot engine parts to carry off the heat. Coolant passages surround each cylinder and are placed in the cylinder head very close to the valve area. Heat from the burning air–fuel mixture passes through the metal of the cylinder head and cylinder wall and enters the cooling passages, where it then passes into the liquid coolant that circulates through the passages. Having entered the liquid coolant, the heat is then dispersed into the air through the radiator.

The main advantage of a liquid cooling system is that it can dispose of more heat than an air cooling system can. An additional advantage is that liquid cooling passages reduce engine noise, so that engine operation is much quieter.

The liquid cooling system (Figure 13–4) is made up of a coolant pump, radiator, thermostatic valve, radiator hoses or pipes, radiator pressure cap, and reservoir tank. The coolant is circulated by an impeller-type pump mounted on the right-hand crankcase and driven by a gear. It is drawn by the pump from the bottom tank of the radiator, directed through the outlet pipe, and discharged around the cylinder and cylinder head through the joint pipe. The coolant passes from the cylinder to the cylinder head through coolant passages and, after circulating around combustion chamber passages, enters the radiator upper tank via the inlet pipe.

The coolant pump drive shaft is driven by a crankshaft-driven gear. The shaft is connected to a small wheel or *impeller* with blades that is located in the coolant passage (Figure 13–5). As the impeller spins, it draws coolant into its center and throws it off the blades by centrifugal force, causing the coolant to be pulled in and pushed out of the pump. The shaft that drives the pump is supported on a bearing which is sealed to prevent coolant from entering. A bypass hole is provided to return any coolant that gets

by a coolant pump seal that is supposed to prevent coolant from getting on the bearing.

Radiator

The heat removed from the hot engine parts by the coolant must then be removed from the coolant itself. This is done by pumping the hot coolant out of the engine and into a heat exchanger, commonly referred to as the *radiator* (Figure 13–6). The radiator removes heat from the coolant so that the coolant may go back through the engine without fear of any engine parts being damaged by heat.

Mounted in front of the engine, the radiator is made up of a top tank, a bottom tank, and a center core or heat exchanger. A radiator cover with air passages is mounted in

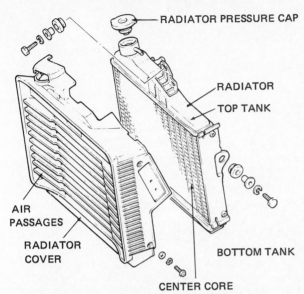

Figure 13–6. The radiator acts as a heat exchanger. *(Yamaha Motor Corp. U.S.A.)*

front of the radiator to protect it and direct air through it. Hot coolant is pumped out of the engine and into the top tank of the radiator. It then enters the radiator core through a large number of small distribution tubes that are made from a metal that is a good heat conductor, usually copper or aluminum. The heat passes out of the liquid and into the wall of the tubes, which are fitted with copper or aluminum air fins. Air circulated through the core past the fins takes the heat from the fins (Figure 13–7). The cooled liquid then runs into the bottom tank of the radiator, where it can be drawn back into the engine to pick up more heat.

Electric fan

As long as the motorcycle is moving through the air, there is adequate circulation of air through the radiator core. During long periods of idle, however, there is no air flow through the core, and the engine may overheat. Some larger engines use an electric motor attached to a fan blade to pull air through the radiator core. The fans typically work on a temperature-sensing system, so they rotate only during idle and warm conditions. A fan is shown in Figure 13–8.

Radiator pressure cap

At atmospheric pressure, water will boil at 212° F (100° C) and a 50–50 antifreeze–water solution will boil at about 226° F (109° C). If allowed to boil, the coolant will turn into steam and expand violently, so that it could easily damage the radiator or engine. The purpose of the radiator pressure cap (Figure 13–9) is to pressurize and raise the boiling temperature of the coolant. Each pound of pressure that the cap ''holds'' will raise the coolant boiling temper-

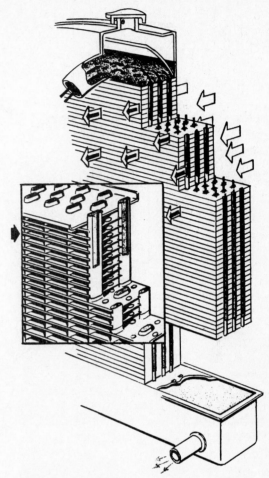

Figure 13–7. Flow of coolant and air through a radiator core. *(E.I. DuPont de Nemours & Co.)*

ature about 3° F. Thus, a cap that places the coolant at 12 pounds pressurization raises its boiling point from 226° F (109° C) to approximately 260° F (126° C).

The radiator pressure cap performs its function through the design and operation of two simple valves: a pressure valve and a vacuum valve. The pressure valve determines the pressure at which the radiator cap will open. The valve presses against a seat in the radiator filler neck under spring tension. The tension of the spring determines the level of pressure required to open the valve. As long as this level is not reached, the pressure valve stays closed. If the valve opens, coolant or steam pressure escapes through the overflow tube into the reservoir tank.

The vacuum valve normally remains closed, sealing the system from the outside air. The system is under constant pressure until the engine is shut down and temperature and pressure descrease. Then the valve opens, allowing air to enter the system. If the valve did not open, the pressure drop would create a vacuum that could collapse the radiator or its hoses.

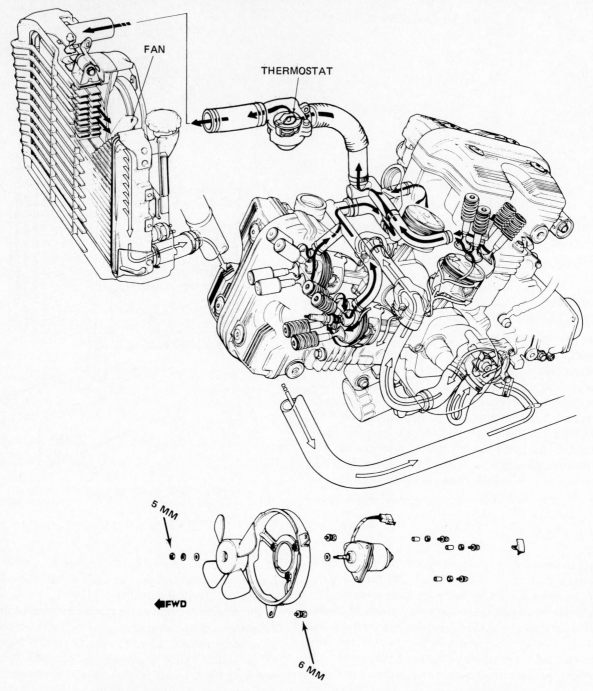

Figure 13–8. Electric fan used to cool the radiator. *(Honda Motor Co., Ltd.)*

The pressure relief valve in the radiator cap is connected to an overflow tube that is hooked to a clear plastic reservoir tank. During pressure relief, the coolant goes through the tube and into the reservoir. When the system has cooled off, the coolant is drawn through the overflow by vacuum and reenters the radiator. Lines on the reservoir tank allow a visual inspection of the coolant level. There is a "full line" and a "low line"; the coolant should be between them (Figure 13–10). A cap on top of the reservoir allows you to add coolant, if necessary.

Thermostat

The thermostatic valve, or thermostat, is a control valve in the coolant system. It senses the coolant temperature and regulates its flow, automatically opening and closing de-

SPECIFIED RELIEF PRESSURE

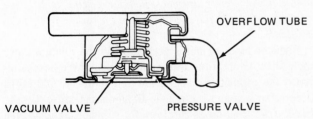

OVERFLOW TUBE

VACUUM VALVE   PRESSURE VALVE

Figure 13–9. Radiator pressure cap. *(Ford Motor Co.)*

CAP

FULL

LOW

Figure 13–10. Reservoir tank allows a visual inspection of coolant level. *(Yamaha Motor Corp. U.S.A.)*

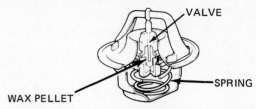

VALVE

WAX PELLET   SPRING

Figure 13–11. A thermostatic valve. *(Ford Motor Co.)*

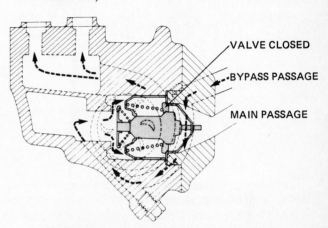

VALVE CLOSED

BYPASS PASSAGE

MAIN PASSAGE

Figure 13–12. Thermostatic valve with main valve closed on a cold engine. *(Yamaha Motor Corp. U.S.A.)*

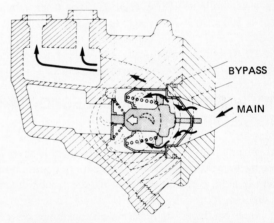

BYPASS

MAIN

Figure 13–13. Thermostatic valve open for a warm engine. *(Yamaha Motor Corp. U.S.A.)*

pending on the temperature of the engine. When the coolant temperature is below minimum, the thermostat remains closed. The coolant recirculates back into the engine through a by-pass passage which is usually located near the thermostat, or, at times, in the thermostat itself.

The most common thermostat in use is the cold expansion wax pellet type, which closes when cold (Figure 13–11). When the engine is cool, the thermostatic valve is closed, but the passage to the by-pass is open. Thus, the coolant does not flow into the radiator, but rather, flows through the bypass hose and the bypass valve into the coolant pump, where it is pumped to the engine cylinder coolant passages (Figure 13–12). As soon as the coolant heats to the temperature at which the thermostat will open, the wax-filled pellet expands, overcomes the spring pressure, and opens the valve for normal cooling action (Figure 13–13). The coolant then flows into the radiator.

The thermostatic valve is installed in the water pump cover. Remove the cover to reach and remove the thermostat (Figure 13–14).

Coolant

The coolant used in most systems is a 50–50 percent mix of distilled water and antifreeze. Plain water is considered an excellent coolant because of its heat-transfer capabilities. However, water freezes at 32° F (0° C) and boils at 212° F (100° C), which limits its use as a coolant. If only water is used, and it does freeze, it will expand about 9% in volume. The pressure of the expanding ice can exert forces that can crack soldered radiator seams. Also, plain water can cause rust formation.

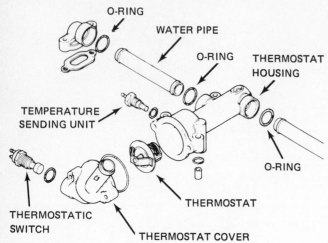

Figure 13–14. Remove the water pump cover to reach the thermostat. *(Honda Motor Co., Ltd.)*

The majority of high-quality antifreezes available are ethylene glycol based, fortified with rust and corrosion inhibitors. A 50% water, 50% ethylene glycol solution lowers the freezing point of water to about −34° F (−37° C).

Ethylene glycol also raises the boiling point of water. Plain water boils at 212° F (100° C), but when ethylene glycol is added to it for protection against freezing down to −34° F (−37° C), the boiling point increases to 226° F (109° C). If boiling does occur, the water boils off first, increasing the concentration of ethylene glycol.

COOLING SYSTEM TROUBLESHOOTING AND SERVICING

Since an air cooling system has no parts, there is never any servicing to perform on such a system. A liquid cooling system is more complex and may require troubleshooting and servicing.

A liquid cooling system that is not operating correctly will allow the engine to overheat. Most liquid cooling systems have a temperature sensor somewhere in them that is connected to a warning light near the tachometer. The warning light comes on when the engine's temperature is too high. Other signs that the engine is overheating are the engine's knocking or pinging under a load and the radiator's venting steam from an overflow.

If you find that your engine is overheating, first check the coolant level. If the level is low, the overheating may be due to a loss of coolant. Make a visual check of the system to find any external leaks. Check all relevant hoses, pipes, and radiator clamps, the radiator core, and the radiator drain.

In general, the coolant level in the radiator should be checked regularly. Overheating due to insufficient coolant

can damage the engine. Check the coolant level when the engine is cold. Cooling systems with a reservoir tank may be inspected for proper coolant level by simply observing the level in the tank. Most tanks are made of a clear plastic, with lines that show the proper coolant level.

When you add coolant, do it through the reservoir cap, not through the radiator cap. You add coolant through the radiator cap only when you have drained and are refilling the system. *(Safety Caution: Remember that the radiator cap keeps the coolant under pressure to raise its boiling point. If the cap is opened when the engine is hot, the coolant may boil and overflow. Open a radiator cap with caution.)*

Radiator pipes or hoses connected to the radiator carry the coolant to and from the engine. If one of the hoses ruptures, the coolant is dumped out very quickly. Old hoses become so stiff and brittle that vibration can cause them to break. Check all hoses carefully for signs of cracks—even a small crack can soon cause trouble. Replace any cracked hose.

Poor coolant flow may be due to a thermostat that fails to open or opens at too high a temperature. Accordingly, the thermostat must sometimes be removed from its housing for testing.

Find out the temperature at which the thermostat will open by checking the shop service manual. Begin testing the operation of the thermostat by putting it inside a container of coolant. (Make sure that it does not rest on the bottom of the container.) Then heat the coolant and check its temperature with a cooking thermometer (Figure 13–15). The thermostat valve should open near its rated temperature. If it fails to open near that temperature or opens far above it, replace the thermostat.

Poor air flow across the radiator core is another cause of the engine's overheating. Radiator fins clogged with bugs, paper, or other debris from the road can reduce air flow.

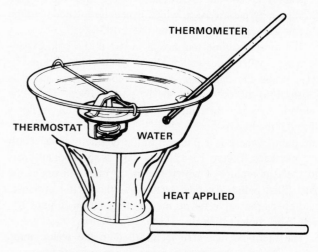

Figure 13–15. Testing a thermostat. *(Honda Motor Co., Ltd.)*

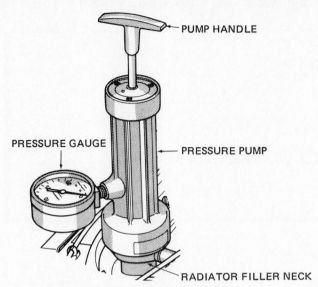

Figure 13–16. Pressurizing the cooling system to check for leaks. *(Chrysler Corp.)*

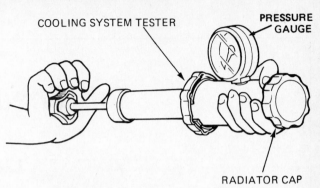

Figure 13–17. Pressure-checking the radiator cap. *(Honda Motor Co., Ltd.)*

Use an air hose to gently blow air out through the radiator from the engine side. *(Safety note: Wear eye protection.)* Bugs and other debris will thereby be forced out. Clearing these passageways at least every few months will greatly improve the operation of the cooling system.

Poor heat flow may result from too much corrosion and scale buildup in the cylinder and cylinder head coolant passages. The heat developed in the cylinders and combustion chambers cannot flow properly through a barrier of corrosion and scale. This condition should be suspected if all of the other troubleshooting procedures fail to reveal the problem.

If visual inspection fails to show the cause of coolant loss, the cooling system must be pressure-tested. Put a cooling system pressure tester on the radiator filler neck (Figure 13–16) and use the handle on it to pump the pressure specified in the shop manual into the system. A gauge on the side of the tester shows the pressure. If the pressure drops on the gauge, there is an internal or external leak. You should then repeat the visual check because, with the system under pressure, it is likely that the source of the leak can be seen.

A radiator pressure cap that fails to hold the specified pressure can cause the coolant to boil off. You can check the pressure cap with the same tester you used to check the system pressure. Place the radiator cap on the end of the tester (Figure 13–17) and pump the handle until the spe-

cified pressure (the pressure written on the cap) is reached on the gauge. If the cap fails to hold the pressure, replace it.

If you do not find any loss of coolant from the system, overheating may be due to poor coolant flow, poor air flow, or poor heat flow. Poor coolant flow may be caused by a bad coolant pump. Check the operation of the coolant pump by running a warm engine while squeezing the return (top) radiator hose. You should feel a surge of pressure as you let go of the hose.

Clogged coolant tubes in the radiator may slow coolant flow, resulting in overheating. Warm up the engine and then turn it off. Test for obstructions by feeling the radiator. It should be hot along the top and warm along the bottom. Cold spots in the radiator mean that sections of it are clogged. Clogged radiators should be replaced or serviced at a radiator shop to remove the obstructions.

To prevent a buildup of scale and corrosion, coolant should be drained periodically and the system filled with fresh, clean coolant. Allow the engine to cool down completely. Then locate the radiator drain plug on the radiator bottom tank, place a pan under the drain plug, and remove the plug. Remove the radiator cap also, in order to provide a vent and allow the system to drain faster. After all the coolant has drained out, replace the drain plug. Mix recommended amount of antifreeze solution and distilled water (usually a 50–50 mix), and refill the system through the radiator filler neck. Then drain the reservoir bottle by disconnecting its bottom hose.

Start the engine, and after it has warmed up, check the system for leaks. Allow the engine to cool down, and then check the coolant level in the reservoir. Add coolant to the reservoir as necessary to bring the system up to the correct level.

Job Sheet 13–1

PRESSURE-TEST A LIQUID COOLING SYSTEM

Before you begin:

Read pp.

Make of Motorcycle _____ Model _____ Year _____

Time Started _____ Time Finished _____ Total Time _____

Flat-rate Time _____

Special Tools, Equipment, Parts, and Materials

Pressure tester

References

Manufacturer's Shop Manual _____

Specifications

Look up the cooling system pressure and write it in the space below:

Pressure _____

Instructor check _____

Procedure

1. Allow the engine to cool off, and remove the radiator cap. *(SAFETY CAUTION: Do not remove a pressure cap if the engine is hot.)*

2. Install the pressure tester on the radiator filler neck.

Instructor check _____

3. Pump the tester up to the specified pressure.

4. Does the pressure:

   Hold steady _____ Drop slowly _____

Instructor check _____

5. Install the radiator pressure cap on the pressure tester.

6. Pump the tester to the pressure rating on the cap.

7. Does the radiator cap:

   Hold the specified pressure _____

   Fail to hold the specified pressure _____

Instructor check _____

8. Remove the tester and reinstall the pressure cap on the radiator.

NOTES

Instructor check _____   Date completed _____

Job Sheet $\boxed{13\text{--}2}$

DRAIN COOLANT AND DEBUG A RADIATOR

Before you begin:

Read pp. _____

Make of Motorcycle _____ Model _____ Year _____

Time Started _____ Time Finished _____ Total Time _____

Flat-rate Time _____

Special Tools, Equipment, Parts, and Materials

Drain pan
Antifreeze coolant
Air hose
Distilled water

References

Manufacturer's Shop Manual _____

Specifications

Look up the following specifications:

Cooling system capacity _____

Mix of antifreeze and water _____

Instructor check _____

Procedure

1. Allow the engine to cool off.

2. Place a pan under the radiator drain plug.

3. Remove the radiator pressure cap. *(SAFETY CAUTION: Make sure the engine is cold to avoid burns from hot coolant.)*

4. Remove the radiator drain plug to drain the coolant. *(SAFETY CAUTION: Coolant solution is poisonous. Swallowing it can cause serious illness or death.)*

5. Allow enough time to completely drain the system. Drain the reservoir tank by removing the bottom hose.

6. Replace the drain plug. Torque the plug if required.

Instructor check _____

7. Using a clean container, mix antifreeze and distilled water in the correct proportions.

8. Pour the coolant mixture into the radiator through the radiator cap opening.

9. Replace the radiator cap and warm up the engine.

10. Check for coolant leakage around the drain plug.

Instructor check _____

11. Stop the engine and allow it to cool off.

12. Add the necessary amount of coolant to the reservoir tank to bring the system up to the correct level.

Instructor check _____

13. Use a shop air hose and gently blow through the radiator core from the engine side out.

14. Check the radiator core to be sure that all bugs have been removed.

NOTES

Instructor check _____   Date completed _____

KEY TERMS

Coolant: liquid used in a liquid cooling system to carry heat away from the engine; usually a mixture of ethylene glycol and water.

Coolant pump: pump used to circulate coolant around hot engine parts.

Cooling fins: metal fins used on air-cooled engine parts to move heat away from the parts.

Cooling system: an engine system used to keep the engine's temperature within limits.

Pressure cap: the cap on the top of the radiator that is used to regulate radiator pressure and vacuum.

Radiator: a large heat exchanger located in front of the engine.

Reservoir tank: a system connected to the radiator that catches overflow and sends it back into the radiator.

Thermostat valve: a device in the cooling system used to control the flow of coolant.

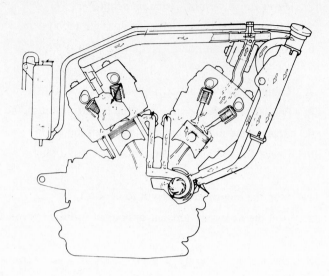

CHECKUP

1. What is the purpose of cooling fins on an air-cooled engine?

2. What is the main advantage of an air cooling system? Identify the parts of the liquid cooling system by writing their names in the spaces provided.

3. _____
4. _____
5. _____
6. _____
7. _____
8. _____
9. _____
10. _____

Identify the parts of the coolant pump by writing their names in the spaces provided.

11. _____
12. _____
13. _____
14. _____
15. _____
16. _____

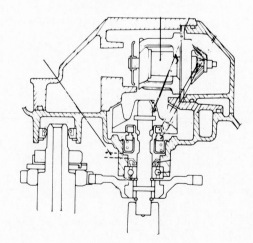

Identify the parts of a radiator by writing their names in the spaces provided.

17. _____

18. _____

19. _____

20. _____

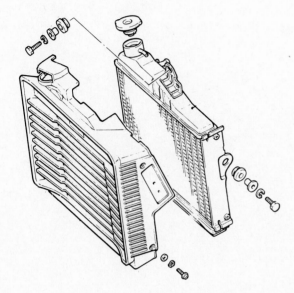

DISCUSSION TOPICS AND ACTIVITIES

1. Using the shop manual for a liquid-cooled motorcycle of your choice, look up its coolant capacity, coolant type, and thermostat heat range.

2. Why do most four-cylinder, in-line motorcycle engines use air cooling?

EXHAUST SYSTEMS AND TURBOCHARGING

When the two-stroke piston uncovers the exhaust port, or when the four-stroke exhaust valve opens, the exhaust gases must be routed out of the engine. The purpose of the exhaust system is to provide for a smooth flow of exhaust to maintain maximum engine performance, while minimizing exhaust noise.

When the hot exhaust gases leave the cylinder under high pressure, the leftover energy in these gases can be used to drive an air pump called a *turbocharger*. The purpose of the turbocharger is to force the air into an engine's cylinders on the intake stroke. If the pressure of the intake system is raised above atmospheric pressure, more air can enter the cylinder. With more air in the cylinder, fuel can be burned more completely and the engine's power output increased. In this unit, we describe the parts and operation of exhaust systems and turbochargers.

JOB COMPETENCY OBJECTIVES

When you finish reading and studying this unit, you should be able to:

1. Describe the parts and operation of a four-stroke exhaust system.

2. Identify the parts and describe the operation of a two-stroke exhaust system.

3. Describe the basic operation of a turbocharger.

4. Identify the parts of a turbocharger.

5. Explain the operation of a wastegate to reduce boost pressure.

FOUR-STROKE EXHAUST SYSTEMS

The exhaust gases on a four-stroke engine must be directed out of the cylinder as smoothly as possible. Any unnecessary bends or restrictions in the system will slow the flow of exhaust out of the engine. We call restrictions in the exhaust system *back pressure*. Back pressure chokes off the flow of exhaust. If not all of the exhaust gases can get out of the cylinder, the leftover exhaust contaminates the fresh intake air–fuel mixture and results in lower power. By contrast, an exhaust system of the correct size and shape can set up flow conditions that actually pull or extract exhaust gases out of the cylinder, resulting in an increase of power.

Motorcycle engineers, of course, well understand the need to design a smooth-flowing exhaust. However, they have a number of other things to consider, e.g., noise levels, space limitations, and ground clearance. These considerations sometimes result in exhaust systems that are less than perfect.

The basic parts of a four-stroke exhaust system are shown in Figure 14–1. The exhaust is attached to the cylinder head through a flange assembly. The exhaust gases flow into the runner pipe, the curves, length, and diameter of which are extremely important for good exhaust flow. The runner pipe is attached to the muffler through a muffler joint assembly. A reducing cone joins the small-diameter runner pipe to the larger diameter muffler.

The purpose of the muffler is to allow the exhaust gases an area over which to expand before they exit the system, and to quiet down the engine noise at the same time. A sectional view of a muffler is shown in Figure 14–2. In the figure, the exhaust gases flow into a large chamber called the *expansion chamber,* where they expand and lose some of their heat and pressure. They are then directed through a set of baffles in which there are holes that quiet the engine noise and shuttle the gases and sound into a silencing chamber. There, the gases make their way through a pipe with holes surrounded by steel wool or fiberglass. The silencing chamber further reduces noise and cuts down or prevents sparks from exiting the pipe.

Twin- and multiple-cylinder engines may direct the exhaust out of the engine in separate exhaust systems. The twin-cylinder engine shown in Figure 14–3 has a separate system each for its left and right cylinders. More commonly, the runners from the left- and right-side systems are joined to a common pipe called a *collector* and go out one muffler, as shown in Figure 14–4. Multiple cylinders typically feed two sets of runners into a collector and muffler on each side of the motorcycle (Figure 14–5). A properly designed collector system can often work to speed up exhaust gases and create an extractor effect.

TWO-STROKE EXHAUST SYSTEMS

The exhaust flow on a two-stroke engine is extremely important to good engine performance. The usual practice is to use individual rather than collector-style exhaust systems on two strokers. The parts of a two-stroke individual exhaust system are shown in Figure 14–6. The exhaust is

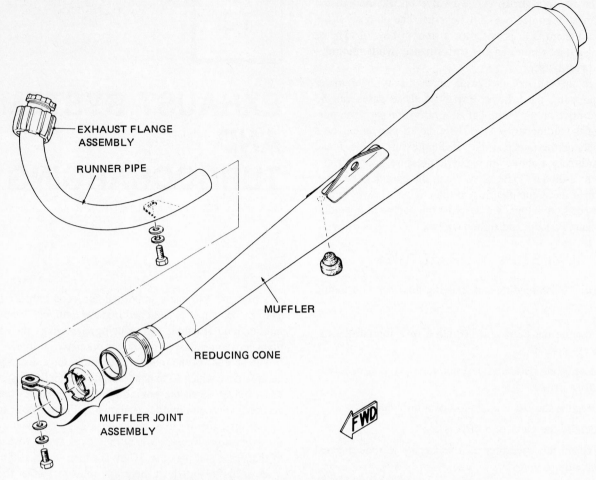

EXHAUST FLANGE
ASSEMBLY

RUNNER PIPE

MUFFLER

REDUCING CONE

MUFFLER JOINT
ASSEMBLY

FWD

Figure 14–1. Four-stroke exhaust system. *(Yamaha Motor Corp. U.S.A.)*

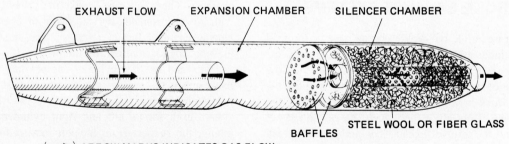

EXHAUST FLOW   EXPANSION CHAMBER   SILENCER CHAMBER

STEEL WOOL OR FIBER GLASS

BAFFLES

(➡) ARROW MARKS INDICATES GAS FLOW

Figure 14–2. Sectional view of a muffler. *(Honda Motor Co., Ltd.)*

RIGHT SIDE SYSTEM   LEFT SIDE SYSTEM

Figure 14–3. A twin with separate exhaust sytems. *(Moto Guzzi)*

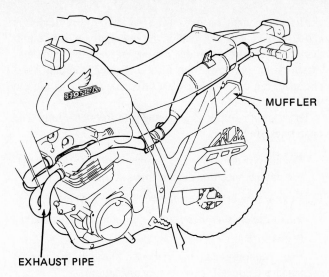

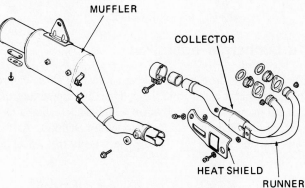

Figure 14-4. The exhaust is connected to a collector and to a muffler. *(Honda Motor Co., Ltd.)*

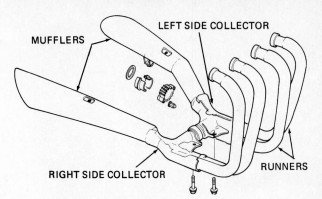

Figure 14-5. Multiple-cylinder engines use a collector and muffler on each side. *(Honda Motor Co., Ltd.)*

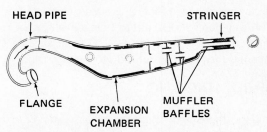

Figure 14-6. Parts of a two-stroke exhaust system. *(Honda Motor Co., Ltd.)*

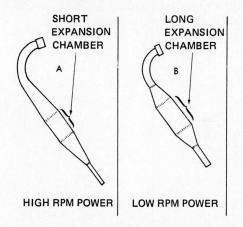

Figure 14-7. Different-length expansion chambers affect engine performance. *(Yamaha Motor Corp. U.S.A.)*

mounted to the cylinder by a flange. Exhaust gases move through a head pipe to an expansion chamber which is part of a muffler with the same basic baffles and steel wool or fiberglass packing that was described for the four-stroke engine. The exhaust gases then exit through a small pipe called the *stinger*.

The expansion chamber is the most important part of the two-stroke exhaust. When the exhaust port first opens, the chamber makes it easier to release the initial high-pressure surge of hot, expanding gas. After the transfer ports open, and during the approximate BDC period, the chamber makes it easier for the fresh gases to be drawn into the entire combustion chamber area.

When the piston starts upward and closes the transfer port, the expansion chamber creates a back pressure against the exhaust port to keep the fresh induction mixture from flowing out into the exhaust pipe. Under extreme conditions, it may even push some of the fresh mixture which has spilled into the exhaust pipe back into the cylinder.

The expansion chamber is designed as a cone or megaphone which merges into a cylindrical area, followed by a convergent cone which tails off into a small-diameter stinger at the end. The exact diameter and length of each part are very critical.

Two different expansion chamber designs are shown in Figure 14-7. Each is specifically designed and constructed for a very special and limited application. The more helpful they are for a special use, however, the more narrow is their power band. For the higher rpm band, a shorter expansion chamber is used (Figure 14-7, left). Conversely, for the lower rpm range, the expansion chamber should be as long as possible (Figure 14-7, right).

Figure 14–8. Two-stroke exhausts must be routed for maximum ground clearance. *(U.S. Suzuki Motor Corp.)*

Because of the need for high ground clearance, most dirt two strokers loop the exhaust and run the stinger up beside the seat, as shown in Figure 14–8. This arrangement is a compromise between power and ground clearance.

TURBOCHARGING

During a four-stroke engine's exhaust stroke, exhaust gases leave the cylinder under high temperature and pressure. There is a great deal of energy in these gases. *Turbocharging* is a method of using the energy in the exhaust gases to force air into the engine's cylinders.

The component used to force air into the cylinder is called a *turbocharger,* which is essentially an air pump that raises or boosts the air pressure entering the cylinders. Increased air pressure from a turbocharger is called *boost pressure*. Figure 14–9 shows a turbocharger set within the whole system.

There are a number of advantages to turbocharging. The main ones are:

- Engine power output can be increased without increasing engine speed or displacement.
- Engine weight per horsepower can be reduced.
- Fuel efficiency is increased by utilizing exhaust energy to improve performance.
- Fuel economy can be increased through the use of smaller engines for the same applications.
- Engine exhaust noise is lowered.

Turbocharger operation

The basics of turbocharger operation are shown in Figure 14–10. Exhaust gases from the cylinder are routed into the exhaust manifold, where a wheel with blades, called a *turbine,* is mounted on a shaft supported by bearings. As the gases hit the blades of the turbine wheel, the wheel is

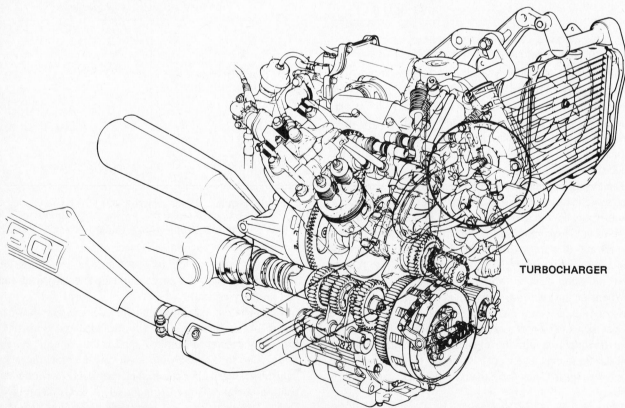

TURBOCHARGER

Figure 14–9. A turbocharger uses exhaust gas energy to force air into the engine's cylinders. *(Honda Motor Co., Ltd.)*

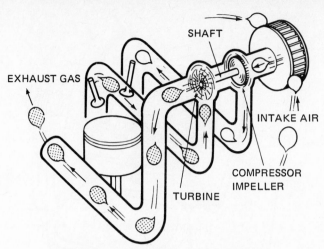

Figure 14–10. Operation of a turbocharger. *(Honda Motor Co., Ltd.)*

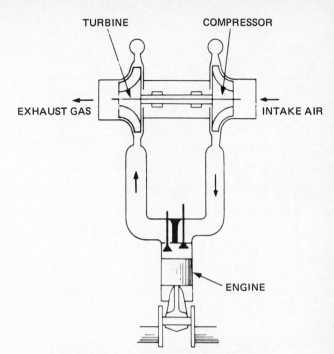

Figure 14–11. The turbine drives the compressor, which raises the pressure of intake air. *(Honda Motor Co., Ltd.)*

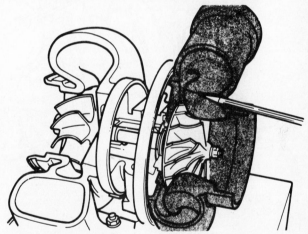

Figure 14–12. The compressor housing. *(Ford Motor Co.)*

forced to turn. The gases then flow through an outlet into the exhaust. The shaft that supports the turbine wheel also supports the turbocharger compressor impeller. This section of the turbocharger works just like any centrifugal pump. Air is pulled into the inlet by the low pressure created by the rotating impeller blades. It is then compressed, pumped out of the housing under pressure, and directed into the engine's cylinders.

In the unturbocharged or naturally aspirated engine, about 40% of the energy generated from fuel combustion is discharged into the atmosphere as heat in the exhaust gases. A turbocharger uses a portion of this energy to drive the turbine and the compressor, which are attached to the same shaft. The compressor increases the pressure of the engine intake air (Figure 14–11) and enables the engine to effectively use a greater mixture of air and fuel. The result is an increase in power output over the naturally aspirated engine.

The power increase resulting from the installation of a turbocharger varies with different engines and turbochargers. The brake horsepower of an engine can typically be increased by approximately 35 to 60 percent over the same displacement for a naturally aspirated engine. This increase is largely due to (1) more complete scavenging of exhaust gases and (2) the presence of a greater amount of air to support complete combustion. Air forced into the cylinder also helps to scavenge or push out burned gases from the cylinder. Since the turbocharger is operated off waste gases, there is no appreciable loss of horsepower, in contrast to a supercharger that is mechanically driven by the engine.

Operation of the turbocharger is dependent on the temperature and flow of exhaust gases. The speed of the turbine will increase as the load on the engine (how hard the engine is working) increases. In other words, the speed of the turbine is more dependent on engine load than on engine speed. Thus, if the engine's speed remains constant, but its load is increased, the speed of the turbocharger will increase, and so will delivery of air to the engine.

Turbocharger components

The main parts of a turbocharger are a compressor housing, compressor impeller wheel, turbine housing, turbine wheel, center housing, and wastegate. The compressor housing (Figure 14–12) contains the compressor impeller

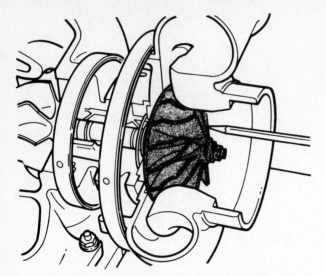

Figure 14–13. The compressor impeller wheel. *(Ford Motor Co.)*

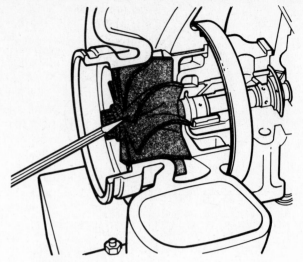

Figure 14–15. The turbine wheel. *(Ford Motor Co.)*

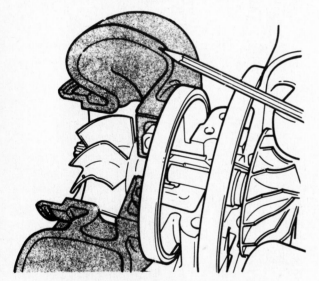

Figure 14–14. The turbine housing. *(Ford Motor Co.)*

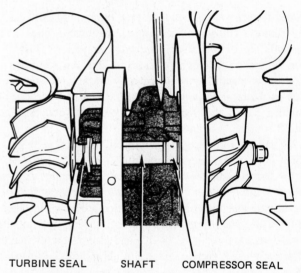

TURBINE SEAL   SHAFT   COMPRESSOR SEAL

Figure 14–16. The center housing. *(Ford Motor Co.)*

wheel and is used to diffuse and compress the flow of air into the intake manifold. The compressor impeller wheel (Figure 14–13) draws air into the housing and directs its flow. The impeller is made of an aluminum alloy so that it can be quickly cooled by incoming air.

The turbine housing (Figure 14–14) contains the turbine wheel. It receives the exhaust gases and directs the flow onto the turbine wheel and into the exhaust system. The turbine wheel (Figure 14–15) is driven by these exhaust gases. Since the turbine is kept hot at around 1,650° F (900° C) by exhaust gases, it is made of special heat-resistant steel.

The center housing (Figure 14–16) contains the shaft and the oil passages that are required to lubricate the bearings that the shaft rides on. It also contains the turbine seal

and the compressor seal. These seals prevent exhaust gases and air from entering the center housing and also prevent oil from entering the turbine housing or the compressor housing. The center shaft is used to connect the turbine wheel to the impeller wheel. As the exhaust gases power the turbine wheel, its rotation is directed to the impeller by the center shaft.

Lubricating oil enters through an oil passage at the top of the center housing and is returned through the bottom into the crankcase (Figure 14–17). The full-floating and thrust bearings are lubricated as the oil flows through.

The center shaft is supported on full-floating-type bearings (Figure 14–18) that are allowed to rotate not only on the shaft but also in their housings. Lubrication is provided

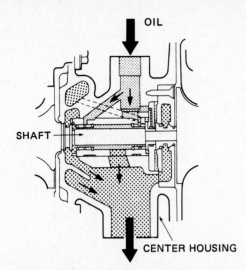

Figure 14–17. Oil flow through the center housing. *(Honda Motor Co., Ltd.)*

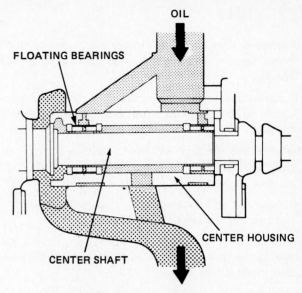

Figure 14–18. The center shaft is supported by floating bearings. *(Honda Motor Co., Ltd.)*

on both sides of the bearings. This design results in longer bearing life and reduced noise and vibration.

Turbocharger control

The turbocharger develops a boost pressure that is directly related to turbine and impeller speed. The faster the turbocharger shaft rotates, the higher the boost pressure into the engine. A control system must be used on the turbocharger to prevent the turbine from overspeeding and to limit boost pressures. Too high a boost pressure could cause engine damage.

Motorcycle turbocharger speed and pressure control are achieved with an exhaust bypass system. An alternate path, which bypasses the exhaust turbine, is provided for the exhaust gases. A valve in the bypass called a *wastegate* controls the flow. The wastegate valve is a simple poppet-style valve.

The parts and operation of a wastegate are shown in Figure 14–19. The wastegate consists of a diaphragm mounted in a housing and connected to the stem of a poppet valve. A part of the boost pressure going to the engine is rotated through a pressure channel to the wastegate diaphragm. As long as the boost pressure is within the safe range, the diaphragm holds the poppet valve in the closed position and all the exhaust gases leaving the engine strike the turbine.

When the boost pressure rises to the predetermined level, the diaphragm is stretched outward, so that it pushes on the stem of the poppet valve and opens it. With the valve open, some of the exhaust gases are routed through a bypass channel and do not strike the turbine. With less exhaust gas striking the turbine, it slows down, lowering the boost pressure. As the boost pressure is lowered, the diaphragm relaxes and the poppet valve closes again. Most motorcycle turbochargers are set to regulate a boost pressure of about 120 kPa (1.2 kg/cm^2).

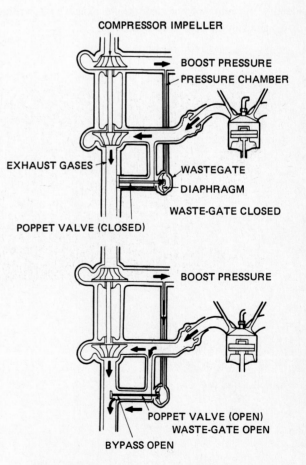

Figure 14–19. Parts and operation of the wastegate valve. *(Honda Motor Co., Ltd.)*

KEY TERMS

Collector: a component of a four-cycle exhaust which brings together individual cylinder exhaust pipes into one pipe.

Expansion chamber: a component of a four- and two-stroke exhaust in which exhaust gases are allowed to expand.

Muffler: a part of a four- and two-stroke exhaust that uses baffles and steel wool or fiberglass packing to reduce the noise of the exhaust.

Turbocharger: an exhaust-driven air pump that is used to force air into the engine's cylinders.

Wastegate: a poppet valve connected to a diaphragm that is used to bypass exhaust gases in order to control turbocharger air output pressure.

CHECKUP

1. Why is the smooth flow of exhaust important in a four-stroke exhaust?

Identify the parts of the four-stroke exhaust by writing their names in the spaces provided.

2. _____

3. _____

4. _____

5. _____

6. _____

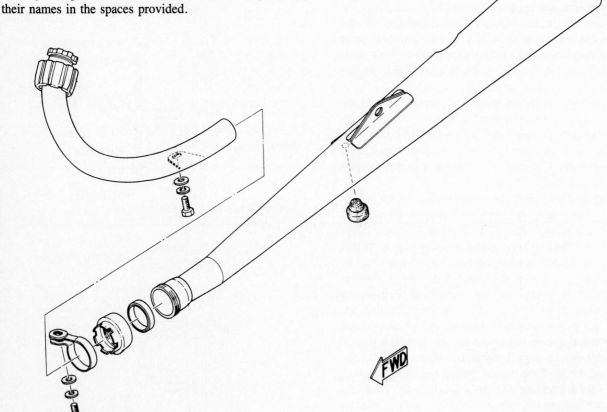

Identify the parts of a muffler by writing their names in the spaces provided.

7. _____

8. _____

9. _____

10. _____

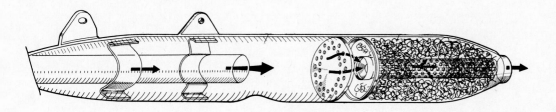

Identify the parts of a two-stroke exhaust by writing their names in the spaces provided.

11. _____

12. _____

13. _____

14. _____

15. _____

16. What is the purpose of the turbocharger?

17. How does the turbocharger use exhaust gases to drive a compressor?

18. What is the purpose of the turbocharger turbine?

19. What is the purpose of the turbocharger compressor?

20. Explain how a wastegate works to control turbocharger boost pressure.

DISCUSSION TOPICS AND ACTIVITIES

1. Mount several two-stroke exhaust systems with different expansion chamber lengths on a bike. Test-ride the bike, and try to determine the relationship between expansion chamber length and performance.

2. What do you think would happen to an engine with a turbocharger wastegate stuck open? Stuck closed?

The purpose of the fuel system is to store enough fuel for several hundred miles of operation, to deliver the fuel to the engine, and to mix the fuel with air in the proper amounts for efficient burning in the cylinder.

The basic parts of a fuel system are shown in Figure 15–1. Fuel (and sometimes oil in a two-stroker) is stored inside the fuel tank. A vented fuel tank cap allows the rider to check and fill the tank. The vent prevents a vacuum from forming in the tank which would prevent fuel flow. The fuel flows from the tank by gravity to a fuel shut-off valve at the bottom of the tank that allows the rider to stop the flow of fuel when the engine is off. A fuel line directs fuel from the fuel tank to the carburetor, which mixes the fuel with air in the correct proportion and then directs it to the crankcase (in a two-stroker) or the intake valve (in a four-stroker). An air filter attached to the carburetor cleans and filters the air before it enters the engine. The carburetor is controlled by a twist-grip hand throttle located on the right handlebar and connected to the carburetor by a throttle cable. In this unit, we describe how the fuel system operates.

JOB COMPETENCY OBJECTIVES

When you finish reading and studying this unit, you should be able to:

1. Describe the purpose of the basic components of a fuel system.

2. Explain the fundamentals of atomization, vaporization, and mixture ratios.

3. Identify the parts and explain the function of a basic carburetor.

4. Explain the operation of the slide throttle valve, carburetor's float, main pilot, and starter metering systems.

5. Describe the parts and operation of a constant-velocity carburetor.

CARBURETOR FUNDAMENTALS

As previously mentioned, the carburetor mixes fuel with air in the proper proportions to burn inside the engine. Carburetors have developed into fairly complex devices. They all have similar parts, however, and operate on the same basic principles. The two basic things a carburetor does are atomize the fuel and meter the fuel into the air flowing into the engine. These jobs are carried out by the carburetor automatically over a wide range of operating conditions, such as changing engine speeds, loads, and operating temperatures.

Before gasoline can be used as fuel for an engine, it must be *atomized*, i.e., broken into fine particles so that it can be mixed with air to form a mixture that will burn.

FUEL SYSTEM OPERATION

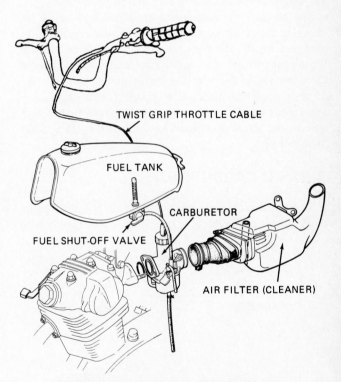

Figure 15–1. Basic parts of the fuel system. (Honda Motor Co., Ltd.)

Gasoline in its liquid state does not burn readily; only gasoline vapor will burn.

Vaporization is the transformation of a substance from a liquid to a gas. Such a transformation occurs only when the liquid soaks up enough heat to boil. In a teakettle, water becomes water vapor or steam when heat is transferred to the water, raising its temperature until it finally reaches the boiling point. At this time it changes to steam.

In a carburetor, gasoline is drawn into the incoming air stream as a spray. The spray is then atomized, or torn into

217

fine droplets, to form a mist, and the resulting air–fuel mixture is drawn into the engine. Since the pressure in the engine is far less than atmospheric pressure, the boiling point of the gasoline is lowered a great deal. At this reduced pressure, heat from the air particles surrounding each drop of fuel causes the gasoline to vaporize.

A correct mixture or ratio of fuel and air is also needed for efficient burning. The carburetor meters or mixes the proper air–fuel ratio for all conditions.

If we analyze the amount of hydrogen and carbon in gasoline, and the amount of oxygen in the air, we would find that it takes just about 15 grams of air to completely burn 1 gram of gasoline. This can be called an air–fuel ratio of 15 to 1. With more fuel, we would have a richer mixture, with less fuel, a leaner mixture. Air–fuel ratios are based upon weight, not volume, because the volume of air and fuel changes with pressure and temperature, while the weight of the mixture is not affected by either.

The air–fuel air ratio must be adjusted to meet the changing needs of the engine for particular conditions of load and speed. The burn ratio of 15 to 1 is an ideal or theoretical mixing ratio, and is, in reality, only achieved for a fraction of the time that the engine is running. Due to the problem of incomplete vaporization of the fuel at low speeds and the requirement of additional fuel at high speeds, the actual operational air–fuel ratio is often richer than 15 to 1.

A BASIC CARBURETOR

In order to understand how a carburetor operates, let us build a basic carburetor (Figure 15–2). We can begin with

a hollow tube or barrel mounted on the engine to permit an airstream to enter and pass through to the cylinder. The fuel is vaporized and mixed into this airstream in the barrel.

A vacuum in the engine causes the airstream. The pistons move down on their intake strokes, creating a vacuum in the combustion chamber (or, in the two-stroker, the piston moves up, creating a vacuum in the crankcase). Since the intake valves are open at this time, the vacuum is also felt in the carburetor barrel. But the air outside the carburetor barrel is at atmospheric pressure. Thus, the pressure difference forces the air through the barrel to fill the vacuum. With the engine operating, there is a continuous stream of air through the barrel.

The carburetor barrel has a restriction in its center called a *venturi* (Figure 15–2). When air flows through the venturi, its speed increases and its pressure decreases. If the venturi is placed near a fuel nozzle, the nozzle works as an atomizer. As the stream of air flows past the nozzle, its pressure falls. But when pressure is reduced at the venturi, atmospheric pressure in the carburetor fuel bowl forces the fuel through the nozzle and into the airstream. Consequently, the fuel atomizes or mists in the airstream. Vaporization is also aided by the reduced pressure.

The size of the venturi opening in our basic carburetor barrel is controlled by a piston-type throttle valve or slide (Figure 15–3). The rider's hand throttle control is connected through a throttle cable to the piston-type throttle valve or slide. When the rider twists the throttle open, the throttle valve moves up out of the barrel, leaving the venturi size larger, so that more air can enter the engine. A strong vacuum is created just above the fuel nozzle, and if we add more fuel, the engine will run faster.

In order to regulate the flow of fuel into the venturi, a tapered jet needle is attached to the throttle valve. When the throttle valve is lifted up, the small part of the tapered jet needle is positioned in the nozzle. A great deal of fuel can then get around the jet needle and into the air stream. The engine runs fast on the large mixture of air and fuel (Figure 15–4).

When the rider twists the hand control closed, the throttle valve moves back into the barrel and less air can get into the engine. At the same time, a larger part of the ta-

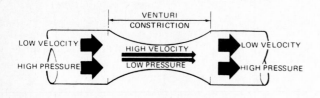

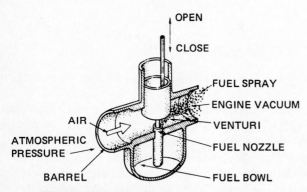

Figure 15–2. Basic parts of a carburetor. *(Top: Kawasaki Motors Corp. U.S.A. Bottom: U.S. Suzuki Motor Corp.)*

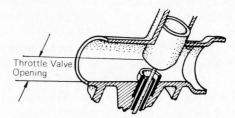

Figure 15–3. The piston-type throttle valve controls venturi size. *(U.S. Suzuki Motor Corp.)*

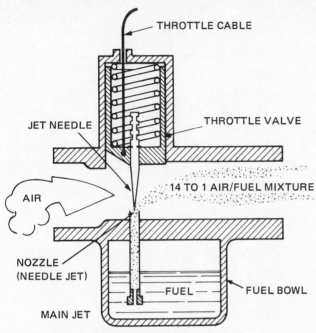

Figure 15–4. The throttle valve controls air and fuel flow.

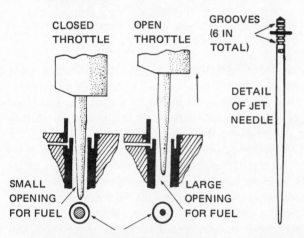

Figure 15–5. The tapered jet needle opens and closes the nozzle. (*U.S. Suzuki Motor Corp.*)

pered jet needle is positioned in the nozzle (Figure 15–5), allowing less fuel to get through the nozzle and into the venturi. With less air and fuel, the engine slows down.

CARBURETOR METERING SYSTEMS

All piston-type throttle valve carburetors have the same basic parts just discussed. In addition, these carburetors have a number of separate systems to supply fuel and air as required. The fuel supply is handled by the *float bowl*. Three separate systems meter the fuel and mix it with the incoming air: the main system for normal running, the pilot sys-

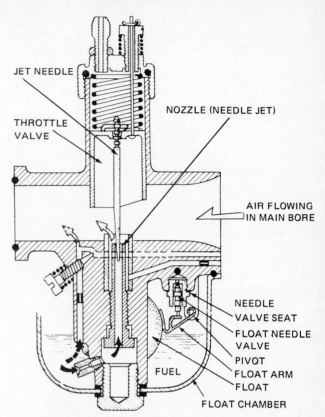

Figure 15–6. The float bowel provides fuel to all the carburetor systems. (*U.S. Suzuki Motor Corp.*)

tem for low-speed running, and the starter system to assist in starting a cold engine. A discussion of these systems and their operation follows.

Float system

The float bowl or chamber (Figure 15–6) is the source of fuel for the other systems that meter the fuel. The float chamber is attached to the bottom of the carburetor. The upper portion of the chamber cavity is vented to the atmosphere, so that the air pressure inside the bowl is the same as that outside the bowl. Some models have a sediment trap in the bottom of the bowl to catch any solid particles which might find their way into the fuel. The sediment trap prevents the solid particles from reaching the carburetor.

Fuel level in the float bowl is controlled by a float (or floats) and a needle valve. The lower end of the needle valve rides on the float arm or tang, and the upper end seals against the needle valve seat. When the level of the fuel in the bowl drops, the float drops slightly and the needle valve moves down, away from the seat (Figure 15–7). Fuel is then allowed to flow from the tank into the bowl. As more fuel enters the bowl, the float rises, pushing the needle valve back into contact with the valve seat and shutting off the flow of fuel (Figure 15–8). The float level is kept almost constant by this continual self-adjustment.

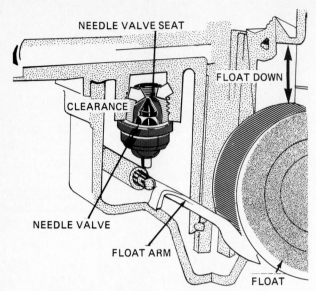

Figure 15–7. When the float drops, the needle valve opens. (Kawasaki Motors Corp. U.S.A.)

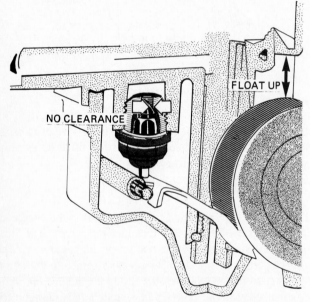

Figure 15–8. The float moves up and closes the needle valve. (Kawasaki Motors Corp. U.S.A.)

The main system

Most of the metering performed by the carburetor is done by the main system whose components are the throttle valve or slide, jet needle, main nozzle, and main jet (Figure 15–9). As soon as there is enough air flow through the venturi to draw fuel up into the nozzle assembly, the main system begins to take effect. The main system components meter fuel from about ⅛ throttle to full throttle.

As previously mentioned, the amount of air entering the carburetor is determined by the throttle valve (slide). The

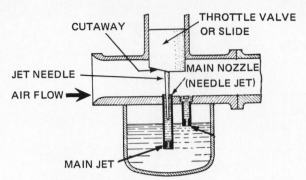

Figure 15–9. Parts of the main system. (U.S. Suzuki Motor Corp.)

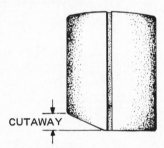

Figure 15–10. The cutaway on the throttle valve (slide) affects air fuel mixtures. (U.S. Suzuki Motor Corp.)

throttle valve rides in a closely fitting bore directly above the venturi in the carburetor body. The up or down movement of the valve is controlled by a cable (or lever) and spring. The higher the valve is lifted, the more air there is that flows through the venturi and into the engine. In the fully closed position, little or no space remains under the slide for the air to flow through the venturi. When the valve is in the lower positions, the valve blocks part of the venturi in the carburetor body, and the area under the valve becomes a venturi inside a venturi. Since the size of the actual venturi changes with the position of the valve, this type of carburetor is sometimes called a *variable venturi* type.

The throttle valve has a cutaway on the edge facing the air flow (Figure 15–10) whose purpose is to provide for adjustment of the air–fuel ratio as the transition is made from idle to the full venturi action of the carburetor.

The cutaway works to affect mixtures at lower throttle positions, usually between ⅛ and ⅓ of total twist-grip rotation. The larger the cutaway, the leaner the mixture will be at a constant throttle position, because the larger cutaway offers less resistance to the incoming air. Since the fuel supply remains relatively constant at any constant throttle position, the additional air results in a leaner mixture. On the other hand, the smaller the cutaway, the greater the airflow resistance, and the richer the mixture.

As mentioned earlier, the jet needle rides in the throttle valve or slide and moves up and down with it. The needle itself is tapered at its lower end and has (usually five) grooves at its upper end. (Refer back to Figure 15–5.)

The top of the needle is fastened to the throttle valve, and the tapered end extends into the needle jet or main nozzle. The needle jet fits in the carburetor body in the center of the venturi. The lower end of the nozzle gets fuel from the float chamber. Since the inside diameter of the nozzle is just fractionally greater than the nontapered section of the needle, the needle effectively blocks the jet when the throttle valve is closed (Figure 15–11) and the needle is all the way down in the nozzle. When the valve is lifted, the needle rises up out of the nozzle, allowing fuel to flow past the tapered section. The effect of the taper is to gradually and progressively increase the clearance between the nozzle and the jet needle as the needle is lifted. The varying amounts of clearance at different throttle positions are shown in Figure 15–12.

As the valve and needle are raised, air flow under the valve creates a low pressure in the venturi. The fuel from the float bowl is drawn by the reduced pressure up into the nozzle and through the clearance area between the nozzle

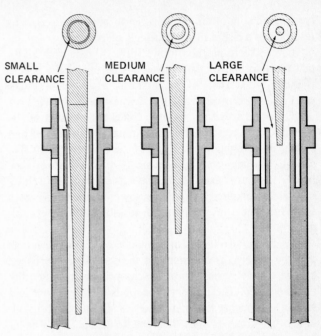

Figure 15–12. As the throttle valve or slide and jet needle are lifted, the opening around the jet needle allows for an increase in fuel flow. *(Kawasaki Motors Corp. U.S.A.)*

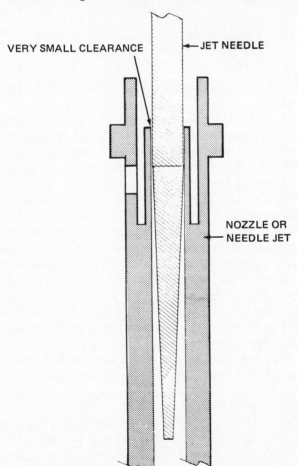

Figure 15–11. When the throttle slide is lowered, the jet needle closes off the nozzle or needle jet. *(Kawasaki Motors Corp. U.S.A.)*

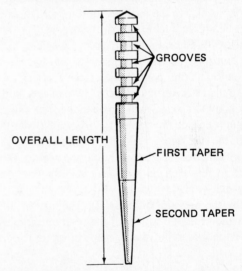

Figure 15–13. Double-tapered jet needle used in some larger two-strokers. *(Kawasaki Motors Corp. U.S.A.)*

and the needle. The greater the clearance as the needle is lifted, the greater is the amount of fuel that can be drawn up into the venturi.

Four-stroke engines and small-displacement two-stroke engines often use a needle with a single taper. Many of the larger two-stroke engines use a needle with two tapered areas called a *double taper* (Figure 15–13). The double taper of the needle helps accelerate the low rate of fuel intake so that the amount of fuel can keep up with the increasing amount of air in the higher throttle positions, thus resulting in a richer mixture at high speeds.

The needle is attached to the valve or slide with a clip that fits into one of the grooves at the top of the needle (Figure 15–5). The air–fuel mixture for the main system can be adjusted by selecting a different groove to attach the needle to the valve by the clip. Since the position of the needle relative to the nozzle determines the amount of fuel available, changing the position of the needle on the valve changes the amount of fuel let in. If the clip goes up, the needle sits lower and the fuel flow is restricted, resulting in a leaner mixture. If the clip is lowered, the needle goes up and the fuel flow is increased, resulting in a richer mixture.

The nozzle also works to atomize the fuel before it gets into the venturi. Atomization of the fuel is accomplished by one of two types of nozzles: the primary type and the air bleed type. The primary type tends to allow more fuel to flow, producing richer mixtures, and is used mostly on larger two-stroke engines. Four-stroke engines and smaller two-strokers usually use the bleed type.

The air bleed type of nozzle (Figure 15–14) has holes around its circumference where some of the air from the front of the carburetor is introduced into the fuel going up the main nozzle. In the air bleed design, air is mixed with the fuel before the fuel exits past the needle. The atomized air–fuel mixture flows readily past the needle.

The primary-type nozzle (Figure 15–15) has a reservoir which surrounds the point at which the fuel exits past the needle. This reservoir is connected by passages in the carburetor body to a very small air jet in the front (away from the engine) end of the carburetor. Air flows into this jet, through the passages, and into the reservoir, where it mixes with the fuel and is drawn into the venturi. Since the entrance to this passage is at near atmospheric pressure, and the exit is subject to the venturi vacuum, air flow is aided (by the pressure differential). The size of the jet is very small, so the air arrives at the reservoir at a high velocity. At the reservoir, the air helps break up the drops of

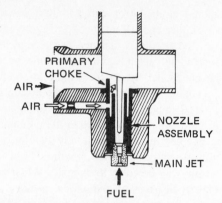

Figure 15–15. Primary-type nozzle assembly. *(U.S. Suzuki Motor Corp.)*

Figure 15–16. Fuel passes into the nozzle through the main jet. *(U.S. Suzuki Motor Corp.)*

fuel as they leave the center metering portion of the nozzle assembly.

A lip extends up into the venturi in front of the needle. This lip generates turbulence, which creates a greater vacuum behind the lip where the reservoir and needle are located. At high rpm, this extra vacuum effect helps pull more fuel up from the float bowl. The lip on the nozzle is known as a *primary choke*. The height of the primary choke determines the amount of turbulence and, consequently, the amount of extra vacuum at the venturi exit of the needle jet. A taller primary choke creates more turbulence and more suction acting on the fuel, leading to enrichment of the mixture at high rpm. Use of a taller primary choke allows a smaller main jet to be used to achieve approximately the same mixture ratio at full throttle. However, a decrease in fuel consumption results in the medium-throttle positions.

Fuel flows into the fuel nozzle from the float chamber through a calibrated hole called a *main jet* (Figure 15–16). The main jet screws into the bottom of the nozzle, as shown in Figure 15–15.

As soon as the main system begins to meter fuel, the throttle valve cutaway, needle, and main jet work together to determine the amount of fuel that should be delivered for the amount of air entering the engine. This working relationship continues until approximately three-fourths throttle. At somewhere around this point, the cross-sectional area of the clearance between the jet needle and the

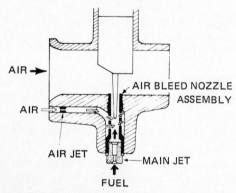

Figure 15–14. An air-bleed nozzle asembly. *(U.S. Suzuki Motor Corp.)*

nozzle becomes greater than the cross-sectional area of the main jet, resulting in no further fuel flow restrictions, and the size of the main jet then determines how much fuel will be available.

The size of the main jet is indicated by the number stamped on the jet. There are three different types of main jets, each with a different numbering system. You should be careful, when changing main jets, to use a replacement of the same type; matching only the numbers can result in an engine that will not run properly.

Pilot or low-speed system

When the rider is operating the motorcycle at a low engine speed and small throttle opening, it is impossible for the main system to provide the proper amount of fuel or air. The reason is because at a low speed and small throttle opening the air flow through the venturi is insufficient to produce enough venturi vacuum to lift the fuel up from the float bowl. The pilot or low-speed system provides the air–fuel mixture for slow engine operation. The parts of the pilot system are a series of passageways in the carburetor body, a pilot jet to meter fuel, and a pilot air screw to meter air (Figure 15–17).

The air for the pilot system enters from the front of the carburetor and is metered by the pilot air screw (Figure 15–17). This screw is tapered to provide a gradual increase in air flow as the screw is backed out. The taper fits in the center of a passageway, and turning the screw all the way in closes the passageway off completely.

The fuel for the pilot mixture is drawn through the pilot jet, which sticks into the float chamber, usually just behind the main system. The pilot jet has a series of holes drilled in its body at the point where the air is introduced from the

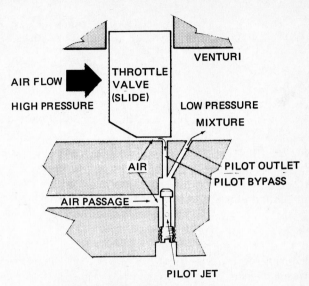

Figure 15–18. Operation of the pilot system. *(Kawasaki Motors Corp. U.S.A.)*

passageways. These holes allow the fuel to be mixed with the air before it enters the venturi through the pilot outlet, which has a very small diameter (Figure 15–18). The air and fuel are blended into an atomized mixture.

Starter or choke system

When the engine is cold, its parts are not hot enough to vaporize the droplets of fuel. Under such circumstances, an even richer mixture than that provided by the pilot system is required to start the engine. To generate these richer mixtures, a starter system or choke system is added to the carburetor.

As shown in Figure 15–19, the starter system consists of a starter jet to meter the fuel and a plunger which opens air passages from the front of the carburetor into the venturi. The plunger is lifted by a cable or lever that is usually mounted on or near the accelerator twist-grip on the handlebar. As the plunger lifts off its seal, it uncovers the fuel passageway. Lifting the plunger further starts to uncover the air inlet passage and the outlet to the venturi, which is on the engine side of the throttle slide. If the throttle slide is closed (as it should be for starting), almost all the air that goes to the engine must come through the starter passageways. When it does, enough suction is created to draw fuel up from the bowl into the chamber below the plunger, where the fuel is mixed with air from the front of the carburetor and drawn into the venturi and the engine.

The process of atomization of fuel for starting is aided by the *emulsion tube,* a long tube which sticks into the fuel and through which the fuel from the starter jet is drawn. This tube has holes drilled in it which allow a small amount of air from the float chamber to be mixed with the fuel before it enters the chamber below the starter plunger.

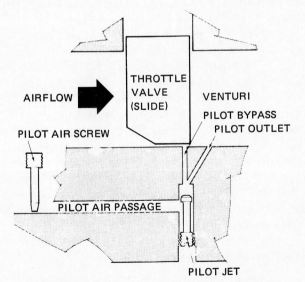

Figure 15–17. Parts of the pilot system. *(Kawasaki Motors Corp. U.S.A.)*

STARTER
CABLE OPEN

THROTTLE VALVE
FULLY CLOSED

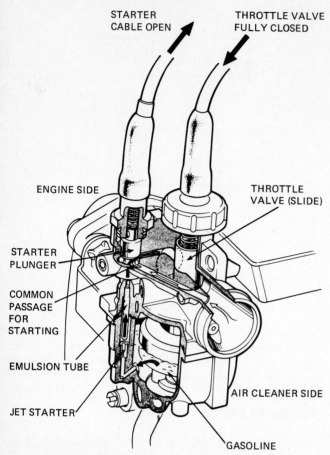

ENGINE SIDE

THROTTLE
VALVE (SLIDE)

STARTER
PLUNGER

COMMON
PASSAGE
FOR
STARTING

EMULSION TUBE

JET STARTER

AIR CLEANER SIDE

GASOLINE

Figure 15–19. The starter system provides a rich mixture for cold starts. *(Honda Motor Co., Ltd.)*

Some four-stroke carburetors use a choke either along with or in place of the starter system. The choke consists of a round butterfly valve mounted on a shaft in the barrel in front of the throttle valve. When the valve is closed by a cable or lever, it reduces air flow through the carburetor, which causes an increase in vacuum within the venturi, which in turn pulls in extra fuel from the pilot and main systems. The extra fuel causes a rich enough mixture to start the cold engine.

CONSTANT-VELOCITY CARBURETORS

A number of the larger street motorcycles use a set of constant-velocity carburetors (one for each cylinder). The constant-velocity carburetor has the accelerator twist-grip connected to a round butterfly valve that is in turn attached to a shaft on the engine side of the venturi (Figure 15–20). It also has a throttle slide and a jet needle, but they are free floating, and not connected to the accelerator twist-grip.

The purpose of a constant-velocity carburetor is to maintain a constant air velocity through the venturi regardless of the amount of throttle opening. This prevents any engine hesitation when the rider snaps open the throttle.

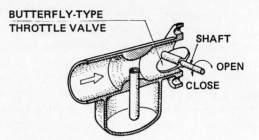

BUTTERFLY-TYPE
THROTTLE VALVE

SHAFT

OPEN

CLOSE

Figure 15–20. Butterfly valve in a constant-velocity carburetor. *(U.S. Suzuki Motor Corp.)*

Main system operation

The parts of a constant-velocity carburetor main metering system are shown in Figure 15–21. The vacuum-operated piston or slide is lifted by the engine vacuum. A flexible rubber diaphragm that is attached to the piston top and housing divides the top part of the carburetor into a vacuum chamber above the diaphragm, and an atmospheric pressure chamber below the diaphragm.

Atmospheric air passes through the atmospheric pressure chamber and occupies the space below the diaphragm. A hole drilled at the bottom of the vacuum piston provides an unobstructed path for air to flow up into the vacuum chamber. As air is pulled past the bottom of the vacuum piston by the engine vacuum, a low-pressure area is created at the bottom of the piston. The piston hole permits this low pressure to fill the vacuum chamber, so that the air pressures on the two sides of the diaphragm are unequal. As a result of the unequal air pressures, atmospheric pressure pushes up on the diaphragm, lifting the vacuum piston. The diaphragm and piston continue to lift until the pressure produced by the force of the vacuum piston return spring and the low air pressure match the pushing atmospheric pressure below.

Air speed through the venturi, which controls the amount of low pressure in the vacuum chamber, is controlled by a butterfly valve (Figure 15–21) to which the throttle grip is directly connected by a cable. Twisting the grip opens the valve. As the valve opens (Figure 15–22), the engine vacuum pulls air through the venturi at a greater speed, which causes a greater drop in air pressure. The lower pressure immediately occupies the vacuum chamber, lifting the vacuum piston higher. The piston will continue to lift as the butterfly is opened further. When the vacuum piston lifts, it also lifts the jet needle, permitting additional fuel to flow up the fuel outlet nozzle or needle jet to the engine (in the standard method of use).

Pilot or idle circuit

Like other carburetors, the constant-velocity carburetor requires a float system, a starter system, and a pilot or idle

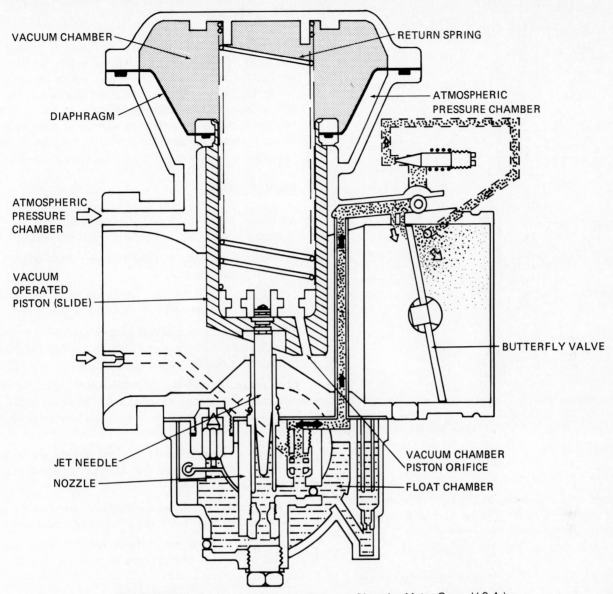

Figure 15–21. Constant-velocity carburetor. *(Yamaha Motor Corp. U.S.A.)*

system. The float and starter systems are the same as those previously described (see Figures 15–6 and 15–19).

The idle or slow-speed system for a constant-velocity carburetor is shown in Figure 15–23. The idle speed is controlled by the position of the butterfly valve. At idling rpm, air pressure in the venturi is not low enough to draw fuel up through the needle jet or main nozzle. So fuel travels up through the main jet to the pilot jet. At the same time, air passes through the pilot air jet down through a drilled passage to the pilot jet, where it mixes with the fuel. The air–fuel mixture passes up through a drilled passage to the pilot outlet at the upper edge of the venturi, just in front of the butterfly. The amount of the mixture sent to the engine is controlled by the pilot screw.

To increase engine rpm, the butterfly valve is opened further (Figure 15–24). The top edge of the butterfly uncovers first one bypass outlet, and then another, permitting more fuel to progressively enter the venturi and to mix with the additional air that begins to flow past the partially opened butterfly valve. In addition, fuel still flows out of the pilot outlet.

CARBURETOR SIZE

Regardless of what type they are, carburetors are classified by size (diameter) of their venturi (Figure 15–25). The venturi of the carburetor regulates the maximum amount of air drawn into the engine, so a carburetor with a large-

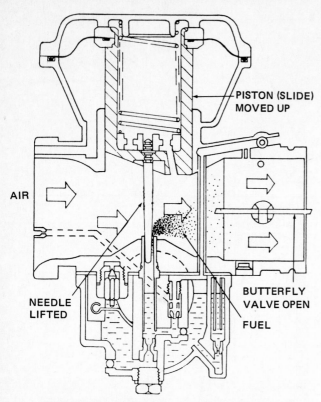

Figure 15–22. Operation of the constant-velocity carburetor when the butterfly valve is opened. *(Yamaha Motor Corp. U.S.A.)*

PISTON (SLIDE) MOVED UP

AIR

NEEDLE LIFTED

BUTTERFLY VALVE OPEN

FUEL

AIR INTAKE

The engine pulls in a tremendous amount of air through the carburetor. To filter dust and dirt out before it enters the engine, the air is routed through an intake box or case which houses an air cleaner. This large housing is located next to the carburetor assembly (Figure 15–26). Inside the housing is a paper or polyurethane foam filter element whose openings are large enough to let air pass through, but small enough to trap dirt and dust (Figure 15–27).

KEY TERMS

Air intake: a large filter assembly mounted above the carburetor to clean the air before it enters the engine.

Atomization: breaking a liquid fuel into small droplets to aid in vaporizing the fuel.

Carburetor: part of the fuel system that mixes air and fuel in the correct amounts to burn in the engine.

Float system: a carburetor system that uses a float-controlled needle valve in a barrel to provide the correct amount of fuel for all the other circuits.

Main system: a carburetor system that uses a piston or slide to control the position of a needle in a fuel nozzle to provide the necessary air–fuel mixture for most operating conditions.

Pilot system: a carburetor system that provides the air–fuel mixture that is required for slow- or low-speed engine operation.

Starter system: a carburetor system that provides the air–fuel mixture that is required for starting a cold engine.

Venturi: a restricted area in the carburetor barrel that is used to develop low pressure to pull in fuel from the nozzle.

Vaporization: turning liquid gasoline into a gas or vapor.

diameter venturi is necessary for large-capacity and high-speed engines. However, if the venturi is so large that maximum output is too high, the response at low speeds gets worse, and the fuel consumption at these speeds is very poor.

The usual practice is to install a carburetor for each individual cylinder of the engine.

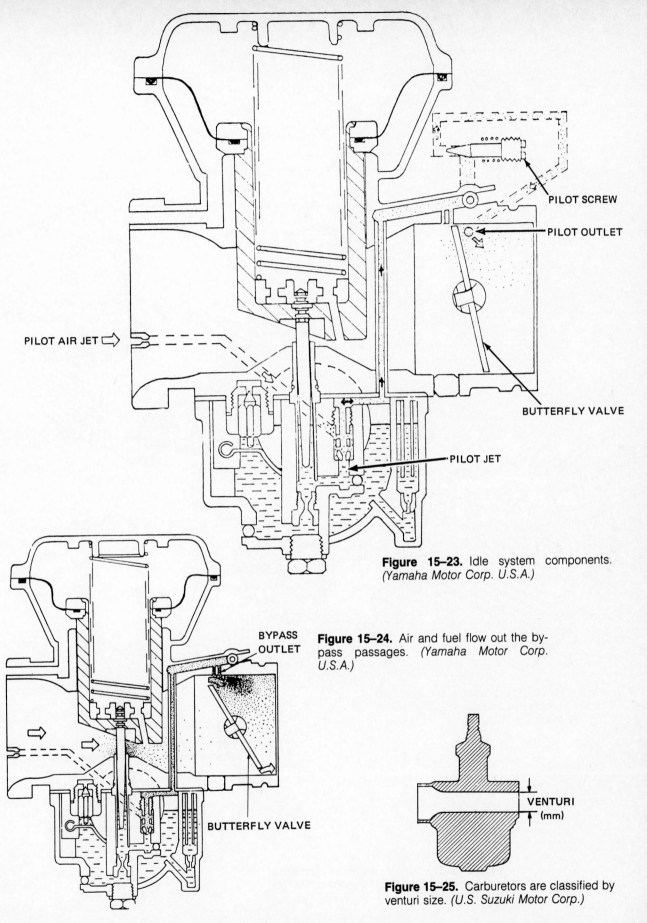

PILOT SCREW

PILOT OUTLET

BUTTERFLY VALVE

PILOT AIR JET

PILOT JET

Figure 15–23. Idle system components. *(Yamaha Motor Corp. U.S.A.)*

BYPASS OUTLET

Figure 15–24. Air and fuel flow out the by-pass passages. *(Yamaha Motor Corp. U.S.A.)*

BUTTERFLY VALVE

VENTURI (mm)

Figure 15–25. Carburetors are classified by venturi size. *(U.S. Suzuki Motor Corp.)*

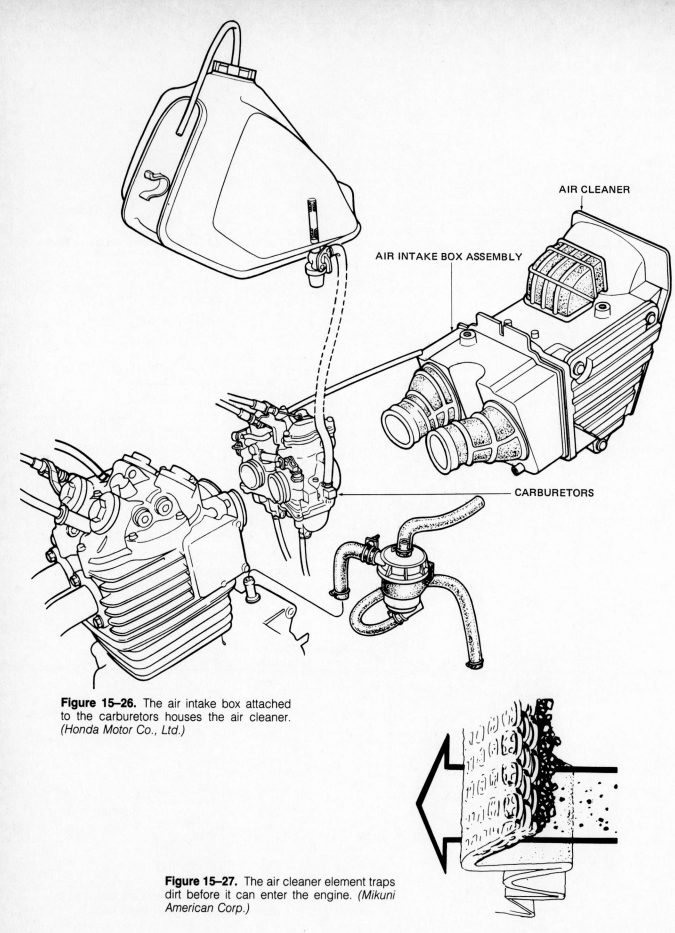

AIR CLEANER

AIR INTAKE BOX ASSEMBLY

CARBURETORS

Figure 15–26. The air intake box attached to the carburetors houses the air cleaner. *(Honda Motor Co., Ltd.)*

Figure 15–27. The air cleaner element traps dirt before it can enter the engine. *(Mikuni American Corp.)*

CHECKUP

Identify the basic parts of a fuel system by writing their names in the spaces provided.

1. _____
2. _____
3. _____
4. _____
5. _____
6. _____
7. _____
8. _____

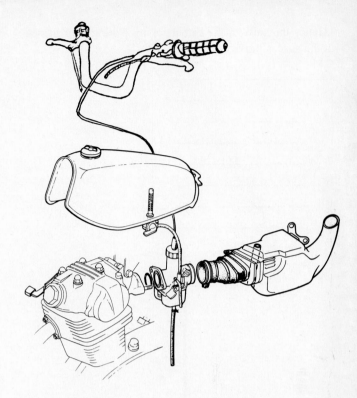

Identify the basic parts of a carburetor by writing their names in the spaces provided.

9. _____
10. _____
11. _____
12. _____

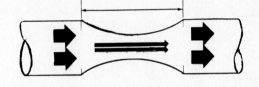

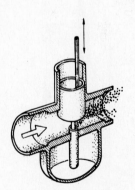

Identify the parts of the carburetor by writing their names in the spaces provided.

13. _____

14. _____

15. _____

16. _____

17. _____

18. _____

19. _____

20. _____

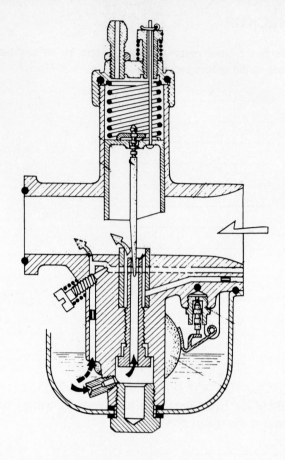

Identify the parts of the constant-velocity carburetor by writing their names in the spaces provided.

21. _____

22. _____

23. _____

24. _____

25. _____

26. _____

27. _____

28. _____

29. _____

30. _____

DISCUSSION TOPICS AND ACTIVITIES

1. Use a cutaway piston slide throttle valve carburetor to trace and identify the float, main, pilot, and starter systems.

2. Use a cutaway constant-velocity carburetor to trace and identify the float, main, pilot, and starter systems.

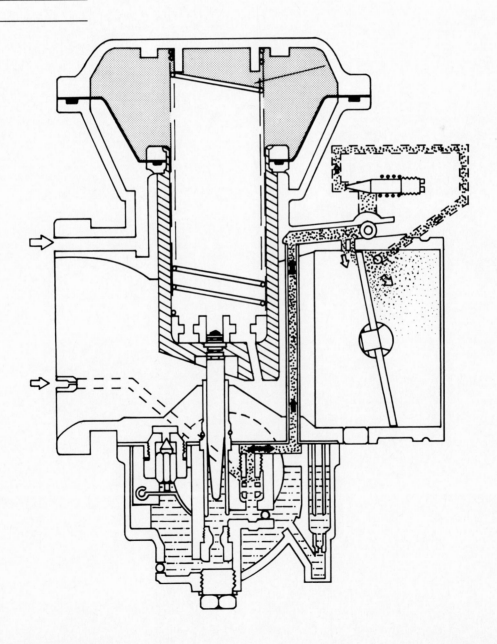

A motorcycle engine must have the correct air–fuel mixture to start and run smoothly. A fuel problem may make the engine hard to start or not even start at all. Too much or too little fuel will cause the engine to run roughly. The problem can be as simple as a carburetor adjustment or a change of air filter. Or it may require a complete carburetor overhaul. In this unit, we describe the troubleshooting and servicing procedures used on the fuel system.

JOB COMPETENCY OBJECTIVES

When you finish reading and studying this unit, you should be able to:

1. Describe how to troubleshoot an engine to determine whether it is running too rich or too lean.

2. Explain how to service an air filter.

3. Explain how to adjust the throttle and starter cables.

4. Explain how to adjust the idle mixture, idle speed, and main mixture.

5. Describe how to synchronize multiple carburetors.

6. Overhaul a carburetor.

FUEL SYSTEM TROUBLESHOOTING

The first step in fuel system troubleshooting is to determine whether the air–fuel mixture is too rich or too lean. A mixture that is too rich can have either too much fuel or not enough air, and a mixture that is too lean can have either too much air or not enough fuel.

The fastest way to determine whether there is a fuel problem is to remove each of the spark plugs. If the mixture has the correct proportions of air and fuel, the firing end of each spark plug will have a light brown or tan color. Also, the spark plugs on twin and multiple cylinders should all have the same color (Figure 16–1). If they do not, there may be a synchronization problem (to be described later).

If the air–fuel mixture is too rich, the fuel will cover the firing end of the spark plug with a black soot, as shown in Figure 16–2. This soot is relatively dry and free of oil, so do not confuse its presence with the presence of excess oil. If the dark deposit on the plug is oily and rubs off easily in your hand, it is not fuel, but oil. Otherwise, if you find a spark plug with fuel on its firing end, the problem is too much fuel or not enough air. On the other hand, if the spark plug end is dry and white in color (Figure 16–3), the problem is too lean a mixture: either the engine is not getting enough fuel, or it is getting too much air.

After determining whether the mixture is too rich or too lean, examine some of the external factors that can affect carburetion. Remember, the fuel system consists of more than just the carburetor. There is also a fuel tank shutoff,

FUEL SYSTEM TROUBLESHOOTING AND SERVICING

fuel lines, an air cleaner, a twist grip, and cables for operation of the throttle and starter system. These all play their part in the proper functioning of the engine.

If the mixture appears rich, check the air cleaner and the cable to the starter system. If the air cleaner is dirty, the entry of air is impaired; if the starter cable is too tight, the starter plunger is allowing extra fuel into the venturi.

Figure 16–1. The correct air–fuel mixture leaves a light tan or brown color on the spark plug. *(Champion Spark Plug Co.)*

Figure 16–2. A black, sooty spark plug means too rich a mixture. *(Champion Spark Plug Co.)*

Figure 16–3. A dry, white spark plug means a lean mixture. *(Champion Spark Plug Co.)*

If the mixture is too lean, the problem might be a clogged fuel shutoff valve. This can easily be checked by disconnecting the fuel line at the carburetor and momentarily turning the fuel shutoff valve to "on" or "prime." When these are done, there should be a strong flow of fuel out of the fuel line. *(Safety Caution: Catch the fuel in a metal container and dispose of it properly.)*

An air leak at the carburetor-to-engine connection (Figure 16–4) can also cause too lean a mixture (too much air). There are two basic types of connections: either the carburetor slips over a metal or neoprene spigot, as shown in Figure 16–5, or it slips into a neoprene socket. In either case the carburetor commonly bolts to an intake pipe or directly to the engine (Figure 16–6).

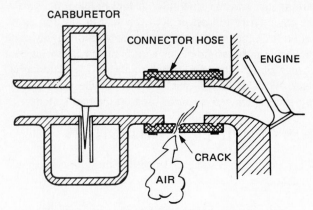

Figure 16–4. Air leaks between the carburetor and engine can cause a lean condition.

Since most of the intake system is at less than atmospheric pressure, any leak will pull in air from outside the intake, generating a lean mixture. For example, a leak can form in the neoprene-type manifold from the cracking of its rubber or the loosening of the nuts which hold it in place. Or, the constant vibration of the engine can pound the phenolic bushing that fits around the metal spigot in one type of carburetor-to-engine connection, pushing the bushing out of shape, and allowing air to leak in past it.

Inspect these areas carefully, and tighten or replace any parts you find to be defective. You can often use duct tape to temporarily seal a suspected air leak and see if engine performance is affected. (The engine will usually slow down when you seal off a leak because it gets less air.)

The operation of the fuel system begins when the rider works the throttle twist grip. Turning the twist grip winds the accelerator cable around a drum, thereby exerting a pulling force at the throttle slide or butterfly valve. The most frequent source of trouble in this system is the cable, which might fray as it exits the twist-grip assembly. Another potential source, particularly on a motorcycle that is not ridden for a period of several weeks or months, is the grease that lubricates the twist-grip–handlebar area. Hardening of this grease causes high throttle effort, slow return to idle, and a generally sluggish feel to the throttle. Simply cleaning the twist grip and the handlebar and applying a new coat of grease should cure this problem.

A fuel starvation problem can sometimes be traced to a plugged fuel tank vent. This vent is located in the fuel tank cap. When it is plugged up, air cannot enter the tank to take the space left by the fuel as it is used, and a vacuum is created in the tank, above the fuel. The problem can be sufficiently serious to slow the flow of fuel enough so that the engine dies while being ridden. If you suspect this problem, replace the fuel tank cap with a new one.

If your external checks fail to uncover the problem, it is time for a test ride. There are several possible symptoms of a rich fuel mixture that may occur under riding condi-

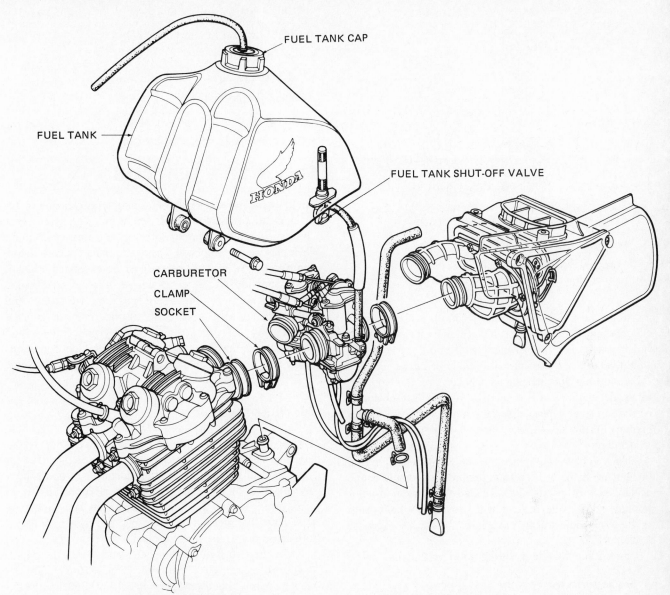

Figure 16–5. Carburetor assembly: spigot or socket connection with clamp. *(Honda Motor Co., Ltd.)*

tions. If the engine runs roughly and/or misses (a condition in a two-stroker known as "four-stroking"), it may be the result of occasionally incomplete combustion caused by too much fuel on the spark plugs.

Look for exhaust smoke—especially black exhaust smoke, caused by an overrich mixture. This is sometimes difficult to determine, since most two-stroke motorcycles smoke anyway and most visible two-stroke exhaust is mostly oil. Oil smoke, however, is blue or white in color.

If the engine is running on too rich a mixture, it will run worse as it warms up. Remember that the mixture must be rich when the engine is cold. As the engine warms up, continued feeding of a rich mixture will cause the warm engine to run poorly.

Try temporarily removing the connector tube to the air cleaner to see if the engine runs better. Even if the air cleaner is clean, it restricts the flow of air to the engine. Eliminating this restriction allows more air into the mixture. If the fuel–air ratio is too rich to begin with, removing the air cleaner from the system will yield a leaner mixture, making the engine run much better.

When an engine is running on too lean a mixture, it will overheat. Overheating, however, is sometimes difficult to determine. Engines with chrome exhaust pipes will show signs of severe blueing near the exhaust port. Also, sometimes an engine that is overheating will smell strongly of hot metal.

A lean mixture can cause the engine speed to fluctuate

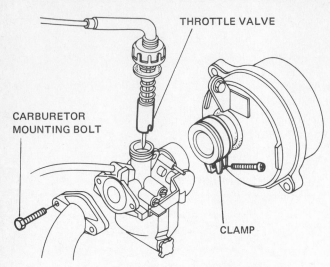

Figure 16–6. Carburetor assembly: bolted to engine. *(Honda Motor Co., Ltd.)*

or "surge" at a constant throttle position, and the engine will consequently lack power. You should not ride the bike hard if you suspect a lean mixture; if you do, the engine could overheat to the point that it could be damaged.

Try pushing the starting or choke lever as you are riding. An engine that is running too lean will run better if the starting lever is pushed because doing so richens up the mixture. Be sure the engine is first warmed up to operating temperature.

When you have determined that the problem is a too rich mixture, or that it is a too lean mixture, you should check the shop service manual for a detailed fuel system troubleshooting guide. The manual will provide a step-by-step service and adjustment procedure to cure a specific problem.

Some of the possible causes of a too rich mixture are:

- needle jet/jet needle worn
- main jet loose
- primary air passage blocked
- fuel level too high in float bowl
- air cleaner clogged
- starter plunger not seated
- pilot jet air bleed blocked
- incorrect pilot air screw adjustment
- incorrect slide needle adjustment

Some of the possible causes of a too lean mixture are:

- carburetor mount loose
- throttle valve worn, allowing air to pass around valve
- pilot jet blocked

- pilot outlet or bypass blocked
- fuel level too low in float bowl
- nozzle blocked
- deposits or dirt on jet needle
- main jet blocked
- incorrect pilot air screw adjustment
- incorrect slide needle adjustment

FUEL SYSTEM SERVICING

Fuel system servicing may be as simple as cleaning or replacing the air filter element, setting the idle speed, synchronizing multiple carburetors, or adjusting cable play. Or it may be as complicated as overhauling the carburetors completely. All of these procedures are explained in detail in the individual service manuals and owner handbooks. Specific settings for the needle position, air screw, and float level are also given in the service manuals and the tuning charts. These settings are recommendations, and some changes may have to be made to suit local conditions or the habits of the rider. In this section we describe some of the general procedures.

Air filter servicing

The air filter must be cleaned or replaced regularly to ensure that only clean, filtered air enters the engine. The air filter element is located in a filter container or box assembly attached to the carburetor intake (Figure 16–7). In some arrangements the filter container has to be removed to remove the filter. In others, a clip or screw is removed to gain access to the filter element.

There are two styles of filter elements: foam and paper. If you are servicing the foam type (Figure 16–8), wash the element gently, but thoroughly, in solvent. Squeeze the excess solvent out of the element and let it dry. Then pour a small quantity of 10W-30 SE motor oil onto the filter and work it throughly into the porous foam material.

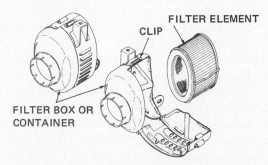

Figure 16–7. The filter assembly is located in the filter container or box. *(Yamaha Motor Corp. U.S.A.)*

FOAM FILTER ELEMENT   CASE

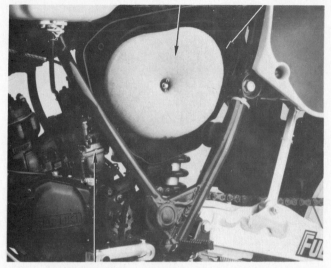

CARBURETOR

Figure 16–8. Foam-type air filter located inside the filter box or case. *(U.S. Suzuki Motor Corp.)*

In order to function properly, the foam element must be damp with oil at all times. It should not, however, be dripping with oil. Coat the upper and lower edges of the filter element with light grease, which will provide an airtight seal between the filter case cover and the filter seat. Reinstall the element assembly and replace the parts that have been removed for access.

If the air cleaner is the dry-paper type, it must not be cleaned with any type of solvent. A dusty air cleaner can be cleaned by blowing compressed air through the element from the inside out. *(Safety caution: Wear eye protection when using compressed air.)* Use low pressure and hold the air nozzle at least three inches from the element to avoid rupturing the element. If the contamination adheres to the filter element, use a soft brush to dislodge the particles, and then blow the filter with air. An extremely dirty or oil-soaked element should be replaced. After cleaning, reinstall the air filter assembly.

Each time filter element maintenance is performed, check the air inlet to the filter case for obstructions. Also, check the air cleaner to the carburetor rubber hose and manifold fittings for an airtight seal. Tighten all fittings thoroughly to avoid the possibility of unfiltered air entering the engine. Never operate the engine with the air filter element removed because doing so allows unfiltered air to enter. Dirt will then cause rapid wear and possible engine damage. Also, operating without the filter element will affect carburetor jetting and cause poor performance and possible engine overheating.

Cable adjustments

Accelerator twist-grip adjustment affects carburetor performance. Always follow the specific adjustment procedure in the shop service manual. A throttle cable that is too tight will cause the engine to idle too fast because the throttle slide cannot return all the way to the closed position. On the other hand, too much play in the cable results in a sloppy feeling at the throttle grip and can very likely cause a decrease in performance because the throttle slides might not completely clear the venturi.

An adjuster and lock nut on top of the carburetor allows the cable housing to be lengthened or shortened (Figure 16–9). Slide the rubber cover off the top of the carburetor and grasp the outer cable housing. Lift it up and feel the slack, which should be about 1 mm (.039″) at the adjuster. If the slack is incorrect, loosen the locknut and turn the adjusting nut in or out as required to achieve the correct slack. Tighten the locknut and reinstall the cap cover.

If the motorcycle has more than one carburetor and the throttle valves are operated by cable (not by a vacuum), you must make sure that each valve is lifted the same amount. You can tell by removing the air filter assembly and watching the valves while someone opens and closes the throttle. The valves should each be at the same height when viewed through the bore (Figure 16–10).

Starter cable play is also important. If there is not enough play, the starter plunger will always be lifted off its seat, allowing extra fuel to enter the venturi, which results in a rich mixture at all throttle positions. The starter cable should also have about 1 mm (.039″) of play. It has an adjuster, just like the throttle valve.

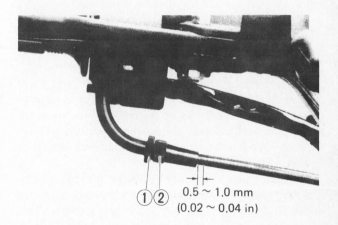

1. LOCKNUT
2. ADJUSTER

Figure 16–9. An adjusting nut for adjusting throttle cable housing play. *(U.S. Suzuki Motor Corp.)*

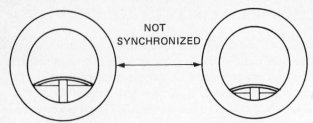

Figure 16–10. These throttle valves (slides) are not lifting the same amount and must be adjusted.

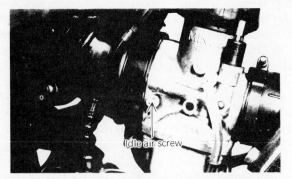

Figure 16–11. Idle air adjusting screw. *(Yamaha Motor Corp. U.S.A.)*

Idle mixture and speed adjustments

One adjustment on the carburetor that affects idle speed and smoothness is an idle mixture adjusting screw, or idle air screw (Figure 16–11). This screw regulates the mixture of air and fuel that is available for idle or low-speed operation and affects how smooth the engine runs.

Different carburetors use different types of mixture adjustments. Most variable-venturi carburetors use a pilot air screw (Figure 16–12) that threads in to the carburetor housing. The end of the screw is tapered and fits into the pilot air passage. When the screw is turned inwards, the tapered end closes off the air flow and changes the idle mixture. A spring on the screw holds it in position.

Constant-velocity carburetors have a tapered screw that regulates an air–fuel mixture which is metered around the closed throttle butterfly valve (Figure 16–13). When the screw is turned inwards, the amount of mixture is decreased; when it is turned outwards, the amount of mixture is increased.

To adjust either type of screw, first get the engine warm and make sure the starter cable is not pushed. Allow the engine to idle. Turn the idle air screw lightly inwards until it is seated. *(Caution: If you overtighten the screw, the tapered end can be damaged.)* Finally, turn the screw outwards until the engine runs smoothly without any hesitation.

The idle speed is usually adjusted with a screw which stops or limits how far the throttle valve can enter the noz-

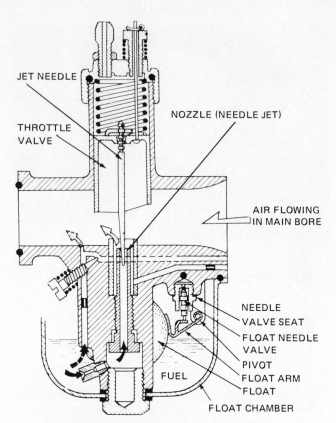

Figure 16–12. The idle mixture on this carburetor is adjusted with a pilot air screw. *(U.S. Suzuki Motor Corp.)*

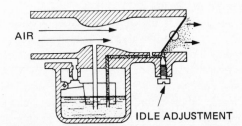

Figure 16–13. Idle mixture adjustment screw on a constant-velocity carburetor.

zle (Figure 16–14). When the screw is turned inwards, the valve is prevented from going as far down as normal. As the screw is turned outwards, the valve can go lower. The position of the valve regulates the amount of air entering the carburetor, which in turn regulates the engine speed.

To adjust the idle speed, first get the engine warm and make sure that the starter cable is not pushed. Make any necessary idle mixture adjustments. Loosen the lock nut, if there is one, on the idle speed screw. Adjust the idle speed as desired by turning the screw inwards or outwards (Figure 16–15), and then retighten the lock nut if it was loosened.

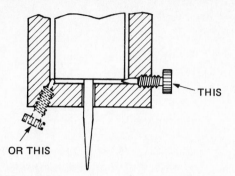

Figure 16–14. The throttle valve (slide) stop screw adjusts idle speed.

THROTTLE STOP SCREW (IDLE SPEED)

AIR SCREW (IDLE MIXTURE)

Figure 16–15. Adjust the idle mixture by turning the screw in or out.

Main mixture adjustment

The air–fuel mixture for the main system is determined by the size of the main jet and the position of the needle on the throttle valve. If the main system is operating too rich or too lean, the needle can be repositioned on the valve.

To change the setting, remove the rubber boot from the top of the carburetor and unscrew the cap. Pull the valve and spring out of the carburetor (Figure 16–16). The needle is attached to the slide with a clip.

The needle usually has five grooves. The needle clip standardly comes in the fourth groove from the top (fourth stage). To lean out the mid-range mixture, move the clip one groove higher (called "dropping the needle"). To enrich the mixture, place the clip one groove lower (called "raising the needle"). Figure 16–17 shows the positions of the clip on the needle. After installing the clip, replace

the slide in the carburetor, screw the top back on, and replace the rubber boot.

Multiple-carburetor synchronization

Twin- and multiple-cylinder engines usually have one carburetor for each cylinder. These carburetors must be synchronized for smooth engine operation. If different cylinders get different amounts of fuel, the engine will run unevenly.

As mentioned earlier, throttle valve action is an important part of carburetor synchronization. Idle mixture and idle speed screws can be synchronized by turning each screw inwards or outwards the same amount of turns on each carburetor. Another technique on twins is to disconnect one spark plug wire and adjust the mixture and speed on the other cylinder, and then reverse the procedure. It may be, however, that when both plug wires are connected, the idle speed is too high. If so, back the idle speed screws off both carburetors the same amount until you get the desired idle speed.

The shop service manual for multiple-cylinder engines usually provides a detailed synchronizing procedure using a vacuum gauge set (Figure 16–18). A vacuum gauge is a dial gauge with a vacuum hose connection. In troubleshooting, the vacuum hose is attached to the engine's intake manifold. The amount of vacuum available is then registered on the face of the dial gauge in inches of mercury (abbreviated as *in. Hg*). Since the amount of vacuum developed by the engine cylinder depends on how fast that cylinder's piston is moving to pump air (to create a vacuum), we can use a set of gauges to see if each carburetor is delivering the same air–fuel mixture.

When using the vacuum gauge set, always follow the procedure in the shop service manual. Run the engine until operating temperature is reached: carburetors must be adjusted with the engine warm and the choke fully open. Attach a bungee cord (stretch cord) to the vacuum gauge mounting plate (Figure 16–19) at the holes provided in the upper corners of the plate. Stretch the cord around the mirrors, suspending the vacuum gauge set across the bike handlebars as shown in Figure 16–19.

Remove the vacuum attachment plug screws (usually found on the carburetor or manifold) from the engine, and install the vacuum hose attachments in these holes (long attachments to the inside, short attachments to the outside).

With the vacuum gauge damping (adjusting) valves closed, start the engine. Open the damping valves until stable vacuum readings are obtained. With proper damping adjustment, the needles will flutter slightly, but should not oscillate more than one graduation on the gauge faces. Synchronize the carburetors according to instructions in the applicable shop manual or service bulletin.

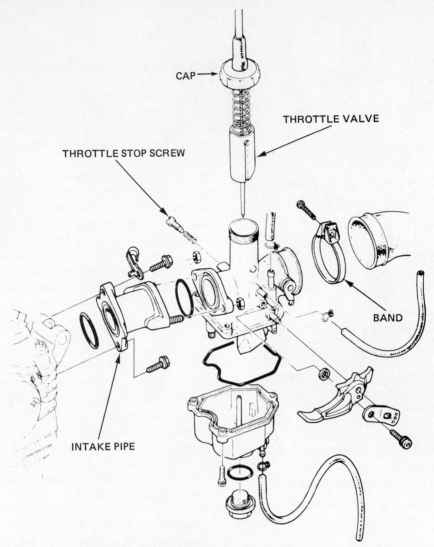

Figure 16–16. Carburetor assembly. *(Honda Motor Co., Ltd.)*

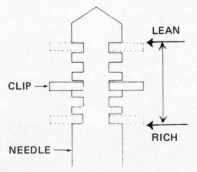

Figure 16–17. The main system mixture can be changed by positioning the needle. *(Yamaha Motor Corp. U.S.A.)*

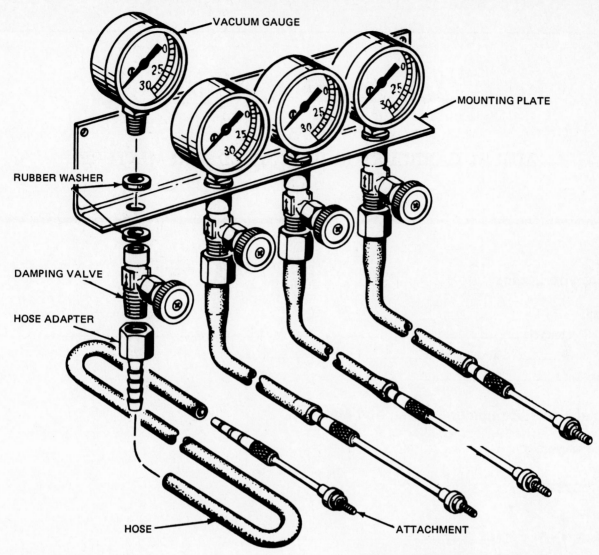

VACUUM GAUGE

MOUNTING PLATE

RUBBER WASHER

DAMPING VALVE

HOSE ADAPTER

HOSE

ATTACHMENT

Figure 16–18. A vacuum gauge set used to synchronize carburetors. *(Honda Motor Co., Ltd.)*

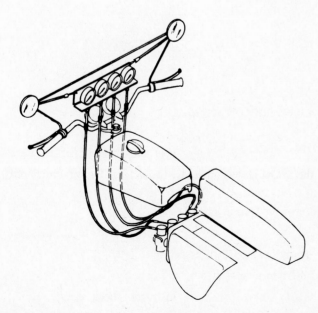

Figure 16–19. Vacuum gauge set attached for carburetor synchronizing. *(Honda Motor Co., Ltd.)*

Job Sheet 16–1

ADJUST CARBURETOR IDLE SPEED AND MIXTURE

Before you begin:

Read pp.

Make of Motorcycle _____ Model _____ Year _____

Time Started _____ Time Finished _____ Total Time _____

Flat-rate Time _____

Special Tools, Equipment, Parts, and Materials

Small screwdriver

References

Manufacturer's Shop Manual _____

Specifications

Procedure

1. Start the engine and allow it to warm up.

2. Locate the pilot or idle mixture adjusting screw.

3. Determine whether the pilot adjusting screw is an air-type or a mixture-type screw.

   Air _____ Mixture _____

   Instructor check _____

4. If the carburetor has an idle mixture adjusting screw, turn the screw slowly inwards, to lean out the mixture, until the engine rpm drops.

5. Turn the screw slowly outwards until the engine smooths out and the rpm levels off.

   Instructor check _____

6. If the engine has a pilot air adjusting screw, turn the screw gently inwards until it seats.

7. Turn the screw outwards until the engine runs smoothly and the rpm levels off.

   Instructor check _____

8. Observe the idle speed and determine whether it should be higher or lower.

9. Locate the idle speed adjusting screw.

10. Turn the idle speed screw inwards or outwards to increase or decrease idle speed, respectively.

Instructor check _____

NOTES

Instructor check _____   Date completed _____

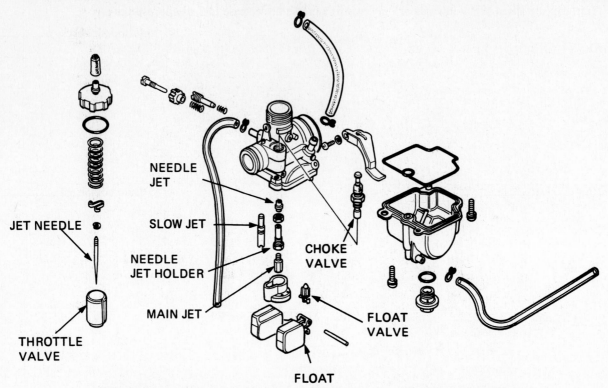

JET NEEDLE

NEEDLE JET

SLOW JET

NEEDLE JET HOLDER

MAIN JET

CHOKE VALVE

FLOAT VALVE

THROTTLE VALVE

FLOAT

Figure 16–20. Exploded views of the carburetor are found in the shop service manual. *(Honda Motor Co., Ltd.)*

Carburetor overhaul

If the carburetor cannot be properly adjusted, and you suspect worn, damaged, or plugged carburetor parts, you might consider overhauling the carburetor. Carburetor overhaul involves disassembly, cleaning, inspection, and reassembly of the carburetor. The shop service manual will provide exploded views (Figure 16–20), as well as disassembly and reassembly procedures.

All the disassembled parts except those made out of fiber or rubber should be cleaned thoroughly in solvent. The best way to clean out all the passages in the carburetor body is by blowing compressed air through them. Compressed air should also be used to clean the main jet, needle jet, pilot jet, float valve seat, and float valve. Never blow compressed air into an assembled carburetor because increasing the pressure in the float chamber will collapse the floats, altering the fuel level and seriously affecting engine performance. *(SAFETY CAUTION: Wear eye protection when using compressed air.)*

After having cleaned the parts, you should inspect them carefully to see if you can find the source of whatever problem caused you to overhaul the carburetor. The bottom of the float bowl should be checked for sediment. If there is dirt or some other sediment in the gasoline, the filter screens in the fuel shut-off valve might be torn or missing. After much mileage, some sediment is expected,

but if you find excessive amounts, you should check out the entire fuel system, starting at the tank.

Carefully check the condition of the float, float valve needle, and float valve seat. Inspect the float for cracks, deformation, or signs of leakage. Especially check the float valve very carefully in the area that contacts the seat (Figure 16–21). If the needle is worn, the seat will also be worn, and both should be replaced with the corresponding size and type. A worn needle and/or seat will usually cause fuel to overflow from the float bowl and flood the engine.

Inspect the throttle valve for any signs of scoring. A worn valve will allow air, and consequently the mixture, to leak past its sides. A worn valve must be replaced with a new one. Make sure that the slide moves freely in the

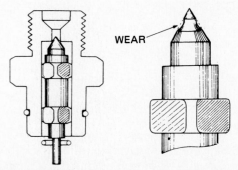

WEAR

Figure 16–21. This float needle valve shows signs of wear. *(U.S. Suzuki Motor Corp.)*

carburetor body with no binding. Check the jet needle for signs of contact. If the needle has been contacting the nozzle (needle jet), both parts will require replacement. A worn nozzle or jet needle will allow too much fuel to enter the engine, resulting in a mixture that is too rich.

Check the main jet and pilot jet for clogging, deformation, and stripped threads. The first two would probably result in lean mixtures, while the last might allow too much fuel through, causing a rich mixture. Also, check the tapered end on the idle air screw for a ridge caused by its having been tightened too much. Replace the air screw if necessary, because a screw that is deformed will make it difficult to adjust the pilot system. Check the pilot air passage, as it, too, might be damaged.

Inspect the starter system plunger to see if it is scored or if the seal on the bottom of the plunger is cracked. Either of these conditions will probably result in decreased performance. Replace the plunger if in doubt.

During reassembly, you will have to check the float level adjustment. The float level determines how high the fuel rises in the float bowl before the float closes the needle valve against the needle seat (Figure 16–22). Too high a float level causes too rich a mixture, while too low a float level causes too lean a mixture.

A specific procedure is provided for adjusting the float level on each model of carburetor. The float is installed, along with a new needle valve and needle seat. The carburetor is usually turned upside down, and a measurement is made between the top end of the float and the surface of the float bowl, as shown in Figure 16–23. The measurement can be made with a rule or special float level gauge.

The float level is adjusted by bending the small metal adjustment tang on the float (Figure 16–24) that pushes on the needle valve. Bending the tang one way will cause an earlier fuel shutoff, resulting in a lower fuel level. Bending it the other way will cause a later shutoff, yielding a higher fuel level.

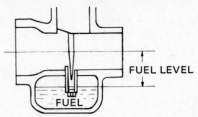

Figure 16–22. The float level determines how high the fuel level in the float bowl will be. *(U.S. Suzuki Motor Corp.)*

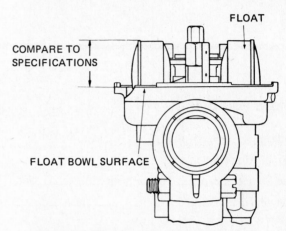

Figure 16–23. Measuring float level adjustment. *(Yamaha Motor Corp. U.S.A.)*

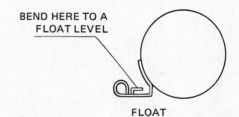

Figure 16–24. Float level is adjusted by bending the tang on the float. *(Yamaha Motor Corp. U.S.A.)*

Job Sheet 16–2

OVERHAUL CARBURETOR

Before you begin:

Read pp.

Make of Motorcycle _____ Model _____ Year _____

Time Started _____ Time Finished _____ Total Time _____

Flat-rate Time _____

Special Tools, Equipment, Parts, and Materials

Cleaning solvent
Compressed air
Float level gauge or rule
Eye protection
Carburetor gasket set

References

Manufacturer's Shop Manual _____

Specifications

Look up the specification for float level and write it in the space below:

Float level _____

Instructor check _____

Procedure

1. Shut off the tank fuel valve and remove the carburetor from the engine.

2. Remove the carburetor top and pull out the return spring, throttle valve (slide), and jet needle assembly.

3. Remove the jet needle retainer and the jet needle from the throttle valve. Be sure to observe in which groove of the jet needle the needle clip is installed.

4. Remove the float bowl screws and the float bowl from the carburetor upper body.

5. Pull out the float pin and float assembly.

6. Remove the needle valve, and then unscrew the needle valve seat.

7. Unscrew the main jet and needle jet from the carburetor upper body.

8. Remove the pilot jet, mixture adjusting screw, and idle speed screw from the upper body.

9. Remove the starter valve assembly from the carburetor.

10. Wash all the parts in solvent. Use compressed air to blow through all the passages. *(SAFETY CAUTION: Wear eye protection when using compressed air.)*

11. Put the parts on a clean rag to dry.

12. Inspect the parts for wear or damage.

Instructor check _____

13. Install the starter valve assembly.

14. Install all the jets and tighten them securely.

15. Install the float needle valve seat assembly and the float.

16. Invert the carburetor and measure the float level setting.
Record your measurement below:

Float level _____

17. Compare your measurement with specifications. If the float level setting requires adjustment, make slight bends in the float tang and recheck.

Instructor check _____

18. Install the float bowl, using a new gasket.

19. Install the jet needle in the throttle valve, making sure that the needle clip is in the proper groove.

20. Replace the throttle valve and jet needle assembly in the carburetor upper body. Make sure that the valve cutaway faces the air intake side of the carburetor.

21. Install the throttle return spring and the carburetor top.

22. Install the pilot air or mixture adjusting screw and the idle speed screw.

Instructor check _____

23. Install the carburetor on the engine and adjust the idle mixture and idle speed.

NOTES

Instructor check _____   Date completed _____

KEY TERMS

Carburetor synchronization: adjusting the idle mixture, idle speed and valve movement in multiple carburetors so that the carburetors work together.

Float level setting: measuring and ajusting the floats so that the fuel level in the float bowl is at the correct level.

Lean mixture: an air–fuel mixture in which there is either not enough fuel or too much air.

Rich mixture: an air–fuel mixture in which there is either too much fuel or not enough air.

CHECKUP

1. Describe how a spark plug looks in an engine that is running too lean.

2. Describe how a spark plug looks in an engine that is running too rich.

3. List three symptoms of a rich fuel mixture.

4. List three symptoms of a lean fuel mixture.

5. List four possible causes of a rich fuel mixture.

6. List four possible causes of a lean fuel mixture.

7. Explain how to service a paper air filter.

8. Explain how to service a foam air filter.

9. How is the twist-grip accelerator cable adjusted?

10. Explain how to adjust a pilot air screw.

11. Explain how to adjust idle speed.

12. How can you change the mixture of the main system?

13. Describe how to synchronize multiple carburetors.

14. List four carburetor parts that should be checked for wear during an overhaul.

15. Explain how to measure the float level setting.

DISCUSSION TOPICS AND ACTIVITIES

1. Disassemble and reassemble a constant-velocity carburetor.

2. Overhaul and synchronize a multiple-carburetor set.

The purpose of the ignition system is to provide a high-voltage spark in each of the engine's cylinders to explode the air–fuel mixture. The high voltage must be distributed to each of the cylinders at just the right time for a power stroke. Motorcycle ignitions are classified as battery coil systems, magneto systems, or capacitor discharge systems (electronic ignition) according to the way in which the high voltage is developed. In this unit, we describe the parts and operation of each of these systems.

JOB COMPETENCY OBJECTIVES

When you finish reading and studying this unit, you should be able to:

1. Describe the parts and operation of a battery coil ignition system.

2. Identify the parts and explain the operation of a magneto ignition system.

3. Describe the parts and operation of a capacitor discharge ignition system.

4. Explain how ignition timing is advanced with a centrifugal timing mechanism.

5. Describe the construction, operation, and technical features of motorcycle spark plugs.

BATTERY COIL IGNITION SYSTEMS

In a battery coil ignition system, a relatively low voltage (6 to 12 volts) is transformed into a momentary charge of high voltage (up to 25,000 volts) that is capable of jumping the spark gap in the cylinder and igniting the air–fuel charge. The parts of the battery coil ignition system are shown in Figure 17–1: battery, ignition coil, ignition switch, engine stop switch, breaker points, and spark plug.

Battery

The battery is the source of power for the battery coil ignition system. The battery provides either 6 or 12 volts of electrical energy. We shall describe the operation of the battery in Unit 20.

Ignition and stop switches

The ignition switch is a key-operated switch that is used to open and close the circuit between the power source and the ignition system. It prevents anyone without a key from starting the motorcycle. The engine stop switch is a push-button switch usually mounted on the right handlebar. When depressed, it interrupts electrical flow in the ignition system and immediately stops the engine. This switch is used for quick shutdown of the engine without the rider having to take his or her hands off the bar.

IGNITION SYSTEM OPERATION

Ignition coil

The ignition coil steps up the low voltage of the battery to a voltage high enough to jump a gap at the spark plug. The coil is made up of two separate windings, the primary winding and the secondary winding (Figure 17–2). The primary winding has approximately 200 turns of relatively heavy copper wire. The secondary winding, which is in the center of the primary winding, has as many as 21,000 turns of very fine copper wire. The two windings are wound around a laminated iron core that concentrates the magnetic field. The winding-and-core assembly is placed into a one-piece steel case upon the top of which is mounted a coil cap of molded insulating material which contains the primary and secondary terminals. A porcelain insulator prevents the winding assembly from touching the grounded case. When the coil is made, it is filled with epoxy to prevent air or moisture from getting in.

There are three terminals at the top of the coil. Two primary terminals are connected to each end of the primary winding and carry low-voltage (sometimes called low-tension) current. The large center terminal carries high-voltage (high-tension) current

When the rider turns on the ignition key (and the breaker points are closed), current flows from the power source through the key switch into the coil primary terminal and through the coil primary winding. Current goes out of the coil through the ignition wire into a switch assembly called the breaker points (Figure 17–3). The current flow in the primary winding creates a magnetic field inside the coil that is concentrated by the laminated core. In a fraction of a second (called saturation or buildup time), the current flow and the magnetic field both reach their maximum.

When the breaker points open, the flow of current through the primary winding is stopped. The magnetic field, which depends upon this flow of current, then rap-

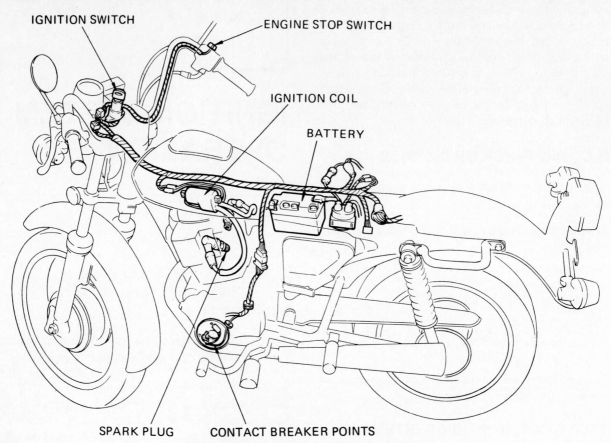

IGNITION SWITCH   ENGINE STOP SWITCH

IGNITION COIL

BATTERY

SPARK PLUG   CONTACT BREAKER POINTS

Figure 17–1. Parts of a battery coil ignition
system. *(Honda Motor Co., Ltd.)*

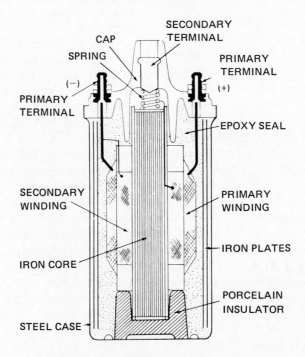

SECONDARY
TERMINAL

CAP

SPRING   PRIMARY
                         TERMINAL

(−)   (+)

PRIMARY
TERMINAL   EPOXY SEAL

SECONDARY   PRIMARY
WINDING   WINDING

IRON CORE   IRON PLATES

                         PORCELAIN
                         INSULATOR

STEEL CASE

Figure 17–2. Sectional view of an ignition
coil. *(U.S. Suzuki Motor Corp.)*

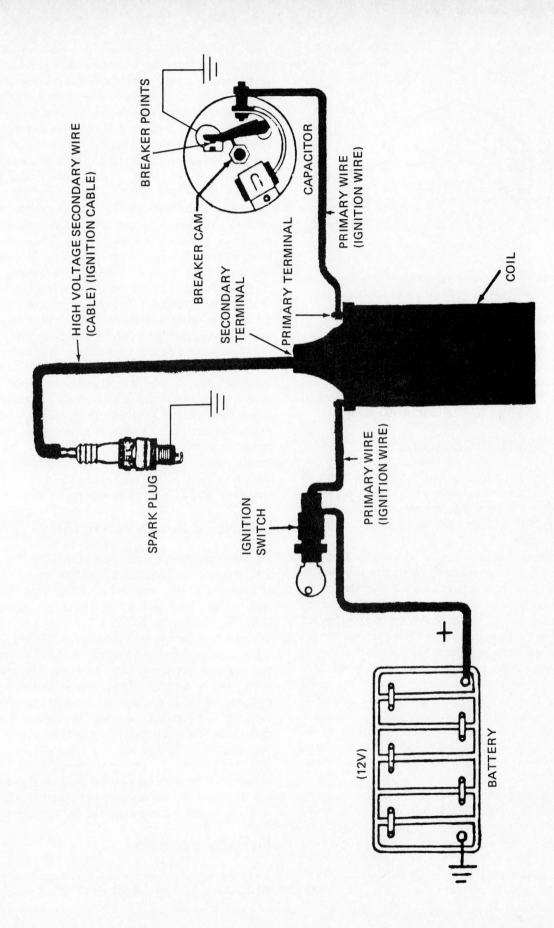

Figure 17-3. Primary circuit wires and components carry low voltage from the battery that is stepped up in the coil to create a secondary high voltage to fire the spark plugs.

BREAKER POINTS

BREAKER CAM

SECONDARY TERMINAL

PRIMARY TERMINAL

CAPACITOR

PRIMARY WIRE (IGNITION WIRE)

HIGH VOLTAGE SECONDARY WIRE (CABLE) (IGNITION CABLE)

SPARK PLUG

COIL

PRIMARY WIRE (IGNITION WIRE)

IGNITION SWITCH

(12V)

BATTERY

251

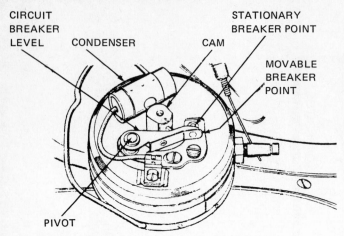

CIRCUIT BREAKER LEVEL   CONDENSER   CAM   STATIONARY BREAKER POINT   MOVABLE BREAKER POINT   PIVOT

Figure 17–4. Breaker point assembly. (Harley-Davidson Motors, Inc.)

idly collapses, inducing a high voltage in every turn of both the primary and secondary windings. In the primary winding the voltage may reach 300 volts, while in the secondary, which has up to 100 times as many turns of wire, the voltage may reach 30,000 volts or even more. The high voltage is then directed out of the secondary terminal through a high-voltage ignition cable to the spark plug.

Breaker points and condenser

The fast buildup and collapse of the primary winding of the coil is made possible by the switching action of the breaker points. The breaker points are usually located behind the flywheel on the left side of the engine, as shown in Figure 17–1.

The primary circuit is opened and closed by a breaker point assembly shown in Figure 17–4. This assembly is opened and closed by a breaker cam that is rotated by the engine crankshaft or attached to the inside of the flywheel.

An insulated rubbing block rides on the breaker cam and is attached to the breaker point set. There are two contact points. The stationary or grounded contact does not move during operation; the movable contact is mounted on a pivot. Rotation of the breaker cam positions a lobe under the rubbing block which causes the movable contact to pivot and separate from the stationary contact. Further rotation of the breaker cam allows the lobe to pass by the rubbing block. A spring, usually made of stainless steel with a copper conductor strip attached, closes the breaker points.

As the breaker points open, the effect of the collapsing magnetic field in the ignition coil also creates some voltage surge in the primary circuit. The capacitor or condenser absorbs this voltage surge and thus helps to prevent the breaker points from arcing as they separate. The condenser is mounted next to the breaker points and connected electrically to the movable breaker point.

The breaker points must be prevented from arcing because arcing causes the points to become pitted and burnt, greatly reducing their service life. Also, arcing allows the primary current to continue to flow for an instant after the points start to open, thus decreasing both the speed with which the coil's magnetic field collapses and the induced voltage in the secondary windings. Use of a capacitor allows the primary circuit to be broken with a minimum of arcing, thereby extending contact point service life and speeding the collapse of the coil's magnetic field.

Twin- and multiple-cylinder ignition systems may use more than one set of breaker points or more than one coil to provide the spark in each cylinder. There are several motorcycles in which a single ignition coil is used to fire two spark plugs, a result achieved by connecting a spark plug to each end of the ignition coil's secondary windings, as shown in Figure 17–5. In this hookup, both spark plugs are wired in series with the secondary coil windings, and both plugs fire simultaneously. Where two spark plugs are fired by a single coil, the plugs are used in cylinders whose firing order is 360° apart. One spark plug will fire while its cylinder is near the top of its compression stroke, and the other spark plug will fire simultaneously while its cylinder is near the top if its exhaust stroke. Spark plugs connected in this way fire twice as often as necessary (no purpose is served by firing on the exhaust stroke), but the design greatly simplifies the ignition system, eliminating the need for a distributor, or for additional sets of contact points, capacitors, and coils for each cylinder.

MAGNETO IGNITION SYSTEMS

On many motorcycles, the spark plug is fired by a magneto, a device that produces its own low voltage with a set of magnets (thus the name) which is then transformed into high voltage. (In a battery coil system, low voltage is of course supplied by the battery.) The magneto has no outside source of electricity to produce the required spark.

To understand how the magneto produces a spark, it is first necessary to understand the relationship between magnetism and electricity. When a wire is moved through a magnetic field so as to cut across the field's lines of force, a current is induced in the wire. The current then flows through the electrical circuit of which the wire is a part. We could wind the wire into a coil and still get the same effect, except that the amount of current produced would be increased in proportion to the number of turns in the coil. It would also be increased in proportion to the speed at which the coil is moved through the magnetic field.

Flywheel magneto

Many magneto systems use a set of magnets attached to the flywheel, as shown in Figure 17–6. An armature-and-

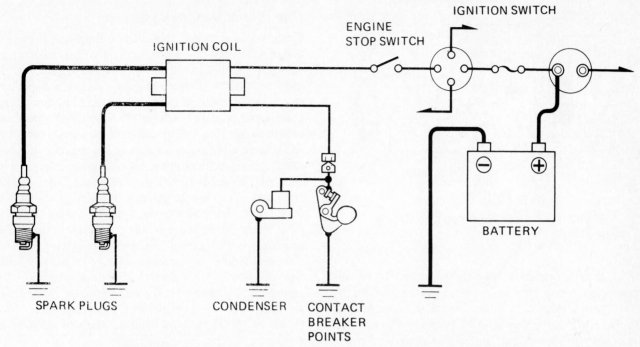

Figure 17–5. Single ignition coil used to provide voltage to two spark plugs. (Honda Motor Co., Ltd.)

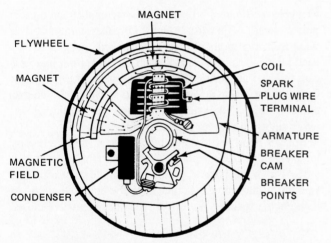

Figure 17–6. Parts of a flywheel magneto. (Champion Spark Plug Co.)

coil assembly is mounted under the flywheel, close to the magnets. The armature, which is made from several thin strips of soft iron that are squeezed tightly together, is used to make a path for the magnetism. The coil is attached to the armature. Inside the coil is a fairly thick wire called the *primary wire* that is wrapped, or coiled, around a part of the armature. One end of the primary wire is attached to the armature; the other end goes to the breaker points.

The coil has a secondary wire wrapped around the primary wire that is much thinner than the primary, and is also wrapped around the armature many more times. One end of the secondary wire is hooked to the armature, while the other end is connected to a terminal where a high-voltage spark plug wire can be attached.

Rotation of the flywheel generates a varying magnetic field in the armature iron core and the coil windings that in turn causes a voltage to be induced and a current to flow in the primary winding. The action in the system is then the same as in a battery coil system. The breaker points, which are timed to open at optimum current flow, open the primary circuit and interrupt the current, causing the magnetic field around the coil to collapse and reverse in direction. (The condenser also aids in this reversal.) At the instant of reversal, a high voltage is induced into the secondary winding of the coil, causing an electrical discharge or spark to occur at the gap of the spark plug.

Rotor-type magneto

Many motorcycles use a rotating magnetic rotor attached to the end of the crankshaft, instead of the flywheel, to develop the primary current. A rotor-type magneto system is shown in Figure 17–7. The rotor is essentially a small-diameter rotating magnet that turns inside a stationary iron core. The iron core or armature provides a path for magnetism to a primary and secondary winding. Rotor type magnetos are divided into high- or low-tension systems.

High-Tension Magnetos

A simplified diagram of a high-tension system, which does not use a separate ignition coil, is shown in Figure 17–8.

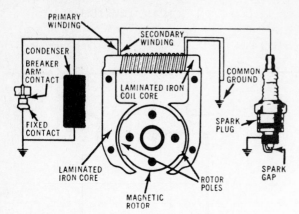

Figure 17–7. Rotor-type magneto. *(Champion Spark Plug Co.)*

Between firing impulses, the breaker points (5) remain closed, completing the primary circuit. As the magneto rotor (1) spins, magnetism causes current to be induced in the magneto primary windings (2). Magnetic lines of force are built up, collapsed, and then built up again in the opposite direction. As the magnetic field in the primary circuit collapses, current is induced in the magneto secondary windings. Since the collapse would not be sufficiently rapid by itself to induce usable ignition voltage, the breaker point cam (6) is timed to open the breaker points just as the magnetic field collapses. Opening the breaker points breaks the primary circuit, speeding the collapse of the magnetic field. Rapid collapse of the magnetic field induces high voltage in the magneto secondary windings (7) which flows through the spark plug (8), causing a spark. The capacitor (4) protects the breaker points and helps to speed the collapse of the magnetic field, as in other ignition systems. When the engine stop switch (3) is closed, the breaker points have no effect: the primary circuit remains unbroken, and the magnetic field will not collapse rapidly enough to induce ignition voltage.

Low-Tension Magnetos

The low-tension system shown in the simplified diagram in Figure 17–9 uses a separate ignition coil to induce high voltage. The breaker points (6) close to complete the primary circuit. The magneto rotor (1) spins, inducing a current in the magneto windings (2) which flows through the ignition coil primary windings (4), establishing a magnetic field in the ignition coil. Because the magneto current flow will reverse direction as the rotor spins, the magnetic field in the ignition coil collapses, but not rapidly enough to induce usable ignition voltage. Accordingly, the breaker point cam (7) is synchronized with the magneto rotor to open the breaker points at the time of collapse, breaking the primary circuit and speeding the collapse of the magnetic field in the ignition coil. Rapid collapse of the magnetic field induces high voltage in the coil secondary windings (8) which flows through the spark plug (9). The capacitor (5) protects the breaker points and helps speed the collapse of the magnetic field. The engine stop switch (3) can be closed to short-circuit the magneto and stop the engine.

CAPACITOR DISCHARGE SYSTEMS

Magneto and battery coil ignition systems that use breaker points have a major disadvantage. Breaker points begin to wear from the moment they are installed. After ten thousand miles or so, the contact points are worn out and ignition failure may result. The wearing of the breaker points and rubbing block changes the time at which the contact points open, which in turn changes the ignition timing, often resulting in poor engine operation.

Breaker point and rubbing block wear make it necessary to change the breaker points to guard against system failure. Also, since breaker points can handle only a limited amount of current, the output from the coil is limited. At high engine speeds, the time the breaker points are closed

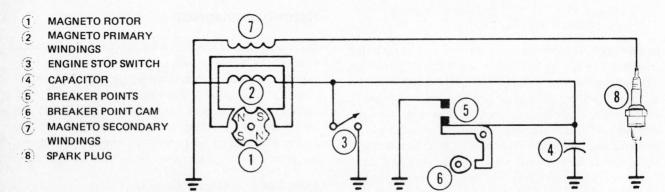

(1) MAGNETO ROTOR
(2) MAGNETO PRIMARY WINDINGS
(3) ENGINE STOP SWITCH
(4) CAPACITOR
(5) BREAKER POINTS
(6) BREAKER POINT CAM
(7) MAGNETO SECONDARY WINDINGS
(8) SPARK PLUG

Figure 17–8. Simplified diagram of a high-tension magneto system. *(American Honda Motor Co.)*

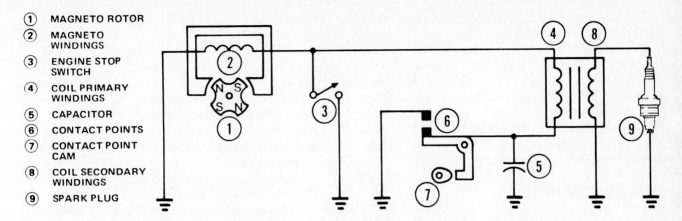

① MAGNETO ROTOR
② MAGNETO WINDINGS
③ ENGINE STOP SWITCH
④ COIL PRIMARY WINDINGS
⑤ CAPACITOR
⑥ CONTACT POINTS
⑦ CONTACT POINT CAM
⑧ COIL SECONDARY WINDINGS
⑨ SPARK PLUG

Figure 17–9. Simplified diagram of a high-tension magneto. *(Honda Motor Co., Ltd.)*

to store energy in the coil is very short, resulting in low-voltage output.

The capacitor discharge, or CD, electronic ignition system was developed to overcome these problems. The principle behind the CD system is that a capacitor (or condenser) has the ability to temporarily store and quickly discharge electrical energy. Any ignition system which discharges a capacitor into the primary windings of the ignition coil for the purpose of inducing secondary voltage is, by definition, a capacitor discharge ignition system. Capacitor discharge ignition comes in many forms and may be incorporated into either battery or magneto systems.

A condenser or capacitor is made of two parallel plates separated by an insulator. When current enters the capacitor, electrons build up on one plate, and their negative charge repels a like number of electrons on the other plate. In this condition, the capacitor is said to be charged—i.e., energy is stored in it. When the current flow is stopped, the energy remains in the capacitor. Only when a conductor is connected across the two plates will it discharge, or regain electron balance. A small capacitor is capable of storing a large electron charge and providing a big discharge.

In a capacitive discharge system, a charged capacitor is placed across the primary winding of an ignition coil. As the capacitor discharges into the primary winding, a strong magnetic field is established that cuts across the secondary winding, inducing a high voltage. Note that energy is not stored in the coil; rather, the coil is used only to step up the voltage from the capacitor. More energy is developed in this way than in a conventional ignition. The capacitor is then disconnected from the coil and recharged, so that the discharge into the primary winding can occur again for the next firing cycle.

A simplified diagram of a CD system is shown in Figure 17–10. Exciter windings (2) in the AC generator (1) produce the alternating current. (How the generator works is described in Unit 20.) Current passes through the diode (5) in the capacitor discharge ignition (CDI) unit (4) to charge the capacitor (6). Because the diode allows current to pass in only one direction, the capacitor is prevented from discharging back through the generator. Alternating current induced in the trigger windings (3) of the generator are used to open and close the electronic switch (7) in the CDI unit.

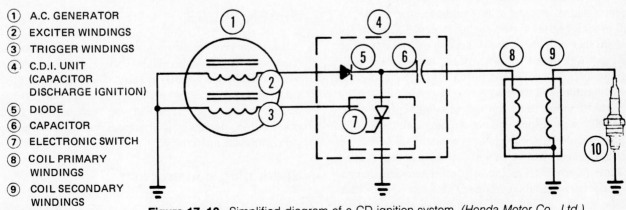

① A.C. GENERATOR
② EXCITER WINDINGS
③ TRIGGER WINDINGS
④ C.D.I. UNIT (CAPACITOR DISCHARGE IGNITION)
⑤ DIODE
⑥ CAPACITOR
⑦ ELECTRONIC SWITCH
⑧ COIL PRIMARY WINDINGS
⑨ COIL SECONDARY WINDINGS
⑩ SPARK PLUG

Figure 17–10. Simplified diagram of a CD ignition system. *(Honda Motor Co., Ltd.)*

The electronic switch remains open while the generator charges the capacitor. When the switch closes, the circuit is completed, grounding one end of the capacitor through the switch, the other end through the ignition coil primary windings (8). The capacitor then discharges through the ignition coil primary windings, causing the rapid buildup of a magnetic field which induces high voltage in the ignition coil secondary windings (9), that flows through the spark plug (10). The location of the CD components on the motorcycle are shown in Figure 17–11.

IGNITION TIMING

Ignition timing is the delivery of the spark to the cylinder at the exact time at which ignition should occur in a combustion chamber. Timing depends upon how long it takes to burn the air–fuel mixture in the cylinder. The time required for complete combustion is affected by several engine design features: the shape of the combustion chamber, the position of the spark plug, and the diameter of the bore. Besides engine design, several other things affect ignition timing. For example, a proper air–fuel mixture burns much faster than one that is too rich or too lean. Also, gasoline with a high octane rating burns much slower than low-octane gasoline. Finally, highly volatile gasoline burns much faster than less volatile gasoline.

Combustion in the cylinder is not instantaneous: ignition must be timed to occur before the end of the compression stroke in order for combustion to be completed in time to drive the piston downward on the power stroke. At idling speed, ignition can be timed to occur quite late in the compression stroke because there is enough time for combustion to be completed as the piston starts its power stroke. At high speeds, ignition must occur earlier in the compression stroke.

Should ignition occur too early (called "too advanced" in the trade) during the compression stroke, combustion will be completed before the piston reaches its top dead center position. The piston will then be forced to move upward against extremely high pressure, and if flywheel momentum cannot overcome this pressure, the engine will stall or kick backward when being started. Excessive ignition advance will result in overheating and loss of power, and may well result in the air–fuel mixture's detonating with an audible knock. The piston may become damaged by overheating and detonation.

Should ignition occur too late (a condition called "too retarded"), combustion will not be completed until the piston has traveled downward on its power stroke. The pressure that propels the piston will then be reduced, resulting in a loss of power. If ignition is further retarded, combustion may not even be completed at the start of the exhaust stroke, and the air–fuel mixture will be discharged into the exhaust port while it is still burning intensely. Overheating

will result, and in four-stroke engines the exhaust valve may even burn.

Some minibikes and dirt bikes have a fixed ignition timing; no automatic advance mechanism is provided. These motorcycles have their ignition timing set permanently in an advanced position, so that timing will be most nearly correct when the engine is running at medium or high speeds. Most motorcycles, however, are equipped with a device which automatically advances ignition timing as engine rpm increases.

The centrifugal advance mechanism is the most commonly used automatic advance system. The centrifugal ignition advance unit (Figure 17–12) rotates with the breaker point cam and is driven by the engine camshaft or crankshaft. An ignition advance unit installed on the end of the camshaft is shown in Figure 17–13. Centrifugally controlled weights mounted to a plate in the advance unit regulate the position of the breaker point cam in relation to the crankshaft.

When the engine is idling, the weights are held inward by spring tension, and the breaker cam is positioned to open the breaker points near the end of the compression stroke. There is enough time at idle speed for combustion before the piston moves down on its power stroke. A small amount of advance provides smooth idling and prevents kickback during starting.

As the rider increases the engine speed, the advance weights fly outward by centrifugal force, rotating the breaker point cam ahead. In the advanced position, the breaker cam opens the breaker points earlier in the compression stroke.

Since capacitor discharge ignition systems do not have contact points, they cannot use a mechanical advance unit. Electronic ignition advance can be provided by taking advantage of the fact that increased rpm induces greater voltage in the trigger windings, which in turn controls the electronic switch that discharges the capacitor. The electronic components can be used to sense this higher voltage and regulate timing thereby.

SPARK PLUGS

Spark plugs provide an air gap in the engine's combustion chamber which the secondary voltage jumps, creating a spark to ignite the air–fuel mixture. There are many different brands and styles of spark plugs, but they all have this one basic job to do. The following sections describe the construction, operation, and various technical features of the motorcycle spark plug.

Spark plug construction

A sectional view of a spark plug is shown in Figure 17–14. Basically, it is a wire, with an air gap at the bottom,

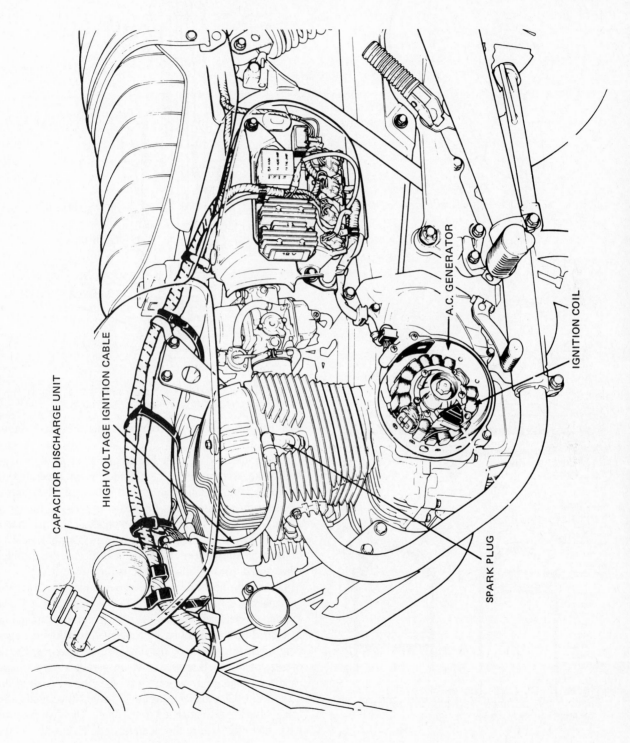

CAPACITOR DISCHARGE UNIT

HIGH VOLTAGE IGNITION CABLE

SPARK PLUG

A.C. GENERATOR

IGNITION COIL

Figure 17–11. Motorcycle with a CD system. *(Honda Motor Co., Ltd.)*

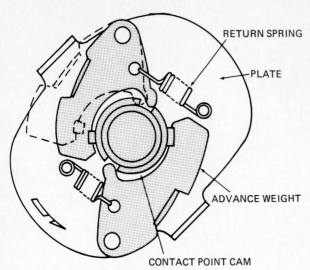

Figure 17–12. Centrifugal advance unit. *(Honda Motor Co., Ltd.)*

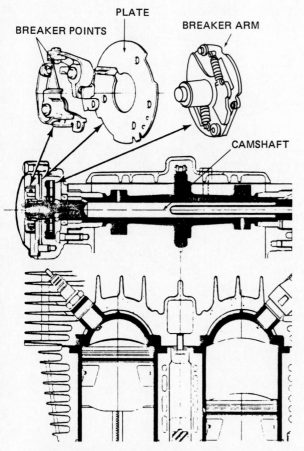

Figure 17–13. Cross section of an engine showing the advance unit attached to the camshaft. *(Honda Motor Co., Ltd.)*

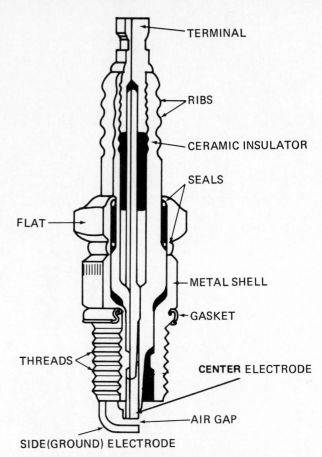

Figure 17–14. Sectional view of a spark plug. *(NGK Spark Plugs (U.S.A.) Inc.)*

The cable-to-spark-plug connection is shown in Figure 17–11.

Center electrodes must be insulated, since they carry high-voltage current into the cylinder. Here, a ceramic insulator is used. The insulator has ribs formed on its outside diameter, which increases the distance between the terminal and the nearest ground. By increasing the distance to the cylinder head, the ribs also help to eliminate leakage of current (flashover). Leakage is especially a problem when the outside of the ceramic is dirty or wet.

The center electrode and the ceramic insulator assembly are attached to a metal shell. The shell is insulated from the center electrode by the ceramic material. Threads are machined on the metal base of the shell to allow the spark plug to be threaded into the combustion chamber. On the outside of the shell are flats, which permit a wrench to be used for installation and removal of the plug. A short distance from the center electrode is a side, or ground, electrode which is also attached to the shell. The distance from the center electrode to the side electrode creates the air gap or spark plug gap that the current jumps to create a spark.

Since spark plugs are subjected to very high pressure, precautions must be taken to prohibit leakage of combustion pressures. Seals are used between the metal shell and

that can be inserted into the engine's combustion chamber. The wire that conducts high voltage into the cylinder is called the *center electrode*. Attached to its top is a terminal that accepts a connector from a high-voltage ignition cable.

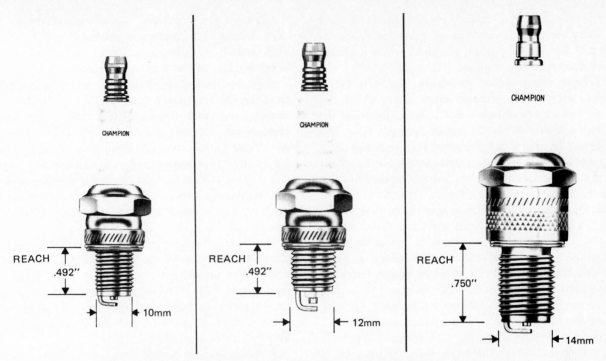

Figure 17–15. Spark plugs are manufactured in different thread and reach dimensions. *(Champion Spark Plug Co.)*

the ceramic insulator and between the center electrode and the ceramic insulator. A metal gasket is used to prevent leakage of combustion pressures around the shell threads.

In order to perform its basic job of providing a high-voltage spark at the proper location in the combustion chamber, a spark plug must exactly match the dimensional requirements of the particular cylinder head in which it is installed.

Spark plugs are made with different shell thread diameters. In the metric system, the threads are measured in millimeters. The threaded section of the shell is also made in different lengths or reaches. There are several common reach dimensions. Spark plugs with different thread diameters and reach dimensions are shown in Figure 17–15. The thickness of the combustion chamber determines the reach of the spark plug. Figure 17–16 (center) shows a spark plug that correctly fits a combustion chamber; spark plugs with too long and too short a reach are shown in Figure 17–16 (left) and Figure 17–16 (right), respectively.

If a spark plug with too long a thread reach is installed, the excessively projected firing end may be hit by the piston and valves, or may overheat and cause engine damage. On the other hand, when a plug with too short a thread reach is installed, engine output may be decreased and the cylinder head threads may become clogged by accumulated deposition. It may be difficult to reinstall a correct thread reach afterwards.

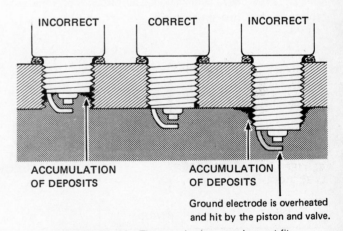

Figure 17–16. The spark plug reach must fit the combustion chamber. *(NGK Spark Plug Co.)*

Spark plug operation and firing end design

To ignite the surrounding combustible mixture of air and fuel in the combustion chamber, secondary high-voltage current flows from the ignition system through the high-voltage ignition cables. This current enters the spark plug at the terminal end of the center electrode and flows down the center electrode to the air gap located in the engine's combustion chamber, where the high voltage has ionized (or prepared) the air–fuel mixture for burning. The current then overcomes the resistance of the gases and jumps the air gap to the side (or ground) electrode, where it creates a spark that ignites the mixture.

Depending upon various conditions, the voltages required to overcome the gap and the resistance of the air–fuel mixture may be different. For instance, the wider the air gap, the higher will be the required voltage. Also, less voltage will be needed if the electrodes are clean and sharp as opposed to their being dirty and eroded. Finally, if the compression pressure is high, the voltage required to overcome the air gap must also be high.

The firing end of the spark plug must be designed to provide a good surface for spark discharge. The problem in motorcycles, especially two-strokers, is that the oil in the fuel tends to burn and collect on the spark plug firing end. This burned oil (called carbon) eventually builds up to the point where it creates too much resistance for current flow or creates a new path for current flow away from the air gap. We call such a condition a *fouled spark plug*.

A number of firing ends have been designed to prevent fouling (Figure 17–17). The conventional gap is used in many motorcycles and is the same as that used in most automobiles. The J-gap is a conventional design that has been modified so that the side electrode extends only midway to the center electrode. The J-gap design requires less voltage, gives better combustion, and offers good fouling protection for a two-stroke engine.

Retracted gap plugs with recessed side electrodes have been designed for combustion chambers that do not provide enough physical room for conventional-type electrodes because of piston or valve interference.

A gold–palladium spark plug with a small-diameter center electrode is available for special requirements. This semiprecious metal alloy makes it possible to provide extra performance, resulting in faster, easier starts; fewer stalls and "false starts"; reduced fouling depoists; and, usually, longer life. The gold–palladium design not only requires less ignition voltage than the conventional electrode types, but also provides more clearance between the shell and the insulator for far better self-cleaning of fuel deposits and less fouling.

The projected-core spark plugs require increased physical clearance between the firing tip and the piston or valves. The incoming air and fuel cools the firing tip at high speeds. At low speeds, the firing tip runs at temperatures higher than those of conventional-type plugs. In this manner, deposits can be burned off the spark plug during long periods of slow-speed running.

A surface-gap spark plug does not have a conventional firing end. Instead, it has a relatively flat sparking surface that arcs between the center electrode and the metal shell which is also exposed within the combustion chamber. Surface-gap plugs are designed for use with capacitor discharge systems, which have the electrical characteristics necessary to take advantage of the surface-gap design.

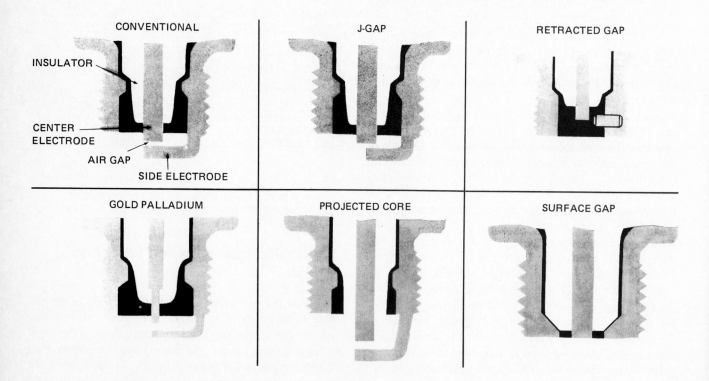

Figure 17–17. Firing-end designs for motorcycle engines. *(Champion Spark Plug Co.)*

Heat range

The spark plug firing end is mounted in the engine's combustion chamber and subjected to very high temperatures, so of course it must be designed to remove this heat. The pathway of the heat is away from the firing end. Heat moves up the ceramic insulator to the metal shell and then out into the engine's cylinder head, to be removed by the air flow or liquid cooling.

Spark plugs are designed to operate within a certain temperature range. *Heat range* describes the ability of a spark plug to conduct heat away from the firing end. It is determined by the distance that heat must flow from the firing end to the metal shell. If the heat path is long, the firing end will maintain a high temperature. The plug is then referred to as a *hot spark plug*. If the heat-flow pathway is short, heat is removed more easily from the spark plug, and the plug is called a *cold spark plug*. Figure 17–18 shows a comparison of cold and hot spark plug heat paths.

The operating temperatures of the spark plug tips are a compromise between carbon and oil fouling on the one hand and preignition and electrode burning on the other. Carbon and oil will not be burned off of the electrodes properly if the temperature of the spark plug tip is too cold. Misfire will probably occur due to deposits that have been built up on the electrodes. On the other hand, if the tip area operates at too high a temperature, the insulator end itself could get hot enough to ignite the air–fuel mixture. This random ignition with no spark is called *preignition*. Preignition is violent and uncontrollable. If continued for a long enough time, it could damage engine components. Electrode burning and corrosion will be accelerated with excessive temperatures at the tip, thus shortening the useful life of the spark plug.

Spark plug codes

The spark plug must be matched correctly to the engine in which it is installed. That is, the plug must have the correct thread diameter, reach, and heat range. Each spark plug manufacturer has developed a code to specify these dimensions, as well as all the other technical features of their spark plugs. The code, a combination of numbers and letters, is printed on the insulator or stamped on the shell. There is no universal code. The catalog for each manufacturer must be consulted to identify a particular spark plug code.

Spark plug inspection

A visual inspection is made of each plug. Disconnect the spark plug cable and unscrew the plug. First, check the spark plug electrodes for wear or damage. The center electrode should be fairly clean and even, and the side electrode should have an even thickness. Then check the ceramic insulator for cracks or chips. Sears should be sound and undamaged. Discard plugs that are fouled or damaged. If the plug appears sound, measure the gap with a feeler gauge, and regap as needed by bending the side electrode.

KEY TERMS

Battery coil ignition system: an ignition system which uses the energy in a battery stepped up by a coil to provide a high-voltage spark.

Breaker points: an assembly that is equivalent to a mechanical switch opened by a cam driven by the engine crankshaft; used to induce a high-voltage current in an ignition coil.

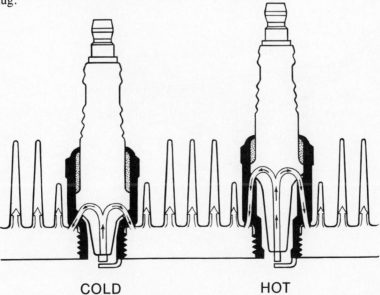

COLD   HOT

Figure 17–18. A hot and cold spark plug. *(Champion Spark Plug Co.)*

Capacitor: an electronic device consisting of alternate plates of conductive and insulative material that is used to store and quickly discharge current.

Capacitor discharge ignition system: an ignition system that uses the energy stored in a capacitor to develop high voltage.

Coil: an electrical device which uses primary and secondary copper windings surrounding an iron core to step up low voltage to high voltage for ignition.

Condenser: an electrical device used in an ignition system to store electrical energy to prevent breaker point arcing.

Magneto ignition system: an ignition system that uses rotating magnets instead of a battery to develop the primary voltage.

Spark plug: the ignition system component which provides an air gap for the high voltage created by the ignition system; the current produced by the high voltage jumps the gap to create a spark in the combustion chamber.

Timing mechanism: a set of weights and springs driven by the engine camshaft or crankshaft; used to move the breaker points into a new position to advance ignition as engine speed increases.

CHECKUP

Identify the parts of the battery coil ignition system by writing their names in the spaces provided.

1. _____
2. _____
3. _____
4. _____
5. _____
6. _____
7. _____

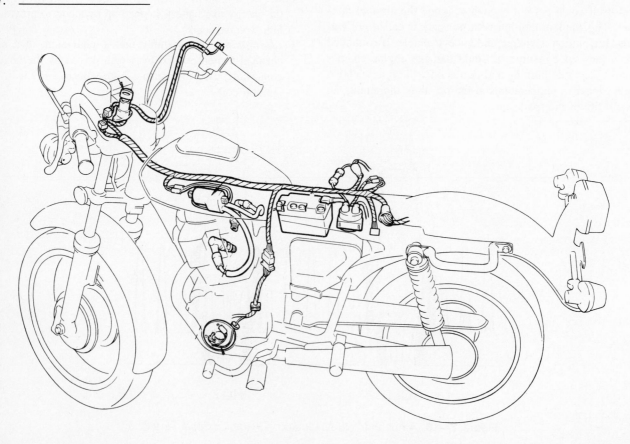

Identify the parts of the ignition coil by writing their names in the spaces provided.

8. _____
9. _____
10. _____
11. _____
12. _____
13. _____
14. _____
15. _____
16. _____
17. _____

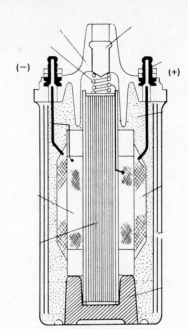

Identify the parts of the magneto ignition by writing their names in the spaces provided.

18. _____
19. _____
20. _____
21. _____
22. _____
23. _____

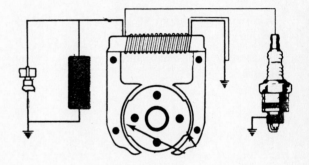

Identify the parts of a spark plug by writing their names in the spaces provided.

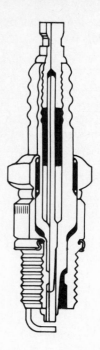

24. _____

25. _____

26. _____

27. _____

28. _____

29. _____

30. _____

31. _____

32. _____

33. _____

34. _____

DISCUSSION TOPICS AND ACTIVITIES

1. Disassemble a battery coil ignition system and identify the parts.

2. Disassemble a magneto ignition system and identify the parts.

A motorcycle with ignition system problems may be hard to start, may run poorly when started, or may not run at all. The ignition system components, especially the spark plugs and breaker points, eventually wear to the point that the system can no longer develop the high voltage required for proper ignition of the air–fuel mixture. To prevent these problems from occurring, the ignition system must be serviced at regular intervals. Servicing the ignition system is usually called an ignition *tune-up*. A good motorcycle technician must be able to determine the cause of an ignition problem and then perform the necessary servicing.

JOB COMPETENCY OBJECTIVES

When you finish reading and studying this unit, you should be able to:

1. Explain how to troubleshoot the ignition system.

2. Remove, clean, regap, and install spark plugs.

3. Remove, replace, and gap breaker points.

4. Adjust ignition timing with a test light, points checker, or timing light.

5. Check high-voltage ignition (spark plug) cables for resistance.

6. Explain how to test an ignition coil.

7. Describe the three condenser tests.

TROUBLESHOOTING THE IGNITION SYSTEM

In order to run, an engine needs compression, fuel, and ignition at the right time. Troubleshooting the ignition system involves making sure that the engine has these basic elements.

The ignition system provides a high-voltage spark in each of the engine's cylinders at just the correct time to burn the air–fuel mixture. An engine that cranks over fast enough to run, but that will not start, may have ignition trouble. Similarly, a motorcycle that loses power and quits on the road is likely to have ignition problems. When either of these malfunctions occurs, first eliminate any obvious potential problem areas. Check the tank to see whether it has fuel. Make a visual inspection of all the primary and secondary wires to make sure a wire has not become disconnected. If the system looks complete, you should then make a spark, or spark intensity, test, which is a quick check to determine whether the ignition system is providing a spark.

To make the test, disconnect the spark plug wire from one of the spark plugs, and then remove the spark plug from the engine. Reconnect the spark plug wire to the spark plug. Hold the spark plug against the cylinder head

IGNITION SYSTEM TROUBLESHOOTING AND SERVICING

so that the shell makes a good grounded contact with the head, as shown in Figure 18–1. *(Safety Caution: Make sure you hold the plug by the insulated spark plug wire boot to avoid getting shocked.)*

Crank or kick the engine. If you see a strong blue spark jump between the center and ground spark plug electrodes, then you have ignition, and the problem lies outside the ignition system. If there is no spark, you know you have an ignition system problem.

If you do not get a good spark, the trouble may involve a spark plug, the fuel system, or engine compression. First, eliminate the spark plug as a possible cause of trouble. Remove each one of the engine's spark plugs, and vis-

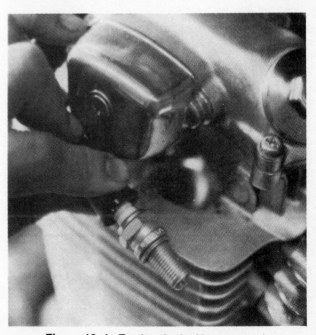

Figure 18–1. Testing the ignition system for spark. *(Champion Spark Plug Co.)*

Normal

Light tan to gray color and slight electrode wear indicate correct heat range.

Change plugs at regular intervals using same heat range.

Core Bridging, Gap Bridging

Combustion particles wedged or fused between the electrodes or the core nose and shell.

Both core bridging and gap bridging are caused by excessive combustion chamber deposits striking and adhering to the spark plug's firing end. They originate from the piston and cylinder head surfaces. These deposits are formed by one or a combination of the following:

Excessive carbon in cylinder. Use of non-recommended oils. Immediate high-speed operation after prolonged low-speed running. Imporper ratio of fuel/oil mixture.

Wet Fouling

Damp or wet, black carbon coating over entire firing end. Forms sludge in some extreme cases.

Wrong spark plug heat range (too cold). Prolonged slow operation. Low-speed carburetor adjustment is too rich. Improper ratio of fuel-to-oil mixture. Worn or defective breaker points, resulting in lack of voltage.

Aluminum Throw-Off

Aluminum deposits on electrodes and insulator core nose.

Caused by first stages of preignition within the cylinder which melts the aluminum alloy of the piston crown. Do not install new plug until piston is examined and the source of preignition is determined.

Overheating

Electrodes badly eroded. Premature gap wear. Insulator has gray or white "blistered" appearance.

Incorrect spark plug heat range (too hot). Ignition timing overadvanced. Consistent high-speed operation.

Preignition

Melted electrodes and/or white insulator indicates sustained preignition. (Insulator may be dirty due to misfiring or debris in the combustion chamber).

Check for correct plug heat range, proper lubrication and/or overadvanced ignition timing. Determine the cause of preignition before putting engine back into service.

Figure 18–2. Spark plugs can be compared to an analysis chart. *(Champion Spark Plug Co.)*

ually inspect the electrode area. If it is excessively wet, there is an excessive supply of fuel, indicating an air–fuel mixture that is too rich. Excessive wetness can also indicate a defective spark plug. Dryness, on the other hand, indicates an air–fuel mixture that is too lean. A spark plug analysis chart (Figure 18–2) may be used to further diagnose problems from the appearance of the spark plugs.

A fouled or improperly gapped spark plug will not ignite the air–fuel mixture in the combustion chamber or will, at best, produce inadequate ignition. On a multiple-cylinder engine, you may find a difference in color of one or more of the spark plugs. If all except one are normal, you can suspect the associated cylinder of misfiring or mechanical damage.

If you do not get a good spark and the ignition system uses breaker points, the points are the most likely source of the problem. The breaker point surfaces must be in good condition and the space between the breaker points must be correct, or the system will not be able to develop any secondary voltage.

Remove the cover over the breaker points and inspect the breaker point surfaces. After a period of time, the points gradually become burnt and pitted (Figure 18–3). Eventually, metal from one point transfers to the other, as shown in Figure 18–4, and the pitting and surface deterioration create enough resistance to prevent good electrical contact. The ignition system then fails to function properly.

Another possibility is that oil may gradually seep past the seal and coat the points or wiring. The oil will burn onto the points, creating an insulating film that must be removed in order for electrical contact to be made.

The fiber cam follower mounted on the pivoting point arm rubs against the cam. Eventually, this cam wears down, resulting in a reduction of the point gap and re-

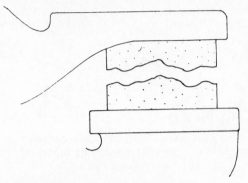

Figure 18–4. Metal from one breaker point can transfer to the other. *(Yamaha Motor Corp. U.S.A.)*

Figure 18–5. Ignition breaker point file.

Figure 18–6. Filing the breaker points.

tarded timing of the affected cylinder. Once this happens, the points must be adjusted to a new gap opening.

In order to get the motorcycle running, you can make a temporary repair by cleaning the breaker points. Breaker points are cleaned with an ignition breaker point file (Figure 18–5). To clean the points, run the file between them (Figure 18–6) until the grey deposits and pits have been removed. Then spray the points with ignition point cleaner and snap them shut on a white business card (or paper of hard texture), repeatedly pulling the card through until no more carbon or metal particles come off on the card.

Check the points to see that they are properly aligned, and that they are not twisted or offset from each other (Figure 18–7). If they are not properly aligned, bend the fixed contact support with either pliers or the recommended special breaker point bending tool. (Never bend the movable breaker arm.) The points should align and be in full, even contact with each other.

After cleaning the points, you will need to reset the gap between them. First rotate the engine until the ignition cam opens the points to their widest position. Then slip a .4-

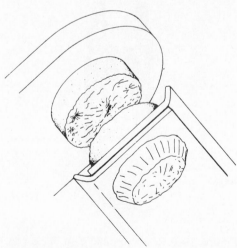

Figure 18–3. Breaker points eventually become pitted and burned. *(Yamaha Motor Corp. U.S.A.)*

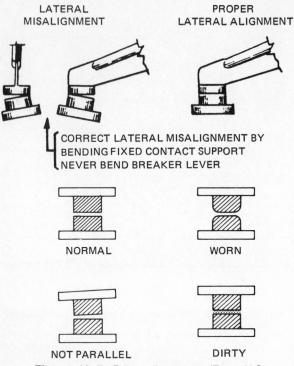

LATERAL MISALIGNMENT   PROPER LATERAL ALIGNMENT

CORRECT LATERAL MISALIGNMENT BY BENDING FIXED CONTACT SUPPORT NEVER BEND BREAKER LEVER

NORMAL   WORN

NOT PARALLEL   DIRTY

Figure 18–7. Point alignment. *(Top: U.S. Navy. Bottom: U.S. Suzuki Motor Corp.)*

mm (.016″) feeler gauge into the gap. It must be a tight slip fit. If an adjustment is necessary, loosen the point lock screw (1 or 2) as shown in Figure 18–8. Insert a screwdriver into the adjustment slots (3 or 4), and open or close the points until the feeler gauge indicates the correct gap. Then retighten the lock screw and recheck the gap. If the ignition uses two sets of breaker points, rotate the cam shaft until the second set of points opens to its widest point. Then perform the same steps over again.

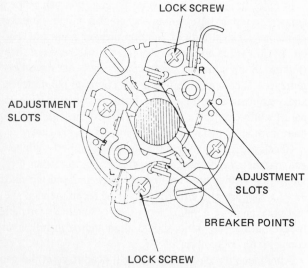

LOCK SCREW

R

ADJUSTMENT SLOTS

L

ADJUSTMENT SLOTS

BREAKER POINTS

LOCK SCREW

Figure 18–8. Adjusting the breaker point gap. *(Yamaha Motor Corp. U.S.A.)*

After regapping the points, check for spark again. If the system now works, the engine should run. If there is still no spark, you will have to perform a complete ignition tune-up as described in the next section.

IGNITION SYSTEM SERVICING

The parts of the ignition system must be serviced at intervals recommended by the motorcycle manufacturer or when there is a problem with the system. Common ignition servicing procedures include cleaning and gapping spark plugs; replacing and adjusting breaker points; setting ignition timing; and performing electrical tests on the coil, condenser, and high-voltage ignition cables.

Spark plug servicing

Spark plug removal and servicing is an important part of every ignition tune-up. Use a 6-point deep spark plug socket (Figure 18–9) for spark plug removal and installation. Spark plug sockets are designed to hold the spark plug firmly so that it may be placed in the socket and started into the cylinder head by hand.

Since, as mentioned earlier, the condition of each spark plug tells a story about the cylinder it was removed from, it is a good idea to keep the plugs in order. An easy method of doing this is to make a spark plug holder from a block of wood (Figure 18–10). Place the plugs in the holder with the terminal end down. They can then be inspected without removing them from the holder. Arrange the plugs in the same order as the cylinders, so that a defective plug can easily be identified with the appropriate cylinder.

After you have removed the plug, closely inspect the insulator and the electrodes. If they are not damaged, you

Figure 18–9. Use a spark plug socket for spark plug removal and installation. Keep in order so you can relate back to the cylinder. *(Champion Spark Plug Co.)*

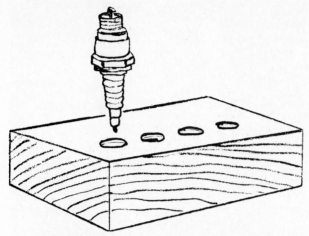

Figure 18–10. As a spark plug is removed, it should be placed in a holder for inspection.

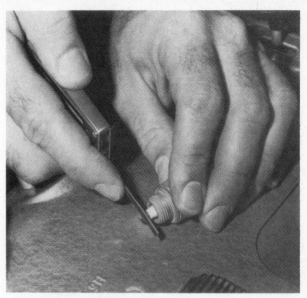

Figure 18–12. Filing the electrodes. *(Champion Spark Plug Co.)*

can clean and regap the spark plugs. However, if the plugs show any damage, have high mileage, or have been cleaned before, they should be replaced with new ones.

Spark plugs that are coated with carbon deposits can be cleaned in a spark plug cleaner (Figure 18–11), which blasts a fine abrasive at the electrode area where the deposits are located. Follow the instructions of the cleaner manufacturer carefully. Plugs should be cleaned until the inside of the shell, the entire insulator, and the electrodes are clean. However, blast cleaning for too long will wear down the insulation and damage the plug. Plugs which cannot be completely cleaned with a reasonable amount of blasting should be replaced. Clean the top insulator and terminal with a cleaning solvent to remove all oil and dirt.

After cleaning, inspect the plug carefully for cracks or other defects which may not have been visible before. If the plug appears to be in good condition, the end of the center electrodes should be filed lightly to provide a flat, square surface.

To file the electrodes, bend the ground electrode away from the center electrode to allow room for a thin ignition breaker point file. File the electrodes of the plug until the surfaces are flat (Figure 18–12). Twenty-five to 40 percent less voltage is required to fire a plug with sharp edges on the center electrode than one with round edges. Do not file the center electrodes of gold–palladium or other fine center wire spark plugs.

After filing, or if you are installing new spark plugs, you must adjust the spark plug electrode gap. A correct gap setting is necessary for efficient firing. Too narrow a gap causes rough running at low speeds; too wide a gap results in the engine missing because voltage is insufficient to jump the gap. The setting is determined for each engine by the motorcycle manufacturer, and it should be maintained. Check the shop service manual for the recommended setting.

A spark plug gapping tool (Figure 18–13) is used to gap the opening. It includes a set of round wire feeler gauges and a bending tool. Round wire gauges provide a more accurate reading for spark plugs than does a flat gauge. The bending tool fits over the ground electrode and allows you to bend it closer or farther away from the center electrode.

To adjust the gap, bend the ground electrode with the bending tool as shown in Figure 18–14. Bend it closer to the center electrode to make the gap smaller and farther away from the center electrode to make it wider. Check the gap by pushing a wire gauge the required thickness through the space. It should fit with a light drag (Figure 18–15).

Figure 18–11. Cleaning a spark plug. *(Champion Spark Plug Co.)*

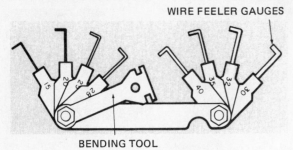

Figure 18–13. Spark plug gapping tool. *(U.S. Navy)*

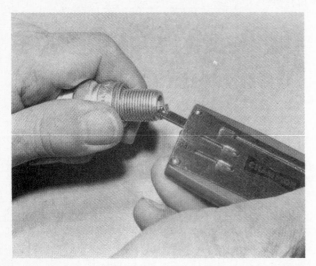

Figure 18–14. Adjusting the spark plug gap. *(Champion Spark Plug Co.)*

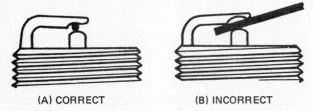

(A) CORRECT   (B) INCORRECT

Figure 18–15. Measuring gap. *(U.S. Navy)*

After cleaning and gapping, the spark plugs are reinstalled. Use the spark plug socket to hold each spark plug, and start the plugs by hand (Figure 18–16). Then use a torque wrench to tighten them to the recommended torque. Using a torque wrench ensures that the spark plug is tightened just the correct amount. If you overtighten the plug, its threads could be stripped; if you don't tighten the plug enough, it could vibrate loose.

Replacing breaker points

Breaker points should be removed and new ones installed at the intervals recommmended by the manufacturer. As mentioned previously, some breaker points are operated by the engine crankshaft, some by the camshaft. Those oper-

Figure 18–16. Start the spark plugs by hand. *(Champion Spark Plug Co.)*

ated by the crankshaft are usually found under a cover on the lower left side of the engine. Those operated by the camshaft are located under a cover on the top cam area of the engine. Some crankshaft-operated breaker points are located behind a flywheel. The flywheel, of course, has to be removed to service these breaker points. Single-cylinder engines use one set of breaker points. Twin- and multiple-cylinder engines use two or more sets of points.

Remove the cover to provide access to the breaker points, and unscrew the point wire securing screw (Figure 18–17). Completely remove the point lock screw and lift the entire point assembly up off the point base plate.

Place the new set of points into position by slipping the point assembly locating pin into the appropriate locating hole in the base plate. Insert and tighten the point lock screw. Then finish the replacement by attaching the point wire to the stationary point and regapping the new point assembly. The point lead wire should not touch the point base plate and should be insulated from the base plate by the insulator washers.

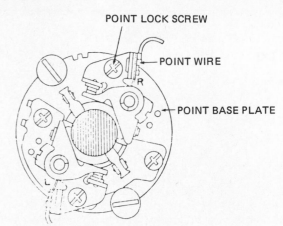

Figure 18–17. Removing and replacing breaker points. *(Yamaha Motor Corp. U.S.A.)*

Be sure not to touch the breaker point surface, as the oil on your hands can cause enough of a resistance to cause misfiring. Some point sets require that the rubbing block be lubricated with high-temperature grease. Check the shop service manual for recommendations.

After installation, the breaker points must be adjusted to the correct gap, as explained in the previous section. Make sure that the feeler gauge you use is perfectly clean. Kick the engine over and observe the point action; the points should meet squarely. If they make contact on only one side, you can gently bend the stationary point into alignment.

Ignition timing adjustment

After the new breaker points are installed, you are ready to check and adjust the ignition timing. The ignition timing is correct when the breaker points open at just the right time in relation to the position of the piston. As explained in Unit 17, the ignition system delivers a spark the instant the breaker points open. Hence, we want to introduce the spark into the cylinder just before the piston reaches top dead center.

The gap between the breaker points affects ignition timing. If the points are spaced too far apart, the cam will open them sooner in the cycle and ignition will occur sooner in relation to piston position. On the other hand, if the points are spaced too close together, the cam will open the breaker points later and ignition will occur later in relation to piston position. These considerations are why gapping the breaker points accurately to specifications is so important. They are also why timing should be checked after the breaker points are serviced.

Timing is adjusted by moving the base plate on which the breaker points (or solid-state components of the CD ignition system) are mounted. Figure 18–18 shows a set of

breaker points mounted to a base plate. The base plate is in turn mounted to the engine by screws which pass through elongated slots in the plate. In Figure 18–18, the breaker point cam is turning clockwise. If we loosen the base plate hold-down screws and rotate the base plate and breaker point assembly counterclockwise, the breaker point rubbing block will contact the cam earlier in the cycle. The spark will then occur earlier in relation to the position of the piston, advancing the ignition timing.

We can also rotate the base plate in the same direction as the cam turns, i.e., clockwise. This will cause the cam to contact the rubbing block later in the cycle. The spark will then occur later in relation to the position of the piston, retarding the ignition timing.

Setting the ignition timing is done in three steps. First, you must position the piston in the cylinder in exactly the place it should be to get ignition, usually just before it reaches top dead center. Second, you must check to see that the breaker points are just starting to open when the piston is in the correct position. Third, if the timing is not correct, you must loosen the base plate and move the breaker point assembly one way or the other to get the points in a position in which they are just barely open.

Timing procedures and specifications are different for different types of motorcycles. Many two-strokers use a procedure which calls for a dial indicator to determine the position of the piston. To use this procedure, you remove a spark plug from the cylinder head and then mount a dial indicator to the top of the head, allowing the dial indicator tracer pin to stick through the spark plug hole and contact the head of the piston (Figure 18–19).

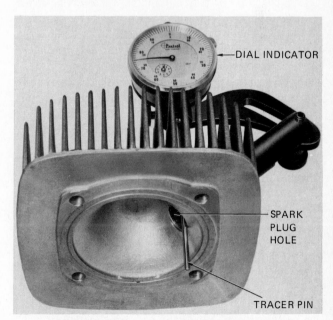

Figure 18–19. A dial indicator mounted with the tracer pin through the spark plug hole. *(Central Tool Co.)*

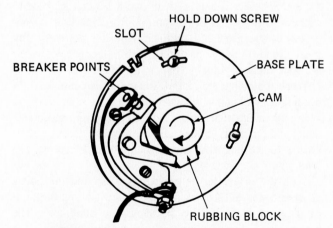

Figure 18–18. Timing is adjusted by moving the base plate in relation to the cam. *(Yamaha Motor Corp. U.S.A.)*

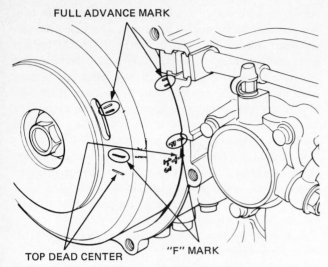

FULL ADVANCE MARK

TOP DEAD CENTER

"F" MARK

Figure 18–20. Ignition timing marks on the flywheel. *(Honda Motor Co., Ltd.)*

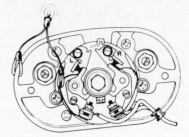

Figure 18–21. A test light used to check breaker point opening. *(Honda Motor Co., Ltd.)*

Rotate the engine until the piston is at top dead center, the highest reading on the dial indicator. Set the zero on the dial indicator face to line up exactly with the dial indicator needle. Rotate the flywheel back and forth to be sure that the indicator needle does not go past zero. Then rotate the engine slowly backwards a recommended number of thousandths of an inch or hundredths of a millimeter on the dial indicator, putting the piston in the proper position just before the top dead center location.

Most four-stroke engines have timing marks to help you get the piston in the correct position. These timing marks are usually on the flywheel, so you will have to remove the left-side engine cover. Different manufacturers use different marks, but those shown in Figure 18–20 are typical. There is a notch on the engine crankcase that is used to align the marks on the flywheel. Two lines are inscribed on the flywheel. The T line stands for the top dead center. When the flywheel is rotated so that the T line lines up with the notch, the piston is at top dead center. Of course, it could be on either compression or exhaust stroke. The best way to tell is to remove a spark plug and put your thumb in the spark plug hole. On the compression stroke, you can feel the high compression in the cylinder.

The F line is the firing or ignition advance line. When the F line is lined up with the notch, and the piston is on a compression stroke (not exhaust stroke), the piston is in the correct position for ignition, usually just before top dead center.

The next step is to determine whether the points are just barely opening. This could be done merely by observing the breaker points, but that is not very accurate. Instead, breaker point opening is better checked with either a test light or a continuity tester, usually called a points checker.

Test Light

A test light is a lightbulb socket with a 12-volt lightbulb connected to two leads which have alligator clips. When properly connected into a circuit, the bulb will light up when there is a voltage in the circuit. The test light can be used to determine when the breaker points open.

A test light that is connected to check breaker point opening is shown in Figure 18–21. One lead is connected to ground and the other is connected to the circuit to the breaker point (either at the connecting wire or the metal breaker arm itself). When the points are closed, the current goes across the closed breaker points to ground, and the light does not light. As the points open, the current can no longer go to ground across the breaker points. Instead, it goes to ground through the test light, and the bulb lights up.

To use the test light, first set the piston in the correct position with the test lamp hooked up. Then rotate the breaker point base plate one way or another until the bulb lights. Finally, tighten the base plate. Check your results by rotating the engine to make sure that the bulb lights as the piston reaches the correct position.

Points Checker

A points checker is a meter with two leads that are used to connect it into a circuit (Figure 18–22). One lead is connected to the grounded stationary breaker point (or any good ground), while the other lead is connected to the movable breaker point (or the circuit feeding it).

When the points are closed, the circuit is continuous. A needle on the points checker shows this continuity by swinging to the right (Figure 18–22, top). As the points open, the circuit is broken and the points checker needle swings to the left, showing no continuity (Figure 18–22, bottom).

With the piston in the correct position and the points checker connected, rotate the base plate back and forth until the points checker needle shows no continuity. The breaker point base is then tightened down. Recheck the setting by rotating the engine and observing the points checker.

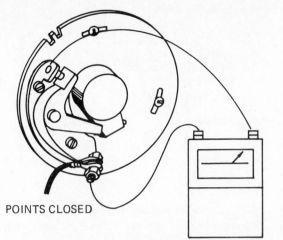

POINTS CLOSED

POINTS CLOSED: CONTINUITY

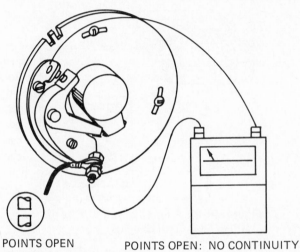

POINTS OPEN

POINTS OPEN: NO CONTINUITY

Figure 18–22. A points checker used to check point opening.

Timing Light

More and more motorcycles are now being timed while running with a timing light (Figure 18–23). This procedure is often called *dynamic timing*.

The typical timing light has a set of leads connected to the motorcycle battery for power. Some are connected into a larger tester or receive power from a 115-volt AC outlet. An induction pickup (shown in Figure 18–23) goes around the high-voltage ignition cable. Other types of timing lights use an adapter that allows the high-voltage ignition cable to be connected to the timing light and the spark plug at the same time. In either type, electrical energy is stored in large capacitors inside the timing light. A high-voltage impulse from the ignition system causes this energy to be discharged into the flash tube of the timing light, creating a bright flash of light. The impulse is received by connecting a lead from the timing light to the spark plug cable for the number-one cylinder.

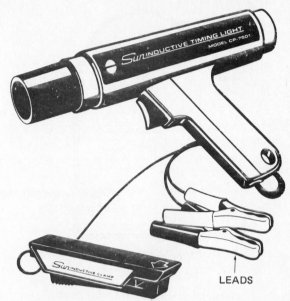

LEADS

Figure 18–23. A timing light used to check dynamic timing. *(Sun Electric Corp.)*

When the engine is running, the ignition impulse causes the timing light to flash each time the number-one spark plug receives high-voltage current. This flashing light is directed at the timing marks on the flywheel, and the strobe effect of the light makes the flywheel marks appear to freeze. It is easy to see whether the marks are aligned. if they are not, the base plate must be moved to correct the timing. In some models, the marks are observed through an inspection plug which must be removed.

Checking spark plug cables

High-voltage ignition cables break down after a period of time. Repeated heating and cooling, combined with extreme moisture and oil exposure, cause the insulation to deteriorate rapidly. If the boot or cable is excessively spongy or brittle, it should be replaced.

You can check a spark plug cable electrically by measuring its resistance with an ohmmeter (Figure 18–24). (Unit 19 explains the use of an ohmmeter.) Calibrate the ohmmeter to the zero line, and turn the range selector knob to the highest scale. Then disconnect one spark plug cable from a spark plug, and disconnect the other end from the coil. Connect one ohmmeter test lead to the spark plug cable terminal and the other lead to the matching metal insert or terminal on the coil end. Then record the resistance, and repeat this procedure for each of the spark plug cables.

Check the readings obtained with the ohmmeter against specifications. Spark plug cable resistance specifications are usually given in ohms per foot. The longer the spark plug cable, the higher the resistance is. The length of the spark plug cable may have to be measured to determine whether it meets specifications. Replace the spark plug ca-

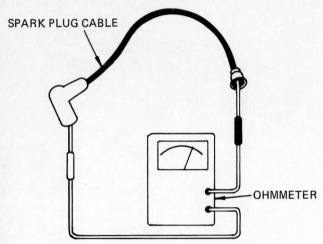

Figure 18–24. Checking spark plug cables for resistance.

bles if the measured resistance is higher than the specifications.

Checking the ignition coil

The best check of the ignition coil is a check for a spark across the spark plug electrode. If you get a good spark, the coil is good. A weak spark can be due to a defective coil. A good way to check is to substitute another, good coil. If you now get a good spark, you know the old core is defective and must be replaced.

Most manufacturers have a coil tester, and most have a test procedure for the resistance of the coil's primary and secondary windings.

Secondary Circuit

The secondary circuit in the ignition coil may also be checked for resistance with an ohmmeter. Remove the primary and secondary wires from the ignition coil. Follow the manufacturer's instructions and calibrate the ohmmeter and turn the range selector knob to the highest scale. Then connect one ohmmeter test lead to the secondary terminal and the other to the grounded frame (Figure 18–25). Check the resistance reading against specifications. If the reading is higher than specifications, replace the ignition coil.

To check the coil's primary circuit, disconnect the primary and secondary wires or leads from the ignition coil. Then calibrate the ohmmeter. Connect one tester lead to the ignition coil primary terminal, and the other lead to the grounded frame (Figure 18–26). Compare the resistance reading from the ohmmeter to specifications. If the resistance is excessive, replace the ignition coil.

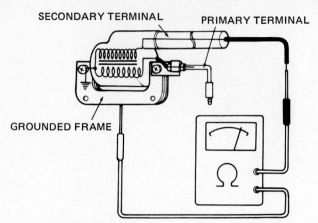

Figure 18–25. Checking secondary windings. *(Honda Motor Co., Ltd.)*

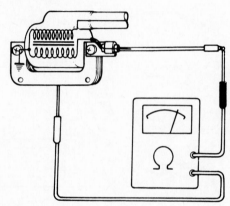

Figure 18–26. Checking the coil primary. *(Honda Motor Co., Ltd.)*

Checking the breaker point capacitor (condenser)

The breaker point capacitor (condenser) instantly stores a static electric charge as the breaker points separate, and the energy stored in the capacitor discharges instantly when the points are closed. If it were not for the capacitor, an electrical charge would arc across the separating breaker points, causing them to burn. The capacitor minimizes the burning of the breaker points, greatly affecting the flow of current in the primary winding of the ignition coil. If the breaker points show excessive wear, or the spark is weak (and the ignition coil is in good condition), check the capacitor. Before checking or testing, however, ground the capacitor to itself, as shown in Figure 18–27, to discharge the stored electrical charge.

The capacitor is tested on a condenser tester (Figure 18–28) for *series resistance*, i.e., the amount of resistance the condenser provides in the primary circuit. Series resistance affects ignition coil output and is tested for leakage; high leakage indicates that the condenser insulation cannot with-

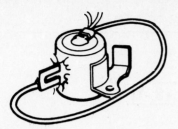

Figure 18–27. Discharge capacitor (condenser) before testing. *(Honda Motor Co., Ltd.)*

stand the demands of the ignition system. The capacitor is also checked for capacitance, which affects point arcing and pitting. Too low or too high a capacitance will cause rapid point pitting.

The manufacturer's instruction manual should be followed when performing capacitor tests. If a condenser fails any one of the tests, it must be replaced. A new condenser should be tested prior to installation to make sure it is in good condition.

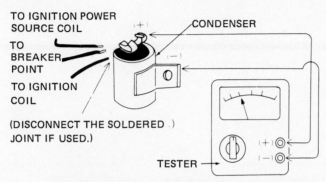

TO IGNITION POWER
SOURCE COIL

TO
BREAKER
POINT

TO IGNITION
COIL

(DISCONNECT THE SOLDERED
JOINT IF USED.)

CONDENSER

TESTER

SET THE ELECTRO-TESTER ON THE "M Ω" POSITION

Figure 18–28. The capacitor is checked on a condenser tester. *(Yamaha Motor Corp. U.S.A.)*

Job Sheet 18–1

REMOVE AND REPLACE SPARK PLUG(S)

Before you begin:

Read pp.

Make of Motorcycle _____ Model _____ Year _____

Time Started _____ Time Finished _____ Total Time _____

Flat-rate Time _____

Special Tools, Equipment, Parts, and Materials

Spark plug socket
Torque wrench
Gapping tool
New spark plugs
Ignition point file
Spark plug cleaner

References

Manufacturer's Shop Manual _____

Specifications

Look up the specifications for spark plug gap and torque and write them in the spaces provided below:

Spark plug gap _____

Spark plug torque _____

Instructor check _____

Procedure

1. Disconnect the high-voltage spark plug cable from the spark plug.
2. Select the proper special spark plug socket to fit the plug hex size.

3. Select the ratchet, extensions, and universals necessary to reach the spark plugs in the engine.

4. Carefully wipe the area around each spark plug to prevent dirt from entering the cylinder.

5. If the engine has aluminum cylinder heads, allow it to cool before removing the spark plugs.

6. Remove each spark plug along with the gasket.

7. As each spark plug is removed, place it in a spark plug holder or tray. The old plugs should be arranged in the holder according to the cylinder and the side of the engine from which they were removed. This procedure will help identify the cylinder when a defect on a particular spark plug is diagnosed.

8. A careful examination of the used spark plugs is helpful in determining engine condition, spark plug heat range selection, and trouble relating to operational conditions.

9. Inspect the side or ground electrode and the center electrode for wear and for any buildup of carbon or oil deposits. Inspect the insulator and shell for blisters or heavy deposits of carbon or oil.

10. If you are going to reuse the spark plugs, blast clean the electrodes, and then file both electrodes flat.

Instructor check _____

11. Each new or cleaned spark plug must have its gap measured and, if necessary, adjusted.

12. To measure the spark plug gap, insert a round, wire-type feeler gauge of the specified gap dimension between the plug electrodes. Do not use a flat feeler gauge because it is not as accurate for this kind of job.

13. Use a special spark plug gapper or bending tool to bend the side (ground) electrode. Bend only the ground electrode.

14. Bend the ground electrode either toward the center electrode to close the gap, or away from the center electrode to open the gap. Do not tap the electrode on a hard surface to adjust the gap. Doing so can break the insulator.

15. When the feeler gauge "snaps through" between the two electrodes, the gap opening is correct.

16. If the feeler gauge cannot pass between the electrodes without your forcing it through, the gap is too close.

17. If the feeler gauge passes through between the electrodes, but does not touch or just touches the electrodes, the gap is too wide.

Instructor check _____

18. With a clean cloth, clean the spark plug seats in the cylinder head.

19. Install the spark plugs finger-tight.

20. Tighten each spark plug to specifications with a torque wrench. Be careful not to place any side pressure on the wrench. Side pressure will tip the socket and break the spark plug insulator.

21. Overtightening the spark plugs can change the gap and cause other damage.

22. Undertightening will cause the plug to overheat and possibly cause preignition.

23. Wipe the plug insulators clean and attach the spark plug cable. Be careful to keep the correct firing order.

Instructor check _____

24. Start the engine and check for proper operation.

NOTES

Instructor check _____   Date Completed _____

Job Sheet 18–2

REMOVE AND REPLACE BREAKER POINTS AND CONDENSER

Before you begin:

Read pp.

Make of Motorcycle _____ Model _____ Year ____

Time Started _____ Time Finished _____ Total Time _____

Flat-rate Time _____

Special Tools, Equipment, Parts, and Materials

Breaker point set with condenser
Feeler gauge
High-temperature ignition lubricant

References

Manufacturer's Shop Manual _____

Specifications

Look up the specification for breaker point gap and record it in the space below:

Breaker point gap _____

Instructor check _____

Procedure

1. Remove the cover from the breaker points.

2. Carefully note the position of all wires connected to the breaker points for correct reassembly.

3. Loosen the leads and remove them from the terminal after noting their relative positions.

4. Remove the screw holding the base of the breaker point set to the base plate.

5. Remove the breaker point assembly from the base plate. Note the locating extrusion on the breaker points that fits into the locating holder of the base plate.

6. To remove the condenser, remove the leads from the primary terminal and loosen the screw holding the condenser bracket to the base plate.

7. The primary lead must be disconnected to remove the condenser. Some types of condensers are connected to the primary terminal by a copper strap which must be released before the condenser can be removed. Others are soldered onto the plate.

Instructor check _____

8. Before either a new breaker point set or a new condenser is installed, the base plate should be cleaned of any dirt, grease, or foreign material.

9. Apply a light coating of high-temperature grease to the breaker cam surface prior to installation of the points. The amount of grease applied should be kept to a minimum to prevent the grease from being thrown off at high speeds and/or at a high temperature.

10. Install the new point set into position on the base plate. Then insert and loosely tighten the attaching screw that holds the breaker point base to the base plate.

11. Carefully replace all condenser and primary leads as they were attached before disassembly. They should be placed so that they will not be struck by the points or cam and so that they will not restrict the movement of the base plate.

Instructor check _____

12. After installing a set of new breaker points, it is necessary to adjust the breaker point opening. Kick the engine over until the point rubbing block is on the peak of the cam lobe. This is the position of maximum point opening.

13. Breaker point opening is then adjusted to the desired specifications by moving the position of the stationary point. Insert a feeler gauge of the correct thickness between the points to determine the correct setting.

14. Use a screwdriver to pry the stationary point base in one direction or the other to change the point opening after the breaker point base screws are loosened. The screws must be tightened securely after the correct point opening is obtained.

Instructor check _____

15. After the breaker points are installed, the point alignment must be checked. Proper alignment is important to breaker point life. If the full faces of the breaker points do not touch each other, the ability of the breaker points to dissipate heat resulting from the primary current is reduced. This will cause excessive point burning. Kick the engine and observe the points for good alignment.

16. The points are aligned laterally by bending the fixed contact support with a bending tool. The movable contact lever must never be bent, or it could be broken.

Instructor check _____

17. Check ignition timing as described in Job Sheet 18–3.

18. Replace the breaker point cover and check the engine for proper operation.

NOTES:

Instructor check _____

Date completed _____

Job Sheet   18-3

ADJUST IGNITION TIMING WITH TEST LIGHT OR POINTS CHECKER

Before you begin:

Read pp.

Make of Motorcycle _____ Model _____ Year _____

Time Started _____ Time Finished _____ Total Time _____

Flat-rate Time _____

Special Tools, Equipment, Parts, and Materials

Test light or points checker

References

Manufacturer's Shop Manual _____

Specifications

Look up the location of the flywheel timing marks and sketch them in the space provided below:

Instructor check _____

Procedure

1. Remove the cover from the breaker points.

2. Remove any plug or cover that might hinder observation of the timing marks.

3. Rotate the engine to line up the timing marks on the compression stroke. *(NOTE: Make sure the engine is not on the exhaust stroke.)*

    Instructor check _____

4. Connect a test light or points checker across the breaker points.

    Instructor check _____

5. Loosen the breaker point base plate.

6. Rotate the breaker point base plate until the light or checker indicates that the breaker points are open.

7. Tighten the breaker point base plate.

8. Rotate the engine and make sure that the light or checker indicates the point opening when the timing marks line up.

Instructor check _____

NOTES:

Instructor check _____   Date completed _____

Job Sheet

CHECK SPARK PLUG CABLE(S) FOR RESISTANCE

Before you begin:

Read pp.

Make of Motorcycle _____ Model _____ Year _____

Time Started _____ Time Finished _____ Total Time _____

Flat-rate Time _____

Special Tools, Equipment, Parts, and Materials

Ohmmeter

References

Manufacturer's Shop Manual _____

Specifications

Look up the specification for resistance of the spark plug cable and write it in the space provided below:
_____ ohms

Instructor check _____

Procedure

1. If you are working on a twin- or multiple-cylinder engine, use masking tape to label each spark plug cable as to which cylinder it goes to. Remove only one cable at a time.

2. Remove the spark plug end of one spark plug cable by first twisting the rubberlike boot back and forth. This twisting breaks the seal that the protective boot forms around the top of the spark plug. Be sure you twist the boot and not the wire. Then, gripping the end of the boot, pull or snap the cable straight out, away from the spark plug.

3. Remove the cable from the end of the coil.

4. Visually check each spark plug cable for dry, cracked insulation, or cuts and breaks in the wires.

5. Wires that are oil- or grease-soaked, dirty or salt-encrusted, should be replaced unless they can be cleaned satisfactorily with a damp cloth and a mild detergent.

Instructor check _____

6. Each cable should be tested for resistance with an ohmmeter. First calibrate the ohmmeter to the × 1000 scale.

7. Connect one tester lead to the spark plug end of the cable. Touch the other tester lead to the terminal on the coil end of the cable.

8. Read the meter and record your readings in the spaces provided below:

Cable number 1 _____

2 _____

3 _____

4 _____

9. Check your readings against specifications to determine whether the cables should be replaced.

10. Twist the cable while you are watching the reading on the ohmmeter. If the needle fluctuates, replace the cable. The fluctuation indicates a broken or partially separated wire within the cable.

Instructor check _____

11. Push the spark plug boots firmly over each spark plug, and push each coil end firmly in place.

12. Check the cable installation to make sure that no cables are out of order.

Instructor check _____

13. Start the engine and check for proper operation.

NOTES:

Instructor check _____   Date completed _____

KEY TERMS

Breaker point gap: the space between the stationary and movable breaker points when they are open to their widest point.

Ignition breaker point file: a small file used to clean breaker point surfaces that are oily or deteriorated.

Spark plug gap: the space between the center and ground electrode of a spark plug.

Spark plug gapping tool: a tool used to adjust and measure the spark plug gap; has feeler gauges and a bending tool.

CHECKUP

1. Describe how to check for spark at the spark plug.

2. How can the spark plug help you determine how the engine is running?

3. How can dirty breaker points prevent the engine from running?

4. How are dirty breaker points cleaned?

5. How is the breaker point gap adjusted?

6. How are spark plugs removed?

7. How are spark plugs cleaned?

8. Why is it important to file spark plug ground electrodes during cleaning?

9. How is a spark plug gap adjusted?

10. Why is the spark plug tightened with a torque wrench?

11. Why must breaker points be adjusted before adjusting timing?

12. How is timing adjusted on most motorcycles?

13. What are two methods used to determine the position of the piston for timing?

14. How is a test lamp used to set ignition timing?

15. What is the position of the breaker points when the test lamp goes out?

16. How is a points checker used to set ignition timing?

17. What is dynamic timing?

18. How can you check a spark plug cable for resistance?

19. Explain two checks to make on an ignition coil.

20. How do you know when the condenser should be checked?

DISCUSSION TOPICS AND ACTIVITIES

1. Check timing with a test light or points checker, and then compare the setting with a timing light. Which is more accurate?

2. Try several different breaker point gaps, and check the timing of each with a timing light. How does the size of the gap affect timing.?

The larger road motorcycles are being produced with more and more electrical and electronic components and accessories. If you want to service these systems and components, you will need a working knowledge of the fundamentals of electricity and electronics. What electricity and electronics are and what they do is basic to understanding an electrical component of a motorcycle. Whether you are working on an ignition, charging, starting, or accessory system, the same principles apply. The fundamentals of electricity and electronics that will be most useful to the motorcycle technician are presented in this unit.

JOB COMPETENCY OBJECTIVES

When you finish reading and studying this unit, you should be able to:

1. Define electricity and explain the flow of electricity.

2. Describe the relationship between voltage, amperage, and resistance.

3. Describe the relationship between magnetism and electricity.

4. Explain the construction and operation of electronic semiconductors.

5. Describe how to read a wiring diagram.

6. Identify the types, and explain the use, of basic electrical test instruments.

ELECTRICITY

The theory of electricity, or the way electricity is thought about and used today, is called the *electron theory*. Even today, we still do not know everything about electricity; however, using the electron theory, we can understand how electricity behaves and how to use it correctly. In order to understand the electron theory, it is necessary to look briefly at what is called the composition of matter.

Everything in the universe except the voids that exist between the sun, stars, and planets is called *matter*. Anything that has weight and takes up space is matter. Even things that cannot be seen, like air, are matter. Matter may be in the form of a solid, a liquid, or a gas. Microscopically speaking, matter is an assembly of select chemical particles called *elements*. Elements are made of *atoms*, the smallest identifiable particles of matter that cannot be further decomposed without changing the properties of the elements of which they are constituents.

Atoms are made up of even smaller particles. An atom is constructed much like our solar system—the sun and the planets that revolve around it. An atom has a center or core called a *nucleus* that is composed of particles called *protons*. Loosely speaking, the nucleus of an atom occupies the same position in the atom as our sun does in the solar

UNIT
19

FUNDAMENTALS OF ELECTRICITY AND ELECTRONICS

system. Small particles called *electrons* circle in orbits around the nucleus just as the planets circle around the sun. (Figure 19–1) Unlike the planets, however, electrons travel at a tremendous rate of speed.

The particles that make up the atom have positive or negative electrical charges, which is where electricity comes from. To say that the charges are positive or negative simply means that there are two charges that are completely opposite to each other. The symbol "+" is used to designate a positively charged particle and "−" to designate a negatively charged particle. Almost everyone has experimented with a set of magnets and found that there are two ends of the magnets that repel each other and two ends that attract. Electrical charges act in much the same way: two positively charged particles repel each other and two negatively charged particles repel each other (Figure 19–2), while a positively charged particle and a negatively charged particle attract each other. It is this mutual attraction that holds atoms together.

The core or nucleus of an atom is composed of positively charged particles. The electrons that orbit in a fixed pattern around the nucleus are negatively charged particles. Different kinds of atoms have different numbers of positively charged particles in the nucleus, and different numbers and spacings of the negatively charged electrons that orbit around the nucleus.

Current flow

The electrons of an atom remain in their orbit around the nucleus because of the electrical attraction between the negatively charged electrons and the positively charged nucleus. This electrical attraction is similar to the gravitational attraction between the sun and the earth in that the electrons that orbit closest to the nucleus (called *bound* electrons) are strongly attracted to it, while the electrons

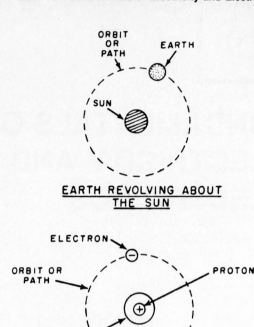

EARTH REVOLVING ABOUT
THE SUN

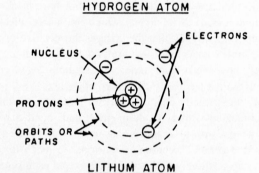

HYDROGEN ATOM

LITHUM ATOM

Figure 19–1. An atom has a central nucleus and orbiting electrons, similar to our solar system with the sun and planets. *(U.S. Air Force)*

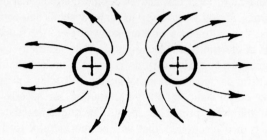

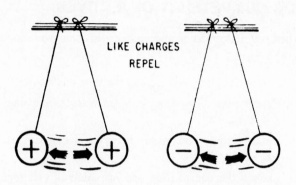

LIKE CHARGES
REPEL

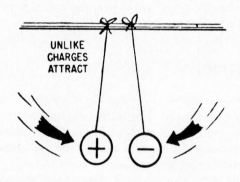

UNLIKE
CHARGES
ATTRACT

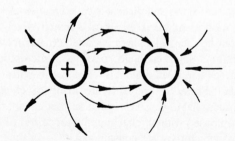

Figure 19–2. Like charges (top) repel each other; unlike charges (bottom) attract each other. *(U.S. Navy)*

that are farther away from the nucleus (called *free* electrons) are weakly attracted to it and can be forced out of their orbits. In fact, free electrons can move from one atom to another, and when they do, we have a flow of (electric) current (Figure 19–3).

We can thus say that electricity is the movement or flow of electrons from one atom to another. In order to have such movement, it is necessary to have a condition of unbalance. In a normal atom, the positively charged nucleus balances the negatively charged electrons and holds them in orbit. If an atom loses electrons, it will have a net positive charge and will then be capable of attracting electrons in order to regain its balance.

The flow of electricity is made possible by causing a quantity of electrons to leave their atoms and gather in a certain area, leaving behind atoms without their normal number of electrons. Science has discovered a number of ways to create this unbalanced condition to start an electron flow. The storage battery and the charging system are two devices that are used for the purpose.

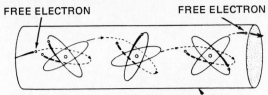

Figure 19–3. Electricity is the movement of electrons from one atom to another. *(U.S. Air Force)*

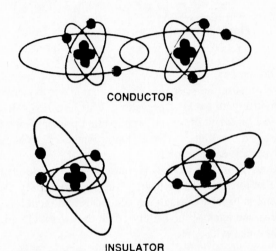

CONDUCTOR

INSULATOR

Figure 19–4. Conductors and insulators. *(Ford Motor Co.)*

Insulators, conductors, and semiconductors

A *conductor* is any material that allows a good electron flow. To be a good conductor, a material must be made of atoms that give off free electrons easily. Also, the atoms must be close enough to each other so that their free-electron orbits overlap (Figure 19–4, top). In the motorcycle's electrical system, copper wires are used to transmit electricity because copper is a good conductor.

An *insulator* is a material whose atoms will not easily part with any of their free electrons (Figure 19–4, bottom). Consequently, insulators will not conduct current. The copper wire in a motorcycle electrical system is covered with an insulator (or *insulation,* as we ordinarily call it) which makes sure that the current does not "leak" out before it gets to its desired destination. Examples of materials that make good insulators are plastic and rubber.

A *semiconductor* is a unique type of material that passes current only under certain conditions. A familiar semiconductor is the diode used in charging systems. It is made of a tiny chip of a pure material with a controlled impurity coating it. The result of this construction is that the diode passes electric current only in one direction. We shall consider the operation of semiconductors in a later section.

ELECTRICAL TERMS

In order to measure and understand electricity, the motorcycle technician must understand the meaning and relationship of a number of electrical terms. These terms are relatively simple, but they are the foundation for all electrical diagnosis and testing.

Voltage (Volt) (V)

We can illustrate electrical voltage by the analogy of water flow. In order to have a flow of water in a water hose, a pressure is necessary. Similarly, in order to have an electron flow in an electrical system, an electrical "pressure" is necessary. This pressure or, to be more technical, potential, that pushes electrons is called *voltage.* Water pressure is measured in pounds per square inch; electrical pressure is measured in volts. The letter symbol for the volt is the letter V.

Voltage is a source of potential energy that exists when unequal numbers of electrons are present in a system. Voltage or volts always describe a *potential difference* existing in an electrical system. To illustrate, the voltage of your house wiring may be 110 volts. This voltage is present even though the household appliances may not be using any of it; the voltage "stands by" until an appliance is switched to the "on" position. Similarly, a motorcycle storage battery provides a voltage potential of 12 volts that exists even when all the electrical devices on the motorcycle are off. Thus, the relation between voltage and electron flow is as follows: voltage can exist without electron flow, but electron flow cannot exist without voltage.

Current (Ampere) (A)

Let's go back to the example of the water hose. A unit of measure of the rate of water flow is gallons per minute (or per hour). In an electrical system we are interested in the rate of electron flow, which is called *current.* Current is measured in *amperes* or *amps,* denoted by the letter A. One ampere is equal to 6.28 billion electrons passing a given point per second. Again, current cannot flow unless a voltage is present.

Resistance (Ohm) (Ω)

The diameter of a water hose affects the amount of water that will be able to flow through it in a given amount of time. A smaller hose will provide more resistance to the flow of water. In a similar fashion, there is a resistance to electron flow in an electrical system. *Resistance* is the opposition offered by a conducting material to the free flow of electrons. The unit of resistance is the ohm, denoted by the Greek letter Ω (uppercase omega).

When current runs into a resistance, the electrons must work harder to get through. This extra work creates heat and reduces flow, since some of the energy is used up as heat.

The relationship between pressure in volts, current flow in amperes, and resistance in ohms is known as *Ohm's law,* which states that, given the values of any two of these parameters, we can calculate the value of the third parameter; i.e.,

Ohm's law
$$\text{Amperes} = \text{volts} \div \text{ohms}$$
$$\text{Volts} = \text{amperes} \times \text{ohms}$$
$$\text{Ohms} = \text{volts} \div \text{amperes}$$

Circuits

A circuit is a path or network of paths that will allow current to flow to do some work. Any circuit, no matter how complicated, is made up of several essential elements. A single circuit is shown in Figure 19–5. A circuit must always have a source of electrical voltage—in this illustration, a battery. Any electrical device in the circuit, like a lightbulb, will offer resistance to the current flow. Wires or conductors connect the battery and light bulb together. In sum, the elements of the circuit are a voltage source (battery), a resistance unit (lightbulb) or other device, and conductors (wires) that connect the voltage to the resistance.

In order for current to flow in a circuit, the path must be unbroken. In Figure 19–5 an unbroken path is created when the two ends of the wire are connected to the battery.

Types of circuits

The two types of electrical circuits commonly used on motorcycles are the *series circuit* and the *parallel circuit.*

Series Circuit

In a series circuit, shown in Figure 19–6, the current flow has only one path to follow. Current flows from the battery through the switch, through the three lamps, and then back

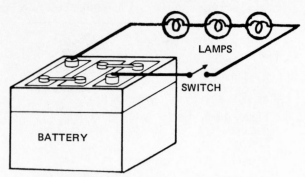

Figure 19–6. A series circuit. *(Honda Motor Co., Ltd.)*

to the battery. Note that in the figure current cannot yet flow because the open switch does not allow the current a complete path back to the battery. This circuit is called an *open circuit* and illustrates an important principle: any time there is a break in the circuit, either intentional or accidental, current cannot flow.

If we close the switch, we provide a complete path for current to flow. The voltage created by the battery causes electrons to flow through the conductors, through the light bulbs, and back to the battery. With the switch closed, the light bulbs will light.

If one of the bulbs should burn out or be removed from its socket, the circuit would be broken and current would not be able to flow. None of the bulbs would then light. This is true of all series circuits: the current must pass through all the electrical devices one after the other; if any device is inoperative, it will act like a switch and open the entire circuit.

Parallel Circuit

A parallel circuit, shown in Figure 19–7, provides two or more paths for current flow. Thus, if one lamp should burn out or be removed from its socket (leaving the circuit path open), the current could still take another path and go through the other lamps, and they would burn normally.

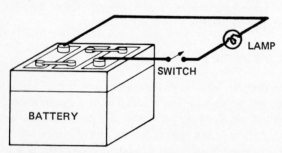

Figure 19–5. A single electrical circuit. When the two ends of the wire are connected to the battery, the bulb will light. *(Honda Motor Co., Ltd.)*

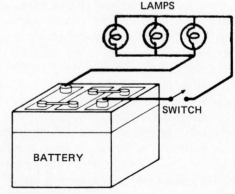

Figure 19–7. A parallel circuit. *(Honda Motor Co., Ltd.)*

Again, of course, the switch must be closed to complete the circuit.

Most motorcycle electrical circuits are a combination of a series and a parallel circuit. Notice that in Figure 19–7 the switch is in series with the complete circuit. The parallel section of the circuit operates like a parallel circuit, and the series section of the circuit functions the same as a series circuit.

One-Wire Circuit

The circuits we have examined so far use two wires to carry current to the battery or to complete the circuit. In motorcycles, however, there is very little need for two wires since the motorcycle frame and engine, which are made of metal, can be used as a single conductor to form a part of a circuit. Thus, most circuits in a motorcycle are constructed from a single wire. One-wire circuits, of course, cut down on the complexity of the wiring. Ground symbols ( ) indicate attachment to the frame or engine. A return wire is necessary only when the electrical components are mounted in such a manner that they are insulated from the frame and engine. A one-wire circuit with a ground connection is shown in Figure 19–8.

MAGNETISM

Magnetism is a force that is involved in the operation of many types of the motorcycle's electrical components. The ignition coil, magneto, and starting and charging systems are just a few examples of electrical components that utilize the fundamental principles of magnetism. A motorcycle technician must understand these principles.

Magnetic fields

You have probably used an ordinary bar magnet to pick up small metal objects. The attractive force which allows the magnet to pick up objects may be described as a *field*. The

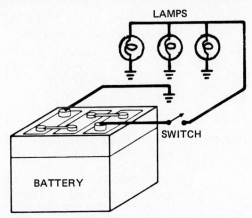

Figure 19–8. A one-wire circuit. *(Honda Motor Co., Ltd.)*

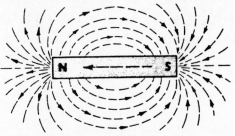

LINES OF MAGNETIC FORCE

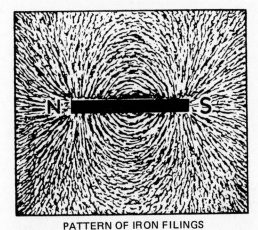

PATTERN OF IRON FILINGS

Figure 19–9. Iron filings (bottom) show the lines of force around a magnet. *(U.S. Navy)*

field surrounding a magnet is invisible, but it may be observed by a simple experiment. If a piece of paper is placed on top of a bar magnet, and iron filings are sprinkled on the paper, the filings will align themselves in a pattern around the bar magnet.

The pattern of the iron filings will show that the magnetic force is strongest at or near the ends of the magnet (Figure 19–9). These areas are called *magnetic poles*. Since one end of the magnet tends to have its lines of force point toward the north, like a compass, it is called the north pole of the magnet. Similarly, the other end is called the south pole of the magnet. If the bar magnet were broken in two, each piece would have its own north and south pole, and this would be true no matter how many times the magnet were broken.

The experiment with iron filings leads to some other important conclusions regarding magnetic fields. The filings show that the magnetic lines of force are closed loops and do not cross each other. The experiment also demonstrates that the magnetic fields will pass through paper. In fact, they will pass through any material: there is no known insulator for magnetic lines of force. Some materials, however, will allow the lines of force to pass through them more readily than others. A material that will not pass lines of magnetic force easily has what is called a *high reluctance;* a material that will allow the easy passage of the

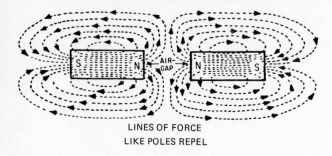

LINES OF FORCE
LIKE POLES REPEL

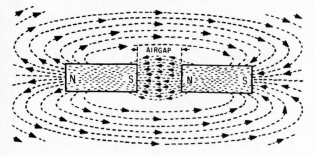

UNLIKE POLES ATTRACT

Figure 19–10. Like poles (top) repel; unlike poles (bottom) attract. Lines of magnetic force are shown. *(U.S. Navy)*

lines of force has a *low reluctance*. Iron is a material with a low reluctance, whereas air has a high reluctance.

Another important characteristic of magnetic lines of force that you have probably observed at one time or another is that if you put two bar magnets close to each other, there is a force of attraction between the two unlike poles and a force of repulsion between the two like poles. This observation is generalized in the principle that unlike or dissimilar poles attract each other and like or similar poles repel each other (Figure 19–10).

Electromagnetism

The relationship between electricity and magnetism is known as *electromagnetism*. From both observation and theory, we find that a conductor that has current passing through it develops a magnetic field. In the case of a wire, as the electric current flows through the wire, it sets up a magnetic field surrounding the wire that is describable as magnetic lines of force encircling the wire, as shown in Figure 19–11.

If we wind the wire in a coil, as shown in Figure 19–12, the magnetic lines of force form a pattern which encircles all adjoining loops of the wire. A magnetic field is established which resembles that of a bar magnet, though many of the lines of force are dissipated between the loops of the coil.

If we were to insert a soft iron core into the wire coil, the lines of magnetic force inside the coil would tend to travel through the iron as shown in Figure 19–13, because it provides a better magnetic path than air. This property of iron, called *permeability,* concentrates the lines of force in the center of the coil, strengthening the magnetic field. The combination of an iron core in a coil wire thus becomes an electromagnet.

When the electric current is switched off, the lines of force collapse and the soft iron core immediately loses its induced magnetism. The reason that a soft iron core is used to produce a temporary electromagnet is because a bar of steel, once magnetized, will retain its magnetism indefinitely. The bar of steel thus becomes a permanent magnet. Soft iron is the conductor of choice for the core of a temporary electromagnet.

ELECTRONICS

Electronics is a branch of electricity concerned with the flow of electrons through semiconductor material. Semiconductors are tiny solid-state devices that are made primarily from crystals of germanium, silicon, boron, and/or phosphorus. In their pure form, these crystals are not good conductors of electricity. The state of the crystals is changed by adding an impurity causing them to become a semiconductor. A semiconductor may be considered half

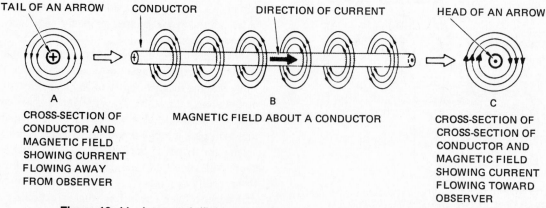

TAIL OF AN ARROW   CONDUCTOR   DIRECTION OF CURRENT   HEAD OF AN ARROW

A
CROSS-SECTION OF CONDUCTOR AND MAGNETIC FIELD SHOWING CURRENT FLOWING AWAY FROM OBSERVER

B
MAGNETIC FIELD ABOUT A CONDUCTOR

C
CROSS-SECTION OF CROSS-SECTION OF CONDUCTOR AND MAGNETIC FIELD SHOWING CURRENT FLOWING TOWARD OBSERVER

Figure 19–11. A magnetic field surrounds a current-carrying wire. *(U.S. Air Force)*

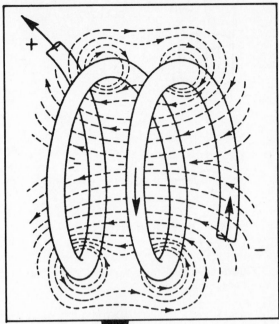

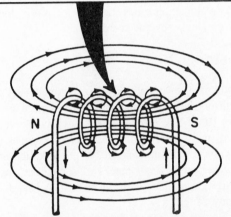

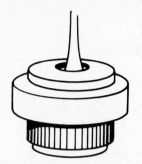

Figure 19–14. A diode. *(U.S. Navy)*

many different types of semiconductor devices, only two types are commonly used in a motorcycle's electrical system: the diode and the transistor.

Diode

A diode (Figure 19–14) is a tiny semiconductor device that will allow current to flow through it freely in one direction, but offers an extremely high resistance to current flow in the opposite direction. Because of this characteristic, diodes may be used to control the direction of current flow, and so they are commonly found in motorcycle charging systems.

A diode is constructed from two wafer-thin chips of semiconductor material. One of the wafers is usually silicon with phosphorus added as an impurity; the other wafer is usually silicon with boron added as an impurity. The two wafers are joined together by a diffusion process. In this process, the semiconductor materials are mounted in a tiny copper case and a connector called a stem is attached to one of the semiconductor wafers at one end and exits the case for connection into an electrical circuit. The other semiconductor wafer is attached to the bottom of the diode case. A cross section of a diode is shown in Figure 19–15.

Figure 19–12. Magnetic field around a coil of wire. The detail shows the field in two adjoining loops of wire.

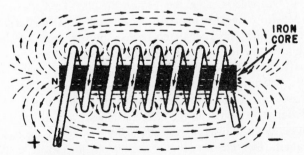

Figure 19–13. Magnetic field in an electromagnet formed by an iron core and a coil. *(U.S. Navy)*

conductor and half insulator. That is, under certain conditions the semiconductor acts like a conductor, and under other conditions it acts like an insulator. While there are

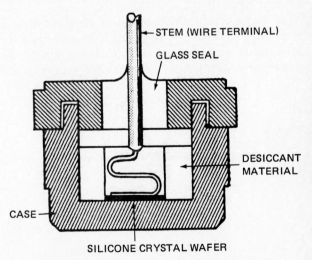

STEM (WIRE TERMINAL)

GLASS SEAL

DESICCANT MATERIAL

CASE

SILICONE CRYSTAL WAFER

Figure 19–15. Cross-sectional view of a diode. *(U.S. Navy)*

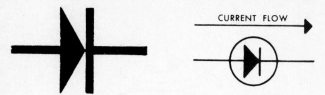

Figure 19–16. The diode symbol shows the direction of current flow.

Since moisture adversely affects the semiconductor material, a moisture-absorbing material called a *desiccant* is located inside the diode case. A glass seal around the diode stem is also used to prevent moisture from entering. During operation, a great deal of heat is developed inside the diode, so the diode case is often mounted to a metal heat sink to dissipate the heat.

Electrically, one of the semiconductor wafers inside the diode is connected into a circuit through the stem, a connection that makes up half of the diode circuit. The other wafer is connected to the case of the diode, forming the other half of the circuit. The only job the diode has is to control the direction of current flow. In Unit 20, we shall examine several circuits in which diodes perform this important function.

The symbol for a diode used in a wiring diagram is shown in Figure 19–16. The arrow on the symbol shows the direction in which the diode will permit current flow. Current will not flow through the diode semiconductor material in the other direction.

Zener diode

The zener diode is a specially designed type of diode that has a large number of extra current carriers that allow it to conduct current in the reverse direction without damage if the proper circuit design is used. A zener diode symbol is shown in Figure 19–17.

The unique operating chracteristic of the zener diode is that it will not conduct current in the reverse direction below a certain predetermined value of reverse voltage. As an example, a certain zener diode may not conduct current

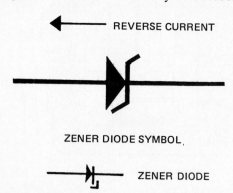

Figure 19–17. Symbol for a Zener diode.

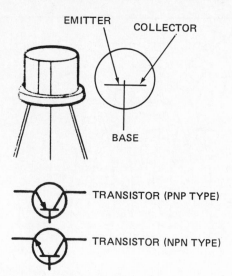

Figure 19–18. A transistor and its symbol. (Top: Ford Motor Co.)

if the reverse voltage is below 12 volts, but when the reverse bias voltage becomes 12 volts or more, the diode suddenly conducts reverse current.

Transistors

A transistor is a very small semiconductor device used to control current flow. A transistor and its symbol are shown in Figure 19–18. A three-element device, the transistor consists of two diodes back to back or two diodes sharing a common base material (Figure 19–19). Like the diode, it is constructed from small pieces of semiconductor material, usually germanium with an impurity such as iridium or antimony added.

The transistor has a base made of very thin material to which a metallic ring is connected. One of the transistor circuit connections is attached to the ring. On either side of the base is another small piece of semiconductor material. One side is called the *emitter*, the other the *collector*. The semiconductor materials are housed in a small case from which three small connectors project: one for the emitter, one for the base, and one for the collector.

The transistor has a special characteristic that makes it very useful in controlling current flow, namely, that the main current in a circuit of which it is a part cannot pass through the emitter to the collector unless a small amount of current is allowed to pass through the emitter to the base circuit. This characteristic makes it possible for a small aount of current to trigger or switch on a larger amount of current.

WIRING DIAGRAMS

Each motorcycle manufacturer provides wiring diagrams to serve as electrical system roadmaps for the motorcycle

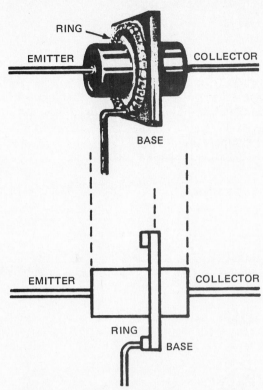

Figure 19–19. Construction of a transistor. *(Delco-Remy Division, General Motors Corp.)*

technician. The diagrams show how the various electrical devices in the motorcycle are connected together with wires, and consequently, they help the motorcycle technician trace or diagnose circuit problems.

Wiring diagrams are usually found in the shop service manual. Some motorcycle manufacturers have a separate manual just for wiring diagrams. The typical wiring diagram book is divided into a section for each motorcycle.

Each wiring diagram is made up of a number of symbols which represent electrical components connected together with lines which represent wires. The diagrams have a color code that corresponds to the color-coded wires on a motorcycle that are used to help the technician trace a circuit. Due to the great number of wires, colors are combined with different-colored stripes, or *tracers*, to designate all the circuits. The wiring diagram may be printed using the same colors as the wires, but, more commonly, it is printed in black and white. It is therefore necessary to print a key on the diagram to explain to the technician what color each wire will be on the motorcycle. On most wiring diagrams, the name of the colors are printed directly on the wire. In the wiring diagram shown in Figure 19–20, the solid-colored wires are identified by one or two letters, such as Gr for green, B for black, and so on; wires identified by letter combinations separated by a slash, such as Y/R, have their solid color denoted by the letter or let-

ters to the left of the slash (Y for yellow) and their tracer (stripe) color denoted by the letter or letters to the right of the slash (R for red).

The electrical components connected together by the wires may be drawn pictorially or may be represented by a symbol. The diagram in Figure 19–20 uses a number of symbols to represent components. Unfortunately, electrical symbols are not standardized from one manufacturer to another. However, the symbols used on most wiring diagrams are sometimes explained on the legend found on the diagram or at the front of the wiring diagram book.

USING BASIC TEST INSTRUMENTS

To troubleshoot most electrical problems, you will need to know how to use a wiring diagram and some basic test instruments. The basic electrical test instruments are jumper wires, test lights, and the multimeter. We shall shortly describe the operation and use of each of these instruments.

Opens, shorts, and grounds

The three problems commonly found in motorcycle electrical systems are described by the terms *open, short* and *ground*. You will be using electrical instruments to determine whether any part of a circuit is open, shorted, or grounded.

A break or interruption in an electrical circuit is called an *open*. A break in the wiring from the source of power to an electrical unit, or within the unit itself, will not allow current to flow. The break results in an open circuit and a complete loss of power in that circuit. An open circuit may occur as the result of a broken wire within a wiring harness, loose connections at terminals of electrical components, broken wiring inside electrical components, or poor connections between component and ground.

When a circuit is accidentally completed so that current bypasses part of the normal circuit, we call it a *short* or *short circuit*. When wiring insulation fails and two wires make contact, there is a short circuit. Then, current that is required to power an electrical component goes to the wrong place, and the component will not operate.

When current bypasses the normal circuit and goes directly to ground, the electrical components in that circuit will not function. A *ground* may be caused by worn insulation on a wire that allows it to touch a metal part on the motorcycle. It may also be caused by deposits of oil, dirt, corrosion, or moisture around connections or terminals. These deposits can provide a path for current to flow to ground.

DS80X

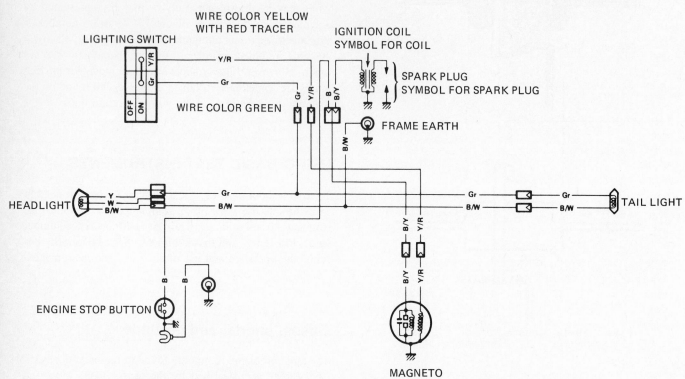

Figure 19–20. Colors of wires are identified on a wiring diagram. This one shows the entire electrical system of a motorcycle. *(U.S. Suzuki Motor Corp.)*

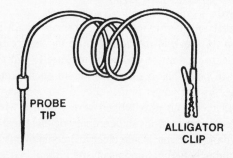

Figure 19–21. A jumper wire. *(Ford Motor Co.)*

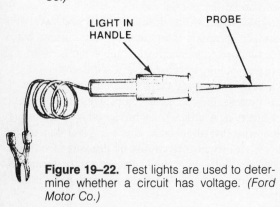

Figure 19–22. Test lights are used to determine whether a circuit has voltage. *(Ford Motor Co.)*

Jumper wire

A jumper wire is the simplest of electrical testing devices, but it can be a very valuable tool. It is merely a wire (Figure 19–21) that is used to bypass or "jump" sections of a circuit. The simplest jumper wire is a length of multistrand wire with an alligator clip at one end and a probe at the other. Most motorcycle technicians have several different styles of jumper wires in several different lengths.

Test light

The test light (Figure 19–22) comes in different styles, but each has three main parts: a groundclip, a probe or alligator clip, and a light. The test light is used by connecting the ground clip to a good ground and the probe or alligator clip wherever it is necessary to detect voltage. The probe is used to penetrate wire insulation and make contact with the wire, without making a large hole in the insulation. If voltage is present, the light in the handle will light; if there is no voltage, the light will not light.

Multimeter

The multimeter is used to measure voltage, resistance, and amperage. There are two basic types of multimeter: the electronic or digital readout type and the movable coil type. The digital readout instrument (Figure 19–23) uses solid-state electronic circuitry to determine readings and display the results in digital form. This type of instrument is the most accurate of all, because no judgment is required on the observer's part. Additionally, most multimeters have such features as automatic range adjustment, automatic polarity adjustment, and accuracy to several decimal points.

The movable coil type of multimeter uses a scale and needle to indicate the measurement (Figure 19–24). Depending on internal wiring and external connection, the meter can be made to indicate volts, ohms, or amperes.

In measuring voltage (with either style of multimeter), first select the voltage or volt setting on the instrument knob. When used as a voltmeter, the instrument must be connected across—i.e., in parallel with—the circuit being tested. There are two wires or leads connected to the multimeter, a black one marked as negative and a nonblack one (usually red) marked as positive. Always connect the negative lead to the negative side of the circuit (to ground or nearest the ground side of the circuit) and the positive lead to the positive side of the circuit (to the power source or nearest the power source).

In measuring amperage, select the amp or amperage setting on the instrument knob and connect the multimeter in a series with a circuit. The multimeter must never be connected in parallel with a battery because the ammeter has a very low resistance and connecting it in parallel like a voltmeter would damage it. Some ammeters have different scales or ranges. A selector switch on the instrument changes the value of the shunt resistor used in the meter circuit. Always start measuring a circuit using the highest range on the meter. To connect the device to the circuit, connect the black or negative lead to the negative side of the circuit and the red or positive lead to the positive side of the circuit.

To measure the resistance of a circuit, select the ohm or ohmmeter position on the multimeter. In ohmmeter mode, the internal circuit of the instrument has a resistance and a power source (usually a battery) that allows a small amount of current to pass through the device being tested. The amount of current that flows through the unit tested is directly related to the amount of resistance, the value of which the meter shows in ohms.

Since the ohmmeter uses its own power source, the device to be tested must always be removed from the circuit. Note that an ohmmeter must never be connected to an external voltage source because it will then be damaged.

Before using the movable-coil-type ohmmeter, the meter

Figure 19–23. A digital-type multimeter. *(Beckman Industrial Corp.)*

Figure 19–24. A movable-coil-type multimeter. *(A.W. Sperry Instruments, Inc.)*

needle must be "zeroed," i.e., calibrated to read zero. Unlike the voltage and amperage scale, the ohms scale reads from right to left. When the meter is not in use, the needle rests against the left or full-scale side of the scale. Consequently when the leads are not connected to a circuit, the needle shows infinite resistance—a full-scale reading (clear to the left).

When the leads are touching, the meter should read zero resistance (clear to the right). To accurately zero the needle, turn the "zero needle," "zero ohms," or "ohms adjust" knob. Now, when the probes are connected to an unknown resistance, current will flow through the needle coil and the needle will register.

KEY TERMS

Atom: a small particle of which all matter is composed.

Circuit: a complete path for electrical current flow.

Conductor: a material that allows electrical current flow.

Current: the flow of electrons in an electrical circuit; measured in amperes.

Diode: a semiconductor that allows current flow in only one direction.

Electricity: the flow of electrons from one atom to another.

Electromagnetism: magnetism produced by an electric current.

Insulator: a material that prevents the flow of electricity.

Resistance: the opposition offered to the free flow of electrons; measured in ohms.

Semiconductor: a tiny, solid-state device that is half conductor and half insulator.

Transistor: a semiconductor device used to control current flow.

Voltage: the source of potential energy in an electrical system; the force that pushes the electrons; measured in volts.

CHECKUP

1. Define electricity.
2. What is an insulator?
3. What is a conductor?
4. What is a semiconductor?
5. What is voltage in an electrical circuit?
6. What is amperage in an electrical circuit?
7. What is resistance in an electrical circuit?
8. What is necessary to have a complete circuit?
9. What are the two basic types of circuits?
10. What is a one-wire circuit and how does it work?
11. Describe a magnetic field.
12. What is an electromagnet?
13. What is the purpose of a diode?
14. What is the purpose of a transistor?
15. How are the wires on a wiring diagram identified?
16. What is the purpose of a jumper wire?
17. What is an open?
18. What is a short?
19. What is ground?
20. What three measurements can be made with a multimeter?

DISCUSSION TOPICS AND ACTIVITIES

1. Use a wiring diagram for a motorcycle and try to identify each wire and electrical part on the motorcycle.
2. Use a battery, wires, switch, and light to build a simple circuit. Can you make the light work? (*Caution:* Use a low-voltage power source—12 volts or less.)

The battery is an electrochemical device that provides a source of stored energy to operate the electrical components of the motorcycle when the engine is not running. Some motorcycles do not require batteries. For example, dirt bikes, especially those which have no lighting equipment, do not require an energy reservoir; their ignition current is supplied by a magneto. Thus, these motorcycles are designed without batteries or starter motors for simplicity and to reduce weight.

A battery is required on all motorcycles equipped with starter motors, because the starter motor must operate when the engine is at rest. A battery is also necessary, or at least helpful, if a large amount of lighting current must be delivered at idle speed. When the engine is running, the charging system takes over. This charging system works to restore the chemical energy used by the battery. It develops all the power required to operate the motorcycle's electrical system once the engine is running. In this unit we describe how the battery and charging system operate and how they are serviced.

JOB COMPETENCY OBJECTIVES

When you finish reading and studying this unit, you should be able to:

1. Describe the construction of the motorcycle storage battery.

2. Explain the chemical operation of the motorcycle storage battery.

3. Describe the parts and operation of the alternator.

4. Explain the purpose of the charging system rectifier and regulator.

5. Perform a visual inspection of the battery and a specific gravity test on it.

BATTERY CONSTRUCTION AND OPERATION

Some time ago it was discovered that if two dissimilar strips of metal conductors or plates were immersed in an acid solution that was also a conductor, the acid would attack one of the plates of metal. As the metal was being eaten away, electrons were released that would enter the acid and become absorbed into the other plate. This discovery led to the development of the battery.

A simple battery or cell may be constructed from a container filled with an acid called an *electrolyte*. The electrolyte is made from sulphuric acid mixed with water. Two metal plates are immersed into the acid, and, as noted, the acid attacks the material in one of the plates. Electrons are then released and transferred to the other plate. The plate that absorbs the excess electrons is called the *negative*

BATTERY AND CHARGING SYSTEM OPERATION AND SERVICING

plate; the plate that looses electrons is called the *positive plate*. Figure 20–1 illustrates a basic, one-cell battery.

When the negative plate is full of electrons, the battery is charged. Because of their mutual negative charge, the electrons on this plate tend to repel each other and attach themselves to (positively charged) atoms which are short of electrons. The battery thus has an electrical potential or voltage: it is capable of providing electrical energy, but not until its electrons are released.

If we connect the plates together with a conductor (Figure 20–2), current flows from one plate through the electrolyte to the other plate, and then through the conductor to complete the circuit. The battery then discharges, converting chemical energy into electrical energy.

As electrons are pulled away from the negative plates, the battery becomes weaker and weaker. Eventually, there will be no more current flow in the conductor because the battery is completely discharged. The chemical action inside the battery is still going on, but as the battery is dis-

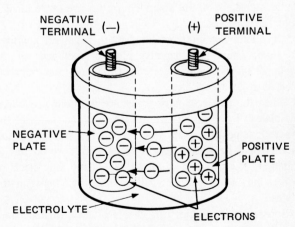

Figure 20–1. A basic one-cell battery. *(Kawasaki Motors Corp. U.S.A.)*

297

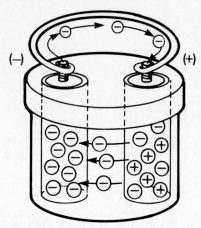

Figure 20–2. When a conductor is connected between the terminals, current flows between the plates. *(Kawasaki Motor Corp. U.S.A.)*

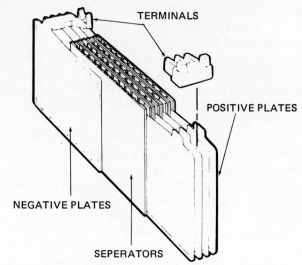

Figure 20–3. Cell plate groups and separators. *(Kawasaki Motor Corp. U.S.A.)*

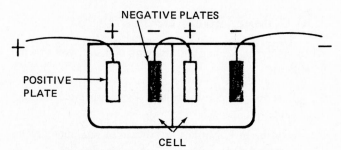

Figure 20–4. Connecting cells in series allows the voltages to add together. *(Ford Motor Co.)*

charged, the electrolyte becomes weaker and weaker. In the process, the negative and positive plates change composition chemically until they are nearly the same composition.

Battery construction

The motorcycle storage battery uses the same principles as described for the basic one-cell battery. However, it is designed to provide 6 or 12 volts of electrical energy and to deliver this energy for the longest possible time. In order to accomplish these tasks, the battery must have more than one cell.

Each cell of the battery consists of a group of positive plates, a group of negative plates, and a set of separators (Figure 20–3). All the negative plates in the cell are connected together and are then connected to a negative terminal. The positive plates are also connected together and then connected to a positive terminal. Plates connected to the negative terminal of the battery are made of plain lead. Plates connected to the positive terminal are made of lead peroxide.

The plates are arranged alternately: negative, positive, negative. There is a negative plate at each side of the group of plates; therefore, the cell has one more negative plate than positive plates.

When the two groups of plates are positioned together, the plates of one group are very close to the plates of the other. If a positive plate were to touch a negative plate, there would be a direct short and the cell would fail to function. The problem is solved by placing thin sheets of porous insulation material called *separators* between the plates.

Separators are made from sheets of resin-treated paper and fiberglass or other nonconductive materials. They are porous to permit the passage of electrolyte, at the same

time insulating the lead plates from each other to prevent short circuiting.

The plate-and-separator assembly is installed in a container called the battery case. When electrolyte is added, the plates, separators, and electrolyte become a cell. No matter how large or small it is, one cell is capable of developing only about 2 volts of electrical potential. But a motorcycle's electrical system requires either 6 or 12 volts. Accordingly, a case is made to hold either three or six cells. In this arrangement, the negative plates of one cell are connected to the positive plates of a neighbor cell by a connector. When the cells are finally connected together in series, as shown in Figure 20–4, their voltages add up. Three 2-volt cells are connected in series to make a 6-volt battery (Figure 20–5), and six 2-volt cells are connected in series to make a 12-volt battery (Figure 20–6).

The case on most motorcycle batteries is made of a clear plastic so that the level of electrolyte can be seen. Terminals exit both ends of the battery (see Figures 20–5 and 20–6) and are identifed as positive or negative by the symbols + or −, or by the abbreviations "Pos." or "Neg."

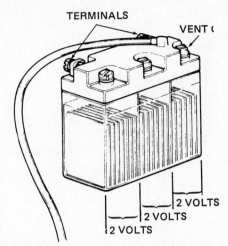

Figure 20–5. Three 2-volt cells connected together to make a 6-volt battery. *(Honda Motor Co., Ltd.)*

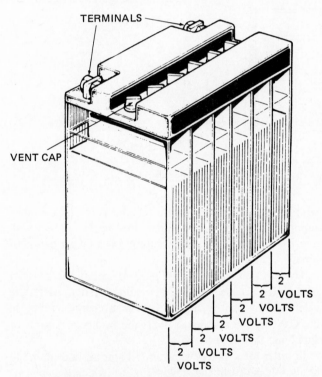

Figure 20–6. Six 2-volt cells connected together for a 12-volt battery. *(Honda Motor Co., Ltd.)*

The markings are typically located on the case, near the terminal.

The top of the battery is covered with a one-piece plastic cover that is bonded to the case by heat sealing. The cover usually has threaded holes over each cell for a vent cap, which may be removed for periodic inspection and refilling of the water in the cells. The cap, which screws into the cover, has a vent that allows hydrogen and oxygen gas to escape during charging.

Battery operation

As mentioned earlier, the battery is an electrochemical device for converting chemical energy into electrical energy. Electrical energy in a battery is produced by chemical reactions between the active materials of the dissimilar plates and the electrolyte.

As we shall see later, some battery servicing techniques are based on an inspection of the battery chemicals. For this reason, a motorcycle technician must understand the basic chemical changes that take place in a battery during charging and discharging.

Chemists assign letters and numbers to different kinds of materials to identify them. The active material in the positive battery plate is lead peroxide. Its chemical symbol is PbO_2. The active material in the negative plate is spongy lead, with a chemical symbol of Pb. The electrolyte in a fully charged battery consists of a mixture of about 36 percent sulphuric acid (H_2SO_4) and 64 percent water (H_2O).

The chemical action in a cell during charging and discharging is shown in Figure 20–7. During the discharge phase, when a load is connected across the positive and negative terminals, the PbO_2 on the positive plate loses its oxygen (O_2) to the hydrogen (H_2) in the acid, resulting in water (H_2O) becoming a larger part of the electrolyte. At the same time, the remaining lead (Pb) on the positive plate combines with the sulfate (SO_4) that remains of the broken-down acid to make lead sulfate ($PbSO_4$). On the negative plate, the abundance of SO_4 liberated by the action of the positive plate is also combining with the lead (Pb) of the negative plate to produce lead sulfate ($PbSO_4$).

As the cell discharges, the plates become more and more the same, and the electrolyte becomes more and more plain water. Electrons are supplied to the negative plate to replace those being drawn off into the circuit as long as the plates are dissimilar and the electrolyte does not revert to water.

When the motorcycle charging system or a battery charger is connected to the battery, the chemical action in the cell is reversed. When a current is applied in reverse direction to the discharge direction, the lead sulfate of both plates again reverts to its original pure lead (Pb) and sulfate (SO_4). Water in the electrolyte is split into hydrogen (H) and oxygen (O), some of which leaves the electrolyte as a gas (the reason batteries sometimes explode). As the SO_4 leaves the plates, it recombined with hydrogen and again become sulfuric acid (H_2SO_4). Free oxygen in the electrolyte combines with lead on the positive plate to form lead peroxide (PbO_2).

The material on the positive plates and that on the negative plates become chemically similar during discharge, as the lead sulfate accumulates. This condition accounts for the loss of cell voltage, since any voltage developed depends upon there being a difference between the two mate-

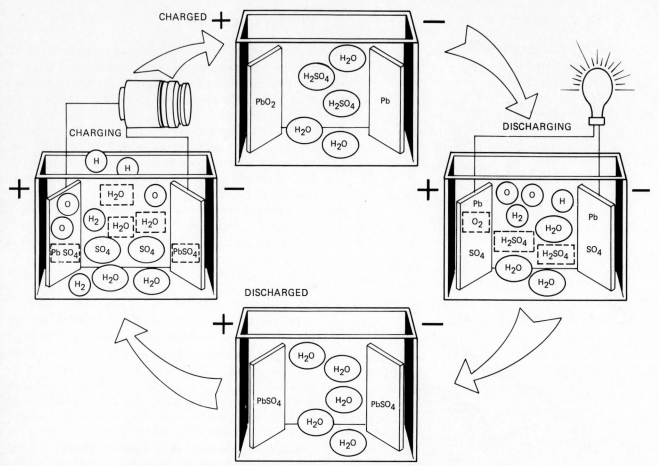

Figure 20–7. Chemical action in a battery during charging and discharging. *(Ford Motor Co.)*

rials. Discharging and recharging the cell over and over again will eventually wear out the components, since the chemical reversals are never 100% effective. Finally, the cell will reach a stage where the plates cannot be made dissimilar through the application of an electric current.

Battery rating

Battery performance is rated according to a variety of laboratory test procedures that have been established by the battery manufacturers. Every manufacturer uses the same procedures so that one manufacturer's battery may be compared with another's. When a battery is replaced, it is important that the replacement battery have a comparable performance rating.

While all three- or six-cell storage batteries have the same voltage, they may differ widely in capacity. *Capacity* is a measure of how long a battery can supply current. The capacity of a battery is determined by the amount of active material and electrolyte in each cell. The number of plates and the size of the plates a battery has will determine how long chemical activity can continue in a cell. A battery

with a few small plates will discharge very quickly when supplying a high current. On the other hand, a battery with many large plates can supply current for a longer period of time.

The most common method used to specify the capacity of a battery is the ampere-hour rating (AHR). AHRs are calculated by multiplying the battery discharge current, in amperes, by the number of hours the battery is capable of supplying that current.

In order for a battery's advertised ampere-hour rating to be useful, the particular time period for which the ampere-hour rating was measured must be known. If a battery is slowly discharged, producing low-amperage current over a period of many hours, it will produce far more ampere-hours of current than if it is discharged at a very rapid rate, such as occurs when it is operating a starter motor.

Most motorcycle batteries are rated on a 10-hour discharge rate. Based on this rate, a 12 ampere-hour battery will deliver 1.2 amperes of electrical current for 10 hours. (1.2 A × 10 hours = 12 ampere-hours.) It is not true, of course, that the battery will deliver 12 amperes for 1 hour; more likely, it would deliver only about 6 amperes for that length of time.

Yuasa 12N12A-4A-1 Battery

Number preceding letter "N" indicates battery voltage. Number immediately following "N" indicates ampere-hour capacity. Other symbols identify the physical construction of the battery.

12N12A-4A-1 CODE INTERPRETATION

12—— Nominal voltage (12 volts)
N —— Initial for Nippon (Japan)
12—— Ampere-hour capacity at 10 hour discharge rate (12 AH)
A —— JIS battery identification symbol
4 —— Terminal position code
A—— Vent tube position code
1 —— Yuasa battery identification number

6N6-3B CODE INTERPRETATION:

6 —— Nominal voltage (6 volts)
N —— Initial for Nippon (Japan)
6 —— Ampere-hour capacity at 10 hour discharge rate (6 AH)
3 —— Terminal position code
B —— Vent tube position code

Figure 20–8. Typical battery identification code. *(Honda Motor Co., Ltd.)*

The rating of a battery is often specified on a code printed on the side of the battery, as are other technical features of the battery. Since each manufacturer has its own code, you must have the technical literature for any particular battery in order to understand it. One manufacturer's code and interpretation are shown in Figure 20–8.

CHARGING SYSTEM OPERATION

The function of the charging system is to generate electrical energy to power the motorcycle's electrical system and to charge the battery. The main components of the charging system are the battery, alternator, rectifier, and voltage regulator (Figure 20–9). The battery works together with the rest of the charging system to supply electrical energy. The charging system as a whole senses the battery's state of charge and works to keep the battery charged.

The *alternator* converts some of the mechanical energy of the engine into electrical energy. It generates electrical energy to supply the demand of the motorcycle's electrical system when the engine is running. In addition, it restores the chemical energy of the battery by sending current through the battery in a direction opposite to the current that flows through it during discharge.

The *rectifier* changes the alternating current developed by the alternator to direct current, which is used to charge the battery and power the electrical equipment.

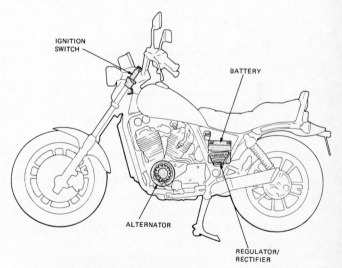

Figure 20–9. Charging system. *(Honda Motor Co., Ltd.)*

The *voltage regulator* senses the output voltage of the alternator and limits it to a safe amount. If this voltage were allowed to become excessively high, the battery and other electrical equipment could be damaged.

The way the battery and alternator work together is shown in Figure 20–10. When the engine is not running, or when its rotational speed is low, the battery is the only source of energy for the electrical system (Figure 20–

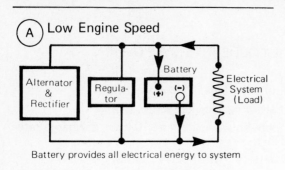

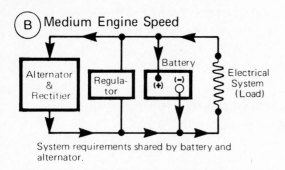

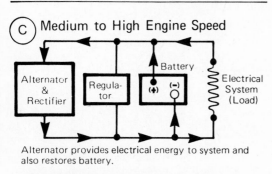

Figure 20–10. The alternator, regulator, and battery work together to power the electrical system. *(Kawasaki Motor Corp. U.S.A.)*

10(a)). As both rotational speed of the engine and the alternator output increase, a speed is reached where the output voltage level of the alternator matches that of the battery. At this point, the battery and the alternator share in providing the current (electrical energy) requirements of the electrical system (Figure 20–10(b)).

During medium to high speed, the alternator supplies energy for the electrical system and also pushes a flow of current through the battery in reverse direction (Figure 20–10(c)). It is this reverse flow of current that enables the battery to be charged during engine operation.

THE ALTERNATOR

The alternator is an alternating-current generator that uses the principles of conductors moving in a magnetic field to

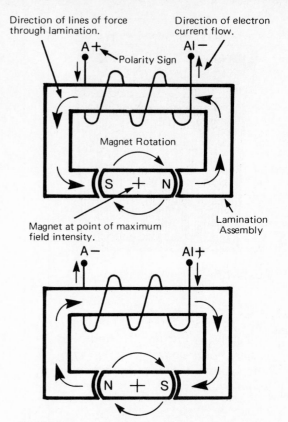

Figure 20–11. A basic alternator. *(Kawasaki Motors Corp. U.S.A.)*

develop electrical energy. The alternator is sometimes called an AC/generator, a dynamo, or a magneto.

Basic principles of the alternator

A basic alternator can be constructed from a single coil of wire wound around a laminated core made up of a number of thin iron strips past which a single magnet is rotated (Figure 20–11). As the magnet turns, the flow of lines of force between the north and south magnetic poles and through the lamination assembly creates a strong magnetic field around the coil windings. The result (as long as the magnet is rotating) is the generation of voltage and current in the coil winding due to the buildup and collapse of the magnetic field with each 180-degree swing of the magnet.

Since the polarity of the magnetic field that builds up and collapses around the coil changes, the direction of current flow through the coil also changes. This is the reason that the current generated by the alternator is called alternating, or AC, current.

Alternator construction

The simple basic alternator just described used a magnet with two poles and a coil of wire with very few turns. In a practical alternator we want to develop more current, so

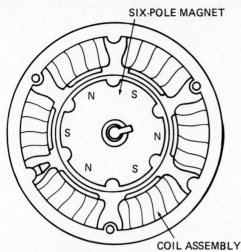

SIX-POLE MAGNET

COIL ASSEMBLY

Figure 20–12. A six-pole alternator. *(Honda Motor Co., Ltd.)*

we use magnets with more poles and coils with many more turns.

If the alternator is equipped with a six-pole rotating magnet and a six-pole soft iron frame, as shown in Figure 20–12, the induced current will reverse every 60 degrees, and a full cycle will be completed every 120 degrees. More current is generated because there are a greater number of generating coils in operation and the magnetic lines of force are cut more frequently.

A motorcycle alternator can be constructed with any even number of poles. It is common practice to use one set of coils to generate ignition current and another set to generate lighting current, or one set of coils to generate the current needed for daytime operation with lights off and additional coils for nighttime operation with lights on.

The alternator consists of two basic parts: a rotating magnet and a set of stationary coils. The rotating magnet assembly is usually driven directly off the end of the crankshaft; the stationary coils are mounted in position next to the rotating magnet. A field coil (Figure 20–13) is used in some alternators. (How the field coil is used to control charging system voltage is described in a subsequent section.)

The alternator can be constructed with the rotating magnet at the center of the coil assemblies or, conversely, with the coil assemblies at the center of the rotating magnet (Figure 20–14). The effect is the same either way.

THE RECTIFIER

As mentioned above, the alternator produces only alternating current and the battery can only be charged by direct current. Consequently, a device called a rectifier (Figure 20–15) that converts alternating current (AC) to direct current (DC) must be installed in the circuit between the alternator and the battery.

Most motorcycle rectifiers are constructed using silicon diodes which act as one-way valves, permitting current flow in one direction and resisting all current flow in the opposite direction. Older rectifiers use selenium plates, which act the same way as a diode.

A single diode inserted in one lead of an alternator circuit (Figure 20–16) is a simple rectifier: current will flow through the load during one half of the AC cycle and will cease during the next half. Since the system rectifies during only half the cycle, we call it a half-wave rectifier. Many motorcycles use half-wave rectifiers.

It is possible to arrange a circuit with four or six diodes to use the current during the entire alternator cycle. The circuit is called a bridge circuit, and the system is called a full-wave rectifier.

A bridge circuit with four diodes is shown in Figure 20–17. When the upper terminal of the alternator coil is at positive (+) polarity, current flows from the bottom (negative) terminal through diode D3, through the load, and then returns to the positive terminal through diode D2. With reversal of current through the coil (change of polarity at the terminals), diodes D1 and D4 start conducting and DC current continues to pass through the load during the second half of the AC cycle.

THE VOLTAGE REGULATOR

The voltage developed by an alternator increases as the speed of the rotor increases. The reason for this relationship is that the lines of force from the rotor cut across the stator windings in the alternator in a shorter period of time. Sufficient voltage must be developed at low speeds to charge the battery and power all the electrical accessories. On the other hand, if unlimited at high speeds, this voltage would increase to a point that the battery would be overcharged and the accessories damaged. The function of the charging system voltage regulator is therefore to limit the alternator voltage to a safe value.

Voltage regulation and the battery

In order for the voltage regulator to protect the battery and accessories, it must sense the battery voltage and limit the alternator voltage accordingly. The voltage regulator, then, senses and is affected by the battery. The battery voltage is in turn affected by a number of things, such as the battery's charging voltage, state of charge, and temperature.

When the battery is being charged by the alternator, the voltage measured across the battery is called the *battery charging voltage*. One component of the battery charging voltage is the *counter-electromotive force*, or CEMF, which is the voltage that is produced within the battery mainly by chemical means. The CEMF opposes the battery charging voltage and is the voltage which the bat-

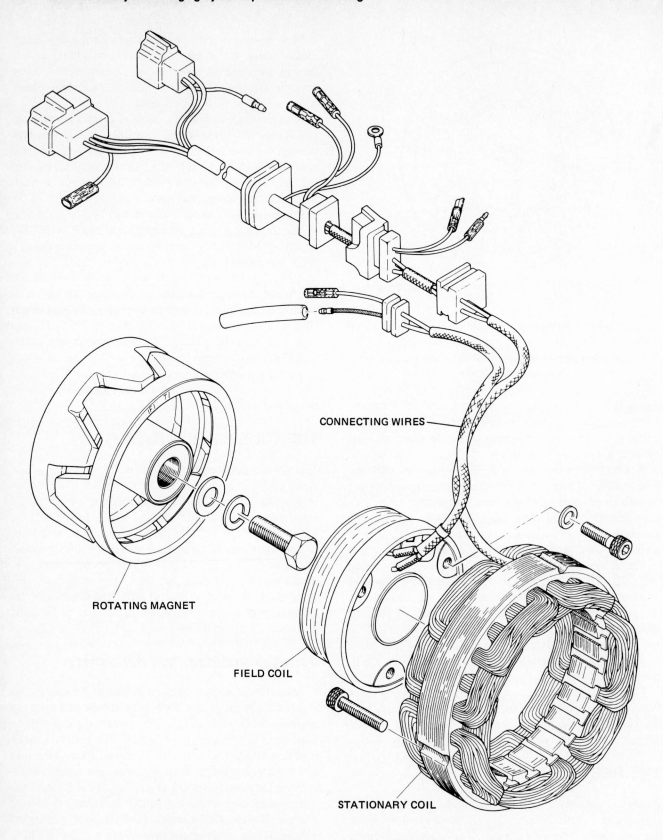

Figure 20–13. Alternator components. *(Yamaha Motor Corp. U.S.A.)*

CONNECTING WIRES

ROTATING MAGNET

FIELD COIL

STATIONARY COIL

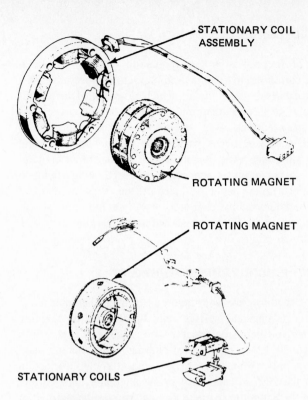

Figure 20–14. Two stationary coil arrangements. *(Honda Motor Co., Ltd.)*

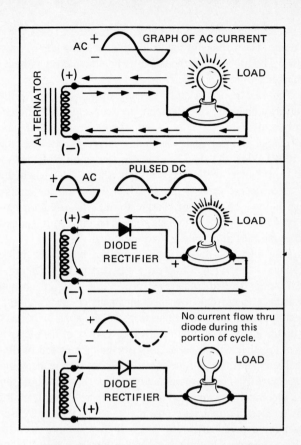

Figure 20–16. A single diode provides half-wave rectification. *(Kawasaki Motors Corp. U.S.A.)*

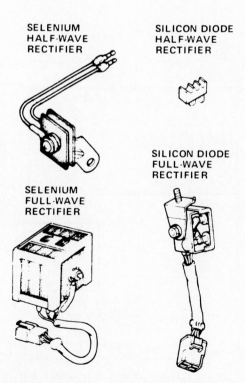

Figure 20–15. A rectifier changes AC current to DC. *(Honda Motor Co., Ltd.)*

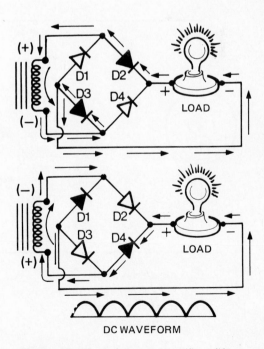

Figure 20–17. A full-wave rectifier. *(Kawasaki Motors Corp. U.S.A.)*

tery charging voltage must overcome in order to charge the battery. The voltage produced by the alternator, then, must always be higher than the CEMF when the battery is being charged.

The CEMF is affected by many factors, including the battery's charging rate, temperature, concentration of electrolyte, plate area in contact with the electrolyte, and state of charge. As the state of charge increases, so does the CEMF. When the state of charge is low, the CEMF is low and the battery will accept a high charge rate; when the state of charge is high, the CEMF is high and the charge rate is low. The state of charge, through its effect on battery CEMF, often establishes the charging voltage and charging rate in a typical charging circuit.

The other component making up the battery charging voltage is the voltage drop caused by the battery's internal resistance. The internal resistance consists of the normal resistance to current flow inherent in the connectors, connector straps, welded connections, plate area in contact with the electrolyte, and electrical resistivity of the electrolyte, together with other factors, including sulfated or discharged plates. One of the more important factors affecting battery resistance is temperature, which has an effect on the electrical resistance or resistivity of the electrolyte. As the temperature decreases, the resistance increases. Consequently, a cold battery having a high resistance will be hard to charge. On the other hand, a hot battery is easy to charge.

Solid-state current limiter

One of the simplest voltage regulation devices is the solid-state current limiter that is used on many motorcycles. This device uses a zener diode, which does not always completely block reverse current. A reverse-biased zener diode will pass current when voltage exceeds a predetermined level, and even then it passes only the amount of current exceeding that level. A solid-state current limiter containing a zener diode is connected in the charging circuit in parallel with the battery to bleed off the excess current that would otherwise overcharge the battery at high rpm. A solid-state current limiter is shown in a charging circuit in Figure 20–18.

Mechanical voltage regulator

Some motorcycles use a field coil in their alternator along with a mechanical voltage regulator to control charging system voltage. An alternator with a field coil is shown in Figure 20–19. In this type of alternator, the rotating magnet is only temporarily magnetized, through interaction with the field coil mounted in the alternator. The current from the battery to the field coil determines the strength of the magnetic field and, in turn, the output of the alternator.

The mechanical voltage regulator limits voltage by controlling the amount of field current in the alternator. The more current that flows in the field winding, the stronger

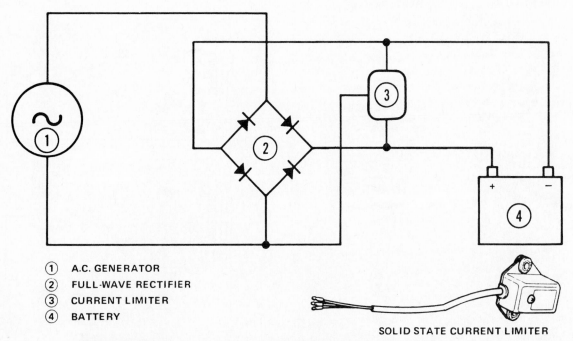

(1) A.C. GENERATOR
(2) FULL-WAVE RECTIFIER
(3) CURRENT LIMITER
(4) BATTERY

SOLID STATE CURRENT LIMITER

Figure 20–18. Charging system with solid-state current limiter. *(Honda Motor Co., Ltd.)*

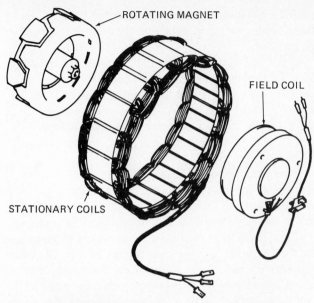

Figure 20–19. An alternator with a field coil. *(Honda Motor Co., Ltd.)*

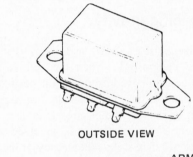

OUTSIDE VIEW

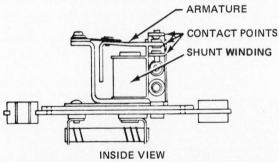

INSIDE VIEW

Figure 20–20. Mechanical voltage regulator. *(Honda Motor Co., Ltd.)*

is the rotating magnetic field. In turn, the stronger the magnetic field, the more lines of force there are that cut across the stationary winding, and the more voltage is created. If the field current is decreased at any given alternator speed, the voltage will be decreased. If the field current is decreased as the alternator speed increases, a balancing effect can be obtained, with the net result being a nearly constant voltage that is regulated by the voltage regulator.

The voltage regulator shown in Figure 20–20 consists of a magnetically operated switch that at appropriate times di-

rects field current through a resistance in order to lower alternator output. Early designs of mechanical voltage regulators utilized a single set of contact points. All late model mechanical regulators utilize double contact points and are sometimes referred to as double-contact voltage regulators.

The regulator consists of a coil of wire wound around an iron core. The winding is usually referred to as a *shunt winding*. The winding and core are assembled together onto a metal frame, to which a flat steel armature is attached by a temperature-sensitive hinge. The hinge bends to allow the armature to move toward the core when it is magnetically attracted by current flowing in the shunt winding. The hinge acts as a pivot point, and the magnetic attraction is opposed by an adjustable helically wound spring expansion located on the other side of the pivot point. Two sets of contact points, an upper and a lower, are insulated electrically from each other and mounted on the armature assembly (Figure 20–20). A stationary set of contacts is located between the upper and lower contacts. With this arrangement, the contact points may be positioned so that either (1) the lower set will be closed, (2) the upper set will be closed, or (3) both sets will be separated. The spring tension holds the lower contacts closed when the regulator unit is not operating.

Current that enters the regulator is directed to the upper contact, where a small part of the current is fed into the shunt winding. Current flow through the shunt winding produces a magnetic field which tends to pull the hinged armature downward. The amount of pull on the armature depends upon the strength of the shunt winding field, which in turn depends upon the amount of system voltage that is pushing current through the winding. When battery current alone is directed to the winding, the voltage is not high enough to cause the armature to be pulled down. Current flows across the closed upper contact set and directly into the alternator field. When the field winding in the alternator is energized by the battery, the alternator will produce voltage when it is operating.

Any time the system voltage is low, the current flows through the upper contacts of the regulator, through the armature, and directly into the alternator field. Since the resistance in this circuit is very low, a maximal field current flows to the field winding, producing a strong magnetic field in the alternator and providing maximum alternator output for any given engine rpm.

When the alternator output increases, the voltage in the system increases, causing the magnetic field of the regulator shunt winding to increase as well. The magnetic pull then becomes strong enough to overcome the spring tension on the armature. Consequently, the hinged armature and the movable contact are pulled away from the upper contact. This relationship of position between the armature and the two contacts is often called the *floating position* because the movable contact does not touch either of the fixed contacts. When the movable contact is in the floating position, current flow is directed through a circuit with a resistor, which is a device that is usually made of metallic wire or of a carbon composition which limits or resists current flow. Current flows through the resistor and then onto the alternator field. Since the resistor reduces current flow, the alternator field strength is also reduced, in turn reducing alternator output.

When a large number of electrical accessories and lights are turned on, the electrical system may demand high alternator output. Under this condition, the combination of shunt winding, magnetic pull, and armature spring tension causes the armature to vibrate between the upper contact and the floating position. This vibration occurs because, with the contacts separated, the rotor field is diverted through the resistor, lowering alternator output. The lowered output in turn causes the magnetic pull created by the shunt winding to decrease. The spring tension then overcomes the magnetism, and the upper contacts reclose. The cycle is repeated as much as 50 times per second.

When few of the electrical accessories are in use and engine rpm is high, the alternator output voltage tends to increase, pushing more current through the shunt winding and creating a very strong magnetic field which pulls the regulator armature down against the lower contact. With the lower contacts closed, there is a direct circuit through the regulator armature to ground through the lower fixed contact. As a result, the alternator field circuit is momentarily bypassed. Consequently, the alternator field starts to collapse, interrupting alternator output. The interruption does not last very long, however. The magnetic field of the shunt winding collapses, allowing the spring to pull the armature and movable contact away from the lower contact. The result is that the movable contact vibrates once more between the floating position and the lower contact. Again, this vibration occurs as many as 50 times per second.

CHARGING SYSTEM SERVICING

Charging system problems are usually evidenced by a battery that is undercharged or a battery that is overcharged. Always begin your troubleshooting of the charging system by inspecting and testing the battery because it is the part that is most subject to failure. If the battery tests out satisfactorily, you can begin a systematic check of the charging system, following the appropriate sections of the shop service manual.

Visual inspection of the battery

The first step in checking out the charging system is to inspect the battery visually. Look for obvious damage, such as a cracked case or loose or broken battery terminals. Look for bulging on the sides of the case which may be caused by hold-down clamps that are too tight. If any of these conditions are in evidence, the battery will need to be replaced.

Inspect the battery cables and terminals for breakage, loose connections, or corrosion. Look for dirt or green crystals on the battery and the connecting parts. If the corrosion is heavy, the battery may be overcharging. Check the battery hold-down to be sure it is tight. A loose hold-down could mean that the battery has vibrated the active material off the plates.

Inspect the top of the battery for dirt or electrolyte. If the top of the battery is not clean, current might flow across the foreign material, which would cause the battery to self-discharge when the motorcycle is not in operation.

Check the level of electrolyte in the battery by observing the fluid level through the case (Figure 20–21). Most batteries have a minimum and maximum line on the case. If any cell fluid level drops below the minimum level, fill the cell with distilled water to the correct height. Check the battery once a month, or even more often in hot weather. Do *not* use tap water.

Checking specific gravity

Once the battery has passed a visual inspection, its state of charge should be determined. When the cell is being charged, lead sulfate is removed from both the positive and the negative plate, and sulfuric acid is again formed. In the process, the water content of the electrolyte is decreased, and the acid content of the electrolyte is increased. Since sulfuric acid is heavier than water, the density of the electrolyte is increased. The *specific gravity* of the electrolyte

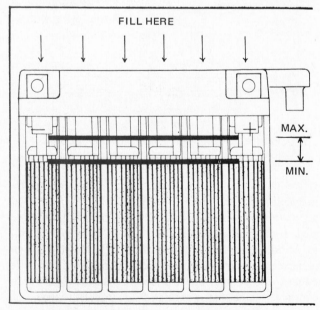

Figure 20–21. Checking cell electrolyte level. *(Yamaha Motor Corp. U.S.A.)*

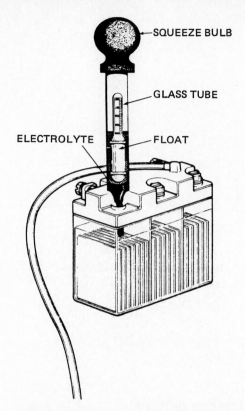

Figure 20–22. A hydrometer used to check specific gravity. *(Honda Motor Co., Ltd.)*

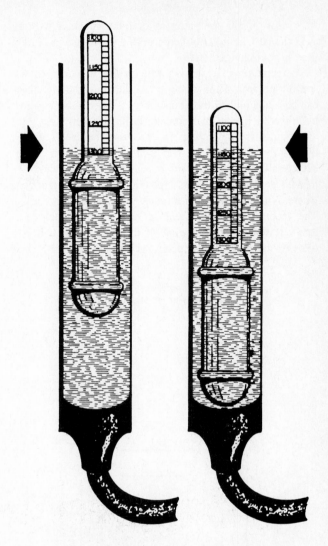

FULL CHARGE **DISCHARGE**

Figure 20–23. The float rises or sinks depending upon the concentration of sulphuric acid. *(Honda Motor Co., Ltd.)*

in the battery is a measure of the density of the electrolyte relative to the density of water. Water has a specific gravity of 1.000.

The cell's state of charge is indicated by the specific gravity of its electrolyte and can be checked with a hydrometer (Figure 20–22). The hydrometer consists of a glass tube with a squeeze bulb attached to one end. The other open end of the hydrometer is inserted into the cell by way of the vent cap hole. As with an eyedropper, the bulb is squeezed and released, suctioning electrolyte from the cell into the glass tube. Inside the tube, a float device shows the level of the electrolyte. The float will not sink too far below the electrolyte level if the electrolyte has a high concentration of sulphuric acid. However, if it is composed primarily of water, the float will sink farther down below the level. This sinking occurs because plain water has a lower specific gravity, or is "thinner," than water mixed with sulphuric acid (Figure 20–23).

The float in the hydrometer has numbered graduations that allow you to determine the level and the specific gravity of the electrolyte. Figure 20–24 shows how to read the scale. The specific gravity must be high enough to promote chemical action in the cell, but not too high, because excessive acid content can shorten the life of the cell. A well-charged cell in a motorcycle battery should have a specific gravity of 1.260 to 1.280. A specific gravity of 1.200 to 1.260 indicates only a partial charge. If the specific gravity

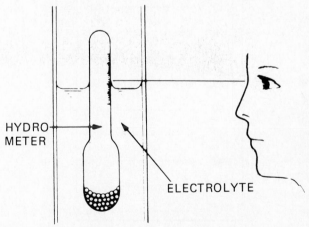

Figure 20–24. Read the scale by sighting at eye level. *(Honda Motor Co., Ltd.)*

falls below 1.200, the battery should be recharged as soon as possible; it should not be permitted to remain for a long time in a discharged state.

Temperature also plays a role in the variation of the specific gravity of the electrolyte. Since accurate readings can be made only if the temperature is fixed at 80°F, most hydrometers have a thermometer built into the side.

Should the temperature rise above or fall below 80°F, the hydrometer must be recalibrated. The reason is because, as the temperature increases, the density of the electrolyte decreases and its specific gravity is reduced, whereas the reverse is true as the temperture decreases. The general formula for making allowances for temperature variation is the following. If the temperature is above or below 80°F, *add* .004 specific gravity for every 10° *over*

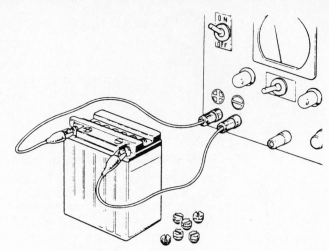

Figure 20–26. Charging the battery. *(Honda Motor Co., Ltd.)*

80°F, and *subtract* .004 specific gravity for every 10° *under* 80°F (Figure 20–25).

Charging the battery

If the battery is discharged, it can be charged by a long ride on the motorcycle or by a shop battery charger. *(CAUTION: Do not use an automotive-type fast charger on a motorcycle battery—the high amperage could cause the battery to overheat and explode. Use only an approved motorcycle battery charger.)*

Follow the directions for using the battery charger. Connect the battery charger positive cable to the battery positive terminal; connect the charger negative cable to the battery negative terminal (Figure 20–26). Remove the caps from each cell to prevent a buildup of pressure. Then set the charger to the lowest possible charging rate, turn the charger on, measure the specific gravity frequently during charging, and stop the process when the battery is fully charged. Discontinue charging if the battery overheats or boils electrolyte out of the cells. *(CAUTION: Remember, as noted in Chapter 2, the hydrogen gas given off during charging is very explosive. Do not smoke or otherwise allow flame or sparks around a battery that is charging.)*

Alternator rectifier/regulator testing

A charging system problem can be caused by a failure of the alternator rectifier or regulator. There are many different types of systems, and all have a different test procedure. When troubleshooting or servicing a charging circuit, always use the specific procedures and testers found in the appropriate shop service manual.

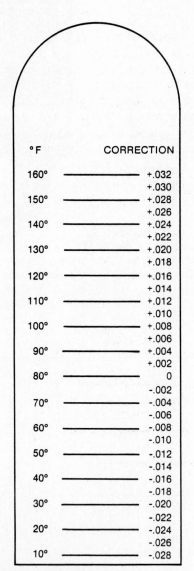

°F	CORRECTION
160°	+.032
	+.030
150°	+.028
	+.026
140°	+.024
	+.022
130°	+.020
	+.018
120°	+.016
	+.014
110°	+.012
	+.010
100°	+.008
	+.006
90°	+.004
	+.002
80°	0
	-.002
70°	-.004
	-.006
60°	-.008
	-.010
50°	-.012
	-.014
40°	-.016
	-.018
30°	-.020
	-.022
20°	-.024
	-.026
10°	-.028

Figure   20–25. Hydrometer   conversion chart. *(U.S. Suzuki Motor Corp.)*

NAME _____ SECTION _____ DATE _____

Job Sheet 20–1

MEASURE SPECIFIC GRAVITY OF BATTERY

Before you begin:

Read pp.

Make of Motorcycle _____ Model _____ Year _____

Time Started _____ Time Finished _____ Total Time _____

Flat-rate Time _____

Special Tools, Equipment, Parts, and Materials

Hydrometer
Battery

References

Manufacturer's Shop Manual _____

Specifications

Procedure

1. *(SAFETY CAUTION: Always wear eye protection when using a hydrometer.)*
2. Remove the cell caps from the battery.
3. Squeeze the bulb on the hydrometer and put the hydrometer tip into the electrolyte in the first cell.
4. Slowly release the bulb until the hydrometer float rises and floats freely. The float should not touch the tube anywhere.
5. Bend over to read the hydrometer. Hold the hydrometer up so that you can read it at eye level, but do not lift it out of the electrolyte (Figure 20–23). Read the scale of the hydrometer float at the level of the electrolyte.
6. Put the electrolyte back into the cell by slowly squeezing the bulb.
7. Repeat steps 2–6 for each of the cells.

8. Record the specific gravity reading of each cell in the spaces provided below:

Cell 1 _____

Cell 2 _____

Cell 3 _____

Cell 4 _____

Cell 5 _____

Cell 6 _____

Instructor check _____

9. A change in temperature will change the specific gravity reading since acid expands with heat and shrinks with cold. So the specific gravity reading you obtain could be wrong at high or low temperatures. To avoid this problem, you need to adjust the specific gravity reading to the temperature.

10. To make the adjustment, first check the temperature of the electrolyte with a thermometer. (In most cases, the thermometer is built into the hydrometer.) Then check the specific gravity with the hydrometer. Subtract .004 from the hydrometer reading for every 10 degrees of temperature below 80°F; add .004 to the reading for every 10 degrees above 80°F.

11. *Example*. If the reading is 1.280 at 70°F:
1.280 (hydrometer reading)
− .004 (for 10 degrees of temperature)
1.276
The true adjusted specific gravity is 1.276.

12. Correct each of your readings for temperature, and record the corrected readings in the spaces provided below:

Cell 1 _____

Cell 2 _____

Cell 3 _____

Cell 4 _____

Cell 5 _____

Cell 6 _____

Instructor check _____

13. Average your corrected readings and compare them with specifications. Indicate below the percentage of charge for the battery:

_____ percent charge.

14. All cells should have the same specific gravity. If there is more than a .050 difference between the cells, the battery will not pick up or hold a charge. Record the difference between the highest and lowest cell in the space below:

_____ difference

Instructor check _____

NOTES

KEY TERMS

Alternator: an alternating current generator used to develop current to charge the battery and power the electrical components on the motorcycle.

Battery: an electrochemical device consisting of alternate plates of different metals in a solution of acid; used to provide a source of stored electrical energy.

Capacity rating: a rating of how long a battery can supply current; usually specified in ampere-hours.

Cell: a basic unit of the battery that is capable of developing about 2 volts.

Current limiter: a solid-state device used to bleed off excessive current on a charging system that does not use a field coil.

Electrolyte: a mixture of sulfuric acid and water used in a battery.

Mechanical voltage regulator: a voltage regulator that uses magnetically controlled switches to control alternator output.

Rectifier: a set of diodes or selenium plates that is used to convert the alternating current from the alternator into direct current.

Specific gravity: a measure of the strength of the electrolyte in a battery cell.

Specific gravity test: a test of the specific gravity in the cells that uses a hydrometer to find out whether the battery is charged.

CHECKUP

Describe the parts and operation of a simple battery cell. Identify the parts of the battery by writing their names in the spaces provided.

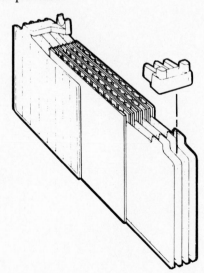

1. _____
2. _____
3. _____
4. _____
5. Why does it take six cells to make a 12-volt battery?
6. Explain the chemical operation of the battery during discharge.
7. Explain the chemical operation of the battery during charging.
8. What is battery capacity?
9. How is battery capacity determined?
10. Explain how the battery and charging system work together to provide power for the electrical system.
11. What is the purpose of the alternator?

Identify the parts of an alternator by writing their names in the spaces provided.

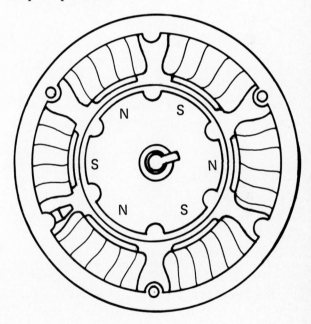

12. _____
13. _____
14. _____
15. _____
16. What is the purpose of the rectifier?
17. What is the purpose of the current limiter?
18. How does the mechanical voltage regulator regulate alternator output?
19. What does specific gravity tell you about a battery?

DISCUSSION TOPICS AND ACTIVITIES

1. Use a hydrometer to test several shop batteries before and after charging. What happens to specific gravity after charging? *(Caution: Wear eye protection.)*

2. Disassemble a shop alternator and see if you can locate and identify all the parts. After identifying the parts, reassemble the alternator.

Most late-model road motorcycles are equipped with an electrical starting system. The large-displacement multicylinder engines are difficult to kick start; the starting system allows the rider to use the energy stored in the battery to power a starter motor to crank the engine. These same motorcycles are also equipped with many accessory systems, such as headlights, turn signals, brake lights, and horns. In this unit, we describe the parts and operation of the starting system and some common accessory systems.

JOB COMPETENCY OBJECTIVES

When you finish reading and studying this unit, you should be able to:

1. Explain the operating principle of a basic starter motor.

2. Describe the construction and operation of a starter motor.

3. Explain the operation of a starter motor drive mechanism.

4. Explain the operation of the headlight, taillight, stoplight and turn signal accessory system.

5. Describe the parts and operation of a motorcycle horn.

THE STARTING SYSTEM

The two basic electrical starting systems in use are shown in Figure 21–1. One cranks the engine with a motor connected to the flywheel ring gear; the other cranks the engine with a motor connected directly to the crankshaft. In the first type, the motor is called the *starter motor,* as it functions in that capacity only. In the second type, the motor is called the *starter/generator* because it functions as the starting motor at the time of engine startup and as a generator after the engine is started.

The starter motor is used on most larger motorcycles and is becoming the most common starting system. The starter/generator is used in the small-sized motorcycles. The starter motor type is so arranged that the starter pinion drives the flywheel ring gear with a high gear ratio, delivering a high torque for big-engine cranking. In the case of the starter/generator, however, the motor is directly coupled with the crankshaft without any reduction in gear ratio. The result is that the cranking power is relatively low. Because of this limited power, the starter/generator is being used less and less.

The starter motor system uses a direct-current motor to transform the battery's electrical energy into the mechanical energy that is needed to crank the engine. Amperage requirements are relatively high, so an electromagnetic switch and heavy-gauge electrical wire leads are used to make the connection between the battery and the starter motor. When the starter motor is actuated, it drives an

STARTING AND ACCESSORY SYSTEMS

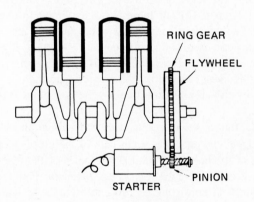

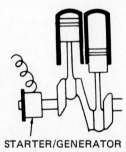

Figure 21–1. Two types of electric starting systems. *(U.S. Suzuki Motor Corp.)*

overrunning starter clutch that has engaged the engine crankshaft. Reduction gears are sometimes used between the starter motor and the starter clutch to multiply the starter motor's torque.

Basic principles of the motor

The starter motor changes the electrical energy of the battery into mechanical energy to crank the engine. It uses the interaction of magnetic fields to convert electric current into torque, or twisting force.

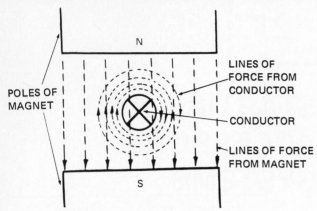

Figure 21–2. Magnetic lines of force from the magnet and conductor. *(U.S. Suzuki Motor Corp.)*

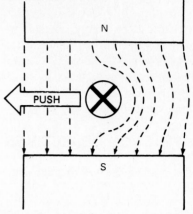

Figure 21–3. The stronger field pushes the conductor to the left. *(U.S. Suzuki Motor Corp.)*

In Unit 19, some of the basic principles of magnetism were described. One of these, very important to electric motors, is that when a straight wire conductor is placed in the magnetic field of a magnet with current flowing through the wire, there will be two separate magnetic fields: the one produced by the magnet, and the one produced by the current flow through the conductor (Figure 21–2).

In the figure, the magnetic lines leave the north pole of one magnet and enter the south pole of the other. The direction of the lines between the two poles of the magnets is downward. The current-carrying conductor produces a magnetic field consisting of concentric circles around the wire in the direction illustrated. The result is a strong magnetic field (a heavy concentration of magnetic lines) on the right-hand side of the wire, and a weak magnetic field (a sparsity of magnetic lines) on the left-hand side of the wire. (On the right-hand side of the wire the magnetic lines are in the same direction and consequently add together, whereas on the left-hand side of the wire the magnetic lines are in the opposite direction and consequently tend to cancel each other out.)

When there is a strong field on one side of a conductor and a weak field on the other side, the conductor will tend to move from the strong to the weak field, or from right to left in the given example. (Figure 21–3). The stronger the magnetic field produced by the magnet and the higher the current flow in the conductor, the greater will be the force tending to move the conductor from right to left. Use of this principle is how electrical energy is converted to torque in all starter motors.

In a simplified starter motor (Figure 21–4), a loop of wire is located between two iron pole pieces and is connected to two separate commutator segments or bars. Riding on the commutator bars are two sliding conducts called *brushes,* which are connected to the battery and to the windings that are located over the pole pieces.

In this basic motor, current flows from the battery through the pole piece windings to a brush and commutator bar, through the loop of wire to the other commutator bar and brush, and then back to the battery. The resulting magnetic fields impart a turning or rotational force on the loop of wire.

As the wire loop turns one-half turn, the commutator bars interchange positions with the two brushes, so the current through the wire loop is in the opposite direction. But since the wire loop has interchanged positions with the pole pieces, the rotational effect will still be in the same counterclockwise direction (Figure 21–4).

The simple motor just described with only one loop and two commutator segments cannot develop much torque because, though the magnetic forces are strong when one leg of the coil is close to a field pole, they drop to zero midway between the poles. Therefore, in practice, motors with many coil loops must be used. As one loop comes into

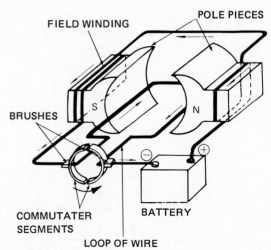

Figure 21–4. Simplified starter motor. *(U.S. Suzuki Motor Corp.)*

play and rotates past a field pole, another immediately takes its place. In this way, the turning motion is made uniform and the torque that is generated is made constant, rather than fluctuating, as it would if only a few loops were used.

Starter motor construction

A starter motor is shown in exploded view in Figure 21–5. The rotating loops (coils) are made from many lengths of heavy-gauge insulated copper wire. The coils are mounted lengthwise on a laminated iron core which not only supports them, but strengthens and concentrates the magnetic field which the field coils (located in the field and frame assembly) produce. The core is laminated to reduce the generation of small opposing voltages called *eddy currents* (CEMF). The ends of each coil are attached to commutator segments. The complete rotating assembly of current-conducting coils and commutator, core, and shaft is called the *motor armature*.

The commutator segments are insulated from each other with an insulation material called mica. The segments themselves are made of a good conductor, usually copper. The hardened-steel shaft, which is pressed through the core laminations, supports the armature in the starter housing and allows it to rotate. The armature loops and commutator are insulated from the shaft.

The magnetic field in the motor is created inside the starter housing (sometimes called the field-and-frame assembly). The field-and-frame assembly consists of field coil windings assembled over iron pole shoes which are attached to the inside of a heavy iron frame. The iron frame and the pole shoes provide not only a place onto which the field coils can be assembled, but also a low-reluctance, or low-resistance path for the magnetic flux that is produced by the field coil windings.

The field coil and pole shoe assembly are mounted to the starter housing by large screws. The field windings are protected by an insulation wrapping. The field coils and the brushes are connected electrically to a terminal usually located at the top rear of the starter housing. The field coils create a magnetic field, while the brushes slide over the rotating armature to deliver current from the battery.

Each end of the starter motor is enclosed by a separate end housing, or end frame. The brushes are usually mounted to the commutator end housing; the other end housing encloses the drive mechanism (to be explained later). Small motors may not require a separate housing on each end of the starter motor.

The brushes are mounted in holders directly over the armature, with the brush springs holding the brushes in contact with the armature. Current from the battery enters the brushes and then passes into the armature. The brushes maintain contact with the armature as it spins to provide a constant path for current flow.

Since the brushes must direct full battery current into the armature, they must be constructed of a material that will provide good electrical contact. Accordingly, they are usually made from various alloys of copper. The brushes are held in position over the commutator by brush holders, which may be attached either to the commutator end frame or to the starter field and frame assembly. A small spring attached to the holder pushes the brush into contact with the commutator.

Starter motor drive mechanisms

In order to crank the engine, the starter drives a large gear called a *ring gear* (Figure 21–6) on the flywheel attached to the engine crankshaft. A small gear on the end of the starter motor, called the *pinion gear,* either meshes with and drives the flywheel ring gear directly or drives the ring gear through a chain. A reduction gear is sometimes used between the pinion gear and the ring gear to increase the turning torque.

The large flywheel ring gear or sprocket and the much smaller starter pinion or sprocket (pinion gear) allow the starter motor to turn at much higher rpm than the engine in order to develop the necessary cranking force. When the engine starts to run, however, the starter motor must be quickly disengaged, or the starter motor would be driven to excessive rpm by the engine and would be seriously damaged.

The starter motor is disengaged by a device called the *overrunning clutch* which allows the starter motor to engage the engine's crankshaft only while the starter motor is operating under a load (cranking the engine). When the engine starts, its increased speed automatically disengages the starter motor. Cross-sectional views of an overrunning clutch used with a chain drive system are shown in Figure 21–7.

The starter motor armature shaft drives the chain and its sprocket. The clutch housing is attached to the engine crankshaft. The starter is engaged by locking the pinion or sprocket to the clutch; disengagement is achieved by unlocking these parts. Spring-loaded rollers in the overrunning clutch housing do the locking and unlocking.

The rollers ride on ramps in the clutch housing. When extended, they wedge the pinion or sprocket hub tightly against the clutch housing. When the rollers are retracted, the pinion or sprocket hub and clutch housing are no longer locked together.

During cranking, the sprocket drives the overrunning clutch housing. The motion of the sprocket hub causes the rollers to extend and lock into the clutch housing. When the engine starts and its rpm increases, the clutch housing rotates at higher rpm than the sprocket or pinion. The rela-

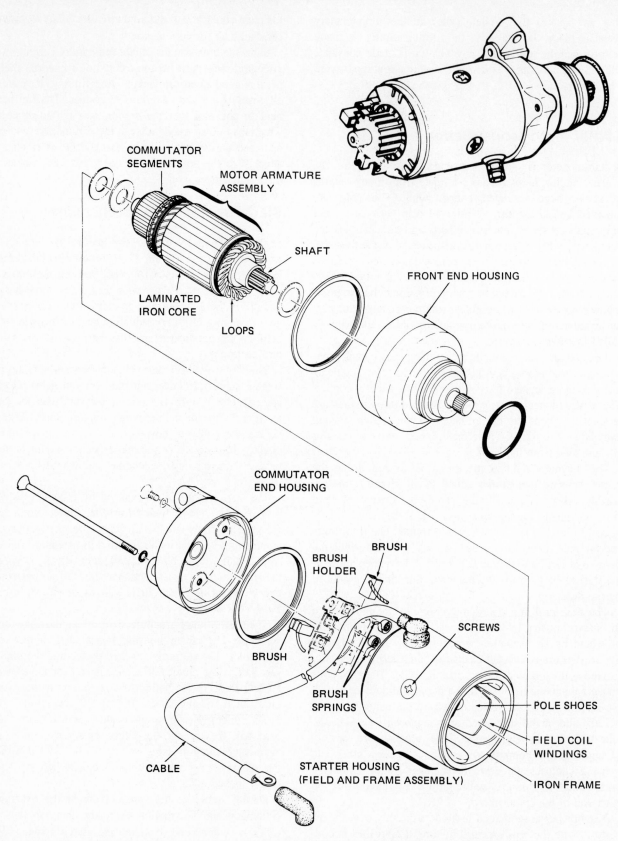

COMMUTATOR
SEGMENTS

MOTOR ARMATURE
ASSEMBLY

SHAFT

FRONT END HOUSING

LAMINATED
IRON CORE

LOOPS

COMMUTATOR
END HOUSING

BRUSH
HOLDER

BRUSH

SCREWS

BRUSH

BRUSH
SPRINGS

POLE SHOES

FIELD COIL
WINDINGS

CABLE

STARTER HOUSING
(FIELD AND FRAME ASSEMBLY)

IRON FRAME

Figure 21–5. Starter motor. *(Top: Honda Motor Co., Ltd. Bottom: Yamaha Motor Corp. U.S.A.)*

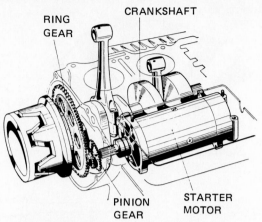

Figure 21–6. Starter motor drive mechanism. *(Honda Motor Co., Ltd.)*

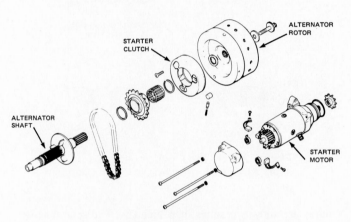

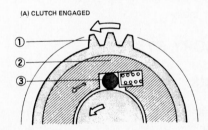

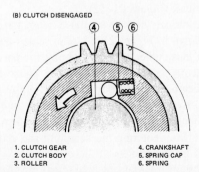

1. CLUTCH GEAR   4. CRANKSHAFT
2. CLUTCH BODY   5. SPRING CAP
3. ROLLER   6. SPRING

Figure 21–7. Starter motor overrunning clutch. *(Top: Honda Motor Co., Ltd. Bottom: Kawasaki Motors Corp. U.S.A.)*

tive motion of these parts retracts the rollers and disengages the starter motor.

Starter motor relay switch

The operation of the starter motor is controlled by a magnetically operated relay switch. The rider controls the operation of the relay with the starter push-button switch. The relay switch is necessary because the starter motor draws more than 100 amperes of current when cranking the engine. Heavy electrical cable and a heavy-duty switch are required to properly handle the current. However, instead of having a heavy cable run up to a large, heavy-duty switch on the handlebar, a small push-button switch on the handlebar activates an electromagnetic relay that connects the battery to the starter motor. This relay switch is usually mounted on the motorcycle frame, near the battery (Figure 21–8).

The construction of a typical relay is shown in cross section in Figure 21–9. The relay has a coil or winding of fine wire that is used to create a magnetic field. When the rider pushes the start button, current flows to the relay winding and the magnetic force is produced. Under the influence of

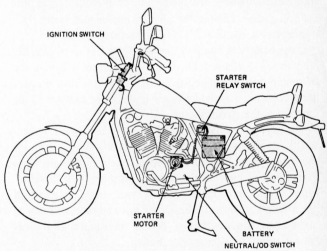

Figure 21–8. Starter motor system. *(Honda Motor Co., Ltd.)*

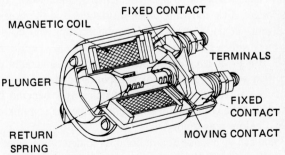

Figure 21–9. Cross-sectional view of a starter relay switch. *(Honda Motor Co., Ltd.)*

this force, a plunger is drawn into the winding, and a moving contact on the other end of the plunger is pressed against the fixed contacts, completing the circuit between the battery terminal and the starter terminal. A return spring is used to ensure that the contacts open when the relay is switched off.

The starting system wiring consists of two separate but related circuits: the starter control circuit and the battery-to-starter-motor supply circuit. The control circuit includes the starter button and the light gauge wire, included in the wiring harness, that connects the button to the relay. The battery-to-starter-motor circuit consists of heavy-gauge cable from battery to relay to starter. The heavy cable carries the higher current that is required to operate the starter motor with minimal losses due to internal resistance.

Starter system servicing

If the starter system fails to operate when the button is pushed, first check the system to make sure that all its wires and cables are attached. The most frequent problem is simply a discharged battery, so check the battery's state of charge with a hydrometer. If the battery is somewhat less than completely discharged, the relay will at least produce an audible click as the plunger moves within the electromagnet. If necessary, charge or replace the battery.

If the battery is charged, the next check is to bypass the relay to see if it is at fault. Use a screwdriver to bridge the two main contacts of the relay. If the engine now cranks, the problem is a faulty relay. If it still does not crank, the problem is the starter motor.

The only parts that get much wear in the starter system are the starter motor brushes and commutator. You can inspect the carbon brushes and replace them if they are worn to the limit of their displacement within the brush holders. Refer to the shop manual for service limits in terms of brush length. Check the brush springs and replace any you find that are weak or broken. Again, refer to the shop manual for spring tension service limits.

Check over the commutator surface to be sure that it is clean and that the copper segments are smooth. Mica insulation must be slightly undercut, as shown in Figure 21–10. Thus, when the copper segments become worn, they no longer stick above the mica insulation, and the brushes will not get good contact. Mica undercutting can be performed with a thin saw blade or a small file (Figure 21–11). Rough or irregular surfaces on copper segments can be filed smooth. The use of sandpaper or emery cloth is not recommended, as abrasive particles may become imbedded in the commutator segments. Wipe the commutator clean before reassembly.

You can also make continuity tests to determine whether a malfunction in the starter motor is due to short circuits or open circuits in the armature or field coils. Test proce-

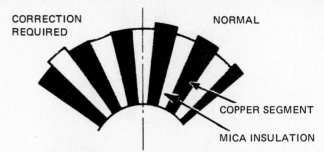

Figure 21–10. Inspecting the starter motor commutator. *(Honda Motor Co., Ltd.)*

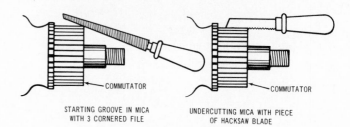

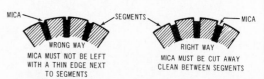

Figure 21–11. Mica undercutting using a small saw or file. *(Harley-Davidson Motors, Inc.)*

dures are shown in some shop manuals. Faulty armatures or field coils usually can be corrected only by replacing the entire starter motor.

ACCESSORY SYSTEMS

Headlights

Almost all motorcycles have a headlight which is normally on whenever the engine is running. There are two basic styles of headlight: the replaceable-bulb unit and the sealed-beam unit (Figure 21–12).

A cross-sectional view of a sealed-beam headlight assembly is shown in Figure 21–13. The sealed-beam headlight has its lens, reflector, and lighting filaments assembled permanently in a sealed unit. Hence, when a filament in a sealed-beam headlight burns out, the entire unit must be replaced. Replacement of a sealed-beam light is more expensive than bulbs, but the airtight seal prevents dust and moisture from entering the headlight and reducing the efficiency of the reflector.

The purpose of the filament is to transform the electrical energy passing through it into light energy. Since the filament emits light in all directions, a reflector is required to

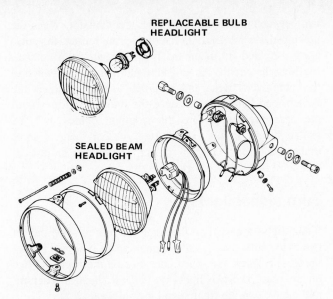

Figure 21-12. Two types of headlight assemblies. *(Honda Motor Co., Ltd.)*

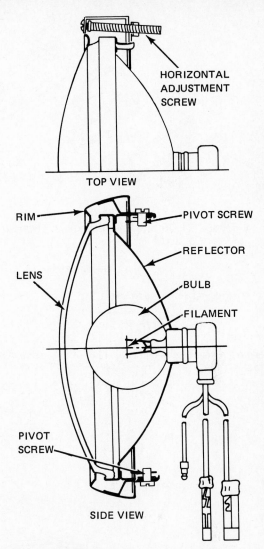

Figure 21-13. Cross-sectional view of a sealed-beam headlight. *(Honda Motor Co., Ltd.)*

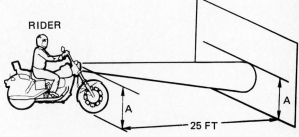

Figure 21-14. Headlamp adjustment. *(Harley Davidson Motors , Inc.)*

redirect the light rays toward the lens at a suitable angle. The inside surface of the lens is composed of many light-refracting segments whose edges are clearly visible from the outside and make it appear as if the lens were ruled off into rectangles. Each lens segment is concave, causing light rays to diverge as they pass through it. In this way, a broad beam of light is made to appear on the road ahead.

Most headlights provide for high and low beam. Dual-beam headlights contain two filaments with just enough difference in position to provide high and low beam angles through the lens. A handlebar-mounted switch enables the rider to light either the high- or the low-beam filaments.

The headlights are mounted to the headlight rim through pivot and horizontal adjustment screws to allow them to be aimed properly for good night vision. Vertical adjustment is done by loosening the headlight mounting bolts and rotating the headlight assembly up or down. Horizontal adjustment is made by turning a horizontal adjustment screw which pivots the headlight in its rim. Always follow the specific adjustment procedure in the shop service manual. Figure 21-14 shows one recommended procedure for adjusting the headlight.

Taillight and stoplight

Most street motorcycles use a taillight which lights up the rear of the motorcycle and includes a light which signals a stop. The taillight assembly (Figure 21-15) contains a two-filament bulb. One filament is wired in parallel with the headlight and comes on when the headlight is on. The other filament is connected to a switch that completes its circuit when the brakes are applied.

The brakelight filament gets its current through the rear brake stoplight switch (Figure 21-16). The rear brake pedal is connected to the operating rod of the switch. When the rider depresses the brakes, the operating rod is pulled down, and the metal tip of the rod completes a cir-

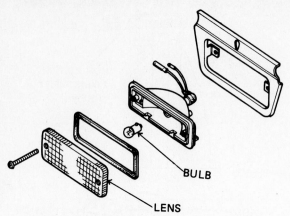

Figure 21-15. Taillight assembly. *(Honda Motor Co., Ltd.)*

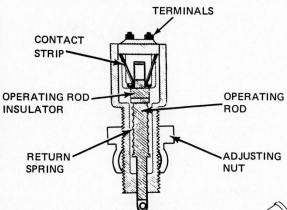

cuit between the contacts, lighting the stoplight. When the brake pedal is released, an internal spring retracts the operating rod, and its metal tip is withdrawn from contact, breaking the circuit. An adjusting nut mounts the switch to the motorcycle frame and is turned to raise or lower the switch, controlling the distance the brake pedal must pull the operating rod before the stoplight comes on. The switch height should be adjusted so that there is some brake pedal free travel and the stoplight comes on just before the brake takes effect.

Turn signal lights

Signal lights are used on the front and rear of some motorcycles to signal turns. A turn signal circuit is shown in Figure 21-17. There are four lights: two on the front and two on the rear. The two lights on the left signal a left turn, and the two on the right signal a right turn.

When the rider turns the turn signal switch on, current flows from the battery through a flasher unit to either the left or right turn signal lights, as determined by the position of the turn signal switch. The flasher unit repeatedly opens and closes the circuit, causing the turn signal lights to blink.

The typical flasher uses a set of breaker points connected to a bimetallic element to open and close the turn signal circuit. A simplified flasher is shown in Figure 21-18. The bimetallic element is formed by attaching two types of

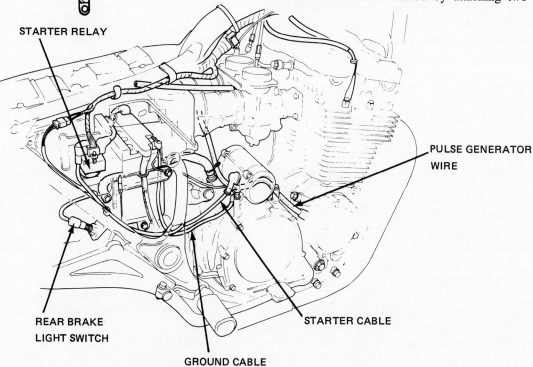

Figure 21-16. Taillight system; brake light switch carries current to the taillight. *(Honda Motor Co., Ltd.)*

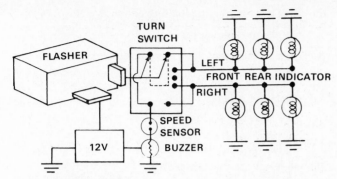

Figure 21-17. Turn signal circuit. *(Honda Motor Co., Ltd.)*

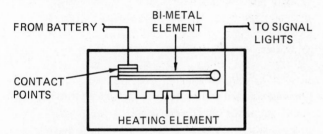

Figure 21-18. Operation of a flasher. *(Ford Motor Co.)*

metals together that have different expansion rates. As the element heats up, the different expansion rates of the metals cause it to bend.

When current flows through the flasher, some of it is directed to ground through a wire heating element, thereby warming the bimetallic strip circuit. The heating element causes the bimetallic strip to open its contacts; all current in the system is shut down, and the turn signal lights go off. As the strip cools, the points close and the lights come back on the cycle again. The cycles will continue until power to the circuit is shut off.

Horn

Many road motorcycles use a horn. The basic principle of the horn, shown in Figure 21-19, is as follows: if an electromagnet is positioned close to a piece of iron sheet (called a diaphragm) that is supported in place at its outside edge, and a current is applied to the coil and turned on and off repeatedly, it causes the iron sheet to vibrate. The vibration then creates a sound whose pitch is determined by the frequency with which the diaphragm vibrates and whose loudness is determined by the extent of motion of the diaphragm.

A cross-sectional view of a typical motorcycle horn is shown in Figure 21-20. When the rider pushes the horn button, current flows from the battery, through contact points, and through an electromagnet. The magnetic field attracts an iron ring on the diaphragm shaft, and the diaphragm is pulled inward. As the diaphragm moves inward,

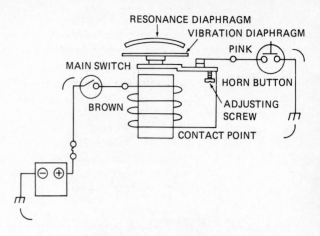

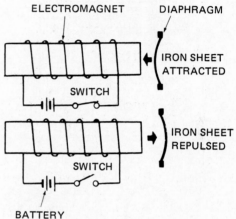

Figure 21-19. An electromagnetic and metal diaphragm can create sound. *(Top: Yamaha Motor Corp. U.S.A. Bottom: U.S. Suzuki Motor Corp.)*

the iron ring strikes an insulator on the movable contact point, separating it from the fixed contact point and breaking the circuit. A return spring then moves the diaphragm shaft and diaphragm forward. The movable contact point is released, the contact points close, and the cycle repeats itself as long as the rider pushes on the horn button.

As shown in the figure, an adjustment screw is attached to the contact point holder. This screw controls the height of the contact point holder in relation to the position of the iron ring on the diaphragm shaft. You can adjust the horn by moving the screw in or out until you get the best sound.

Fuses

Fuses are used to protect the motorcycle circuits. They consist of a small glass tube with metal caps on each end (Figure 21-21). Inside the tube, a small strip of metal allows current to flow. If the current flow through the circuit is excessive, the metal strip melts, immediately stopping the flow. Because the tube is glass, the technician can see whether the metal strip is severed (Figure 21-21, right).

① BATTERY
② MAIN SWITCH
③ FIXED CONTACT POINT
④ MOVABLE CONTACT POINT
⑤ CONTACT POINT INSULATOR
⑥ RESONATOR PLATE
⑦ DIAPHRAGM
⑧ IRON RING
⑨ ELECTROMAGNET
⑩ DIAPHRAGM SHAFT
⑪ RETURN SPRING
⑫ ADJUSTMENT SCREW
⑬ CONTACT POINT HOLDER
⑭ PUSH BUTTON SWITCH

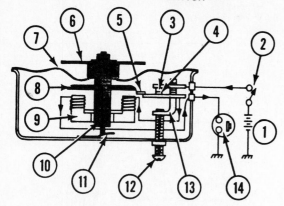

Figure 21-20. Cross-sectional view of a horn. *(Honda Motor Co., Ltd.)*

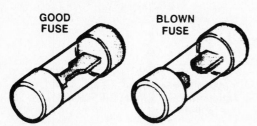

Figure 21-21. Motorcycle fuses. *(Ford Motor Co.)*

Whatever source of difficulty there might be with the circuit, it should be located before a new fuse is installed.

When a fuse blows, it should be replaced with a fuse of the same amperage rating, never with one of a higher rating. Fuses are rated according to the amperage they can withstand. Generally, the longer the fuse, the higher the amperage rating. The rating (in amps) is marked on the fuse. A "30," for instance, means that the fuse is rated and operates successfully at 30 amperes.

Troubleshooting accessory systems

When lights or a horn are completely inoperative, it indicates that the circuit is broken somewhere. If all systems are dead, there is very likely no current flowing from the battery—the battery is completely discharged or disconnected.

If the switch is on and a light or the horn does not work at all, make these checks:

1. Check to see that the bulb is not burnt out.
2. Check for a blown fuse.
3. Check to see that the battery is supplying power.
4. Check for a broken wire.
5. Check for a faulty switch.

If the lights come on, but only very dimly, probably the battery is low or there is resistance in the circuit.

If the headlight beam does not operate when the hi-lo switch is turned on, check to see if the bulb filament is burned out. Also, check the switch.

KEY TERMS

Brushes: the sliding contacts that deliver battery current into the rotating armature.

Commutator: the contact surface on the starter motor armature on which the brushes ride.

Field winding: the part of the starter motor that creates a magnetic field.

Motor armature: the part of the starter motor that is rotated by a magnetic field.

Overrunning clutch drive: a starter motor drive mechanism that uses an overrunning clutch to disconnect the drive pinion from the flywheel ring gear.

Pinion: the gear or sprocket driven by the starter motor that rotates the flywheel.

Ring gear: the gear or sprocket formed by the teeth on the outside of the flywheel.

Relay: a magnetic switch that controls the circuit between the starter motor and the battery.

Starter motor: an electric motor connected to the engine's crankshaft by a gear or chain system; used to crank the engine for starting.

CHECKUP

1. Explain the principle of magnetism that asserts why a conductor moves in a magnetic field.

Identify the parts of a simplified starter motor by writing their names in the spaces provided. (See art on next page.)

2. _____
3. _____
4. _____
5. _____
6. _____

Identify the parts of a starter motor by writing their names in the spaces provided. (See art on page 326.)

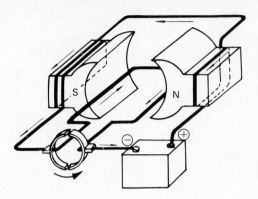

7. _____

8. _____

9. _____

10. _____

11. _____

12. _____

13. _____

14. _____

15. _____

16. _____

17. _____

18. _____

19. _____

20. What is the purpose of the starter overrunning clutch?

21. What is the purpose of the starter relay?

22. What are the two types of headlights?

23. How is the brake light activated?

24. How does a flasher work to cause signal lights to flash?

25. How does a horn create sound?

DISCUSSION TOPICS AND ACTIVITIES

1. Disassemble a starter motor and identify all the parts.

2. Disassemble a relay, identify its parts, and explain its operation.

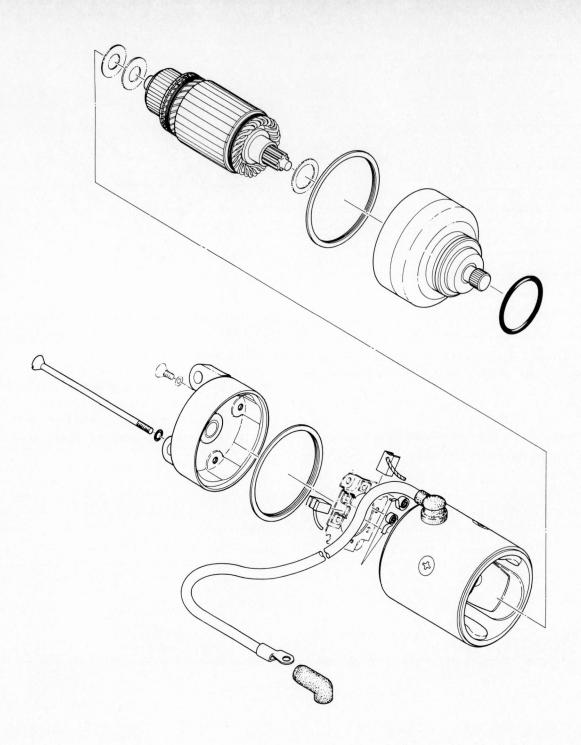

After the engine develops its power, the power must be delivered to the rear wheel of the motorcycle. This delivery is the job of an assembly of parts called the *drive train*. The components of the drive train are shown in the sectional view of an engine in Figure 22–1. The power developed by the engine enters the power train through a set of primary gears located in a primary case. One of the primary gears is attached to the crankshaft, the other to the clutch. The purpose of the primary gears (or sprocket and chain) is to effect an increase of torque and reduction of speed into the drive train. The clutch is used to connect (engage) and disconnect (disengage) the engine's power from the drive train. From the clutch, power flows into the transmission, which provides the rider with a selection of different gear ratios to match engine power output with motorcycle speed. The transmission delivers power to the final drive, which in turn delivers the power to the rear wheel through a chain and sprocket or shaft assembly. In this unit, we begin the study of the drive train with a consideration of the primary drive and clutch.

JOB COMPETENCY OBJECTIVES

When you finish reading and studying this unit, you should be able to:

1. Describe the relationship between torque and gear ratio.

2. Identify the parts and explain the operation of a primary drive.

3. Identify the parts and explain the operation of a multiplate clutch.

4. Adjust the freeplay on a multiplate clutch.

5. Disassemble, inspect, and reassemble a multiplate clutch.

GEARS (SPROCKETS) AND TORQUE

The purpose of the drive train is to get the power of the engine to the rear wheel and to help the engine by increasing its torque through a system of gears. Before examining the individual components of the drive train, however, let us consider some of the basics of gears and torque.

As we have learned, the burning of fuel takes place in the engine's cylinder, where the pistons and connecting rods force the crankshaft to turn. This rotary unit of force is called *torque*. One of the main purposes of the power train is to increase the torque developed by the engine.

We can define torque as a turning or twisting effort. For example, when you use a wrench to tighten a nut (Figure 22–2), you apply torque to tighten the nut. When the nut is tight, you may not be able to turn it anymore, even though you are still exerting an effort. In that case, you are

PRIMARY DRIVE AND CLUTCH OPERATION AND SERVICING

still applying torque. Torque, then, is a force that tends to produce rotation.

On the motorcycle, the drive train and the engine work as a team to start the cycle moving from a standstill up to road speed. The rear wheel of the motorcycle rotates to drive the motorcycle; the twisting or turning effort needed to rotate the tire is torque. Torque is developed by the engine, but the engine alone cannot develop enough torque to get the motorcycle moving quickly from a standstill.

In Unit 6 the torque curve developed by a motorcycle engine was described. It was pointed out there that different engines describe different curves, but they are all similar in that at low engine rpm, torque is low. As engine rpm increases, torque increases up to a point in the rpm range at which the engine will have trouble "breathing in" enough air and fuel. At this point the torque curve will begin to drop off.

The drive train works to overcome low torque at low rpm. It allows the engine to operate at higher speeds while the motorcycle is operating at low speeds so that the engine can operate at, or near, its best torque range. An important job of the drive train is *torque multiplication*, that is, multiplying the engine's low initial torque to get the motorcycle moving and to meet varying road conditions. The drive train multiplies engine torque by means of either gears or sprockets and chain. Both of these operate in the same basic way.

Two gears are shown connected together (in mesh with each other) in Figure 22–3. Both gears have the same number of teeth and are of the same diameter, so that both turn at the same speed. The gear ratio is therefore 1:1. In Figure 22–4, there are also two gears in mesh, one with 12 teeth and the other with 24 teeth. The smaller gear will revolve twice as fast as the larger gear. When the smaller gear drives, the gear ratio between the two thus is 24:12,

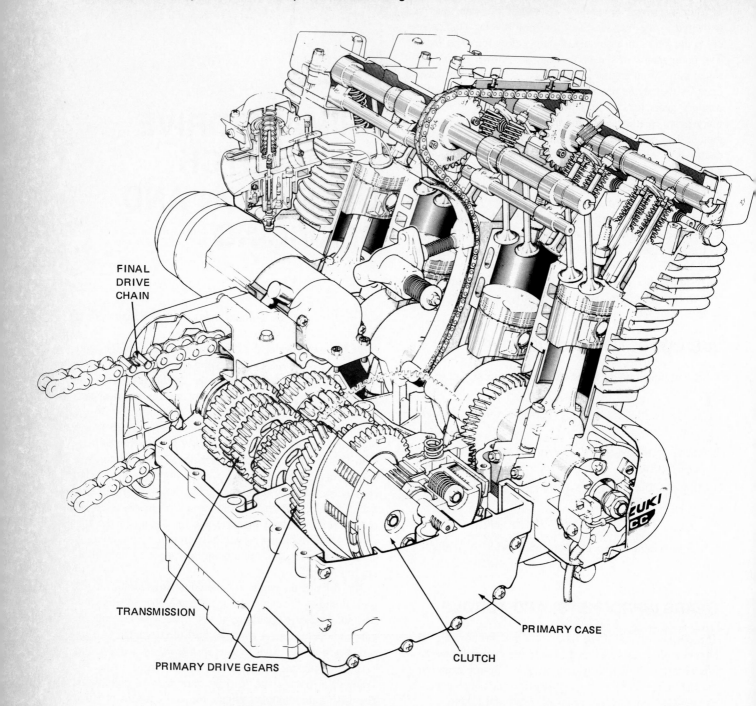

Figure 22–1. Parts of the drive train. *(U.S. Suzuki Motor Corp.)*

or 2:1. In general, the gear ratio between two meshing gears is the relative speeds, or rpm, at which they turn.

Notice in Figure 22–3 and 22–4 that when the two gears are in mesh, they turn in opposite directions. If we want the direction of rotation to be the same, we must use three gears. Thus, if we place a gear between two gears, as shown in Figure 22–5, we can get the outside gears to turn in the same direction. In that case, the gear in the middle

is called an *idler,* i.e., it is free to turn on an idler shaft. When gear A is turned counterclockwise, the idler gear turns clockwise and drives gear B counterclockwise. The idler gear does not affect the gear ratio between gears A and B.

Sprockets and chain are used instead of gears in many motorcycle drive trains. Sprockets and chain work just like two gears in mesh: the number of teeth on the two sprock-

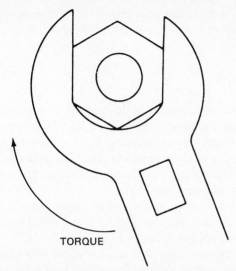

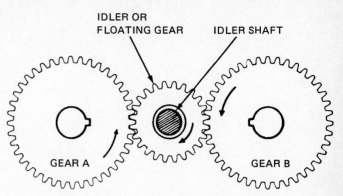

Figure 22–5. An idler gear allows gears to turn in the same direction. *(Chrysler Corp.)*

Figure 22–2. Torque is applied to a nut with a wrench. *(Yamaha Motor Corp. U.S.A.)*

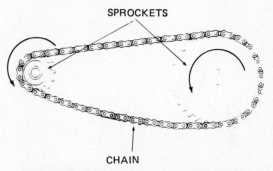

Figure 22–6. Sprockets and chain work like gears, except that the direction of rotation is the same. *(U.S. Suzuki Motor Corp.)*

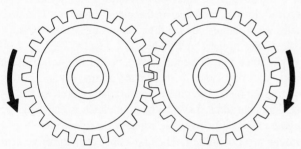

Figure 22–3. Meshing gears with a 1:1 ratio. *(U.S. Army)*

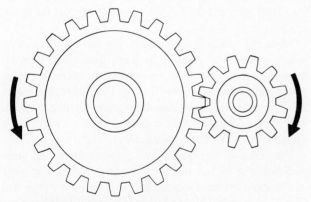

Figure 22–4. Meshing gears with a 2:1 ratio. *(U.S. Army)*

ets determines a gear ratio between them. The only difference is that the two sprockets, driven by a chain, turn in the same direction, as shown in Figure 22–6.

Both gears and sprockets and chain can be used to increase torque or to provide a mechanical advantage. You have probably used a lever to raise a heavy object. If a box is too heavy to be lifted by hand, a lever can be used to

lift it, as shown in Figure 22–7 (top). With the lever placed as shown, only half as much force is required to raise the box as would be required to raise it by hand. For example, suppose that a lifting force of 200 pounds is required to raise the end of the box. With the lever arranged as shown, only a 100-pound downward push is needed on the lever to do the same job. The farther out on the lever you put your hand (away from the pivoting point, or fulcrum), the less downward push is required. However, the farther away the pivot point, the farther your hand must move downward to raise the box. The mechanical advantage of the lever is the ratio between the two distances from the fulcrum—in Figure 22–7, 2:1.

We can compare the mechanical advantage in levers with the mechanical advantage in gears. When one end of a lever is twice as far from the fulcrum as the other end, the first end moves twice as far as the other. Similarly, when two gears are meshed and one has twice as many teeth as the other (as, for example, in Figure 22–7 (bottom)), the smaller gear will rotate twice for each revolution of the larger gear. In other words, the mechanical advantage between the two gears would be 1:2 when the larger gear drove the smaller gear. If the smaller gear drove the larger gear, the mechanical advantage would be 2:1, since the smaller gear would have to exert half the force over twice the distance.

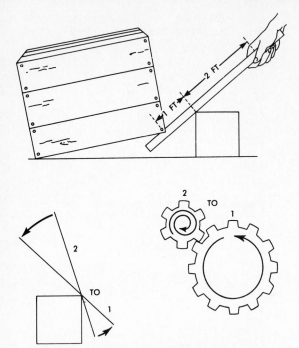

Figure 22–7. Gearing provides a mechanical advantage or torque multiplication. *(U.S. Army)*

The amount of torque multiplication we get from two gears or two sprockets varies with the mechanical advantage that is with the gear ratio of the driving to the driven gear or sprocket. For example, when a small gear drives a larger gear, the speed is reduced, but the torque delivered by the larger gear is increased.

PRIMARY DRIVE

The first set of gears or sprockets in the drive train is called the *primary drive* (Figure 22–8). The primary drive consists of a small gear or sprocket attached to the crankshaft and a large gear or sprocket attached to the clutch assembly. The components of the primary drive and clutch are housed inside the primary case. Figure 22–8 shows the relationship of the small crankshaft gear to the large clutch gear.

The ratio between the small crankshaft gear and the larger clutch gear is usually about 3:1 (Figure 22–9). This ratio provides a torque increase for the engine and a speed reduction for the torque entering the drive train. In other words, the clutch gear is turning only one-third as fast as the engine. The engine is thus allowed to run fast to achieve the best part of its torque curve.

Most late-model motorcycles use a gear-type primary drive. Many older motorcycles, and some still made today, use a chain-type primary drive. A chain-type drive is shown in Figure 22–10. A small sprocket is attached to the crankshaft and a large sprocket is attached to the clutch. A special wide chain with three sets of links side by side is

used for strength and quiet operation. A chain adjustor is used to take up any slack in the chain and to prevent excessive noise.

CLUTCH

The clutch is positioned in the primary case between the engine and the transmission (Figure 22–11). It allows the rider to disengage or disconnect the flow of power from the engine into the transmission. The rider disconnects the engine from the transmission when shifting the transmission from one gear to the next.

Most motorcycles use a type of clutch called a *multiplate* or *multiple disc wet clutch*. An exploded view of a multiplate clutch is shown in Figure 22–12.

The clutch consists of a number of friction discs and steel plates stacked alternately and held tightly together by springs under pressure. The friction discs are the drive plates, the steel plates the driven plates. The friction discs have radial tabs on their outer edges that interlock with vertical slots on the edge of the clutch housing. The steel plates have radial tabs on their inner edges that interlock with splines in the clutch hub.

The clutch hub or center is attached to the transmission input shaft and rides in the center of the clutch housing when assembled. The clutch housing is centered on the input shaft, but turns freely. When the clutch is engaged, the engine crankshaft drives the primary drive crankshaft gear through a set of splines. The crankshaft primary drive gear in turn rotates the clutch housing, the clutch housing drives the friction discs, the friction discs turn the steel plates because the springs force them together, the steel plates turn the clutch hub, and finally, the clutch hub drives the transmission.

When the clutch is disengaged, the release mechanism is activated and the plates move away from each other, allowing them to slip. With the two sets of plates slipping, power cannot be transmitted through the clutch. The plates are covered with oil so that during the slipping they are well lubricated and do not overheat. The oil covering is the reason why the clutch is called a wet clutch.

The clutch is disengaged by removing the spring pressure from the friction discs and the steel plates. The parts of the clutch release mechanism are shown in exploded view in Figure 22–13 and in sectional view in Figure 22–14. A push rod connected to the clutch linkage enters the center of the clutch assembly. A round pushing device called a *crown* is attached to the end of the push rod. The push crown is positioned next to the pressure plate, which is attached to the clutch springs.

When the rider squeezes the clutch lever, the linkage moves the push rod inward so that the crown pushes on the pressure plate. The pressure plate then compresses the springs and moves them away from the clutch hub. With-

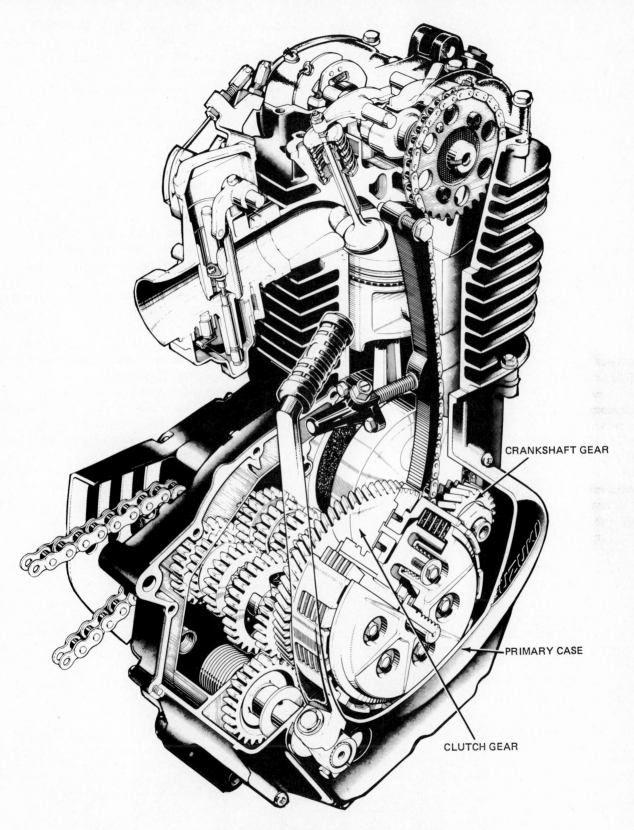

CRANKSHAFT GEAR

PRIMARY CASE

CLUTCH GEAR

Figure 22–8. A gear-type primary drive.
(U.S. Suzuki Motor Corp.)

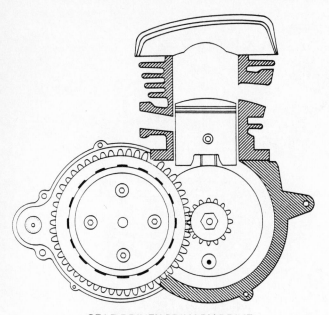

GEAR-DRIVEN PRIMARY DRIVE

Figure 22–9. The small crankshaft gear drives the larger clutch gear at a ratio of 3:1. *(U.S. Suzuki Motor Corp.)*

out spring pressure, the clutch discs are not held together by friction, and the clutch is disengaged.

The typical clutch is activated by a clutch lever on the handlebar. Squeezing the handle causes a cable that is connected to the handle to move. The motion is then transferred through the cable to the primary case, where a linkage arrangement changes the pulling motion of the cable into a pushing motion to move the clutch push rod.

Many clutch mechanisms use a screw-type release mechanism (Figure 22–15). The unit works like a bolt and nut. The inner part (the bolt) has external threads and is connected to a lever that is attached to the clutch cable. When the clutch cable is pulled, the lever turns the inner screw. The outer part has internal threads like a nut and is attached to the clutch push rod. When the inner screw turns, it pushes the outer section and push rod inward to release the clutch.

Another popular release mechanism is the ball and cam plate (Figure 22–16). In this arrangement, three steel balls are placed between the dents on the clutch lower plate and the clutch release plate. A roller pin is inserted through the center holes of the two plates and is connected to the clutch push rod. When the clutch lever plate is turned by the clutch cable, the steel balls jump out of the dents in between the flat portion of the clutch release plate and the clutch lever plate. This action separates the two plates and moves the roller pin and the clutch push rod so that the clutch is disengaged.

Some small motorcycles use an automatic clutch that works just the opposite of a regular clutch. That is, the clutch springs force the clutch apart to disengage it, so that at rest, the clutch is disengaged. On the other hand, when the engine speed is in excess of a certain rpm, the centrifugal force pushes the steel balls outward and away from the unit. Then, as the balls move outward, they climb a sloping ramp, which in turn pushes the clutch plates together. With an increase in engine speed, the clutch is completely engaged. It will then disengage if engine speed drops. This type of clutch uses no clutch lever or release mechanism.

Figure 22–10. Chain-type primary drive. *(Harley Davidson Motors, Inc.)*

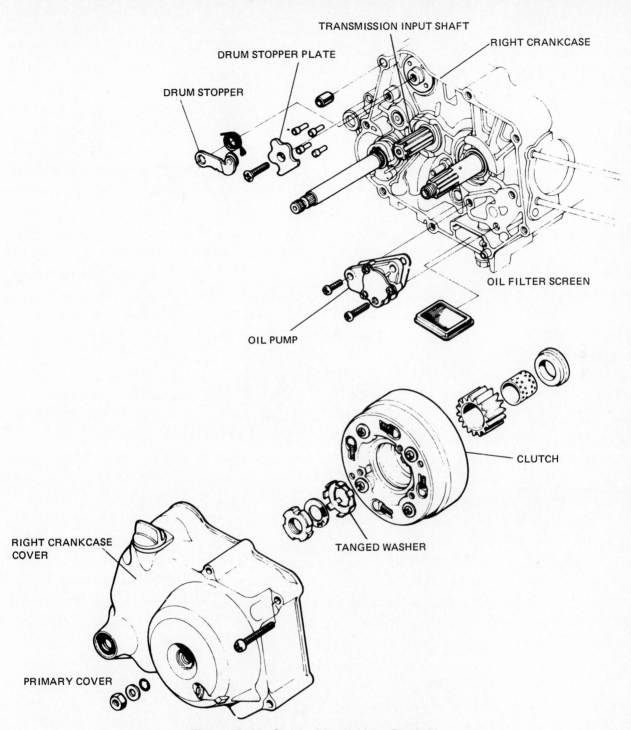

DRUM STOPPER

DRUM STOPPER PLATE

TRANSMISSION INPUT SHAFT

RIGHT CRANKCASE

OIL FILTER SCREEN

OIL PUMP

CLUTCH

TANGED WASHER

RIGHT CRANKCASE COVER

PRIMARY COVER

Figure 22–11. Clutch. *(Honda Motor Co., Ltd.)*

PRIMARY DRIVE TROUBLESHOOTING AND SERVICING

Noises are the most frequent problem in the primary drive area. Abnormal gear whine or clunking noises coming out of the primary case area can signal a problem. Always begin your diagnosis by checking the lubricant level in the primary case. If necessary, fill the case to the correct level with the recommended type of lubricant.

Gear-type primary drives rarely cause any problems. Chain-type primary drives may suffer from excessive chain wear, sprocket wear, or damage to the chain tensioner. If you hear abnormal primary drive noises from a bike with a chain system, remove the primary case cover and inspect

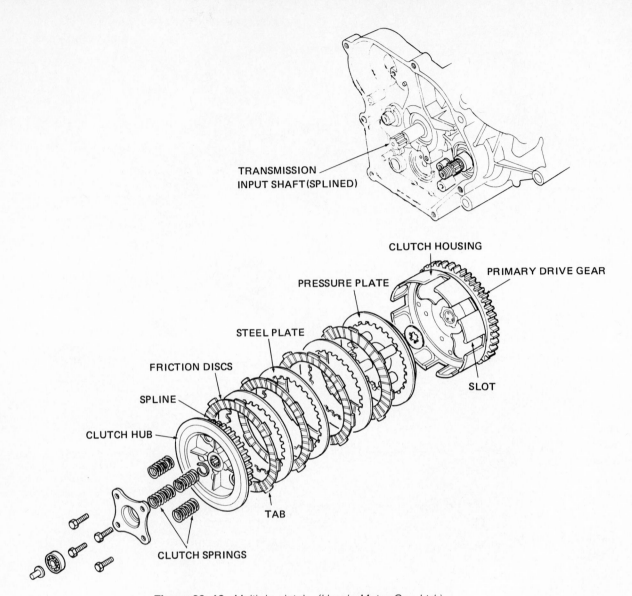

Figure 22–12. Multiple clutch. *(Honda Motor Co., Ltd.)*

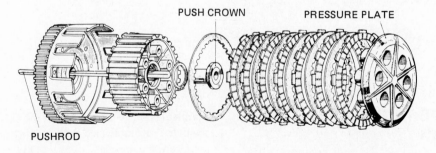

Figure 22–13. Parts of the clutch release mechanism. *(Honda Motor Co., Ltd.)*

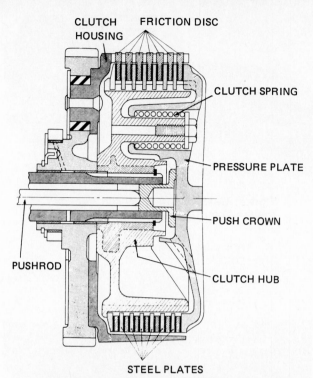

CLUTCH HOUSING   FRICTION DISC
CLUTCH SPRING
PRESSURE PLATE
PUSH CROWN
CLUTCH HUB
PUSHROD
STEEL PLATES

Figure 22–14. Sectional view of a clutch release mechanism. *(Honda Motor Co., Ltd.)*

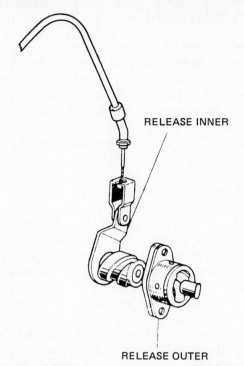

RELEASE INNER
RELEASE OUTER

Figure 22–15. A screw-type clutch release mechanism. *(Yamaha Motor Corp. U.S.A.)*

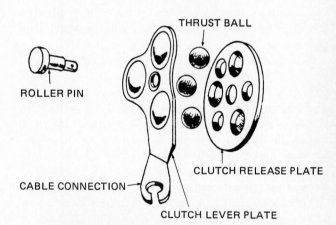

THRUST BALL
ROLLER PIN
CLUTCH RELEASE PLATE
CABLE CONNECTION
CLUTCH LEVER PLATE

Figure 22–16. A ball and cam plate clutch release mechanism. *(Mid America Vocational Curriculum Consortium)*

these parts. Check for worn parts or a chain that is tensioned improperly. The shop service manual is your best guide for chain adjustment.

CLUTCH TROUBLESHOOTING AND SERVICING

Clutch problems may show up in several ways. The rider may have a problem engaging the clutch, or it may slip when it is engaged. There is an engagement problem when you release the clutch lever and the bike acts like it is not in gear. Slipping is evident when you accelerate the bike and hear the engine rev up without any power going to the rear wheel.

The most common problems that can prevent engagement or cause slipping are:

- Weak or broken pressure springs
- Seized cable, push rod, or linkage
- Bent or damaged push rod
- Worn friction discs or steel plates
- Clutch out of adjustment (not enough free play in clutch linkage)

The opposite problem is when the clutch will not disengage—that is, when you cannot disconnect the engine from the transmission even though you have squeezed the clutch

lever. The most common problems that can cause the clutch not to disengage are:

- Binding clutch plates and friction discs
- Warped or distorted clutch plates or friction discs
- Worn clutch release mechanism
- Stretched or misadjusted clutch cable
- Clutch out of adjustment (too much free play in clutch linkage)

Clutch adjustment

The most common service job performed on a clutch is an adjustment. A clutch linkage that is out of adjustment can cause slipping, nonengagement, or failure to disengage. The clutch release mechanism requires periodic lubrication for proper operation, and adjustment to compensate for wear on the clutch plates.

Most bikes have a clutch cable length adjustor and a clutch mechanism adjustor. The cable length adjustor is used to take up slack from cable stretch and to provide sufficient free play for proper clutch operation under various operating conditions (Figure 22–17). The clutch mechanism adjustor is used to provide the correct amount of clutch push rod movement or "throw" for proper disengagement. Normally, once the mechanism is properly adjusted, the only adjustment required is for maintenance of free play at the clutch handle lever.

Free play in the cable is determined by the amount of free movement you can feel at the clutch lever. As you move the lever, you will find that it moves easily at first and then has more resistance as it starts to work the release mechanism. The amount of free movement is compared with specifications to see if the clutch free plate should be adjusted.

To adjust the free play, loosen the handle lever adjustor lock nut. Then turn the length adjustor either in or out until proper lever free play is achieved (Figure 21–18).

If the cable's free play is way out of specifications, or if you have a problem with clutch operation, you should check the adjustment on the clutch release mechanism. This adjustment determines how far the clutch push rod is pushed in when the handlebar lever is squeezed. Different models use different adjustments. Some use a cable adjustor located near the primary case (Figure 22–19), while others use a screw in the primary case which lengthens or shortens the release mechanism (Figure 22–20).

After loosening a lock nut, turn the screw in until you feel a slight resistance. When you do, all the play is out of

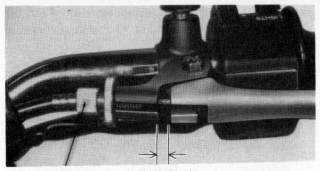

ADJUSTER   LEVER PLAY

Figure 22–18. Adjusting clutch free play. *(Honda Motor Co., Ltd.)*

1. LOCK NUT
2. ADJUSTER

Figure 22–19. Clutch cable adjustment at the primary case. *(Honda Motor Co., Ltd.)*

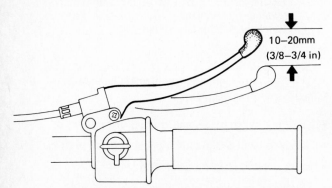

10–20mm
(3/8–3/4 in)

Figure 22–17. Clutch cable free play is measured at the clutch lever. *(Honda Motor Co., Ltd.)*

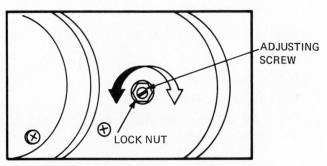

ADJUSTING SCREW

LOCK NUT

Figure 22–20. Adjusting screw on primary cover. *(Mid American Vocational Curriculum Consortium)*

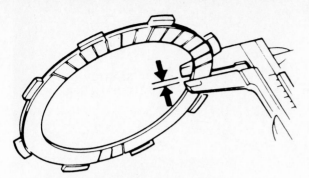

Figure 22–21. Measuring clutch friction discs for wear. *(Honda Motor Co., Ltd.)*

bent section of welding rod, remove the friction discs and metal plates. Stack the plates as they are removed so that you will be able to replace them in their original position. Some clutches can be removed as a unit after the release mechanism and a large nut or snap ring are removed. Clean all the clutch parts in cleaning solvent, and allow them to air dry.

Look the friction discs over carefully because, of all the parts, they usually wear the most. Look all surfaces over for any signs of discoloration or peeling; these are signs that the plates have overheated. Check the tabs for wear. Measure the thickness of the friction plates with calipers and compare it with shop service manual specifications (Figure 22–21). If necessary, install a full set of new discs.

the release mechanism. Then back the screw off a specified number of turns to set the clearance.

Clutch repair

If a clutch problem cannot be cured with an adjustment, the clutch will have to be disassembled and inspected, and new parts will have to be installed. Always follow the specific procedure in the shop service manual.

The first step in removing the clutch is taking off the primary cover that protects it. Drain the oil from the primary case before you remove it; there is an oil drain plug on the bottom of the case. Once the clutch is exposed, there will be nuts or screws that hold the springs in place. After you remove the clutch springs, lift off the pressure plate, exposing the clutch plate. Using a hooked tool, such as a

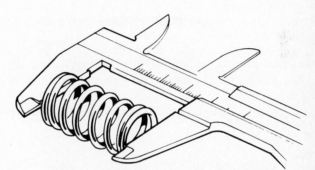

Figure 22–23. Measuring clutch spring height. *(Honda Motor Co., Ltd.)*

You should never replace just one or two discs, as the old discs will put unwanted pressure on the new disc's tabs. The steel plates and the friction discs should also be checked for flatness. Put the plate on a flat surface and, using the specified feeler gauge, try to insert the gauge between the plate and the surface. If it fits, the plate is warped (Figure 22–22). Also, check the plate tabs for wear. The clutch springs should be checked for their heights with a caliper (Figure 22–23). Compare your measurement with specifications. Never replace one spring— always use a completely new set.

Coat all the parts, especially the new plates, with oil. Then install the new springs and plates in order (Figure 22–24). Align the splines on the plates by rotating the clutch center back and forth. To be sure that there is uniform pressure on the plate, tighten all the springs evenly. Rotate the clutch housing and look for any high spots in

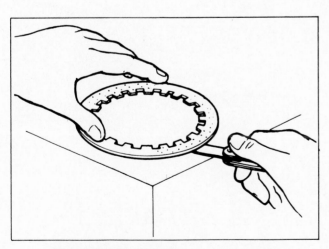

Figure 22–22. Checking the clutch plate. *(Honda Motor Co., Ltd.)*

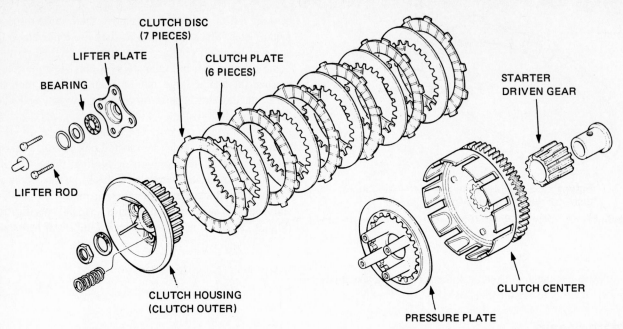

Figure 22–24. Install the friction discs and steel plates in order. *(Honda Motor Co., Ltd.)*

the clutch parts as the housing revolves. Finally, turn the spring adjustor that is closest to the high spots, and test for rotation.

When the clutch is reassembled, install the primary cover and fill the primary case with the recommended type of lubricant. Adjust the clutch release mechanism and the free play. Then check the clutch to see whether it operates properly.

Job Sheet 22–1

ADJUST A CLUTCH

Before you begin:

Read pp.

Make of Motorcycle _____ Model _____ Year _____

Time Started _____ Time Finished _____ Total Time _____

Flat-rate Time _____

Special Tools, Equipment, Parts, and Materials

Steel rule
Eye protection

References

Manufacturer's Shop Manual _____

Specifications

Look up the specification for clutch lever free play and write it in the space below:

Free play _____

Instructor check _____

Procedure

1. Look up the procedure for clutch adjustment in the shop service manual.

   Instructor check _____

2. Loosen the clutch cable and adjustor lock nuts at each end of the cable, at the hand lever end, and at the primary cover end (if such a cover is used).

3. Rotate the clutch cable adjustor clockwise as far as possible to give maximum cable slack.

4. Loosen the clutch adjusting screw lock nut on the primary drive.

Instructor check _____

5. Rotate the adjusting screw clockwise until you can feel a slight resistance. Rotating the screw in this direction decreases the free play.

6. Rotate the adjusting screw the specified turns counterclockwise (check the shop service manual) and tighten the lock nut.

7. Rotate the clutch cable adjustors at the primary side cover and the hand lever counterclockwise until the proper cable free play is obtained.

8. As you make the adjustment, measure the free play with a rule and compare it with specifications.

9. Tighten the cable lock nuts at the hand lever end and the primary cover end.

10. Test the clutch for correct operation. It should engage and disengage properly.

Instructor check _____

NOTES

Date completed _____   Instructor check _____

Job Sheet | 22–2 |

DISASSEMBLE, INSPECT, AND REASSEMBLE A CLUTCH

Before you begin:

Read pp.

Make of Motorcycle _____ Model _____ Year _____

Time Started _____ Time Finished _____ Total Time _____

Flat-rate Time _____

Special Tools, Equipment, Parts, and Materials

Eye protection
Calipers
Feeler gauge
Drain pan

References

Manufacturer's Shop Manual _____

Specifications

Look up the following specifications and write them in the spaces below:

Friction disc thickness _____

Steel plate warpage _____

Clutch spring height _____

Instructor check _____

Procedure

1. Look up the procedure for clutch disassembly and reassembly in the shop service manual.

   Instructor check _____

2. Drain the oil from the primary case.

3. Remove the primary cover.

4. Remove the pressure plate mounting screws and the pressure springs.

5. Remove the pressure plate and the push crown.

6. Remove the clutch hub retaining snap ring or large nut.

7. Remove the clutch assembly from the transmission input shaft.

8. Remove the clutch hub, discs, and plates from the clutch housing.

9. Separate the discs, plates, and clutch hub.

Instructor check _____

10. Inspect the friction discs for excessive wear and overheating.

11. Measure the friction disc lining thickness with a micrometer or caliper, and compare the value with service manual specifications. Are the discs worn _____ acceptable _____

Instructor check _____

12. Inspect the clutch's steel plates for excessive wear and overheating.

13. Place the clutch plates on a flat surface one at a time, insert a feeler gauge between the clutch plate and the surface to check for warpage, and compare the results with service manual warpage allowances. Are the plates warped _____ acceptable _____

14. Measure the free length of the pressure springs with a vernier caliper and compare the measured value with service manual specifications. Are the springs worn _____ acceptable _____

15. Coat the friction discs with the recommended type of oil, and assemble the discs and clutch plates onto the clutch hub.

16. Install the plate, disc, and hub assembly into the clutch housing.

17. Install the clutch assembly on the transmission input shaft, and tighten the connection with a clutch hub snap ring or a large nut. If using a nut, tighten it to the specified torque.

18. Install the push crown into the end of the transmission input shaft.

19. Install the pressure plate onto the clutch hub, and tighten the connection with mounting screws and pressure springs.

20. Install the primary cover and fill the unit with the recommended type and amount of oil.

21. Check the clutch for proper operation.

Instructor check _____

NOTES

Date completed _____   Instructor check _____

KEY TERMS

Clutch free play: the space in the clutch release mechanism, measured at the clutch hand lever, that is used to provide clearance on clutch engagement.

Clutch release mechanism: a screw-type or ball-and-cam-plate mechanism used to relieve spring pressure on the clutch plates in order to disengage the clutch.

Gear (sprocket) ratio: a ratio determined by the number of teeth on two gears in mesh or two sprockets connected by a chain.

Multiplate clutch: a clutch that uses alternate plates of friction and steel pushed together by spring pressure when they are engaged.

Primary drive: a set of gears or sprockets and chain that delivers power from the engine to the clutch and provides for a gear reduction.

Torque: a rotary unit of force; a turning or twisting effort used to rotate the rear wheel of the motorcycle.

CHECKUP

Identify the parts of the drive train by writing their names
in the spaces provided.

1. _____

2. _____

3. _____

4. _____

5. _____

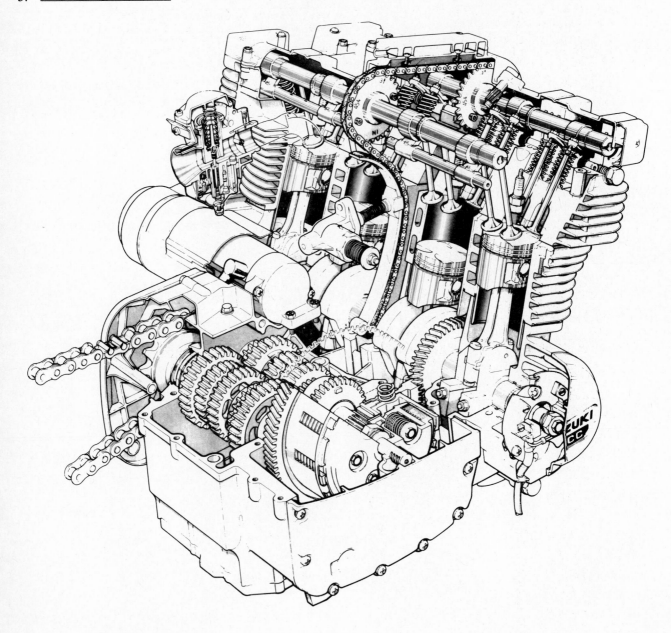

Identify the parts of the primary drive by writing their names in the spaces provided.

6.  _____

7. _____

8. _____

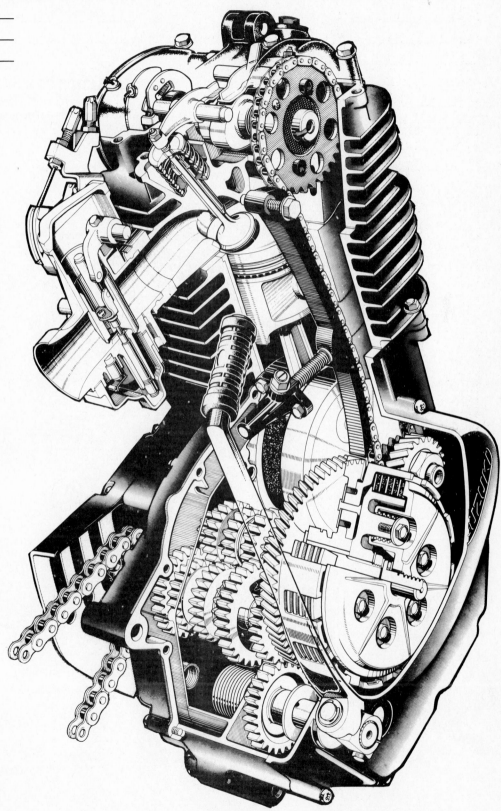

Identify the parts of the multiplate clutch by writing their names in the spaces provided.

9. _____

10. _____

11. _____

12. _____

13. _____

14. _____

15. _____

16. _____

17. _____

18. _____

19. _____

20. _____

DISCUSSION TOPICS AND ACTIVITIES

1. Count the teeth on the gears of a shop engine primary drive. Calculate the gear ratio.

2. Disassemble and reassemble a shop multiplate clutch. How many of the parts can you identify?

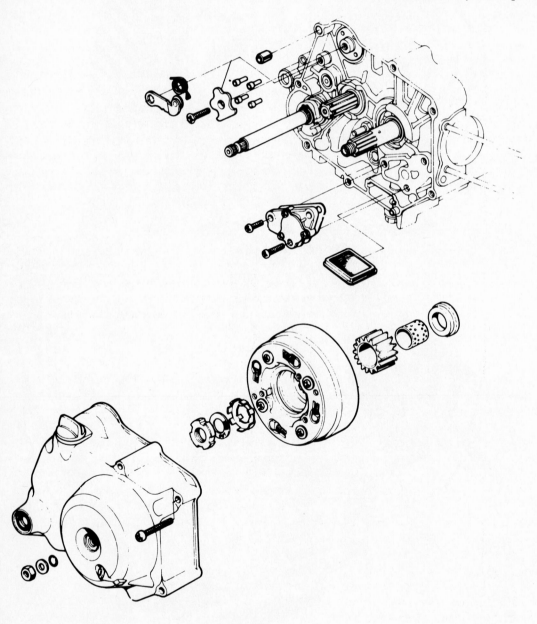

The motorcyle engine is efficient only when it is operating at fairly high rpm. A transmission is necessary to keep the engine operating at high enough rpm while it is being ridden at slow speeds. The transmission provides the rider with a selection of four, five, or six gear shifts that allow him or her to match the engine speed to riding conditions. Each shift provides a different gear ratio and results in a different amount of mechanical advantage between the engine and the rear wheel.

The torque must be multiplied by the transmission and directed to the rear wheel to push the motorcycle down the road. A set of sprockets and chain or a shaft system called the *final drive* is used to deliver the torque from the transmission to the rear wheel. In this unit we describe the parts and operation of the transmission and final drive.

TRANSMISSION AND FINAL DRIVES

JOB COMPETENCY OBJECTIVES

When you finish reading and studying this unit, you should be able to:

1. Describe the parts of a transmission and trace the flow of power through it.

2. Identify the parts and explain the operation of a chain and sprocket final drive.

3. Identify the parts of a shaft drive and trace the power flow through it.

4. Clean, lubricate, and measure a final drive chain.

5. Adjust the tension and alignment of a final drive chain.

TRANSMISSION

The transmission (Figure 23–1) is located inside the engine cases behind the crankshaft. It is made up of two parallel shafts, each with a set of gears. Each shaft is supported on each end in ball bearings so that it can turn freely. One shaft, variously called the *input shaft, driveshaft,* or *main shaft,* receives the torque of the engine through the clutch. The other shaft, called the *output shaft, countershaft,* or *layshaft,* delivers the engine's torque out to the final drive sprocket (or shaft drive).

There is a set of gears on the input shaft and a set of gears on the output shaft. Each gear on the input shaft is in mesh with a gear on the output shaft. Each of these sets of gears represents a transmission speed. Each pair of gears remains meshed all the time, so the transmission is sometimes described as being in constant mesh. There are four, five, or six different-size gears on each shaft, and a gear set for each shift or speed the transmission has. During operation, only one set of gears is used to transmit the power from the engine to the rear wheel. As we shall see, the other gears spin freely on their shafts.

Using different-size gears on the input and output shafts allows the rider to vary the gear ratio between the engine input and the drive-sprocket output. When the rider selects low gear, there is a very large drop in rpm at the output of the transmission; when high gear (fourth, fifth, or sixth gear) is selected, there is usually a straight connection through the transmission. There is always, however, a 3-to-1 reduction provided by the primary gears.

Transmission gear types

There are several basic types of gears inside the transmission. The exploded view of a transmission in Figure 23–2 shows these different types. Those that can spin on their shaft are called *idler gears.* They have a bushing on their inside surface so that they can rotate freely as the shaft spins inside them. An idler gear is always in mesh with a gear that is attached to its shaft.

Gears can be attached to a shaft in one of two ways: mechanically, as part of the shaft, or with splines. When they are machined as part of the shaft, we call them *integral gears.* When splines are cut on the inside of the gear to match splines on the outside of the input or output shaft, the gears are called *splined gears.*

As already stated, the gears on the input shaft are always in mesh with the gears on the output shaft. In all cases, one of the gears will be attached to the shaft, and the other will be freewheeling. In order to use or deliver torque through any gear set, we have to lock the freewheeling gear to its shaft. Locking and unlocking are done with gears called *sliding gears,* or *sliders.*

How a sliding gear works is shown in Figure 23–3. The sliding gear has a set of tabs on its side called *dogs,* which may be square or round in shape, and a groove around one side. A shift fork (to be explained in detail later) attached to the transmission shifter engages this groove. The slider

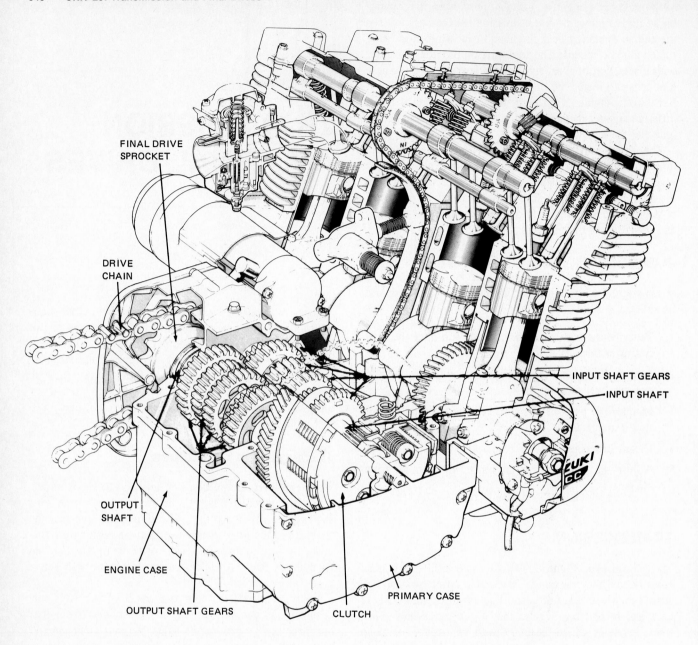

FINAL DRIVE
SPROCKET

DRIVE
CHAIN

INPUT SHAFT GEARS

INPUT SHAFT

OUTPUT
SHAFT

ENGINE CASE

OUTPUT SHAFT GEARS

CLUTCH

PRIMARY CASE

Figure 23–1. Transmission. *(U.S. Suzuki Motor Corp.)*

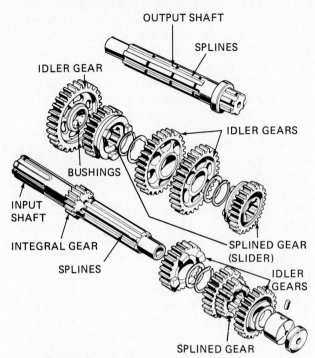

Figure 23–2. Types of transmission gears. *(Honda Motor Co., Ltd.)*

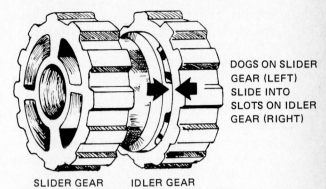

Figure 23–3. Operation of a sliding gear: slider gear (left) is engaged in slots of idler gear (right). *(Mid American Vocational Curriculum Consortium)*

can then be moved a short distance along its shaft (sliding on its splines) until the dogs engage in slots, holes, or other dogs in the freewheeling idler gear next to it.

When the two gears are engaged, the idler gear is solidly attached through the slider gear to its shaft. Since the idler gear is in mesh with another gear that is already locked to its shaft, power can flow from one shaft to another through the two gears.

The slider gear has to move only a small amount to engage its dogs. It does not move enough to get out of mesh with its companion gear on the opposite shaft. Only one set of gears can be locked to the shaft at one time, or the whole transmission would be locked up. Remember that when the slider moves to lock up the gear next to it, the two gears are locked to each other and to their shaft.

Power flow

We are now ready to describe the way torque or power flows through a typical transmission. The transmission (Figure 23–4) has an input shaft and an output shaft. Since

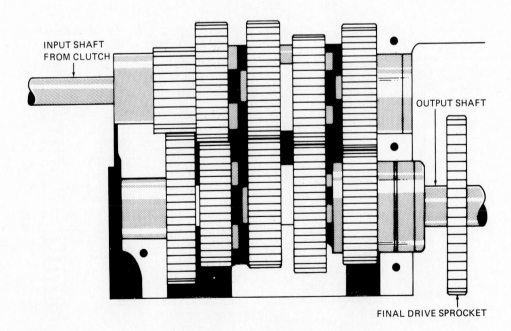

Figure 23–4. Transmission in neutral.

each has five gears, the transmission has five speeds. Each gear on the input shaft is a different size and is in mesh with a different-size gear on the output shaft.

In Figure 23–4, all the sliding gears are positioned so that none of the dogs are engaged. Since none of the freewheeling gears are locked to a slider, there is no power flow through the transmission. We call this shift position neutral. If the clutch is engaged, the input shaft turns but none of the gears on the output shaft are driven.

When the rider shifts into low gear or first gear (Figure 23–5), the smallest gear on the input shaft is used. This gear is usually the integral type. The first gear on the input shaft is in mesh with the largest gear (first gear) on the output shaft. A sliding gear next to the first gear is moved to the left, and the first gear of the output shaft is locked to it and to the output shaft. Power then flows across these two gears. Since a small gear is turning a large gear, there is a large reduction in speed and increase in torque.

As the bike picks up speed, the rider will shift into second gear. The power flow through the transmission in second gear is shown in Figure 23–6. Power from the clutch flows across the input shaft to the second gear, which is splined to the shaft. The second gear of the output shaft is freewheeling until the slider next to it is moved to the left and locks it to the shaft. At the same time, the sliding gear which was used to lock up the first gear is now moved to unlock it. With both second gears now locked to the shaft, power can flow across them. Again, since a small gear is turning a large gear, speed decreases and torque increases.

When the rider shifts into third gear, the shift mechanism disengages the slider that is currently holding the transmission in second gear. A slider is then moved to the right to attach the third gear to the output shaft. As shown in Figure 23–7, power now flows across the input shaft to the third gear, which is attached to the input shaft. Power then flows into the output shaft third gear, which normally freewheels but is now locked to the slider, and then through the slider to the output shaft. Again, since the gear on the input shaft is smaller than the gear on the output shaft, there is a reduction in speed and an increase in torque. Notice, however, that this time there is less of a reduction and increase, respectively, because there is less of a difference in gear sizes as we go through the shifts.

As the rider shifts into fourth gear, a slider on the input shaft is moved to the left, engaging the freewheeling fourth gear and locking it to its shaft. Power now flows across the input shaft to the slider into the input shaft fourth gear, and across to the fourth gear on the output shaft, which is splined to the output shaft. The power flow in fourth gear is shown in Figure 23–8. Since there is only a slight difference in the size of the two fourth gears, there is only a slight reduction in speed and increase in torque.

When the motorcycle is up to highway speed, the rider shifts into the top gear—in the example under consideration, fifth gear (Figure 23–9). At this point the bike is moving fast enough that there is no longer a need for a gear reduction (beyond that provided by the primary gears and the final drive). Fifth gear on the input shaft and out-

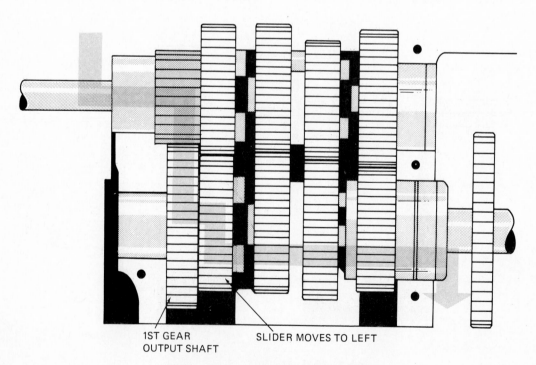

1ST GEAR
OUTPUT SHAFT   SLIDER MOVES TO LEFT

Figure 23–5. Power flow in first (low) gear.

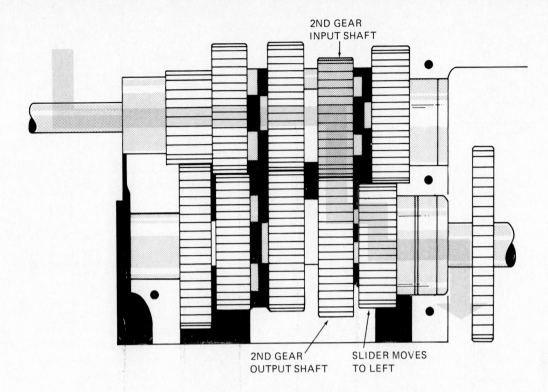

2ND GEAR
INPUT SHAFT

2ND GEAR
OUTPUT SHAFT

SLIDER MOVES
TO LEFT

Figure 23–6. Power flow in second gear.

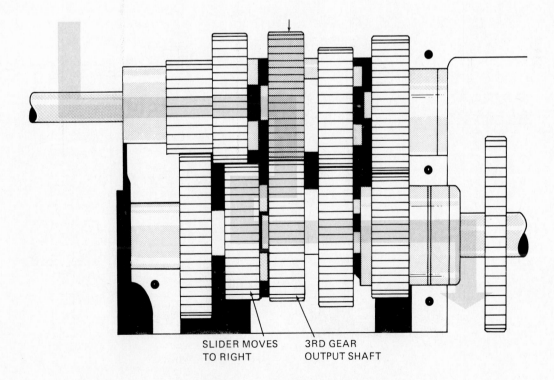

SLIDER MOVES
TO RIGHT

3RD GEAR
OUTPUT SHAFT

Figure 23–7. Power flow in third gear.

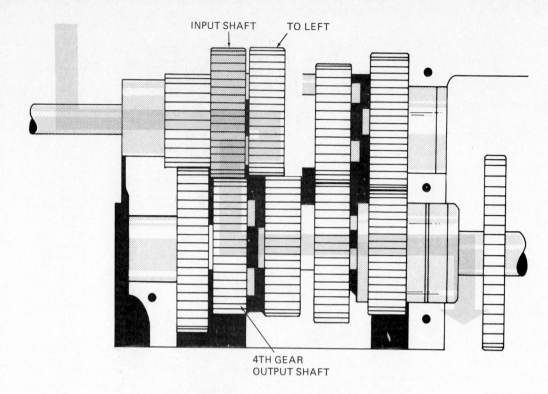

Figure 23–8. Power flow in fourth gear.

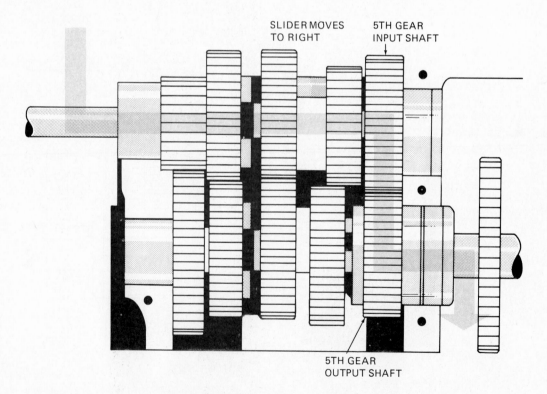

Figure 23–9. Power flow in fifth gear.

put shaft are the same size. Thus, when the slider on the input shaft is moved to the right, it engages the freewheeling fifth gear and locks it to the input shaft. This fifth gear then drives the fifth gear on the output shaft at a 1:1 ratio. Consequently, there is no reduction in speed or increase in torque.

Shift mechanism

As has been discussed, the transmission shifts into different gears by having sliding gears move inside it. This shifting is accomplished by the rider's moving a foot-operated shift lever. A shift mechanism is required to transfer the outside motion of the rider's shift lever to motion inside the transmission.

The gear shift mechanism is located inside the transmission directly over the gears (Figure 23–10) and is connected to the gear shift pedal on the outside of the transmission. The parts of a gear shift mechanism are shown in Figure 23–11. The mechanism consists of a set of gear shift forks that are engaged to the sliders, a gear shift drum, a gear shift pedal, and a gear shift camplate.

The shift forks are moved by the shift drum, which has slots along its outside surface in which pins from the forks ride. The positions of the forks are controlled by the slots in the drum. When the drum rotates, the forks are moved sideways to shift the gears. Just a few degrees of rotation is enough to move the slider and change gears.

In order for the drum to move the forks, it has to be rotated. Accordingly, the gear shift pedal is connected to the shift linkage and then to a camplate. The camplate changes the up and down motion to rotary motion and turns the drum enough to engage the correct gear (Figure 23–12).

Transmission troubleshooting and servicing

Transmission problems generally fall into one of two categories: noise and poor shifting. Noise inside the transmission can be caused either by worn-out bearings which support the input and output shafts or by worn gears. In order to service most transmissions, the engine must be disassembled and the cases split. This much work means that you should be very sure of your diagnosis. Many times a clutch problem or engine noise is confused with a transmission problem. On the other hand, any time the engine is disassembled for service, the transmission should be inspected for wear.

The transmission shafts can usually be lifted out when the engine cases have been split. Always follow the specific shop manual procedure for disassembling and reassembling the gears.

Transmission parts should be cleaned in solvent and inspected for wear or for gears that do not engage properly.

Hard shifting can be caused by damage or wear to the shift forks or shift mechanism, by a clutch not releasing completely, by low transmission lubricant level, by scored or damaged shaft splines, or by a binding shift drum or camplates.

If the transmission jumps out of gear, the problem is usually caused by worn dogs that do not fully engage or by a worn or damaged shift linkage.

A transmission that will not shift at all probably has either a broken shift linkage or a shift pedal that is loose on the shift shaft.

Check each gear for chipped gear teeth. Check sliders for worn, broken, or chipped dogs (Figure 23–13).

The most common wear problem is a worn shift fork. Hence, check the contact area of the fork for wear (Figure 23–14). There is often a micrometer or caliper specification for the thickness of the fork. Also, check the shift fork groove for scoring, which is evidence of wear.

As you reassemble the transmission components, follow the procedure in your shop service manual exactly. As you assemble the gears, remember that splined, integral, and fixed gears always mesh with free-spinning gears. Also, round dogs match against round holes, square dogs against square holes. Be aware that double sliding gears need two free-spinning gears on the other shaft and that sliding gears or fixed gears usually alternate with free-spinning gears.

Kickstarter

The kickstarter assembly allows the rider to spin the engine over with his or her foot for starting. It is housed inside the transmission (Figure 23–15). A starter pinion gear is in mesh with one of the gears on the input shaft or, on some models, with the clutch primary gear. A spindle attached to the kickstart pedal is splined to a drive ratchet that has teeth which fit into teeth on the starter pinion.

When the rider kicks down on the kickstarter pedal, the spindle turns. The teeth of the drive ratchet are shaped to drive the starter pinion, which spins the engine through the transmission gears. As soon as the engine starts, the drive ratchet must be pushed out of mesh; otherwise the kickstarter pedal could swing around and injure the rider. The shape of the ratchet teeth on the starter pinion prevents it from driving the ratchet. The teeth are angled and can only drive in one direction, as shown in Figure 23–15. A kick spring returns the spindle to position after each kick start.

FINAL DRIVES

As mentioned previously, the purpose of the final drive assembly is to deliver engine torque from the transmission to the gear wheel. There are two types of final drive: the chain and sprocket, and the shaft. The chain and sprocket is the oldest and by far the most common type.

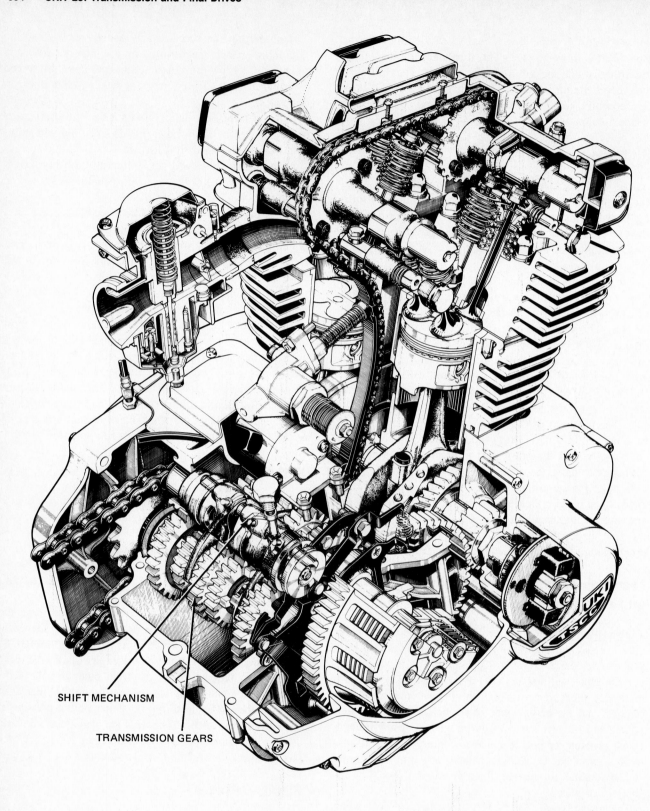

SHIFT MECHANISM

TRANSMISSION GEARS

Figure 23–10. The gear shift mechanism is located above the gears in the transmission. *(U.S. Suzuki Motor Corp.)*

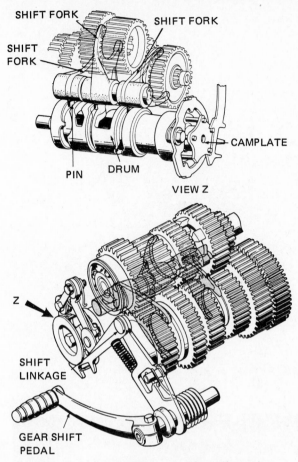

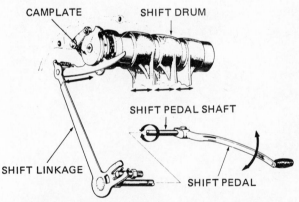

Figure 23–11. Components of a shift mechanism. *(Honda Motor Co., Ltd.)*

Figure 23–12. Operation of the shift mechanism. *(Honda Motor Co., Ltd.)*

Chain-and-sprocket drive

A chain-and-sprocket final drive system is shown in Figure 23–16. In this system, a sprocket is attached to the output shaft of the transmission, a driven rear sprocket is attached to the hub (center) of the rear wheel, and a chain connects the two sprockets together. When the engine is running

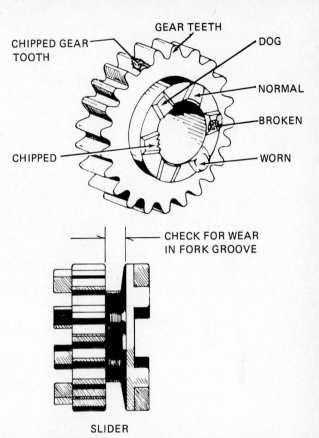

Figure 23–13. Checking for gear wear. *(Mid American Vocational Curriculum Consortium)*

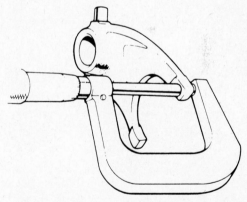

Figure 23–14. Check shaft fork for wear. *(Honda Motor Co., Ltd.)*

and the transmission is in gear, the driving sprocket turns, driving the chain, which in turn drives the rear sprocket.

The rear sprocket is attached to the rear wheel and moves up and down with the rear suspension. The flexible chain allows for this up-and-down movement.

The front drive sprocket is much smaller than the rear sprocket, providing a final reduction in speed and increase in torque to the rear wheel. The numbers of teeth on the two sprockets, of course, determine the final drive ratio.

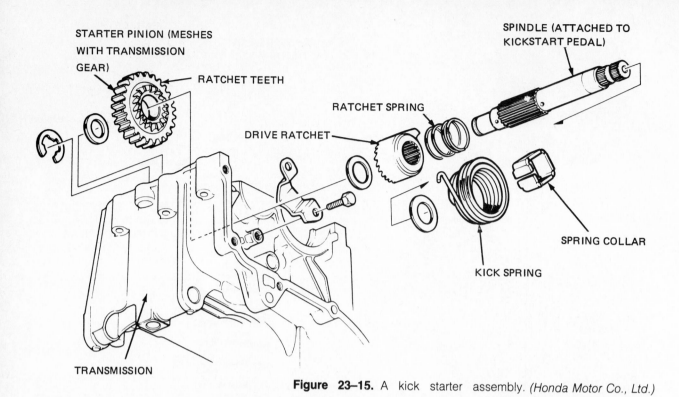

Figure 23–15. A kick starter assembly. *(Honda Motor Co., Ltd.)*

Figure 23–16. Chain-and-sprocket final drive system.

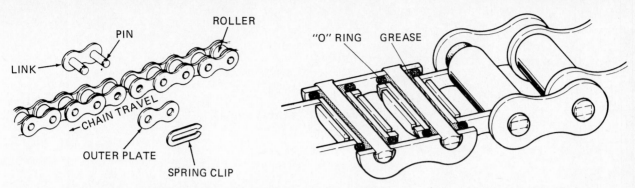

Figure 23–17. Roller chain construction. *(Left: Harley Davidson Motors, Inc. Right: U.S. Suzuki Motor Corp.)*

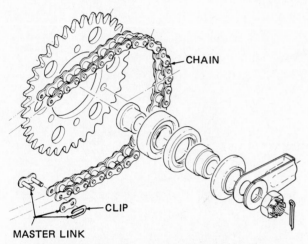

Figure 23–18. The master link allows the chain to be separated. *(Yamaha Motor Corp. U.S.A.)*

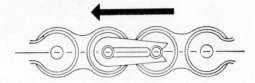

DIRECTION OF TRAVEL

Figure 23–19. The closed end of the clip faces the direction of chain travel. *(Yamaha Motor Corp. U.S.A.)*

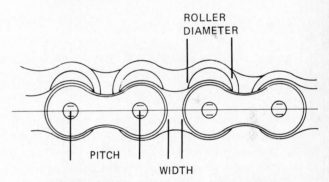

Figure 23–20. Chain size measurements. *(Mid American Vocational Curriculum Consortium)*

The size (number of teeth) of the rear sprocket can be changed for different kinds of riding, such as dirt or street riding.

The rear sprocket may be bolted directly to the rear hub, or it may be bolted to a rear hub damper. The damper is made from a flexible material which absorbs some of the shock of the final drive when the clutch is engaged and engine torque reaches the rear wheel.

The chain used in most applications is a roller-type chain. The construction of a roller chain is shown in Figure 23–17. Inner and outer plates, held together by steel pins, form chain links. Pins are attached to the outer plates, bushings to the inner plates; the pins fit through the inside of the bushings. Rollers which fit around the outside of the bushings roll around the pins to form a bearing between the pin and the sprocket teeth.

In order to remove the chain from the motorcycle, it must be separated. Most chains have a master link like the one shown in Figure 23–17 and 23–18. The master link has a set of pins with a groove cut in their end. When the link is assembled, a clip fits into the grooves to hold the link together. When the clip is removed, the link can be removed from the chain. When you install a clip, make sure that the closed end is facing the normal direction of chain rotation (Figure 23–19).

If the chain does not have a master link, a chain-breaking tool must be used to push one of the pins out of one of the outer plates. The same tool is then used to push the pin back into position for reassembling the chain.

Chains are constructed in different sizes according to the power the transmission requires. Chain sizes are most frequently specified by the diameter of the roller, the width between links, and the distance (pitch) between the center lines of the pins (Figure 23–20). Chains must always be replaced with chains of the same size and must also match the size of the sprocket teeth.

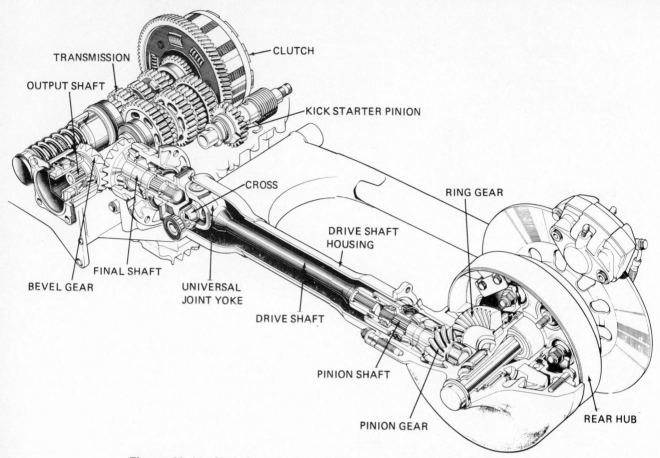

TRANSMISSION

OUTPUT SHAFT

CLUTCH

KICK STARTER PINION

CROSS

RING GEAR

DRIVE SHAFT HOUSING

FINAL SHAFT

BEVEL GEAR

UNIVERSAL JOINT YOKE

DRIVE SHAFT

PINION SHAFT

PINION GEAR

REAR HUB

Figure 23–21. Shaft final drive assembly. *(U.S. Suzuki Motor Corp.)*

Shaft drive

The chain drive system is relatively simple and does an efficient job of transferring torque. Chains, however, have certain built-in disadvantages. For example, they are hard to lubricate and tend to pick up dirt and abrasives which accelerate their wear. Also, they are noisy and prone to developing a certain amount of vibration. To avoid these problems, some of the larger road motorcycles have gone to a shaft drive assembly.

A shaft drive assembly is shown in Figure 23–21. The transmission and clutch are essentially the same as in a chain drive assembly, except that the output shaft is attached to a bevel gear instead of a sprocket. When the output shaft turns, the bevel gear turns, driving another bevel gear that is meshed with it. Power flows through these two bevel gears to a short shaft called the final shaft.

From the final shaft, power flows to a universal joint assembly. The universal joint is basically a Y-shaped yoke whose prongs (the upper, forked part of the Y) are connected by a crossmember called a *cross* or *spider* which is itself shaped like an X. The yoke is free to move up and down in relation to the cross, allowing torque to be transferred through the universal joint when the yoke is posi-

tioned at an angle. The universal joint allows the drive assembly to move up and down as the rear wheel goes up and down on the suspension.

The universal joint yoke is attached to a shaft called the *drive shaft* or *propeller shaft*. This shaft, which is enclosed and protected by a housing, delivers power to another short shaft called the *pinion shaft* that is located at the rear wheel. A pinion gear is attached to the second gear of the pinion shaft.

In mesh with the pinion gear is a large bevel gear called the *ring gear*. As the pinion gear turns, it causes the ring gear to turn. Since the ring gear is attached to the rear wheel hub, it then causes the rear wheel to turn. The number of teeth on the pinion and ring gears provides a final drive gear ratio, just as the sprockets in a chain drive do.

Final drive inspection and servicing

Shaft Drive Servicing

The shaft drive assembly is normally lubricated with gear oil. Since the system is fully enclosed, it does not get contaminated with dirt; therefore, periodic inspection and servicing is not normally required. Any required shaft drive inspection or servicing should be done following the specific instructions in the shop service manual.

Chain-and-Sprocket Inspection and Servicing

The chain-and-sprocket system is exposed to road dirt; hence, the system requires constant attention for lubrication, wear, and adjustment.

One of the most important things a rider can do to increase the service life of his or her chain is to keep it clean and lubricated. The three main areas of the chain that require lubrication are between the pin and the bushing, between the bushing and the roller, and between the overlapping side plates. The most important area is between the pin and the bushing, because that area is the most heavily stressed part of the chain. Lubrication between the bushing and the roller is important to provide a cushion against the forces that arise as the chain engages a tooth on the sprocket.

Chain lubrication cannot be achieved by pouring oil onto the outside of the chain. Oil on the outside of the rollers will serve no useful purpose because chains and sprockets are designed so that the roller seats into the sprocket tooth-pocket without any rolling or sliding. Beyond the small amount of oil required to prevent rust, oil on the outside of a chain serves only to collect dirt and sand, which accelerate wear.

For proper lubrication, oil must be present inside the chain. In order to get inside to the working parts of the chain, the oil must travel between the overlapping side plates and into the bushing/roller area. A dilemma arises, however, in that in order for the lubricant to make its way between the side plates and into the chain, it must be thin, whereas if the internal chain components are to be properly protected, it must be thick.

To resolve the dilemma, manufacturers have produced a number of special spray lubricants for motorcycle chains. These chain lubricants contain solvents which thin them, allowing them to penetrate the working parts of the chain more easily. At the same time, however, after application, the solvent evaporates, leaving the lubricant thick enough for protection. Figure 23–22 shows lubricant being sprayed on the chain.

Regardless of the type of lubricant, it will eventually become contaminated. Therefore, for long life, the chain must be cleaned and relubed on a regular basis. Spray-on cleaners are available for the purpose, or the chain may be removed and soaked in solvent or kerosene (Figure 23–23). All the solvent must be removed before the chain is lubricated.

To remove the chain, first determine whether it has a master link. If it does, use a small screwdriver to remove the spring clip. Then remove the outer plate and push the link out. If the chain does not have a master link, use a removing tool to push a link pin out of the side plate, as

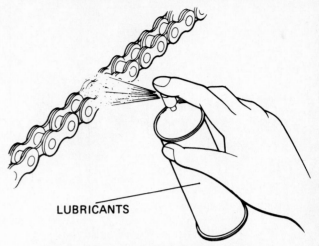

LUBRICANTS

Figure 23–22. Spray lubricant is used to lubricate a chain. *(Honda Motor Co., Ltd.)*

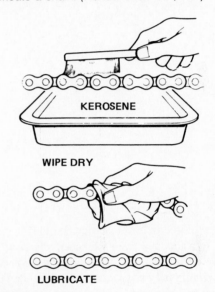

KEROSENE

WIPE DRY

LUBRICATE

Figure 23–23. Cleaning the chain. *(Honda Motor Co., Ltd.)*

shown in Figure 23–24. Use the same tool to push the pin back in for assembly.

A good time to check the chain for wear and possible replacement is when it is removed from the bike for lubrication. Chain wear is measured by determining the percent of elongation or stretch that has occurred. As the chain works, the pins and bushings wear, resulting in stretching in each of the links of the chain. Chain wear is then determined by calculating how much stretch has occurred. Note that bowing a chain sideways is not an accurate method of estimating wear.

To measure the chain, first clean it in solvent to remove the old lubricant. Then lay the chain out flat on a bench or the floor. Starting at one end, push each of the chain links together and measure the overall length of the compressed chain. Next, holding one end of the chain and pulling on

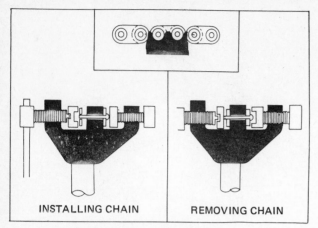

Figure 23–24. Use a special chain removing tool to push out link pins to remove the chain. *(Yamaha Motor Corp. U.S.A.)*

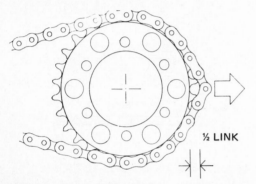

Figure 23–25. Checking for chain wear. *(Yamaha Motor Corp. U.S.A.)*

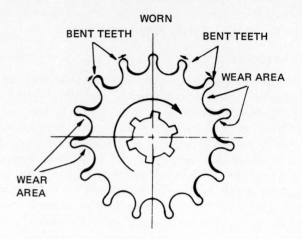

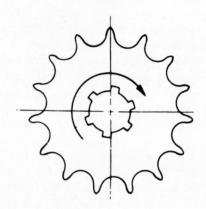

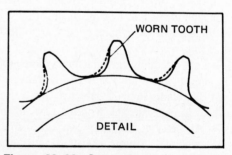

Figure 23–26. Comparison of a worn and good sprocket. *(Yamaha Motor Corp. U.S.A. Detail: U.S. Suzuki Motor Corp.)*

the other, measure the overall stretched length. Then subtract one measurement from the other, divide this difference by the normal length of the chain (the number of links times the pitch), and multiply the result by 100. This figure is the percent elongation. The chain is considered excessively worn when the elongation approaches 3 percent.

You can inspect the chain and sprockets visually without disassembling the chain. With the chain still on the motorcycle, lift the chain away from the rear wheel sprocket as shown in Figure 23–25. A chain is defective if it can be pulled away from the sprocket more than half the length of a link.

A worn drive sprocket may result in abnormal noise and shorten the life of the chain. Accordingly, check the sprocket teeth for wear and deformation. Look the sprocket over for any of the problems shown in Figure 23–26 (top). Sprocket-and-chain wear can be caused by operating in excessively dirty conditions, or by improper tension, improper alignment, and poor lubrication.

Anytime the chain has been removed and installed, it should be checked for tension and alignment. The amount of tension (tightness) a chain has is determined by grabbing the chain at its longest span (between the two sprock-

ets) and moving it up and down (Figure 23–27). The amount of up-and-down movement is called *free play*. After measuring the free play, compare your measurements with specifications. Generally, the free play should be about ½ to ¾ of an inch.

Chain tension is adjusted by moving the rear wheel assembly with the rear sprocket back or forward. An elongated slot is provided for the rear axle at the rear frame (Figure 23–28). The rear axle shaft is held in position in the elongated slot by the rear axle nuts and the drive chain

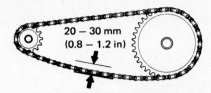

Figure 23–27. Checking the chain for tension. *(U.S. Suzuki Motor Corp.)*

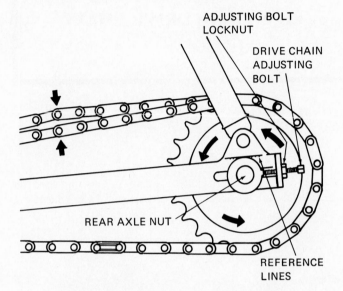

Figure 23–28. Chain tension adjusting mechanism. *(Mid American Vocational Curriculum Consortium)*

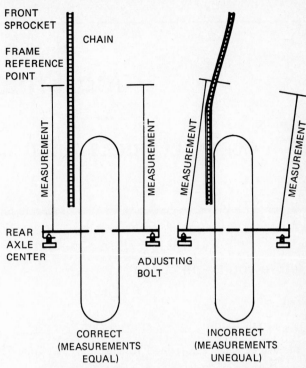

Figure 23–29. Checking rear wheel alignment. *(Mid American Vocational Curriculum Consortium)*

adjusting bolts (one on each side). Reference lines are sometimes provided at each axle to help you keep the wheel square to the frame as you make adjustments.

To make an adjustment, loosen the rear axle nut, the adjusting bolt locknuts, and the adjusting bolts. Turn both adjusting bolts in or out until proper free play is obtained. Both bolts should be turned an equal amount to maintain correct alignment; if reference marks are present, be sure

that the same marks are in alignment. Finally tighten the axle nut, the adjusting bolt locknuts, and the adjusting bolts.

After adjusting chain tension, you should check the alignment of the rear wheel. Use a tape measure to measure from the center of the rear axle to some point on the motorcycle frame, and then repeat the measurement on the other side. Be careful to use the same point both times. If your measurements are not the same, the wheel is not pointing straight and you will have to make an adjustment on one side of the axle to correct the alignment (Figure 23–29).

Job Sheet 23–1

CLEAN, LUBRICATE, AND MEASURE A FINAL DRIVE CHAIN

Before you begin:

Read pp.

Make of Motorcycle _____ Model _____ Year _____.

Time Started _____ Time Finished _____ Total Time _____

Flat-rate Time _____

Special Tools, Equipment, Parts, and Materials

Cleaning solvent
Cleaning brush
Cleaning pan
Safety glasses
Tape measure

References

Manufacturer's Shop Manual _____

Specifications

Look up the specifications for chain stretch and write them in the space below:

Chain stretch _____

Instructor check _____

Procedure

1. Remove the master link clip and the chain master link.

2. Pull the chain off the drive and the driven sprockets.

3. Soak and wash the chain thoroughly in a pan of cleaning solvent. Use the cleaning brush to get out all the dirt between the link plates.

4. Remove the chain from the solvent and hang it up so the solvent will drain off. Allow the chain to air-dry long enough to get rid of all the solvent.

5. Wipe off both sprockets and inspect the teeth for wear. Are the sprockets:

Worn _____ Acceptable _____

Instructor check _____

6. Lay the chain on a flat surface, stretch it to its full length, and then measure its length with a measuring tape.

7. Compress the chain as much as possible without bending or kinking it, and measure it again.

8. Subtract the shortened length from the stretched length.

9. The difference in your two measurements is the amount of stretch. Write your measurements below:

Extended measurement _____

Compressed measurement _____

_____

Difference (stretch) _____

10. Compare the amount of stretch you found with specifications. Is the chain:

Worn _____ Acceptable _____

11. Spray chain lubricant over the chain several times and then wipe off the excess.

12. Install the chain over the sprockets and assemble the master link. Make sure that the clip is oriented correctly (closed end toward the direction of travel).

NOTES

Date completed _____

Instructor check _____

Job Sheet [23–2]

ADJUST FINAL DRIVE CHAIN TENSION AND ALIGNMENT

Before you begin:

Read pp.

Make of Motorcycle _____ Model _____ Year ____

Time Started _____ Time Finished _____ Total Time _____

Flat-rate Time _____

Special Tools, Equipment, Parts, and Materials

Measuring Tape
Eye protection

References

Manufacturer's Shop Manual _____

Specifications

Look up the specification for chain tension (free play) and write it in the space below:

Chain free play _____

Instructor check _____

Procedure

1. Use a tape measure to measure the chain's free play between the drive and the driven sprockets. Write your measurement below:

   Chain free play _____

2. Compare your measurement with specifications. Is the chain tension:

   Correct _____ Too loose _____ Too tight _____

   Instructor check _____

3. If you need to adjust the tension, loosen the rear axle nut, the adjusting bolt locknuts, and the adjusting bolts.

4. Turn both adjusting bolts in or out until you get the proper free play.

5. As you turn the adjusting bolts, be sure that you turn them an equal amount to maintain correct alignment. The same marks should be in alignment on both sides of the wheel.

Instructor check _____

6. Tighten the axle nuts and the adjusting bolt locknuts.

7. Measure from the axle center line to a common reference point on both sides of the frame.

8. If both measurements are the same, the wheel is in alignment. If the measurements are different, the wheel is misaligned. Are your measurements;

Same _____ Different _____

Instructor check _____

9. If necessary, reposition one or the other side of the axle for alignment and remeasuring.

NOTES

Date completed _____   Instructor check _____

KEY TERMS

Chain-and-sprocket drive: a final drive system in which a sprocket attached to the transmission output shaft is connected to a sprocket at the rear wheel by a chain.

Chain free play: the amount of slack in the final drive chain; used to determine chain tension.

Final drive: the components that deliver engine torque from the transmission to the rear wheel.

Shaft drive: a final drive system in which torque is directed to the rear wheel through a drive shaft instead of a chain.

Transmission: a system of parallel shafts and gears used to multiply engine torque to get the motorcycle moving.

CHECKUP

Identify the parts of a transmission by writing their names in the spaces provided:

1. _____
2. _____
3. _____
4. _____
5. _____
6. _____
7. _____
8. _____

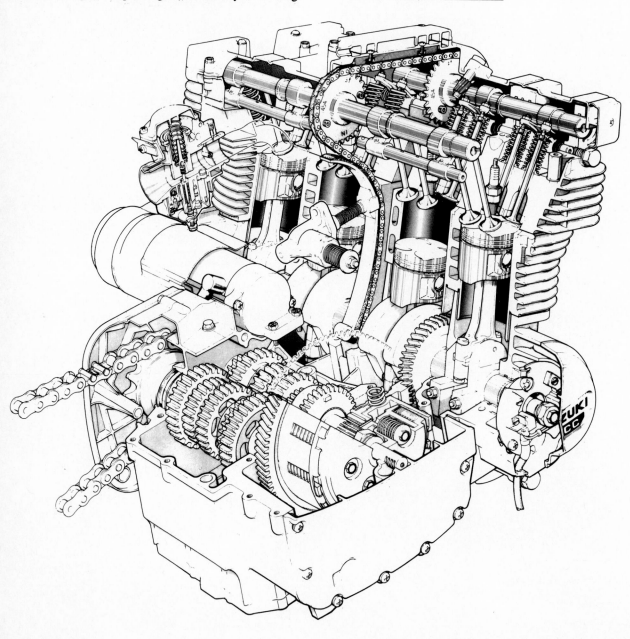

9. How are transmission gears attached to a shaft?

10. Why are fixed gears always in mesh with freewheeling gears?

11. Explain how dogs work to lock a freewheeling gear to its shaft.

Identify the parts of a gear shift mechanism by writing their names in the spaces provided.

12. _____
13. _____
14. _____
15. _____
16. _____
17. _____
18. _____

Identify the parts of a chain by writing their names in the spaces provided.

19. _____
20. _____
21. _____
22. _____
23. _____
24. _____

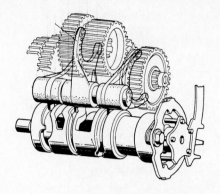

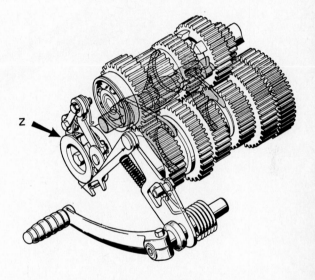

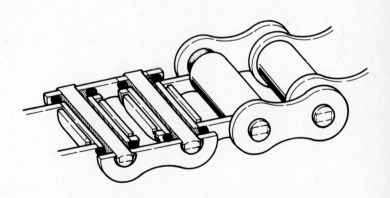

Identify the parts of a shaft drive by writing their names in the spaces provided. (See art on page 368.)

25. _____
26. _____
27. _____
28. _____
29. _____
30. _____

DISCUSSION TOPICS AND ACTIVITIES

1. Use a disassembled shop transmission to trace the flow of power through each transmission shift. Turn the input shaft to simulate power flow.

2. Calculate the final gear ratio in each speed through a transmission considering primary drive, transmission gears, and final drive.

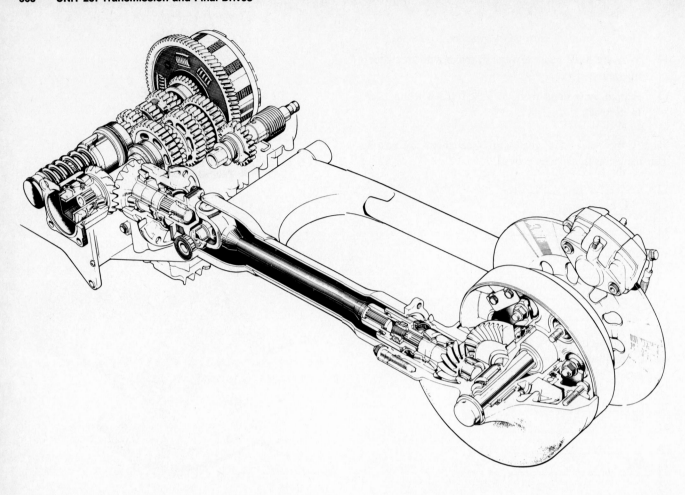

FRAME AND SUSPENSION

Up to this point, we have studied those components of the motorcycle which develop power and transfer it to the bike's rear wheel. These components would be useless if they were not held in the relationship necessary for them to function as a unit. Holding them in that manner is the purpose of the motorcycle frame. Working with the frame to smooth out the ride and provide the rider with good control or handling is the suspension system, a series of springs, linkages, and hydraulic dampening devices. In this unit, we describe the components, operation, and servicing of the frame and suspension system.

JOB COMPETENCY OBJECTIVES

When you finish reading and studying this unit, you should be able to:

1. Describe the parts and operation of the frame and steering system.

2. Identify the parts and explain the operation of the front and rear suspension systems.

3. Change front fork hydraulic oil.

4. Disassemble, inspect, and reassemble a front fork.

5. Check a rear swing arm for wear.

6. Check rear coil springs and shock absorbers.

FRAME

The purpose of the frame is to hold all the motorcycle parts in the correct relationship so that the bike can operate as a complete unit. The engine power train and rear wheel must be held in position so that power can be delivered to the road. The rider's controls, handlebars, and footpegs must be positioned so that they are comfortable. The frame holds the front and rear wheels in line for good handling and provides the brackets for all the parts that must be attached to it, such as the fuel tank, seat, fenders, electrical parts, lights, oil tanks, and battery. The frame also must be able to support the weight of all the motorcycle's components and one or two riders, at the same time withstanding all the forces of the road or trail, such as bumps and potholes.

The frame must be designed to be not only strong enough to support all the necessary weight and absorb all the necessary stresses, but also as light as possible and with just the right amount of flexibility.

There are two basic types of frame in use. The *stamped-steel* frame (Figure 24–1) is used on many mopeds and very small motorcycles. It is made from a structure that is stamped or pressed from steel parts and then welded together.

The stamped-steel frame provides the needed rigidity and strength for very small motorcycles. The engine,

which is bolted to the frame, also adds structural support. The basic advantage of this type of frame is that it is inexpensive to manufacture.

All larger motorcycles use a *tubular* frame (Figure 24–2). This type of frame is made from a series of tubes welded together to form the finished structure. The design makes for a very light, yet very strong frame.

Some of the main tubes of the tubular frame have names. The basic structure is formed by the top main tube, front down tube, and center tube. (See Figure 24–2.) The steering system (to be described later) is attached to a short tube in front called the head tube. To these basic tubes, a number of smaller tubes and braces are fitted to form the final structure or assembly.

Steering system

One of the most important parts of the frame is the head tube, which provides the mounting for the steering system.

FRAME

Figure 24–1. Small mopeds and motorcycles use a stamped-steel frame. *(Batavus U.S.A.)*

TOP MAIN TUBE

HEAD TUBE

CENTER TUBE

FRONT
DOWN TUBE

Figure 24-2. Tubular frame assembly. *(Honda Motor Co., Ltd.)*

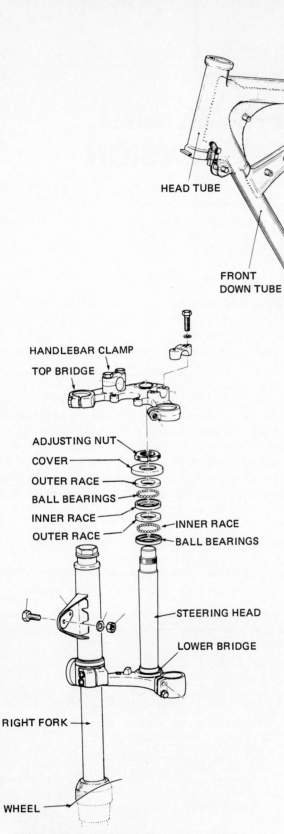

HANDLEBAR CLAMP

TOP BRIDGE

ADJUSTING NUT

COVER

OUTER RACE

BALL BEARINGS

INNER RACE

OUTER RACE

INNER RACE

BALL BEARINGS

STEERING HEAD

LOWER BRIDGE

RIGHT FORK

WHEEL

Figure 24-3. Exploded view of the steering head assembly. *(Yamaha Motor Corp. U.S.A.)*

The steering system allows the rider to move the front wheel left or right to guide the motorcycle.

The front wheel is attached to the front forks, which are in turn attached to the steering head assembly. An exploded view of the steering head assembly is shown in Figure 24-3. Only the right fork is shown.

A part called a fork leg holder, lower crown, or lower bridge is clamped around both the forks. A shaft called the steering head is attached to the lower bridge and passes through the frame head tube. Figure 24-4 shows the forks in relation to each other and to the mounting components.

The steering head must be designed both to withstand the forces of braking and to support the weight of the front end of the motorcycle. At the same time, it must be free to turn. To fulfull these requirements, it has two sets of bearings, one at the bottom to support the weight and one at the top to absorb the forces of braking. The bearings are either ball bearings or tapered roller bearings. On each end of the steering head are two races, separated from each other by roller or ball bearings that roll on the races to reduce friction. The balls and races are made of very hard steel to enable them to withstand the forces they encounter.

The steering-head-and-bearing assembly is installed through the frame head tube. A cover and an adjusting nut are installed to hold the steering head in position. A top bridge is then installed which clamps around the top of the forks and provides a mount for the handlebar.

A typical handlebar clamp assembly is shown in Figure 24-5. The clamp assembly fits over the bar and holds it in

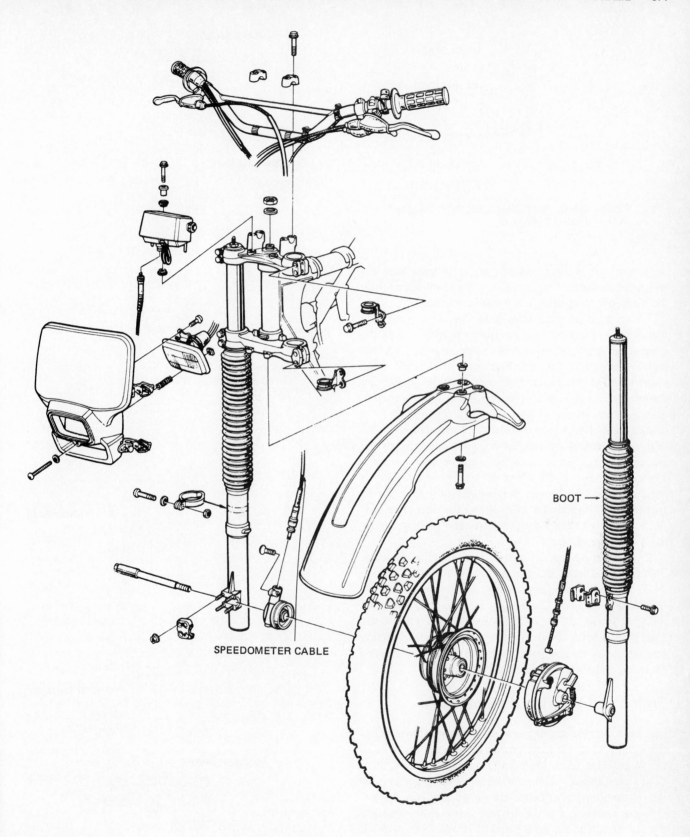

BOOT →

SPEEDOMETER CABLE

Figure 24–4. Front steering assembly.
(Honda Motor Co., Ltd.)

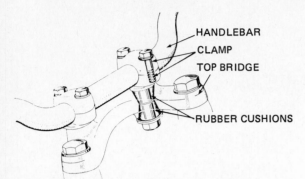

Figure 24–5. Handlebar-to-steering-bridge mount. *(Honda Motor Co., Ltd.)*

the top bridge. Rubber cushions are sometimes used between the clamps and the bridge to prevent vibrations from the front fork from being felt in the handlebar.

If vibrations or oscillations from the front wheel are transferred to the handlebar, the rider will have to fight the steering to keep the motorcycle going straight. Accordingly, some type of dampening device is used to lessen the effect of these vibrations. One common type of steering damper, shown in Figure 24–6, consists of a set of friction discs located on the lower bridge and connected by a bracket to the frame. Some of the discs are attached to the bridge, and others are attached to the frame through the bracket. The friction between the discs prevents unwanted vibration. A knob at the top of the handlebar assembly is attached to a long damper bolt which goes down to the friction discs. Turning the knob allows the rider to set different amounts of tension on the discs and thereby change the dampening effect.

A hydraulic damper is used on many steering systems. This type of damper has two parts: a center shaft (Figure 24–7) attached to the lower bridge, and an outer body attached to the frame. The damper is filled with hydraulic fluid and works like a shock absorber. That is, the center shaft propels hydraulic fluid in the body through restricting passages, moving the shaft back and forth, and thereby providing a dampening effect on the steering.

Frame and steering dimensions

The frame and the steering system are designed together to make the motorcycle easy for the rider to control. A number of common terms are used to describe some of these design relationships. Some of these terms, together with the relationships they denote, are shown in Figure 24–8.

Ground clearance is the distance between the road and the lowest component in the middle of the motorcycle. It is important that the weight of the motorcycle be as low as possible for good cornering. Otherwise, the motorcycle would be top heavy and difficult to control. On off-road

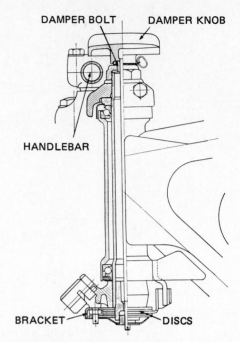

Figure 24–6. Sectional view of a steering damper assembly. *(Honda Motor Co., Ltd.)*

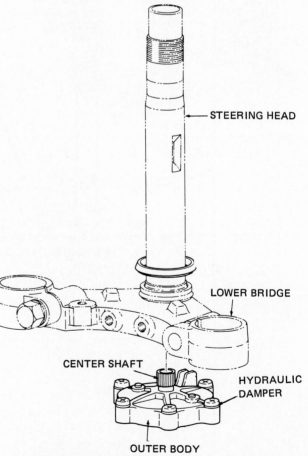

Figure 24–7. A hydraulic steering damper. *(Yamaha Motor Corp. U.S.A.)*

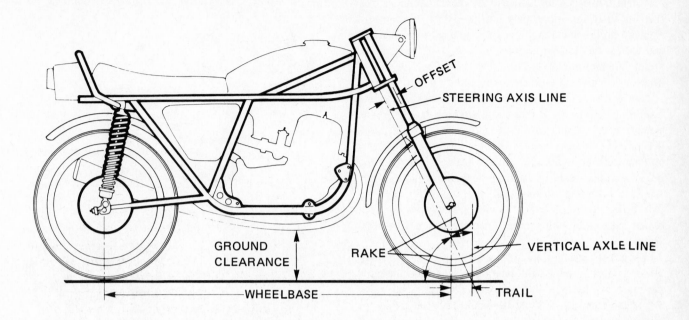

Figure 24–8. Frame and steering relationships. *(Kawasaki Motors Corp. U.S.A.)*

dirt bikes, the ground clearance must be very high so that the motorcycle can clear obstacles.

The distance between the center of the front axle and center of the rear axle is called the *wheelbase,* which also denotes the length of the motorcycle. The length of the motorcycle has a lot to do with how it handles. A long wheelbase is slower handling because it reacts less rapidly to a steering change than does a shorter wheelbase, which also reacts more quickly to a shift in the rider's position.

Small dirt bikes often have a short wheelbase for a quick steering response. Larger, heavier road bikes have a longer wheelbase to provide a more stable feel on the highway.

Steering feel is also affected by a design feature called *trail.* Trail is the distance between the points of intersection of two lines with the plane surface of the ground. One of the lines, called the steering axis, runs down the center of the steering head to the ground. The other line is a vertical line from the center of the front axle to the ground. The steering axis intersection point with the road lies ahead of the other point, which is in the center of the tire's road contact point—i.e., the center of the tire contact point trails the steering axis road intersection point. This relationship gives the front wheel a tendency to follow, or self-correct. Thus, if the front wheel is deflected by a bump, the friction of the road on the tire contact point behind and to one side of the steering axis pushes the tire around until

the center of the contact point is once again directly behind the steering axis.

How much trail a motorcycle has is determined by two factors: the rake and the fork offset. The *rake* is the angle of the steering axis from the vertical; the *offset* is the distance that the fork tubes are placed forward of the steering axis.

Frame and steering system servicing

Frame damage and steering system wear can cause poor handling. If the frame is twisted or bent so that the wheels and suspension components are not in the proper relationship to each other, motorcycle handling is affected: the rider will have a difficult time controlling the bike.

Normally, the only way a frame gets damaged is as a result of a crash. If the frame is bent, cracked, broken, or otherwise distorted by a crash, handling will suffer. Cracks or breaks in the frame are relatively easy to find. After a crash, check all the welds for cracks, especially around the steering head. Chipped or peeling paint is an indication of a possible problem. Wash the frame thoroughly to make any cracks easy to see. The frame can be inspected with magnetic or fluorescent crack detection equipment. Diagnosis and repair is normally done by experts adept in the use of this special equipment.

A bent frame is a lot harder to diagnose than cracks. A small bend in the frame may not be visible but can still alter the cycle's handling. The only sure way to diagnose and correct this kind of a problem is to completely disassemble the motorcycle and have the frame checked and, if necessary, corrected on the manufacturer's test fixture.

The steering system requires periodic maintenance and inspection, especially if there is a handling problem. The steering head bearings are subject to damage from unexpectedly high shock loadings, such as might be caused by accidents. In order to have smooth steering, the steering head bearings require cleaning and lubrication. They should be removed, cleaned, and checked for damage before being coated generously with a heavy, waterproof grease such as lithium grease. Then they should be reassembled.

When the steering head is disassembled, check for obvious broken or crumbled ball bearings. Look for dimples in the races and pits, or dull spots on the races and balls. While the steering head is disassembled, check that the steering stem is straight by placing it on a flat surface. If you remove the bearing races, they must be reset solidly and squarely in position in the steering head tube and on the bottom end of the bridge. If they are loose, the steering bearings will go out of adjustment quickly. If they are cocked slightly, the steering will bind, and the bearings may be destroyed completely.

The most important part of steering head reassembly is the bearing adjustment, which, if done properly, will avoid fast wear and loss of control. To adjust the bearings, tighten the adjustment nut until the bearings bind, and then back off the nut until the forks swing easily from side to side. The bearings must be loose enough so that the front wheel will fall to either side when the bike is on a center stand with the front wheel off the ground. At the same time, they must be tight enough so that there is no back-and-forth play in them.

To check for play, leave the motorcycle on the center stand and grab both front forks. Then try to pull the front wheel back and forth. If you are able to feel any movement at all, the bearings are too loose.

SUSPENSION

The suspension system is a set of linkages, springs, and hydraulic damping devices that are used to suspend or hold up the weight of the motorcycle and rider. The suspension system also connects the wheels to the frame. The most important function of the suspension is to cushion the motorcycle and rider from the bumps on the road. If the suspension does its job, the wheels of the motorcycle can go up and down as they roll over bumps without the motorcycle's bouncing (Figure 24–9).

An often overlooked fact is that the tires (see Unit 26) are an important part of the suspension. The tires are filled

Figure 24–9. The suspension lets the wheels bounce while preventing the bike from bouncing. *(Kawasaki Motors Corp. U.S.A.)*

with air under pressure and also have some elasticity. Thus, the air in the tires can be compressed, and the motorcycle can bounce up and down on the tires.

The typical motorcycle has front and rear suspensions to support the front and rear tires, respectively. While suspension systems have many minor variations, they all operate in essentially the same manner.

Front suspension

The front suspension system consists of a set of telescoping front forks (Figure 24–10). The front wheel, through its axle, is attached to the bottom end of the front forks. The frame is attached to the other end through the steering

Figure 24–10. The front suspension consists of a set of telescoping front forks. *(U.S. Suzuki Motor Corp.)*

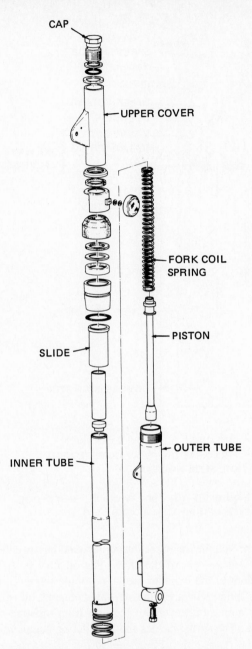

Figure 24–11. Exploded view of a telescoping front fork. *(Yamaha Motor Corp. U.S.A.)*

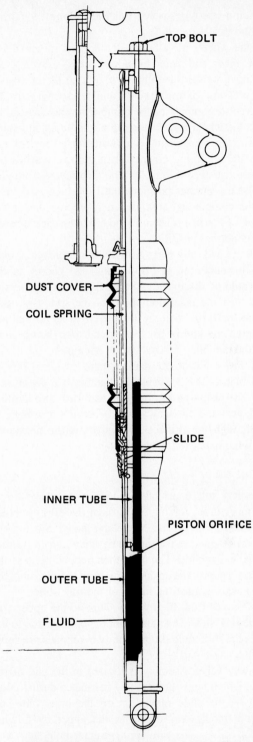

Figure 24–12. Front fork assembly. *(Kawasaki Motors Corp. U.S.A.)*

system. Each fork is constructed from an inner and outer tube that can telescope in on each other, allowing the forks to get longer or shorter as the front wheel moves up and down.

Basically, each fork is a tubular hydraulic damper or shock absorber with an internal or external spring to support the motorcycle. The forks work to support the motorcycle without transferring road shocks to it and the rider. An exploded view of a front fork is shown in Figure 24–11, and a sectional view is shown in Figure 24–12.

The front fork is divided into the inner tube (connected to the frame) and the outer tube (connected to the wheel). With the inner tube inserted into the outer tube, both tubes move up and down in a sliding motion. A slide located on top of the outer tube provides the sliding surface. The vertical motion of the tubes is controlled by a long coil spring and by fluid inside the unit.

When the wheels hit a bump, the springs mounted between the inner and outer tubes compress, allowing the forks to move upward to follow the contour of the bump. The compression of the springs and telescoping of the forks prevent the impact of the bump from moving up the frame. As the wheel reaches the top of the bump and starts back down, the bike continues upward for an instant and then also starts coming down. When the tire reaches the level surface, it stops falling, but the motorcycle continues down, past the normal position, until the increased pressure of the compressed springs can overcome the downward force of the bike. Then the bike moves back upward towards its normal position.

If the forks had only coil springs, the motorcycle would continue to bounce up and down until the energy in the springs would be dissipated. But the hydraulic dampers in the forks slow the extension speed of the springs so that they cannot push the motorcycle up beyond its normal position. When the spring tries to extend after being compressed, the damping unit resists the attempt.

A sectional view of the damper parts inside a fork is shown in Figure 24–13. Inside the damper is a piston in a cylinder. The piston pushes oil back and forth through tiny orifices (holes) and one-way valves. The oil's resistance to flowing through the orifices and valves is the resistance that slows the extension of the spring.

Compression

When the fork telescopes, the slide moves up and down over the inner tube, forcing oil through the oil flow holes in the cylinder, valve plate, and valve body. Since these parts are all fastened to the inner tube, they remain stationary relative to the slide. The oil is then trapped because the piston seals against the inside of the inner tube, and the inner tube seals against the inside of the fork slide.

The oil moves from the lower volume to the upper volume as the fork slide rises, and from the upper to the lower volume as the fork slide drops. The two volumes are separated by the valve parts.

A one-way valve assembly is located in the end of the inner tube which helps prevent any resistance during compression. As the slide moves up on the inner tube, oil moves from the lower volume to the upper by flowing through the valve. The tiny spring cannot hold the valve against the valve plate because of the oil pressure.

During this time, the oil is also allowed to move from the lower volume through the center of the cylinder to the spring chamber above the piston. This translation is necessary because the total volume of the upper and lower volumes decreases during the compression stroke of the fork. The reason for the decrease in volume is because the inner tube takes up more room inside the fork slide. On the other

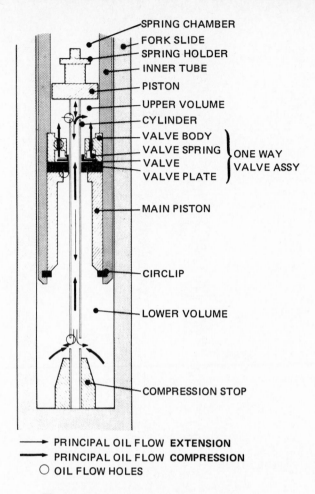

PRINCIPAL OIL FLOW **EXTENSION**
PRINCIPAL OIL FLOW **COMPRESSION**
○ OIL FLOW HOLES

Figure 24–13. Fork hydraulic dampening system. *(Kawasaki Motors Corp. U.S.A.)*

hand, the volume increases during rebound because the inner tube moves out of the slide. The oil flow holes near the bottom of the cylinder are large to allow free oil flow to the spring chamber during the compression stroke, thereby aiding in preventing the unit from resisting compression. The spring carries the load during compression.

Rebound

During the rebound stroke, oil flows from the upper volume to the lower, as the size of the upper volume decreases. The valve shuts against the valve plate immediately because now the oil pressure is helping the spring close it. The oil can get out only through the tiny oil flow hole at the top of the cylinder.

The oil in the spring chamber flows easily down through the cylinder, out the large oil flow holes at the bottom, and into the lower volume. The rebound oil flow speed, which is controlled by the size of the small oil flow holes at the top of the cylinder, determines the amount of resistance the forks will have to being extended by the springs. If the small oil flow holes at the top of the cylinder were even

Figure 24–14. Swing arm rear suspension system. *(Harley Davidson Motors, Inc.)*

smaller, there would be more rebound damping (controlling spring oscillation by a hydraulic piston assembly).

Rear suspension

Like the front wheel, the rear wheel must be allowed to move up and down independently of the frame. The rear suspension system consists of a swing arm assembly controlled by coil springs and hydraulic shock absorbers. The rear wheel is attached to the end of the swing arm. The unit gets its name from the fact that it allows the wheel to swing up and down (Figure 24–14).

The swing arm is mounted to the rear of the frame on a set of bearings or bushings so that up-and-down movement is possible. An exploded view of a typical swing arm suspension is shown in Figure 24–15. A pivot shaft fits through the frame and the swing arm tube. A long bushing fits into the swing arm tube and supports the center of the swing arm. Smaller frame bushings support the pivot shaft in the frame. When the rear wheel moves in the vertical direction, the part of the swing arm which is mounted to the frame on bushings becomes the pivot point, and the rear wheel moves in an arc.

Movement of the swing arm is controlled by one or two coil springs and one or two shock absorber units. In Figure 24–15 each side of the swing arm has a coil spring, and in the middle of the coil spring is a shock absorber. This design is called a *twin-shock design*.

Other motorcycles use what is called a *monoshock design*, in which one large spring and shock absorber is attached to the center of the swing arm. A monoshock system is shown in Figure 24–16.

The rear spring or springs and shocks are similar, in principle, to the forks. The springs support the weight of the motorcycle and are on the outside of the suspension unit. This arrangement allows the use of a longer spring than would otherwise be possible. The external spring has another advantage in that it is cooled by the surrounding air. Heating of the spring is caused by the energy of contraction and expansion.

The rear shock absorber or twin-shock absorbers dampen spring action just as the front fork units do. The shock or damper is located inside the coil spring, as shown in Figure 24–17. The rear shock absorbers or dampers have an arrangement of one-way valves and small oil flow orifices that give them the desired damping characteristics. On most motorcycles, the rear units cannot be disassembled or repaired, so we shall not present a detailed description of how they work.

Most rear springs have a provision for changing the spring rate. This spring adjuster is shown in Figure 24–17. The bottom of the coil spring sits on the spring adjuster, whose position is controlled by a spring seat on the shock absorber. Turning the adjuster allows you to select a high or low slot in it for the spring seat. The slots increase or decrease the spring tension, as the case may be. You may want to change tension if you normally carry a passenger.

Suspension travel

Suspension travel is the distance that the front or rear wheels can move up and down relative to the rest of the motorcycle. Because the wheels must move up and down to go over bumps, the greater the suspension travel, the larger a bump or the deeper a hole that the wheel can travel over without disturbing the rider. As the wheels rise and fall, however, they change the other basic dimensions of the motorcycle, such as the wheelbase and the steering trail.

If the motorcycle has a chain-type final drive, the chain tension is also affected by the action of the swing arm (Figure 24–18). The chain tightens and loosens as the distance between the two sprockets changes with wheel travel. Too much suspension travel is as much a problem as too little, which is why correct chain tension is important.

Suspension system servicing

Front or rear suspension problems may show up as poor handling, or too stiff or soft suspension action. After a crash, the front forks and rear trailing arm must be checked for breaks, cracks, and bends. Damage to the front forks or the rear swing arm can make the bike difficult to steer and control. The same techniques as are used to locate a frame problem will work for suspension system components.

Worn coil springs or worn hydraulic components can cause the suspension to fail to control the motorcycle wheels properly. The bike will start to feel too soft, or, if the parts are binding, it may start to feel too stiff. When hydraulic parts fail, the damping effect of the springs is lost: the bike will begin to bounce excessively after a

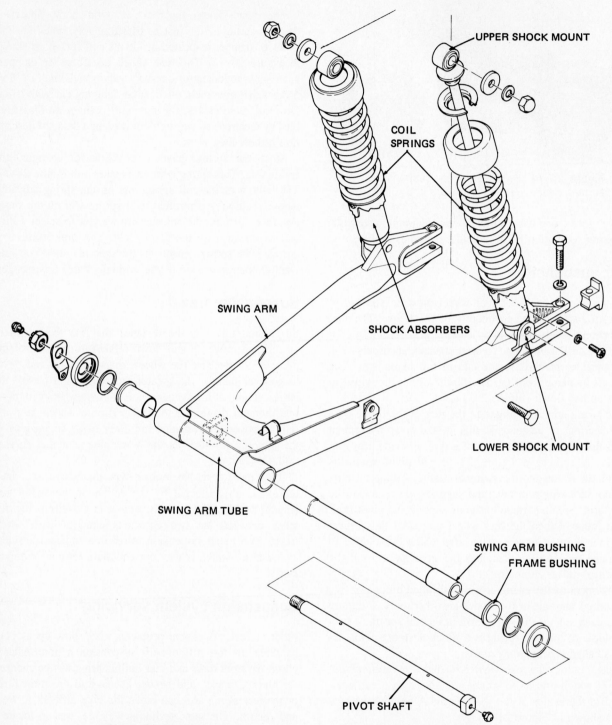

Figure 24–15. Rear swing arm assembly. *(Yamaha Motor Corp. U.S.A.)*

bump. If you experience any of these problems, you will have to service the front or rear suspension.

Front Fork Servicing

Sometimes front fork problems can be cured by a change of hydraulic oil in the hydraulic dampers. The fluid can get contaminated with dirt, especially if the fork dust boot gets torn. Or worn seals can allow the hydraulic oil to escape. If you have poor front fork action, a good first step is to try a change of fluid.

To change the fluid, place a drain pan under the drain bolt (Figure 24–19) on one of the forks. Then remove the

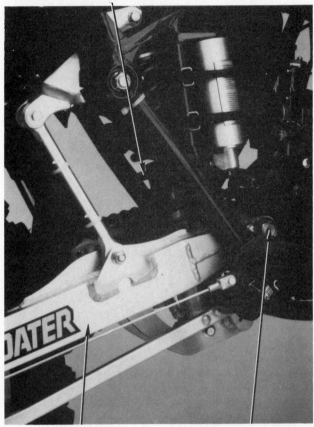

MONO SHOCK AND SPRING

SWING ARM   SWING ARM PIVOT

Figure 24–16. The mono shock system uses one shock and coil spring. *(U.S. Suzuki Motor Corp.)*

fill plug at the top of the fork and the drain plug at the bottom of the fork. Allow the oil to drain out of the fork. To push any remaining oil out of the fork, apply the front brake while you push up and down on the forks. Next, replace the drain plug and use a funnel to add the recommended type and amount of oil to the fork through the fill plug. Finally, replace the fill plug. Repeat the procedure for the other fork and test-ride the bike, checking it for good suspension performance.

If a change of fluid does not result in good suspension performance, you will need to disassemble the forks, inspect them for wear, and replace any worn parts. To remove the forks, securely block the motorcycle up with the front wheel off the ground, and then follow the specific procedure in the shop service manual for the motorcycle you are working on. The following procedures are typical.

Disconnect the speedometer cable (Figure 24–20; see Figure 24–4 for details.) Then disconnect the brake calipers and remove the front wheel. Place a wooden wedge or other object into the caliper assemblies to keep the brake pads from falling out (more on this in Unit 25). Remove the front fender.

Loosen the pinch bolts on the steering stem and bridge, and remove the forks. Remove the fork tube caps, spring clips, and oil drain screws. (Refer to Figure 24–19.) Drain the fork oil as described earlier. You can then hand pump the fork to remove any remaining fluid (Figure 24–21).

Remove the Allen bolt from the bottom of the fork assembly, and pull the inner tube out of the outer tube.

To remove the fork seal, first pull off dust cover and remove the set ring or circlip over oil seal (Figure 24–22) with a screwdriver. Then pry out the oil seal, being careful not to damage the fork tube. A bad oil seal is a common front fork problem. The seals wear out frequently, allowing fluid to escape from the fork. Pull the remaining parts out of the tube.

Clean all the parts in cleaning solvent and allow them to dry. Inspect each part for evidence of damage or wear. Examine the inner tube of the fork for scratches and straightness. If the tube is scratched severely or bent, it should be replaced. You can check for any bends by rolling the tube over a flat surface. If the tube is bent anywhere, you should be able to see it hop as it rolls.

Check the outer tube for dents. If any dent in the outer tube causes the inner tube to "hang up" during operation, the outer tube should be replaced.

Check the coil spring by measuring its free length with a measuring tape. If it is shorter than specifications, it is worn out and should be replaced.

Apply hydraulic oil to the fork seal, and install the seal spacer and seal by driving them in with a seal driver. Install the snap ring.

Install the inner tube inside the outer tube. Then install the dust cover and install and tighten the Allen bolt and washer. Assemble the inside components in the order you disassembled them. Be sure to follow the shop manual instructions.

When you install the fork springs, the greater pitch (the space between the spring coils) should be at the bottom (Figure 24–23).

Install the fork assemblies into the bridge and steering assemblies. Be sure to torque all clamp bolts to specifications. Install the wheel and brake assemblies, as well as any accessories (e.g., the fender and the speedometer cable) that you removed. Fill the forks with the recommended type and amount of oil and then remove the motorcycle from its blocks and test the suspension action.

Rear Suspension Servicing

Wear in the rear suspension occurs chiefly at three points: the swing arm pivot bushings, the coil spring, and the shock absorbers. Wear in the swing arm pivot bushings or bearings causes poor swing arm action. Wear in the coil spring results in too soft a ride and the possibility of rear wheel hop. Finally, if the shock absorbers wear out, they

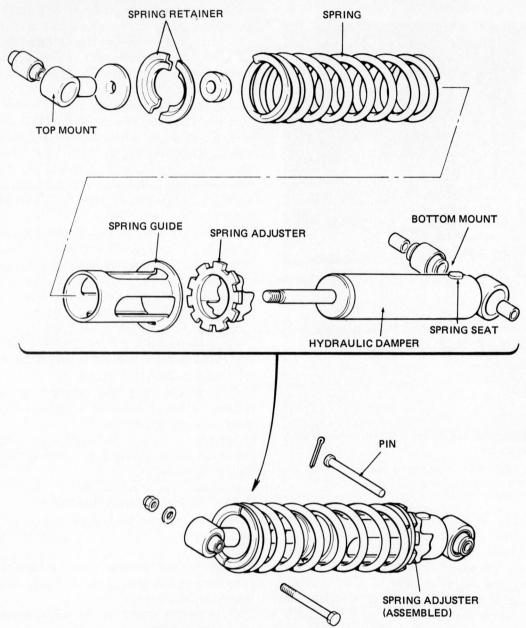

Figure 24–17. The shock absorbers are located inside the coil springs. *(Yamaha Motor Corp. U.S.A.)*

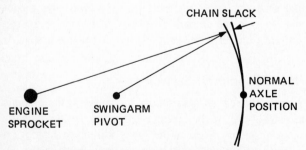

Figure 24–18. Wheel travel is limited by a final drive chain. *(Kawasaki Motors Corp. U.S.A.)*

will fail to dampen the springs properly, resulting in a bike that bounces excessively.

To check the rear swing arm, you will have to unbolt the shock absorbers from the bottom of the arm. First, lift and support the rear of the motorcycle. Remove the rear wheel assembly, and grab the swing arm and try to move it from side to side. There should be no noticeable side play. Then move the swing arm up and down. The arm should move smoothly, without tightness, binding, or rough spots that might indicate damaged bushings or bearings.

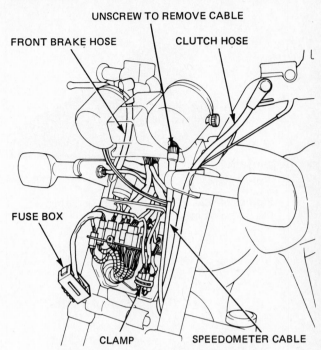

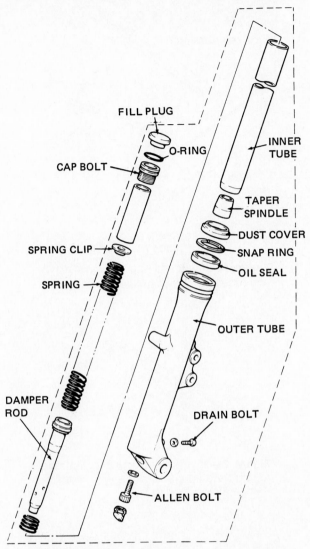

Figure 24–19. Location of the drain and fill plugs on a front fork. *(Yamaha Motor Corp. U.S.A.)*

Figure 24–20. Disconnect the speedometer cable. *(Honda Motor Co., Ltd.)*

Figure 24–21. Pump fork to remove remaining fluid. *(Honda Motor Co., Ltd.)*

If you find a problem, remove the pivot bolt (Figure 24–24), and then remove the swing arm. Replace all bushings or bearings. Then lubricate the new bushings or bearings and reinstall the swing arm.

In order to check the coil spring, it will have to be removed from the shock absorber. (*SAFETY CAUTION: The coil spring is under tension. Do not remove it from the shock absorber without a compressing tool. Wear eye protection.*) Using the recommended tool, compress the coil spring (Figure 24–25) until the spring retainers can be removed.

Use a measuring tape to measure the free length of the coil spring. If it is shorter than specifications, replace the spring.

The shock absorber can be checked visually for signs of fluid leakage or a bent tube or rod. On the other hand, it

is extremely difficult to test a shock absorber for good damping action by working it by hand. The best rule is that if the rear wheel has been bouncing or hopping, replace the shock absorbers.

Replace the coil spring on the shock absorber, using the same compressing tool you used to remove it. (*SAFETY CAUTION: Wear eye protection.*) Mount the shock-and-coil-spring assembly back on the bike. Finally, reinstall the rear wheel assembly and test the rear suspension for proper operation.

1. OIL SEAL RING
2. OIL SEAL

Figure 24–22. Remove set ring or circlip. *(Kawasaki Motors Corp. U.S.A.)*

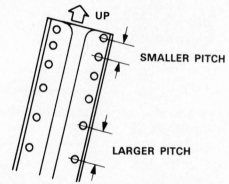

Figure 24–23. Install coil springs with wide pitch toward the bottom. *(Yamaha Motor Corp. U.S.A.)*

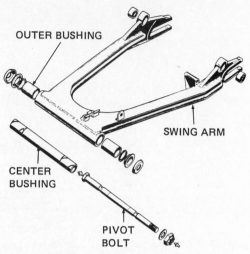

Figure 24–24. Rear swing arm disassembly and assembly. *(Honda Motor Co., Ltd.)*

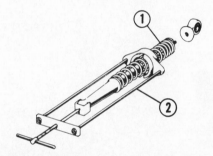

Figure 24–25. Using a spring compressor to remove a spring from a shock absorber. *(Honda Motor Co., Ltd.)*

Job Sheet 24–1

CHANGE FRONT FORK HYDRAULIC OIL

Before you begin:

Read pp.

Make of Motorcycle _____ Model _____ Year ____

Time Started _____ Time Finished _____ Total Time _____

Flat-rate Time _____

Special Tools, Equipment, Parts, and Materials

Drain pan
Replacement oil
Eye protection
Measuring container
Funnel

References

Manufacturer's Shop Manual _____

Specifications

Look up the type and amount of oil for each front fork, and write them in the spaces below:

Oil type _____   Oil amount _____

Instructor check _____

Procedure

1. Remove the filler caps at the top of the fork.

2. Place a drain pan under the fork and remove the drain plug.

3. Apply the front brake and pump the forks to remove any additional oil in the fork.

4. Install the drain plug.

5. Repeat steps 1–4 at the other fork.

Instructor check _____

6. Measure out the correct amount of oil for the fork.

7. Using a funnel, pour the correct amount of oil in the fork.

8. Replace the filler cap.

9. Repeat steps 6–8 for the other fork.

Instructor check _____

10. Check the forks for good suspension action.

NOTES

Instructor check _____

Date completed _____

Job Sheet 24–2

DISASSEMBLE, INSPECT, AND REASSEMBLE A FRONT FORK

Before you begin:

Read pp.

Make of Motorcycle _____ Model _____ Year _____

Time Started _____ Time Finished _____ Total Time _____

Flat-rate Time _____

Special Tools, Equipment, Parts, and Materials

Measuring tape   Fork overhaul parts
Seal driver   Eye protection
Drain pan
Funnel
Replacement oil

References

Manufacturer's Shop Manual _____

Specifications

Look up the specification for coil spring free length and write it in the space below:

Coil spring free length _____

Instructor check _____

Procedure

1. Block the motorcycle up safely, with the front wheel off the ground.
2. Remove the front wheel.
3. Remove the speedometer cable.
4. Disconnect the front brake calipers and remove the front wheel.
5. Remove the front fender.

6. Loosen the bridge clamp bolts and remove the forks from the motorcycle.

Instructor check _____

7. Drain the oil from the forks.

8. Remove the Allen bolt from the bottom of the fork assembly.

9. Pull the inner tube out of the outer tube.

10. Remove the fork seal snap ring and seal.

11. Clean all parts in cleaning solvent.

Instructor check _____

12. Examine all parts for wear or damage.

13. Measure the free length of the coil spring and compare your measurements with specifications. Is the spring:

Acceptable _____ Too short _____

Instructor check _____

14. Lubricate all the components with hydraulic oil.

15. Install a new seal with a seal driver, and replace the snap ring.

16. Install the parts in the fork assembly in the correct order.

Instructor check _____

17. Install the assembled forks on the motorcycle.

18. Fill the forks with the correct amount of recommended oil.

19. Install all the accessories you removed during disassembly.

20. Remove the bike from the blocks and check the front forks for correct suspension action.

NOTES

Instructor check _____   Date completed _____

Job Sheet 24–3

CHECK A REAR SWING ARM FOR WEAR

Before you begin:

Read pp.

Make of Motorcycle _____ Model _____ Year _____

Time Started _____ Time Finished _____ Total Time _____

Flat-rate Time _____

Special Tools, Equipment, Parts, and Materials

Drift punch
Grease
Eye protection

References

Manufacturer's Shop Manual _____

Specifications

Procedure

1. Block the rear of the motorcycle so that the rear wheel is raised off the floor.
2. Unbolt the lower mounts of the shock absorber from the swing arm.
3. Remove the master link and disconnect the drive chain.
4. Disconnect the rear brake rod if the motorcycle has one.
5. Remove the rear wheel assembly.
6. Move the swing arm side to side to check for side play. Is there:

   Noticeable side play _____ Zero side play _____
7. Move the swing arm up and down to check for smooth movement. Is the movement:

   Smooth _____ Rough _____

Instructor check _____

8. If the bushings or bearings are worn, remove the pivot shaft nut and withdraw the pivot shaft. A hammer and a drift punch may be needed to drive the pivot shaft out.

9. Separate the swing arm from the frame.

10. Drive or press out all bushings, bearings, seals, and spacers from the swing arm.

Instructor check _____

11. Inspect the bushings or bearings, pivot shaft, and swing arm for wear.

12. Reassemble the swing arm, replacing old components with new ones as necessary.

13. Test the swing arm for smooth operation.

Instructor check _____   Date completed _____

Job Sheet   24-4

CHECK REAR COIL SPRINGS AND SHOCK ABSORBERS

Before you begin:

Read pp.

Make of Motorcycle _____ Model _____ Year _____

Time Started _____ Time Finished _____ Total Time _____

Flat-rate Time _____

Special Tools, Equipment, Parts, and Materials

    Coil spring compressor
    Eye protection
    Measuring tape

References

Manufacturer's Shop Manual _____

Specifications

Look up the specification for rear coil spring free length and write it in the space below:

Coil spring free length _____

Instructor check _____

Procedure

1. Remove the coil-spring-and-shock-absorber assembly by removing the upper and lower retaining bolts.

2. Using a coil spring compressor, compress the shock absorber spring until the spring retainers can be removed. *(SAFETY CAUTION: Wear eye protection when doing this job.)*

3. Release the spring tension and remove the spring and other parts from the shock.

Instructor check _____

4. Inspect the hydraulic shock absorber for oil leakage and obvious damage.

5. Check the shock's resistance to compression and extension by moving the shock in and out by hand.

6. Measure the free length of the coil spring and compare it with specifications. Is the length:

Correct _____ Too short _____

Instructor check _____

7. Using the compressor, reassemble the coil spring onto the shock absorber and lock the assembly in place with spring retainers.

8. Reinstall the coil-and-shock-absorber assembly on the motorcycle.

NOTES

Instructor check _____

Date completed _____

KEY TERMS

Coil spring free length: the length of a coil spring when it is not compressed; used to determine whether the spring is worn.

Shock absorber: a hydraulic device connected to the frame at one end and to the wheel at the other end; used to control spring oscillations.

Stamped-steel frame: type of frame used on small motorcycles and mopeds; welded from pressed steel.

Suspension: system of linkages, springs, and hydraulic dampers used to suspend the front and rear wheel of the motorcycle.

Swing arm: motorcycle rear suspension system that uses a pivoting rear fork that is attached to the rear wheel and controlled by a coil spring and shock absorber.

Telescoping forks: motorcycle front suspension consisting of a set of inner and outer tubes that are controlled by a coil spring and hydraulic damping.

Tubular frame: a common type of frame constructed from tubes welded together for a strong, light structure.

CHECKUP

Identify the parts of the frame by writing their names in the spaces provided.

1. _____

2. _____

3. _____

4. _____

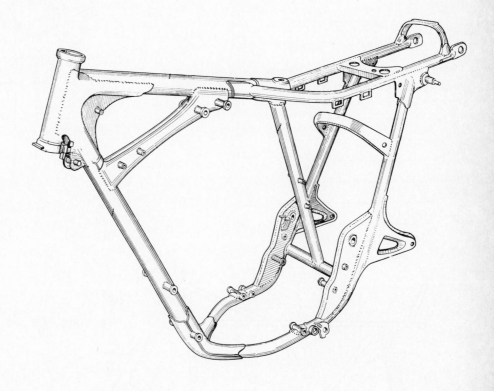

Identify the parts of the steering head assembly by writing their names in the spaces provided.

5. _____

6. _____

7. _____

8. _____

9. _____

10. _____

11. _____

12. _____

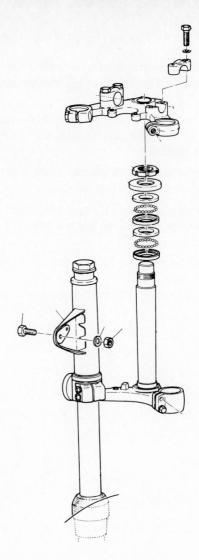

Identify the frame and steering dimensions by writing their names in the spaces provided.

13. _____

14. _____

15. _____

16. _____

17. _____

18. _____

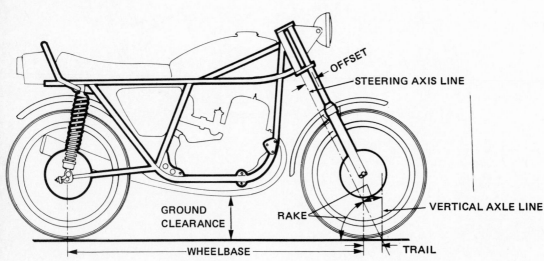

Identify the parts of the front fork by writing their names in the spaces provided.

19. _____

20. _____

21. _____

22. _____

23. _____

24. _____

25. _____

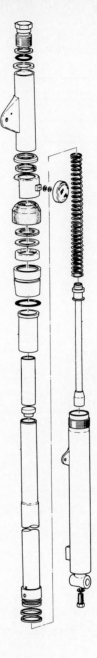

Identify the parts of the rear swing arm by writing their names in the spaces provided.

26. _____

27. _____

28. _____

29. _____

30. _____

DISCUSSION TOPICS AND ACTIVITIES

1. Change the rear coil spring settings on a motorcycle. How do the riding characteristics change as the coils get stiffer?

2. Measure the suspension travel on a road bike and on a dirt bike. Which has the most travel? Why?

The purpose of the motorcycle brake system is to slow down the rotation of the wheels to allow the rider to slow or stop the bike. The system has a lever which is squeezed by the hand or pushed by the foot, producing a force that is transferred to the wheel brakes, which develop friction to slow the motorcycle. There are two basic types of brake systems in use: the mechanical drum brake and the hydraulic disc brake. In this unit, we describe the operation and servicing of both types of brakes.

JOB COMPETENCY OBJECTIVES

When you finish reading and studying this unit, you should be able to:

1. Describe the parts and operation of mechanical drum brakes.

2. Describe the parts and operation of hydraulic disc brakes.

3. Adjust mechanical drum brakes.

4. Service a mechanical drum brake.

5. Service a master cylinder.

6. Service a disc brake caliper.

MECHANICAL DRUM BRAKES

Mechanical drum brakes are the oldest type of brakes used on motorcycles. This brake system uses the mechanical advantage gained by a hand lever or foot pedal to push a set of brake shoes into contact with a rotating brake drum. Mechanical drum brakes are commonly used on small street motorcycles and dirt bikes.

Brake lever

Brake action starts with the hand- or foot-operated brake lever, which acts to multiply the strength of the rider, enabling him or her to exert the necessary force on the brake itself. The lever is designed so that with a small effort at the lever, the rider can exert a much larger force at the brake.

A hand-operated brake lever is shown in Figure 25–1. The long lever swings on a pivot to pull on a brake actuating cable. With a 1-inch distance from the pivot to the cable junction, and a 5-inch distance from the pivot to the center of hand pressure, the lever provides a mechanical advantage of 5 to 1. Thus, if the rider squeezes the lever with a force equal to 10 pounds, there will be a force of 50 pounds applied to the brake cable.

The front brake is mounted on the bottom of the telescoping forks (Figure 25–2) and is operated by a cable connected to a hand lever on the handlebar. Normal suspension travel varies the distance between the brake and

BRAKE SYSTEM OPERATION AND SERVICING

the lever by several inches, so a cable is used to provide needed flexibility.

The rear brake is often operated by a foot-pedal lever (Figure 25–3) connected to a rod which is in turn connected to the rear wheel brake mechanism. A rod can be used at the rear brake because the distance between the brake lever and the rear brake does not change much as the wheel goes up and down. The foot-operated brake pedal lever provides the same kind of leverage to increase the mechanical advantage.

Wheel brake mechanism

The rod or cable is attached to another lever located on the wheel brake mechanism. This lever again multiplies the rider's effort to give additional mechanical advantage. The lever is attached to a part called the *brake backing plate* (Figure 25–4), which is mounted at the wheel and anchored so that it is stationary (does not turn with the wheel). The backing plate provides the platform on which the rest of the nonrotating brake components are mounted. A return spring is attached from the lever to the backing plate and is used to return the lever to its position after the pedal or hand lever is released.

The lever on the backing plate is connected to a cam device on the other side (Figure 25–5). The cam is an eccentric that, when turned, is used to push brake shoes out and into contact with a rotating brake drum. The brake shoes have a friction lining which contacts the surface of the rotating brake drum.

An exploded view of a wheel brake mechanism is shown in Figure 25–6. The mechanism is essentially the same whether it is used on the front or rear wheel. The brake drum is attached to the rotating wheel; the friction between the brake shoes and drum slows and stops the wheel. The backing plate, upon which all the other compo-

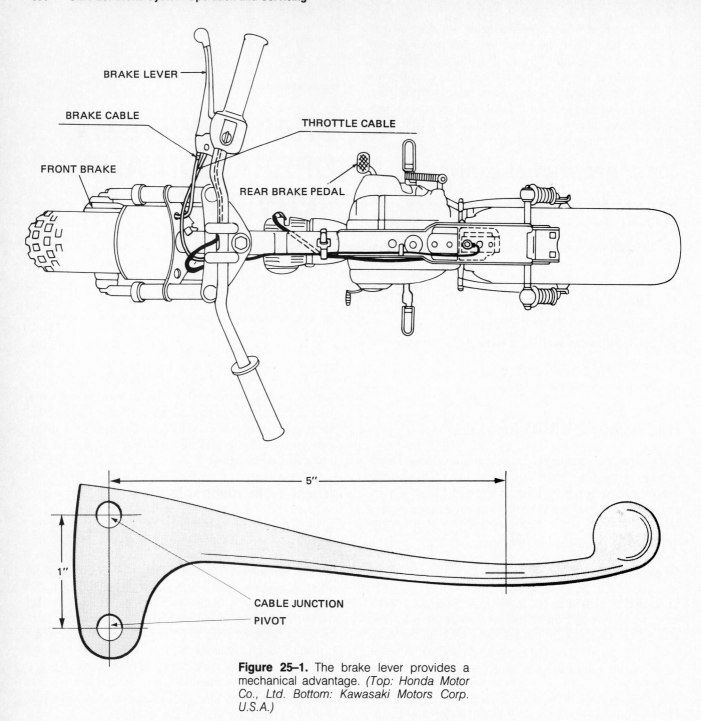

Figure 25–1. The brake lever provides a mechanical advantage. *(Top: Honda Motor Co., Ltd. Bottom: Kawasaki Motors Corp. U.S.A.)*

nents except the drum are mounted, is prevented from rotating by being firmly anchored to the frame. The brake cam lever, which receives the movement from the brake lever, actuates the cam, which then rotates and forces the brake shoes outward; the shoes contact the drum at one end. A pivot point supports one end of the brake shoes and is not acted upon by the cam. A set of return springs pulls the shoes away from the drum when the brake lever is released.

Single leading shoe brakes

There are two basic types of wheel brake mechanisms: single leading shoe brakes and double leading shoe brakes. They differ in the way they are designed to use the rotational force of the drum to help apply the brakes. Use of this rotational force is called the *self-energization* or *self-actuation principle*.

How the self-energization principle works is shown in

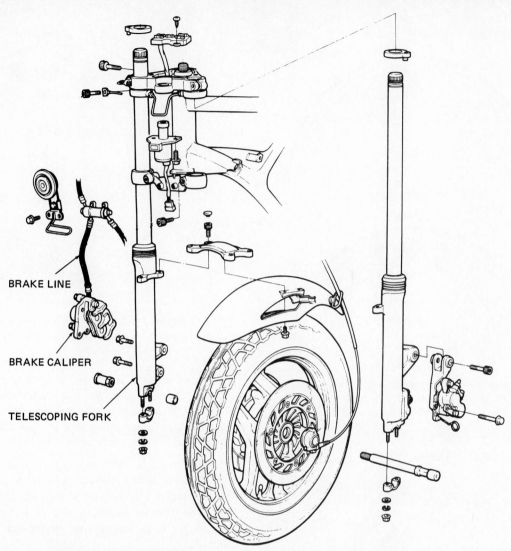

Figure 25–2. Front wheel and brake assembly. *(Honda Motor Co., Ltd.)*

BRAKE LINE

BRAKE CALIPER

TELESCOPING FORK

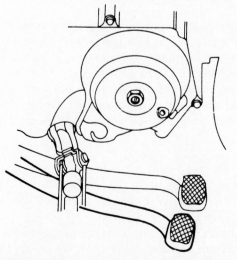

Figure 25–3. Rear brake. *(Honda Motor Co., Ltd.)*

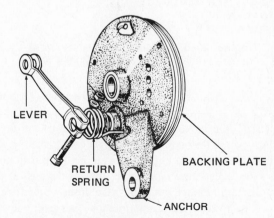

LEVER

RETURN SPRING

BACKING PLATE

ANCHOR

Figure 25–4. Backing plate and lever assembly. *(Kawasaki Motors Corp. U.S.A.)*

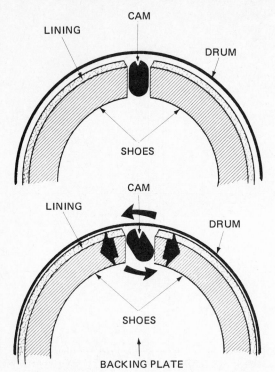

Figure 25–5. Lever-operated cam pushes brake shoes out against the rotating brake drum. *(Kawasaki Motors Corp. U.S.A.)*

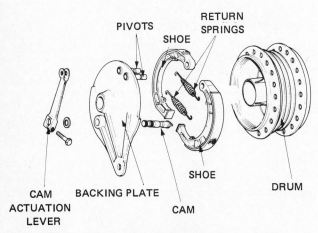

Figure 25–6. Exploded view of a wheel brake mechanism. *(Kawasaki Motors Corp. U.S.A.)*

Figure 25–7. The drum rotates toward the front of the motorcycle as long as the bike is going forward. When the cam turns, the brake shoes are forced against the drum. With a pivot at the bottom and a single cam at the top, one of the shoes is pushed in the direction the drum is turning. This shoe, called the *leading shoe,* utilizes the push it gets from the cam to move out against the drum, around which it tries to rotate. The drum rotation, however, acts to wedge the shoe tight against the drum and the pivot, providing a good deal of added braking action.

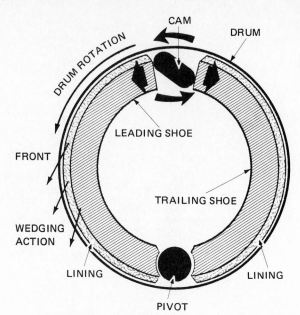

Figure 25–7. Drum rotation helps force the leading shoe into the brake drum. *(Kawasaki Motors Corp. U.S.A.)*

The other shoe is called the *trailing shoe.* It moves against drum rotation, provides no self-energization, and does not do as much to stop the bike.

Since it has one leading shoe and one trailing shoe, this type of wheel brake mechanism is called a single leading shoe mechanism. Although only one shoe is self-energized, if the motorcycle were stopped on a hill and began rolling backwards, the trailing shoe would become a leading shoe (because the drum rotation is reversed). For this reason, the single leading shoe mechanism is often used on dirt bikes.

Double leading shoe brakes

The double leading shoe brake is designed to use the self-energizing principle on both brake shoes. The components of this type of brake are similar to those of the single leading shoe brake, but with an important difference: on the double leading shoe brake, the brake cam actuating lever is connected to a second actuating lever and cam. The connecting linkage and the second cam are shown in Figure 25–8.

Each brake shoe in the double leading shoe mechanism has its own brake cam, and each shoe is a leading shoe. Each shoe is forced out in the direction of drum rotation by the brake drum, as shown in Figure 25–9, and the net braking force is greatly increased.

The double leading shoe brake provides greater stopping power because both shoes have self-energization. The system is about one-and-a-half times as powerful as a single leading shoe system of the same size and is used where

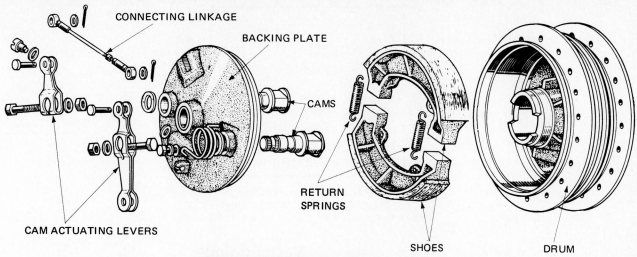

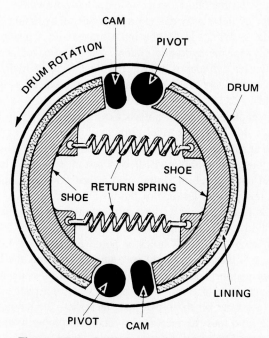

Figure 25–8. Exploded view of a double leading shoe brake. *(Kawasaki Motors Corp. U.S.A.)*

Figure 25–9. Operation of the double leading shoe brake. *(Kawasaki Motors Corp. U.S.A.)*

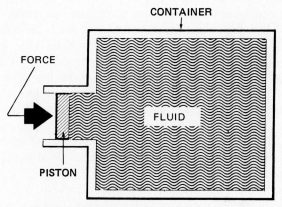

Figure 25–10. Since liquids are not compressible, the piston cannot move. *(Kawasaki Motors Corp. U.S.A.)*

this increased braking power is required, usually on the front wheel of a road machine. The forward weight transfer during braking places most of the braking load on the front wheel.

HYDRAULIC DISC BRAKES

While mechanical drum brakes work well enough for lighter, slower bikes, large, fast road bikes require more stopping power. The hydraulic disc brake system was de-

signed to provide the stopping performance required for these bikes.

Principles of hydraulics

The hydraulic disc brake system uses the principles of hydraulics to multiply the rider's force in applying the brakes and to transfer motion from the hand lever to the wheel brake mechanism. The principles of hydraulic operation of these brakes are relatively simple, but quite important. *Hydraulics* is the science of liquids. The fact that no liquid, e.g., water or brake fluid, can be compressed has important practical consequences. Consider, for example, a cylinder filled with a liquid and sealed with a piston at one end, allowing no leakage. (See Figure 25–10.) With no outlets for the liquid to escape, the piston will be unable to move, because in order to move it would have to compress the liquid.

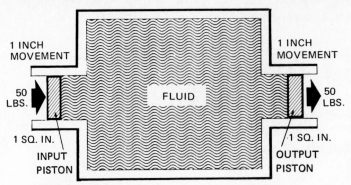

Figure 25–11. Movement of one piston causes movement of the other. *(Kawasaki Motors Corp. U.S.A.)*

If we put an opening at the other end of the container and place a piston there as well (Figure 25–11), force can be transferred between the pistons. For example, a 1-inch movement at the first (input) piston would give a 1-inch movement at the second (output) piston. This is how motion travels from one part of the brake system to another.

Suppose, now, that the area of the first piston in Figure 25–11 is 1 in^2 and the force pushing it is 50 lb. Then the pressure in the cylinder will be 50 lb/in^2, or 50 psi. This means that every square inch of surface inside that system has 50 lb of pressure pushing on it. If the area of the outlet piston at the other end of the cylinder is 1 in^2, the force on the second piston will be 50 lb/in$^2 \times 1$ in$^2 = 50$ lb. This scenario illustrates a second important principle of hydraulics: pressure in any part of the system is transmitted equally throughout the system.

We can use this principle to provide a multiplication of force in the brake system. In Figure 25–12, we have the same cylinder as before, but with an output piston that measures 2 in^2. If the same 50 lb/in^2 of pressure is applied by the input piston, *each* of the two square inches of the output piston has 50 lb of pressure upon it. Therefore, the net force on the output piston is 50 lb/in$^2 \times 2$ in^2, or 100 lb. Remember that each square inch has 50 lb of pressure upon it. We use the same idea in the brake system to increase the rider's force.

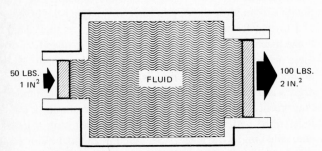

Figure 25–12. How force is multiplied in a hydraulic system. *(Kawasaki Motors Corp. U.S.A.)*

Master cylinder

The brake lever on a disc hydraulic brake system is connected to a hydraulic device called a *master cylinder*. The master cylinder provides (1) a reservoir of hydraulic fluid for the system, and (2) the input force (with a piston assembly) for the hydraulic system. The force developed by the master cylinder is transferred by means of hydraulic lines to the disc brake mechanisms on the wheels (Figure 25–13).

An exploded view of a master cylinder is shown in Figure 25–14. When the rider pulls the brake lever, it exerts force against the back of a piston assembly in the cylinder. This piston assembly consists of a piston, two major seals called cups, a return spring, and a dust boot to keep out dust and prevent leakage of fluid.

The piston assembly rides in a cylinder above which is the fluid reservoir. The fluid reservoir is connected to the cylinder by two small holes or ports (Figure 25–15). The largest of these is a supply port which is towards the back of the piston. The other, smaller port is a pressure relief port which is in front of the piston when the piston is at rest. As wear on the brake pads increases, the amount of brake fluid must be increased to maintain proper hydraulic pressure. The reservoir tank supplies this brake fluid. To prevent air from entering the brake line when the brake fluid level lowers, especially on a rough road or in an inclined position, a compensating diaphragm (Figure 25–14) which rises and lowers with the fluid level is provided for the reservoir tank.

When the rider pulls the brake lever, the piston moves forward easily until the first seal, called the primary cup, passes the pressure relief port. At this point, there is nowhere for the fluid in front of the piston to escape to, and the pressure begins to build up in the system. The pressure is exerted evenly along the inside of the whole system (Figure 25–16) and is transmitted through a hydraulic line to the disc brake mechanism at the wheel (Figure 25–17).

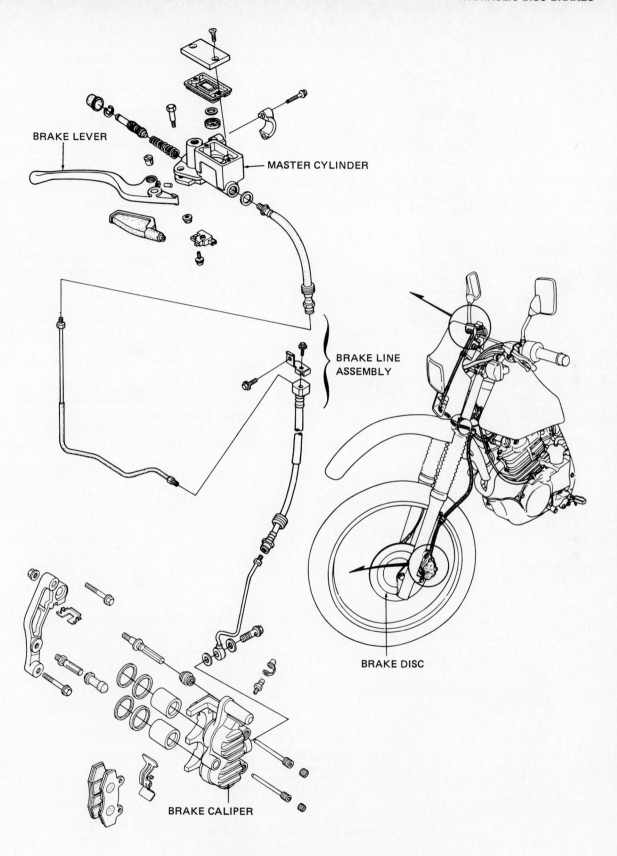

BRAKE LEVER

MASTER CYLINDER

BRAKE LINE
ASSEMBLY

BRAKE DISC

BRAKE CALIPER

Figure 25–13. Master cylinder. *(Honda Motor Co., Ltd.)*

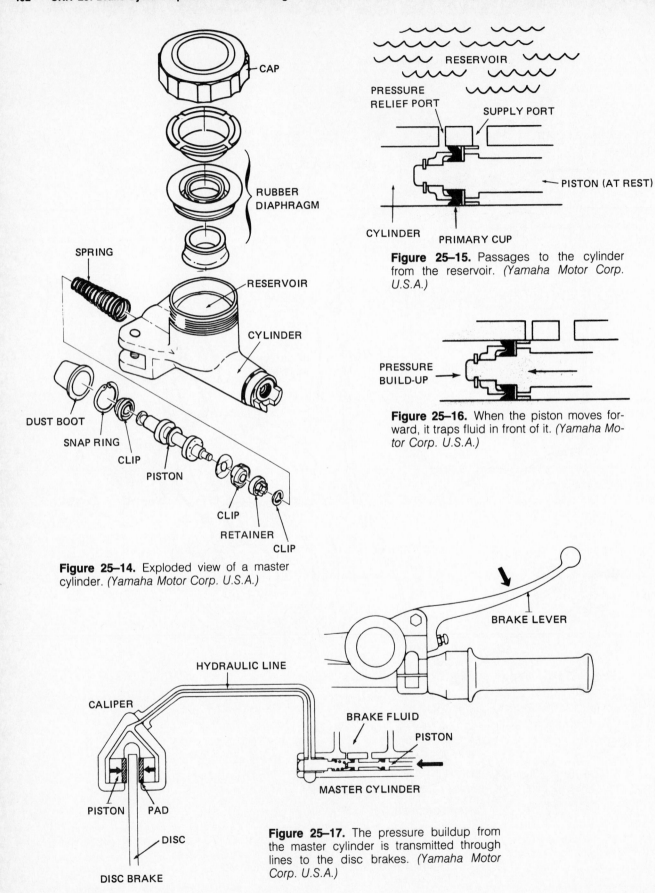

Figure 25–14. Exploded view of a master cylinder. *(Yamaha Motor Corp. U.S.A.)*

Figure 25–15. Passages to the cylinder from the reservoir. *(Yamaha Motor Corp. U.S.A.)*

Figure 25–16. When the piston moves forward, it traps fluid in front of it. *(Yamaha Motor Corp. U.S.A.)*

Figure 25–17. The pressure buildup from the master cylinder is transmitted through lines to the disc brakes. *(Yamaha Motor Corp. U.S.A.)*

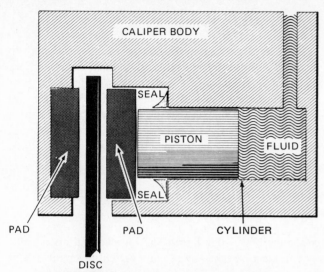

Figure 25–18. Cross-sectional view of a simplified caliper. *(Kawasaki Motors Corp. U.S.A.)*

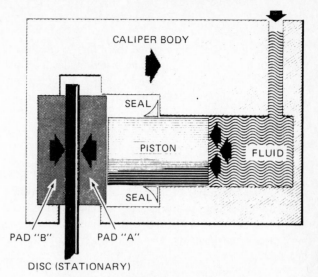

Figure 25–19. Operation of the caliper during braking. *(Kawasaki Motors Corp. U.S.A.)*

Caliper assembly

As Figure 25–18 shows, the fluid pressure from the master cylinder is transferred by means of a hydraulic line to another hydraulic component called the brake caliper. The pressure forces the brake pads against the brake disc to slow and stop the rotation of the wheel.

A simplified cross-sectional view of a caliper is shown in Figure 25–19. The caliper body has a cylinder for a piston. A seal which is held in the caliper body fits around this piston. The two brake pads, each with frictional material, ride on each side of the rotating disc, which is attached to the wheel and rotates with it.

The caliper assembly is mounted on two shafts which hold it onto the front fork or rear suspension. The caliper is thus free to move sideways on the shafts to keep the disc centered between the pads.

When pressure builds up in the caliper cylinder, the piston is pushed towards the disc. Between the piston and the disc is the brake pad (A). As the piston moves toward the disc, it pushes the pad ahead of it. When the pad touches the disc, which has no side-to-side play, the pad and piston can go no further. The caliper assembly then slides in the direction opposite to that of piston movement. As the caliper slides over, another pad (B), which is firmly mounted in the caliper half opposite the piston, moves into contact with the disc as shown in Figure 25–19. As more pressure is applied, the disc is squeezed between the pads and the wheel stops. The total distance the caliper moves is but a fraction of a millimeter, so the braking action is almost instantaneous.

There are no return springs in the caliper. The piston seal is designed to move the piston back to its return position by making use of its torsional movement after the

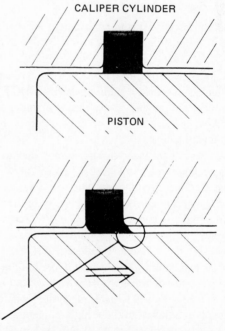

THE FRICTION BETWEEN PISTON SEAL AND PISTON AND ELASTICITY OF THE SEAL CAUSE THE PISTON TO RETURN TO ITS POSITION.

Figure 25–20. The piston seal acts like a return spring. *(Yamaha Motor Corp. U.S.A.)*

brake lever is released (Figure 25–20). The torsional movement is produced by the frictional force and elasticity of the piston seal. The piston seal also serves as an automatic adjuster of the clearance between the disc and the pad.

Disc

The brake disc (sometimes called the rotor) is attached to the hub of the wheel assembly. The disc provides the brake surface for the friction pads. The caliper is mounted over the disc. A caliper-and-disc mounting is shown in exploded view in Figure 25–21.

Brake fluid

The hydraulic fluid used in the brake system is called brake fluid. The performance of the hydraulic disc brake system is highly dependent upon proper performance of the brake fluid used. Brake fluid is a specially formulated liquid that must meet strict standards. The most important of these are that the fluid must:

• Flow freely at low and high temperatures

• Have a high boiling point (over 400° F, or 200° C)

• Not cause metal or rubber brake parts to deteriorate

• Lubricate metal and rubber parts

• Be able to absorb moisture that enters the hydraulic system

Brake fluid is rated by the Department of Transportation. The fluid is assigned a number, such as DOT 4, in which the higher the number, the higher is the fluid's boiling point. Always use the type of fluid specified by the motorcycle manufacturer.

In hot weather, under heavy usage, some brake components reach temperatures of 500 to 650° F (260 to 345° C), although the fluid itself rarely gets this hot. Even at these high temperatures, the correct type of brake fluid will not boil when the brake is applied, because of the tremendous pressure inside the system. As soon as the brake is released, however, the pressure is reduced, and the effects of temperature can be felt. A fluid with a low boiling point will turn to gas and not work properly in the system.

Any water that is allowed to enter the system will vaporize immediately if exposed to these high temperatures. For this reason, it is very important that water and other impurities be kept out of the brake fluid. Brake fluid must always be stored in clean, dry containers. Because it is hygroscopic—that is, it attracts moisture—it must be kept tightly sealed and away from dampness. Brake fluid should also be protected from contamination, especially oil, grease, and other petroleum products. It should never be reused. *(CAUTION: Never use gasoline, kerosene, motor oil, transmission fluid, or any fluid containing oil to clean brake system components; these fluids will cause the rubber cups and seals in the master or caliper units to soften, swell, and distort, resulting in brake failure.)*

BRAKE SERVICING

A brake problem usually shows up as either difficulty in stopping or noise. In the first case, you may notice, for example, that the brake lever may have to be moved a great deal further than usual to get the motorcycle to stop. Or you may get the feeling that the bike uses a lot more road to slow down. In the second case, noise is usually noticed in the wheel brake mechanism. If you have either of these problems, you will have to adjust, inspect, or service the brake system before long.

Drum brake adjustment

When the brake shoe linings on a mechanical drum brake system wear, it takes more hand or foot lever movement to apply the brakes. Periodically, the brake cable or brake rod has to be shortened to compensate for lining wear.

The rear brake is adjusted by first determining the amount of free play at the brake pedal. As you move the pedal up and down (Figure 25–22), you will feel the pedal first move easily and then meet resistance as the rear shoes contact the drum. The amount of easy movement is the free play. Use a tape measure to measure this free play, and then compare it with specifications.

If there is too much free play, the rear brakes need adjusting. To adjust the rear brake, you must turn the adjusting nut provided at the end of the brake rod where it connects to the backing plate lever. Turning the nut in a direction that shortens the rod will decrease free play and adjust the brakes so that they are tighter (Figure 25–23).

Front mechanical drum brake free play is checked and adjusted at the hand brake lever. The free play is measured at the brake lever pivot point, as shown in Figure 25–24. An adjusting nut is provided on the end of the cable. If the freeplay is excessive, turn the adjuster so that it tightens the cable until the amount of free play is correct. Sometimes there are additional adjusters on the brake backing plate.

Brake inspection

If, after adjusting the brakes, the problem is not solved, or if the problem is noise from the brakes, you should inspect the brakes.

Mechanical drum brakes are inspected by disassembling the drum from the backing plate. The procedure is basically the same on both the front and the rear. You will have to safely block the bike front or rear wheel off the ground. Since the wheel must be removed, you must remove the brake cable or rod attachment. On a front wheel, you will also have to remove the speedometer cable. To remove the axle and spacers on a rear wheel, you will have

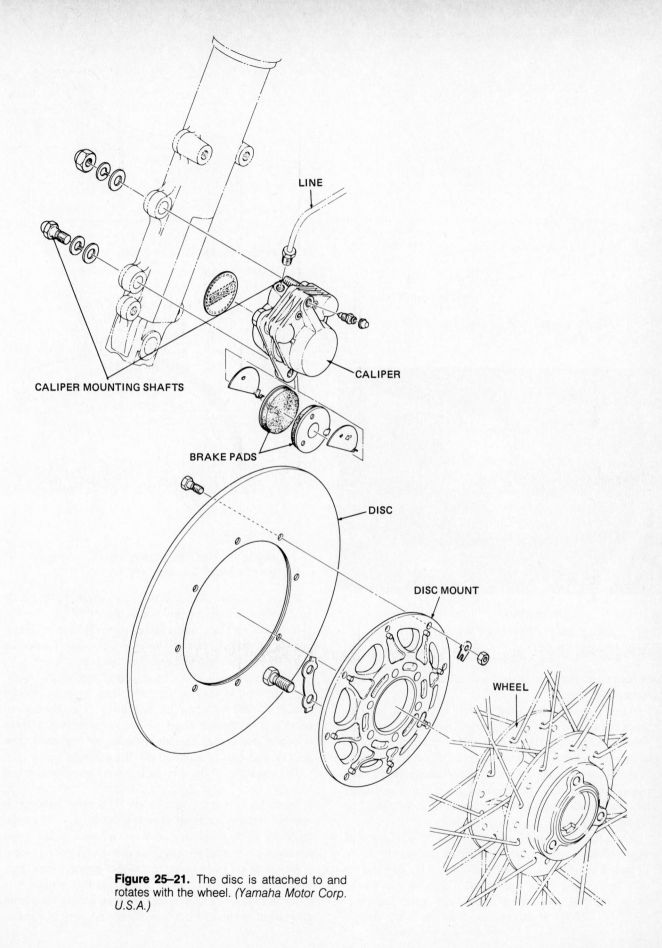

LINE

CALIPER MOUNTING SHAFTS

CALIPER

BRAKE PADS

DISC

DISC MOUNT

WHEEL

Figure 25–21. The disc is attached to and rotates with the wheel. *(Yamaha Motor Corp. U.S.A.)*

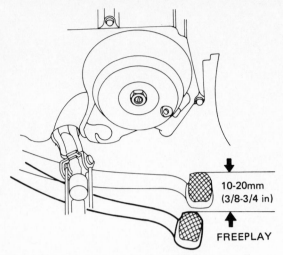

Figure 25–22. Rear brake. *(Honda Motor Co., Ltd.)*

ADJUSTING NUT

Figure 25–23. Rear brake adjustment.

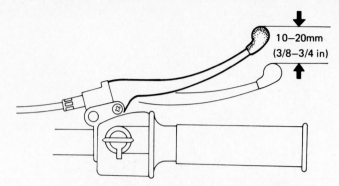

Figure 25–24. Checking free play. *(Honda Motor Co., Ltd.)*

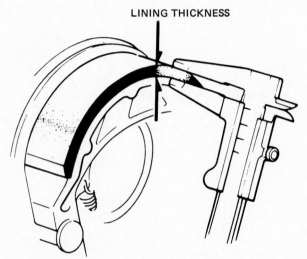

LINING THICKNESS

Figure 25–25. Measuring brake lining. *(Honda Motor Co., Ltd.)*

to disconnect the final drive chain and axle nuts, and then remove the wheel.

When you have the wheel removed, you can separate the backing plate assembly from the drum. Look the brake shoes over carefully; the friction lining material is riveted or bonded to the metal brake shoe. Measure the thickness of the lining and compare it with specifications in the shop manual (Figure 25–25). Generally, if the lining is thinner than the metal support behind it, the brake shoes should be replaced.

While the drum is off, check for any obvious signs of wear or broken parts. The brake drum surface should be clean and smooth. Look for broken return springs and for signs that parts may be overheated. Grease or dirt on the lining material can cause noise and poor stopping. (*SAFETY CAUTION: Brake dust from the brake linings*

can have asbestos. Do not blow brake parts off with an air hose; asbestos is dangerous to breathe.)

If the brakes show wear, the system will require servicing, as described later. If not, you can reassemble the brake mechanism and reinstall it on the bike.

Disc brakes can usually be inspected without disassembly. The disc is easy to see. Just look it over carefully (Figure 25–26) for any signs of scoring. The best way to check it is to run your fingernail across the surface. If there is a score that is deep enough to catch your fingernail, then the disc will require replacement or machining.

The condition of the disc brake pads can be determined visually. Look inside the caliper where the brake pads are located. Each brake pad consists of a steel backing to which a friction pad is attached (Figure 25–27). When the thickness of the friction pad is worn down to the same thickness as the steel backing, the pads should be replaced.

As the brake pads wear, the caliper piston moves outward to a new position. The piston seal then works on a different part of the piston and the area behind the piston gets larger and holds more brake fluid. You will notice that

Figure 25–26. The disc can be checked visually for scoring. (*U.S. Suzuki Motor Corp.*)

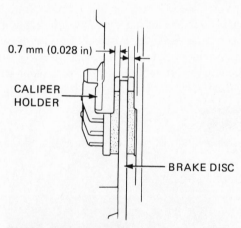

Figure 25–27. Checking disc brake pads. (*Honda Motor Co., Ltd.*)

the master cylinder reservoir gets lower as the brake pads wear. Add more brake fluid, as needed.

Mechanical drum brake servicing

Front or rear mechanical drum brake servicing involves the replacement of the brake shoes and return springs. Remove the wheel and brake drum as explained earlier. Then remove the cam levers and the connecting rod. Remove the return springs and shoes by folding the shoes inward.

Remove the brake cams and check them for thickness and for whether they are bent or warped. Check the return springs for signs of overheating. It is a good idea to re-

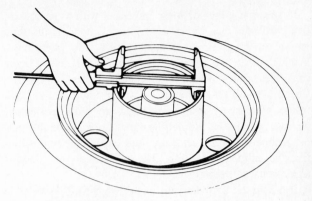

Figure 25–28. Measuring brake drum. (*Honda Motor Co., Ltd.*)

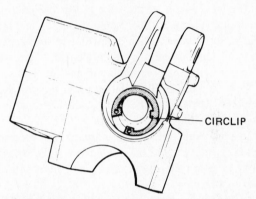

Figure 25–29. Remove the master cylinder circlip or snap ring. (*Kawasaki Motors Corp. U.S.A.*)

place the springs each time you replace the brake lining.

Use a vernier caliper or a large telescoping gauge to measure the brake drum to determine whether it is oversize or out of round (Figure 25–28). If the drum is worn, oversize, or out of round beyond specifications, it will have to be replaced. Small scratches or glazed areas can be removed with sandpaper.

Reassemble the new shoes and hardware on the backing plate. Install the brake backing plate in the drum, and the wheel assembly back on the motorcycle. Make an adjustment to the free play as described previously.

Hydraulic disc brake servicing: Master cylinder

A problem in a hydraulic disc brake system may be due to the hydraulic system itself or to the mechanical parts of the pads and disc.

A hydraulic problem can occur at either the master cylinder, the hydraulic line, or the piston and seal in the caliper. A pressure leak at any of these spots will result in a spongy feeling at the brake lever; if the leak is a bad one, the lever will have no resistance and there will be no brake action at all.

If you find either of these problems with your brakes, first check the resevoir in the master cylinder. If the fluid is gone or the level has dropped rapidly, the system has a leak. (Rember, the level does go down slowly as the brake pads wear, but the reservoir should never be empty.) Check over all the hydraulic lines and connections. Look inside the master cylinder dust boot; any fluid here means that the cylinder is definitely leaking. Look inside the caliper around the piston seal; any fluid outside the seal means that the caliper is leaking. The most likely problem is leaky seals in the master cylinder.

If the master cylinder is at fault, a repair kit is available to replace the piston and seals. Remove the master cylinder dust boot. Remove the circlip or snap ring with snap ring pliers (Figure 25–29). Remove the piston and pull out the return spring (Figure 25–30). Remove the clip and remove the piston cup retainer. Then remove the piston cups.

Clean all reusable metal parts in alcohol or clean brake fluid. Immerse the parts in the liquid and brush them with a parts cleaning brush. Blow out all passages, orifices, and valve holes. Then allow the parts to dry thoroughly on a clean paper or a lint-free clean cloth. (*SAFETY CAUTION: Wear eye protection when using shop air. Do not use gasoline, kerosene, or any other cleaning fluid having the slightest trace of mineral oil, as this will cause damage to rubber parts.*)

If the bore is excessively scratched, the cylinder should be replaced. Brake hoses are available for cleaning cylinder bores, but they must be used carefully to prevent honing the bores oversize. Dip the new cups in clean brake fluid and install them on the piston. Then install the retainer and cup, and insert the spring into the bore.

Check the piston surfaces and cup surfaces (Figure 25–31) for scratches, and then insert the piston into the cylinder. Avoid forcing the piston—the cylinder wall may become scratched, allowing the brake fluid to leak past. Install the snap ring, and install the boot in the master cylinder groove. Then install the master cylinder back into position. After making sure that the bolts are torqued to specifications, install the hydraulic line.

After the cylinder is installed, fill the reservoir and remove the air by bleeding, as explained below.

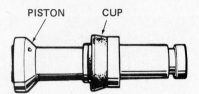

Figure 25–31. Check the piston surfaces for scratches. *(Kawasaki Motors Corp. U.S.A.)*

Bleeding the hydraulic system

Bleeding hydraulic brakes removes any air that is trapped in the system. Air enters the system when any of its hydraulic parts are disconnected or if the brakes are operated when the fluid level in the master cylinder is too low.

A bleeding valve is provided on the brake caliper to remove the air. Connect a vinyl tube to the caliper bleed screw tightly, so that no brake fluid will spill. Use a container to catch the brake fluid at the end of the vinyl tube (Figure 25–32). (*NOTE: Do not reuse brake fluid that has been emitted during bleeding, or in general, any old brake fluid.*)

Apply the brake lever slowly a few times. With the lever squeezed, loosen the bleed screw. As fluid and air escape, the lever will close. Tighten the bleed screw before the lever bottoms on the handlebar grip. When bleeding the air, do not operate the brake lever quickly because the air will then turn into fine bubbles and make the bleeding difficult. Keep bleeding the air until the air bubbles completely disappear in the vinyl tube. Refill the reservoir with fresh

Figure 25–32. Bleed the brakes. *(Harley Davidson Motors, Inc.)*

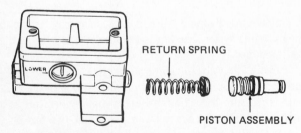

Figure 25–30. Pull out the return spring. *(Kawasaki Motors Corp. U.S.A.)*

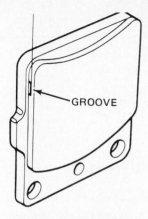

LEFT HAND SHOWN
(RIGHT HAND OPPOSITE)

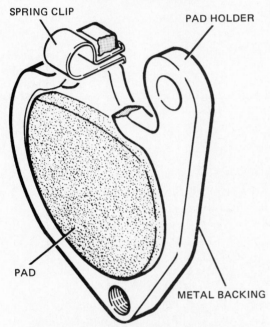

Figure 25–33. Check brake pads for wear depth. *(Top: Honda Motor Co., Ltd. Bottom: Harley Davidson Motors, Inc.)*

brake fluid so that the level will again reach the specified line.

Take care that neither dust nor water contaminates the new brake fluid; don't change the brake fluid outside in a rain or high wind. Also, always use fresh fluid from a closed container; an open container may collect water or dust. If water is mixed with brake fluid, it will lower the boiling point of the fluid. If brake fluid is spilled on a painted surface, clean the surface immediately; brake fluid can damage it.

Hydraulic disc brake caliper servicing

Worn brake disc pads can usually be installed without disassembling the brake caliper. Remove the wheel-and-disc assembly. Usually the pads are held in with clips, so remove the clips to remove the old pads. Some brake pads have a mark or groove to indicate depth of wear (Figure 25–33). Replace both pads if one or both are worn down to the service limit groove. (*CAUTION: Use brake fluid or alcohol to clean brake parts, other than the brake pads or the disc. Do not use gasoline or motor oil, as they destroy rubber parts. Take care that no oil or brake fluid gets on the brake pads or the disc; they should be cleaned with a special solvent to remove any oily residue.*)

When you install new pads, it is necessary to push back the piston so that the pads can be easily installed. When the piston is pushed back, and the compensating port is open, the brake fluid level in the reservoir tank will rise. Loosen the bleed screw if necessary, and bleed off the excess brake fluid. Watch that you do not cause the fluid in the reservoir to overflow.

Install the new pads and install the cups that hold the shoes. Then reinstall the disc-and-wheel assembly.

A hydraulic problem in the caliper usually means that the seal is worn out. The caliper must be removed from the bike to service the seal. The pads are removed, and the piston is pulled out of its bore. The bore and piston must be cleaned in clean brake fluid. If either are scratched or scored, the caliper assembly must be replaced.

Pull the old seal out using a sharp piece of wood or plastic so that you do not scratch the bore. Lubricate the new seal with brake fluid, and install it in position. Then install the piston. Finally, reassemble the caliper and mount it on the bike. Bleed the system as previously described.

Job Sheet 25–1

ADJUST MECHANICAL DRUM BRAKES

Before you begin:

Read pp.

Make of Motorcycle _____ Model _____ Year _____

Time Started _____ Time Finished _____ Total Time _____

Flat-rate Time _____

Special Tools, Equipment, Parts, and Materials

    Measuring tape
    Eye protection

References

Manufacturer's Shop Manual _____

Specifications

Look up the brake foot pedal and hand lever free-play specifications and write them in the spaces below:

Hand lever free play _____ foot pedal free play _____

                                     Instructor check _____

Procedure

1. Move the brake pedal back and forth to feel the free play in it.

2. Use a measuring tape to measure the free play.

3. Use a wrench to turn the rear brake rod adjuster to lengthen or shorten the brake rod.

4. Adjust the rod to set the free play to specifications.

                                     Instructor check _____

5. Squeeze the hand lever back and forth until you can feel the free play at the pivot.

6. Measure the pivot free play with a measuring tape.

7. Adjust the cable nut backwards or forwards to set the free play to specifications.

Instructor check _____

NOTES

Date completed _____   Instructor check _____

Job Sheet   25–2

SERVICE A MECHANICAL DRUM BRAKE

Before you begin:

Read pp.

Make of Motorcycle _____ Model _____ Year _____

Time Started _____ Time Finished _____ Total Time _____

Flat-rate Time _____

Special Tools, Equipment, Parts, and Materials

Eye protection
Measuring tools

References

Manufacturer's Shop Manual _____

Specifications

Look up the specification for minimum brake lining thickness and write it in the space below:

Minimum brake lining thickness _____

Instructor check _____

Procedure

1. Raise and support the front or rear of the motorcycle on a stand and blocks.

2. Disconnect the brake cable or rod.

3. Disconnect the speedometer cable, if there is one.

4. Remove the brake backing plate anchor arm, if there is one.

5. Remove the wheel axle and spaces. Disconnect the final drive chain if you are servicing a rear wheel. Remove the wheel-and-brake assembly.

6. Separate the backing plate assembly from the brake drum.

7. Remove the cam levers and connecting rod.

8. Remove the return springs and shoes by folding the shoes inward.

9. Remove the brake cams and check them for thickness and bent or warped conditions.

10. Check the return springs for evidence of overheating.

11. Inspect the brake drum for scoring or distortion.

Instructor check _____

12. Measure the thickness of the brake lining and compare it to specifications. Is the lining:

    Acceptable _____   Worn _____

13. Measure the brake drum for out-of-round and oversize. Compare your measurement to specifications. Is the drum:

    Acceptable _____   Worn _____

Instructor check _____

14. Reassemble the brake unit, replacing old parts with new ones where required.

15. Reinstall the wheel and brake unit on the motorcycle.

16. Adjust the brake cable or rod to obtain proper free play.

Instructor check _____

17. Check the brakes for proper operation.

NOTES

Instructor check _____   Date completed _____

Job Sheet   25–3

REPAIR A MASTER CYLINDER

Before you begin:

Read pp.

Make of Motorcycle _____ Model _____ Year _____

Time Started _____ Time Finished _____ Total Time _____

Flat-rate Time _____

Special Tools, Equipment, Parts, and Materials

Master cylinder repair kit
New brake fluid
Eye protection
Drain pan

References

Manufacturer's Shop Manual _____

Specifications

Procedure

1. Disconnect the hydraulic brake line from the master cylinder, making sure to catch the brake fluid in a drain pan.

2. Remove the master cylinder mounting bolts, and remove the cylinder from the motorcycle.

3. Empty the brake fluid from the cylinder into the drain pan.

4. Remove the dust boot.

5. Using suitable snap ring pliers, remove the snap ring.

6. Withdraw the piston, piston cups, and return spring from the cylinder.

Instructor check _____

7. Wash all the parts in clean brake fluid.

8. Inspect the master cylinder bore for scratches, scores, and pits.
   Is the bore:

   Damaged _____ Acceptable _____

   Instructor check _____

9. Using parts from the repair kit, reassemble the master cylinder. Lubricate all rubber pads with brake fluid.

   Instructor check_____

10. Remount the master cylinder to the motorcycle and connect the hydraulic line.

11. Fill the reservoir with new, clean fluid.

12. Bleed the brake system.

13. Check the brakes for proper operation.

NOTES

Instructor check _____   Date completed _____

Job Sheet

SERVICE A DISC BRAKE CALIPER

Before you begin:

Read pp.

Make of Motorcycle _____ Model _____ Year _____

Time Started _____ Time Finished _____ Total Time _____

Flat-rate Time _____

Special Tools, Equipment, Parts, and Materials

Eye protection
Drain pan
Brake fluid
Repair kit

References

Manufacturer's Shop Manual _____

Specifications

Procedure

1. Disconnect the brake line from the caliper body and catch the fluid in a drain pan.

2. Remove the caliper from its mounting bolts.

3. Remove the caliper assembly from its mounting on the fork or frame.

4. Remove the caliper bolts and separate the caliper bodies.

5. Remove the brake pads.

6. Remove the piston boot and piston.

Instructor check _____

7. Wash all metal parts (except the pads) in clean brake fluid.

8. Inspect the caliper bore for signs of scoring, scratching, and pitting. Is the bore:

Worn _____ Acceptable _____

9. Inspect the thickness of the pad friction material and compare it to the thickness of the metal backing. Are the pads:
   Worn _____ Acceptable _____

   Instructor check _____

10. Coat the parts with brake fluid and install piston seal in the caliper body.
11. Coat the piston with brake fluid and push it slowly into the cylinder.
12. Install the brake pads into the caliper body halves.
13. Reinstall the caliper bolts using new dust seals.

    Instructor check _____

14. Reinstall the caliper assembly on the motorcycle, torquing all the bolts to specifications.
15. Reconnect the brake line.
16. Bleed the system to remove all the air.
17. Check the brake system for proper operation.

NOTES

Instructor check _____   Date completed _____

KEY TERMS

Bleeding: removing air from a hydraulic brake system.

Brake drum: the part of the wheel brake assembly that is attached to the wheel.

Brake pads: the shoes or friction linings used on disc brake systems.

Brake shoes: the friction lining used on drum brake systems.

Caliper: a housing for the hydraulic components of a disc brake system.

Disc: the part of the disc brake system that turns or rotates with the wheels.

Disc brakes: brakes that use a rotor attached to the wheel, and a caliper with brake pads to stop the wheel.

CHECKUP

Identify the parts of a drum wheel brake mechanism by writing their names in the spaces provided.

1. _____
2. _____
3. _____
4. _____
5. _____
6. _____
7. _____

Identify the parts of the double leading shoe brake by writing their names in the spaces provided.

8. _____
9. _____
10. _____
11. _____
12. _____

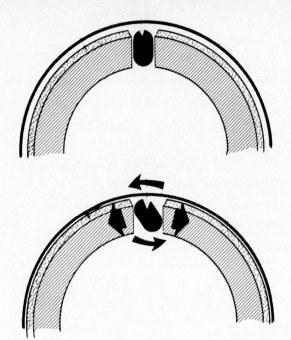

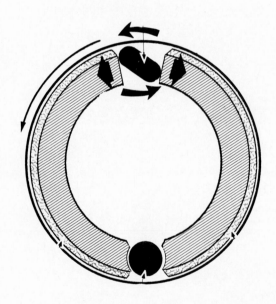

Identify the parts of a master cylinder by writing their names in the spaces provided.

13. _____

14. _____

15. _____

16. _____

17. _____

18. _____

19. _____

20. _____

21. _____

22. _____

23. _____

24. _____

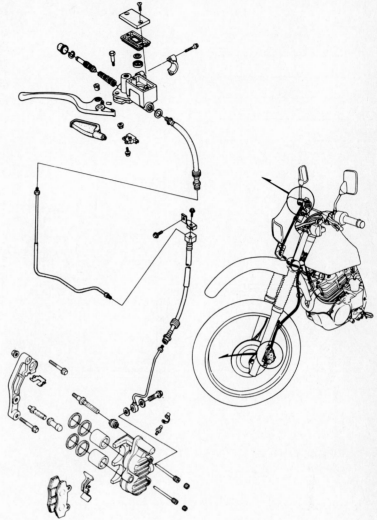

Identify the parts of a caliper by writing their names in the spaces provided.

25. _____

26. _____

27. _____

28. _____

29. _____

30. _____

DISCUSSION TOPICS AND ACTIVITIES

1. Following the procedures in this chapter, check the condition of the brakes on the motorcycle you ride. Do they need replacement?

3. Disassemble a shop master cylinder. Inspect the condition of all the parts, and then reassemble the cylinder.

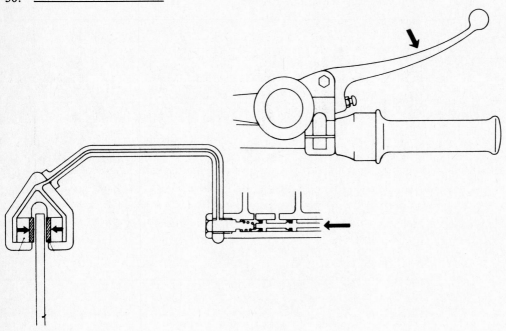

The tires and the wheel assembly are an important part of the motorcycle. The tires and wheels support the weight of the motorcycle and allow it to move down the road. The front tire and wheel provide directional control. The rear tire and wheel deliver the engine's power to the road to push the motorcycle forward. In this unit, we describe the parts, operation, and servicing of the tires and the wheel assembly.

JOB COMPETENCY OBJECTIVES

When you finish reading and studying this unit, you should be able to:

1. Identify the parts and explain the operation of a tire and a wheel assembly.

2. True a wheel for lateral and radial runout.

3. Replace a broken spoke.

4. Remove and replace a rim.

5. Disassemble, clean, lubricate, and install wheel bearings.

TIRES

Tires have two basic functions. First, they provide a cushion between the road and the motorcycle wheels to absorb shocks transmitted by rough roads. Tires flex, or give, as bumps are encountered to reduce the effect of the shock on the rider. Second, the tires provide frictional contact between the wheels and the road for good traction. Good traction enables the motorcycle to transmit power through the tires to the road for rapid acceleration, to resist the tendency of the bike to skid on turns, and to come to a quick stop when the rider applies the brakes.

Tire parts and construction

While it is common to think of a tire as made of rubber, it is really constructed of a number of parts made from different materials. A tire is shown in cross section in Figure 26–1.

The main structural element of a tire is its two wire beads. Each bead is formed by wrapping together several steel wires for a continuous hoop.

The basic strength of a tire is determined by its internal structure, called its *carcass* or *casing*. The carcass consists of layers of rubberized metal or fabric called plies and belts. Each ply is a layer of rubber with metal or fabric cords imbedded in its body. The cords may be made from a variety of materials, such as rayon, nylon or polyester, fiberglass, steel, or aramid. The type of material used determines the tire's stability and resistance to bruises, fatigue, and heat. The plies are wound at their ends around the beads and bonded into the sides of the tire.

TIRE AND WHEEL OPERATION AND SERVICING

The tread section of the tire provides the area of traction with the road. The tread is designed to allow air flow to cool the tire and to channel out water during wet weather. Treads are made of a rubber compound that is highly resistant to abrasion. The thick layer of tread rubber is specially compounded to withstand road wear and provide traction. The spaces between the treads permit distortion of the tire on the road without rubbing that would accelerate wear. Most street tires have *wear bars* or *tread wear indicators* (TWI) between the treads. These are raised sections moulded into the tire tread. An arrow on the tire sidewall points to the locations of TWIs. When the tire wears down, the tread wear indicators come flush to the surface, signalling that a new tire should be purchased.

The sidewalls are made of a different grade of rubber that is designed to help absorb irregularities in the road and to protect the cord plies from damage. The sidewall rubber, which does not touch the road, is not as thick as the

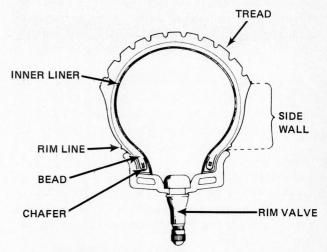

Figure 26–1. Cross-sectional view of a tire. *(Honda Motor Co., Ltd.)*

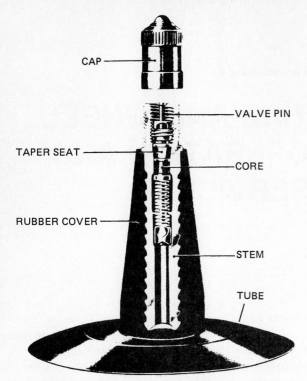

Figure 26–2. Tube valve assembly. *(U.S. Army)*

Figure 26–3. A valve cap with a screwdriver tip can be used to remove a core. *(U.S. Army)*

tread but is made of an abrasion-resistant rubber to provide maximum protection for the structural plies. Inflation pressure and the stiffness of the cords account for the rigidity of sidewalls; the sidewall rubber has almost nothing to do with it. In general, the more plies a tire has, the stiffer the sidewalls, and, therefore, the less cushioning the tire gives the rider.

The tire is filled with air. Most motorcycles use a separate inner tube to hold the air inside the tire. A rubber rim strip is used between the wheel rim and the inner tube to protect the tube. Some motorcycle tires are tubeless. The air in them is contained inside the tire carcass, sealed by the bead area between the rim and the tire.

Tubes are inflated by air under pressure. Air is forced into the tube through the valve, which automatically prevents the air from escaping (Figure 26–2). The valve stem is threaded inside and out at the end to accommodate the valve core and cap.

The core is a spring-loaded seal that prevents air from escaping. A pin on the core allows air to enter under pressure and to escape when it is depressed (for lowering air pressure). The core can be unscrewed out of the valve for quick tire deflation.

The valve cap keeps the core clean and serves as the final seal. The screwdriver-type of cap has a forked tip which can be used to remove and replace valve cores (Figure 26–3).

Motorcycle tires are manufactured in many different sizes and designs. Tire sizes are determined by the diameter of the rim that the tire fits on. Common tire rim diameters are 16, 17, 18 and 19 inches. The diameter of the tire used is determined by the size and use of the motorcycle.

Tire tread designs have been developed for different types of motorcycles and different riding conditions. A selection of tire tread designs is shown in Figure 26–4. Knobby treads are used for off-road riding because they provide good traction in the dirt. Rib treads are used on the front (never the rear) of road bikes because they provide good directional control. A number of tread patterns, called universal treads, are used on the rear of road bikes.

Tire markings

Tire manufacturers have adopted a tire marking system that provides information about the construction, size, pressure, and speed ratings, as well as other important information, for motorcycle tires. An example of a tire marking system is shown in Figure 26–5. Each of the markings on the side of the tire tell something about the tire. One of the most important items is the direction in which the tire should rotate, which is shown with an arrow. The speed markings, when referred to a speed chart, tell how fast the tire can be safely ridden. The load index is a numerical code that tells how much weight a tire can support.

Tire pressure

Correct tire pressure is necessary for safe driving, good tire mileage, and responsive steering. Tires should be checked frequently to make sure that they are at the recommended pressure. Tire pressure should be checked with an accurate pencil- or dial-type gauge; service station air gauges are frequently inaccurate from rough use and should not be depended upon for an accurate pressure reading.

To check the pressure, remove the valve cap from the tire valve and push the tire gauge check firmly over the valve. The pencil-style gauge scale extension will then pop out of the gauge (Figure 26–6), at which time you can read the pressure on the scale. The dial-type gauge has a needle that points to the tire pressure.

The specifications for correct tire pressure are provided in the motorcycle owner's manual and the shop service manual. Correct inflation (Figure 26–7, right) permits full tread contact on the pavement with relatively even force

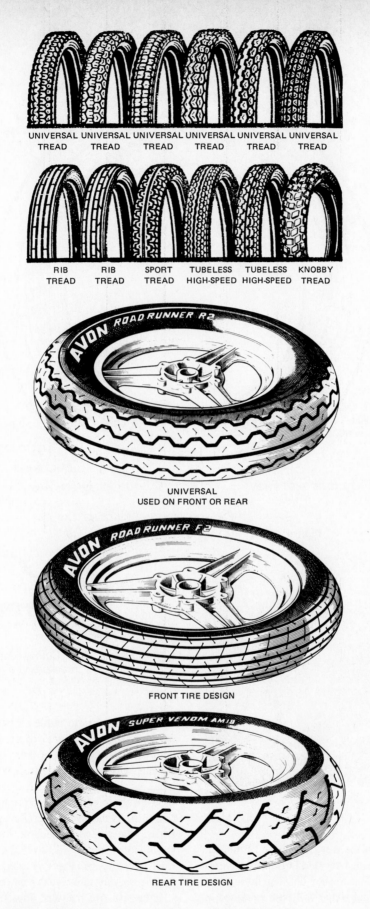

UNIVERSAL TREAD UNIVERSAL TREAD UNIVERSAL TREAD UNIVERSAL TREAD UNIVERSAL TREAD UNIVERSAL TREAD

RIB TREAD RIB TREAD SPORT TREAD TUBELESS HIGH-SPEED TUBELESS HIGH-SPEED KNOBBY TREAD

UNIVERSAL
USED ON FRONT OR REAR

FRONT TIRE DESIGN

REAR TIRE DESIGN

Figure 26–4. Tire tread designs. *(Avon Tyres Ltd.)*

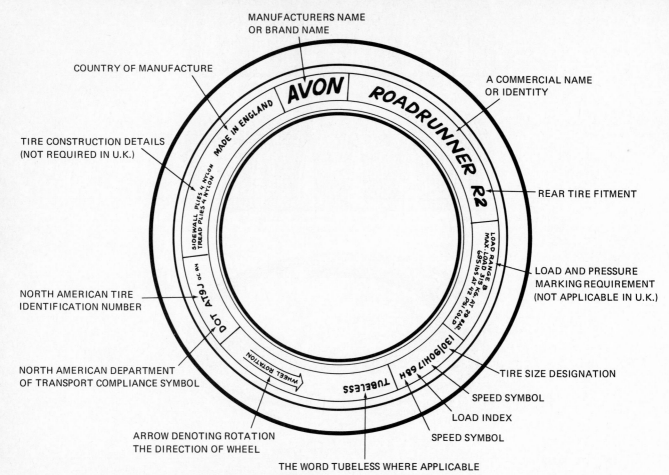

MANUFACTURERS NAME
OR BRAND NAME

COUNTRY OF MANUFACTURE

A COMMERCIAL NAME
OR IDENTITY

TIRE CONSTRUCTION DETAILS
(NOT REQUIRED IN U.K.)

REAR TIRE FITMENT

NORTH AMERICAN TIRE
IDENTIFICATION NUMBER

LOAD AND PRESSURE
MARKING REQUIREMENT
(NOT APPLICABLE IN U.K.)

NORTH AMERICAN DEPARTMENT
OF TRANSPORT COMPLIANCE SYMBOL

TIRE SIZE DESIGNATION

SPEED SYMBOL

LOAD INDEX

ARROW DENOTING ROTATION
THE DIRECTION OF WHEEL

SPEED SYMBOL

THE WORD TUBELESS WHERE APPLICABLE

Figure 26–5. Tire markings. *(Avon Tyres Ltd.)*

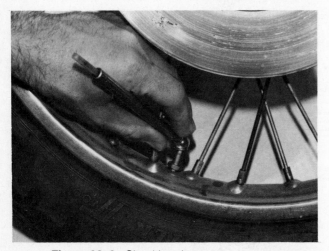

Figure 26–6. Checking tire pressure.

Uneven wear slips, Uneven wear
on pavement

Figure 26–7. Comparison of high, low, and correct air pressure in a tire. *(Kawasaki Motors Corp. U.S.A.)*

When a tire has too little air pressure to properly support the load, the central area of the tread rises upward at the point of road contact, as the sidewalls flex. This motion concentrates tremendous stress on the outside edges of the tread, as shown in Figure 26–7 (center), causing maximum wear on those edges and minimum wear at the center portion of the tread. Moreover, low pressure allows the tire to flatten, the sidewalls become more flexible, and the rim shifts from side to side over the center of the tread. The rider feels these changes as a slight side-to-side instability: the motorcycle feels mushy when turning corners.

Excessive tire pressure does not allow the tire tread to flatten out at the point of road contact. The central portion

throughout the full width of the tread. A properly inflated tire offers maximum resistance to skidding and provides greatly extended tire life. The tread will wear throughout its full width, and the original shape will be maintained at each edge of the tread.

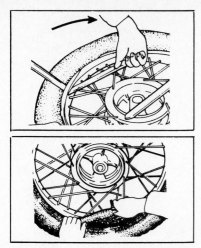

Figure 26–8. Dismounting the tire and removing the tube. *(Yamaha Motor Corp. U.S.A.)*

of the tread then wears heavily (Figure 26–7, left). High pressure produces hard riding characteristics and reduces the ability of the tire to grip the pavement. It also makes the tread bend up away from the road on the side. The tire becomes stiffer, but less rubber is in contact with the road, so the tires can skid more easily under heavy braking for cornering.

Tire repair

One of the most common tire problems is a flat tire. When a tire is punctured, it must be dismounted from one side of the rim, and the tube must be pulled out. The tube can then be patched or replaced.

To remove the tire, first unscrew the valve cup and remove the valve core. When all the air is out of the tube, separate the tire bead from (both sides of) the rim by stepping on the tire with your foot. Use two tire removal irons (with rounded edges) and begin to work the tire bead over the edge of the rim, starting 180 degrees opposite the tube stem (Figure 26–8). Take care to avoid pinching the tube as you work.

After you have worked one side of the tire completely off the rim, you can slip the tube out. Be very careful not to damage the stem while pushing it back out of the rim hole. If you are changing the tire itself, finish the removal by working the tire off the same rim edge.

Once the tire is off the rim, examine its inside for signs of damage. A ply separation near a puncture or other injury may not be easy to see; probing is the only way to detect separation. If the damage is not great, you can patch, or boot, the inside of the tire.

A puncture in the tube can be located by putting air in the tube and holding it under water. The tube can then be patched or replaced, depending upon its condition.

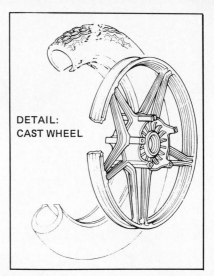

DETAIL: CAST WHEEL

Figure 26–9. Motorcycle equipped with cast wheels. *(Top: U.S. Suzuki Motor Corp. Detail: Honda Motors Co., Ltd.)*

The tire assembly is reinstalled by reversing the disassembly procedure, with one difference: right after the tube has been installed, but before the tire has been completely slipped onto the rim, inflate the tube. Inflation removes any creases that might exist. Then release the air and continue with reassembly. Right after the tire has been completely slipped onto the rim, check to make sure that the stem is squarely in the center of the hole in the rim.

WHEEL ASSEMBLY

The wheel assembly supports the tire and provides for a center mounting on the motorcycle through an axle.

There are two types of wheel in use: the spoked wheel and the cast wheel. The cast wheel (Figure 26–9) is becoming the more popular for the larger road bikes. In this type of wheel, the wheel hub center and rim are cast as one piece from an alloy of aluminum or magnesium. This construction makes for a very strong and light wheel that requires very little maintenance.

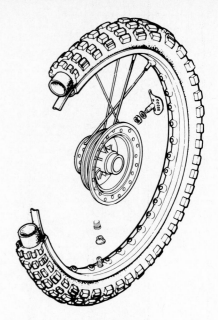

Figure 26–10. A motorcycle with a spoke-type wheel. *(Top: Kawasaki Motors Corp. U.S.A. Detail: Honda Motor Co., Ltd.)*

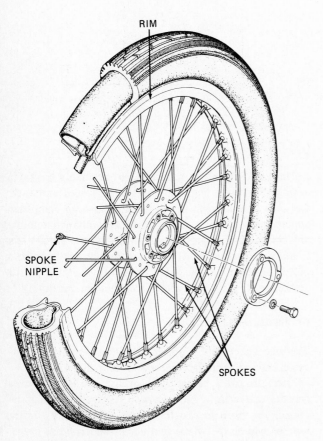

Figure 26–11. Parts of a spoke wheel. *(Yamaha Motor Corp. U.S.A.)*

The spoke wheel is the oldest type of motorcycle wheel (Figure 26–10). It is still used on most small and medium-size motorcycles. The wheel (Figure 26–11) is made up of three basic components. The outside of the wheel is formed by a round rim made of steel or an aluminum alloy. The center of the wheel provides the mounting for the axle (to be discussed shortly). The hub and rim both have holes drilled in them to accept spokes. The spokes fit through holes in the hub and go out to the rim, where they are held in position with threaded nipples that fit through holes in the rim.

The spokes are arranged in an overlapping pattern. Once they are installed (called lacing the wheel) and tensioned properly, the resulting wheel is extremely light, yet extremely strong.

Most wheels have either 36 or 40 spokes. Several patterns are used to lace the wheel according to which wheels are described as cross 1, 2, 3, or 4. The rationale of the patterns is as follows. Each spoke in the wheel is installed at an angle from the hub to the rim. The angular position of the spoke allows it to absorb power transmission and braking forces. In forming its particular angle, each spoke may cross over a number of other spokes (on the same side of the hub) on its way to the rim. If it crosses over one spoke only, it is a cross 1 pattern (Figure 26–12). If it crosses over two spokes, it is a cross 2 pattern, and so on. Cross 1 and cross 2 use very short spokes, resulting in a very light wheel. Cross 3 and cross 4 use longer spokes, providing a heavier, more rigid wheel.

Spokes are manufactured from high-quality steels and are usually chrome plated. Each spoke has a head, blade,

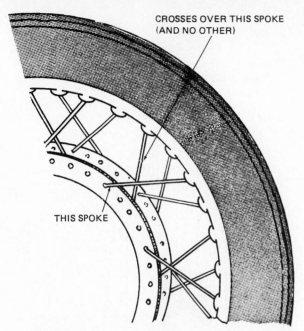

Figure 26–12. The spokes cross over one spoke on the same side of the hub in a cross 1 pattern. *(Mid American Vocational Curriculum Consortium)*

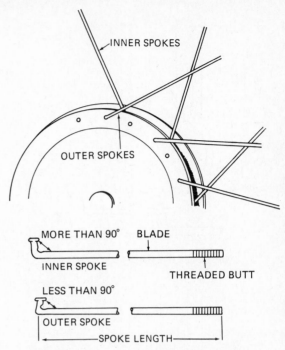

Figure 26–13. Spoke parts and types. *(Mid American Vocational Curriculum Consortium)*

and threaded butt (Figure 26–13). The length of the spoke is measured from the head to the end of the threaded area, with the head fitting through the holes in the hub. The spokes used on the inside of the hub are called *inner spokes* and have a head angle of more than 90 degrees. The spokes used on the outside of the hub are of course *outer spokes* and have a head angle less than 90 degrees. The different head angles are necessary to aim the spoke around the hub and directly at the rim.

Truing a wheel

A new wheel with a perfectly round rim and properly tensioned spokes will rotate without either up-and-down variation (called *radial runout*) or side-to-side variation (called *lateral runout*). If the wheel hits an obstacle hard enough, the rim can get damaged and spokes can eventually begin to loosen up. When this happens, the wheel may begin to show either or both kinds of runout (Figure 26–14).

Correcting a wheel for lateral or radial runout is called *truing* a wheel. The wheel is removed from the bike, and the tire dismounted. The wheel is then installed on a truing stand (Figure 26–15), which supports it in its center hub and allows you to rotate it. An adjustable pointer on the stand is adjusted near the wheel and is used to visually determine the amount of runout (Figure 26–14). Some stands have a dial indicator for very accurate runout measurements.

The wheel is trued by first determining where the lateral or radial runout is located and then tensioning the spokes to correct the runout. The spokes are tensioned with a spoke wrench (Figure 26–16), which fits over the spoke nipple. The nipple is turned to tighten or loosen the spoke tension.

When you spin the wheel on the stand and observe side-to-side movement in relation to the pointer, lateral runout (Figure 26–17) is present. As you spin the rim, it will be obvious whether the rim is out of true to the left or to the right. If it is out to the left, you need to pull it back into the right; if it is out to the right, you need to pull it to the left.

As you look at your wheel, notice that half of the spokes fit into the left side of the hub and the other half fit into the right side of the hub (Figure 26–18). Find the runout area in the wheel and mark it with chalk or a grease pencil. Suppose, for example, it is off to the left. Then you can pull the rim to the right in any area by tightening the spokes just opposite that area on the left side of the hub. Tighten several of the left-side spokes just slightly and keep checking to see how the rim is responding. You can also loosen spokes on the right side to get the same effect. The trick is to make small corrections, tightening and loosening, and end up with spokes that are all tensioned about the same.

Correcting radial runout is a lot harder. As you spin the wheel, look for up-and-down movement or hop between

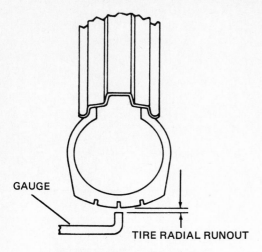

GAUGE

TIRE RADIAL RUNOUT

CHECKING TIRE RADIAL RUNOUT

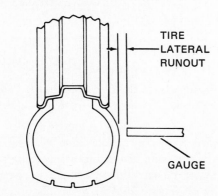

TIRE
LATERAL
RUNOUT

GAUGE

CHECKING TIRE LATERAL RUNOUT

Figure 26–14. Wheel radial and lateral run-out. *(Harley-Davidson Motors, Inc.)*

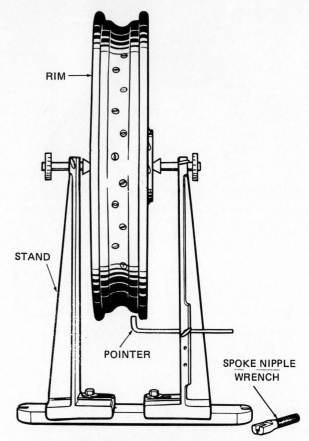

RIM

STAND

POINTER

SPOKE NIPPLE WRENCH

Figure 26–15. Wheels are trued in a wheel truing stand. *(Harley Davidson Motors, Inc.)*

Figure 26–16. Spokes are tensioned with a spoke wrench. *(Yamaha Motor Corp. U.S.A.)*

the pointer and the rim (Figure 26–19). First, try to determine whether the hop is due to a high spot or a low spot. If a high spot is the problem, the side of the wheel on which the high spot is located has to be made lower. To do so, tighten a group of spokes on that side of the wheel, and loosen a group of spokes on the exact opposite side, as shown in Figure 26–20.

Anytime you correct a rim for one type of runout, you should recheck it to make sure you have not created the other type. Keeping the spokes properly tightened during truing is an art. Good wheel builders twang the spokes with their fingernail and listen to the pitch. This tells them how tight or loose a spoke is. This kind of knowledge, of course, takes a good deal of experience.

Replacing a spoke

A severe tire impact can cause one or more spokes to bend or break. Damaged spokes will cause a severe runout condition. To replace a spoke, you will usually have to remove the wheel from the motorcycle and dismount the tire.

Pull the broken spoke head end out of the hub, and unthread the nipple from the blade end. Get a replacement spoke of the correct length and diameter, and then push this spoke through its hole in the hub in the same direction you removed it. Following the pattern of the rest of the spokes, direct the spoke over to its place on the rim. Start the nipple on the threaded end of the spoke, and tighten the nipple until there are as many threads uncovered as you can observe on the other spokes.

Finally, install the wheel in a truing stand and true the wheel as previously described.

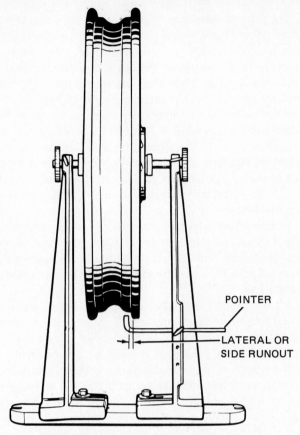

Figure 26–17. Wheel with lateral (side-to-side) runout. *(Harley Davidson Motors, Inc.)*

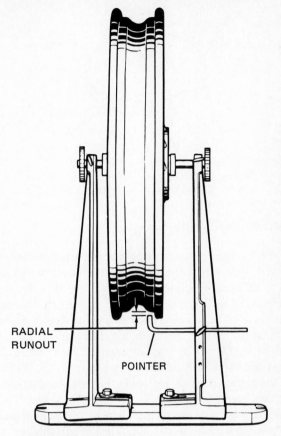

Figure 26–19. Locating radial runout. *(Harley Davidson Motors, Inc.)*

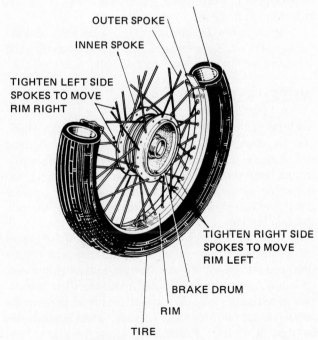

Figure 26–18. Correcting lateral runout. *(Kawasaki Motors Corp. U.S.A.)*

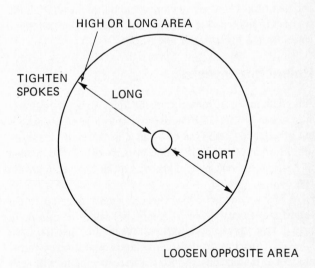

Figure 26–20. Correcting radial runout. A high or long area is corrected by tightening long spokes and loosening short spokes.

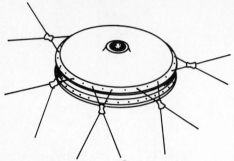

Figure 26–21. Taping the spokes to prevent mixup. *(Mid American Vocational Curriculum Consortium)*

Replacing a rim

A severely bent rim cannot be properly trued without excessive tightening of the spokes. Instead, the rim will need to be replaced. To do so, first remove the wheel from the motorcycle and dismount the tire. Then locate the valve stem hole in the rim and, in direct alignment with it, make a reference on the hub with a grease pencil. Tape the spokes together with masking tape in parts where they cross and form an X, as shown in Figure 26–21. Remove all the nipples from all the spokes, and then carefully work the rim free of the spokes.

Make sure your replacement rim has the same number of spoke holes as the old one. Then, place the new rim back over the hub and spokes, aligning the valve stem hole with the reference mark you made on the hub. Start at the valve stem hole and carefully work one taped pair of spokes at a time through the rim holes, and then screw the nipples on just a few turns. Continue this procedure until all the spokes are inserted and each nipple is started. Then, starting at the valve stem hole, tighten each nipple about one-half turn. Continue to work around the rim until all the spokes are tightened to the same tension. Put the complete wheel on the truing stand and true it.

Balancing wheels

Any shaking or vibration that the rider feels at highway speeds can be caused by a tire and wheel assembly that is out of balance. Being out of balance is caused by there being different densities in different parts of the tire, which in turn causes one part of the tire to be heavier than the rest of it.

At highway speeds, the wheel assembly develops great centrifugal force. If the assembly is heavier at one point than at any others, vibrations will result. Because the front wheel is connected to the steering and suspension systems, any condition causing the front wheel to vibrate will seriously affect the life of all of the suspension and steering parts. In addition, the bike will be unsafe and uncomfortable to ride.

The tire and wheel can be balanced on the wheel truing stand. Mount the wheel as you would to true it, and then spin it slowly and wait for it to stop rotating. When it stops, mark the bottom of the tire with a piece of chalk. Now spin it again. If the chalk mark ends up on the bottom, the wheel is heavier there and is out of balance.

A tire and wheel are in balance when the weight of the wheel-and-tire assembly is distributed equally around the axis of rotation of the wheel (the axle). If the tire and wheel are balanced, the wheel will have no tendency to rotate by itself, regardless of its position. If they are not balanced, the wheel will always rotate until the heaviest spot is at the bottom.

A motorcycle wheel is balanced by putting corrective wheel balance weights that are commercially available on the spokes or on the rim opposite the heavy spot in the wheel. Spoke-type weights can be made by the amateur from solder.

When you find the heavy part of the wheel, put two wheel weights of equal mass on the fifth spoke on either side of the point opposite the heavy point (Figure 26–22, top). If the heavy point stays where it is, increase the mass of the weights or move them closer together. If the heavy point moves to the opposite side of the wheel, the weights are too heavy. In that case use lighter weights. When you cannot find a heavy spot, the wheel is balanced. If you use two weights to oppose the heavy part of the wheel, the total mass is spread out, preventing overstress to any one part of the wheel. You also get greater accuracy by moving the weights toward or away from the light point. Use the same approach when using rim weights (Figure 26–22, bottom).

Computerized wheel balancers are available that spin the wheel and sense any unbalance. The operator can then add corrective weight to balance the assembly.

WHEEL HUB ASSEMBLY

The wheel hub assembly is an important part of the wheel. On spoke-type wheels, it serves as the support for the head end of the spokes. The rotation hub provides the mounting for the brake drum or brake disc. On the rear wheel, the hub serves as the mount for the rear sprocket of the final drive. The hub also provides for the mounting of the axle and axle bearings.

A cross-sectional view of a front hub is shown in Figure 26–23; the brake parts shown in the illustration have been described previously. An axle that passes through the center of the hub is mounted in the front forks. The hub rotates in relation to this stationary axle. In order to make the rotation as free of friction as possible, wheel bearings are installed in the hub. The bearings allow the axle to turn while supporting the weight of the motorcycle. The rear hub assembly is very similar.

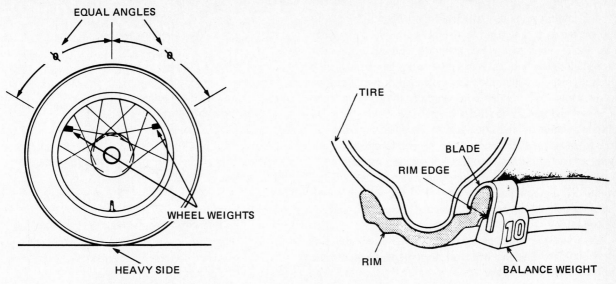

Figure 26-22. Balancing a wheel. *(Kawasaki Motors Corp. U.S.A.)*

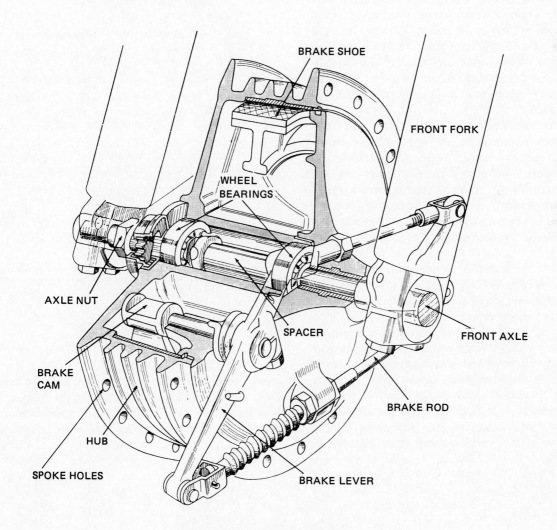

Figure 26-23. Cross-sectional view of a front hub. *(Honda Motor Co., Ltd.)*

Most motorcycles use ball bearings (Figures 26–24) to support the axle. The bearing assembly consists of an outer race and an inner race which supports the balls. The outer race fits into the hub and has a groove or channel in which several precision balls ride. The balls also fit into a groove in the inner race, whose bore supports the axle. A cage supports and spaces the balls apart. The inside race can turn in relation to the outside race because the balls are free to rotate in both races. With proper lubrication, this type of bearing allows excellent low-friction rotation.

Both the front and rear bearings are close to the road and eventually get contaminated with dirt. Accordingly, they must periodically be removed, cleaned, inspected, and lubricated.

To service the wheel bearings, first safely block the motorcycle up so that the wheel to be worked on is off the ground. Then remove the wheel assembly.

Next, remove the axle nut and pull out the axle. Some bearings have a set of seals on each end of the hub to prevent dirt and moisture from getting into the bearings. These seals can be removed by prying them out with a pry bar. (It is a good idea to use new seals during reassembly.)

Drive out the wheel bearings and spacer (Figure 26–25). Use a hammer and brass drift or bushing driver, and carefully drive on the outer race of the bearing to avoid damaging the ball cage.

Wash all the parts in clean solvent. (*NOTE: Some bearings are sealed and cannot be repacked with lubricant; do not wash this type of bearing.*) Wipe excess cleaning solvent off of bearings and other parts with shop towels, and allow them to dry. Then inspect the bearing races and balls for pits or roughness. As you spin the bearing by hand, you should feel a smooth movement between the parts. Replace any bearing that runs rough, is noisy, or has excessive play.

The axle can be checked for bending in V-blocks or on a flat surface (Figure 26–26). Check the specification for allowable runout on the axle shaft. If you detect any bending, the axle should be replaced.

Use the type of wheel bearing grease recommended in the manual and pack the bearings with grease. Then, placing some grease in the palm of your hand, hold the bearing between the thumb and fingertips of your other hand and force grease between the balls by pressing the bearings against the palm of your hand into the grease. Be sure to coat the outside of the cage and balls with grease.

Reinstall the bearings with the drift or bushing driver,

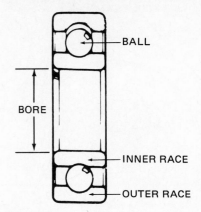

Figure 26–24. Ball bearing. *(Honda Motor Co., Ltd.)*

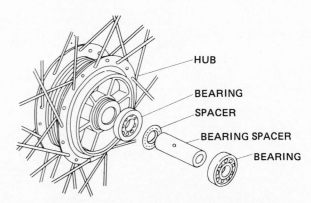

Figure 26–25. Removing axle bearings from the hub. *(Yamaha Motor Corp. U.S.A.)*

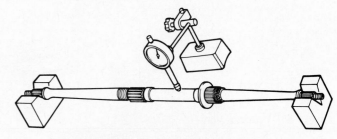

Figure 26–26. Check axle shaft for trueness. *(Honda Motor Co., Ltd.)*

being careful to drive only on the outer race. Then replace the seals and install the axle. It may be necessary to adjust how tightly the axle nut bears against the bearings and spacer. Check the shop service manual for this procedure. Finally, install the wheel in the motorcycle.

Job Sheet 26–1

TRUE A WHEEL

Before you begin:

Read pp.

Make of Motorcycle _____ Model _____ Year ____

Time Started _____ Time Finished _____ Total Time _____

Flat-rate Time _____

Special Tools, Equipment, Parts, and Materials

Spoke nipple wrench
Truing stand
Tire irons
Grease pencil
Eye protection

References

Manufacturer's Shop Manual _____

Specifications

Procedure

1. Remove the wheel from the motorcycle.

2. Dismount the tire and tube from the rim.

3. Mount the wheel in a wheel truing stand.

4. Adjust the truing stand pointer to indicate lateral runout.

5. Spin the wheel and make a grease pencil mark at the point of greatest runout.

6. Correct any lateral runout by loosing the spokes on the marked side of the rim by one-half turn and tightening the spokes opposite the marked side of the rim by one-half turn.

7. Clean off the grease pencil mark from the rim, and continue checking and adjusting until runout does not exceed $\frac{1}{32}$ of an inch.

Instructor check _____

8. Adjust the truing and pointer to indicate radial runout.

9. Spin the wheel and make a mark at the point of maximum radial runout.

10. Correct any radial runout by loosening the spokes directly opposite the marked area by one-half turn and tightening the spokes at the marked area by one-half turn.

11. Clean off the grease pencil mark from the rim and continue adjusting until runout does not exceed $\frac{1}{32}$ of an inch.

12. Since you have just adjusted the radial runout, recheck and readjust the lateral runout, if necessary.

NOTES

Instructor check _____   Date completed _____

Job Sheet 26–2

REMOVE AND INSTALL A WHEEL RIM

Before you begin:

Read pp.

Make of Motorcycle _____ Model _____ Year _____

Time Started _____ Time Finished _____ Total Time _____

Flat-rate Time _____

Special Tools, Equipment, Parts, and Materials

Spoke nipple wrench
Grease pencil
Masking tape
Eye protection

References

Manufacturer's Shop Manual _____

Specifications

Procedure

1. Remove the wheel from the motorcycle.

2. Dismount the tire and tube from the wheel.

3. Make a reference mark on the hub in alignment with the rim valve stem hole.

4. Use masking tape to tape the spokes together in pairs where they cross.

5. Use the spoke nipple wrench to remove the nipples from all the spokes.

6. Carefully work the rim free of the spokes.

Instructor check _____

7. Place the new rim back over the hub and spokes, aligning the valve stem hole with the reference mark on the hub.

8. Start at the valve stem hole and carefully work one taped pair of spokes at a time through the rim holes. Then screw the nipples on a few turns.

9. Continue installing spokes until all the spokes are in place and each nipple is on a few turns.

10. Begin at the valve stem hole and tighten each spoke nipple one-half turn with the spoke nipple wrench.

11. Go all the way around the rim until all the spokes are tightened to the same tension.

Instructor check _____

12. True the wheel for radial and lateral runout.

Instructor check _____

13. Mount the tire and inflate it to specifications.

14. Install the wheel on the motorcycle.

NOTES

Instructor check _____   Date completed _____

Job Sheet 26–3

DISASSEMBLE, CLEAN, LUBRICATE, AND INSTALL AXLE BEARINGS

Before you begin:

Read pp.

Make of Motorcycle _____ Model _____ Year _____

Time Started _____ Time Finished _____ Total Time _____

Flat-rate Time _____

Special Tools, Equipment, Parts, and Materials

Wheel bearing grease
New seals
Eye protection

References

Manufacturer's Shop Manual _____

Specifications

Procedure

1. Remove the wheel from the motorcycle.

2. Remove the axle nut and pull out the axle.

3. Use a pry bar to remove the wheel bearing seals from each end of the hub.

4. Use a hammer with a brass drift or bushing driver to drive the bearings out of the hub. (*NOTE: Drive on the outer race only, or you could damage the bearing.*)

5. Wash all parts in cleaning solvent and allow them to dry.

6. Inspect the bearing balls and races for any pits or roughness. Are the bearings:

   Damaged _____ Acceptable _____

7. Check the axle by rolling it on a flat surface for bending. Is the axle:

   Straight _____ Bent _____

Instructor check _____

8. Pack the bearings with the recommended type of wheel bearing grease.

9. Install the bearings in the hub with a brass drift or bushing driver.

10. Install new seals in either end of the hub.

11. Install the axle and axle nut.

Instructor check _____

12. Install the wheel on the motorcycle.

NOTES

Instructor check _____   Date completed _____

KEY TERMS

Lacing: the construction of a spoked wheel by installing the spokes in a crossing pattern.

Lateral runout: the side-to-side movement of a spoked wheel as it spins.

Radial runout: the up-and-down movement of a spoked wheel as it spins, caused by high and low areas in the wheel.

Truing: the correction of spoke tension to remove the radial and lateral runout from a wheel.

Wheel balance: the correction of a heavy spot on one side of a wheel by installing corrective weights on the other side.

CHECKUP

Identify the parts of the tire by writing their names in the spaces provided.

1. _____
2. _____
3. _____
4. _____
5. _____
6. _____
7. _____
8. _____
9. _____

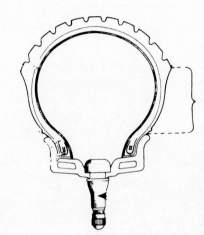

Identify the parts of a spoke by writing their names in the spaces provided.

10. _____
11. _____
12. _____
13. _____

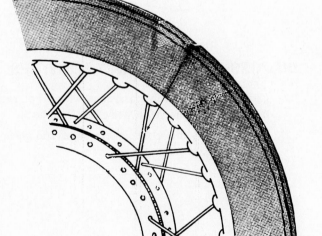

Identify the parts of a hub assembly by writing their names in the spaces provided.

14. _____

15. _____

16. _____

17. _____

18. _____

19. _____

20. _____

21. _____

22. _____

23. _____

24. _____

Identify the parts of a wheel bearing by writing their names in the spaces provided.

25. _____

26. _____

27. _____

28. _____

29. _____

30. _____

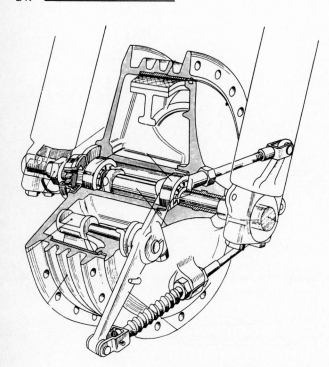

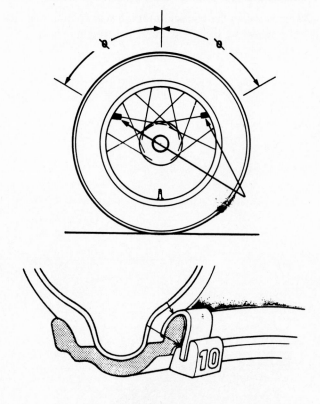

DISCUSSION TOPICS AND ACTIVITIES

1. Completely disassemble a spoked wheel. Following a pattern on a complete wheel, lace the wheel.

2. Try to identify the spoke pattern on several types of spoked wheels.

INDEX